THE GREAT GANGSTER PICTURES

by

JAMES ROBERT PARISH

and

MICHAEL R. PITTS

Editor: T. Allan Taylor

Research Associates:
John Robert Cocchi; Edward Connor;
Florence Solomon; Vincent Terrace

The Scarecrow Press, Inc.

Metuchen, N.J.   1976

Library of Congress Cataloging in Publication Data

Parish, James Robert.
    The great gangster pictures.

    1. Gangster films--History and criticism.
I. Pitts, Michael R., joint author. II. Title
PN1995.9.G3P36   791.43'0909'353   75-32402
ISBN 0-8108-0881-1

To

Elisha Cook, Jr.

TABLE OF CONTENTS

AUTHORS' NOTE and ACKNOWLEDGMENTS

As the complexities, styles, and focuses of life have changed over the decades, so has the shape and scope of that violence-prone film genre, the gangster movie.

While we were researching the possible entries for this volume, we came across many likely motion pictures produced throughout the world. However, because the gangster feature is so peculiarly parochial to the American film scene, we have decided to forego discussion of most of these "foreign" productions, which, according to the scholarship of Pierre Guinle in Brussels, could fill a volume of its own. Rather, we narrowed our entries to mainly U.S.-produced features which examine the criminal in a variety of milieus: in his pre-lawbreaking days, as the proverbial thug, as the incarcerated convicted man, or as the jailbreaker or lawfully released ex-prisoner. We have deliberately omitted discussion of such revenge-style ("an eye for an eye") movies as Death Wish (1974), which may be violent and gory and classify as thrillers but are certainly not within the scope of the (un)traditional gangster motion picture. Much harder to separate from the genre of gangster movies have been the detective movies. Obviously there could be no sleuth studies on camera if the (amateur) gumshoe did not have a criminal case of one sort or another to solve for a client. But in this latter type of film, the focus is generally on the detective himself and/or his relationship with his clients, rather than on depicting the underworld ambience of the racketeers, the hoodlums, the thugs, the molls, and everything that we have come to accept as part of the gangster life.

Naturally the authors would be most grateful to learn the reaction of readers to this second in a series of books dealing with assorted film genres.

Grateful acknowledgment of their helpfulness is given to Anderson (Ind.) Newspapers, Inc., Richard Braff, David Bucove and the staff of the Anderson (Ind.) Public Library, Morris Everett, Jr., Filmfacts, Film Fan Monthly, Films in Review, Pierre Guinle, Louis Harrison, Ken D. Jones, Doug McClelland, Albert B. Manski, Alvin H. Marill, Jim Meyer, Peter Miglierini, Norman Miller, Movie Poster Service (Bob Smith), Carolyn Mudd, Screen Facts, Charles Smith, Mrs. Peter Smith, Charles K. Stumpf, and Steven Whitney.

And special thanks to Paul Myers, curator of the Theatre Collection at the Lincoln Center Library for the Performing Arts, and his staff: Monty Arnold, David Bartholomew, Rod Bladel, Donald Fowle, Maxwell Silverman, Dorothy Swerdlove, Betty Wharton; and Donald Madison, Photographic Services.

James Robert Parish
300 E. 56th St. #9b
NYC 10022

Michael R. Pitts
604 Hendricks Street #1
Anderson, Indiana 46016

GANGSTERS OF THE SCREEN

by Edward Connor

A stick-up job, a gum-chewing moll, a bulging suit jacket covering a shoulder holster, the one-way-ride, a snarling, cigar-chewing kingpin, the masked bandits, the nightclub smoke and chatter, the tommygun, the speakeasy, a body weighed with cement or chains and tossed into the river, the gaming house, the Senate Rackets Committee's hearings, the Mafia family, the kiss of death, the prison riot, the death row cellblock, the big break-out. These are some of the terms, ambiances, situations we have come to associate with the word "gangster."

The American film industry, always seeking new grist for its production mills, has long been fascinated with the world of the law-breaker. One of the more interesting phenomena in this century has been U. S. filmmakers' reliance on the gangster motif as the basis for countless photoplays, serials, radio and television shows, and stage plays (not to mention the continuing rash of gangster-focused pulp fiction).

What is a so-called gangster film? By definition "gangster" is a colloquialism for "a member of any gang." However, the word did not come into general use until the Roaring Twenties (with Prohibition) when it became solidly identified with those who fought the police--and one another--for the manufacture, sale, and control of bootleg liquor. By extension the word then came to apply to all who operate outside the law (especially in gambling, narcotics, prostitution, or the protection rackets), whether operating in gangs or as "loners."

The Girl and the Gangster (1914) was one of the few silent films to use the word in a title, although there were certainly other films of the period to incorporate the hoodlum theme into the story-line. One of the pathfinding efforts was D. W. Griffith's Musketeers of Pig Alley (1912), which gave a flavor of the disreputable type who moves in social circles unmindful of law and order. While Griffith was busy at his new base, Mutual, Selig produced The Making of Crooks (1914), which used the pool hall as the den of hoodlums and juvenile delinquents, and detailed the corruption of youths. Griffith returned to thug-exploiting with the modern story sequence of his mammoth film Intolerance (1916). In his very moralistic way, the famed director was pointing the way to the future course of the genre.

1

The Charleston, bathtub gin, the flapper, and the rising stock market were not the only subjects to claim the headlines during the Twenties. Exposés of gangland doings in Chicago and other big cities filled the newspapers, giving a hint of what was to come in the turbulent Thirties, when the Depression spawned a siege of lawlessness. Strangely, Hollywood, where the film industry in America had become centered, remained rather aloof from the gangster motif. When one considers how many features/serials/shorts were devoted to love stories, spy tales, Western adventures, etc., it seemed almost as if filmmakers were too genteel to cope with the world of punks, henchmen and underlings of crime czars, and the nefarious goings-on of the times.

Lon Chaney, that "man of a thousand faces," made several excursions into underworld melodramas. It was not that he had any altruistic outlook to offer on the subject, but that the portrayal of the criminal offender provided him with a perfect theme: the loner, the tough guy, the man who could brave any physical obstacle, but who had no power when swayed by the love for a beautiful girl. So it was that in Outside the Law (1921), Big City (1928), and While the City Sleeps (1928) Chaney explored the plotline gimmick of the beast and the beauty.

Interestingly enough, it was Josef von Sternberg, the craftsman genius who would remain best known for his Thirties' excursion into the esoteric with Paramount's Marlene Dietrich, who brought to the still-forming gangster genre a very essential lesson. In Underworld (1927) he depicted the shadowy sphere inhabited by the denizens of crime. The silent cinema seemed the perfect medium to express this brooding atmosphere which bred the gangster and his molls, and everything that one was beginning to associate with the criminal's way of life. But like so much of the 1920s--in films or elsewhere-- it was largely illusory, more fantasy than a depiction of reality.

Other more conventional exercises in the species came with Dressed to Kill (1928), Me, Gangster (1928), The Racket (1928), and Romance of the Underworld (1929). Me, Gangster featured a very young and lovely Carol(e) Lombard in her pre-comedy stardom days while The Racket, which would be remade in 1951, was a production of Howard Hughes.

The Jazz Singer (1927), starring Al Jolson, was the feature which did so much to usher in the commercial feasibility of the sound film era. It also led the way for Lights of New York (1928) Warner Bros.' contribution to the industry as the first all-talking film. Director Bryan Foy took Helen Costello, Cullen Landis, Mary Carr, and Eugene Pallette through their paces as two country rubes hit the big city and found it a lot tougher to survive, let alone succeed, than they had ever imagined. Before long they are involved with a bootleg operation and a racketeer. The granddaddy of the screen gangster film was released in 1929 by Universal. Broadway derived from the stage show of the same title, and in its talkie and silent versions established all the celluloid clichés that would haunt

the business for decades to come: the nightclub atmosphere, the
gangland rivals, the sudden shootings, the chorine who loves the
wholesome hero, the girl who witnesses a killing, an innocent party
almost jailed for a crime committed by another, the rough, smart,
fast talk. With art imitating real life, ex-hoofer/ex-underworld
frequenter George Raft would star in a remake of Broadway in 1942,
by which time the clichés had become so well-worn that they were
considered nostalgia.

With the coming of sound and the new decade, Hollywood went
wild with the possibilities of exploiting the gangster theme. If all-
talking, all-singing, all-dancing musicals were becoming passé, here
was a new fertile field to explore. Each film of a famous trio of
features would establish its male lead as a Hollywood star and typecast him for the remainder of his screen career--a high price for
fame.

The first was Mervyn LeRoy's production of Little Caesar
(1931), which some feel is a highly over-rated film. Those who
pay it high tribute tend to overlook the very slow pace and the long
stretches of little action. Many "seasoned" film buffs are surprised
to learn that this was not Edward G. Robinson's first film, nor his
initial excursion in the underworld milieu on camera. (He had made
the crime melodrama Hole in the Wall in 1929). However, as Rico,
the Little Caesar of the title, the actor gave a highly-charged performance that insured him a special place in moviegoers' hearts and
convinced Warner Bros. that here was the perfect performer to play
such roles ad infinitum.

On the other hand, Public Enemy (1931) does fully live up to
its reputation, even according to today's standards. More so than
Little Caesar, the film moves right along. It is jammed with action,
and has enough violence, blood, and gore to satisfy the most bloodthirsty audience. The final scene never fails to shock. It was
James Cagney's fifth feature film and his second as a gangster. (It
is intriguing to observe that both Cagney and Robinson, who would
become the leading progenitors of the screen racketeers, were each
pleasant, mild-mannered individuals off camera, and physically short
and unassuming--it was their dramatic presence which made them
tower).

Then in 1932, Howard Hughes produced and Howard Hawks
directed Scarface: The Shame of a Nation. If it were available for
rescreening today, it would still hold up with its violent depiction of
hoods, gang wars, etc. Although Paul Muni (who had been in films
since The Valiant in 1929) is called Tony Camonte in the movie,
he is really playing out a version of Al Capone's career. (It would
be some time before gangsters were called by their real names on
the screen.)

Other gangster films of equal or superior quality were being
made at about the same time--all of them practically forgotten today. Doorway to Hell (1930) pulls no punches in its graphic detail-

ing of the rise of a baby-faced hood (Lew Ayres) to become head of
his own gang (which includes James Cagney), his victories over rival gangs, and his eventual downfall.

The 1931 entry, Corsair, a well-made melodrama directed by
Roland West, is one of the more amoral movies on the books, spell-
ing out in large letters the message that crime DOES very much pay.
All criminals herein get away scot free at the end, loaded down with
their ill-gotten gains. Night Nurse, also 1931, is not primarily a
gangster film, but is every bit as amoral as Corsair. Whenever
"hero" Ben Lyon gets into trouble, he simply telephones his underworld pals who promptly go into action for him, and no justice is
meted out to them or to Lyon at the finish.

Even The Secret Six (1931), with Wallace Beery in a
Capone-type role, is, for some, more actionful than the much-
touted Little Caesar. MGM's The Secret Six had a remarkable cast:
Beery, Lewis Stone, John Mack Brown, Jean Harlow, Clark Gable,
Ralph Bellamy, Marjorie Rambeau, Paul Hurst, John Miljan, et al.

Although Edward G. Robinson and James Cagney were to play
many more gangster roles in their screen careers (the former even
playing a Chinese gangster in 1932's Hatchet Man), it is amazing
how many times they also appeared, and most convincingly, on the
right side of the law. Cagney's G-Men (1935), which would start
a new trend in idolizing the lawman, not the lawbreaker, is still
frequently shown on TV, along with Robinson's I Am the Law (1938)
and Vice Squad (1953). It is also interesting to note that it was
only after some of these good guy roles that both appeared in their
most bloodthirsty gangster assignments: Cagney in White Heat (1949),
Robinson in Key Largo (1948), Black Tuesday (1954), and Hell on
Frisco Bay (1955).

After Scarface, the prestigious Paul Muni did not play a gangster on screen until the fantasy picture Angel on My Shoulder (1946)
in which he is shot in the first reel, goes to hell, then is told by
the Devil (Claude Rains) to return to earth and bring about the downfall of a district attorney. However, Muni became a Depression-
victim convict in I Am a Fugitive from a Chain Gang (1932) and he
would be very much involved with thugs in Dr. Socrates (1935).

George Raft, who had a small role in Scarface but had already played criminal types in such earlier entries as Hush Money
(1931), would later make a career of playing gangster roles. The
other big figure of the genre would be Humphrey Bogart, who after
a see-saw career on Broadway and in Hollywood, would establish
himself as the prototype of the hardened public enemy in The Petrified Forest. When this stage success was transferred to the screen
in 1936, with Leslie Howard and Bette Davis co-starred, Bogart was
hired to re-enact his role of Killer Duke Mantee. It set him on the
professional path that would dog his future years in moviemaking.
However, both Raft and Bogart also made surprising excursions to
the side of the law and were as convincing as Robinson and Cagney.

In fact, Bogart as the hero of Crime School (1938) was repeating
Cagney's role in Mayor of Hell (1933).

Barton MacLane, that featured player who was such a staple
of Thirties' thrillers, played the gang boss in such films as G-Men
and Dr. Socrates, but also took time out to play Lieutenant Steve
McBride in some of the Torchy Blane series, as well as a tough detective in The Maltese Falcon (1941).

Jack LaRue was typecast as a gangster right through the Thirties and into the Forties, with just a brief time out to play the priest
in A Farewell to Arms (1932). LaRue received a great deal of publicity when he took over the top gangster role refused by George
Raft in Paramount's The Story of Temple Drake (1933), starring
Miriam Hopkins. However, like MacLane, LaRue never achieved
star status. (In 1948, he would travel to England to star in No
Orchids for Miss Blandish, which was adapted from James Hadley
Chase's adaptation-novel of William Faulkner's Sanctuary, from
which The Story of Temple Drake had derived.)

With every major and minor film studio turning out underworld dramas by the score in the Thirties there was plenty of room
for a wide variety of featured performers to shine as the nasty villains. George Bancroft, who had starred in the silent era as Josef
von Sternberg's leading hoodlum type, returned to the form in Columbia's Racketeers in Exile (1937). Other mob bosses were played by
the likes of Ralph Ince, Edwin Maxwell, C. Henry Gordon, Otto Kruger, Akim Tamiroff, Bruce Cabot, and Cesar Romero. Surrounding
these "big boys" were a whole flock of actors playing hoods, stooges,
stool pigeons, and hired killers who would not have been found dead
on the side of the law (but frequently were). They included such
people as Paul Fix, Noel Madison, Stanley Fields, Maurice Black,
William Pawley, Edward Pawley, Al Hill, Paul Guilfoyle, Harold
Huber, Marc Lawrence, Joseph Dowling, et al. Then there were
the intentionally funny gangsters, e.g., Warren Hymer, Allen Jenkins, Edward Brophy, and the unintentionally amusing mobster, like
Ernie Adams.

On the other side of the law--protecting the public--in most
gangster films of the Twenties and Thirties were Thomas Jackson
(first brought to the screen in 1929 to repeat his stage role of detective in Broadway) and Robert Elliott. Each played the detective
in exactly the same way--slow, laconic, unsmiling, self-assured,
speaking in a drawling voice--to such an extent that either could
have taken over the other's role in any film. However, Jackson
played a crook in Fall Guy (1931) and, if Elliott never fell from
grace in his unwavering devotion to the police department, he still
used highly questionable, unorthodox methods to get rid of mobster
Ben Bard in Romance of the Underworld (1928).

The actor most seen as the cop on the beat was Robert Emmett O'Connor, moving his great bulk around with comparative ease
and constantly stretching what seemed to be a permanently stiff neck.

But even he wavered in his screen morality. In Public Enemy, he played the minor hood who started Cagney and Edward Woods on their path of crime. Other regular patrolmen on the cinema beat were Willard Robertson, Robert Homans, Frank Sheridan, DeWitt Jennings, and James Burke [the latter remembered most for Dead End (1937)].

At meetings of the celluloid Grand Jury, where the gangsters' fates would surely be sealed, the foreman was almost certain to be Edward LeSaint, who also sat on the judge's bench many times, alternating with George Irving, Edwin Stanley, Selmer Jackson, and Paul Stanton.

Women were certainly not excluded from the field of crime. One of the earlier examples of the female wrongdoer was Madame Racketeer (1932) starring Paramount's Alison Skipworth, that bulky but effective character actress. She was a good-natured con artist like May Robson in Lady for a Day (1933), the latter film a version of a Damon Runyon story about Apple Annie, a colorful fleecer. [Bette Davis, of all people, would star in the remake, Pocketful of Miracles (1961).] Just as there had been the molls, hangers-on, chorines and spongers in the silent cinema, so the talkies spawned their repertory of such love interests and diversions for the on-camera tough guys. Whether it was Joan Blondell, Glenda Farrell, Ruth Donnelly, Wynne Gibson, Mayo Methot, Veda Ann Borg, or Natalie Moorhead, they were a tough bunch of babes on camera. Perhaps none was tougher than Barbara Stanwyck in Ladies They Talk About (1933), a rough and tumble gal who knew how to hold her own in and out of prison. A more genteel, sympathetic type was the wrongdoer as played by Sylvia Sidney. Whether one of the Ladies of the Big House (1932), Mary Burns, Fugitive (1935), the wife-accomplice of You Only Live Once (1937), or the ex-convict in You and Me (1938) with George Raft her co-star, the doe-eyed Miss Sidney was the decade's most famous distaff troublemaker.

Just as the Hot Twenties and Prohibition had supplied the basis for bootleggers/speakeasies (and the plotlines for dozens of screen thrillers), so the Thirties and the Depression set up a new motif and created new stars of the genre. While Cagney, Robinson, and others were mowing down their rivals and barking out orders to their accomplices, such melodramas as City Streets (1931) and Dead End, both starring Sylvia Sidney, were showing that environment had its effects in creating the hardened criminal. Living in tenements and coping with poverty was not only morale-crushing, but it often set right-thinking individuals on the path to crime.

Thus, in its own way Dead End was pathfinding. It provided the screen debut of the Dead End Kids (Leo Gorcey, Huntz Hall, Billy Halop, et al.) and started these youngish actors on their road to movie fame as participants in scores of tenement dramas in which they admired and worked for or against the underworld. Rising out of this heap as the male answer to Sylvia Sidney's (criminal) victim of society, was John Garfield. They Made Me a Criminal (1939),

a remake of Douglas Fairbanks, Jr.'s The Life of Jimmy Dolan
(1933), perhaps says it all with its title. With the proverbial chip
on his shoulder and a scowl on his face, Garfield's screen character
has no use for the breadline of yore, or the relief payroll of the
Thirties. He wants his just share of happiness, and, if it requires
his going bad to achieve this happiness, then that is okay by him.
Long after Franklin D. Roosevelt's anti-Depression program had
merged into World War II prosperity, plucky Garfield would be ex-
ercising his way on camera with the same stereotype of the environ-
mental-bred punk, or ex-reform school alumnus.

While there were loads of features dealing with the gangster
field, so there was a high percentage of motion picture serials--
silent and sound--concerning gangsters. Usually the cliffhanger's
chief villains (mysteriously cloaked in bizarre costumes to hide their
identity until the final chapter) headed large compliant gangs and,
therefore, had hordes of minions to do their most trivial bidding.
Several such chapterplays stand out in this field, such as Universal's
Gang Busters (1942), starring Kent Taylor and based on a widely
popular radio series.

Dick Tracy (Ralph Byrd) took on four gangs in as many Republic serials: the Lame One's group in Dick Tracy (1937), Pa
Stark's mob in Dick Tracy Returns (1938), foreign agent Zarnoff's
gang in Dick Tracy's G-Men (1939), and the Ghost's outfit in Dick
Tracy Vs. Crime Inc. (1941). Most impressive was the last, in
which the mysterious masked Ghost (capable of invisibility) headed
the gigantic enterprise, Crime Inc., after the death of his brother,
Rackets Reagan.

The Green Hornet (1940) (Gordon Jones and, later, Warren
Hull) fought organized crime in two serials, as did The Spider (Hull)
(1941), Secret Agent X-9 (1939, 1945 & serials) (first Scott Kolk and
then Lloyd Bridges), Superman (Kirk Alyn), and even the Dead End
Kids in Junior G-Men (1940) and Junior G-Men of the Air (1942).

Don Terry, who had been in gangster melodramas of the late
Twenties and had thereafter been in such program features as Paid
to Dance (1937), Columbia's minor exposé of the dance hall rackets,
took on The Scorpion and his thugs in Don Winslow of the Navy
(1942) and Don Winslow of the Coast Guard (1943). A different kind
of Scorpion and gang was opposed by heroes of other serials: the
1927 and the 1937 versions of Blake of Scotland Yard, and the exciting Adventures of Captain Marvel (1941) with Tom Tyler.

The Clutching Hand, in the 1936 independently-made serial of
the same name, was a master criminal whose gang members reported to him via television.

When the momentum ran out of the genre after Little Caesar,
Public Enemy, and Scarface had initiated a host of imitation entries,
the filmmakers turned to other subjects; but in 1935 came James
Cagney's G-Men, which found a new gimmick for re-introducing the

tommygun slaughter, fast-racing getaway cars, and the rugged action
and talk of earlier films. The once neurotic gangster hero was now
the villain, while the usually subservient law enforcer was the star.
Even this gambit had its inventive limitations, and by the late Thirties, the movie studios had generally relegated the underworld drama
to the "B" film. Thus, seemingly countless assembly-line productions hit the American film market in a wide variety of directions,
pacings, and slants, hoping to stir up some audience interest in
these double-bill items. Monogram's Federal Bullets (1937) found
Zeffie Tilbury as an old lady running a hoodlum gang; Warner Bros.'
Alcatraz Island (1937) featured John Litel as a hoodlum in prison
who is framed there for the murder of another inmate; and Republic's Gangs of New York (1938) offered Charles Bickford as a policeman posing as a hood because he is a look-alike for his criminal counterpart. On a rather higher budget than was its custom, Monogram
produced a series of Jackie Cooper dramas, including Boy of the
Streets (1937) and Gangster's Boy (1938), which were essentially
spin-off conglomerations of themes used in the Dead End Kids (a. k. a.
Little Tough Guys) movies.

A rather sophisticated group of low-budget crime dramas was
produced by Paramount in the mid to late Thirties, many of them
based upon J. Edgar Hoover's book, Persons in Hiding. Using the
studio's marvelous stock company, Paramount produced Daughter of
Shanghai (1937), King of Gamblers (1937), Dangerous to Know (1938),
Tip-off Girls (1938) and, of course, Persons in Hiding (1939). Others cranked out by the same studio were King of Alcatraz (1938),
King of Chinatown (1938), Prison Farm (1938) with Shirley Ross,
Illegal Traffic (1938), Federal Offense (1938), Paroles for Sale (1938),
and the following year's Undercover Doctor, Ambush (with opera
singer Gladys Swarthout), Island of Lost Men and Grand Jury Se-
crets.

King of Alcatraz, running a bare fifty-eight minutes, had the
full advantage of the studio's contract players. Headed by Lloyd
Nolan, Robert Preston, Gail Patrick, Porter Hall, and veteran Harry Carey, the cast also included J. Carrol Naish as the title character. (Few moviegoers will ever forget his entrance, boarding a
ship disguised as a gentle, grandmotherly old lady.) Tough guys
surrounding Naish were Anthony Quinn, Tom Tyler, Gustav von Seyffertitz, Harry Worth, Paul Fix, and Clay Clements. Other members of this really sensational cast were Eddie Acuff, Stanley Blystone, Nora Cecil, Buddy Roosevelt, and John Hart. This was the
Golden Age of Hollywood, when any kind of economy fare, especially
a gangster yarn, had built-in parts for many rising or declining
players.

The coming of a new decade, the Forties, did not change the
film scene as if by magic. But the entrance of America into World
War II did bring some new wrinkles to the genre and the parts
played by the established types in the genre. Of course, there were
still the run of typical programmers. Warners made Lady Gangster
(1942) with Faye Emerson, and PRC turned out City of Silent Men

(1942), in which ex-criminals try to lead normal lives in a rural
community. There was even Baby Face Morgan (1942), another
PRC entry in which Richard Cromwell was a country boy posing as
a big-shot hoodlum. The eerie Bela Lugosi returned to the format
in Bowery at Midnight (1942), a Monogram production in which Lugosi was a hoodlum running a mission as a front for his gang.
Ralph "Dick Tracy" Byrd was a reporter who goes to prison to
work on an exposé in Broadway Big Shot (1942), while Men of San
Quentin (1942) was yet another study of the penitentiary and what it
did to men. (This was filmed on location, but still did not give it
the zest of 1930's The Big House or 1932's The Last Mile or 1933's
20,000 Years in Sing Sing or 1939's Each Dawn I Die, each in its
way superior essays on jail life and the routines/fates/attitudes of
a variety of convicts.)

Two films of 1942 showed that gangsters could have patriotic
souls, and each starred a very contrasting type of screen tough guy.
Humphrey Bogart led his mob against Nazi fifth columnists in All
Through the Night (1942), while in Lucky Jordan (1942), short,
trench-coated Alan Ladd abandoned his on-screen capering with Veronica Lake long enough to be a lawbreaker drafted into the Army
who goes A.W.O.L. and comes to grips with Axis agents in the
U.S. These attempts seemed to prove that old canard of Damon
Runyon's, that crooks did have hearts of gold--especially when, as
here, they were inspired by patriotism.

The breakthrough in calling gangsters by their real names
seemed to be Roger Touhy, Gangster (1944). In spite of a large
and competent cast headed by Preston Foster and Victor McLaglen,
and a semi-documentary style used by competent Robert Florey (who
directed King of Alcatraz), the film is a strange and unconvincing
mish-mash. It is often spoken of as "heavily censored," but without back-up evidence of just what was censored and why. It was
followed by Dillinger (1945), with Lawrence Tierney starring, a feature that played fast and loose with the facts but proved a financial
bonanza for lowly Monogram. [Different sets of facts were presented in Young Dillinger (1965) with Nick Adams and Dillinger
(1973) with Warren Oates.]

Mickey Rooney starred in Baby Face Nelson (1957), Charles
Bronson in Machine Gun Kelly (1958), Ray Danton in The Rise and
Fall of Legs Diamond (1959), and John Chandler in Mad Dog Coll
(1959). Perhaps most impressive in this rogue's gallery of cinema
bad guys was Al Capone (1959), with Rod Steiger in dress and makeup that convincingly simulated the famous mobster, although there
was the standard juggling of facts for entertainment purposes. Neville Brand portrayed Capone in the teleseries, "The Untouchables,"
and again in The George Raft Story (1961), and managed to suggest
the famous mobster despite the lack of any real resemblance. On
the other hand, no resemblance of any kind was found in the Capone
part played by Jason Robards, Jr. in Roger Corman's The St. Valentine's Day Massacre (1967), and in Corman's Capone (1975) with
Ben Gazzara in the lead role.

Another favorite cinema hero-hood was Pretty Boy Floyd.
John Ericson played the wanted man in a 1959 entry of that name.
His "life" was done again by singer Fabian in A Bullet for Pretty
Boy (1970), and yet again as the primary focus in a telefeature with
Martin Sheen, The Story of Pretty Boy Floyd. The three actors
were far handsomer than the real Floyd, whose nickname must have
been a comparative one, a tribute to his fair looks in the midst of
gangland's pug-uglies.

When Bonnie and Clyde burst upon the scene to tumultuous
acclaim in 1967, people were surprised to learn there had been an
earlier The Bonnie Parker Story (1958) and that it was already on
the late, late show. It was a cheaply made American International
product compared to the Warren Beatty-Faye Dunaway project, but
not totally without merit. The Fifties' version had Dorothy Provine
in the lead while Clyde Barrow, as played by Jack Hogan, was re-
named Guy Darrow.

The infamous Ma Barker was played to the hilt by Shelley
Winters in Bloody Mama (1970), a film geared more to incest than
violence, while Blanche Yurka played a thinly disguised version of
the same character in Queen of the Mob (1940). Somewhat in the
same mold was Judith Anderson's Lady Scarface (1941), a cheapie
churned out in 1941. An often overlooked rendition of the distaff
criminal theme was Lurene Tuttle's performance in Ma Barker's
Killer Brood (1960).

Proper ladies who came in contact with gangsters, to either
their detriment or improvement, have been played by Fay Bainter
in Lady and the Mob (1939), Katie Johnson in The Ladykillers (1955),
and Brenda de Banzie in Too Many Crooks (1958).

The last two were, of course, British releases. In the main
the earliest British gangster films were those based on Edgar Wallace novels, with gangs operating under leaders (generally masked)
with such colorful names as The Frog, The Professor, and The Pan-
da. Some of the Wallace books have had a longer "international"
history on the screen. The Fellowship of the Frog, for instance,
was filmed in Hollywood in 1928 as a ten-chapter Pathé serial,
Mark of the Frog (the locale changed from London to New York
City), then was used as the source for three different features
made in England: The Frog (1931 and 1937) and Return of the Frog
(1939). It would then be remade in Germany as Face of the Frog
(1959).

While members of The Frog's gang would have the image of
a frog tattooed on their forearms, more bizarre was the gang of
blind peddlers operating under a mastermind criminal, who are bilk-
ing insurance companies in Wallace's Dark Eyes of London (1938),
with Bela Lugosi in a dual role. (The film would be retitled The
Human Monster when released in the U.S.) The Germans would
resurrect the Wallace story for their Dead Eyes of London (1961).
Actually, the German filmmakers had a fondness for Wallace's under-

world thrillers. They made Puzzle of the Red Orchid (1962), based
on the author's When the Gangs Came to London, in which Scotland
Yard and the F. B. I. come between American and British racketeers.
Christopher Lee, Klaus Kinski, and Fritz Rasp were in the cast.
The plot of the latter entry is reminiscent of Sherlock Holmes (1932),
in which the nefarious Professor Moriarity (Ernest Torrence) at-
tempted to bring gangster methods into England, the better to oppose
Scotland Yard and Sherlock Holmes (Clive Brook).

Perhaps the best of the British underworld films of the Fifties was Night and the City (1950), which relied on American stars
for its box-office appeal.   In the plotline, seedy, smalltime pro-
moter Richard Widmark tries to take on "big boss" Herbert Lom.
The film, which co-starred Gene Tierney, is filled with believable
lowdown characters.

Earlier, in 1948, the British had attempted a realistic Amer-
ican-type gangster film, No Orchids for Miss Blandish (as detailed
before).   Linden Travers, Zoe Gail, Hugh McDermott, and Percy
Marmont played American types.   Jack LaRue was imported from
the U. S. to play the sleazy but fascinating gangster, as he had previously in The Story of Temple Drake.   While No Orchids was a
big commercial hit in its country of origin, in America it was practically laughed off the screen.

It is surprising how soon in its history the gangster film
started kidding itself.   The Little Giant (1933) had ex-beer baron
Edward G. Robinson seeking culture and respectability and being
"taken" by the society crowd.   Robinson again sought respectability
in A Slight Case of Murder (1938), but what could he do when four
gangster corpses were left sitting around a card table in his summer home?   He and his friends decided to deposit the bodies on
other hoodlums' doorsteps.   This film is arguably the funniest gangster comedy ever made in Hollywood.   However, it lost most of its
laughs when remade as Stop, You're Killing Me (1953) with Broderick Crawford.

An early comic plot gimmick was to have an ineffectual,
meek and mousy individual mistaken for a tough gang boss, with
predictable results.   This was done by El Brendel in Mr. Lemon
of Orange (1931), by Charles Butterworth in Baby Face Harrington
(1935) and by Edward G. Robinson in John Ford's The Whole Town's
Talking (1935).

But whether or not blood and comedy can mix successfully
was much more of a question in Some Like It Hot (1959).   Here
Jack Lemmon and Tony Curtis witness the St. Valentine's Day Massacre (presented in gory, realistic fashion).   They then disguise
themselves as women so that they can leave town with an all-girl
orchestra.   Some found the feature very funny, others thought the
central transvestite theme, apart from the blood bath used as a
comedy aid, in bad taste.

The plots of early gangster films graduated from the story of
a single operator on his way to becoming boss of the gang (e.g.,
Doorway to Hell), to that of two buddies doing the same thing (e.g.,
Public Enemy), and then went in for a switch on the latter theme:
the two boyhood friends who grow up on opposite sides of the law.
The one on the right side generally became the District Attorney
who prosecutes the lawless one [e.g., Manhattan Melodrama (1934)]
or the priest who walks the condemned pal to the electric chair
[e.g., Angels with Dirty Faces (1938)].   Another favorite gimmick
was to depict the falling out between two brothers in the police service [e.g., Beast of the City (1932)] or father and son [e.g., Sergeant Madden (1939)], the weak one getting involved with gangsters
and then trying to redeem himself at the end.

Intermingled with these formula plot devices were a few films
with highly unusual storylines which were neither imitated nor caused
any real trends.   The Amazing Dr. Clitterhouse (1938) based on a
successful play, had Edward G. Robinson as the title character who
believes crime is a "disease" and wishes to analyze the medical
symptons (pulse, heart beat, temperature) of hoodlums in on-the-job
action.   Brother Orchid (1940) again starred Robinson, but this
time as a mobster who is sheltered in a monastery to which he returns, but only as a completely "converted" man by the finale.

Another unique item, although it did not quite come off, was
Joe Macbeth (1955), filmed in England.   It retold the Shakespearean
plot in a modern gangster setting with Paul Douglas as the ambitious
mobster who kills gang leader Dutch (Harry Green) to help fulfill
the prophecy of greatness given him by a card-reading fortune teller.

The year 1955 also saw the release of Samuel Goldwyn's Guys
and Dolls, an underworld "operetta" in color and CinemaScope, in
which the mobsters constantly burst into song (something they did
not do in the 1929 or 1942 versions of the musical Broadway).   In
Guys and Dolls, derived from Damon Runyon stories, Frank Sinatra
sang on pitch but Marlon Brando did not.

There were trends in gangster films in the Fifties which gave
employment to many actors.   One was the exposé feature which could
be elaborate and well-handled--from the study of the corrupt longshoreman's union in On the Waterfront (1954), which won several
Academy Awards, to the tacky New Orleans Uncensored (1955).
Spurred on by the Senator Kefauver crime hearings, such pictures
attempted, with good or bad results, to yank from the headlines
stories of big-scale graft, corruption, and violence as masterminded
by highly organized crime syndicates.   It seemed that no city in
America was sacred from such underworld control, and, in the mid-
Fifties, most major cities served as sites and title names for such
crime melodramas.

The other trend was put into gear by the enduringly popular,
French-made Rififi (1954), which set out the parameters of the so-
called heist film.   This Jules Dassin-directed feature, which un-

leashed its own series of sequels as well as countless imitations all
around the globe, told of a group of thieves who plan and execute a
carefully-mapped out robbery. No casual on-the-spot decision, the
crime would be painstakingly planned, analyzed, and executed. The
finale gimmick to Rififi, and to most of its successors, would be
the quirk of fate or human act that would lead the successful perpetrators of the heist to lose their ill-gotten gains. Seven Thieves
(1960) with Edward G. Robinson and Rod Steiger, Dead Heat on a
Merry-Go-Round (1966) with James Coburn, and Topkapi (1964) are
just a few of the many such entries. The latter, also directed by
Jules Dassin, benefited from a wry tongue-in-cheek quality, plus
beautiful on-location photography in Constantinople. Other films
played the heist gambit much more for laughs, as in the case of the
British-made The Lavender Hill Mob (1950) with Alec Guinness.

   With nearly every country in the world producing feature
films there was bound to be an attempt to blend the American-style
gangster yarn with storylines related to local customs and atmos-
pheres. The greatest influence on the underworld melodrama from
the Sixties onward was the Italian-American Mafia linkage. There
had been such offbeat studies as The Black Hand (1950) turned out
by MGM, with Gene Kelly starring in a turn-of-the-century study of
the Sicilian crime organization's influence in Manhattan. But that
was a rarity, as was the Italian-produced Mafia (1949). With changing mores in Hollywood's censorial boards, and particularly after the
phenomenal success of the teleseries "The Untouchables," anything
became possible. Moviemakers, it seemed, were now ready to
tackle the dreaded, deadly subject of the Mafiosa, the Cosa Nostra,
and other such similar criminal cartels based on Continental traditions. Thus came Murder Inc. (1960), Inside the Mafia (1959),
Mafioso (1962), The St. Valentine's Day Massacre (1967), Hail!
Mafia (1967), Mafia (1970), and the grandest picture of them all,
The Godfather (1972). This blockbuster, an Academy Award-winning
feature, managed to avoid using the word "Mafia" throughout its
scenario, but everyone was aware of what "The Family" was in the
film. The word "Mafia" was also frequently used in Crazy Joe
(1974), an Italian-American co-production. This Peter Boyle-Fred
Williamson feature had amazing parallels to real-life Mafia members, even to the extent of using newsreel footage of a Columbus
Day rally at which one leader was shot and the black gunmen im-
mediately dispatched. The restaurant where the title character
meets his end was correctly named, but, in a surprising throwback
to films of the early Thirties, the surnames of all characters were
altered (to protect the guilty?).

   Before, contemporary with, and after The Godfather, the
gangster film enjoyed a resurgence not seen since the Fifties. In
America, there were a seemingly unending flow of black exploitation
features which combined the detective-gangster-thriller genres with
minimum effect, except to clog up the screen with meaningless gore.
Meanwhile in Italy, a cycle started that threatens to outdo anything
engendered by the Sergio Leone Spaghetti Westerns of the Sixties.
Dino De Laurentiis, who later moved his operations (appropriately

enough) to New York, was a prime mover in this area with his The
Valachi Papers (1972) and The Stone Killers (1973), both starring
Charles Bronson.   Among other such entries churned out in Europe
were: Sicilian Connection (1973), about the drug trade from Italy to
New York and starring Ben Gazarra; Kiss Thy Hand (1973), with
Arthur Kennedy and John Saxon; Mafia Junction (1973); My Brother
Anastasia (1973), with Richard Conte as Alberto Anastasia; Love
and Death in a Women's Prison (1974), about the Mafia and sex-
starved women, etc., etc.   The French turned out Borsalino & Company (1973), a sequel to Borsalino (1970), with Alain Delon repeating his role in a further "nostalgia" study of Gallic gangsterism in
the Thirties.

A fondness for hoodlums of bygone decades has swept American filmaking.   Tony Curtis starred as Louis "Lepke" Buchalter in
Lepke (1975) and Ben Gazzara was tough guy Capone (1975) for
Roger Corman.   On the production charts are Hit the Dutchman, the
story of Dutch Schultz, a study of ex-mobster Mickey Cohen, and,
among others, Peter Bogdanovich's Bugsy (Siegel).   And capping the
cycle where it once began, there is now talk of a new rendition of
Little Caesar, to be scripted by W. R. Burnett, the original author
of the story.   It would be titled Caesar's Last Days.

While all these major trends continue, such sub-trends as the
crooked policeman or detective move forward as well.   In early gangster films this type of character did not get used very much until
played by Barry Kelley in The Asphalt Jungle (1950).   The end of
this picture, which would be remade three times (once even as a
Western!), detailed the melancholy and paradoxical message: better
a police force with crooked cops on it than no police force at all.
(As if the possible choices ended there.)   The number of men in the
department "on the take" increased in subsequent films until finally
THEY took over and the hero was no less than a cop or detective
"loner" (Frank Sinatra, Clint Eastwood, Al Pacino, John Wayne, Elliott Gould) who spends as much time fighting the department (its
bureaucracy as well as its dishonest members) as he does crime.
Eventually--according to the current formula--he despairs, gives up
and leaves the force.

Things were less complicated in the early Thirties and far
less confusing to the average moviegoer who, watching a film like
Prime Cut (1972) today, suddenly realizes with horror part-way
through that the cruelest, most amoral gang character in it (Lee
Marvin) is also the "hero."

Audiences did not need a score card in the old days to tell
the good guys from the bad guys.   Today one needs not only a score
card but intuition, ESP, and faith!

THE GREAT GANGSTER PICTURES

A BOUT DE SOUFFLE (Imperia, 1959)   90 min.

Producer, Georges de Beauregard; director, Jean-Luc Godard; idea, François Truffaut; screenplay, Godard; assistant director, Pierre Rissient; artistic supervisor, Claude Chabrol; music, Martial Sotlal; sound, Jacques Maumont; camera, Raoul Coutard; editors, Cecile Decugis, Lila Herman.

Jean-Paul Belmondo (Michel Poiccard, alias Laszlo Kovacs); Jean Seberg (Patricia Franchini); Daniel Boulanger (Police Inspector); Jean-Pierre Melville (Parvulesco); Liliane Robin (Minouche); Henri-Jacques Huet (Antonio Berrutti); Van Doude (The Journalist); Claude Mansard (Claudius Mansard); Michel Fabre (Plainclothes Policeman); Jean-Luc Godard (An Informer); Roger Hanin (Carl Zombach); Jean Domarchi (The Drunk); Richard Balducci (Tobnatchoff).

U.S. release: Breathless (Films Around the World, 1961) 89 min.

New wave director Jean-Luc Godard created quite a stir in France with this story of amoral young people. In America, the critical reaction was mixed; the acceptance of the new French cinema style was a few years off. The then ultra-conservative Films in Review lambasted it: "The sickness of Western culture is all too well exemplified in this jejune film from France. The story is intellectual juvenile delinquency par excellence."

On the other hand, Bosley Crowther (New York Times) lowered his guard sufficiently to admit, "Powerful--not in a strong, heroic way, not in a rich accumulation of a stunning philosophy ... but in its harsh illumination of a stratum of modern young folks, who here happen to be Parisians but who might be matched in a metropolis of the Western world." Variety quite rightly noted, "This film shows the immediate influence of Yank actioners and socio-psycho thrillers. This adds up to a production resembling such past Yank pix as Gun Crazy, They Live By Night and Rebel Without a Cause. But it has local touches in its candor, lurid lingo and frank love scenes."

What do underworld figures do when they are not engaged in crime or paying for their misdeeds? Very often their lives are as sedentary and boring as the average, law-abiding person's. In A Bout De Souffle, Godard, in his first feature-length film, examines with theatrical reality the hum-drum existence of Michel Poiccard (Belmondo), a loafer who nominally treats his life as if he were Humphrey Bogart in one of those 1940s movies. He has no scruples,

15

no strong desires, no charitable thoughts of others. Part of his
life-style includes his liaison with American Patricia Franchini (Seberg) who sells the Herald-Tribune on the Champs-Elysées. En
route from Marseilles to Paris to see Patricia, he steals a car,
engaged in reckless driving, and, when cornered by the law, shoots
down a policeman in cold blood. Living for the moment, he mugs
and robs a Parisian to pay for his evening with Patricia. When he
refuses to show any concern about the fact that he has made her
pregnant, the American expatriot, in a fit of anger, informs on him
to the police, and then regrets her hasty action. But he refuses to
show alarm, and even when he is ambushed by the law enforcers
and is lying dying, he merely smiles up at her, calls her--affection-
ately--"a little bitch, " and then dies.

     Just as Nicholas Ray's (gangster) thrillers had had an enor-
mous influence on Godard, so Godard and his A Bout de Souffle
would exert an evident effect on the course of the genre. Filmmakers thereafter would perceive that there was boxoffice gold, as well
as artistic integrity, in portraying the lawbreaker as a common man,
a character whose appeal (romantic image?) derives from a nihilis-
tic rather than an antagonistically destructive point of view.

AL CAPONE   (Allied Artists, 1959)   105 min.

     Producers, John H. Burrows, Leonard J. Ackerman; direc-
tor, Richard Wilson; based on the life of Al Capone; screenplay,
Malvin Wald, Henry Greenberg; music, David Raksin; art director,
Hilyard Brown; set decorator, Joseph Kish; assistant directors,
Lindsley Parsons, Jr., Phil Rawlins; makeup, Dave Grayson; wardrobe, Russell Hanlin, Forrest T. Butler, Sabine Manella; special effects, Dave Koehler; sound, Charles Schelling, Tom Lambert, Joe
Keener; camera, Lucien Ballard; editor, Walter Hannemann; montage
editor, Neil Brunnenkant.

     Rod Steiger (Al Capone); Fay Spain (Maureen Flannery); Mur-
vyn Vye (Bugs Moran); James Gregory (Sergeant Schaeffer); Nehe-
miah Persoff (Johnny Torrio); Lewis Charles (Hymie Weiss); Joe De
Santis (Big Jim Colosimo); Martin Balsam (Mack Keely); Louis
Quinn (Joe Lorenzo); Raymond Bailey (Mr. Brancato); Robert Gist
(O'Bannion); Peter Dane (Pete Flannery); Al Ruscio (Tony Genero);
Ron Soble (Tony); Lewis Charles (Weiss); Roy Jenson (Customer);
Allen Jaffe (Bodyguard); Jim Bacon (Reporter); Robert Christopher
(Man); Joseph D. Sargent (Buell); Clegg Hoyt (Lefty); Mason Curry
(Tailor); Jack Orrison (Police Clerk); Sam Scar (Louie); John Mitch-
um (Photographer).

     The gigantic success of the teleseries "The Untouchables"
revived great interest in Al Capone and in the Chicago gang era of
the 1920s. The ganglord's family attempted to stop, obviously without success, the production of this film-biography of the famous
hoodlum.

     The picture was made in a documentary style. It followed
Brooklyn hoodlum Capone (Rod Steiger) from his arrival in Chicago
in 1920. He first becomes a bouncer for Johnny Torrio's (Nehemiah

Al Ruscio, Rod Steiger and Louis Quinn in a publicity pose from
<u>Al Capone</u> (1959).

Persoff) gaming joint. Ambitious for power, Capone urges Torrio
to murder his uncle (Joe De Santis) and to take over the area during
this lucrative Prohibition era. Later, when Torrio retires, Al rises
to the post of criminal kingpin of Chicago, with a yearly intake of
over $100 million. The chronicle concludes with Capone's intern-
ment at Alcatraz on a federal income tax evasion charge, and his
later release and death (on January 25, 1947, of paresis).

"A flashback to the kind of gangster film that Warners did
so well in the early thirties, Capone shares their sense of pained
dedication to rousing the public conscience, as if the studio would
have made the picture even if it did not know that such revelations
of vice and violence generally paid off handsomely" (Saturday Review). The television-style montage-editing may have mitigated
against the film's production values, but the depiction of violence
and gore was so vividly handled that it mattered to few. Among
the violent highlights are the Chicago gang wars, including the infamous St. Valentine's Day massacre (where Capone tried to eradicate Bugs Moran's boys), and the murder of newspaper reporter
Mack Keely (Martin Balsam). (Balsam's unorthodox newsman was
based on real-life reporter Jack Lingle, whose slaying in Chicago's
La Salle Street tunnel did rouse public indignation and led to a federal investigation.)

The psychological analysis of Capone was emphasized in the
film, such as the effect of his scarred face and his attraction to nifty
clothes. Although one may wish the film had told more about the
criminal's motivation, Steiger's bravuro performance has its own
spellbinding allure. Particularly engaging is his attraction to Maureen Flannery (Fay Spain), the widow of one of his early victims.
Powerful with his confederates, he finds himself all too often at her
mercy. As Films in Review decided, "... [Steiger's] success in
the part does not derive from the creation of an image in the audience's mind, but from leaving undisturbed an image of which the
audience is already possessed."

Almost a vintage piece in its day, Al Capone added no new
dimensions to the genre. While it did not glamorize the arch criminal, neither did it follow yellow journalism by becoming a devastating pictorial critique of the notorious Chicago gangland baron.

ALGIERS (United Artists, 1938) 95 min.

Producer, Walter Wanger; director, John Cromwell; based on
the story Pepe le Moko by Detective Ashelbe; screenplay, John Howard
Lawson, James M. Cain; art director, Alexander Toluboff; music,
Vincent Scott, Mohammed Igorbouchen; song, Scott, Igorbouchen, Ann
Ronell; camera, James Wong Howe.

Charles Boyer (Pepe le Moko); Sigrid Gurie (Ines); Hedy
Lamarr (Gaby); Joseph Calleia (Slimane); Gene Lockhart (Regis);
Johnny Downs (Pierrot); Alan Hale (Grandpere); Mme. Nina Koshetz
(Tania); Joan Woodbury (Aicha); Claudia Dell (Marie); Robert Greig
(Giroux); Stanley Fields (Carlos); Charles D. Brown (Max); Ben
Halls (Gil); Koliz L'Arbi (Sergeant); Walter Kingsford (Louvain);
Paul Harvey (Janvier); Bert Roach (Bertier); Luana Walters (Wait-
ress).

"Come with me to the Casbah" is the famous dialog snippet
attributed to this film. However, like most enduring screen lines,
it really did not get uttered in this picture.
Taken from Detective Ashelbe's novel Pepe le Moko, Algiers
was producer Walter Wanger's American remake of the highly-re-
garded French film (q. v.) of 1937. For this moody, slow moving
and exotic Hollywood rendition, Charles Boyer was cast as Pepe.
As long as Pepe remains in the sanctuary of the Casbah section of
Algiers he is free from legal capture. For the love of the beautiful and tempestuous Gaby (Hedy Lamarr), however, he leaves the
native girl (Sigrid Gurie) who loves him, and meets his demise.
"Algiers is one of those naturals in pictures, having action,
romance, strange places and predicaments, and the peg of character
to hang it on" (New Republic). For those who enjoyed fantasies
about crooks and the criminal milieu, Algiers added greatly to their
romantic distortions. To start with, the mysterious, unfamiliar native quarters of Algiers provided great charm and intrigue. The
atmosphere was intensified by the interplay of the lead characters
who moved in and out of the shadows and sunlight, as if gliding in
a world of make believe (which it was).
Boyer's jewel thief had a dual nature. He could be hard,
fast, and sinister when the occasion demanded, but he preferred the
guise of the romantic, a man engulfed in his own fantasies. Ironically, in his great passion for Gaby, to whom he sings "C'est la
Vie, " he confuses the lovely creature with his long-lost city of Paris.
At one point he informs the limpid-eyed beauty that to him she not
only represents Paris but even that city's subways.
On a slightly more realistic level is the interplay between the
underworld and the native police. The latter, including Slimane (Joseph Calleia), have an understanding with their adversaries, biding
their time until the gangsters tip their hands or move outside the
sanctuary of their quarter. When the weak-willed Regis (Gene Lockhart) turns stool-pigeon, he is punished according to criminal ethics.
Dark-haired Lamarr became an American movie star "over-
night" with this film, and Boyer solidified his popularity as a top
screen lover. Their screen love affair, which obscured the gangster elements of the film, was termed "sensational" by Variety and
the public. The New York Times judged Algiers as "... one of the
finest directorial jobs, one of the most rewarding in its performances, clearly one of the most interesting and absorbing dramas of
the season.... few films this season, or any other, have sustained
their mood so brilliantly. "
Those movie viewers who had seen the French film original
could easily discern how Hollywood had diverted the bitter-sweet
point of view of the former into one of romantic optimism-fatality.
Nine years after the release of Algiers, Universal would remake the
story as Casbah (q. v.), with Tony Martin as a singing Pepe.

ALIBI (United Artists, 1929) 8, 167'

Presenter, Joseph M. Schenck; producer-director, Roland
West; based on the play Nightstick by John Griffith Wray, J. C.

Nugent, Elaine S. Carrington; screenplay-titles-dialog, West, C.
Gardner Sullivan; art director, William Cameron Menzies; music
arranger, Hugo Riesenfeld; choreography, Fanchon; camera, Ray
June; editor, Hal Kern.
      Chester Morris (Chick Williams); Harry Stubbs (Buck Back-
man); Mae Busch (Daisy Thomas); Eleanor Griffith (Joan Manning);
Irma Harrison (Totts the Cabaret Dancer); Regis Toomey (Danny
McGunn); Al Hill (Brown); James Bradbury, Jr. (Blake); Elmer Ballard (Soft Malone the Cab Driver); Kernan Cripps (Trask the Plainclothesman); Purnell B. Pratt (Pete Manning the Police Sergeant);
Pat O'Malley (Detective Tommy Glennon); DeWitt Jennings (Policeman O'Brien); Edward Brady (George Stanislaus David); Edward Jar-
don, Virginia Flohri (Singers in Theatre).

      Chester Morris was one of the first big stars to evolve out
of the talkies, having come from the initiation of the Broadway stage.
His fine speaking voice, mannerisms, and good looks kept him a top
name throughout the 1930s.   One of his first Hollywood efforts was
a top crime thriller, Alibi, which focused on the rather unpleasant
topic of a hood (Morris) taking advantage of the girl who loved him
and using her as a shield for his criminal activity.
      Alibi made good use of its new found sound technique to pre-
sent the story of Chick Williams (Morris), a gangster who marries
the daughter (Eleanor Griffith) of a policeman.   He uses her as his
alibi for a robbery he commits during a theatrical intermission.
The girl thinks the man she loves is law-abiding.   Later, the police
sneak an agent (Regis Toomey) into Chick's gang, but he is uncovered and Chick kills him.   The climax occurs when Williams is cornered by the police in his own home.
      Little seen today, Alibi was justly popular during its initial
release.   However, it must have been dated even a few years after
its issuance due to the rapid advances in sound technology and acting standards.   Still the film remains as one of the first gangster
epics of the sound era and is certainly worthy of occasional revival.

ALL THE WAY   see   THE JOKER IS WILD

THE AMAZING DR. CLITTERHOUSE   (Warner Bros. , 1938)   87 min.

      Associate producer, Robert Lord; director, Anatole Litvak;
based on the play by Barre Lyndon; screenplay, John Wexley, John
Huston; assistant director, Jack Sullivan; music, Max Steiner; art
director, Carl Jules Weyl; camera, Tony Gaudio; editor, Warren
Low.
      Edward G. Robinson (Dr. Clitterhouse); Claire Trevor (Jo
Keller); Humphrey Bogart (Rocks Valentine); Gale Page (Nurse Ran-
dolph); Donald Crisp (Inspector Lane); Allen Jenkins (Okay); Thurston
Hall (Grant); John Litel (Prosecuting Attorney); Henry O'Neill (Judge);
Maxie Rosenbloom (Butch); Curt Bois (Tug); Bert Hanlon (Pal); Ward
Bond (Rabbitt); Vladimir Sokoloff (Popus); Billy Wayne (Candy); Rob-
ert Homans (Lieutenant Johnson); Georgia Caine (Mrs. Updyke);

Romaine Callender (Butler); Mary Field (Maid); Bob Reeves, Ray
Dawe (Policemen); Winifred Harris (Mrs. Ganswoort); Wade Bote-
ler (Captain MacLevy); Libby Taylor (Mrs. Jefferson); Joyce Wil-
liams (Patricia); Hal K. Dawson (Pedestrian); Monte Vandergrift,
Jack Mower (Detectives); Vera Lewis (Juror); Irving Bacon (Jury
Foreman); Edward Gargan (Sergeant); Thomas Jackson (Connors);
Bruce Mitchell (Bailiff); Susan Hayward (Patient); Ronald Reagan
(Announcer's Voice).

  The criminal mind has always fascinated psychology researchers. Occasionally films are made on the subject of the amoral or
anti-social individual, The Bad Seed (1955) probably being one of
the most definitive of its type. The Amazing Dr. Clitterhouse also
used this theme, but the result was only a slick melodrama with an
implausible finale. In later years, co-star Humphrey Bogart would
refer to the film deprecatingly as "The Amazing Dr. Clithoris."
  Edward G. Robinson starred as Dr. Clitterhouse, a professor writing a detailed volume on criminal mentality who becomes a
gang member to study better his subjects. He masterminds several jewel robberies and meets a female fence (Trevor) who works for
hood Rocks Valentine (Bogart). The professor later joins Rocks'
gang and annotates their reactions to situations, including those of
Valentine who becomes jealous of Clitterhouses's attentions to attractive Jo Keller. The racketeer locks the doctor in a cold storage
vault during a robbery, but the latter is saved by another hood (Rosenbloom). When Clitterhouse completes his exhaustive studies he
breaks away from the gang, but Rocks demands that he fleece his
rich friends or else be exposed for his recent criminal activities.
Clitterhouse, whose mind has been more affected by his anti-social
associates than he realizes, decides he needs a chapter on the rationale and the act of homicide. He poisons Rocks and coolly observes and records the crook's reactions as he dies. Later the
educator is arrested for the crime. However, a jury acquits (!)
him because he claims he was sane (and not insane as he first
pleaded) during the crime.
  In its day--this was the golden age of Hollywood--The Amazing Dr. Clitterhouse never received its full credit as the deft study
of criminality and its allure that it was. The New York Herald-
Tribune granted that it was "an intriguing and farcical photoplay"
and the New York Times admitted the picture was "smooth and satisfactory." But it remained for Otis Ferguson (The New Republic)
to perceive, "The story is ingenious, but Anatole Litvak and his
producing-acting crew have so thoroughly kept the lark mood of it
while setting up the necessary undercurrent of interest and suspense
that it is hard to see where conception leaves off and the shaping
into motion begins."
  What wouldn't motion picture producers give today for such
a cast as is in this film? It included Robinson, Bogart, Trevor,
Donald Crisp, Allen Jenkins, Thurston Hall, John Litel, Henry
O'Neill, Vladimir Sokoloff, and Curt Bois. But, in 1938, most of
these figures were "merely" just part of the Warner Bros. stock
company. As for Robinson's lead role of the Jekyll-Hyde figure,
he had yet to escape the image of Little Caesar (1930), q.v., and

all that entailed. Thus film critics insisted that he was not the
proper figure to play this title role and that Sir Cedric Hardwicke
had handled the characterization more subtly on stage.

A good deal of credit for this film must go to both director
Anatole Litvak, who ably explored the movie medium with his subject matter, and scenarists John Wexley and John Huston, who
added so many wry touches to the potentially stereotyped mobster
characters.

THE ANDERSON TAPES (Columbia, 1971) C-98 min.

Producer, Robert M. Weitman; associate producer, George
Justin; director, Sidney Lumet; based on the novel by Lawrence
Sanders; screenplay, Frank R. Pierson; music-music conductor,
Quincy Jones; production designer, Benjamin J. Kasazkrow; art di-
rector, Philip Rosenberg; set decorator, Alan Hicks; makeup, Saul
Meth; assistant director, Alan Hopkins; technical consultant, Roger
G. Battle; sound, Dennis Maitland, Jack Fitzstephens, Al Gramag-
lia; camera, Arthur J. Ornitz; editor, Joanne Burke.

Sean Connery (Duke Anderson); Dyan Cannon (Ingrin Ever-
leigh); Martin Balsam (Tommy Haskins); Ralph Meeker (Captain
Delaney); Alan King (Pat Angelo); Christopher Walken (The Kid); Val
Avery (Socks Parelli); Dick Williams (Spencer); Garrett Morris
(Everson); Stan Gottlieb (Pop); Anthony Holland (Psychologist); Con-
rad Bain (Dr. Rubincoff); Scott Jacoby (Jerry Bingham); Paula True-
man (Nurse); Margaret Hamilton (Miss Kaler); Judith Lowry (Mrs.
Hathaway); Max Showalter (Bingham); Janet Ward (Mrs. Bingham).

"Had the film restricted itself to its own Rififidom, it would
have remained as airtight as a legit alibi. But Lumet aims for
nothing less than political satire.... Unfortunately, failed comedy
and vigorous suspense are handcuffed together for the entire trip."
(Time). Professional safecracker, Duke Anderson (Connery) upon release from a ten-year prison sentence, visits his ex-girl Ingrid
Everleigh (Cannon) who now resides in a plush Fifth Avenue and
91st Street apartment building in New York City. He almost im-
mediately decides upon a heist to be carried out on Labor Day.
Having recruited his staff, which includes an electronics whiz (Walk-
en), an antique dealer (Balsam), and the resolute Pop (Gottlieb),
the plot is put into action. What none of the participants realizes
is that they are all under electronic surveillance for one or another
federal, state, or personal reasons. The caper is pulled off neatly, but a foul-up leads to a police blockade, with the gang being
killed or apprehended one by one. At the finish, the assorted wiretapping agents destroy their taped evidence to prevent prosecution
for their illegal acts.

With ex-James Bond star Connery (without toupee) at the
helm, The Anderson Tapes, filmed largely on location in Manhattan,
did a great deal to restore the dying heist genre. As Newsweek
analyzed this type of film, "The crime caper offers the straight-
forward pleasure of watching professionals ply their trade under

pressure. We are transfixed by the sweet methodology of safecrack-
ing or seduced by the complicated choreography of a bank. The
camera details each artful step as the tension builds and we shelve
our demands for higher meaning to enjoy an exercise in style and
suspense. "
         There was a good deal of commotion at the time this film
was lensed when it was learned that the downbeat ("crime does not
pay") ending had been contrived in order to make a future television
sale more viable.

ANGEL ON MY SHOULDER (United Artists, 1946) 100 min.

         Producer, Charles R. Rogers; associate producer, David W.
Siegel; director, Archie Mayo; story, Harry Segall; screenplay, Segall, Roland Kibbee; music-music director, Dimitri Tiomkin; art
director, Bernard Herzbrun; set decorator, Edward G. Boyle; costume designer, Maria Donovan; men's wardrobe, Robert Martien;
sound, Frank Webster; special effects, Harry Redmond, Jr. ; cam-
era, James Van Trees; editors, George Arthur, Asa (Boyd) Clark.
         Paul Muni (Eddie Kagle); Anne Baxter (Barbara Foster);
Claude Rains (Nick); Onslow Stevens (Dr. Matt Higgins); George
Cleveland (Albert); Erskine Sanford (Minister); Hardie Albright
(Smiley Williams); Marion Martin (Mrs. Bentley); James Flavin
(Bellamy); Murray Alper (Jim); Joan Blair (Brazen Girl); Fritz
Leiber (Scientist); Kurt Katch (Warden); Sarah Padden (Agatha, the
Minister's Wife); Maurice Cass (Lucius); Addison Richards (Big Har-
ry); Ben Welden (Shaggsy); Joel Friedkin (Malvola); Lee Shumway
(Bailiff); Russ Whiteman (Interne); Chester Clute (Kramer); Noble
Johnson (Trustee); Archie Twitchell (Police Sergeant).

         Issued in the fall of 1946, this Archie Mayo-directed gang-
ster-fantasy might have been fresh and witty had it not been so similar to the earlier film, Here Comes Mr. Jordan (1941). Both
films were scripted by Harry Seagall. Said New York Times critic
Bosley Crowther, "... the story is so imitative--and is repeated
so dutifully--that it's hard to feel any more towards it than a mildly nostalgic regard. "
         The film tells of a hoodlum (Paul Muni) who makes a pact
with the devil (Claude Rains) so that he can return to Earth and liquidate the man who cheated and killed him. In exchange he must
take over and disgrace the body of a good, honest judge. In the
latter assignment, Eddie Kagle falls for the judge's fiancée (Anne
Baxter) and later refuses to do the devil's bidding. He and the
"bee-zell-bub" make a fresh pact. Nick will allow the judge to live
out his natural life in peace and Eddie will be made a trustee in
Hell.
         While the film was badly dated in execution and was a box-
office dud, it did provide some interesting speculations on the criminal mind/soul. For example, when Muni's Eddie returns to Earth
and takes over for the judge, he finds to his amazement that despite everything, his primitive nature is essentially honest and humanitarian. Then, too, if Eddie Kagle, typical of many uncultured

criminals was such a corrupt soul, how come he could wage a moral battle (and win a draw at least) with Hades' diplomat? It was all another step in society's gradual realization that the lawbreaker could not be stereotyped as a purely evil person.

ANGELS WASH THEIR FACES   (Warner Bros., 1939)   76 min.

Director, Ray Enright; idea, Jonathan Finn; screenplay, Michael Fessier, Niven Busch, Robert Buckner; music director, Adolph Deutsch; camera, Arthur L. Todd; editor, James Gibbons.

Ann Sheridan (Joy Ryan); Ronald Reagan (Pat Remson); Billy Halop (Billy Shafter); Bonita Granville (Peggy Finnegan); Frankie Thomas (Gabe Ryan); Bobby Jordan (Bernie); Bernard Punsley (Sleepy Arkelian); Leo Gorcey (Leo Finnegan); Huntz Hall (Huntz); Gabriel Dell (Luigi); Henry O'Neill (Remson, Sr.); Eduardo Ciannelli (Martino); Berton Churchill (Mayor Dooley); Minor Watson (Maloney); Margaret Hamilton (Miss Hannaberry); Jackie Searle (Alfred Goonplatz); Bernard Nedell (Kroner); Cy Kendall (Hynes); Dick Rich (Shuffle); Grady Sutton (Gildersleeve); Aldrich Bowker (Turnkey); Marjorie Main (Mars. Arkelian); Robert Strange (Simpkins); Egon Brecher (Mr. Smith); Sibyl Harris (Mrs. Smith); Frank Coghlan, Jr. (Boy); Charles Trowbridge (Superintendent); Eddy Chandler (Cop); Ed Keane (Defense Attorney); Jack Wagner (Marsh); William Hopper (Photographer); John Ridgely, John Harron (Reporters); Harry Strang (Assistant Turnkey).

It is an accepted fact in Hollywood that sequels rarely match their originals. Angels with Dirty Faces (1938), q.v., had been such a superior entry that it would require a great deal for the successor to match it or improve upon the formula. None of the major technical talent associated with the first picture was involved with the second, and the lessened production values were very obvious in the results.

As directed by competent, but uninspired, Ray Enright, the movie told of a slum boy (Billy Halop) who is falsely accused of homicide by local crooked politicians. They wish to divert attention from their own nefarious deeds in an arson-set fire. When the boy's pals, the "Dead End Kids," take over the reins of government during Boys Week, the criminals are rounded up and Billy Shafter is set free. For romantic interest, the Kids also play cupid for Billy's sister Joy (Ann Sheridan) who, by the fadeout, weds Pat Remson (Ronald Reagan), the son of the district attorney (Henry O'Neill).

ANGELS WITH DIRTY FACES   (Warner Bros., 1938)   97 min.

Producer, Sam Bischoff; director, Michael Curtiz; story, Rowland Brown; screenplay, John Wexley, Warren Duff; art director, Robert Haas; music, Max Steiner; song, Fred Fisher and Maurice Spitalny; orchestrator, Hugo Friedhofer; costumes, Orry-Kelly; dialog director, Jo Graham; assistant director, Sherry

Shourds; makeup, Perc Westmore; sound, Everett A. Brown; camera, Sol Polito; editor, Owen Marks.

James Cagney (Rocky Sullivan); Pat O'Brien (Jerry Connelly); Humphrey Bogart (James Frazier); Ann Sheridan (Laury Martin); George Bancroft (Mac Keefer); Billy Halop (Soapy); Bobby Jordan (Swing); Leo Gorcey (Bim); Bernard Punsley (Hunky); Gabriel Dell (Pasty); Huntz Hall (Crab); Frankie Burke (Rocky as a Boy); William Tracy (Jerry as a Boy); Marilyn Knowlden (Laury as a Girl); Joe Downing (Steve); Adrian Morris (Blackie); Oscar O'Shea (Guard Kennedy); William Pawley (Bugs the Gunman); Edward Pawley (Guard Edwards); Earl Dwire (Priest); John Hamilton (Police Captain); Theodore Rand, Charles Sullivan (Gunmen); The St. Brendan's Church Choir (Themselves); William Worthington (Warden); James Farley (Railroad Yard Watchman); Pat O'Malley (Railroad Guard); Harry Hayden (Pharmacist); Dick Rich, Stevan Darrell (Gangsters); Charles Wilson (Buckley the Police Chief); Frank Coghlan, Jr., David Durand (Boys in Poolroom); Charles Trowbridge (Norton J. White the Press Editor); Lane Chandler (Guard); Jack Perrin (Death Row Guard); Poppy Wilde (Girl at Gaming Table); Eddie Brian (Newsboy); Vera Lewis (Soapy's Mother).

Always quick to embrace any marketable fad, Warner Bros. contracted the immensely popular boys, The Dead End Kids, from United Artists' Dead End (1937), q.v., and rushed them into Angels with Dirty Faces. Fattening the cast with James Cagney, Ann Sheridan, Humphrey Bogart, Pat O'Brien, and George Bancroft, the resultant feature was one of that studio's top grossers of 1938.

Angels with Dirty Faces, "one of the year's best titles" (Time), was basically a reworking of Manhattan Melodrama (1934), q.v. Two boyhood pals break into a boxcar. One escapes and grows up to become the local (Lower East Side) priest Father Jerry Connelly (O'Brien), while the other, Rocky, goes to reform school and maturates into a crook (Cagney). Years later in the old neighborhood, the paroled hood takes up with his tomboy tease (Sheridan) of the past. He becomes the idol of the neighborhood kids, threatening to undermine everything Father Connelly is trying to accomplish.

Meanwhile, Rocky attempts to retrieve $100,000 for an old job from his crooked lawyer (Bogart), now a club owner hooked up with a dishonest politician (Bancroft). When they refuse to give Cagney his financial due, he kidnaps Mac Keefer and threatens to reveal everything to the authorities. To save themselves, the gangsters form an uneasy alliance with Rocky. After Father Connelly starts a campaign to rid the city of criminals, Frazier and Keefer plan to have him killed. Sullivan, however, eradicates the duo to save the priest. Later, convicted of the crime, Rocky, at the clergyman's request, pretends to be afraid of dying and goes screaming to the electric chair. This about-face of the supposedly tough ·hero reduces his image in the eyes of the street kids, who no longer want to grow up to emulate him.

The New York Times called the film "a savage melodrama," while the New York Daily Mirror said it was "a rousing, bloody, brutal melodrama." Michael Curtiz, who would direct James

James Cagney and Pat O'Brien in Angels with Dirty Faces (1938).

Cagney in some of his most flavorful screen work, such as Jimmy
the Gent (1934) and Yankee Doodle Dandy (1942), was at the helm,
guiding veteran Cagney through the elaborate backlot and soundstage
sets.   Throughout the film, it was hard to decide whether to sym-
pathize with, hate or admire Cagney's Rocky.   The cocky young
man, who was a product of his environment, was clearly good at
heart, bright, and very responsive to his ambience.   He could ban-
ter with feisty Laury Martin (Sheridan, the widow of a taxi driver-turned
crook), joke with the priest, urge on the neighborhood kids to more
worthwhile projects, and accept life as it was.   Yet, and this was
the morally redeemable aspect of his character that was stressed,
when confronted by corruption and evil his was not an equally cor-
roded soul responding in like kind.   Instead, it was the pugnacious
response of a life-whipped mug who is experienced in the art of
survival and conquest.   It is fascinating to note that in 1938, some
thirty-five years before the shame of Watergate, the public noncha-
lantly accepted the presence on camera of dishonest politicos and
attorneys.
      With the blockbuster response to Angels with Dirty Faces,
it was obvious to the brothers Warner that a sequel was merited.
Hence, Angels Wash Their Faces (1939), q. v.

ANY NUMBER CAN WIN   see   MELODIE EN SOUS-SOL

THE ASPHALT JUNGLE   (MGM, 1950)   112 min.

Producer, Arthur Hornblow, Jr.; director, John Huston;
based on the novel by W. R. Burnett; screenplay, Ben Maddow,
Huston; art directors, Cedric Gibbons, Randall Duell; camera, Har-
old Rosson; editor, George Boemler.
Sterling Hayden (Dix Handley); Louis Calhern (Alonzo D. Em-
merich); Jean Hagen (Doll Conovan); James Whitmore (Gus Minissi);
Sam Jaffe (Dr. Erwin Riedenschneider); John McIntire (Police Com-
missioner Hardy); Marc Lawrence (Cobby); Barry Kelley (Lieutenant
Ditrich); Anthony Caruso (Louis Ciavelli); Teresa Celli (Maria Cia-
velli); Marilyn Monroe (Angela Phinlay); William Davis (Timmons);
Dorothy Tree (May Emmerich); Brad Dexter (Bob Brannon); Alex
Gerry (Maxwell); Thomas Browne Henry (James X. Connery); James
Seay (Janocek); Don Haggerty (Andrews); Henry Rowland (Franz
Schurz); Helene Stanley (Jeannie); Raymond Roe (Tall Boy); Chuck
Courtney (Red); Jean Carter (Woman); Strother Martin (Doldy); Hen-
ry Corden (Smith); Frank Cady (Night Clerk); Judith Wood (Fat Wom-
an); Patricia Miller (Thin Girl); Eloise Hardt (Vivian); Gene Evans,
Jack Stoney, Wesley Hopper (Policemen); Mary Anderson, J. J.
Smith, Ethel Lyons, Harry G. Burcher (Police Broadcasters).

"That Asphalt Pavement thing is full of nasty, ugly people
doing nasty, ugly things. I wouldn't walk across the room to see
a thing like that." Thus spoke Louis B. Mayer, then head of MGM,
about his studio's 1950 production, The Asphalt Jungle, which was
directed by John Huston. Critic James Agee, on the other hand,
thought Huston "... [made] a silk purse out of a sow's ear," while
New York Times called the film an "electrifying crime melodrama."
Taken from W. R. Burnett's novel, the film told the story
of the hiring of a gang of jewel thieves, the complex story of the
heist, the police action in arresting the hoodlums, and presented a
stirring critical examination of how crime affects society.
Nearly the last really good film directed by Huston to date,
The Asphalt Jungle is, considering the standards of the day, a rendition with no compromise. It shows the disgusting side of crime
and the measures that must be taken to thwart it. Huston personally selected Sterling Haydn, Sam Jaffe, Louis Calhern, and Marilyn
Monroe for their roles, and he won the Screen Directors Guild
Award for this feature.
Participating in the sordid dealings were a mild-mannered
ex-convict (Jaffe), a fast-shooting rough guy (Hayden) who wants
money to buy back the family's farm in Kentucky, the moll (Hagen)
who loves him, the evil lawyer (Calhern) who poses as a fence, and
such underlings as Gus Minissi (Whitmore), Louis Ciavelli
(Caruso), and bookie Cobby (Lawrence). The latter finances the operations. Not to be overlooked, especially in retrospect, is Marilyn Monroe as Angela Philay. In her eleventh-billed role, she was
the "niece" of Calhern, a euphemism for censorship-taboo mistress.

Louis Calhern, Sterling Hayden, Jean Hagen and Sam Jaffe in a pose
for The Asphalt Jungle (1950).

"If there should be a qualification about the picture, it is
that crime does not flourish in our day as it did when The Public
Enemy was shown to a somewhat shocked public twenty years ago.
Much of the plot seems more fabricated than realistic and the strands
of the melodrama have a tendency to unravel." Evidently Howard
Barnes of the New York Herald-Tribune was not very prophetic about
the criminal aspect of American society. The following year, Senator Estes Kefauver's investigations would reveal widespread criminal
activities throughout the U.S.
        So germane was the theme of The Asphalt Jungle that it would
serve as the basis for a teleseries, "The Asphalt Jungle" (1961),
and three additional theatrical film remakes: The Badlanders (1958),
an Alan Ladd Western; Cairo (1962) with George Sanders; and Cool
Breeze (1972), q.v., a black exploitation actioner.

BABY FACE HARRINGTON   (MGM, 1935)   61 min.

        Producer, Edgar Selwyn; director, Raoul Walsh; based on the
play Something to Brag About by Selwyn, William LeBaron; screenplay, Nunnally Johnson, Edwin H. Knopf; art directors, Cedric Gibbons, Howard Campbell; set decorator, Edwin B. Willis; music,
Sam Wineland; camera, Oliver T. Marsh; editor, William S. Gray.

Charles Butterworth (Willis); Una Merkel (Millicent); Harvey Stephens (Ronald); Nat Pendleton (Hawk); Eugene Pallette (Uncle Henry); Donald Meek (Skinner); Ruth Selwyn (Dorothy); Dorothy Liaaire (Edith); Edward J. Nugent (Albert); Robert Livingston (George); Stanley Fields (Mullens); Raymond Brown (McGuire); Wade Boteler (Flynn); Bradley Page (Dave); Richard Carle (Judge Forbes); G. Pat Collins (Hank); Claude Gillingwater, Sr. (Colton); Galon Gough (Gangster); Carl Stockdale (Mr. Tunney); Sherry Hall (Harry); Walter Maher, Donald Kerr (Reporters); Charles C. Wilson (City Editor); Paul Porcasi (Headwaiter).

The gangster film was going through another one of its declines as a screen cycle when this modest satire came along.   A petty clerk (Butterworth) harassed by his wife (Merkel) is mistakenly believed to be Public Enemy #2.   The naive, guileless soul proceeds to become involved with a gang and jail life; as the final event, he captures the big gangster.   Proclaimed a hero, he returns home to his nagging but loyal wife.   She has known all along that his rightful place is by the hearthside with his feet is a mustard bath. As they jokingly (?) admit, the only "public enemy" in their home has been the influenza germ.

BABY FACE MORGAN   (Producers Releasing Corp. , 1942)   60 min.

Producer, Jack Schwartz; director, Arthur Dreifuss; story, Oscar Brodney, Jack Rubin; screenplay, Edward Dein, Jack Rubin; camera, Art Reed; editor, Dan Miller.
Mary Carlisle (Virginia Clark); Richard Cromwell ("Baby Face" Morgan); Robert Armstrong ("Doc" Rogers); Chick Chandler (Oliver Harrison); Charles Judels ("Deacon" Davis); Warren Hymer (Wise Willie); Vince Barnett (Lefty Lewis); Ralf Harolde (Joe Torelli); Hal Dawson (J. B. Brown); Pierce Lyden (Gap).

From the nearest of low, low economy producers on poverty row came this minor effort.   Despite everything, it had an engaging comedy premise.   Rural son (Cromwell) of an ex-racketeer is made the nominal head of a city mob which wants to bring back the good old days.   The gang reasons that since the F.B.I. is so busy ensnaring spies and saboteurs, the coast will be clear for their own illegal activities.   It is a shame that the paltry but promising feature had such stagnant handling.

BABY FACE NELSON   (United Artists, 1957)   85 min.

Producer, Al Zimbalist; associate producer, Byron Roberts; director, Donald Siegel; screenplay, Daniel Mainwaring; camera, Hal Mohr; editor, Leon Barschke.
Mickey Rooney (Lester Gillis [Baby Face Nelson]); Carolyn Jones (Sue); Sir Cedric Hardwicke (Doc Saunders); Chris Dark (Jerry); Ted de Corsia (Rocca); Emile Meyer (Mac); Anthony Caruso (Hamilton); Leo Gordon (John Dillinger); Dan Terranova (Miller);

Mickey Rooney and Leo Gordon in <u>Baby Face Nelson</u> (1957).

       Shot on a nineteen-day filming schedule by director Don Sie-
gel and producer Al Zimbalist, this retelling of the story of the
psychopathic hoodlum Baby Face Nelson (Rooney) closely followed
the events in the criminal's life.   Budgeted at $175,000, the film
was a good moneymaker.   Rooney and Jack Elam (as Fatso) received the equivalent of the French Academy Award for their performances and the black-and-white picture wàs widely shown in
Europe.   One of the film's chief assets was Daniel Mainwaring's
script, which detailed Nelson's mental deterioration from psychosis
to insanity.
       The film opens with Nelson already an adult and mentally
disturbed.   When released from prison, having served time for an
earlier misdeed, he is offered a contract by a hoodlum (Ted de
Corsia) to kill a union leader.   He refuses.   Instead, Nelson seeks
out his girl (Carolyn Jones).   Later, when he returns to his hotel,
the police arrest him for the union head's murder, a crime committed with his gun.   On the way to prison, Sue helps Nelson to
escape and he murders his betrayer, but is then shot himself in a
robbery.   He is treated by a doctor (Cedric Hardwicke) who is attracted to Sue.   While at the hospital Baby Face meets a member

of the Dillinger gang. At the time Dillinger (Leo Gordon) is
teamed with a robbery expert, Fatso. During one heist Nelson guns
down six guards. When Dillinger is later killed, Nelson takes over
the gang, kills the physician, and embarks on a murder-robbery
rampage. Finally the F.B.I. surround his hideout and he is injured in the shootout. He persuades Sue to complete the job. He
eggs her on by telling her he planned to kill two small boys who
may have squealed on him. The girl shoots him and he dies in a
small graveyard.

   At the time, establishment newspapers in the U.S. passed off
Baby Face Nelson as an artistic bust: "... [it] is a thoroughly
standard, pointless and even old-fashioned gangster picture, the
kind that began going out along with the oldtime sedans" (New York
Times). However, in subsequent years, many critical sources
would agree that this Siegel film was a turning point in the genre,
leading directly to such later psychological gangster studies as
Bonnie and Clyde (1967), q.v., and Bloody Mama (1970), q.v.

BATTLING BELLHOP   see   KID GALAHAD (1937)

THE BEAST OF THE CITY   (MGM, 1932) 87 min.

   Director, Charles Brabin; story, W. R. Burnett; screenplay,
John L. Mahin; camera, Norbert Brodine; editor, Anne Bauchens.
   Walter Huston (Captain Jim Fitzpatrick); Jean Harlow (Daisy
Stevens); Wallace Ford (Ed Fitzpatrick); Jean Hersholt (Sam Bel-
monte); Dorothy Peterson (Mary Fitzpatrick); Tully Marshall (Attor-
ney Michaels); John Miljan (District Attorney); Emmett Corrigan
(Bert the Police Chief); Warner Richmond (Tom); Sandy Roth (Mac);
J. Carrol Naish (Pietro Cholo); Lieutenant Edward Coppo (Finger-
print Expert); George Chandler (Reporter); Clarence Wilson (Coroner); Charles Sullivan (Cop in Hall); Morgan Wallace (Police Captain); Mickey Rooney (Mickey Fitzpatrick); Nat Pendleton (Abe the
Gunman); Arthur-Hoyt (Witness); Robert Homans (Desk Sergeant);
Ed Brophy (Police Announcer); Julie Haydon (Blonde); Chuck Hamilton, Tom London (Cops).

   One of the most prolific writers of gangster novels and
scenarios was W. R. Burnett, and in 1932 Metro-Goldwyn-Mayer
filmed The Beast of the City, based on one of his stories and directed by Charles Brabin. The New York Post said, "... it is a
well written story, brilliantly directed and its excitement seems to
spring from natural causes rather than any artificialities imposed
on them by the author." The New York Times enthused, "... [it]
is endowed with vitality and realism, the various characters being
exceptionally true to life." Such compliments would be valued by
any producing studio. But that MGM, a studio never noted for
graphic realism on screen, should receive such praise was noteworthy indeed.
   An honest cop (Huston) tries to jail a racketeer (Hersholt)
but cannot catch him in any misdeeds. Instead, Jim Fitzpatrick is

assigned to a quieter precinct. When he makes headlines by capturing two holdup men, a reform commission appoints him police chief.
In his new post he rushes to arrest Sam Belmonte and, in so doing,
upsets many powerful people. Another problem is that his dishonest
brother (Ford) is on the payroll of local hoodlums and goes with
Daisy Stevens (Harlow), a girl connected with Belmonte. Later Ed
is jailed for his participation in a money shipment robbery, but
scare tactics cause a jury to pronounce him innocent. Jim then decides to take a dozen of his best men and have a showdown with
Belmonte. Ashamed of his past, Ed sides with his brother and is
later killed by Belmonte. A Bloody gun battle ensues and most of
the hoodlums and cops are killed, including Daisy.

The Beast of the City never attained the public popularity of
Metro's earlier The Secret Six (1931), q.v., or Dance, Fools, Dance
(1931), q.v., for it was too uncompromising in its study of gangland versus law enforcer practices, without the usual overdose of
romantic interest.

BIG BAD MAMA   (New World, 1974)   C-83 min.

Producer, Roger Corman; associate producer, Jon Davison;
director, Steve Carver; screenplay, William Norton, Frances Doel;
art director, Peter Jamison; music, David Grisman; costumes, Jac
McAnelley; sound, Robert Gravenor; camera, Bruce Logan; editor,
Tina Hirsch.

Angie Dickinson (Wilma McClatchie); William Shatner (Wil-
liam J. Baxter); Tom Skerritt (Fred Diller); Susan Sennett (Billy
Jean McClatchie); Robbie Lee (Polly McClatchie); Noble Willingham
(Barney); Joan Prather (Jane Kingston); Royal Dano (Reverend John-
son); William O'Connell (Preacher); Ralph James (Sheriff); Shannon
Christie (Stripper); Sally Kirkland (Bit).

Processed for the exploitation market, this film was labeled
a rip-off by some trade papers. Variety, for example, charged the
scripters with a "cynical contempt for the audience." As the same
journal reasoned, Big Bad Mama "... is mostly rehashed Bonnie
and Clyde with a bit more blood and Angie Dickinson taking off her
clothes for sex scenes with the crooks in her life...." The Hollywood Reporter was more indulgent, judging the movie to have
"... enormous vitality and genuine visual flair as it affectionately
displays the radiant warmth of its star, Angie Dickinson."

Within its compressed screen time, this "R"-rated feature
follows Wilma (Dickinson) who decides that a poverty-filled life in
Paradise, Texas, 1932-style, is no fit existence for her two daughters (Sennett and Lee). Almost before they know it, and apparently
almost by accident, the trio become bank heisters. Later, they
establish a "family" with professional bank robber Fred Diller and
bad-luck gent William J. Baxter.

The gangster genre has long been fodder for the exploitation-
type feature, but rarely has the emphasis been so geared to sexual
titillation as in Big Bad Mama. Interesting character moments are

provided by Shannon Christie as a stripper, Joan Prather as the
kidnapped heiress, and Ralph James as the doughnut-gouging sheriff.

THE BIG BANKROLL   see   KING OF THE ROARING TWENTIES

THE BIG CITY   (MGM, 1928)   6,838'

Director-story, Tod Browning; screenplay, Waldemar Young;
titles, Joe Farnham; set designer, Cedric Gibbons; wardrobe, Lucia
Coulter; camera, Henry Sharp; editor, Harry Reynolds.

Lon Chaney (Chuck Collins); Marceline Day (Sunshine); James
Murray (Curly); Betty Compson (Helen); Matthew Betz (Red); John
George (The Arab); Virginia Pearson (Tennessee); Walter Percival
(Grogan); Lew Short (O'Hara); Eddie Sturgis (Blinkie).

Although Josef von Sternberg is largely given credit for creating the first definitive gangster films (The Dragnet, Underworld,
Thunderbolt), the team of producer-director-writer Tod Browning
and actor Lon Chaney have to their credit a number of gangster features, some of which predate Sternberg's Paramount trilogy.

Nine years after Chaney and Betty Compson became stars in
The Miracle Man, the duo appeared together in The Big City. In
it, Chuck Collins operates a cabaret as a front for his fence operation of rare jewels. His girl (Compson) manages a costume shop
which is used by Chuck for his criminal activities. When Collins
finds a rival gang fleecing his cabaret customers, he develops a
scheme whereby the rival hood (Betz) unknowingly turns over his
loot to members of Chuck's gang. Finally, in retribution, an employee (Day) of Helen's convinces Chuck and his partner (Murray) to
go straight while Red goes to jail.

Rather naive in its concept, this eight-reeler provided the
popular Chaney with an opportunity to play a non-makeup role as
the gangster. Instead of his usual emphasis on the freakish, Chaney
spotlighted his hood characterization with a slick appearance and
flashy clothes.

THE BIG COMBO   (Allied Artists, 1955)   89 min.

Producer, Sidney Harmon; director, Joseph H. Lewis; screenplay, Philip Yordan; production designer, Rudi Feld; set decorator,
Jack McConaghy; makeup, Larry Butterworth; music, David Raksin;
assistant directors, Mack Wright, Robert Justman; sound, Earl Snyder; camera, John Alton; editor, Robert Eisen.

Cornel Wilde (Detective Lieutenant Diamond); Richard Conte
(Brown); Brian Donlevy (McClure); Jean Wallace (Susan Cabot); Rob-
ert Middleton (Peterson); Lee Van Cleef (Fante); Earl Holliman
(Mingo); Helen Walker (Alicia); Jay Adler (Sam Hill); John Hoyt
(Dreyer); Ted De Corsia (Bettini); Heleen Stanton (Rita); Roy Gordon
(Audubon); Whit Bissell (Doctor); Steve Mitchell (Bennie Smith; Bruce
Sharpe (Detective); Donna Drew (Miss Hartleby); Rita Gould (Nurse).

Cornel Wilde and Ted De Corsia in The Big Combo (1955).

Director Joseph H. Lewis' final foray into the gangster film
genre came with The Big Combo, from Philip Yordan's script.   The
New York Times called it a "sputtering, misguided antique. "   But
there is far more to the film than is evident on first glance.   (In
The Velvet Light Trap, #11, 1974, Tom Flinn presents a lengthy
discussion of both The Big Combo and The Big Heat, q.v.)   In its
buckshot presentation, the picture has a lot to say on the subject of
big business crime, circa 1950, as well as that perpetually intriguing aspect of underworld life, the link between criminal behavior
and sexuality.   Taking such below-the-surface aspects into account,
a critic can only be very hesitant to agree with the same Times
critic who further added, "... [the film] isn't very big or good ...
a shrill, clumsy and rather old-fashioned crime melodrama with all
hands pulling in opposite directions. "
     A heavily violent film, The Big Combo concerns a detective
(Wilde) who tries to get evidence against a vicious hoodlum (Conte)
while both men are at odds over the same girl (Wallace).   Full of
mayhem, including six killings, the film leaned very heavily on its
theme of brutality.   The cast was uniformly good, especially Conte
and Donlevy, the latter as the former's quiet, sadistic henchman.
Only a distinct lessening in the enforcement of the film industry's
production code could have allowed the unstated but evident homosexual relationship (Van Cleef, Holliman) to exist in the film, as

well as the bizarre alliance between Conte's Brown and Wallace's
Susan Cabot, a tie bordering on the masochistic.
    To be noted especially is the de-emphasis of the Italian Ma-
fia stereotype, with Conte's "Brown" angling for a very American
look.

THE BIG HEAT (Columbia, 1953) 90 min.

    Producer, Robert Arthur; director, Fritz Lang; based on the
novel by William P. McGivern; screenplay, Sidney Boehm; art di-
rector, Robert Peterson; set decorator, William Kiernan; music,
Daniele Amfitheatrof; assistant director, Milton Feldman; camera,
Charles Lang, Jr.; editor, Charles Nelson.
    Glenn Ford (Sergeant Dave Bannion); Gloria Grahame (Debby
Marsh); Jocelyn Brando (Katie Bannion); Alexander Scourby (Mike
Lagana); Lee Marvin (Vince Stone); Jeanette Nolan (Bertha Duncan);
Peter Whitney (Tierney); Willis Bouchey (Lieutenant Ted Wilkes);
Robert Burton (Gus Burke); Adam Williams (Larry Gordon); Howard
Wendell (Commissioner Higgins); Chris Alcaide (George Rose); Mi-
chael Granger (Hugo the Cop); Carolyn Jones (Doris); Dorothy Green
(Lucy Chapman); Ric Roman (Baldy); Dan Seymour (Atkins); Edith
Evanson (Selma Parker); Donald Kerr (Cabby); Laura Mason (B-Girl);
Rex Reason (Bit); Norma Randall (Jill); Sid Clute (Bartender); Joe
Mell (Dr. Kane the Autopsy Surgeon); Linda Bennett (Joyce Bannion);
Herbert Lytton (Martin); Ezelle Poule (Mrs. Tucker); Mike Rose
(Segal); Ted Stanhope (Butler); Kathryn Eames (Marge); Harry Laut-
er (Hank O'Connell); John Crawford (Al); John Doucette (Mark Rein-
er); Celia Lovsky (Mrs. Lagana--Portrait).

    Columbia Pictures' Harry Cohn might have been slow to re-
alize it, but The Big Heat proved to be one of the definitive films
of the 1950s, blazening the screen with a taut account of post-World
War II America.   It was a film filled with brutality, sordidness,
and the seaminess of the unlawful.
    The storyline was simple in structure.   It dealt with a police
lieutenant (Ford) who doggedly attempts to discover why a fellow policeman committed suicide.   He soon learns that the man's wife and
the police force want him to halt the investigation.   Only his own
wife (Brando) supports him, but she meets a violent death in their
car from a bomb intended for her husband.   Her demise further
spurs Dave Bannion to his hunt and he uncovers that big time criminal Mike Lagana (Scourby) operates as an average well-to-do businessman.   Bannion also encounters Lagana's sadistic henchman
(Marvin) and the latter's moll (Grahame).   Eventually the police
force join Bannion and the hoodlums are arrested.
    Taken from William P. McGivern's novel, also serialized in
the Saturday Evening Post, the film was "... a skillful and violent
film that has well-integrated theme" (Paul Jensen, The Cinema of
Fritz Lang, 1969).
    Director Fritz Lang has his own rationale for the enduring
fascination of The Big Heat: "... [it] is an accusation against
crime.   But it involves people--unlike other good pictures against

Glenn Ford and John Doucette in The Big Heat (1953).

crime which only involve gangsters.... Glenn Ford is a member
of the police department and his wife gets killed. The story becomes a personal affair between him and crime. He becomes the
audience. "

The "highlights" of The Big Heat are two sequences of action
and reaction: Vince Stone tossing boiling coffee into Debby March's
face, and her later revenge when she returns the gesture. Gordon
Gow commented in Hollywood in the Fifties (1971), "Considered in
isolation, such palpable violence would be highly suspect. Contained
as it was by a sharp little plot and sensible psychology, as well as
the brilliant light-and-shadow play which typified the high style of
Lang at his post-expressionist best, even in these dog days of his
Hollywood career, the sensation was justifiable and possibly, for
some, cathartic. "

Another valid aspect of The Big Heat was that it presented
the master criminal as an average guy, not as a leering monster,
madman, or inarticulate sadist. Scourby's Mike Lagana therefore
was more underplayed. Despite excessive violence in the overall
film, this portrayal was in many ways far more frightening than a
Rico or a Scarface.

THE BIG HOUSE (MGM, 1930) 86 min.

Director, George Hill; story-screenplay, Frances Marion; additional dialog, Joe Farnham, Martin Flavin; art director, Cedric Gibbons; sound, Robert Shirley, Douglas Shearer; camera, Harold Wenstrom; editor, Blanche Sewell.

Chester Morris (Morgan); Wallace Beery (Butch); Lewis Stone (Warden); Robert Montgomery (Kent); Leila Hyams (Anne); George F. Marion (Pop); J. C. Nugent (Mr. Marlowe); Karl Dane (Olsen); DeWitt Jennings (Wallace); Mathew Betz (Gopher); Claire McDowell (Mrs. Marlowe); Robert Emmett O'Connor (Donlin); Tom Kennedy (Uncle Jed); Tom Wilson (Sandy); Eddie Foyer (Dopey); Roscoe Ates (Putnam); Fletcher Norton (Oliver).

Over the years prison pictures have had their vogues, many times trying to improve conditions of prison life, usually without much success. One of the first, biggest, and most successful of this particular sub-genre was Metro-Goldwyn-Mayer's The Big House, written by Frances Marion and filmed in four languages. The American version was directed by George Hill with the German and French versions by Paul Fejos and the Spanish version by Ward Wing.

The Big House centered on three men sent to prison: Morgan (Morris), a forger; Butch (Beery), a killer; and Kent Marlowe (Robert Montgomery), convicted of manslaughter due to a traffic accident. The trio become cellmates and eventually Morgan escapes and goes to Marlowe's sister (Hyams), with whom he falls in love. He is later recaptured, but now decides to go straight for the girl's sake. Back in prison he learns that Butch is planning an escape and that other prisoners plan to join him due to the bad jail conditions. Marlowe tips off the warden of the proposed plan. A riot ensues. Morgan intervenes and quells the riot, for which he is paroled.

In some areas of the U.S. The Big House is still one of the most constantly revived early talking films seen on television. A good script, excellent direction which brought out the stark prison life, and fine performances by the three leads highlight the movie. The film set a trend in prison pictures which continues to this date, although the genre may have been watered down by numerous "B" imitations in the '30s, '40s, and '50s.

THE BIGGEST BUNDLE OF THEM ALL (MGM, 1968) C-105 min.

Producer, Joseph Shaftel; associate producer, Sy Stewart; director, Ken Annakin; story, Shaftel; screenplay, Sy Salkowitz; music, Riz Ortolani; assistant director, Victor Merenda; art director, Arrigo Equini; camera, Piero Portalupi; editor, Ralph Sheldon.

Robert Wagner (Harry Price); Raquel Welch (Juliana); Godfrey Cambridge (Benjamin Brownstead); Vittorio de Sica (Cesare Celli); Edward G. Robinson (Professor Samuels); Davy Kaye (Davy Collins); Francesco Mule (Antonio Tozzi); Victor Spinetti (Captain Giglio); Yvonne Sanson (Teresa); Mickey Knox (Joe Ware); Femi Benussi (Uncle Carlo's Bride); Andrea Aureli (Carabiniere); Carlo Croccolo

(Franco); Piero Gerlini (Captain Capuano); Giulio Marchetti (Lieutenant Naldi); Nino Musco (Chef); Calisto Calisti (Inspector Bordoni).

Although given good exploitation in America when issued in
1968, The Biggest Bundle of Them All proved to be no more than
a run-of-the-mill heist melodrama which marked Edward G. Robinson's final effort of any note in the gangster genre.
With shades of The Happening (1967), q. v., this Italian-
lensed feature focused on a group of novice criminals who kidnap a
deported U. S. hoodlum (de Sica) in Italy and demand a ransom.
None of his underworld pals, however, will underwrite the rescue.
As an alternative, Celli (de Sica) agrees to train the gang so they
can undertake a five million dollar platinum robbery.   Celli enlists
the aid of "The Professor" (Robinson) to plan the heist.   After
much bungling, the group accomplish the robbery.   But as their
plane is making its getaway, the bomb doors open and the loot falls
into the hands of the police waiting below.
Many a naive filmgoer assumed that the movie's title re-
ferred to co-star Raquel Welch, or at least to a portion of her well-
publicized anatomy.

THE BIG SHOT   (Warner Bros., 1942)   82 min.

Producer, Walter MacEwen; director, Lewis Seiler; screen-
play, Bertram Millhauser, Abem Finkel, Daniel Fuchs; music,
Adolph Deutsch; orchestrator, Jerome Moross; dialog director,
Harold Winston; assistant director, Art Lueker; art director, John
Hughes; gowns, Milo Anderson; makeup artist, Perc Westmore;
sound, Stanley Jones; camera, Sid Hickox; editor, Jack Killifer.
Humphrey Bogart (Duke Berne); Irene Manning (Lorna Flem-
ing); Richard Travis (George Anderson); Susan Peters (Ruth Carter);
Stanley Ridges (Martin Fleming); Minor Watson (Warden Booth);
Chick Chandler (Dancer); Joseph Downing (Frenchy); Howard da Sil-
va (Sandor); Murray Alper (Quinto); Roland Drew (Faye); John
Ridgely (Tim); Joseph King (Toohey); John Hamilton (Judge); Vir-
ginia Brissac (Mrs. Booth); William Edmunds (Sarto); Virginia Sale
(Mrs. Miggs); Ken Christy (Kat); Wallace Scott (Rusty).

Humphrey Bogart's last "B" gangster film at Warner Bros.
was The Big Shot, "a brisk melodrama" (New York Times) which
teamed him with Irene "Yankee Doodle Dandy" Manning under Lewis
Seiler's direction.
Three-time loser Duke Berne (Bogart) tries to operate legitimately but finally joins a holdup gang led by lawyer Martin Fleming (Ridges).   Ridges' wife, Lorna (Manning), was once Duke's
mistress and she keeps him out of the upcoming robbery.   Fleming
learns of the situation and has Duke framed.   Berne is sentenced
to prison but later escapes.   He and Lorna have a brief respite
from reality in a mountain lodge, but when he hears that his buddy
(Travis) is to be tried for a murder Duke committed, he decides to
clear him of the "rap. "   On the way back from their hideout, the
police ambush Duke and Lorna and she is killed.   Berne escapes,

finds Travis, and kills him.   In the encounter he is shot, but he
lives long enough to clear Anderson.
    Made on a modestly-budgeted scale, The Big Shot was quite
lively, with Bogart and Manning making a plausible screen team.
Several scenes were well handled, especially the sequences of the
lovers in their log cabin retreat and the chase in which they are
attacked by the police.
    Even in this pre-Casablanca (1943) entry, Bogart's law-
breaker was more well-intentioned than evil-doing.

BLACK CAESAR   (American International, 1973)   C-87 min.

    Executive producer, Peter Sabiston; producer, Larry Cohen;
co-producer, Janelle Cohen; associate producer, James P. Dixon;
director-screenplay, Larry Cohen; production designer, Larry Lurin; music, James Brown; song, Bodie Chandler and Barry De Vor-
zon; technical adviser, Paul Stader; sound, Alex Vanderkar; camera, Fenton Hamilton, James Signorelli; editor, George Folsey, Jr.
    Fred Williamson (Tommy Gibbs); D'Urville Martin (Reverend
Rufus); Gloria Hendry (Helen); Art Lund (John McKinney); Val Avery
(Cardoza); Minnie Gentry (Mama Gibbs); Julius W. Harris (Mr.
Gibbs); Phillip Roye (Joe Washington); William Wellman, Jr. (Al-
fred Coleman); Myrna Hansen (Virginia Coleman); Omer Jeffrey
(Tommy--as a Boy); James Dixon (Bryant); Cecil Alonso (Motor);
Allen Bailey (Sport); Larry Lurin (Carlos).
    British release: The Godfather of Harlem (Gala, 1974)
C-84 min.

    After having enjoyed success with film biographies of vari-
ous white hoodlums and making big money with a black horror film,
Blacula (1972), American International Pictures invaded the gangster movie field with Black Caesar, written-produced-directed by
Larry Cohen.
    With location filming in Harlem, good photography, and a
soundtrack written by soul singer James Brown, the action-aimed
film told of the rise of a Harlem black (Williamson) who ruthlessly
takes over the Mafia in his part of town.   However, he is later
gunned down for his troubles.   Nevertheless, before he dies he
takes revenge on his assassin, who, at the finale, is beaten to
death by a group of neighborhood punks.
    Reaction to this ethnic film, which grossed $2.2 million
domestically, was mixed.   Films in Review found it "absurd" but
the exhibitor-tradepaper, Greater Amusement, said it was a "better
than average black action film. "   Variety opined it was a "strongly-
premised crime meller ... [it] fits patly into [the] current trend of
violent black pix. "   In England, the British Monthly Film Bulletin
reasoned, "Less hysterical and less offensively violent than many
black movies ... [it] sets out to prove that absolute black power
corrupts absolutely, and in doing so, invests its hero with unusually
sympathetic characteristics. ...   this is a welcome attempt to move
black films off the beaten track. "

BLACK FRIDAY   (Universal, 1940)   69 min.

Producer, Burt Kelly; director, Arthur Lubin; story-screenplay, Curt Siodmak, Eric Taylor; art director, Jack Otterson; set
decorator, Russell Gausman; music director, Hans J. Salter; makeup, Jack Pierce; costumes, Vera West; special effects, John P.
Fulton; camera, Elwood Bredell.

Boris Karloff (Dr. Ernest Sovac); Bela Lugosi (Eric Marnay);
Stanley Ridges (Professor George Kingsley/Red Cannon); Anne Nagel
(Sunny Rogers); Anne Gwynne (Jean Sovac); Virginia Brissac (Mar-
garet Kingsley); Edmund MacDonald (Frank Miller); Paul Fix (Kane);
Murray Alper (Bellhop); Jack Mulhall (Bartender); Joe King (Police
Chief); John Kelly (Taxi Driver); Harry Hayden (Bit).

One of the less popular of the Boris Karloff-Bela Lugosi co-
starring vehicles was Black Friday. It was actually a well-con-
structed film but, upon discovering it was a gangster picture and
not the horror entry they had anticipated, many fans were disap-
pointed. Although a science fiction plot about a brain transplant is
the crux of the film, the basic action and motivations of the story
are those of a gangster thriller.

College professor-doctor Ernest Sovac (Karloff) operates on
a kindly colleague (Ridges) after he has been badly hurt when hit by
a speeding car driven by gangsters. The underworld kingpin has
already died as a result of a broken back from the crash. To save
his friend, who has brain damage, Sovac removes part of the gangster's brain and implants it in his friend's skull. Professor Kingsley recovers and seems fine until a trip to New York, and to the
gangster's hideout, brings out the evil personality of the criminal,
which leads to eventual tragedy.

Originally Lugosi was set to play Ridges' part, but a last-
minute casting switch had him portraying a definitely supporting role
(with star billing) of the rival gangster who caused the accident. It
is Lugosi's unique performance, however, which holds the film's
greatest interest and his death scene is most realistic. He also
enjoys some good comedy lines. In one scene, for example, he is
talking to moll Sunny Rogers (Nagel) who has been visited by the
professor/crook. She explains that the man did not look like her
former boyfriend or sound like him but it was "really him!" Lugosi's Eric Marnay looks at her with raised eyebrow and intones in
a thick, Hungarian accent, "He's dead. How did he get here, in a
hearse?"

THE BLACK HAND   (MGM, 1950)   92 min.

Producer, William H. Wright; director, Richard Thorpe;
story, Leo Townsend; screenplay, Luther Davis; art directors, Cedric Gibbons, Gabriel Scognamillo; music, Alberto Colombo; camera, Paul C. Vogel; editor, Irving Warburton.

Gene Kelly (Johnny Columbo); J. Carrol Naish (Louis Lorel-
li); Teresa Celli (Isabella Gomboli); Marc Lawrence (Caesar Xavier
Serpi); Frank Puglia (Carlo Sabballera); Barry Kelley (Captain

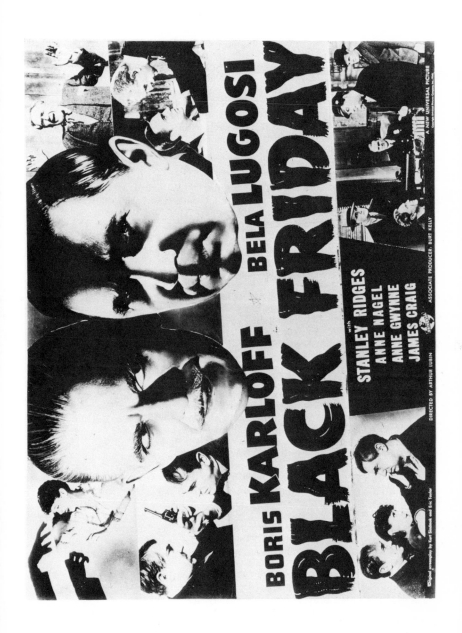

Advertising poster for <u>Black Friday</u> (1940).

Thompson); Mario Siletti (Benny Danetta); Carl Milletaire (George
Allani); Peter Brocco (Roberto Columbo); Eleanora Mendelssohn
(Maria Columbo); Gracia Narcisco (Mrs. Lanetta); Maurice Samuels
(Moriani); Burke Symon (Judge); Bert Freed (Prosecutor); Mimi
Aguglia (Mrs. Sabballera); Baldo Minuti (Bettini); Carlo Tricoli
(Pietro Riago); Marc Krah (Lombardi); Jimmy Lagano (Rudi Gom-
boli); Phyllis Morris (Mary the Shamrock); Alfred Linder (Rat Type);
Felix Romano (Hunchback) Vincent Renno (Editor); Raymond Malkin
(Johnny Columbo at Age Fourteen) Anna Demetrio (Manageress);
John Marlin (Customer); Ray Bennett (Policeman); Jim Pierce (Bail-
iff); Almira Sessions, Lillian Bronson (Tourists); Bobby Blake (Pas-
quale the Bus Boy); Robert Malcolm (Firechief).

Gene Kelly's most exacting non-musical film role of his MGM
years came in this nice little thriller. Kelly and J. Carrol Naish
made an effective team and, together with director Richard Thorpe's
work and the fitting urban background, The Black Hand had "...
more to recommend it than a good, adventurous gangster plot" (New
York Times).
Set in New York City's "Little Italy" at the turn of the century, the film tells of a crusading young man (Kelly) who, with the
aid of a veteran police detective (Naish), tries to rid the neighborhood of Mafia terrorists and extortionists. The Luther Davis-scripted
story was especially good in its depiction of how organized crime can
hold and corrupt the poor.
Over the years, there have been several celluloid exposés of
"The Black Hand," such as La Mano Nera, an Italian-Spanish co-
production of 1973 starring Lionel Stander and Philippe Leroy.
Most such entries, however, lacked the historical perspective necessary to give the delineated brutality of Mafia life any sense of
balance.
On re-seeing Kelly's The Black Hand a viewer may legitimately wonder how, after so many maulings, the star is capable of
hurling the knife which kills the underworld kingpin. But no matter! "The stalking of victims through darkened alleys, sluggings,
shootings and knifings are what make the picture a vivid production"
(New York Herald-Tribune).

BLACK TUESDAY (United Artists, 1954)   80 min.

Producer, Robert Goldstein; director, Hugo Fregonese; story-
screenplay, Sydney Boehm; assistant director, Sam Wurtzel; art director, Hilyard Brown; set director, Al Spencer; music, Paul Dunlap; sound, Tom Lambert; camera, Stanley Cortez; editor, Robert
Golden.
Edward G. Robinson (Vincent Canelli); Peter Graves (Peter
Manning); Jean Parker (Hatti Combest); Milburn Stone (Father Slo-
cum); Warren Stevens (Joey Stewart); Jack Kelly (Frank Carson);
Sylvia Findley (Ellen Norris); James Bell (John Norris); Victor Perrin (Dr. Hart).

One of Edward G. Robinson's forays into the type of

conscienceless hoodlum that made him famous as Little Caesar, was
the role of Vincent Canelli in <u>Black Tuesday</u>. The film was a "B"
picture throwback to the Warners' gangster epics of the Thirties,
with an overabundance of needless violence tossed into the fray.

On the day ("Black Tuesday") he is scheduled to go to the
electric chair for a killing accomplished during a bank robbery,
Canelli is helped to escape from prison by a guard whose daughter
has been kidnapped by Canelli's gang and his moll (Parker). The
escape procedure uses a gang member disguised as a newsman who
is thus able to give Vincent a gun just before the planned execution.
Together they shoot their way out of prison and, in so doing, the
guard is killed. Canelli and his gang hide at a warehouse and hold
several hostages for ransom. The money from the bank robbery is
retrieved from a deposit box by Canelli's partner (Graves) who has
been wounded in the breakout. His trail of blood leads the police
to the gang's hideaway. Surrounded, Canelli threatens to kill the
hostages if the police attack. To prove his point he murders one
of the captives. When he plans to shoot a priest (Stone) next, Manning turns on him and kills Vincent. As Manning leaves the warehouse he, in turn, is shot by the advancing police.

BLIND ALLEY (Columbia, 1939) 61 min.

Director, Charles Vidor; based on the play by James Warwick; screenplay, Philip MacDonald, Michael Blankfort, Albert Duffy; music director, Morris W. Stoloff; camera, Lucien Ballard;
editor, Otto Meyer.

Chester Morris (Hal Wilson); Ralph Bellamy (Dr. Anthony
Shelby); Ann Dvorak (Mary); Joan Perry (Linda Curtis); Melville
Cooper (George Curtis); Rose Stradner (Doris Shelby); John El-
dredge (Dick Holbrook); Ann Doran (Agnes the Maid); Marc Law-
rence (Buck); Stanley Brown (Fred Landis); Scotty Beckett (Davy
Shelby); Milburn Stone (Nick); Grady Sutton (Holmes the Student);
Eddie Acuff (State Trooper); John Hamilton (Warden).

As one of the earlier films successfully to intermingle the
fields of psychology and gangsters, <u>Blind Alley</u> produced better results than might be expected. According to the <u>New York Sun</u>, "It
is an extraordinary and, as the picture presents it, a completely
credible melodrama, with psychology used for the first time as a
weapon stronger than a gun. " The <u>New York Daily News</u>, in its
three star review, was even more enthusiastic about the picture's
plot gimmick. "<u>Blind Alley</u> is as un-Hollywood as anything that has
come from France this year. "

The story concerns a killer gang which is led by Hal Wilson
(Morris), a man haunted by a recurring nightmare. Due to his
fears of insanity, Hal is more than eager to talk about his problems
with Dr. Anthony Shelby (Bellamy) whose country home he has ap-
propriated as part of his getaway plan. While waiting for the escape boat, Shelby takes advantage of the situation by drawing out
Hal's past and, later, reducing the gangster to a helpless physical
state. The gangster's past experiences are shown on screen through

negative filming techniques. The doctor then helps Hal to understand the causes of his nightmares, and perhaps, to fathom the
rationale for his criminal life.
Clever direction and performances by Morris and Bellamy,
along with Ann Dvorak as Morris' moll, a girl afraid she will lose
her man if he becomes normal, added to the excellence of the film.
Columbia would remake Blind Alley as The Dark Past (1948),
q. v. , but despite a bigger budget it was not up to the original.

BLONDE CRAZY (Warner Bros. , 1931) 74 min.

Director, Roy Del Ruth; story-screenplay, Kubec Glasmon,
John Bright; music director, Leo F. Forbstein; songs, E. A. Swan;
Gerald Marks and Buddy Fields; Roy Turk and Fred Ahlert; Sidney
Mitchell, Archie Gottler, and George W. Meyer; makeup, Perc
Westmore; camera, Sid Hickox; editor, Ralph Dawson.
James Cagney (Bert Harris); Joan Blondell (Ann Roberts);
Louis Calhern (Dapper Dan Barker); Noel Francis (Helen Wilson);
Guy Kibbee (A. Rupert Johnson, Jr.); Raymond Milland (Joe Rey-
nolds); Polly Walters (Peggy); Charles Lane (Desk Clerk); William
Burress (Colonel Bellock); Peter Erkelenz (Dutch); Maude Eburne
(Mrs. Snyder); Walter Percival (Lee); Nat Pendleton (Hand); Russell
Hopton (Jerry); Dick Cramer (Cabbie); Wade Boteler (Detective);
Ray Cooke, Edward Morgan (Bellhops); Phil Sleman (Conman).

After his success in The Public Enemy (1931), q. v. , and his
teaming with Edward G. Robinson for Smart Money (1931), q. v. ,
James Cagney was given his first solo starring vehicle in Blonde
Crazy.
Cagney impersonated a bootlegging and blackmailing bellhop
who falls for a con artist blonde (Blondell). Bert (Cagney) attempts
to win the girl a job at his hotel as a chambermaid, and is slapped
by her for his troubles. They do get together, however, and team
their dishonest resources. Beginning to enjoy their new-found rich-
es, they move westward. Then they are fleeced by Dapper Dan
(Calhern) who sells Bert good money and pretends it is bogus stuff.
Later he steals it back. Since he seems to know most of the tricks
of the trade, Bert tries his own con game. Posing as a jeweler's
representative, he steals a diamond bracelet from a rich girl by
claiming he has come to retrieve the wrong gems delivered for the
lady's wedding. Eventually Bert and Ann take revenge on Dapper
Dan, but the novelty of their life together has worn thin. She marries a broker (Milland) while Bert plans to head for Europe, but
instead is caught and sent to jail. When Ann learns of his incarceration she visits him, tells him she is divorcing the broker,
and will wait for him to serve out his sentence.
The film's working title was Larceny Lane and it introduced
the song "When Your Lover Has Gone" by E. A. Swan, which would
be popularized by Kate Smith. Blondell replaced Marian Marsh as
the feminine lead. Blondell and Cagney had already appeared in
three pictures together (besides their joint Broadway foray with

Sinner's Holiday) but Blonde Crazy was the real beginning of the
Cagney-Blondell screen team.

As for the film itself, the New York Times rated it "lively
and cleverly acted" while Time called it "... a chipper, hardboiled,
amusing essay on petty thievery." In its compact seventy-four minutes, the movie managed to maintain a swift pace and be alternating-
ly naughty, tongue-in-cheek, melodramatic, and tough. Its greatest
charm, as with so many films of the early 1930s, was its lack of
pretension. Despite its reformation ending, this pre-Code feature
did very little prosletyzing, and was satisfied merely to entertain
its viewers with its slice-of-gangster/con artist life.

BLOODY MAMA (American International, 1970) C-90 min.

Executive producers, Samuel Z. Arkoff, James H. Nicholson;
producer, Roger Corman; co-producer, Norman T. Herman; director, Corman; story, Robert Thom, Don Peters; screenplay, Thom;
music-music director, Don Randi; title song, Randi, Guy Hemric,
and Bob Silver; costumes, Thomas Costich; sound, Charles Knight;
special effects, A. D. Flowers; camera, John Alonzo; editor, Eve
Newman.

Shelley Winters (Kate "Ma" Barker); Pat Hingle (Sam Adams
Pendlebury); Don Stroud (Herman Barker); Diane Varsi (Mona Gib-
son); Bruce Dern (Kevin Dirkman); Clint Kimbrough (Arthur Barker);
Robert De Niro (Lloyd Barker); Robert Walden (Fred Barker); Alex
Nicol (George Barker); Michael Fox (Dr. Roth); Scatman Crothers
(Moses); Stacy Harris (Agent McClellan); Pamela Dunlap (Rembrandt);
Lisa Jill (Young Kate); Steve Mitchell (Sheriff); Roy Idom (Ferryboat
Passenger).

Shelley Winters had a tour de force as "Ma" Barker, the
matriarch of a gang of hoodlums who terrorized America's south-
land during the 1930s. Filmed on location in the Ozark country of
Arkansas by producer-director Roger Corman, Bloody Mama indul-
gently exploited the "basic" facts behind the Ma Barker gang.

Although this was not the first time Ma had been portrayed
on camera, Miss Winters (who had starred as Ma on the "Batman"
teleseries) certainly took the part as her own. "It's a free country,
but unless you're rich you ain't free. I aim to be freer than the
rest of the people." This is the credo Winters' Ma imparts to her
four weak-willed sons, one of whom is a drug addict. She gleefully
leads her willing sons down the path of robbery, kidnapping, and
murder, and onward to eventual death. Along the way one of the
boys' sluttish girlfriends (Varsi) joins the gang, making it one of the
most famous and colorful of its era.

Over the years, Corman had produced and/or directed several minor gangster entries, along with the documentary-like The
St. Valentine's Day Massacre (1967), q.v., but this work for his
old studio, American-International, was one of the biggest grossers
of his productive career. (The picture had been planned for filming
a year or more earlier, but had been temporarily shelved when this
country underwent a temporary anti-violence spree regarding movies

and television programming.) The main credit for Bloody Mama's
success, however, must go to the bravura performance of Shelley
Winters in the pivotal role. The once sex siren seemed to revel
in the perversities of the part, galloping through the picture with a
strident scream ("You gotta fight the bastards always, boys"), outrageous costumes, and unbridled mugging.

"What I can't understand," pondered Newsweek's Joseph Mor-
genstern, "is how critics who are supposed to know a bit more than
the commonest man can discuss such a movie as anything but a
shrewd commercial exercise." But many a reviewer delved deep to
extract meaning from this essential potboiler. For example, the
British Monthly Film Bulletin's critic observed, "Ma Barker's independent way of life, totally at odds with the rest of society and
as a result isolated and incestuous, is instantly reminiscent of its
many predecessors in Corman's work. The superior sensitivity of
Roderick Usher, the painfully unique vision of Dr. James Xavier,
the leaping ambitions of Joseph Curwen, the obsessive sexuality of
Verden Fell: each of these--quite apart from the direct legacies of
Machine Gun Kelly, Joe Sante and Al Capone--find their echoes in
the Bible-thumping career of Kate as she steams through the Arkansas countryside with God, Lindbergh, the Ku-Klux-Klan and Aimee
Semple McPherson on her side. Like the tormented misanthropists
before her, Ma Barker is as much a product of contemporary ma-
laise as of the disorders of her historical time; Corman's world
cries out to be destroyed before it can be saved, and Bloody Mama
illustrates once more how the processes of destruction are still
stronger than those of salvation."

Unfortunately, not a great deal of accurate history was transformed to the screen in Bloody Mama. Only three of the four sons
of the real-life Ma Barker were actually hoods (one committed suicide in 1927) and only "Doc" was gunned down along with Ma in a
fierce gun battle with federal officers in 1935. The portion of the
film concerning the kidnapping of a multi-millionaire (played by Pat
Hingle in the film) was somewhat truthful. However, Corman tended
to insert a good deal of psychology into the film, including a scene
where the libido-oriented Ma gives one of her adult sons (Stroud) a
caressing bath!

As was to be expected (with the possibility that Corman was
baiting such a reaction), there was a good deal of outcry at the
"unnecessary" violence and sexuality within the film, which includes
murder by boot on the throat, a bathtub drowning, prison perver-
sions, gang rape, incest, and, as a "bonus," the torture of a
squeeling piglet.

BODY AND SOUL   (United Artists, 1947)   104 min.

    Director, Robert Rossen; screenplay, Abraham Polonsky;
art director, Nathan Juran; set decorator, Edward J. Boyle; music,
Hugo Friedhofer; music director, Rudolph Polk; songs, Johnny Green
and Edward Heyman; Robert Sour and Frank Eyton; assistant director, Robert Aldrich; sound, Frank Webster; camera, James Wong
Howe; editor, Francis Lyon.

Lloyd Gough, John Garfield and Lilli Palmer in Body and Soul (1947).

John Garfield (Charlie Davis); Lilli Palmer (Peg Born); Hazel Brooks (Alice); Anne Revere (Anna Davis); William Conrad (Quinn); Joseph Pevney (Shorty Polaski); Canada Lee (Ben Chaplin); Lloyd Gough (Roberts); Art Smith (Davis); James Burke (Arnold); Virginia Gregg (Irma); Peter Virgo (Drummer); Joe Devlin (Prince); Shimen Ruskin (Grocer); Mary Currier (Miss Tedder); Milton Kibbee (Dan); Tim Ryan (Shelton); Artie Dorrell (Jack Marlowe); Cy Ring (Victor); Glen Lee (Marine); John Indrisano (Referee); Dan Tobey (Fight Announcer); Wheaton Chambers (Doctor).

This melancholy fight-romance film was the first picture to be made by star John Garfield's own production company, Enterprise Studios. Garfield received an Academy Award nomination for his role as a boxer who fights to the top of his profession and along the way deserts the girl (Palmer) who leaves him for the attentions of a social tramp (Brooks). Eventually he realizes hoodlums are using him but it is not until a black buddy (Lee), an ex-pug, goes crazy and dies from a beating that he really wakes up to his situation. At the finale, Charlie (Garfield) doublecrosses racketeers by winning the fight he was supposed to lose. Faced with retribution from the gangsters, he snarls at them, "What can you do, kill me? Everybody dies."

Filmed at the time sports "fixing" was being investigated in

New York, the movie had pertinent appeal.   James Wong Howe won
an Oscar for best cinematography on this picture.
     There had been, and would be, other films dealing with the
criminal stranglehold on the boxing world (i. e. Champion, The Set-
Up, The Harder They Fall), but Body and Soul is the one most people recall.   Time observed, ". . . a good deal of the picture has
the cruelly redolent illusion of reality that distinguished many of
the movies of low life made in the thirties. " James Agee, on the
other hand, insisted that the movie ". . . [which] gets very bitter
and discreetly leftish about commercialism in prize fighting--is
really nothing much, I suppose, when you get right down to it. "
(Body and Soul scripter Abraham Polonsky would be among those
nearly suffocated during the anti-Red craze in Hollywood in the early 1950s).
     For the record, the film's title is derived from the popular
torch song of the Twenties, made famous by Helen Morgan.   The
tune is used effectively throughout the picture, especially in the
Charlie Davis-Peg Born scenes.

BONNIE AND CLYDE   (Warner Bros. -Seven Arts, 1967)   C-111 min.

     Producer, Warren Beatty; director, Arthur Penn; screenplay,
David Newman, Robert Benton; art director, Dean Tavoularis; set
decorator, Raymond Paul; music, Charles Strouse; title theme sung
by Rudy Vallee; background music, Lester Flatt, Earl Scruggs; costumes, Theadora Van Runkle; makeup, Robert Jiras; assistant direc-
tor, Jack N. Reddish; sound, Francis E. Stahl; special effects, Dan-
ny Lee; camera, Burnett Guffey; editor, Dede Allen.
     Warren Beatty (Clyde Barrow); Faye Dunaway (Bonnie Parker);
Gene Hackman (Buck Barrow); Michael J. Pollard (C. W. Moss);
Estelle Parsons (Blanche); Denver Pyle (Frank Hamer); Gene Wilder
(Eugene Grizzard); Evans Evans (Velma Davis); Dub Taylor (Moss);
James Stiver (Grocery Store Owner); Clyde Howdy (Deputy); Garry
Goodgion (Billy); Ken Mayer (Sheriff Smoot); Martha Adcock, Sadie
French (Bank Customers); Ada Waugh, Frances Fisher (Bonnie's
Aunts); Ann Palmer (Bonnie's Sister); Harry Appling (Bonnie's Un-
cle); Mabel Cavitt (Bonnie's Mother); Russ Marker (Bank Guard);
Gibson W. Brice (Grocery Clerk).

     A recent film buff's publication called this blockbuster gang-
ster picture (it grossed over $22 million in distributors' domestic
rentals alone) a "rip-off" and, despite its popularity in the late Sixties, the movie has aged badly.   Close scrutiny shows that director
Arthur Penn and his scripters borrowed heavily from earlier films
such as Deadly Is the Female (1949), q. v. , You Only Live Once
(1937), q. v. , and Young Dillinger (1964), q. v.   Exceedingly popular
when it was first issued (it even graced the cover of Time), the
film failed to win the Academy Award as best picture of 1967 and
afterward began to drop both in popularity and critical regard.   Recent TV showings of Bonnie and Clyde over CBS-TV in 1973-74
showed a slightly cut but slow and basically disjointed production
whose once "sharp" edge has been hewn by time.

Warren Beatty and Faye Dunaway in <u>Bonnie and Clyde</u> (1967).

In The Gangster Film (1970) John Baxter discusses the real
life Clyde Barrow (1910-1934) and Bonnie Parker (?-1934), pointing
out "It was left to Arthur Penn to set the legend firmly in ascend-
ancy over the truth, perpetuating it in an age weary of legends by
stressing its modern aspects. "

The film's scenario kept close to the basic facts, without revealing very many facts of the actual life of the duo.   The movie
opens in 1930 when Clyde Barrow (Beatty), a "half-wit" with a prison record, meets waitress Bonnie Parker (Dunaway) and they begin
their career in petty crime.   Along the way they team up with another low-mentality figure, C. W. Moss (Pollard).   The latter's
actual sexual character was stunted in the film version.

One scene has Bonnie and Clyde joining in with destitute
farmers, including a black man, in shooting out windows on govern-
ment-owned property in rebellion against the Depression.   It was
just another example of outlaws being presented as modern day Robin Hoods, which in reality they were not.

In December, 1932, the trio joins with Clyde's brother Buck
(Hackman) and his hysteria-prone wife, Blanche (Parsons).   They
continue their killing and robbery spree until Buck is fatally injured
in July, 1933.   Now an object of national attention and an F.B.I.
manhunt, Bonnie, Clyde, and C. W. are ambushed and mercilessly
murdered by a law party headed by Texas Ranger Hamer (Pyle),
the latter having been previously humiliated by the gang.

To insure generous boxoffice returns, little of the cold, cal-
culated viciousness of the lawbreakers was presented in the film.
Bonnie and Clyde, unfortunately, set a trend whereby a whole slew
of whitewashed hoodlums were presented on celluloid.

On the plus side, Bonnie and Clyde was a finely photographed
feature which beautifully recaptured the Depression era.   Direction
by Penn, however, was static and the film was gratuitously over-
violent.   Performances varied, with Beatty's work as impotent as
the character he portrayed while Dunaway showed flashes of solid
acting as his helpmate.   Hackman provided the movie's best performance, while Parsons earned a Supporting Actress Oscar for
her characterization.

After the film's steamrolling release, a lawsuit was filed
against the producer, Warren Beatty, by Sheriff Hamer.   He claimed
his character had been treated badly in the film.   History actually
shows that Hamer gave the gangsters verbal warning before the final shootout, which was not the savage ambush depicted oncamera. *
Bonnie Parker's sister made a recording for RCA Victor, post-
Bonnie and Clyde, which reportedly told the actual events of the
criminal duo in contrast to the story used for the film.   Singer Rudy
Vallee threatened to sue Beatty, but declined after the film failed to
win an Oscar.   His complaint was that Beatty had offered him no

---

*Actual newsreel footage taken a few minutes after the shootout was
shown in the documentary Crime Does Not Pay, which also covered
the lives of John Dillinger, Machine Gun Kelly and Pretty Boy Floyd.
Other screen uses of the Bonnie and Clyde story were in Persons in
Hiding (1938), q. v. , Guns Don't Argue (1957), q. v. , and The Bonnie
Parker Story (1958) q. v.

money or screen credit for the use of "Deep Night, " a song Vallee
co-authored and the 1929 RCA recording of which was used as the
film's title theme under the opening credits.

  Hollis Alpert (Saturday Review) offered the following post-
script to the lucrative Bonnie and Clyde saga. "The conviction that
crime pays at the box office is firmly entrenched in Hollywood, and
it is a melancholy fact that far more of our nation's gangsters and
wild ones have been enshrined cinematically than our more worthy
historical figures. Few indeed are the films built around philan-
thropists, pacifists, and scientific wonder-workers, but from Billy
the Kid to Dillinger, a long line of antiheroes has stalked the
screen, guns in hand. "

THE BONNIE PARKER STORY   (American International, 1958)
79 min.

  Executive producers, James H. Nicholson, Samuel Z. Ar-
koff; producer, Stanley Shpetner; director, William Witney; screen-
play, Shpetner; music-music conductor, Ronald Stein; assistant di-
rector, Robert Agnew; special effects, Thol Simionson; camera,
Jack Marta; editor, Frank Keller.
  Dorothy Provine (Bonnie Parker); Jack Hogan (Guy Darrow);
Richard Bakalyan (Duke Jefferson); Joseph Turkel (Chuck Darrow);
William Stevens (Paul); Ken Lynch (Restaurant Manager); Douglas
Kennedy (Tom Steel); Patti Huston (Chuck's Girl); Joel Colin (Bobby);
Jeff Morris (Marv); Jim Beck (Alvin); Stanley Livingston (Little Boy);

Jack Hogan and Dorothy Provine in The Bonnie Parker Story (1958).

Carolyn Hughes (Girl); Karl Davis (Texan); Raymond Guth (Louisiana Sheriff); Vince Williams (Narrator); Frank Evans (Announcer).

"Obviously an exploitation item, but it is capably constructed and intelligently carried out" (Variety).

Dorothy Provine who would be more noted for playing giddy heroines on television, was exceptionally appropriate as the notorious Bonnie Parker, here presented as an abused soul of Depression-weary America. When she weds Duke Jefferson (Bakalyan) she is unaware that he is a bank robber. Later he is captured and sentenced to life in prison. Thereafter she teams with Guy and Chuck Darrow (Hogan and Turkel), and together they engage in a wild melee of lawlessness. After Chuck's death, she becomes the gang's head and, in between bank robberies, manages to get her husband out of jail. As in the latter Bonnie and Clyde (1967), q.v., she meets her end in 1934, when gunned down by Texas Rangers.

Much more than Faye Dunaway's Bonnie Parker, Miss Provine's Bonnie is presented, after her marriage to Duke, as a very hardened, cigar smoking dame. A tommy gun and not a purse is her favorite accoutrement. While her initial decline into amorality is seasoned by reaction to her environment, once she becomes a criminal, there is little attempt to soften her suddenly violent nature.

BORDER G-MAN   (RKO, 1938)   60 min.

Producer Bert Gilroy; director, David Howard; screenplay, Oliver Drake; camera, Joseph H. August; editor, Frederic Knudston.

George O'Brien (Jim Galloway); Laraine Johnson (Day) (Betty Holden); Ray Whitely (Luke); John Miljan (Louis Rankin); Rita LaRoy (Rita Browning); Edgar Dearing (Smoky Joslin); William Stelling (Leslie Holden); Edward Keane (Colonel Christie); Ethan Laidlaw (Curly); Hugh Sothern (Matt Rathburn); Bobby Burns (Sheriff).

Western hero Jim Galloway (O'Brien), his pal Luke (Ray Whitely), and their musical group battle a group of hoodlums who are selling horses and guns to enemy agents in this nicely photographed (by Joseph August), strong entry in the RKO-O'Brien Western series.

"More westerns like this would be pleasantly received," Variety stated. Its gimmick of combining two genres (i.e. the Western and the Gangster film) was an appealing notion hastened by the approach of World War II and America's rekindled interest in world affairs. To be more topical, sagebrush tales turned to racketeers and espionage agents in order to spruce up their plotlines. This high class "B" film was one of the first, and one of the best to do so.

Among the picture's highlights were a stampede sequence, good seacoast camerawork, and a top-notch climax which finds Jim Galloway, the G-man incognito, lassoing villain Louis Rankin (Miljan) off his getaway boat and pulling him back to shore. Musicians

Luke and the boys sang "Back in the Saddle Again" to add flavor to
the proceedings.

BORN RECKLESS   (Fox, 1930)   82 min.

Presenter, William Fox; associate producer, James K. Mc-
Guinness; director, John Ford; stager, Andrew Bennison; based on
the novel Louis Beretti by Donald Henderson Clarke; screenplay,
Dudley Nichols; art director, Jack Schulze; assistant director, Edward O'Fearna; sound, W. W. Lindsay; camera, George Schneider-
man; editor, Frank E. Hull.
Edmund Lowe (Louis Beretti); Catherine Dale Owen (Jean
Sheldon); Warren Hymer (Big Shot); Marguerite Churchill (Rosa Ber-
etti); Lee Tracy (Bill O'Brien); William Harrigan (Good News Bro-
phy); Frank Albertson (Frank Sheldon); Paul Page (Ritzy Reilly);
Ferike Boros (Ma Beretti); Paul Porcasi (Pa Beretti); Joe Brown
(Needle Beer Grogan); Eddie Gribbon (Bugs); J. Farrell MacDonald
or Roy Stewart (District Attorney Cardigan); Yola D'Avril (French
Girl).

BORN RECKLESS   (Twentieth Century-Fox, 1937)   78 min.

Producer, Sol M. Wurtzel; associate producer, Milton H.
Feld; director, Malcolm St. Clair; story, Jack Andrews; screenplay,
John Patrick, Robert Ellis, Helen Logan; art director, Chester Gore;
music director, Samuel Kaylin; camera, Daniel B. Clark; editor,
Alex Troffey.
Rochelle Hudson (Sybil Roberts); Brian Donlevy (Bob "Hurry"
Kane); Barton MacLane (Jim Barnes); Robert Kent (Lee Martin);
Harry Carey (Dad Martin); Pauline Moore (Dorothy Collins); Chick
Chandler (Windy Bowman); William Pawley (Mac); Francis McDonald
(Louie); George Wolcott (Danny Horton); Joseph Crehan (District At-
torney).

Outside of the fact that both films were produced by the Fox
Film Corporation and each dealt with the world of gangsters, the
two films had little in common.
Edmund Lowe, who was still thriving on his What Price
Glory? tough guy reputation, was cast as Louis Beretti in the 1930
Born Reckless.   Convicted on a robbery charge, he is sent overseas
to fight in World War I.   When he returns to New York, he turns
to his old criminal way of life, but manages to redeem himself by
shooting it out with Big Shot (Hymer), the underworld figure who has
kidnapped Jean Sheldon's (Owen) child.   Coursing through this programmer were Damon Runyonesque-type comedy hoods.
The 1937 Born Reckless was less elaborate, satisfied to be
merely a double bill item.   The New York Times branded it "mentally retarded and incurably lame" in its account of racketeers working in a taxi protection association which instigates warfare among
cab drivers.   Like many "B" films of the period, about the only
thing this little entry had going for it was an impressive cast.

BORSALINO (Paramount, 1970) C-126 min.

Producer, Alain Delon; associate producer, Pierre Caro; director, Jacques Deray; based on the book Bandits à Marseille by Eugene Soccomare; screenplay, Jean-Claude Carriere, Claude Sautet, Jacques Deray, Jean Cau; art director, François de Lamothe; music, Claude Bolling; costumes, Jacques Fonteray; sound, Jacques Maumont; camera, Jean-Jacques Tarbes; editor, Paul Cayatte.

Jean-Paul Belmondo (Capella); Alain Delon (Siffredi); Michel Bouquet (Rinaldi); Catherine Rouvel (Lola); Francoise Christophe (Mme. Escarguel); Corinne Marchand (Mme. Rinaldi); Julien Guiomar (Boccase); Arnoldo Foa (Marello); Nicole Calfan (Ginette); Christian de Tiliere (The Dancer); Mario David (Mario); Andre Bollet (Poli); Laura Adani (Siffredi's Mother); Daniel Ivernel (Police Inspector); Denis Berry (Nono); Helene Remy (Lydia); Mireille Darc (Whore).

Produced by star Alain Delon and directed by Jacques Deray on an elaborate budget, this film was geared to appeal to the international film market. Its popularity brought back the vogue in gangster films in France and Europe, although it was less successful in the U.S. It did, however, meet with popular acclaim from critics. The clothing styles of the Thirties presented herein started a minor fashion revolution on both sides of the Atlantic.

Somewhat tongue-in-cheek, the film recounted the underworld life in Marseilles in the early 1930s. Two crooks (Delon and Belmondo) work their way through protection rackets to become the kingpins of prostitution and gambling, besides controlling the wholesale meat and fish trades of the port city. Along the way, of course, there is excessive murder, violence, mayhem, and sex.

Despite its colorful storyline and a distinct turn toward comedy the well-mounted feature was rugged but not cohesive, and its pacing was dull (unlike the bouncy Claude Bolling score). New York Times critic Roger Greenspun found it "decadent because it is so deliberately drained of vitality." Other critics disagreed. The New Yorker found it "... sumptuous! A little Easy Rider here, a little Bonnie and Clyde there," while Cosmopolitan thought it was "dazzlingly chaotic." British writer F. Maurice Speed said the film was "a quite outstanding gangster movie ... brutal ... but made with a tongue-in-cheek manner which brought it to the edge of farce on occasions."

Quite naturally, moviegoers brought to this screen exercise a preformulated preference for either Delon or Belmondo. The two stars themselves conducted a subtle on-camera rivalry (and a very blatant contest off-camera). Drenched in its period flavor, Borsalino was as much an exercise in ambience as screen thriller tactics.

Four years later Borsalino & Co., infra, appeared.

BORSALINO & CO. (CIC, 1974) C-110 min.

Executive producer, Julien Derode; producer, Alain Delon; director, Jacques Deray; screenplay, Pascal Jardin, Deray; music,

Claude Bolling; camera, Jean-Jacques Tarbes; editor, Henri Lanoe.
    Alain Delon (Roch); Catherine Rouvel (Lola); Ricardo Cuciolla
(Volpone); Reinhardt Kolidehoff (Sam); Daniel Ivernel (Inspector).

    With the resounding success of Borsalino (1970), supra, it
took little prompting for producer-star Alain Delon to package this
follow-up. This time, Jean-Paul Belmondo, who had had many dis-
agreements with his co-star, is not part of the action. (Besides,
his character had been killed off in the earlier film).
    Set in the early 1930s in France, the overlong story details
an underworld gang rivalry, with one of the sides being backed by
the Nazis and French Fascists. Roch (Delon) is spurred into action
to revenge the death of his partner (Belmondo). When he loses the
tug of war, initially, he reacts by burying his depression in drinking, ending up in an asylum (!). Later he escapes to Italy and
thereafter returns to eradicate the opponents. Along the way he
rescues Lola (Rouvel) from a bordello where she is one of the girls,
eliminates a corrupt police commission, and then heads off to America (for yet another sequel?).
    Despite the lavish production values, Variety complained,
"... pic looks like a foreign attempt to emulate Yank gangster epics
of the '30s without their rooting in social and economic times or the
breezy flair of those pix. " Belmondo's tongue-in-cheek presence
was sorely missed in this episode. Fierce gunplay and lots of corpses were not adequate compensation.

BOXCAR BERTHA (American International, 1972) C-92 min.

    Presenters, James H. Nicholson, Samuel Z. Arkoff; producer,
Roger Corman; associate producer, Julie Corman; director, Martin
Scorsese; based on characters in Sister of the Road, the autobiogra-
phy of Boxcar Bertha Thompson as told to Dr. Ben L. Reitman;
screenplay, Joyce H. Corrington, John William Corrington; music,
Gib Guilbeau, Thad Maxwell; music conductor, Herb Cohen; assis-
tant director, Paul Rapp; costumes, Bob Modes; sound, Don F.
Johnson; camera, John Stephens; editor, Buzz Feitshans.
    Barbara Hershey (Boxcar Bertha); David Carradine (Big Bill
Shelley); Barry Primus (Rake Brown); Bernie Casey (Von Morton);
John Carradine (H. Buckram Sartoris); Victor Argo, David R. Oster-
hout (The McIvers); Ann Morell (Tillie Stone); Grahame Pratt (Emeric
Pressburger); Marianne Dole (Mrs. Mailler); Chicken Holleman (M.
Powell); Harry Northup (Harvey Saunders); Joe Reynolds (Joe Dreft).

    After the success of Bonnie and Clyde (1967), q.v., Ameri-
can International, which had produced numerous cheap gangster flicks
since the late 1950s, joined the bandwagon with a series of classy,
well-produced gangster yarns based on fact, such as Bloody Mama
(1970), q.v., and Dillinger (1973), q.v. These films would experience good playoff engagements in smaller houses and at drive-in
theatres. In the summer of 1972, the studio released Boxcar Bertha.
    Barbara Hershey (before she became implanted with the soul
of a seagull and changed her name) starred in the title role of a

hobo girl of the Depression era who joins another hobo (David Carradine) and a black lad (Casey) to stage a series of bank and train robberies.   Made in a new tongue-in-cheek manner with an obvious attempt to imitate the winning style of <u>Bonnie and Clyde</u>, this film suddenly climaxes with a very austere finale.

The best part of the film is a fine recreation of the 1930s period and an excellent picturization of how the economy slump affected rural folk, many of whom became homeless.   One of the results of the Depression, it seems, was the production of an endless assortment of hoodlums, among whom Boxcar Bertha was certainly of the minor variety.   Yet her adventures were souped-up by AIP and, like that studio's predecessors in the species it found its boxoffice market.

One could only wish that in the course of films like this, the director-scripters might find some reason for examining the decades-old question of whether heredity or environment was the cause of the subjects' anti-social behavior.   Such sturdiness of purpose, while not as audience-grabbing as having Big Bill Shelley literally crucified oncamera, might have engendered more meat and purpose for furthering the genre.

BREATHLESS   see   A BOUT DE SOUFFLE

BRENDA STARR, REPORTER   (Columbia, 1945) 13 chapters.

Director, Wallace W. Fox; based on the comic strip by Dale Messick; screenplay, Andy Lamb, George H. Plympton.
Joan Woodbury (Brenda Starr); Kane Richmond (Lieutenant Larry Farrel); Syd Saylor (Chuck Allen); Joe Devlin (Tim); George Meeker (Frank Smith); Wheeler Oakman (Joe Heller/Lew Heller); Cay Forester (Vera Harvey); Marion Burns (Zelda); Lottie Harrison (Abretha); Ernie Adams (Charlie); Jack Ingram (Kruger); Anthony Warde (Muller); John Merton (Schultz); Billy Benedict (Pesky).
Chapters: 1) Hot News; 2) The Blazing Trap; 3) Taken for a Ride; 4) A Ghost Walks; 5) The Big Boss Speaks; 6) Man Hunt; 7) Hideout of Terror; 8) Killer at Large; 9) Dark Magic; 10) A Double-Cross Backfires; 11) On the Spot; 12) Murder at Night; 13) The Mystery of the Payroll.

Films dealing with the newspaper profession have long included the stereotypes of the demanding city editor, the clatter of the newsroom and the daredevil reporter (male, female, or both). All these "The Front Page" plot contrivances were firmly welded into this thirteen-chapter Columbia cliffhanger which proved to be milder in entertainment values than it should have been.
Reporter Brenda Starr (Woodbury) and a photographer (Saylor) cover a fire in an old house and find a dying gangster (Oakman) who is being sought for stealing $250,000.   Joe Heller tells the girl someone took the money from him and he gives her a coded message before he dies.   The killer (Ingram) finds the satchel but it contains only paper, not the loot, and his gang captures Brenda.   They try

to make her talk. She is saved by Chuck Allen and police lieutenant
Larry Farrel. When the message is decoded, the money is located
and the gang goes to jail.

Had Republic made this serial derived from the popular cartoon strip, the action would have been swifter-paced and the special
effects more intricate. As with most action entries of this type,
the gangster's henchmen were presented as brawny dim-wits who do
nothing but sit about staring blankly at walls until their boss calls
them into action. (Do they ever sleep, eat, or think with minds of
their own?) Many agree that this is one of the worst sound serials
ever made, even for Columbia.

BROADWAY (Universal, 1929) 9,661' (color sequences)

Presenter, Carl Laemmle; producer, Carl Laemmle, Jr. ;
director, Paul Fejos; based on the play by Jed Harris, Philip Dunning, George Abbott; screenplay, Edward T. Lowe, Jr. , Charles
Furthman; dialog, Edward T. Lowe, Jr. ; titles, Tom Reed; art director, Charles D. Hall; synchornization-score, Howard Jackson;
songs, Con Conrad, Archie Gottler, and Sidney Mitchell; choreography, Maurice L. Kusell; costumes, Johanna Mathieson; sound, C.
Roy Hunter; special effects, Frank H. Booth; camera, Hal Mohr;
editors, Robert Carlisle, Edward Cahn.

Glenn Tryon (Roy Lane); Evelyn Brent (Pearl); Merna Ken-
nedy (Billie Moore); Thomas Jackson (Dan McCom); Robert Ellis
(Steve Crandall); Otis Harlan ("Porky" Thompson); Paul Porcasi
(Nick Verdis); Marion Lord (Lil Rice); Fritz Feld (Mose Levett);
Leslie Fenton ("Scar" Edwards); Arthur Housman (Dolph); George
Davis (Joe); Betty Francisco (Mazie); Edythe Flynn (Ruby); Florence
Dudley (Ann); Ruby McCoy (Grace); Gus Arnheim & His Coconut
Grove Ambassadors (Themselves).

BROADWAY (Universal, 1942) 91 min.

Producer, Bruce Manning; associate producer, Frank Shaw;
director, William A. Seiter; based on the play by Phillip Dunning,
George Abbott; screenplay, Felix Jackson, John Bright; art director,
Jack Otterson; music director, Charles Previn; costumes, Vera
West; assistant director, Seward Webb; songs, Joe Young, Sam Lew-
is, and Harry Akst; Ben Bernie, Kenneth Casey, and Maceo Pinkard;
Noble Sissle and Eubie Blake; Shelton Brooks; Gus Kahn and Walter
Donaldson; B. D. DeSylva, Lew Brown, and Ray Henderson; chore-
ography, John Mattison; camera, George Barnes.

George Raft (George); Pat O'Brien (Dan McCorn); Janet Blair
(Billie); Broderick Crawford (Steve Crandall); Marjorie Rambeau (Lil);
Anne Gwynne (Pearl); S. Z. Sakall (Nick); Edward S. Brophy (Porky);
Marie Wilson (Grace); Ralf Harolde (Dolph); Arthur Shields (Pete Dai-
ley); Iris Adrian (Maisie); Elaine Morey (Ruby); Dorothy Moore (Ann);
Nestor Paiva (Rinati); Abner Biberman (Trado); Damian O'Flynn
(Scar Edwards); Mack Gray (Himself); Benny Rubin, Anthony Warde,
Charles Jordan, Sammy Stein, Larry McGrath, Charles Sullivan,

S. Z. Sakall, Pat O'Brien, Ralf Harolde, Ed Brophy and Broderick Crawford in Broadway (1942).

Tony Paton, Jimmy O'Gatty (Gangsters); Jennifer Holt (T.W.A. Hostess); Tom Kennedy (Kerry the Cop); John Sheehan (Oscar); Eve March (Mary); Fern Emmett (Will's Wife); Henry Roquemore (Will); Kernan Cripps (Morgue Attendant).

Universal had a sure-fire property when it decided to film Broadway as a sound musical. The 1926 stage show had enjoyed a 603-performance run in New York City, which insured that the general moviegoing public would be well aware of the vehicle's history when it played in their local cinema palace.

In retrospect, the simplistic plot of two nice entertainers (Tryon and Kennedy) who become involved with a bunch of gangsters is rather naive. However, in its day, it was considered fresh enough to support a full blown musical. As an added bonus for this talking picture, the studio expanded the budget to provide for color sequences.

Nick Verdis (Porcasi) runs the Paradise Night Club. When he is killed by a rival gang leader (Ellis), the latter has Roy Lane (Tryon) arrested for the crime, so he can have Billie Moore (Kennedy) for himself. Billie, however, had witnessed the homicide and supports Roy's cause. Thereafter, Verdis' mistress (Brent) shoots Crandall when she finds out he killed her man. The finale finds Roy and Billie free to get married and look forward to a life of happiness.

Although First National's The Show of Shows and MGM's The Broadway Melody (which won the Academy Award) were considered the big musicals of the year, Broadway, with its "daring" gangster flavor, had its own coterie of admirers.   The New York Times complimented it on the "... modernistic decorations, impressive photography and other frills" and declared it "... a handsome entertainment, in which much of the drama of the original survives." As for the sound reproduction, the Times critic was generally pleased, although he observed "... there are moments when there is a distinct change in volume...." " (Simultaneously, a silent version was released to those theatres not yet equipped for sound.)

To offset the rough talk and action of the underworld ambience, there were the nightclub musical interludes, providing occasions for such numbers as "Hot Footin' It," "Hittin' the Ceiling," "Sing a Little Love Song," etc.

While today the speakeasy of the 1920s is a cliché accepted by even the most uninitiated, this world of night spots held a special aura of attraction for Prohibition America.   People were just beginning to equate nightclubs with the underworld, a mysterious linkage that made nocturnal outings to such entertainment spots all the more "fast and loose." Broadway with its hoodlum types, its babes-in-arms chorines and perennially ambitious entertainers, established prototypes that would soon become bland stereotypes in both the movies and the Broadway stage itself.

Thirteen years later Universal dusted off Broadway.   As a gimmick to give new life to the warhorse play, the studio had George Raft portraying himself and telling the story in flashback (thus a period setting could still be used).   Fourteen song numbers were interwoven into the 91-minute feature.

Set primarily in the 1920s (save for the 1942 "modern" sequences), the new Broadway finds George (Raft) and his dance partner (Blair) appearing in a speakeasy run by bootlegger-racketeer Steve Crandall (Crawford).   Crandall becomes Billie's protector when he kills a rival (O'Flynn) and persuades her to try to forget what she has witnessed.   When George is framed for the killing, however, Billie, after prodding from police officer Dan McCorn (O'Brien), tells the truth and frees George.   Later, another dancer (Gwynne) shoots Crandall.   In his report closing out the case, McCorn states the incident was a suicide.

Although full of songs and some action, the 1942 Broadway did not fully develop Raft's screen character, which seemed to stay in the background, although he and Blair did dance the tango.   Despite the relatively rich trappings, the remake of Broadway could not escape its now hackneyed formula.

Naturally, when Universal released its 1940s Broadway it took full, if unsubtle, occasion to exploit the well-known fact that star Raft had been a closer part of the speakeasy-underworld scene than most of the other established screen tough guys, such as Edward G. Robinson, James Cagney, or Paul Muni.

BROADWAY THRU A KEYHOLE   (United Artists, 1933)   90 min.

   Producers, William Goetz, Raymond Griffith; director, Lowell
Sherman; story, Walter Winchell; screenplay, Gene Towne; songs,
Mack Gordon and Harry Revel; choreography, Jack Haskell; camera,
Barney McGill; editor, Maurice Wright.
   Constance Cummings (Joan Whelan); Russ Columbo (Clark
Brian); Paul Kelly (Hank Rocci); Blossom Seeley (Sybil Smith);
Gregory Ratoff (Max Mefoofski); Texas Guinan (Tex Kaley); Hugh
O'Connell (Chuck Haskins); Hobart Cavanaugh (Peanuts Dinwiddle);
C. Henry Gordon (Tim Crowley); William Burress (Thomas Barnum);
Helen Jerome Eddy (Esther); Lucille Ball, Ann Sothern (Girls at
Beach); Eddie Foy, Jr. , Abe Lymam & His Orchestra, Frances
William (Specialties).

   Syndicated columnist Walter Winchell wrote the story on
which this potpurri film was based, and it was the second film for
the fledgling Twentieth Century Pictures.   As an added attraction,
the film had good songs composed by Harry Revel and Mack Gordon,
and a lineup of popular performers that included Russ Columbo,
Blossom Seeley, and Texas Guinan.
   The plot concerns a tough New York hoodlum (Kelly) who
runs a posh club and falls for singer Joan Whelan (Cummings) whom
he makes the star of the establishment.   Hoping she will marry him,
he stops his gang war activities.   When a rival (Gordon) threatens

Paul Kelly, Constance Cummings, Gregory Ratoff, Blossom Seeley,
Hugh O'Connell and Texas Guinan in Broadway Thru a Keyhole
(1933).

the well-bred girl, he sends her to Florida in the care of Sybil Smith (Seeley), who works at his club. In Florida, Joan meets crooner Clark Brian (Columbo) and they, of course, fall in love. When Hank learns of the romance, he orders the trio back to New York where the previously dovish Clark defends his love. In a moment of generousness, Hank steps down and leaves the lovers to their happiness.

With its club background and some well staged music numbers, the film proved rather popular. Singing idol Columbo, who had a pleasing personality, might well have become a major film star had he not died in an accident the next year. In the film Columbo sang one of his more popular tunes, "You're My Past, Present and Future."

The film, which like many another movie, owed a lot to Broadway (1929), q. v. , gave Paul Kelly an opportunity to play a gangster in a class "A" production. In subsequent years he would play many such roles, but, like Lloyd Nolan, he was usually relegated to doing his bit in programmer films. Watch for Lucille Ball and Ann Sothern in fleeting bits in the Florida beach scene.

BROTHER ORCHID (Warner Bros. , 1940) 91 min.

Executive producer Hal B. Wallis; associate producer, Mark Hellinger; director, Lloyd Bacon; story, Richard Connell; screenplay, Earl Baldwin; assistant director, Dick Mayberry; art director, Max Parker; music, Heinz Roemheld; special effects, Byron Haskin, Willard Van Enger; camera, Tony Gaudio; editor, William Holmes.

Edward G. Robinson ("Little John" Sarto); Ann Sothern (Flo Addams); Humphrey Bogart (Jack Buck); Ralph Bellamy (Clarence Fletcher); Donald Crisp (Brother Superior); Allen Jenkins (Willie the Knife Corson); Charles D. Brown (Brother Wren); Cecil Kellaway (Brother Goodwin); Joseph Crehan (Brother MacEwen); Wilfred Lucas (Brother MacDonald); Morgan Conway (Philadelphia Powell); Richard Lane (Mugsy O'Day); John Ridgely (Texas Pearson); Dick Wessel (Buffalo Burns); Tom Tyler (Curley Mathews); Paul Phillips (French Frank); Dan Rowan (Al Muller); Granville Bates (Pattonsville Superintendent); Nanette Vallon (Fifi); Paul Guilfoyle (Red Martin); Tim Ryan (Turkey Malone); Joe Caits (Handsome Harry Edwards); Pat Gleason (Dopey Perkins); Tommy Baker (Joseph); John Qualen (Mr. Pigeon); Leonard Mudie, Charles Coleman (Englishmen); William Hopper, George Haywood, Creighton Hale (Reporters); Mary Gordon (Mrs. Sweeney the Landlady); Harlan Briggs (Thomas A. Bailey); Sam McDaniel (Janitor); Frank Orth (Waiter); Frank Faylen (Superintendent of Service).

By 1940 Warner Bros. seemed almost to have played out the gangster cycle and, in order to inject new life into the genre, combined serious drama with farce in Brother Orchid.

"Little John" Sarto (Robinson) abandons his criminal milieu to go abroad to acquire culture and status. He returns home to find a rival (Bogart) has usurped his leadership of the mob. "Little John" forms another gang and tries to combat Jack Buck, but he is

captured and taken for a one-way ride. Nearly killed and certainly
left for dead, he is taken to a nearby monastery where the brothers
grow flowers, sell them, and give the proceeds to the poor. There
he slowly adjusts to the unique atmosphere. He finds a peaceful
way of life at the cloisters, taking enormous pleasure in growing
orchids. When he later learns that his girl (Sothern) plans to wed
a rancher (Bellamy) he returns to the outside world. He soon discovers that Flo is really in love with this Clarence Fletcher. When
he is informed that Buck and the boys are out to take over the monastery's flower business, he decides it is time to fight Buck to the
finish. Having accomplished his mission, he returns to the monastery, having found "real class."

The New York Herald-Tribune said the film was the "gayest
variation of the gangster film since A Slight Case of Murder ...
frequently hilarious," while the New York Times labeled it a "lively
farce."

Taking a cue from the flavorful Damon Runyon, Brother Orchid is not only often very funny indeed, but is also frequently
touching. Near the end of the film, "Little John" plans to return
to the monastery and has no need for the several hundred dollars
on his person. He asks an old scrub woman if she has anyone to
care for her. She says she does not, and he gives her the cash.
Could this really be "Little Caesar"?

THE BROTHERHOOD (Paramount, 1968)   C-96 min.

     Producer, Kirk Douglas; director, Martin Ritt; screenplay,
Lewis John Carlino; music, Lalo Schifrin; art director, Tambi Lar-
sen, Toni Sarzi-Braga; set decorators, Robert Drumheller, Giorgio
Postiglione; scenic artist, Murray Stern; costumes, Ruth Morley;
makeup, Martin Bell; assistant director, Peter Scoppa; sound, Jack
C. Jacobsen; camera, Boris Kaufman; second unit camera, Americo
Gengarelli; editor, Frank Bracht.
     Kirk Douglas (Frank Ginetta); Alex Cord (Vince Ginetta);
Irene Papas (Ida Ginetta); Luther Adler (Dominick Bertolo); Susan
Strasberg (Emma Ginetta); Murray Hamilton (Jim Egan); Eduardo
Ciannelli (Don Peppino); Joe De Santis (Pietro Rizzi); Connie Scott
(Carmela Ginetta); Val Avery (Jake Rotherman); Val Bisoglio (Cheech);
Alan Hewitt (Sol Levin); Barry Primus (Vido); Michele Cimarosa
(Toto); Louis Badolati (Don Turridu).

     Unfortunately for this mediocre Mafia melodrama, it pre-
dated The Godfather (1972), q.v., and had relatively little effect at
the boxoffice (despite a promotional campaign which featured Kirk
Douglas and Alex Douglas engaged in a "kiss of death").
     "... [B]lunt, square and sentimental" is how the New York
Times pegged this Kirk Douglas vehicle. (He was both producer
and star.) In unflattering terms, Martin Ritt directed this cloying
account of Frank (Douglas), a middle-aged member of a Mafia family
whose ideas clash with the rest of the family's. He is immersed
in the old regime and opposes new attempts by the family to branch
out into syndicate operations. His brother, Vince (Cord), however,

Alex Cord and Kirk Douglas in The Brotherhood (1968).

favors the plans, and is eventually assigned to murder Frank.
        In The Films of Kirk Douglas (1972), Tony Thomas pinpointed
the problems with The Brotherhood. 'No matter how human the
hoods are at home and no matter how businesslike their dealings,
the film strains the interest and sympathy of the viewer.... The
film tacitly invites sympathy from the audience for the one [old]
style against the other [new one], and in siding with the old rogues,
who appear to have all the personality and all the chivalry, however
warped, the viewer leaves the picture with a certain confusion, if
not guilt. "
        The addition of such veteran gangster actors as Eduardo
Ciannelli and Luther Adler did not save the effort. Ciannelli, however, did have one good scene in Douglas' warehouse where he and
his men arrive to give Douglas the assignment of killing an informer.

THE BROTHERS RICO (Columbia, 1957) 91 1/2 min.

        Producer, Lewis J. Rackmil; director, Phil Karlson; based
on the novel by Georges Simenon; screenplay, Lewis Meltzer, Ben
Perry; art director, Robert Boyle; music director, Morris Stoloff;
music, George Duning; camera, Burnett Guffey; editor, Charles
Nelson.
        Richard Conte (Eddi Rico); Dianne Foster (Alice Rico);

Richard Conte, Jane Easton, Peggy Maley and Richard Bakalyan in
The Brothers Rico (1957).

Kathryn Grant (Norah); Larry Gates (Sid Kubik); James Darren
(Johhny Rico); Argentina Brunetti (Mrs. Rico); Lamont Johnson (Pe-
ter Malaks); Harry Bellaver (Mike Lamotta); Paul Picerni (Gino
Rico); Paul Dubov (Phil); Rudy Bond (Gonzales); Richard Bakalyan
(Vic Tucci); William Phipps (Joe Wesson); Mimi Aguglia (Julia Rico);
Maggie O'Byrne (Mrs. Felici); George Cisar (Dude Cowboy); Peggy
Maley (Jean); Jane Easton (Nellie); James Waters (Laundry Truck
Driver); George Lewis (El Camino Desk Clerk); Betsy Jones More-
land (Looping Voice).

        A "gangbuster nightmare" is how Time described this adap-
tation of a Georges Simenon novel, while Newsweek carped, "...
the movie is fully short of good suspense from a lack of inspired
directing." (Director Phil Karlson would later become something
of a minor cult figure in the late 1960s, admired for his ability to
handle action sequences.)
        Eddie Rico (Conte), a one-time major accountant for the syn-
dicate, has gone legitimate, and now has a wife, a family, and a
nice home. A syndicate leader, however, tells him he must help
to find Johnny Rico (Darren). Eddie does not know that Johnny had
bolted after participating in a murder, and that the crime ring now
wants to liquidate him. Before the action is completed in this swift-
moving feature, Eddie's other brother (Picerni) has been killed, and
Eddie, with the help of a district attorney, has turned on his former
bosses.

Very effective is Larry Gates as Sid Kubik, the "hit" man
who shadows Eddie's every step, keeping the organization posted on
this key figure.

BRUTE FORCE   (Universal, 1947)   98 min.

Producer, Mark Hellinger; associate producer, Jules Buck;
director, Jules Dassin; story, Robert Patterson; screenplay, Richard
Brooks; art directors, Bernard Herzbrun, John F. De Cuir; set
decorators, Russell A. Gausman, Charles Wyrick; music, Miklos
Rozsa; assistant director, Fred Frank; sound, Charles Felstead,
Robert Pritchard; special camera, David S. Horsley; camera, Wil-
liam Daniels; editor, Edward Curtiss.
Burt Lancaster (Joe Collins); Hume Cronyn (Captain Munsey);
Charles Bickford (Gallagher); Sam Levene (Louis); Howard Duff
("Soldier"); Roman Bohnen (Warden Barnes); Art Smith (Dr. Walters);
John Hoyt (Spencer); Richard Gaines (McCallum); Frank Puglia (Fer-
rara); Jeff Corey ("Freshman"); Vince Barnett (Muggsy); James Bell
(Crenshaw); Yvonne De Carlo (Gina); Ann Blyth (Ruth); Ella Raines
(Cora); Anita Colby (Flossie); Jack Overman (Kid Coy); Whit Bissell
(Tom Lister); Sir Lancelot ("Calypso").

Despite all the gangster films which had preceded Brute
Force, this was the most important picture to depict prison conditions as they might well be in too many of America's penal institutions.   It gave even the most blase and cynical observers cause to
ponder whether the punishment being meted out to lawbreakers was
more severe than necessary.   For moviegoers Brute Force, while
engaging in its own brand of pretentiousness and stereotypes, did
help to dispel the clichés of the 1930s Warner Bros. prison dramas,
where every maximum security cell had such "star" convicts as
James Cagney, Humphrey Bogart, John Garfield, Edward G. Robinson, Joe Sawyer, et al., every guard was a carbon copy of tough
Barton MacLane, and every warden as genteel and humanitarian as
Pat O'Brien or Henry O'Neill.
Thus it was surprising that Bosley Crowther (New York
Times) could so matter-of-factly say of Brute Force, 'Not having
intimate knowledge of prisons or prisoners, we wouldn't know whether the average American convict is so cruelly victimized as are the
principal inmates [here] ....   But to judge by this 'big house' melodrama, the poor chaps who languish in our jails are miserably and
viciously mistreated and their jailers are either weaklings or brutes. "
(Other critics noted that the inmates are all good guys, the guards
all villains.)
In this line-up of convicts versus law enforcers, there are
prisoners Joe Collins (Lancaster), aging Gallagher (Bickford), Louie
(Sam Levene), "Soldier" (Duff), "Freshman" (Corey), and assorted
others.   Through flashbacks, their individual stories are retold,
giving an overly generous interpretation to the forces that led them
to a prison cell.   On the other hand, there is little kindly explana-
tion to explicate the ineffectualness of Warden Barnes (Bohnen), the
drunken doctor (Smith) or, least of all, the sadistic captain of the
guards (Cronyn).

In addition, unfortunately, there are the standard scenes of the prison exercise yard, the mess-hall, the men at occupational therapy, the prisoners corralled into their iron-barred cells, and assorted byways where recalcitrant convicts are punished. There is the expected riot, the retribution against the cruel jailers, and the inevitable slaughter of innocent and guilty alike before the uprising is quelled. But whether because of the thoughtful performance of Bickford as Gallagher, who runs the prison newspaper, or the sensitive acting of other actor-convicts, every viewer of this film can derive new insights into the actuality of prison life. One begins to sense that the on-camera criminal who flirts so dangerously with unlawful acts is not usually equipped to cope with the deadening effect of imprisonment.

An interesting observation on both Brute Force and The Criminal (1960), q. v., is that each of the films' directors (Dassin and Joseph Losey) was a victim of the anti-Red purge of late-1940s Hollywood. Perhaps it was not so strange that two of the best features on American-British jails should have been directed by these leftist-oriented film helmers.

A BULLET FOR JOEY   (United Artists, 1955)   85 min.

Producers, Samuel Bischoff, David Diamond; director, Lewis Allen; story, James Benson Nablo; screenplay, Geoffrey Homes, A. I. Bezzerides; music, Harry Sukman; assistant director, Bert Blazer; camera, Harry Neumann; editor, Leon Barsha.

Edward G. Robinson (Inspector Raoul Leduc); George Raft (Joe Victor); Audrey Totter (Joyce Geary); George Dolenz (Carl Macklin); Peter Hanson (Fred); Peter Van Eyck (Eric Hartman); Karen Verne (Mrs. Hartman); Ralph Smiley (Paola); Henri Letondal (Dubois); John Cliff (Morrie); Joseph Vitale (Nick); Bill Bryant (Jack Allen); Stan Malotte (Paul); Toni Gerry (Yvonne Temblay); Sally Blane (Marie); Steven Geray (Garcia); John Alvin (Percy); Bill Henry (Artist).

The teaming of George Raft and Edward G. Robinson in Manpower (1942), along with Marlene Dietrich, resulted in good boxoffice. In 1955 United Artists attempted to rekindle that popularity with the two aging gangster stars being placed opposite each other in the Cold War-espionage-gangster opus, A Bullet for Joey. The results were more nostalgic than hard-hitting.

The rather complex plotline has deported hoodlum Joe Victor (Raft) being brought from Lisbon to aid in the kidnapping of a Canadian atomic physicist (Dolenz). A U.S. agent (Robinson) begins to connect three murders with the scientist's disappearance and soon stumbles onto the kidnapping plot, which is led by the leader of the spy ring (Van Eyck). Joe calls in his former henchmen (Bryant) and his girl (Totter), but the spies kill the scientist's secretary (Gerry) and Joyce falls in love with Macklin. After the kidnapping is staged, Inspector Leduc traces the gang to a ship and a gun battle ensues. During the subsequent interplay, Joe discovers just how un-American the gang is and, just as Alan Ladd did in Lucky Jordan

Steven Geray and George Raft in A Bullet for Joey (1955).

(1942), q.v., he double-crosses his associates. For his "patriotic" efforts he is killed, but not before he has helped the River Patrol corral the enemy agent gang.

Because this mixed-breed genre piece is not enough of one species or another, it failed to find its proper marketplace, except as a quickly forgotten item on the action film circuit. Said Bosley Crowther (New York Times) of this mishmash, "There are things Mr. Raft and Mr. Robinson can act with their eyes shut and sometimes do."

A BULLET FOR PRETTY BOY (American International, 1970)
C-89 min.

Producer-director, Larry Buchanan; story, Enrique Touceda, Buchanan; screenplay, Henry Rosenbaum; music, Harley Hatcher; music supervisor, Al Simms; costumes, Ron Scott; sound, Lawrence Gianneschi, Sr., Lynn Brooks; camera, James R. Davidson; editor, Miguel Levin.

Fabian Forte (Charles "Pretty Boy" Floyd); Jocelyn Lane (Betty); Astrid Warner (Ruby); Michael Haynes (Ned Short); Adam Roarke ("Preacher"); Robert Glenn (Hossler); Anne MacAdams (Beryl); Camilla Carr (Helen); Jeff Alexander (Wallace); Desmond Dhooge (Harvey); Bill Thurman (Huddy); Hugh Feagin (Jack Dowler); Jessie Lee Fulton (Mrs. Floyd); James Harrell (Mr. Floyd); Gene Ross (William); Ed Lo Russo (Boy); Charlie Dell (Charlie); Eddie Thomas (Ben Dowler); Frank De Benedett (Lester Floyd); Ethan Allen (Seth); Troy K. Hoskins (Sheriff Taylor).

One of the more notorious criminals of the 1930s was Charles Arthur "Pretty Boy" Floyd, who was gunned down by federal officers in 1934. Just how much of a criminal he really was is still subject to debate. He definitely robbed one bank. However, myth (a song by Woody Guthrie) and local sentiment built him up to the ranks of John Dillinger (with whom he supposedly worked) and other big-name criminals of the Thirties. The cinema/television has occasionally borrowed the character of "Pretty Boy" for a supposed biography: in 1959 with John Ericson, with Fabian Forte in 1970, and in 1974 with Martin Sheen.

The Fabian version, A Bullet for Pretty Boy, had little to do with reality but was another in American International's series of 1970s films romanticizing criminals of the 1930s. Harry Rosenbaum's script depicted Pretty Boy as more of a knight in shining armor to the poor folks of the South than a bank robber. AIP strengthened the proceedings with plenty of color and action, which resulted in good payoffs at secondary cinemas and drive-in theatres.

As Pretty Boy, who earned the nickname not because of his looks but for his continual combing of his hair, Fabian, billed as Fabian Forte, was surprisingly effective, despite the script's lack of convincing motivation.

Director-producer-co-story-creator Larry Buchanan had previously helmed such AIP-TV remakes as Zontar, The Thing from Venus, The Eye Creatures, and Creatures of Destruction.

BULLETS OR BALLOTS (First National, 1936) 81 min.

Associate producer, Louis F. Edelman; director, William Keighley; story, Martin Mooney, Seton I. Miller; screenplay, Miller; assistant director, Chuck Hansen; art director, Carl Jules Weyl; music, Heinz Roemheld; sound, Oliver S. Garretson; special effects, Fred Jackman, Jr., Warren E. Lynch; camera, Hal Mohr; editor, Jack Killifer.

Edward G. Robinson (Johhny Blake); Joan Blondell (Lee Morgan); Barton MacLane (Al Kruger); Humphrey Bogart (Nick "Bugs" Fenner); Frank McHugh (Herman); Joseph King (Captain Dan McLaren); Richard Purcell (Ed Driscoll); George E. Stone (Wires); Louise Beavers (Nellie LaFleur); Joseph Crehan (Grand Jury Spokesman); Henry O'Neill (Bryant); Gilbert Emery (Thorndyke); Henry Kolker (Hollister); Herbert Rawlinson (Caldwell); Rosalind Marquis (Specialty); Norman Willis (Vinci); Frank Faylen (Gatley); Alice Lyndon (Old Lady); Victoria Vinton (Ticket Seller); Addison Richards

Barton MacLane, Humphrey Bogart, Edward G. Robinson and Joan
Blondell in <u>Bullets or Ballots</u> (1936).

(Announcer's Voice); Harry Watson, Jerry Madden (Kids); Herman
Marks, Benny the Gouge, Al Hill, Dutch Schlickenmeyer (Men);
Eddie Shubert (Truck Driver); Max Wagner (Actor Impersonating
Kruger); Milton Kibbee (Jury Foreman); Ed Stanley (Judge); Ralph
M. Remley (Kelly); Anne Nagel, Gordon "Bill" Elliott (Bank Secre-
taries); Carlyle Moore, Jr. (Kruger's Secretary).

On the right side of the law for a change, Edward G. Robinson was cast as cop Johnny Blake who joins a New York City mob
as a secret operative for a crime investigator (King).   Later Blake
rises to power, after he persuades the group to go into the numbers
rackets which his girl (Blondell) operates.   The move proves successful but the gang leader (MacLane) is murdered by a power-
hungry rival (Bogart).   Blake is now forced into a position of taking
over the mob's operations.   He eventually learns the identities of
the dishonest bankers.   Just at this point, Nick Fenner unmasks
his true identity.   In the ensuing gun battle both Blake and Fenner
are killed, but not before Johnny relays the names of the bosses to
the proper authorities.
        Once again, Warners succeeded at the boxoffice by yanking a
story from the headlines.   Efficiently directed by William Keighley,
the production benefitted from the studio's stock company, the members of which were well attuned to performing in such gangster melodramas.   The <u>New York Times</u> rated it "crisp, cohesive, " while

the New York Herald-Tribune judged it "taut and compelling. "
Bullets or Ballots remains a favorite with Humphrey Bogart fans.

BULLITT   (Warner Bros. -Seven Arts, 1968)   C-114 min.

        Executive producer, Robert E. Relyea; producer, Philip
D'Antoni; director, Peter Yates; based on the novel Mute Witness
by Robert L. Pike; screenplay, Alan R. Trustman, Harry Kleiner;
art director, Albert Brenner; set decorators, Ralph S. Hurst,
Philip Abramson; music, Lalo Schifrin; costumes, Theadora Van
Runkle; assistant directors, Tim Zinnemann, Daisy Gerber; sound,
John K. Kean; special effects, Sass Bedig; camera, William A.
Fraker; editor, Frank P. Keller.
        Steve McQueen (Detective Lieutenant Frank Bullitt); Robert
Vaughn (Walter Chalmers); Jacqueline Bisset (Cathy); Don Gordon
(Detective Delgetti); Robert Duvall (Weissberg the Cab Driver);
Simon Oakland (Captain Bennet); Norman Fell (Captain Baker); George
Stanford Brown (Dr. Willard); Justin Tarr (Eddy the Informer); Carl
Reindel (Detective Stanton); Felice Orlandi (Ross the Decoy); Victor
Tayback (Pete Ross); Robert Lipton (Aide); Ed Peck (Wescott); Pat

Steve McQueen and Robert Vaughn in Bullitt (1968).

Renella (Johnny Ross [Renick]); Paul Genge (Hired Killer); John
Aprea (Killer); Al Checco (Desk Clerk); Bill Hickman (Phil).

'Reminiscent in style of the good old Warner Bros. crime
films of the '40s, Bullitt is given a distinct touch of Now by Director Peter Yates. The movie is full of gritty city details and has
a streaking pace... " (Time). Other critics called the film 'bright,
diamond-hard and glittering. " The public responded to this feature
in a big way; it earned over $19 million in distributors' domestic
rentals.

Besides containing one of the fastest, most exciting and best
produced chase sequences in film history, Bullitt is notable for its
sharp depiction of the anti-hero, a deadpan lead character who displays as little emotion in dangerous situations as in bed with the
girl of the moment.

Taken from Robert L. Pike's engaging novel, Mute Witness,
the storyline is translated by the filmmakers into action cinematic
terms. San Francisco police detective Frank Bullitt (McQueen) dis-
obeys his ambitious political superior (Vaughn) and tracks down and
kills a Chicago hoodlum who has stolen a fortune and who was promised a deal if he would testify before a Senate Committee.

Typical of this cynical study of the uneasy alliance between
police and politicians (as well as between public officials and the
underworld) is the finale, which finds politician Chalmers riding off
into the mist in his luxuriant car, a sticker on his bumper stating,
"Support Your Local Police. "

Frank P. Keller won an Oscar for the film's editing.

BUNNY O'HARE (American International, 1971) C-92 min.

Executive producers, James H. Nicholson, Samuel Z. Arkoff;
co-producer, Norman T. Herman; producer-director, Gerd Oswald;
story, Stanley Z. Cherry; screenplay, Cherry, Coslough Johnson;
music, Billy Strange; wardrobe, Phyllis Garr; makeup, Beau Wilson;
creative consultant, John Astin; assistant director, Rusty Meek;
sound, Howard Warren; camera, Loyal Griggs, John Stephens; second unit camera, Michael Dugan; editor, Fred Feitshans, Jr.

Bette Davis (Bunny O'Hare); Ernest Borgnine (Bill Green
[Gruenwald]); Jack Cassidy (Lieutenant Horace Greeley); Joan De-
laney (R. J. Hart); Jay Robinson (John C. Rupert); John Astin (Ad);
Reva Rose (Lulu); Robert Foulk (Commissioner Dingle); Brayden
Linden (Frank); Karen Mae Johnson (Lola); Francis R. Cody (Rhett);
Hank Wickham (Speed); J. Rob Jordan (Policeman Nerdman); Darra
Lyn Tobin (Elvia); Governor David Cargo (Himself).

How could it miss? A modern day Bonnie and Clyde with
veteran Oscar winners Bette Davis and Ernest Borgnine as an older
generation couple robbing banks and getting away on a motorcycle.
But the best laid plans of mice, men, and American International
sometimes go astray. The only results of Bunny O'Hare were bad
reviews, poor business, and a lawsuit filed by Miss Davis.

With much publicity, Davis and Borgnine, who had co-starred

in The Catered Affair (1956), were reunited to play a dispossessed grandmother and a bank robber joined together to relieve banks of money for better causes.   Quickly turning into hippie freaks, the superannuated couple are constantly pursued by a young cop, get involved in a shoot-out, and eventually head for the Mexican border and safety, as in The Getaway.

At the time Miss Davis signed for the part she stated it was a good comedy role and one she would enjoy. She did not enjoy the on-location shooting, nor the final release print distributed by AIP. The actress promptly sued the film company for five million dollars, claiming "fradulent misrepresentation." Director Gerd Oswald agreed with his star, saying the released film was "... a different film from the one we had conceived."

With all the talent involved, it is a shame that the film could not have focused a little less on the slapstick comedy elements and a good deal more on the offbeat situation of a middle-aged citizen turning to a life of crime.

BUY ME THAT TOWN (Paramount, 1941) 70 min.

Producer, Sol C. Siegel; associate producer, Eugene Zukor; director, Eugene Forde; based on a story by Harry A. Gourfain, Murray Boltinoff, Martin Rackin; screenplay, Gordon Kahn; art directors, Hans Dreier, Haldane Douglas; camera, Theodor Sparkuhl; editor, William Shea.

Lloyd Nolan (Rickey Deane); Constance Moore (Virginia Paradise); Albert Dekker (Louis Lanzer); Sheldon Leonard (Chink Moran); Vera Vague (Henrietta Teagarden); Edward Brophy (Ziggy); Warren Hymer (Crusher); Horace McMahon (Fingers); Richard Carle (Judge Paradise); Rod Cameron (Gerard); Russell Hicks (Malcolm); Charles Lane (J. Montague Gainsborough); Edwin Maxwell (P. V. Baxter); Pierre Watkin (Carlton Williams); Jack Chapin (Tom); Keith Richards (Harry); Trevor Bardette (George); John Harmon, Si Jenks (Hecklers); Lillian Yarbo (Nancy); Ann Doran, Jane Keckley, Grace Hayle (Women).

"Although the cycle of snarling gangster films has gone to seed, it still blossoms up here and there in such unpretentious little comedies as Buy Me That Town..." (New York Times).

Moviegoers who caught this little item got their money's worth. Rather dopey but good-natured crook Rickey Deane (Nolan) and his cronies take over a hamlet, pulling the community out of bankruptcy. What is their scheme? A group of affluent law manipulators want immunity from prosecution of heavier charges elsewhere and persuade Rickey and the boys to keep them in the local jail under minor charges.   Fine, but the fee is $1,000 a week per capita, a sum which the tycoons willingly pay.

Lay enforcers must have rejoiced to find that on one occasion, at least, it was the bad guys, not the good guys, who were mentally dense.

Constance Moore, Lloyd Nolan and Albert Dekker in <u>Buy Me That Town</u> (1941).

CAGED (Warner Bros. , 1950) 96 min.

　　　　Producer, Jerry Wald; director, John Cromwell; story-screen-play, Virginia Kellogg, Bernard C. Schoenfeld; art director, Charles H. Clarke; music, Max Steiner; camera, Carl Guthrie; editor, Owen Marks.
　　　　Eleanor Parker (Marie Allen); Agnes Moorehead (Ruth Benton); Ellen Corby (Emma); Hope Emerson (Evelyn Harper); Betty Garde (Kitty Stark); Jan Sterling (Smoochie); Lee Patrick (Elvira Powell); Olive Deering (June); Jane Darwell (Isolation Matron); Gertrude Michael (Georgia); Sheila [MacRae] Stevens (Helen); Gertrude Hoffman (Millie); Queenie Smith (Mrs. Warren); Esther Howard (Grace); Edith Evanson (Miss Barker); Ann Tyrell (Edna); Taylor Holmes (Senator Donnolly); Ruth Warren (Miss Lyons).

　　　　It was not all peaches and cream to be the moll of a gang-ster, or even to be a distaff criminal. As <u>Caged</u> dramatically (and theatrically) depicts, prison is hell on earth for most female con-victs.
　　　　Co-scripter Virginia Kellogg did on-the-spot research for the

Eleanor Parker and Agnes Moorehead in Caged (1950).

scenario by spending several months as a planted prisoner in assorted state penitentiaries. The result was a gripping screen drama, a bit too showy, but quite gritty in its revelation of life behind
the big bars.

If sociologists/psychologists/psychiatrists are still uncertain
about what makes a person a criminal in the first place, most everyone is convinced that incarceration in prison can turn the most
innocent soul into a hardened, "unregenerated social outcast."

To provide the plot thrust, there is Marie Allen (Parker),
the young woman whose husband is killed in the process of robbing
a gas station. She is implicated in the crime and sentenced to a
jail term. Once inside the big walls, she becomes susceptible to
all the tough forces (sadistic matrons, cruel prisoners, the monotonous life of deprivation and humiliation) that rob her of her essential goodness. She has her child within the prison, but the future
holds only bleakness for the now-corrupted inmate.

Besides the large array of cameo performances of actress
"inmates" there is Hope Emerson as Evelyn Harner, the hulking,
vicious prison guard, and Agnes Moorehead as Ruth Benton, the
humanitarian warden who must cope with the corrupt forces in order to push through her reform program.

It is interesting to contrast this post-World War II study with The Snake Pit (1948), the Olivia de Havilland study of a mental asylum. Each reveals aspects of American institutionalization at its worst.

CASBAH (Universal, 1948) 94 min.

Producer, Nat G. Goldstone; associate producer, Erik Charell; director, John Berry; based upon the novel Pepe Le Moko by Detective Ashelbe (Henri La Barthe); screenplay, Ladislas Bush-Fekete, Arnold Manoff; musical story, Charell; art directors, Bernard Herzbrun, John F. DeCuir; set decorators, Russell A. Gausman, Oliver Emert; music, Harold Arlen; music director, Walter Scharf; choreography, Bernard Pearce; costumes, Yvonne Wood; makeup, Bud Westmore; assistant director, Jack Voglin; sound, Leslie I. Carey, Jack A. Bolger, Jr.; special effects, David S. Horsley; camera, Irving Glassberg; editor, Edward Curtiss.

Yvonne De Carlo (Inez); Tony Martin (Pepe Le Moko); Peter Lorre (Slimane); Marta Toren (Gaby); Hugo Haas (Omar); Thomas Gomez (Louvain); Douglas Dick (Carlo); Katherine Dunham (Odette); Herbert Rudley (Claude); Gene Walker (Roland); Curt Conway (Maurice); Andre Pola (Willem); Barry Bernard (Max); Virginia Gregg (Madeline); Will Lee (Beggar); Harris Brown (Pierre); Houseley

Tony Martin and Hugo Haas in Casbah (1948).

Stevenson (Anton Duval); Robert Kendall (Ahmed); Rosita Marstini
(Woman); Jody Gilbert, Kathleen Freeman (American Women);
George J. Lewis (Detective); Major Sam Harris, Kathryn Wilson
(British Tourists); Katherine Dunham Dance Troupe with Eartha Kitt
(Themselves); Barry Norton (Pilot); Robert Lorraine (Tourist).

Fond memories of the French-made Pepe le Moko (1937),
q. v. , and the American remake, Algiers (1938), q. v. , sparked
Universal to translate the popular tale into a new movie musical.
Casbah had too much gloss to live up to the first two versions, but good performances, especially by Tony Martin and Peter
Lorre (respectively as the charming jewel thief and the determined
police inspector) gave the production some body.   Unfortunately an
inexperienced Marta Toren played the role of Gaby, which should
have gone to Yvonne De Carlo (stuck with the stereotyped native
girl's part).
Besides bouyant Martin, the other strong point of Casbah is
a romantic score by Harold Arlen and Leo Robin.   Using an oldie,
"Hooray for Love, " the writers added three lush romantic tunes,
"For Every Man There's a Woman, " "It Was Written in the Start, "
and "What's Good about Goodbye. " A very romantic scene occurs
when Martin's Pepe and Toren's Gaby walk along the rooftops of the
Casbah as the former intones a musical love chant.
But all in all Casbah was a far cry from the Gallic original:
the bite of the initial story was lost in fable-esque fabrication.
Moreover, the duality of a criminal's life, on the one hand daring
and invigorating, on the other drab and depressing, was cast aside
in favor of Hollywood concepts of romantic thieves.   One could almost imagine this as a vehicle for Maria Montez and Jon Hall.

CASTLE ON THE HUDSON (Warner Bros. , 1940) 76 min.

Associate producer, Samuel Bischoff; director, Anatole Lit-
vak; based on the book 20,000 Years in Sing Sing by Warden Lewis
E. Lawes; screenplay, Seton I. Miller, Brown Holmes, Courtenay
Terrett; camera, Arthur Edeson; editor, Thomas Richards.
John Garfield (Tommy Gordon); Ann Sheridan (Kay Manners);
Pat O'Brien (Warden Walter Long); Burgess Meredith (Steven Rock-
ford); Jerome Cowan (Ed Crowley); Henry O'Neill (District Attorney);
Guinn Williams (Mike Cagle); John Litel (Prison Chaplain); Edward
Pawley (Black Jack); Grant Mitchell (Psychologist); Margot Steven-
son (Ann Rockford); Willard Robertson (Ragan); Nedda Harrigan (Mrs.
Long); Wade Boteler (Mac--Principal Keeper); Billy Wayne (Pete);
Joseph Downing (Gangster); Barbara Pepper (Goldie); Robert Strange
(Joe Harris); Walter Miller, Pat O'Malley (Guards); Pat Flaherty
(Stretcher Attendant); Ed Kane (Club Manager); Frank Faylen (Guard
Who Is Slugged); Eddie Acuff (Bill the Clerk); Adrian Morris (Pris-
oner); William Hopper (Reporter); Lee Phelps (Guard in Visitor's
Room).

Despite stage success, John Garfield was badly misused by
Warner Bros. during the early years of his film career.   Often he

was assigned to remakes such as this feature, an economical retelling of Warden Lewis E. Lawes' book 20,000 Years in Sing Sing, filmed earlier (1933), q.v., under the book's title with Spencer Tracy, Bette Davis, and Lyle Talbot.

Far more so than the earlier edition, this version stressed the concept of the criminal as a victim of his environment. (Who better played the Depression-abused young man than Garfield?) In the course of the film, Garfield's Tommy Gordon expostulates on just how fate (not moral indifference) has done him dirt. He barks that he was arrested on a Saturday, sentenced on a Saturday, taken to prison on a Saturday, given a bum murder rap for a Saturday's mistake, and come to think of it, he was even born on a Saturday. (Interestingly, that same year Garfield starred in Warners' Saturday's Children, based on the Broadway play.)

With Tommy Gordon as a swaggering criminal and Kay Manners (Sheridan) as his teary girl friend, the formula-induced story was completed by having considerate Pat O'Brien cast as Warden Walter Long. The latter is the thoughtful supervisor who allows Tommy permission to leave jail long enough to visit dying Kay. Will this allegedly socially-unconscionable young man return to prison? Yes! He has grown to respect the warden and does not want him to lose his job at the hands of his political enemies. At the finale, he goes to the electric chair, wisecracking all the way.

As far as depicting the scope and depth of prison life, Castle on the Hudson was as guilty as almost every other picture of the period in delineating the (stock) type of prisoner, guard, and prison conditions. Rising above the stereotype, a bit, was Burgess Meredith as Steven Rockford, the college graduate convict who commits suicide when his jailbreak attempts fail.

CELL 2455, DEATH ROW (Columbia, 1955) 77 min.

Producer, Wallace MacDonald; director, Fred F. Sears; based on the book by Caryl Chessman; screenplay, Jack De Witt; assistant director, Eddie Saeta; art director, Robert Peterson; music director, Mischa Bakaleinikoff; camera, Fred Jackman, Jr.; editor, Henry Batista.

William Campbell (Whit); Robert Campbell (Whit as a Boy); Marian Carr (Doll); Kathryn Grant (Jo-Anne); Harvey Stephens (Warden); Vince Edwards (Hamilton); Allen Nourse (Serl); Diane De Laire (Hallie); Paul Dubov (Al; Tyler MacDuff (Nugent); Buck Kartalian (Monk); Jimmy Murphy (Sonny); Jerry Mickelson (Tom); Bruce Sharpe (Bud); Wayne Taylor (Skipper Adams).

Based on the real life-death of Caryl Chessman, whose bouts with stays of executions and retrials, and whose eventual execution led to tremendous public concern about the rationale of capital punishment, this feature attempted to present a low-keyed version of this "lover's lane" killer. Unfortunately, due to poor production values and rather sleazy acting, it resulted in a hackneyed prison drama, nowhere near as powerful as Susan Hayward's I Want to

Live (1958), q.v., or the similar, but rightly unheralded Terry
Moore variation, Why Must I Die? (1960).

CHARLIE CHAN ON BROADWAY   (Twentieth Century-Fox, 1937)
68 min.

        Producer, John Stone; director, Eugene Forde; based on the
character created by Earl Derr Biggers; story, Art Arthur, Robert
Ellis, Helen Logan; screenplay, Charles S. Belden, Jerry Cady;
camera, Harry Jackson; editor, Al De Gaetano.
        Warner Oland (Charlie Chan); J. Edward Bromberg (Murdock);
Joan Marsh (Joan Wendall); Louise Henry (Billie Bronson); Joan
Woodbury (Marie Collins); Donald Woods (Speed Patton); Douglas
Fowley (Johnny Burke); Harold Huber (Inspector Nelson); Keye Luke
(Lee Chan); Leon Ames (Buzz Moran); Marc Lawrence (Thomas Mitchell); Toshia Mori (Ling Tse); Charles Williams (Meeker); Creighton
Hale, Billy Wayne (Reporters); Lon Chaney, Jr. (Desk Man--Report-
er); James Blaine (Detective); Sam Ash (Waiter); Lee Shumway (Po-
liceman); Robert Middlemass (Police Official); Edwin Stanley (Labo-
ratory Expert).

        Earl Derr Biggers' Oriental sleuth battled many types of
criminals and, as in Charlie Chan at the Racetrack (1936), was occasionally pitted against organized crime.
        Here Chan (Oland) and number one son Lee Chan (Luke) are
in New York to attend a police testimonial banquet.   Soon they are
involved in a murder on the Great White Way, a hidden diary, and
even Lee being accused of murder.   Among the film's cast of potential red herrings are Speed Patton (Woods), a scandal reporter;
Murdock (Bromberg), his tough editor; Johnny Burke (Fowley), head
of a nightclub and the gangland henchman of Buzz Moran (Ames),
the kingpin of a crime syndicate.

THE CHASE   (United Artists, 1946)   86 min.

        Producer, Seymour Nebenzal; associate producer, Eugene
Frenke; director, Arthur Ripley; based on the story The Black Path
of Fear by Cornell Woolrich; screenplay, Philip Yordan; music,
Michel Michelet; music director, Heinz Roemheld; music supervisor,
David Chudnow; art director, Robert Usher; set decorators, Victor
A. Gangelin, Edward Mann; assistant director, Jack Voglin; sound,
Carson Jowett; special camera effects, Ray O. Binger; camera,
Franz F. Planer; editor, Ed Mann.
        Robert Cummings (Chuck Scott); Michele Morgan (Lorna Ro-
man); Peter Lorre (Gino); Steve Cochran (Eddie Roman); Lloyd Cor-
rigan (Johnson); Jack Holt (Commander Davidson); Don Wilson (Fats);
Alexis Minotis (Lieutenant Acosta); Nina Koshetz (Madame Chin);
Jimmy Ames (The Killer); James Westerfield (Detective Lacca);
Shirley O'Hara (Manicurist); Martin Garralaga (Cabman); Yolanda
Lacca (Midnight); Alex Montoya (Detective); Florence Auer (Lady
Barber).

Following the success of <u>Black Angel</u> (1946) the works of
Cornell Woolrich began to appear with more frequency on the screen
and, in 1946, United Artists issued <u>The Chase</u>, based on the author's story <u>Black Path of Fear</u>. A strange, dark, and moody film,
the picture attempted to integrate gangster and fantasy films into a
cohesive unit, but became a very uneven and mystic-like product.
The production was held together by good performances rather than
basic plot motivations.

Within the story, derelict Chuck Scott finds a wallet and returns it to hoodlum Eddie Roman (Cochran), who rewards him by
making him his chauffeur. Eddie is a sadist and his wife (Morgan)
falls for Chuck. They plan to flee together. Later, in a Havana
night spot, Lorna is stabbed to death. Chuck runs away but before
he can prove his innocence Eddie and his henchman (Lorre) kill him.

At this vital juncture, Chuck wakes up to discover the previous events were all a part of a bad dream and that he is still in
Eddie's house. He and Lorna, however, do carry out their plan to
escape. As the movie concludes, they are seen entering the nightclub where the girl was stabbed in the dream.

CHICAGO CONFIDENTIAL (United Artists, 1957) 75 min.

Producer, Robert E. Kent; director, Sidney Salkow; screenplay, Raymond T. Marcus; music, Emil Newman; camera, Kenneth
Peach, Sr.; editor, Grant Whytock.

Brian Keith (Jim Fremont); Beverly Garland (Laura); Dick
Foran (Blane); Beverly Tyler (Sylvia); Elisha Cook (Candymouth);
Paul Langton (Jake Parker); Tony George (Duncan); Douglas Kenne-
dy (Harrison); Gavin Gordon (Dixon); Jack Lambert (Smitty); John
Morley (Partos); Phyllis Coates (Helen); Jim Bannon (Pilot); Linda
Brent, Lynne Storey, Nancy Marlowe ("B" Girls).

Capitalizing on the Senatorial Crime Hearings, this was yet
another example of the mid-Fifties tough, resolute expose-style
feature. It "... sets such a wild pace that there is neither incli-
nation nor time to pick up loose ends. The errors of omission are
fatal to any semblance of realism... " (New York Daily News).

That seemingly undying breed of mobsters is back on the
scene, this time trying to take over a big Chicago union by elim-
inating the group's president on a murder rap. State's attorney
Jim Fremont (Keith) almost convicts the innocent man, but later
realizes his error, and then goes after the racketeers.

As in so many underworld melodramas, it seemed that the
good guys always triumphed over the bad forces, something that
often does not happen in real life.

CITY FOR CONQUEST (Warner Bros., 1940) 101 min.

Producer, Anatole Litvak; associate producer, William Cagney; director, Litvak; based on the novel by Aben Kandel; screenplay, John Wexley; dialog director, Irving Rapper; assistant

director, Chuck Hansen; makeup, Perc Westmore; costumes, Howard
Shoup; music, Max Steiner; music director, Leo F. Forbstein; orchestrator, Hugo Friedhofer; choreography, Robert Vreeland; art director, Robert Haas; sound, E. A. Brown; camera, Sol Polito,
James Wong Howe; editor, William Holmes.

James Cagney (Danny Kenny); Ann Sheridan (Peggy Nash);
Frank Craven (Old Timer); Donald Crisp (Scotty McPherson); Arthur
Kennedy (Eddie Kenny); Elia Kazan (Googi); Frank McHugh (Mutt);
George Tobias (Pinky); Jerome Dowan (Dutch); Anthony Quinn (Mur-
ray Burns); Lee Patrick (Gladys); Blanche Yurka (Mrs. Nash);
George Lloyd (Goldie); Joyce Compton (Lilly); Thurston Hall (Max
Leonard); Ben Welden (Cobb); John Arledge (Salesman); Ed Keane
(Gaul); Selmer Jackson, Joseph Crehan (Doctors); Bob Steele (Cal-
lahan); Billy Wayne (Henchman); Pat Flaherty (Floor Guard); Sidney
Miller (M. C.); Ethelreda Leopold (Dressing Room Blonde); and:
Lee Phelps, Howard Hickman, Ed Gargan, Murray Alper, Ed Paw-
ley, William Newell, Margaret Hayes, Lucia Carroll, Bernice Pi-
lot.

Since the 1920s, the fight game and the underworld have been
linked together in films. In City for Conquest, an elaborately-
budgeted feature, this theme is subverted to an Our Town-like the-
sis in which environment has a very strong influence on the characters' actions. In fact, Frank Craven, who had played the narrator
in Thornton Wilder's classic story on Broadway and in the movies,
was used here as Old Timer, the observer who informs the moviegoers of the implications of the plot development. (When the film
was reissued, his scenes were nearly all deleted.)

In a role that might have been better suited to John Garfield,
James Cagney functioned as Danny Kenny, a tenement youth who has
made a name in the fight ring, but quits, preferring a less hazardous occupation. However, when his childhood sweetheart Peggy
Nash (Sheridan), now the dance partner of Murray Burns (Quinn),
taunts him for his failure to achieve material success, he returns
to the canvas, determined to become a champ at any cost. At this
juncture he becomes involved with underworld elements, the latter
insistent that the only good fight is a fixed one.

If moviegoers of the day objected to the preachy sentiment
provided by scripter John Wexley and delivered largely by Craven's
Old Timer, there were many realistic film fans who found the finale
too saccharine for its own good. Danny, almost blind (the gangsters'
stooge had earlier thrown rosin into his eyes during a match), runs
a local newsstand. It is evening. He has turned the radio on to
hear a broadcast of his younger brother's symphony which is having
its premiere performance. Suddenly, out of the mist comes Peggy.
Danny, by dint of memory, can almost fathom her features. The
two stand together, happy at last, having found simplicity.

CITY STREETS (Paramount, 1931) 82 min.

Producer, E. Lloyd Sheldon; director, Rouben Mamoulian;
story, Dashiell Hammett; screenplay, Oliver H. P. Garrett, Max

Marcin; adaptor, Marcin; music-orchestrator, Sidney Cutner; sound, J. A. Goodrich, M. M. Paggi; camera, Lee Garmes, William Shea.

Gary Cooper (The Kid); Sylvia Sidney (Nan Sooley); Paul Lukas (Big Fellow Maskal); William "Stage" Boyd (McCoy); Guy Kibbee (Pop Cooley); Stanley Fields (Blackie); Wynne Gibson (Aggie); Betty Sinclair (Pansy); Terry Carroll (Esther March); Bob Kortman (Servant); Barbara Leonard (Girl); Edward LeSaint, Hal Price (Shooting Gallery Patrons); Robert E. Homans (Inspector); Willard Robertson (Detective); Ethan Laidlaw (Killer at Prison); George Regas (Machine Gunner); Leo Willis, Nick Thompson (Henchmen); Allan Cavan (Cop); Matty Kemp (Man Stabbed with a Fork); Norman Foster (Extra on Midway); Bill Elliott (Dance Extra); Bill O'Brien (Waiter);

Already having made a successful directorial debut in films with Applause (1929), Rouben Mamoulian was ready to helm Dashiell Hammett's only original screenplay, City Streets, when, due to a personal crisis, Clara Bow dropped out of the project. Paramount chose cinema fledgling Sylvia Sidney to replace the It Girl. As a result, this rather arty gangster film, with excellent camera work, launched the doe-eyed Miss Sidney on a long and successful screen career.

This film, which was described by Mordaunt Hall (New York Times) as "all melodramatic and incredible, " Sidney appeared as Nan, a girl whose stepfather (Kibbee) works for a beer-running racketeer (Boyd); Nan falls in love with "The Kid" (Cooper), who works for a carnival. She urges The Kid to get into the rackets to make more money, but initially he refuses. Meanwhile Pop Cooley bumps off a hoodlum (Fields) because McCoy wants his girl (Gibson). McCoy confirms an alibi for Pop.

Nan is railroaded into prison when she will not pinpoint her stepfather as a murderer. While she is serving time, The Kid joins the rackets in hopes of getting evidence to set her free. When she is released from jail, Nan cannot get The Kid to leave the rackets. She goes to McCoy to beg him to expel The Kid from his gang. During the argument, however, Aggie shoots McCoy and blames the crime on Nan. The gang takes Nan for a ride, but at the finale she is rescued by The Kid.

Few times in cinema history has the gangster picture been so richly treated by camera and direction as in City Streets. Many of the camera shots, such as one of Nan and The Kid walking on the beach, predate the "new wave" of European films which featured such characteristic shots more than two decades later. Typically rough and tough in the Hammett style, the film stands alone in the 1930s as the arty attempt to dignify the gangster genre. As such, and because of its own intrinsic entertainment value, City Streets is a picture that will not be forgotten even by future generations.

LE CLAN DES SICILIENS (THE SICILIAN CLAN) (Fox-Europa/Les Films du Siecle, 1968) C-120 min.

Producer, Jacques E. Strauss; director, Henri Verneuil; based on the novel by Auguste Le Breton; screenplay, Verneuil,

Yves Lefebvre, Alain Delon and Philippe Baronnet in Le Clan des Siciliens (1968).

Jose Giovanni, Pierre Pelegri; art director, Jacques Saulnier; set decorator, Charles Merangel; music, Ennio Morricone; music director, Bruno Nicolai; sound, Jean Rieul; camera, Henri Decaë; editor, Albert Jurgenson.

Jean Gabin (Vittorio Manalese); Alain Delon (Roger Sartet); Lino Ventura (Inspector Le Goff); Irina Demick (Jeanne Manalese); Amedeo Nazzari (Tony Nicosia); Sydney Chaplin (Jack); Elise Cegani (Maria Manalese); Karen Blanguernon (Therese); Marc Porel (Sergio Manalese); Yves Lefebvre (Aldo Manalese); Philippe Baronnet (Luigi); Leopoldo Trieste (Stamp Expert); Cesar Chauveau (Roberto); Danielle Volle (Monique Sartet); Ed Meeks (Pilot); Jacques Duby (Rovel).

After quickly becoming the biggest grosser in French cinema history, this 1968 heist film surprisingly did over two million dollars' worth of boxoffice business in the U.S. in an English language edition.

Starring French superstar Jean Gabin, popular Alain Delon, and Italian favorite Lino Ventura, this glossy "A" production told of French-headquartered Mafia chief Vittorio Manalese (Gabin) who plans to return to Sicily to pull off one last big job. His scheme is to steal a collection of priceless gems from a Rome exhibit. Realizing security measures are too great, he enlists the aid of a condemned killer (Delon), whom he helps to escape from jail. Together they plan the heist, with the robbery to occur while the jewels are aboard an American-bound plane.

Along with a well-written story, good direction, and crisp

photography, the feature greatly benefitted by the powerful presence of Gabin as the aging boss of the operation. The actor's capacity to grip an audience again proved his durability. Others in the cast included Irina Demick as Jeanne Manalese, Vittorio's loose-living daughter-in-law.

A highlight of the film occurs when the thieves force the jet's crew to make an unscheduled landing along a superhighway. This bit of business is guaranteed to leave the audience breathless.

COFFY   (American International, 1973)   C-91 min.

Executive producer, Salvatore Billitteri; producer, Robert A. Papazian; director-screenplay, Jack Hill; art director, Perry Ferguson; set decorator, Charles Pierce; music-music director-songs, Roy Ayers; stunt coordinator, Bob Minor; sound, Don Johnson; special effects, Jack DeBron; camera, Paul Lohmann; editor, Charles McClelland.

Pam Grier (Coffy); Booker Bradshaw (Brunswick); Robert DoQui (King George); William Elliott (Carter); Allan Arbus (Vitroni); Sid Haig (Omar); Barry Cahill (McHenry); Morris Buchanan (Sugar-Man); Lee de Broux (Nick); Bob Minor (Studs); John Perak (Aleva); Ruben Moreno (Ramos); Carol Lawson (Priscilla); Linda Hayes (Meg); Lisa Farringer (Jeri).

With such black heroes as Shaft, Superfly, and Charleston Blue established, it was only natural that a black girl should also be presented in the black gangster craze. In 1973 writer-director Jack Hill (responsible for such films as Spider Baby and Pit Stop) presented Pam Grier in the title role of Coffy. Filled with a plethora of violence, four-letter words, and a consistently near-nude Ms. Grier, this R-rated thriller couped $2.6 million in domestic rentals.

To avenge her eleven year old sister (whose mind has been destroyed by drugs) nurse Coffy poses as a drug addict in order to infiltrate the dope operations and hunt out the culprits in charge. She later kills a white hoodlum (Arbus) who has taken over a black gangster's (DoQui) territory, and murders her dishonest lover (Bradshaw) who was hooked up with a crooked politician who had beaten up another of her lovers (Elliott).

"What distinguishes this superficially rough and routine effort from the run of the black sexploitation mill is its all-embracing grimness. Its moral blackness, in fact. Coffy is shown to inhabit a world where exploitation, both sexual and political, is simply the norm; and just as the film seems about to incorporate a serious discussion of a way out of the appalling heroin impasse, it quite casually reveals the one person in a position to give voice to the radical policies the situation demands, and to implement them, to be totally corrupt himself" (British Monthly Film Bulletin).

Interestingly, the plot resembles Cornell Woolrich's The Bride Wore Black, only here the "bride" is black!

COLD SWEAT see DE LA PART DES COPAINS

COLLEGE CONFIDENTIAL see HIGH SCHOOL CONFIDENTIAL

COLORADO TERRITORY see I DIED A THOUSAND TIMES

COME BACK CHARLESTON BLUE see COTTON COMES TO HARLEM

THE CONCRETE JUNGLE see THE CRIMINAL

CONFESSIONS OF BOSTON BLACKIE (Columbia, 1941) 65 min.

Producer, William Berke; director, Edward Dmytryk; based upon the character created by Jack Boyle; story, Paul Yawitz, Jay Dratler; screenplay, Yawitz; music director, Morris W. Stoloff; camera, Philip Tannura; editor, Gene Milford.
Chester Morris (Boston Blackie); Harriet Hilliard (Diane Parrish); Richard Lane (Inspector Farraday); George E. Stone (The

Walter Sande, Richard Lane and Chester Morris in <u>Confessions of Boston Blackie</u> (1941).

Runt); Lloyd Corrigan (Arthur Manleder); Joan Woodbury (Mona);
Walter Sande (Sergeant Mathews); Ralph Theodore (Joe Buchanan);
Kenneth MacDonald (Caulder); Walter Soderling (Joseph Allison);
Billy Benedict (Ice Cream Man); Mike Pat Donovan (Cop); Jack Clif-
ford (Motor Cop); Eddie Laughton (Express Man); Ralph Dunn (Offi-
cer McCarthy); Harry Hollingsworth (Plainsclothes Man); Martin
Spellman (Jimmy Parrish); Eddie Kane (Auctioneer); Herbert Clifton
(Albert the Butler); Eddie Fetherstone (Cabby); Stanley Brown (In-
terne); Betty Mack, Dorothy Curtis (Bidders).

After a man is murdered at an art auction, Boston Blackie
(Morris) is accused of the crime and is forced to prove his innocence (or else there would be no plot).   To do so, he must flee the
law and determine the linkage between an art theft racket and the
homicide.
Of the dozen entries in this popular Columbia series produced
throughout the 1940s, this was the only segment in which fast-talking
Blackie dealt with organized crime, here a rather refined group of
criminals.   This was the best of the series.

COOGAN'S BLUFF   (Universal, 1968)   C-94 min.

Executive producer, Richard E. Lyons; producer, Donald Siegel; associate producer, Irving Leonard; director, Siegel; story,
Herman Miller; screenplay, Miller, Dean Riesner, Howard Rodman;
art directors, Alexander Golitzen, Robert C. MacKichan; set decora-
tors, John McCarthy, John Austin; music, Lalo Schifrin; music supervisor, Stanley Wilson; costumes, Helen Colvig; assistant director,
Joe Cavalier; sound, Waldon O. Watson, Lyle Cain, Jack Bolger;
camera, Bud Thackery; editor, Sam E. Waxman.
Clint Eastwood (Deputy Sheriff Walt Coogan); Lee J. Cobb
(Detective Lieutenant McElroy); Susan Clark (Julie); Tisha Sterling
(Linny Raven); Don Stroud (Ringerman); Betty Field (Mrs. Ringerman);
Tom Tully (Sheriff McCrea); Melodie Johnson (Millie); James Ed-
wards (Jackson); Rudy Diaz (Running Bear); David F. Doyle (Pushie);
Louis Zorich (Taxi Driver); Meg Myles (Big Red); Marjorie Bennett
(Mrs. Fowler); Seymour Cassel (Young Hood); John Coe (Bellboy);
Skip Battyn (Omega); Albert Henderson (Desk Sergeant); James Mc-
Callion (Room Clerk); Syl Lamont (Manager); Jess Osuna (Prison
Hospital Guard); Jerry Summers (Good Eyes); Antonia Rey (Mrs.
Amador); Marya Henriques (Go-Go Dancer); Kristoffer Tabori, Don
Siegel (Elevator Passengers).

What and how much will a law enforcer do to bring a criminal to justice?   Coogan's Bluff examines this issue by dressing up
a standard Western theme in big city, contemporary guises.
Arizona sheriff Walt Coogan (Eastwood) is sent to New York
to bring back criminal Ringerman (Stroud) to meet his legal obligations.   Strapping Coogan, a renegade type even in the Western desert, finds himself at odds in the metropolitan atmosphere.   His
mission is not helped by Detective Lieutenant McElroy (Cobb) who
finds Coogan as strange as the other finds him.   Impatient to get

his job completed, the sheriff undertakes to speed up the course of
action subverting McElroy's orders.   He takes time out to romance
social worker Julie (Clark), makes love to Ringerman's girl (Sterling) to find out necessary information, and, for all his trouble,
gets badly beaten by three hoods.   Ringerman escapes Coogan's
surveillance, and the latter has to be hospitalized, albeit temporarily.   Eventually, determined Coogan completes his task of corraling
Ringerman and returning him to Arizona.   However, he also asks
Julie to join him out West.

One of the side points detailed in this thriller, as well as in
other Clint Eastwood films, is the capacity for the individual lawman to exercise ingenuity rather than rote response in coping with
the particular mentality of a wanted man or organized gang.

Early in 1970, NBC-TV presented a telefeature, McCloud:
Who Killed Miss U. S. A. ? with Dennis Weaver as a New Mexico
sheriff who comes to New York City in pursuit of a prisoner.   The
similarity in plotlines resulted in a lawsuit from the producers of
Coogan's Bluff, although the Weaver pilot eventually spawned a long-
running TV series.

COOL BREEZE   (MGM, 1972)   C-101 min.

Producer, Gene Corman; director, Barry Pollack; based on
the novel The Asphalt Jungle by W. R. Burnett; screenplay, Pollack;
music, Solomon Burke; orchestrator, Gene Page; art director, Jack
Fisk; assistant director, Arne Schmidt; sound, Jeff Wexler; camera,
Andy Davis; editor, Morton Tubor.

Thalmus Rasulala [Jack Crowder] (Sidney Lord Jones); Judy
Pace (Obalese Eaton); Raymond St. Jacques (Bill Mercer); Jim Wat-
kins (Travis Battle); Lincoln Kilpatrick (Lieutenant Brian Knowles);
Sam Laws (Stretch Finian); Margaret Avery (Lark); Pamela Grier
(Mona); Paula Kelly (Martha Harris); Wally Taylor (John Battle);
Rudy Challenger (Roy Harris); Stewart Bradley (Captain Lloyd Har-
mon); Edmund Cambridge (Bus Driver); Stack Pierce (Tinker); Biff
Elliot (Lieutenant Carl Magers); Tracee Lyles (Vivian); Lee Weaver
(Father Blue); Jovita Bush, Linda Sexton, Rita Ford (Beauty Con-
testants).

The specious version of The Asphalt Jungle (1950), q. v., won
no plaudits from any quarter.   "This sleazy remake ... is cast primarily with blacks, but the men who made it--Scenarist-Director
Barry Pollack, Producer Gene Corman--are white.   Their interest
is not so much in reaching the new-found black audience as in exploiting it.   The color they really care about is folding green"
(Time).

Ostensibly told from the black point of view, this reworking
of the W. R. Burnett novel has a black gang in Los Angeles executing a jewel robbery in order to finance a black people's bank.
After the robbery, however, the hoodlums break up among themselves and a fence (St. Jacques) loses the jewels which fall into the
hands of an underworld leader (Rasulala).

Instead of focusing the action on taut sequences, the

filmmakers opted for emphasis on scantily clad and sex-hungry young ladies. "Most film heists are long and ingenious; this one is brief and hair-brained" (San Francisco Chronicle).

COPS AND ROBBERS (United Artists, 1973) C-89 min.

Producer, Elliott Kastner; associate producer, George Pappas; director, Aram Avakian; screenplay, Donald E. Westlake; art director, Gene Rudolf; set decorator, Kenneth Fitzpatrick; scenic artist, Bruno Robotti; music-music director, Michel Legrand and Jacques Wilson; Legrand, Chilton Ryan, and Buddy Butler; sound, Chris Newman, William Gramaglia; technical adviser, Garo Jon; camera, David L. Quaid; editors, Robert Q. Lovett, Richard Cirincione.

Cliff Gorman (Tom); Joe Bologna (Joe); Dick Ward (Paul Jones); Shepperd Strudwick (Mr. Eastpoole); Ellen Holly (Mrs. Wells); John P. Ryan (Patsy O'Neill [Pasquale Aniello]); Nino Ruggeri (Mr. Joe); Gayle Gorman (Mary); Lucy Martin (Grace); Lee Steel (Hardward Store Owner); Jacob Weiner (Thief); Frances Foster (Bleeding Lady); Arthur Pierce, Martin Cove (Ambulance Attendants); Jim Ferguson (Liquor Store Clerk); Walter Gorney (Wino); Frank Gio (Rocco); Jess Ossuna (Ed); Joseph Spinell (Marty); George Harris II (Henry); Charlene Dallas (Secretary); Randy Jurgensen (Randy); Delphi Lawrence (Rich Lady); Frank Scioscia (Picnic Hood); Joseph Sullivan (Jack); Robert W. Miller, Walter J. Klavun, Albert Henderson (Cops); Charles Bergansky, Cliff Cudney (Perpetrators).

Another in the long line of police films to show action. in New York City, Cops and Robbers was a bit different in that it was somewhat of a comedy and that the major crime perpetrated in the story was committed by the two cops who were the alleged heroes of the picture!

Shot on location, the film told of two average policemen (Gorman and Bologna) stuck in their New York City middle class lives who want something better for themselves and their families. They plan a caper to steal a large sum of bearer bonds on the day a huge parade will be honoring a returning astronaut. They raid a Wall Street office and carry out their goal, departing somewhat from their original plans.

The film had the added attraction of (what else?) a good chase sequence through Central Park. New York Times' critic Roger Greenspun said, "... it is uncommonly well acted ... and it is the first movie in a long time to understand, rather than merely to exploit, its NYC locales."

Ironically, on August 25, 1973, as the film was playing the UA Eastside Cinema, a robber took $5,000 in receipts from the theatre's boxoffice.

COTTON COMES TO HARLEM (United Artists, 1970) C-97 min.

Producer Samuel Goldwyn, Jr.; director, Ossie Davis; based

on the novel by Chester Himes; screenplay, Arnold Perl, Davis; assistant director, Domenic D'Antonio; second unit director, Max Kleven; art director, Manuel Gerard; set decorator, Bob Drumheller; music, Galt MacDermot; songs, MacDermot and Joseph S. Lewis; MacDermot and Davis; MacDermot and William Dumaresq; MacDermot and Paul Laurence Dunbar; choreography, Louis Johnson; costumes, Anna Hill; titles, F. Hillsberg, Inc.; sound, Newton Avrutis; special effects, Sol "Stosh" Stern; camera, Gerald Hirschfeld; second unit camera, Gil Geller; editors, Robert G. Lovett, John Carter.

Godfrey Cambridge (Gravedigger Jones); Raymond St. Jacques (Coffin Ed Johnson); Calvin Lockhart (Reverend Deke O'Malley); Judy Pace (Iris); Redd Foxx (Uncle Bud); John Anderson (Captain Bryce); Emily Yancy (Mabel); J. D. Cannon (Calhoun); Mabel Robinson (Billie); Dick Sabol (Jarema); Theodore Wilson (Barry); Eugene Roche (Anderson); Frederick O'Neal (Casper); Vinette Carroll (Reba); Gene Lindsey (Luddy); Van Kirksey (Early Riser); Arnold Williams (Hi Jenks); Leonardo Cimino (Tom).

Many films had been made about white America's crime syndicates, the Italian Mafia and other international cartels, but at this point (1970) little had found its way to the screen concerning criminal activities in Harlem by blacks against blacks. This picture, softened by its comic approach, moved into relatively new cinematic territory, an area that would soon explode with the advent of the black exploitation violence picture.

In a very ethnic manner (having been written by a black, directed by a black, and starring blacks), this feature tells of the exploits of two unorthodox Harlem police detectives, Gravedigger Jones (Cambridge) and Coffin Ed Johnson (St. Jacques), and how they become involved with one Reverend Deke O'Malley (Lockhart). The latter sponsors a huge barbecue in the heart of Harlem to collect funds for his "Back to Africa" movement. He plans to abscond with the proceeds. Before he can make his planned getaway, however, an ex-con (Cannon) runs off with the money. When the two detectives catch up with him the money is gone and an all-out search for the loot begins.

Director-co-scripter Davis used the same ploy in this film as he had in Gone Are the Days (1966), that of making his black characters into stereotyped jokes. He reasoned that by the mid-twentieth century most of his soul brothers with any sensibilities would be far enough removed from the original types to appreciate the joke. An added attraction of this near-farce was blue comic Redd Foxx as a junk dealer, a part he would later make famous on television's "Sanford and Son."

Two years after the initial film, Cambridge and St. Jacques reprised their Himes' characters in a sequel, Come Back Charleston Blue. In this more complex, confused and less funny sequel, the two sleuths are at odds with a black hoodlum (Peter De Ande) who intends to take over the Harlem drug trade with a bloody purge of the Mafia establishment. This less popular followup ended any movie plans to continue the Himes book series.

CRAZY JOE   (Columbia, 1973)   C-100 min.

Presenter, Dino De Laurentiis; executive producer, Nino E. Kriksman; director, Carlo Lizzani; story, Nicholas Gage; screenplay, Lewis John Carlino; art director, Robert Dundlach; sound, Dennis Maitland; camera, Aldo Tonti.

Peter Boyle (Crazy Joe); Paula Prentiss (Anne); Fred Williamson (Willy); Charles Cioffi (Coletti); Rip Torn (Richie); Luther Adler (Falco); Fausto Tozzi (Frank); Franco Lantieri (Nunzio); Eli Wallach (Don Vittorio); and: Louis Guss, Henry Winkler, Sam Coppola, Adam Wade, Ralph Wilcox, Peter Savage, Nella Dina.

With the new interest in gangland films spawned by The Godfather (1972), q. v. , scripter Lewis J. Carlino (Honor Thy Father) q. v. and producer Dino De Laurentiis (The Valachi Papers) q. v. joined with director Carlo Lizzani to bring forth the supposed true story of Joseph "Crazy Joe" Gallo (1929-72). The resulting Crazy Joe was only a 100-minute "B" movie given "A" bookings due to its theme and cast.

Peter Boyle was cast as Crazy Joe, an intellectual type Mafia leader who was shot at a clam house in Little Italy on April 7, 1972 for allegedly attempting to expand his holdings at the expense of other Mafia families. (At one point in the loosely constructed tale he joins forces with Harlem blacks led by Fred Williamson's Willy.) Boyle was acceptable in his role, but an episodic storyline, tied together only by gratuitous violence (e. g. , tossing a victim into a cement mixer, but first cutting off his hand for identification purposes) complicated his performance. He had little with which to work by way of character development or motivation. Others in the cast included a distracted Paula Prentiss as Joe's hysterically possessive girl, Williamson as the handsome black mobster, Rip Torn as Joe's childish brother, and Eli Wallach as a Mafia don (complete with pseudo Italian accent and gestures).

Produced by Italians, Crazy Joe's only claim to boxoffice fame seems to be its origins with the country where the Mafia began. Certainly the delineation of Brooklyn-born Crazy Joe Gallo (once known as Joe the Blond) is of limited depth. It was a quickly forgotten biography about a basically second-string mobster.

CRIME WAVE   (Warner Bros. , 1953)   73 min.

Producer, Bryan Foy; director, Andre de Toth; based on the story by John and Ward Hawkins; adaptor, Bernard Gordon, Richard Wormser; screenplay, Crane Wilbur; music, David Buttolph; assistant director, James McMahon; camera, Bert Glennon; editor, Thomas Reilly.

Sterling Hayden (Detective Lieutenant Sims); Gene Nelson (Steve Lacey); Phyllis Kirk (Ellen); Ted de Corsia ('Doc" Penny); Charles Buchinsky [Bronson] (Hastings); Jay Novello ('Dr. " Otto Hessler); James Bell (Daniel O'Keefe); Dubb Taylor (Gus Snider); Gayle Kellogg (Kelly); Mack Chandler (Sully); Richard Benjamin (Mark); Timothy Carey (Johnny).

Parolee Steve Lacey (Nelson) would like to go straight, but when three crooks (de Corsia, Buchinsky, and Carey) escape from San Quentin, they pressure Steve into joining them on a bank heist. Toothpick-chomping law enforcer Sims (Hayden) is on hand to put matters right, but not before the escapees are wiped out.

As Invisible Stripes (1940), q.v., pointed out, it is not easy for an ex-convict to readapt to the outside world, especially when his old ties are reinforced.

THE CRIMINAL   (Anglo-Amalgamated, 1960)   97 min.

Producer, Jack Greenwood; associate producer, James P. O'Connolly; director, Joseph Losey; story, Jimmy Sangster; screenplay, Alun Owen; music-music conductor, Johnny Dankworth; art director, Scott MacGregor; production designer, Richard MacDonald; sound, Sidney Rider, Ronald Abbott; camera, Robert Krasker; editor, Reginald Mills.

Stanley Baker (Johnny Bannion); Margit Saad (Suzanne); Sam Wanamaker (Mike Carter); Gregoire Aslan (Frank Saffron); Jill Bennett (Maggie); Laurence Naismith (Mr. Town); Noel Willman (Prison Governor); Patrick Magee (Chief Warder Barrows); Edward Judd (Young Warder); Dorothy Bromiley (Angela); Jack Rodney (Scout); Nigel Green (Ted); Rupert Davies (Edwards); Tom Bell (Flynn); Keith Smith (Hanson); Larry Taylor (Charles).

U.S. release: The Concrete Jungle (Fanfare, 1962) 85 min.

So much has been filmed, true and otherwise, about prison conditions in the U.S. that the rare feature dealing with incarceration English-style deserves comment. In The Criminal, director Joseph Losey digs resolutely to present a compelling study of the "dank, sleazy, claustrophobic prison atmosphere" (Variety). This certainly proved to be the counterpart to Hollywood's Brute Force (1947), q.v.

Johnny Bannion (Baker) is serving a three-year prison term. During his sentence he maps a detailed plot for robbing a race track. Once released, he and his cohort (Wanamaker) undertake the job and escape with $100,000 of loot. Later he is betrayed by a former girlfriend and is sentenced again to prison. He refuses to tell the police where he has secreted the loot. Meanwhile, Carter arranges for Johnny to join in a jail break. An overzealous associate of Carter kills Johnny before he has led them to the whereabouts of the buried money. Johnny dies and a frantic Carter is left holding an empty bag.

"What is most potently fascinating in [The Concrete] Jungle (U.S. release title of The Criminal) is also most subtle: U.S.-born director Joseph Losey's vision of the world of crime as a self-contained universe without external points of reference. Normal society judges and humanizes itself from ethical and spiritual vantage points that are above society. The terror of criminal society, as Losey presents it, is that it is a kingdom of one-eyed men, whose lack of ethical depth perception prevents them from seeing, knowing, or redeeming themselves" (Time).

As James Leahy points out in The Cinema of Joseph Losey (1967), "The prison is, at one and the same time, a compelling general symbol of those who have given up the struggle to find purpose in life, retreating into a defensive shell, and, at the same time, a reproach to the society which allows it to exist. Its inadequacies symbolise society's lack of concern with essentials.... "

THE CRIMINAL CODE   (Columbia, 1931) 97 min.

Producer, Harry Cohn; director, Howard Hawks; based on the play by Martin Flavin; screenplay, Seton I. Miller, Fred Niblo, Jr.; art director, Edward Jewell; sound, Glenn Rominger; camers, James Wong Howe, L. William O'Connell; editor, Edward Curtiss.

Walter Huston (Warden Brady); Phillips Holmes (Robert Graham); Constance Cummings (Mary Brady); Mary Doran (Gertrude Williams); De Witt Jennings (Captain Gleason); John Sheehan (McManus); Boris Karloff (Gats Galloway); Otto Hoffman (Jim Fales); Clark Marshall (Runch); Arthur Hoyt (Leonard Nettleford); Ethel Wales (Katie Ryan); John St. Polis (Dr. Rinewulf); Paul Porcasi (Tony Spelvin); James Guilfoyle (Detective Doran); Lee Phelps (Detective Doherty); Hugh Walker (Lew the District Attorney's Aide); Jack Vance (Reporter); Tetsu Komai (Convict); Andy Devine (Convict-- Kitchen Worker); Russell Hopton (State's Attorney); Al Hill (Gary-- Food Deliverer).

Martin Flavin's play, The Criminal Code, won the Theatre Club Trophy of America in 1929 as the year's best play and the production was brought to the screen by Columbia in 1931.

The movie told of a young man (Holmes) who comes to New York. There he takes a girl to a club for dinner and, after a dispute over her honor, he kills the man with whom he was arguing. Brady, the district attorney (Huston) railroads him into prison. Later Brady becomes the warden of that institution and he makes Graham (Holmes) chauffeur for his daughter (Cummings). When two convicts attempt an escape, a stoolie (Marshall) turns them in and is murdered. Only Graham knows the killer's identity but he follows the code of criminals and refuses to tell. The warden puts him in solitary despite Mary's pleadings to the contrary. He is later pardoned, however, when the real killer confesses.

One of the most impressive performances in this Howard Hawks-directed film was that of Boris Karloff as Ned Galloway, a convict-trustee turned killer. His good reviews brought the actor better screen roles and led directly to his part of the monster in Frankenstein (1931) which made him famous. (Scenes of Karloff in The Criminal Code were utilized in the actor's later feature, Targets) (1968).

The Criminal Code would be remade twice by Columbia, as Penitentiary (1938) and Convicted (1950). Neither edition had the same gutsy impact as the stark 1931 version.

Yvonne De Carlo and Dan Duryea in <u>Criss Cross</u> (1949).

CRISS CROSS   (Universal, 1949)   87 min.

Producer, Michel Kraike; director, Robert Siodmak; based
on the novel by Don Tracy; screenplay, Daniel Fuchs; art directors,
Bernard Herzbrun, Boris Leven; set decorators, Russell A. Gausman, Oliver Emert; music, Miklos Rozsa; costumes, Yvonne Wood;
makeup, Bud Westmore; assistant director, Fred Frank; sound, Leslie I. Carey, Richard DeWeese; special effects, David S. Horsley;
camera, Frank Palmer; editor, Ted J. Kent.

Burt Lancaster (Steve Thompson); Yvonne De Carlo (Anna);
Dan Duryea (Slim Dundee); Stephen McNally (Pete Raimrez); Richard
Long (Slade Thompson); Esy Morales (Orchestra Leader); Tom Pedi
(Vincent); Percy Helton (Frank); Alan Napier (Finchley); Griff Barnett
(Pop); Meg Randall (Helen); Joan Miller (The Lush); Edna M. Holland
(Mrs. Thompson); John Doucette (Walt); Marc Krah (Mort); James
O'Rear (Waxie); John Skins Miller (Midget); Robert Osterlch (Mr.
Nelson); Vincent Renno (Headwaiter); Charles Wagenheim (Waiter);
Tony Curtis (Gigolo); Beatrice Roberts, Isabel Randolph (Nurses);
Stephen Roberts (Doctor); Garry Owen (Johnny); Kenneth Patterson
(Bently the Guard); Vitto Scotti (Track Usher); John Roy (Bartender);
Kippee Valez (Girl Friend).

The engaging, tough story of Steve Thompson (Lancaster) who returns home to the desolation of the big city and renews an affair with his ex-wife (De Carlo) who has married a crook (Duryea). Convincing Steve that she still loves him, she persuades him to join with her new husband, Slim Dundee, in the robbery of a money truck which Steve is driving for a living. He agrees but finds out that Anna will double-cross him. He realizes too late that the robbery will be blamed on him, that Anna and Dundee will get the loot, and that he has been a complete fool. In retaliation, he double-crosses them. Quick-thinking Anna then makes an about-face, proclaiming her basic love for him. At the finale, slimy Slim finds the two together. Panicky Anna renounces Steve, but Dundee kills them both. He then waits for the police to arrest him.

A dark, somber film, Criss Cross was doubly good because of its fine direction by Robert Siodmak and a taut script by Daniel Fuchs from Don Tracy's book. Adding to the overall effect was low-keyed photography and a strong cast. Particularly memorable was De Carlo's conniving Anna. Of this character, Steve's mother observes that in some ways she "... knows more than Einstein." Still caught in his casting mold of the 1940s, Duryea was his sleazy, tough, sadistic screen self: a perfect foil to the physically strong, but emotionally confused, Lancaster.

As a point of interest, Tony Curtis made his screen debut in this film, dancing with De Carlo.

CRY OF THE CITY (Twentieth Century-Fox, 1948) 95 min.

Producer, Sol C. Siegel; director, Robert Siodmak; based on the novel by Henry Edward Helseth; screenplay, Richard Murphy; art directors, Lyle Wheeler, Albert Hogsett; set decorators, Thomas Little, Ernest Lansing; music, Alfred Newman; orchestrator, Herbert Spencer; music director, Lionel Newman; assistant director, Jasper Blystone; makeup, Ben Nye, Harry Maret, Pat McNally; costumes, Bonnie Cashin; sound, Eugene Grossman, Roger Heman; special effects, Fred Sersen; camera, Lloyd Ahern; editor, Harmon Jones.

Victor Mature (Lieutenant Candella); Richard Conte (Martin Rome); Fred Clark (Lieutenant Collins); Shelley Winters (Brenda); Betty Garde (Mrs. Pruett); Berry Kroeger (Niles); Tommy Cook (Tony); Debra Paget (Teena Riconti); Hope Emerson (Rose Given); Roland Winters (Ledbetter); Walter Baldwin (Orvy); June Storey (Miss Boone); Tito Vuolo (Papa Roma); Mimi Aguglia (Mama Roma); Konstantin Shayne (Dr. Veroff); Howard Freeman (Sullivan); Dolores Castle (Rosa); Claudette Ross (Rosa's Daughter); Vito Scotti (Julio); Robert Karnes, Charles Tannen (Internes); Emil Rameau (Dr. Niklas); Kathleen Howard (Mrs. Pruett's Mother); Jane Nigh (Nurse); George Magrill, Ed Hinton (Cops).

The decades-old tale of the two boys who grow up on opposite sides of the law was re-exploited in Cry of the City, a stout melodrama expertly helmed by Robert Siodmak. The director's capacity to delineate underworld characters on celluloid was at its best in this film, especially his direction of Hope Emerson as a masseuse

Betty Garde and Victor Mature in Cry of the City (1948).

and Berry Kroeger as a corrupt lawyer.

Taken from Henry Edward Helseth's book, The Chase for Martin Rome, the feature told of an honest cop (Mature) who gives chase to childhood pal Martin Rome (Conte), the latter a wounded hoodlum suspected of murdering another policeman.

Told against the cold, depressing ambience of a big city at night, the Twentieth Century-Fox film was "... another taut and grimly realistic melodrama ... [it] emerges as a starkly tough yarn with its heart and civic pride in the proper place" (New York Times).

In Hollywood in the Forties (1968), writers Charles Higham and Joel Greenberg judged the film superior for sequences which were "... powerfully realized and charged with an oppressive coldness."

During the 1930s the gangster film was primarily the forte of Warner Bros. and the independent studios. However, by the World War II era, other studios were delving into the genre not only with increasing regularity but also with more forcefulness. Equally underrated actors, Mature and Conte offered well-fulfilled characterizations in this feature which demonstrated that Darryl F. Zanuck's studio was capable of producing entertainment above and beyond Betty Grable Technicolor musicals.

CRY TOUGH (United Artists, 1959) 83 min.

Producer, Harry Kleiner; director, Paul Stanley; based on
the novel by Irving Shulman; screenplay, Kleiner; music, Laurino
Almedia; art director, Edward Carrere; set decorators, Russell A.
Gausman, William Tapp; assistant director, Philip Bowles; sound,
Leslie I. Carey, Don McKay; camera, Philip Lathrop, Irving Glass-
berg; editor, Frederic Knudtson.

John Saxon (Miguel Estrada); Linda Cristal (Sarita); Joseph
Calleia (Señor Estrada); Harry Townes (Carlos); Don Gordon (Incho);
Perry Lopez (Toro); Frank Puglia (Lavandero); Penny Santon (Señora
Estrada); Joe de Santis (Cortez); Barbara Luna (Tina Estrada); Ar-
thur Batanides (Alvears); Paul Clarke (Emilio); John Sebastian (Al-
berto); Nira Monsour (Dolores);

When released in 1959 this "routine gangster melodrama"
(New York Times) attracted some excitement due to its inclusion of
brief nude love scenes between John Saxon and Linda Cristal. The
scenes, however, were deleted in most U.S. showings, although they
were restored for European distribution.

Besides the sex notoriety, the movie had little to offer except a downbeat tale of a Puerto Rican youth (Saxon) who fights with
his girl and joins a rackets gang. Later he tries to take over the
organization. Both his father (Calleia) and a Cuban dance hall gal
(Cristal) attempt to reform him, but the influence of gang leader
Cortez (de Santis) is too strong.

Once again, the usual theme of "crime does not pay" was
used; at the finale Saxon is labeled a turncoat by his fellow gang
members and chased across tenement rooftops, and falls to his
death.

Trend-conscious Time was distinctly unimpressed with this
entry. "With a pretense of social protest, the film tries for realism as it pans in on Spanish Harlem and enters slums where children sleep on pallets and adults line up nine-deep to use the bath-
room. But what the cameras actually record is little more than a
Puerto Ricochet from the smallest-bore gangster plot in the film
maker's gun cabinet...."

THE CRY-BABY KILLER (Allied Artists, 1958) 62 min.

Executive producer, Robert Corman; producers, David Kramar-
sky, David March; director, Jus Addiss; story, Leo Gordon; screenplay, Gordon, Melvin Levy; music, Gerald Fried; camera, Floyd
Crosby; editor, Irene Morra.

Harry Lauter (Porter); Jack Nicholson (Jimmy); Carolyn
Mitchell (Carole); Brett Halsey (Manny); Lynn Cartwright (Julie);
Ralph Reed (Joey); John Shay (Gannon); Barbara Knudson (Mrs. Max-
ton); Jordon Whitfield (Sam); Claude Stroud (Werner); Ruth Swanson
(Mrs. Wallace); Frank Richards (Gambelli); Ed Nelson (Rick);

"... for dramatic value there should have been more motivation than is given for the boy's actions" (Variety). However, this

very early Jack Nicholson feature does delve into the personality of a youthful gunman who thinks he has killed two other teenagers in a scuffle.   He later is trapped by the police in a storeroom of a drive-in restaurant, where he is persuaded eventually by the law to surrender.

Although technically Jimmy's character is not a gangster or part of a real mob, the feature, in its minor way, does reflect what happens to the lawbreaker when he is on his own against the police.   The pressures exerted on him parallel those experienced by Edward G. Robinson in Little Caesar (1931), q. v. , et al.   The only difference is a matter of degree.

CZAR OF THE SLOT MACHINES   see   KING OF GAMBLERS

DAMN CITIZEN   (Universal, 1958)   88 min.

Producer, Herman Webber; director, Robert Gordon; screenplay, Stirling Silliphant; music, Henry Mancini; camera, Ellis W. Carter; editor, Patrick McCormack.
Keith Andes (Colonel Francis C. Grevemberg); Maggie Hayes (Dorothy Grevemberg); Gene Evans (Major Al Arthur); Lynn Bari (Pat Noble); Jeffrey Stone (Paul Musso); Edward C. Platt (Joseph Kosta); Ann Robinson (Cleo); Sam Buffington (DeButts); Clegg Hoyt (Sheriff Lloyd); Kendall Clark (Colonel Thomas Hastings); Rusty Lane (Inspector Sweeney); Charles Hoevath (Lieutenant Palmer); Carolyn Kearney (Nancy); Aaron M. Kohn, Reverend J. D. Grey, Richard R. Foster (Themselves); Tiger Flowers (News Commentator); John Schowest (Satchel Man).

This true life story was more rambling than convincing. Former World War II hero Francis C. Grevemberg (Andes) becomes the superintendent of the state police in Louisiana to combat crime and corruption.   There are the usual raids on gambling halls, attempts to close down houses of prostitution, alliances between racketeers and dishonest police, etc.
The on-location filming around New Orleans gave the feature some verisimilitude.   The film, like the real-life character, is praiseworthy for the zealous attempt to show that crime can be fought by a one-man crusade.   The Christian Science Monitor lauded the picture for its "documentary directness and editorial trenchancy. "

THE DAMNED DON'T CRY   (Warner Bros. , 1950)   103 min.

Producer, Jerry Wald; director, Vincent Sherman; story, Gertrude Walker; screenplay, Jerome Weidman, Harold Medford; art director, Robert Hass; music, Daniele Amfitheatroff; camera, Ted McCord; editor, Clarence Kolster.
Joan Crawford (Ethel Whitehead); David Brian (George Castleman); Steve Cochran (Nick Prenta); Kent Smith (Martin Blackford); Hugh Sanders (Grady); Selena Royle (Patricia Longworth); Jacqueline

de Wit (Sandra); Morris Ankrum (Mr. Whitehead); Sara Perry (Mrs. Whitehead); Richard Egan (Roy); Jimmy Moss (Tommy); Edith Evanson (Mrs. Castleman).

A frustrated housewife (Crawford) leaves her commonplace husband (Egan) and her small factory town existence (the death of her only child in a traffic accident was the final blow). She seeks more out of life in the big city. Working at a cigar counter she spurs a drab accountant (Smith) onto a better career and then becomes a model and a high class call girl. Blackford is still beguiled by Ethel and she, in turn, continues to encourage his career. She introduces him to a club owner, and he becomes the man's accountant. Then, Ethel and Blackford are introduced to crime kingpin George Castleman. Ethel urges Martin to become his accountant, and he does so, against his better judgment. Thereafter Ethel becomes George's mistress. Castleman hires Patricia Longworth as Ethel's companion and to teach her class. Although Ethel has a strong love for Castleman, he uses her to set up Nick Prenta for a killing. When Ethel meets Nick, who is George's chief rival, she falls for him and delays Castleman's deadly plans. Sensing a doublecross, Castleman comes West and kills Nick. Blackford persuades the gangster not to take revenge on Ethel. Meanwhile, Ethel runs back to her old home town. Castleman and Blackford follow. A gun battle ensues and Blackford kills Castleman. Ethel is left to her unhappy future.

Undoubtedly, this Jerry Wald production had one of the most engaging film titles in the annals of American cinema. The producer hoped that he could follow up Crawford's earlier Warner Bros. success, Mildred Pierce (1945), and the lurid, but engaging Flamingo Road (1949) with another strident melodrama that would stimulate box-office interest in the faltering post-World War II market. The role of Ethel Whitehead was a part that Oscar-winner Crawford might better have portrayed two decades earlier, but the actress gave the somewhat obvious role tremendous intensity.

As a new-style study of the mobster scene in the U.S.A., The Damned Don't Cry was a shade too flabby. The New York Herald-Tribune thought the film's "... theme is shabby and the incidents too violent for complete plausibility." Some, such as Bosley Crowther (New York Times) took issue with Crawford's portrayal, insisting that "... a more artificial lot of acting ... could hardly be achieved."

Both Cochran and Brian had an affinity for hoodlum roles and excelled in their parts, making the rather cornball drama far more plausible than the script warranted.

DANCE, FOOLS, DANCE (MGM, 1931) 82 min.

Director, Harry Beaumont; story, Aurania Rouverol; screenplay, Richard Schayer; dialog, Rouverol; songs, Frank Crumit and Lou Klein; Dale Winbrow and L. Cornell; Roy Turk and Fred Ahlert; Dorothy Fields and Jimmy McHugh; camera, Charles Rosher; editor, George Hively.

Joan Crawford (Bonnie Jordan); Lester Vail (Bob); Cliff Edwards (Bert Scranton); William Bakewell (Rodney Jordan); William Holden (Stanley Jordan); Clark Gable (Jake Luva); Earl Foxe (Wally); Purnell B. Pratt (Parker); Hale Hamilton (Selby); Natalie Moorhead (Della); Joan Marsh (Sylvia); Russell Hopton (Whitey); James Donlan (Police Reporter); Tommy Shugrue (Photographer).

Loosely based on the Chicago murder of reporter Jake Lingle by the underworld, interpolated with the St. Valentine's Day Massacre, this Harry Beaumont-directed melodrama has a socialite (Crawford) joining a newspaper after her wealthy father loses his fortune in the 1929 stock market crash. She is unaware that her no-good brother (Bakewell) is making a living as a bootlegger and that he drove a car used for the machine-gunning of a rival gang. When another reporter (Edwards), who was investigating the murders, is killed, the girl romances a gangster (Gable) to ferret out information on the underworld. Barely escaping with her life, she exposes the racketeers.

With the glittery production values of Metro-Goldwyn-Mayer supporting the storyline, Dance, Fools, Dance was yet another screen example of the cinema's most frolicsome flapper (Crawford) portraying the put-upon young lady who rises above her unfortunate circumstances to triumph. Any early 1930s film with the effervescent Joan Crawford was bound to have a resilient pace, as she bounced from one scene to another. Her dramatic conviction might have been lacking, but her enthusiasm was undeniable. Thus, despite the efforts of the scripters to base the plotline on gory fact, the photoplay emerged more as an entertainment than a realistic representation of the crime world.

This film would be the first of seven features to team Crawford with the up-and-coming Clark Gable, cast here once again as the somewhat oily gangster. He is the ruthless guy who menaces both Bakewell and Crawford before meeting his "just" fate.

DANGEROUS FEMALE   see   THE MALTESE FALCON (1931)

DANGEROUS TO KNOW   (Paramount, 1938)   70 min.

Director, Robert Florey; based on the book and play, On the Spot by Edgar Wallace; screenplay, William R. Lippmann, Horace McCoy; camera, Theodor Sparkuhl; editor, Arthur Schmidt.

Anna May Wong (Madam Lan Ying); Akim Tamiroff (Stephen Recka); Gail Patrick (Margaret Van Kase); Lloyd Nolan (Inspector Brandon); Harvey Stephens (Philip Easton); Anthony Quinn (Nicholas Kusnoff); Roscoe Karns (Duncan); Porter Hall (Mayor Bradley); Barlowe Borland (Butler); Hedda Hopper (Mrs. Carson); Hugh Sothern (Harvey Greggson); Edward Pawley (John Rance).

During the 1930s, Akim Tamiroff enjoyed a brief reign as a gangster star at Paramount and this Robert Florey-directed melodrama was one of the films made (on a low budget) to exploit this

Harvey Stephens, Anna May Wong and Akim Tamiroff in a pose for
Dangerous to Know (1938).

fine performer.   Taken from a work by the late Edgar Wallace, the
film was too quickly dismissed by the New York Times as "... a
second rate melodrama hardly worthy of the talent of its generally
capable cast. "
        The story revolves around Stephen Recka (Tamiroff), the
cultured head of a rackets operation.   He enjoys classical music,
although he has no qualms about sending his henchmen out to perpetrate horrors on his enemies and the public.   After a time, Recka
begins to yearn for society girl Margaret Van Kase, a desire which
results in his ultimate downfall.
        This film contains at least two interesting scenes.   In one
Recka plays a bit of Tchaikovsky while his distraught mistress (Wong)
proceeds to disembowel herself.   The other "rare" moment occurs
earlier in the programmer where Madam Lan Ying plays "Thanks
for the Memory" to Recka.   It was all a bit of in-house publicity for
the studio since the song was the hit number from Paramount's The
Big Broadcast of 1938.

DARK CITY (Paramount, 1950) 88 min.

        Producer, Hal B. Wallis; director, William Dieterle; based

on the story No Escape by Larry Marcus; screenplay, Leonardo
Bercovici, John Meredyth Lucas; art director, Franz Bachelin; mu-
sic, Franz Waxman; camera, Victor Milner; editor, Warren Low.
Charlton Heston (Danny Haley); Lizabeth Scott (Fran); Viveca
Lindfors (Victoria Winant); Dean Jagger (Captain Garvey); Don De-
Fore (Arthur Winant); Jack Webb (Augie); Ed Begley (Barney); Hen-
ry Harry Morgan (Soldier); Walter Sande (Swede); Mark Keuning
(Billy Winant); Mike Mazurki (Sidney Winant); Stanley Prager (Sam-
my); Walter Burke (Bartender); Byron Foulger (Motel Manager);
Greta Granstedt (Margie); Stan Johnson (Room Clerk); John Bishop
(Fielding); James Dundee (Detective); Dewey Robinson (Gambler);
Edward Rose (Shoeshine Boy); Jay Morley (MacDonald);

After being very popular in the late 1940s, the vogue of the
crime thriller which exploits the betrayal of a man by a woman or
his friends was coming to an end.   This Hal B. Wallis production,
from Larry Marcus' story No Escape, was one reason for the spe-
cie's demise.
Charlton Heston made his Hollywood film debut as the card-
sharp leader of a gambling gang who fleeces a victim (De Fore) for
his bankroll.   Afterwards the loser commits suicide.   The dead
man's crazed brother (Mazurki) demands revenge, and stalks the
group.   Meanwhile, the nightclub thrush Fran (Scott), who has a
yen for Danny Haley (Heston), tries to help him in his plight.   Also
on hand to confuse the plotline are the dead man's embittered spouse
(Lindfors) and Captain Garvey (Jagger), the latter as the cop who
eventually solves the caper.
The only real action in this anemic thriller was in the location shots which switched from Los Angeles to Las Vegas during
the tepid proceedings.   At the finale, Danny and Fran end up in
Vegas, hardly a locale suitable for the reformation of a crooked
gambler.

DARK PASSAGE   (Warner Bros. , 1947)   106 min.

Producer, Jerry Wald; director, Delmer Daves; based on the
novel by David Goodis; screenplay, Daves; art director, Charles H.
Clarke; set decorator, William Kuehl; music, Franz Waxman; music director, Leo F. Forbstein; assistant director, Dick Mayberry;
sound, Dolph Thomas; special camera effects, H. F. Koenekamp;
camera, Sid Hickox; editor, David Weisbart.
Humphrey Bogart (Vincent Parry/Narrator); Lauren Bacall
(Irene Jansen); Bruce Bennett (Bob); Agnes Moorehead (Madge Rapf);
Tom D'Andrea (Sam the Cabby); Clifton Young (Baker); Douglas Ken-
nedy (Detective); Rory Mallinson (George Fellsinger); Houseley
Stevenson (Dr. Walter Coley); Richard Walsh, Bob Farber (Police-
men); Clancy Cooper (Man on Street); Pat McVey (Taxi Driver);
Tom Fadden (Cafe Waiter); Mary Field (Mary the Lonely Woman);
Lennie Bremen (Ticket Clerk); Ross Ford (Ross the Bus Driver);
Craig Lawrence (Bartender).

This was a "... grim story that has plenty of killings and

Lauren Bacall and Humphrey Bogart in <u>Dark Passage</u> (1947).

suspense" (Variety). Teaming Humphrey Bogart and Lauren Bacall
for the third time, this lesser Jerry Wald production pushed Bogart
back into the gangster genre as a man who escapes from prison
where he has been sent (falsely) for the murder of his wife.
    After the break-out, a San Francisco girl (Bacall) picks him
up and it develops that she has followed his trial and believes him
to be innocent. Her boyfriend (Bennett) is married and his wife
(Moorehead) proves to be the friend of Vincent's late wife. In fact,
it was her damning testimony which sent him to prison. Staying
with Irene, Vincent arranges to have plastic surgery so that with a
new guise he can find out who actually killed his wife. A petty
crook (Young) finds out about the operation and tries to blackmail
Vincent but he is accidentally killed by the convict. In the process
Parry learns that it was actually Madge Rapf who was his wife's
killer. He confronts her and she confesses, but then she falls to
her death from a window. With no chance to clear himself, Vince
heads for South America, where Irene will join him.
    While fairly entertaining, Dark Passage was more of a mys-
tery than a gangster epic and its niche in cinema history must come
from the fact that Bogart's character did not die at the end of the
film. (It was an indication that the once-strict Production Code
could be circumvented with an ingenious plotline.) Another then still
unusual aspect of cinema technique which was used in Dark Passage
was having the camera act as a subjective eye for Vincent. Not until after his operation is his face revealed to the camera. (This
gimmick had been used with equal effect by Robert Montgomery in
Lady in the Lake, 1946.)

THE DARK PAST (Columbia, 1949) 75 min.

    Producer, Buddy Adler; director, Rudolph Mate; based on the
play Blind Alley by James Warwick; screenplay, Philip MacDonald,
Michael Blankfort, Albert Duffy; adaptators, Malvin Wald, Oscar
Saul; art director, Gary Odell; set decorator, Frank Tuttle; music,
George Duning; music director, Morris W. Stoloff; makeup, Clay
Campbell; costumes, Jean Louis; assistant director, Milton Field-
man; sound, George Cooper; camera, Joseph Walker; editor, Viola
Lawrence.
    William Holden (Al Walker); Nina Foch (Betty); Lee J. Cobb
(Dr. Andrew Collins); Adele Jergens (Laura Stevens); Stephen Dunne
(Owen Talbot); Lois Maxwell (Ruth Collins); Barry Kroeger (Mike);
Steven Geray (Professor Fred Linder); Wilton Graff (Frank Stevens);
Robert Osterloh (Pete); Kathryn Card (Nora); Bobby Hyatt (Bobby);
Ellen Corby (Agnes); Charles Cane (Sheriff); Robert B. Williams
(Williams); Phil Tully (Cop); Harry Harvey, Jr. (John Larrapoe);
Edward Earle (McCoy); Pat McGeehan (Commentator).

    In 1949 Columbia remade James Warwick's play, Blind Alley,
q. v. , which had been produced for the screen nine years earlier under its
original title with Chester Morris. The first screen version had
been highly successful considering its limited budget. The new edition, while not up to the original, was a "... lucid, taut and adult

melodrama" (New York Times).

Hoodlum Al Walker (Holden) and his gang take over a psychiatrist's (Cobb) home and hold him and his family captives while they await a getaway. The doctor, however, begins to probe into the mind of the hoodlum to trace the cause of his recurring nightmares. He begins to lift the veil surrounding the man's past, finding, among other problems, that Al suffers from an Oedipus complex.

Despite Holden's ingratiating performance in Golden Boy (1939), he had yet to display much dramatic range in his subsequent screen work. Mostly he was cast as the good-natured, wholesome young man, literally the all-American. As the law breaker here, he was overshadowed by more adept acting from Cobb as the physician and especially by Nina Foch as Betty, the attractive moll.

The Dark Past did receive a few compliments. Jack Thompson in the New York Sunday Mirror magazine reported, "The idea that adult crime would be drastically reduced if juvenile delinquents were treated by psychiatry has been made into an absorbing thriller."

DE LA PART DES COPAINS   (Corona-Fair, 1970)   C-94 min.

Executive producer, Serge Lebeau; producer, Robert Dorfman; associate producer, Maurice Jacquin; director, Terence Young; based on the novel Ride the Nightmare by Richard Matheson; screenplay, Shimon Wincelberg, Albert Simonin; art director, Tony Roman; music, Mic el Magne; camera, Jean Rabier; editor, Johnny Dwyre.

Charles Bronson (Joe Martin); Liv Ullmann (Fabienne Martin); James Mason (Ross); Jill Ireland (Moira); Michel Constantin (Whitey); Jean Topart (Katanga); Yannick Delulle (Michele Martin); Luigi Pistilli (Eausto).

U.S. release: Cold Sweat (MGM, 1974).

Shot on location in the South of France, this Terence Young-directed thriller has little to offer beyond the attractive scenery and a delightfully hammy performance by James Mason as a crook.

Cruise boat owner Joe Martin (Bronson) and his wife Fabienne (Ullmann) are marked by a hit man, whom Joe kills as he invades their home. It is later revealed that Joe was once in a military prison (for hitting an officer). He and the deceased and the latter's gang had broken out of confinement together, but Martin had deserted them after they murdered a guard. He escaped, but the others were recaptured. It soon becomes evident that the gang is now at large and they gravitate to Martin's home. The leader, a southerner named Ross (Mason), informs Joe he will use his boat to take them to safety. Their destination is to be an Arab cruiser, which actually is used for drug transport in the area. Joe, however, doublecrosses the group and hijacks Ross' young girlfriend (Ireland), holding her hostage in return for the safety of his wife and twelve year-old step-daughter. Then begins the chase within the chase, and the double-cross on top of another double-cross.

Despite the popularity of superstar Bronson during the 1970s,

this film, which again co-starred him with his wife (Jill Ireland),
has very little artistic merit, let alone entertainment value.   The
flip, cynical dialog cannot compensate for the paper-thin characterization or the sense that the picture was tossed out as product fill-
er.   None of the potential of an examination of the criminal psyche
was explored.

DEAD END   (United Artists, 1937)   93 min.

        Producer, Samuel Goldwyn; associate producer, Merritt Hub-
burd; director, William Wyler; based on the play by Sidney Kingsley; screenplay, Lillian Hellman; dialog director, Edward P. Good-
now; assistant director, Eddie Bernoudy; art director, Richard Day;
set decorator, Julie Heron; costumes, Omar Kiam; music director,
Alfred Newman; sound, Frank Maher; special effects, James Basevi;
camera, Gregg Toland; editor, Daniel Mandell.
        Joel McCrea (Dave Connell); Sylvia Sidney (Drina Gordon);
Humphrey Bogart (Joe "Baby Face" Martin [Marty "Johnson"]); Allen
Jenkins (Hunk); Wendy Barrie (Kay Burton); Claire Trevor (Francey);
Gabriel Dell (T. B.); Billy Halop (Tommy Gordon); Huntz Hall (Dip-
py); Bobby Jordon (Angel); Leo Gorcey (Spit); Bernard Punsley (Mil-
ty); Charles Peck (Philip Griswold); Minor Watson (Mr. Griswold);
Marjorie Main (Mrs. Martin); James Burke (Mulligan the Cop);
Marcelle Corday (Governess); Ward Bond (Doorman); George Hum-
bert (Pascagli); Esther Dale (Mrs. Fenner the Janitress); Elisabeth
Risdon (Mrs. Connell).

        The desperation and futility of slum life was brought to life
in Sidney Kingsley's Broadway success, Dead End.   Lillian Hellman
adapted the strong drama for the screen, altering characterization
and emphasis to suit the demands of the film industry's production
code.
        Set on New York's east side, Dead End is concerned with all
aspects of that proverbial slice of life.   It tells of the residents of
waterfront tenements and of a group of boys who idolize a hood
(Bogart) who comes back to the old neighborhood to see his flinty
mother (Main) and his ex-girl (Trevor).   Also present is Dave
(McCrea), a frustrated architect, who cares for two girls, Drina
(Sidney) and Kay (Barrie).   The former is a shop girl who wants to
get out of the slums with her younger brother (Halop), while the
latter is the mistress of a rich man.   Joe Martin's mother denounces
him and he finds that Francey has become a streetwalker.   More
disgusted with life than ever, but totally committed to his criminal
ways, Martin plans to kidnap a rich boy.   Dave tries to stop him
and is shot and left for dead.   Later, Dave traps Martin and kills
him.   He then uses his reward money to defend Tommy Gordon who
is accused of knifing Mr. Griswold (Watson).
        Long considered a classic, this Samuel Goldwyn film, which
displays William Wyler's fine directorial touches, is a sturdy tract
on the force of environment in shaping the future of an individual.
In retrospect, one may find Bogart's snarling Baby Face Martin too
simplistic and Sidney's teary-eyed proletarian too sentimental, but

the flavor of the grimy city is all there (amazingly, since the film was largely shot on a soundstage set), with Rockefeller Center facing the wrong way. Perhaps the most memorable scene in the film occurs when the rugged, no-nonsense Mrs. Martin renounces her infamous son, ordering him out of her life.

And, of course, for better or worse, Dead End was the film project responsible for starting the Dead End Kids (a. k. a. Little Tough Guys, East Side Kids, the Bowery Boys) on their decades-long movie careers.

DEAD HEAT ON A MERRY-GO-ROUND (Columbia, 1966) C-107 min.

Producers, Carter De Haven, Bernard Girard; director-script, Girard; assistant director, William Kissel; art director, Walter M. Simonds; camera, Lionel Lindon; editor, William Lyon.
James Coburn (Eli Kotch); Camilla Sparv (Inger Kundson); Aldo Ray (Eddie Hart); Nina Wayne (Frieda Schmid); Robert Webber (Milo Stewart); Rose Marie (Margaret Kirby); Todd Armstrong (Alfred Morgan); Marian Moses (Dr. Marion Hague); Michael Strong (Paul Feng); Severn Darden (Miles Fisher); James Westerfield (Jack Balter); Phillip E. Pine (George Logan).

This amusing crime caper starred James Coburn as Eli Kotch, a con artist who plans a big heist in between romancing a bevy of ladies. The scheduled job is to rob a bank at the Los Angeles International Airport. The arranged date coincides with the arrival of the Russian premier, which should, Kotch hopes, create its own blend of confusion at the airport. Kotch works out the details while still in prison, then persuades a female psychiatrist to maneuver his jail release. Along the way he even marries a comely secretary (Sparv) who takes part in the film's twist ending after Kotch and crew have successfully carried out the robbery.

There were two opposing reactions to this picture. On one hand, Time asserted, it "... just fills the space between a frisky title and a tricky TV-comedy ending, but doesn't fill it with any revels that require a viewer's complete attention. " In contrast, Joseph Gelmis of Newsday decided, "... the mystique of this sort of film is just to submerge yourself in the moment-to-moment adventure, trust to the director to get a reasonable conclusion and enjoy yourself along the way. " This book's authors favor the latter point of view. As A. H. Weiler (New York Times) noted, the movie "... has the refreshing temerity to thumb its nose figuratively at laws and gaily get away with it. "

DEAD RECKONING (Columbia, 1947) 100 min.

Producer, Sidney Biddell; director, John Cromwell; story, Gerald Adams, Biddell; adaptor, Allen Rivkin; screenplay, Oliver H. P. Garrett, Steve Fisher; assistant director, Seymour Friedman; art directors, Stephen Goosson, Rudolph Sternad; music, Marlin

Skiles; song, Allan Roberts and Doris Fisher; music director, Morris Stoloff; camera, Leo Tover.

Humphrey Bogart (Rip Murdock); Lizabeth Scott (Coral Chandler); Morris Carnovsky (Martinelli); Charles Cane (Lieutenant Kincaid); William Prince (Johnny Drake); Marvin Miller (Krause); Wallace Ford (McGee); James Bell (Father Logan); George Chandler (Louis Ord); William Forrest (Lieutenant Colonel Simpson); Ruby Dandridge (Hyacinth).

In the post-World War II period, the gangster film no longer had the slickness and the pat characters of pre-war days; instead, they became far more realistic and brutal. These films were replete with sleazy characters, beatings, and quick, violent gunplay. Instead of bootlegging and vice, they tended to center around gambling and, with even more freedom, explored such topics as narcotics and sports.

Dead Reckoning is a bizarre love story which forever ends the innocence of the leading lady in the gangster film. Bogart was cast as Rip Murdock, a former paratrooper who tries to find out why his buddy was murdered. He stumbles into the underworld milieu and frequents a club run by Martinelli (Carnovsky) with Coral Chandler (Scott) as his chirp. Rip's buddy was supposed to have killed her husband. Without too much adieu, Rip falls in love with Coral. He is beaten by hoods and learns that it was Coral who killed her spouse, allegedly in self-defense. Supposedly, it was Rip's late service pal who had saved her. It is later unearthed that Martinelli is blackmailing Coral. She and Rip go to the crook to retrieve the murder weapon. In the midst of the confrontation, she kills him. Trying to use her seductive powers (à la Mary Astor in The Maltese Falcon), Coral attempts to persuade Rip not to turn her in to the law. He refuses and she tries to kill him as they drive to the police station. Instead she causes a wreck which takes her life.

A bleak, depressing film, Dead Reckoning has its champions who find sturdiness in Scott's brand of emoting as the femme fatale. Outstanding in the cast was Marvin Miller as Krause, one of Martinelli's goons.

DEADLY IS THE FEMALE (a. k. a. GUN CRAZY) (United Artists, 1949) 87 min.

Producers, Frank and Maurice King; director, Joseph H. Lewis; based on the story Gun Crazy by MacKinlay Kanton; screenplay, Kantor, Millard Kaufman; music, Victor Young; song, Young and Ned Washington; camera, Russell Harlan; editor, Harry Gerstad.

Peggy Cummings (Annie Laurie Starr); John Dall (Bart Tare); Barry Kroeger (Packett); Morris Carnovsky (Judge Willoughby); Anabel Shaw (Ruby Tare); Harry Lewis (Clyde Boston); Nedrick Young (Dave Allister); Trevor Bardette (Sheriff Boston); Mickey Little (Bart Tare at Age Seven); Rusty Tamblyn (Bart Tare at Age Fourteen); Paul Frison (Clyde Boston at Age Fourteen); Dave Bair (Dave Allister at Age Fourteen); Stanley Prager (Bluey-Bluey); Virginia Farmer

(Miss Wynn); Anne O'Neal (Miss Sifert); Frances Irwin (Danceland Singer); Don Beddow (Man from Chicago); Simen Ruskin (Cab Driver); Harry Hayden (Mr. Mallenberg).

With each passing year, this "B" budgeted feature tends to grow in popularity. When it was issued it was termed "pretty cheap stuff" by the New York Times. Today, however, the production enjoys a cult following and many people who see it after viewing the more highly commercial Bonnie and Clyde (1967), q.v., often prefer this Joseph H. Lewis-directed melodrama from which the producers of Bonnie and Clyde borrowed heavily.

Produced by Frank and Maurice King, who had presented such previous genre pieces as Dillinger and The Gangster, this entry was essentially an updated recounting of the story of Bonnie Parker and Clyde Barrow. Fictionalized names and settings were utilized.

John Dall appeared as Bart Tare, a World War II veteran who had suffered from shock, and who had had a lifelong fascination with guns ever since he killed a pet as a boy. After his service discharge, he meets a petite, pretty carnival markswoman (Cummings) and through their mutual attraction to firearms they fall in love. Scheming Annie Laurie Starr induces Bart to embark on a robbery spree. This crime wave eventually leads them to murder. The duo become the most hunted couple in the country and they meet a gruesome death. Trying to escape from the law, they are shot down in a swamp.

What holds the movie together so well and makes it forever timely is Lewis' smooth direction, buoyed by well-modulated performances from the leads. As Bart, Dall is just seedy and slightly paranoid enough to be believed, while Cummings creates a definitive study of the devious woman who uses a weak man at her will and for her own gain. Lewis keeps the film moving at a fast pace. Near the finale, the lovers dance to "Laughing on the Outside, Crying on the Inside" at a roadhouse. The song interlude is full of irony because as the tune concludes, the two realize that the law has caught up with them. With commendable subtlety, Lewis engineers the film's final thrust as they make a last desperate but vain attempt to flee.

In The American Cinema (1968), Andrew Sarris correctly judges this genre classic as Lewis' "... one enduring masterpiece ... a subtler and more moving evocation of the gun cult in America than the somewhat overrated Bonnie and Clyde."

DEPORTED (Universal, 1950) 89 min.

Producer, Robert Bucker; director, Robert Siodmak; story, Lionel Shapiro; screenplay, Bucker; art directors, Bernard Herzbrun, Nathan Juran; music, Walter Scharf; camera, William Daniels; editor, Ralph Dawson.

Marta Toren (Countess Christine di Lorenzi); Jeff Chandler (Vic Smith); Claude Dauphin (Vito Bucelli); Marina Berti (Gina Carapia); Richard Rober (Bernardo Gervaso); Silvio Minciotti (Armando

Sparducci); Carlo Rizzo (Guildo Caruso); Mimi Aguglia (Teresa Spar-
ducci); Michael Tor (Ernesto Pampilione); Adraino Ambrogi (Father
Genaro); Erminio Spalla (Benjamino Barda); Dino Nardi (Donati);
Guido Celano (Aldo Brescia); Tito Vuolo (Postal Clerk).

    By 1950 Hollywood was in sad shape and desperate to try
any gambit to recoup its dwindling cinema audience. Shooting films
abroad was one means of combating inflationary production prices in
California and of offering moviegoers on-the-spot location back-
grounds.
    This shoddy melodrama was one of the earlier attempts of
the new decade to bring foreign locales into focus on the American
movie screens. The results were negligible, particularly in comparison to the sturdy crime-oriented thrillers of the 1930s and 1940s.
But at this point, reviewers were far more indulgent (their bid to
help Hollywood in its time of need?): thus the New York Sunday
Mirror magazine could rate this film ''... a fast-action thriller
made more enjoyable by the great beauty of its Italian background. ''
    Deported unreeled a tale of a U. S. gangster (Chandler) who
is deported to Italy. Once there, the troublemaker becomes involved in black-market operations. Soon, however, he comes under
the spell of the Countess Christina di Lorenzi (Toren) who is the
patroness of the small town where Vic Smith has settled. As expected, heel Vic abandons his plans to fleece the villagers and the
Countess, and instead settles for her love.
    One could speculate on the trend, which would increase in
later years, of Italian-origin gangsters returning to their homeland
and turning over a surprising new leaf. Just what special interest
groups were at work in the fashioning of such films?

THE DESPERATE HOURS (Paramount, 1955) 112 min.

    Producer, William Wyler; associate producer, Robert Wyler;
director, William Wyler; based on the novel and play by Joseph
Hayes; screenplay, Hayes; assistant director, C. C. Coleman, Jr.;
art directors, Hal Pereira, Joseph MacMillan Johnson; set decorators, Sam Comer, Grace Gregory; music, Gail Kubik; costumes,
Edith Head; makeup, Wally Westmore; sound, Hugo Grenzbach, Winston Leverett; special effects, John P. Fulton, Farciot Edouart;
camera, Lee Garmes; editor, Robert Swink.

    Humphrey Bogart (Glenn Griffin); Fredric March (Dan Hilliard);
Arthur Kennedy (Jesse Bard); Martha Scott (Eleanor Hilliard); Dewey
Martin (Hal Griffin); Gig Young (Chuck); Mary Murphy (Cindy Hilliard);
Richard Eyer (Ralphie Hilliard); Robert Middleton (Sam Kobish); Alan
Reed, Michael Moore, Don Haggerty (Detectives); Whit Bissell (Car-
son); Ray Collins (Masters); Bert Freed (Winston); Beverly Garland
(Miss Swift); Ann Doran (Mrs. Walling); Walter Baldwin (Patterson);
Ric Roman (Sal); Pat Flaherty (Dutch).

    ''Maybe I'm getting too old to play hoodlums, '' Humphrey Bo-
gart told director William Wyler after seeing The Desperate Hours.
The film, in fact, was the last time Bogie played the type of screen

Martha Scott and Humphrey Bogart in The Desperate Hours (1955).

role that had made him famous.

Although the film version of the book and stage-hit pleased critics, it was never quite as successful as promised. The story line had a typical family home being used as a hideout for three gangsters, with shades of The Petrified Forest (1936) q. v. all too evident. The hoods (Bogart, Martin, Middleton) permit the husband (March) and daughter (Murphy) to carry on their everyday routines to avoid suspicion while the mother (Scott) and son (Eyer) are kept captive. The gangsters have yet to receive their getaway money and must remain undetected for the time being. Finally, suspicion grows among the family's friends and neighbors. The police surround the house and one by one the convicts are killed.

A "polished production" said Hollis Alpert in Saturday Review, while Time opined, "... to melodrama fans, it may prove one of the most pleasurably prostrating evenings ever spent in a movie house...."

Unfortunately the Cold War, internal unrest and the boob tube all united to antiquate the interest of the three hardly original hoods, led by an aging Bogart. After all, it had all been seen before in countless "B" films--and could now be seen for nothing on the tube.

Jan Wiley, Ralph Byrd and Michael Owen in <u>Dick Tracy vs. Crime,</u>
<u>Inc.</u> (1941).

DICK TRACY VS. CRIME, INC.   (Republic, 1941) fifteen chapters

   Associate producer, W. J. O'Sullivan; directors, John Eng-
lish, William Witney; based on the cartoon strip by Chester Gould;
screenplay, Ronald Davidson, Norman S. Hall, William Lively,
Joseph O'Donnell, Joseph Poland; music, Cy Feuer; special effects,
Howard Lydecker; camera, Reggie Lanning.
   Ralph Byrd (Dick Tracy); ????? (The Ghost); Ralph Morgan
(Morton/Metzicoff); Jan Wiley (June Chandler); Michael Owen (Bill
Carr); Kenneth Harlan (Lieutenant Cosgrove); Jack Mulhall (Wilson);
John Dilson (Weldon); Robert Frazer (Brewster); Robert Fiske (Cab-
ot); John Davidson (Lucifer); Anthony Warde (Corey); Chuck Morris-
on (Trask); Frank Alten (Drage); Hooper Atchley (Trent); Marjorie
Kane (Cigarette Girl); Max Waizman (Telegrapher); C. Montague
Shaw (Dr. Jonathan Martin); Edmund Cobb (Kelly); Selmer Jackson
(Marine Officer); Griff Barnett (Watchman); Stanley Price (Jackson);
Nora Lane (Ella Gilbert); Howard Hickman (Stephen Chandler); Wal-
ter McGrail (Marine Captain).
   Chapters: 1) The Fatal Hour; 2) The Prisoner Vanishes 3)
Doom Patrol; 4) Dead Man's Trap; 5) Murder at Sea; 6) Besieged;
7) Sea Racketeers; 8) Train of Doom; 9) Beheaded; 10) Flaming

Peril; 11) Seconds to Live; 12) Trial by Fire; 13) The Challenge;
14) Invisible Terror; 15) Retribution.

Two years after starring in Dick Tracy's G-Men, q.v., Republic for the fourth time cast Ralph Byrd as the famed law enforcer in Dick Tracy vs. Crime, Inc., a fifteen-chapter cliffhanger
again directed by William Witney and John English. This entry,
in spite of the stock footage from the earlier serials, was a superior one from Republic's Golden Age of Serials. It sported a fine
musical score by Cy Feuer, his last for a chapterplay, and all in
all, provided plenty of action for serial fans.
    The plot had the chief villain, The Ghost (billed as "?????"
on-screen) as a clandestine member of the Council of Eight, a
group formed to rid the nation's capital of crime. Tracy (Byrd) is
called in to stop the master criminal who works with the evil Lucifer (Davidson), the latter having a machine which cloaks The
Ghost in invisibility. The Ghost liquidates six of the council's
eight members. When the detective later discovers at a crime
scene a medal which is given only to council members, he suspects
a group member of being a part of the arch criminal's gang. Finally Tracy uses bloodhounds to track down the troublesome Ghost.
The latter is electrocuted as he crosses some high tension wires.
His identity is known only through Tracy's talking thereafter to the
last surviving member of the Council of Eight in the climactic
scene.
    When shown on-camera The Ghost wore a rubber face mask
to conceal his identity. He spoke with actor Ralph Morgan's voice,
but was Republic cheating or not!!!!
    The serial was re-issued as Dick Tracy vs. Phantom Em-
pire in 1952.
    For the record, Chapter One makes use of disaster footage
(showing a tidal wave engulfing NYC) form The Deluge (1933).

DICK TRACY VS. PHANTOM EMPIRE   see   DICK TRACY VS.
CRIME, INC.

DICK TRACY'S G-MEN   (Republic, 1939)   fifteen chapters

    Associate producer, Robert Beche; directors, William Wit-
ney, John English; based on the cartoon character created by Chester
Gould; screenplay, Barry Shipman, Franklyn Adreon, Rex Taylor,
Ronald Davidson, Sol Shor; music, William Lava; camera, William
Nobles; editors, Edward Todd, William Thompson, Bernard Loftus.
    Ralph Byrd (Dick Tracy); Irving Pichel (Zarnoff); Ted Pear-
son (Steve); Phylis Isley (Gwen); Walter Miller (Robal); George
Douglas (Sandoval); Kenneth Harlan (Anderson); Robert Carson (Scott);
Julian Madison (Foster); Ted Mapes, William Stahl, Robert Wayne
(G-Men); Joe McGuinn (Tommy); Kenneth Terrell (Ed); Harry Hum-
phrey (Warden Stover); Harrison Greene (Baron).
    Chapters: 1) The Master Spy; 2) Captured; 3) The False
Signal; 4) The Enemy Strikes; 5) Crack-Up!; 6) Sunken Peril; 7)

Tracking the Enemy; 8) Chamber of Doom; 9) Flames of Jeopardy;
10) Crackling Fury; 11) Caverns of Peril; 12) Flight in the Sky 13)
The Fatal Ride; 14) Getaway; 15) The Last Stand.

For its third full-length serial based on the famous cartoon
strip, Republic again cast Ralph Byrd as the square-jawed Dick
Tracy. It was the story of a master international spy, and was
full of melodrama, science fiction, and gangster film clichés. The
blend was handled by veteran serial directors William Witney and
John English. Adding to the plus values of the chapterplay was the
interpolation of actual newsreel footage, especially of the Hindenburg
disaster, into the action. William Lava contributed a rousing film
score.

The narrative concerned the head of a spy ring, one Zarnoff
(Pichel), who is captured by F.B.I. agent Tracy (Byrd). Zarnoff
is convicted of assorted crimes, including murder, and is sent to
the gas chamber. Later his body is stolen and he is revived by a
rare drug. Tracy and pal Steve Lockwood (Pearson) soon find out
that their arch enemy is still alive. The G-men chase Zarnoff's
gang to their mountain hideout. There the villain tries to board
his private plane in order to flee the country. But Tracy races
aboard, knocks down the pilot and captures Zarnoff (yet again).
The two head West. Engine trouble, however, forces them to land
in the desert where they journey on foot and nearly die of thirst.
Coming to a water spring, Zarnoff knocks out Tracy, ties him to a
tree, and drinks his fill. The G-men soon arrive on the scene and
save Tracy. What of Zarnoff? He dies in the desert. It seems
the water he drank came from an "arsenic spring."

An excellent serial, firmly in the Republic tradition, the
chapterplay was re-issued in 1955. By that time cast member
Phylis Isley was a famous superstar-Oscar winner, better known as
Jennifer Jones.

DILLINGER (Monogram, 1945) 74 min.

Producer, Maurice and Franklin King; director, Max Nosseck; screenplay, Phil Yordan; dialog director, Leon Charles; music, Dimitri Tiomkin; assistant director, Frank Fox; technical director, Herman King; sound, Thomas Lambert; camera, Jackson
Rose; editor, Edward Mann.

Edmund Lowe (Specs); Anne Jeffreys (Helen); Lawrence Tier-
ney (Dillinger); Eduardo Cianelli (Murph); Marc Lawrence (Doc);
Elisha Cook, Jr. (Kirk); Ralph Lewis (Tony); Ludwig Stossel (Otto);
Else Jannsen (Mrs. Otto); Hugh Prosser, Dewey Robinson (Guards);
Bob Perry Proprietor); Kid Chisel, Billy Nelson (Watchmen); Lou
Lubin (Walter); Constance Worth (Blonde).

DILLINGER (American International, 1973) C-107 min.

Executive producers, Samuel Z. Arkoff, Lawrence A. Gordon; producer, Buzz Feitshans; associate producer, Robert Papazian;

Warren Oates in Dillinger (1973).

director-screenplay, John Milius; assistant directors, Donald C.
Klune, Ronald Martinez; art director, Trevor Williams; set decora-
tor, Charles Pierce; music, Barry Devorzon; costumes, James
George, Barbara Siebert; stunt coordinator, Max Kleven; sound,
Don Johnson, Kenny Schwarz; special effects, A. D. Flowers, Cliff
Wenger; camera, Jules Brenner; editor, Fred Feitshans, Jr.

Warren Oates (John Dillinger); Ben Johnson (Melvin Purvis);
Michelle Phillips (Billie Frechette); Cloris Leachman (Anna Sagel
[The Lady in Red]); Harry Dean Stanton (Homer Van Meter); Steve
Kanaly (Lester "Pretty Boy" Floyd); Richard Dreyfuss (George "Ba-
by Face" Nelson); Geoffrey Lewis (Harry Pierpont); John Ryan
(Charles Mackley); Roy Jenson (Samuel Cowley); John Martino (Eddie
Martin); Read Morgan ("Big Jim" Wollard); Frank McRae (Reed
Youngblood); Jerry Summers (Tommy Carroll); Terry Leonard (The-
odore "Handsome Jack" Klutas); Bob Harris (Ed Fulton).

Eleven years after John Dillinger was gunned down* in front

*Some sources insist that the famed Indiana bandit was not the man shot
on July 22, 1934 in Chicago, but that the F. B. I. gunned down someone
else and allowed the public to believe it had been the wanted criminal.

of the Biograph Theatre in Chicago after viewing <u>Manhattan Melo-drama</u>, q. v. poverty row studio producers Maurice and Frank King re-leased their exploitation thriller about the gangster through Mono-gram. The production claimed to follow the life (1903-?) of the famous hoodlum and "folk" hero. Little accuracy could be found in this wooden, little film. Due to its subject matter and the heavy exploitation campaign, <u>Dillinger</u> garnered good playdates, which was a bit unusual for a Monogram product.

Philip Yordan received an Academy Award nomination for the film's script, which had Dillinger (Tierney) robbing a grocer to please a pickup. He is later caught and sent to jail. There he meets Specks (Lowe) a big-time bank robber, who has his own gang on the outside as well as pals on the inside. Dillinger agrees to help Specks and his fellow convicts break out of jail, once he has been paroled and can organize an escape for them from a road gang detail. The scheme is a success. The gang then embarks on a series of successful robberies with Dillinger slowly taking over the reins of leadership from Specks. In the interim, Dillinger is at-tracted to Helen, a girl he once robbed at a movie box-office booth. It is she who later urges him onward in his life of crime. Even-tually, hard times fall on the gang and they hide out with a mem-ber's (Cook, Jr.) "folks." When Specks doublecrosses Dillinger, the latter kills him and is forced to seek sanctuary in a rundown hotel. Helen, tired of running and of being with her notorious lover, leads him to his death outside a movie theatre, wearing red to let the G-men know who to gun down.

The extensive search for the proper actor to play Dillinger led to stardom for Lawrence Tierney, who still works occasionally in the genre in Europe. Lowe, however, turned in the film's best performance and Jeffreys was luscious. She was more than capa-ble of imparting color to her role as the pseudo "lady in red."

Unfortunately, this film, which was banned in Chicago, looked as though it was made on the cheap (which it was). It contained far too much obvious stock footage, including the robbery sequence from <u>You Only Live Once</u> (1937), q. v. As <u>Variety</u> observed at the time, "Somehow, the pic smacks of the same intensity imparted to gang-land pictures of the '30s, when such films seemed the boxoffice rage. But in 1945, <u>Dillinger</u>, as most such pix, seems passé." (Ironically, this film remains one of the few Monogram pictures to have extensive TV playdates even in the 1970s.)

The American International 1973 version, marking screen-writer John Milius' directorial debut, was hardly a remake of the earlier film. This colorful, violent actioner tried to follow closely the "facts" of the Dillinger case, even to casting an excellent War-ren Oates (a Dillinger look-alike) in the lead. The chronicle fol-lowed the hoodlum's exploits and rise to fame with an almost tongue-in-cheek humor that rather accurately revealed that Dillinger may have grossed over $250,000 from his capers (with no taxes to pay).

Co-starred with Oates was Ben Johnson, who was resilient but too old to portray G-man Melvin Purvis properly. After the 1933 Kansas City Massacre which encompassed the death of three lawmen, Purvis vowed to round up all hoodlums. (Dillinger had not participated in that exploit.) Crosscutting throughout, the film

showed Purvis tracking down each of the most wanted hoodlums.
As his field of prey narrows, his chase for Dillinger becomes more
determined.

The 1973 version does include the legend of Dillinger teaming with Homer Van Meter (Stanton), Pretty Boy Floyd (Kenaly) and
Baby Face Nelson (Dreyfuss).   The character of Billie Frechette
(Phillips) appeared as the criminal's sexy girlfriend.   A number of
incidents, including Dillinger's breakout from the Crown Point, Indiana, jail with a hand-carved revolver, are colorfully retold.   One
poignant scene had Dillinger, near the end of his tether, driving to
his parents' rural home but not stopping.   There is a memorable
long shot of his flivver driving away on a long-winding gravel road.

"The outlaws and G-men are defined with extravagant flour-
ishes, but Milius never balances the comic book heroics with subtler, quieter moments.   As a result, the characters become almost
indistinguishable; they all seem to be vain, brash, belligerent loud-
mouths" (Stephen Farber, writing in the New York Times).   On the
other hand, Films in Review called the film "an exciting period
piece with fine performances by Oates and Phillips. "   Use of period
music did a good deal to highlight the film.   This Dillinger contained some well-staged shootouts.   The final scenes with the "woman in red" (Leachman) turning in Dillinger and marking him for the
F.B.I. gundown were particularly good.

DIRTY HARRY   (Warner Bros. , 1971)   C-101 min.

Executive producer, Robert Daley; producer, Don Siegel;
associate producer, Carl Pingitore; director, Siegel; story, Harry
Julian Rin, Rita M. Fink; screenplay, Harry Julian Fink, Rita M.
Fink, Dean Riesner; art director, Dale Hennesy; set decorator,
Robert DeVestel; music, Lalo Schifrin; sound, William Randall;
camera, Bruce Surtees; editor, Carl Pingitore.

Clint Eastwood (Harry Callahan); Harry Guardino (Lieutenant
Bressler); Reni Santoni (Chico); John Vernon (The Mayor); Andy
Robinson (Killer); John Larch (Chief); John Mitchum (De Georgio);
Mae Mercer (Mrs. Russell); Lyn Edgington (Norma); Ruth Kobart
(Bus Driver); Woodrow Parfrey (Mr. Jaffe); Josef Sommer (Rothko);
William Paterson (Bannerman); James Nolan (Liquor Proprietor);
Maurice S. Argent (Sid Kleinman); Jo de Winter (Miss Willis); Craig
G. Kelly (Sergeant Reinke).

Following the success of Coogan's Bluff (1968), q. v. , producer-director Don Siegel and star Clint Eastwood made Dirty Harry for Warner Bros.   (Eastwood had been a replacement for ailing
Frank Sinatra, and for not-interested Paul Newman.)   The film,
which grossed over $16. 4 million in distributors' domestic rentals,
was shot on location in San Francisco.

Dirty Harry further promoted the image of the rebel cop who
can and will twist the laws to suit his purpose--the capture of
criminals.   Most critics regarded the movie as fine on an action
level but rather implausible in its storyline.   Pauline Kael of the
New Yorker called the film "a right-wing fantasy ... an almost

perfect piece of propaganda for para-legal police power...." Others
felt that this film reflected the new morality of the mid-twentieth
century, in which it seems difficult always to decide who is on the
right side of the law.

The rapid-fire story focuses on a mad killer (Robinson) who
shoots a number of people from a rooftop and promises to quit for
a ransom of $200,000. Dirty Harry Callahan (Eastwood), a racist
cop on the case, and his partner (Santoni) try to capture the killer
but fail. Afterward Harry comes upon a bank robbery and shoots
the robbers while the Killer murders a ten year old boy and kidnaps
an adolescent girl, demanding ransom. The mayor agrees and Harry is assigned to deliver the loot, but the Killer leads the cop on a
merry chase around the city. They finally meet in a park where
the Killer beats Harry and tells him the girl is dead. Chico arrives
on the scene and the Killer injures him, but Harry stabs the Killer
in the leg. He tails him later to the latter's room at Kezar Stadium, where he is a groundskeeper, and shoots and beats him. The
kidnapped girl is found dead, but the police have to let the Killer
go because Harry violated the man's civil rights to the point of de-
stroying the state's case. Harry's superior (Guardino) chastises
him and the Killer thereafter has himself beaten and puts the blame
on Harry. With Harry off his trail--for the moment--the Killer
kidnaps a busload of children and threatens to kill them. He wants
getaway money and a plane with which to leave the country. The
mayor again agrees, but Harry gets onto the bus, turns it off the
main road, chases the Killer and then kills him. At the finale, because he disobeyed police orders, Harry throws away his badge.

Critics throughout America had a field day lambasting the
structure of Dirty Harry, but this, as indicated above, had little ad-
verse effect on the box-office. The Washington Post exclaimed,
"The premise is developed along such a simplistic right-wing line
.... Movie action melodramas, like action comic strips, tend to
have a slightly sub-fascist fantasy element, glorifying supermen or
thugs on the right side of the law. What makes Dirty Harry insup-
portable and eventually laughable is that it lacks even that much so-
phistication and stylization."

In 1974, Warner Bros. released Magnum Force, directed by
Ted Post and again starring Clint Eastwood as Dirty Harry Callahan.
This time the unorthodox law enforcer is pitted against his superior
(Hal Holbrook) who, it develops, is heading a group of vigilante police who have decided to rid San Francisco of undesirables by sum-
marily executing them. The overabundance of violence did not compensate for waning audience interest in such genre pieces.

DISBARRED (Paramount, 1939) 58 min.

Associate producer, Stuart Walker; director, Robert Florey;
story, Harry Sauber; screenplay, Lillie Hayward, Robert Presnell;
art directors, Hans Dreier, William Flannery; music director, Boris Morros; camera, Harry Fischbeck; editor, Arthur Schmidt.

Gail Patrick (Joan Carroll); Robert Preston (Bradley Kent);
Otto Kruger (Tyler Cradon); Sidney Toler (G. L. "Hardy" Mardsen);

Robert Preston, Gail Patrick and Otto Kruger in a pose for
Disbarred (1938).

Edward Marr (Harp Harrigan); Charles D. Brown (Jackson); Helen
Mac Kellar (Abbey Tennant); Clay Clement (Attorney Roberts);
Frank M. Thomas (G. H. Blanchard the District Attorney); Virginia
Dabney (Gita La Rue); John Hart, Harry Worth (Reporters); Ruth
Robinson (Aunt Marion); Virginia Vale (Stewardess); Philip Warren,
Sheila Darcy (Secretaries); Henry Roquemore (Passenger); Robert
Frazer (Brimmer); Jim Pierce (Bailiff); Guy Usher, Edward J. Le
Saint (Judges); Stanley Blystone (Schaeffer); Paul Fix (Bomb Throw-
er); Jack Knoche (Reporter); Pop Byron (Jury Foreman); Wheaton
Chambers (Ballistic Expert); Harry Tyler (Cashier); Dick Elliott
(Small Town Character).

This miniature crime thriller was typical of the unpretentious
supporting bill features that Robert Florey turned out for Paramount
in the late 1930s. In it Joan Carroll (Patrick) appears as the country lawyer who is brought to the big city to defend a gangster. She
is paid by a big time crook (Kruger). Her client is accused of
pointing a lethal weapon at a state's witness and Joan's goal is to
prove he did not own the weapon in question. All ends well, however, when a young assistant district attorney (Preston) sets Joan
on the right course. He proves the criminal leanings of her client

and, of course, also of Tyler Cradon.

Patrick and Preston, both of whom had appeared in Florey's King of Alcatraz (1938), q. v. , made an attractive duo. Kruger was his usual smooth criminal self, while Sidney Toler, who was becoming famous as a screen Charlie Chan, contributed a solid performance as a hoodlum involved in the case.

THE DOCKS OF NEW YORK   (Paramount, 1928)   7,202'

Associate producer, J. G. Bachmann; director, Josef von Sternberg; story, John Monk Saunders; adaptor, Jules Furthman; titles, Julian Johnson; set designer, Hans Dreier; camera, Harold Rosson, editor, Helen Lewis.

George Bancroft (Bill Roberts); Betty Compson (Sadie); Olga Baclanova (Lou); Clyde Cook (Sugar Steve); Mitchell Lewis (Third Engineer); Gustav von Seyffertitz (Hymn Book Harry); Guy Oliver (The Crimp); May Foster (Mrs. Crimp); Lillian Worth (Steve's Girl).

This film was one of the several gangster melodramas directed by Josef von Sternberg for Paramount.   It helped to establish the pattern and flavor that would become so essential to the underworld drama of forthcoming years.

Tramp steamer stoker Bill Roberts (Bancroft) saves waterfront tramp Sadie (Compson) from suicide.   Later, while drunk, Bill weds Sadie.   The following morning he leaves her and returns to his ship.   When a boat engineer (Lewis) attempts to make love to Sadie, he is killed by his wife Lou (Baclanova).   Sadie is charged with the crime, but Lou later confesses.   Meanwhile Bill realizes he loves Sadie and jumps ship.   He returns ashore just in time to prevent Sadie from being sentenced for having stolen the clothes he gave her to be wed in.   He saves her by truthfully admitting to the theft himself.   As he is led off to serve his two months' sentence, he promises to return to Sadie.

In Josef von Sternberg (1967), Herman G. Weinberg records, "Sternberg conjured up a section of the Hoboken waterfront in the studio, complete with a dirty tramp steamer tied up to the dock.... Except for a fleeting glimpse of the New York skyline and oil slicks on the lapping waters of the bay, The Docks of New York was wholly studio-made.   The director felt that only on the studio stages could he control the infinite shades of black-and-white photography, which he had developed by this time to an art in itself. "

The London Daily Telegraph would sense the rationale behind the pictorially beautiful feature.   'It conveys, quite unobtrusively, a great moral lesson.   By a hundred deft touches, Sternberg makes us poignantly aware of some vague, inarticulate longings for something better that may haunt human souls seemingly depraved beyond redemption. "

Perhaps most importantly, films such as The Docks of New York helped to set new concepts in moviegoers' minds regarding the emotional make-up of the so-called criminal element: that such people were not all black-and-white, that there could be some good or evil in everyone.

Olga Baclanova and George Bancroft in <u>The Docks of New York</u> (1928).

DR. BROADWAY (Paramount, 1942) 68 min.

Producer, Sol C. Siegel; associate producer, E. D. Leishin;
director, Anthony Mann; based on a story by Borden Chase; screen-
play, Art Arthur; art directors, Hans Dreier, Earl Hedrick; camera,
Theodore Sparkuhl; editor, Arthur Schmidt.
Macdonald Carey (Dr. Timothy Kane); Jean Phillips (Connie
Madigan); J. Carrol Naish (Jack Venner); Richard Lane (Patrick
Doyle); Eduardo Ciannelli (Vic Telli); Joan Woodbury (Margie Dove);
Arthur Loft (Captain Mahoney); Warren Hymer (Maxie the Goat).

Anthony Mann made his directorial debut with this mini-film.
It was a would-be comic melodrama involving a Times Square doctor
(Carey) who is persuaded to do a final favor for a dying gangster.
He later runs into trouble with a rival gang and the law.   Screen
newcomer Carey proved likeable as the hero and gave some dimension to the premise that professional men other than law enforcers
and detectives can come into close association with the underworld.

DOCTOR SOCRATES (Warner Bros. , 1935) 69 min.

Producer, Robert Lord; director, William Dieterle; based on
the story by W. R. Burnett; screenplay, Robert Lord, Mary C. Mc-
Call, Jr.; camera, Tony Gaudio; editor, Ralph Dawson.
Paul Muni (Dr. Lee Caldwell); Ann Dvorak (Josephine Gray);
Barton MacLane (Red Bastian); Raymond Brown (Ben Suggs); Ralph
Remley (Bill Payne); Hal K. Dawson (Mel Towne); Grace Stafford
(Caroline Suggs); Samuel Hinds (Dr. McClintock); Marc Lawrence
(Lefty); Sam Wren (Chuck); Hobart Cavanaugh (Floyd Stevens); Henry
O'Neill (Greer); Mayo Methot (Muggsy); Carl Stockdale (Abner Cluett);
Helen Lowell (Ma Ganson); John Eldredge (Dr. Burton); Ivan Miller
(Doolittle); Adrian Morris (Beanie); Robert Barrat (Dr. Ginder);
John Kelly (Al).   Leo White (Tailor); Harry Harvey, Jack Gardner
(Photographers); Jack Norton, Huey White (Drunks); Marie Astaire,
Lucille Collins (Molls); Al Hill, Robert Perry, Larry McGrath,
James Dundee, Frank McGlynn, Jr. (Gangsters); Milton Kibbee (Bank
Teller).

Paul "Scarface" Muni starred in this medium-key thriller as
the physician of the title who becomes involved with hoodlums after
they break into his home following a job.   One of the group is injured and the doctor is forced to operate on him and then shelter
the gang.   He also protects a girl hitchhiker (Dvorak).   Soon the
townspeople become suspicious of the happenings at the doctor's
house, especially after the arrival of Josephine Gray, whom they
assume is the mob's moll.   When the gang threatens to hurt Josephine, Dr. Caldwell takes action by convincing them they have contracted yellow fever.   He injects them with serum which puts them
to sleep and thus thwarts a gang shootout with G-men.   The law enforcers round up the gang as they slumber.
The New York Times acknowledged this "a pleasant enough
melodrama" and, writing about Muni's career in Films in Review,

Paul Coster said it ".. . was cleverly and excitingly plotted and the sets unusually good. "

Doctor Socrates would be remade by Warner Bros. in 1939 as King of the Underworld, q.v., nominally starring Kay Francis, but with Humphrey Bogart as the focal gangster figure.

THE DON IS DEAD (Universal, 1973) C-117 min.

Producer, Hal B. Wallis; associate producer, Paul Nathan; director, Richard Fleischer; based on the novel by Marvin H. Albert; screenplay, Albert; adaptators, Christopher Trumbo, Michael Philip Butler; assistant directors, David Hall, Tom Blank; art director, Preston Ames; set decorator, Don Sullivan; music, Jerry Goldsmith; song, Jerry and Carol Goldsmith; stunt co-ordinator, George Sawaya; sound, John Kean, Waldon O. Watson, Ronald Pierce; camera, Richard H. Kline; editor, Edward A. Biery.

Anthony Quinn (Don Angelo Dimorra); Frederic Forrest (Tony Fargo); Robert Forster (Frank Regabulto); Al Lettieri (Vince Fargo); Angel Tompkins (Ruby Dunne); Charles Cioffi (Luigi Orlando); Jo Anne Meredith (Marie); J. Duke Russo (Don Bernardo); Louis Zorich (Mitch); Anthony Charnota (Johnny Tresca); Ina Balin (Nella); Joe Santos (Joe Lucci); Frank de Kova (Giunta); Abe Vigoda (Don Tolusso); Victor Argo (Augie the Horse); Val Bisoglio (Peter Lazatti); Robert Carricart (Spada); Frank Christi (Harold Early); Sid Haig (The Arab); Maurice Sherbane (Corsican); George Skaff (Vito); Vic Tayback (Ralph Negri).

Hal B. Wallis returned to Hollywood-based production, after several years in Britain, with this Richard Fleischer-directed melodrama loosely adapted from Marvin H. Albert's novel.

This specious film, which pandered to every cliché of the genre and to every stereotype of the Mafia system, dealt with an inner-family feud between Mafia leaders after an old Don dies. Don Angelo Dimorra is given half the dead man's territory in New York while Luigi Orlando (Cioffi), the consigliori for Don Bernardo (Russo), retains control of the other segment. Orlando hopes to gain control of the whole territory before Don Bernardo is released from jail. To foment trouble between Dimorra and his protege, Frank Regabulto (Forster), Orlando introduces Ruby Dunne (Tompkins) to the don. As is hoped, Dimorra becomes infatuated with Ruby, not knowing she is Frank's girl. Frank returns to town and, infuriated by his idol's "betrayal," enlists the aid of triggermen to avenge this insult. The battle wages back and forth among Frank's men, Dimorra's group, and the trouble-instigating Orlando. Before the peace is restored, Frank and Orlando are killed, Dimorra has been reduced to a helpless cripple, and Don Bernardo, released from prison, becomes the big shot of the district.

The British Monthly Film Bulletin, observing this American-oriented feature, commented that it had ".. . an appropriate B-thriller air of total fantasy, and there is some discreetly precise, non-starry characterisation: the dismal vulgarity of the Machiavellian schemer ... and the non-clichéd rendering of the cliched partnership

of the muscle-headed brother with the dissatisfied dreamer, by Al
Lettieri and Frederic Forrest. The result is still solid formula
stuff rather than a St. Valentine's Day Massacre display of gangsters caught in the toils of their own rituals.... "
   On the other hand, U.S. critics quickly dismissed the film
as a faltering exploitation of a shop-worn formula; a poor imitation
of The Godfather, and, really, just plain lousy entertainment. (The
film earned less than one million dollars in distributors' domestic
rentals.) Alvin H. Marill in Films in Review had an interesting
cast observation: "In some ways, The Don Is Dead is a lavishly-
produced updating of the type of thing Quinn used to make nearly 30
years ago at Paramount, except that Quinn is now playing the role
then taken by J. Carrol Naish, and Robert Forster grunts menac-
ingly through an old Anthony Quinn-type character. "

THE DOORWAY TO HELL   (Warner Bros. , 1930)   78 min.

   Director, Archie Mayo; based on the story A Handful of
Clouds by Rowland Brown; screenplay, George Rosener; music di-
rector, Leo F. Forbstein; makeup, Perc Westmore; sound, David
Forrest; camera, Barney McGill; editor, Robert Crandall.
   Lew Ayres (Louis Ricarno); Charles Judels (Sam Marconi);
Dorothy Mathews (Doris); Leon Janney (Jackie Lamar); Robert El-
liott (Captain O'Grady); James Cagney (Steve Mileway); Kenneth
Thomson (Captain of Military Academy); Jerry Mandy (Joe); Noel
Madison (Rocco); Bernard "Bunny" Granville: (Bit); Fred Argus
(Machine Gunner); Ruth Hall (Girl); Dwight Frye, Tom Wilson, Al
Hill (Gangsters).

   The frequent uselessness of a gangster's life and the fatalism
exhibited by such a person were often the themes of Thirties' underworld films. One of the earliest with such a plotline was The
Doorway to Hell. Today it is remembered only as one of James
Cagney's first gangster film appearances. However, at the time of
its release, the New York Herald-Tribune termed it "... an excellent gangster film. "
   The story focused on the rise and fall of a beer baron, with
Lew Ayres cast as a big-time hoodlum who controls the bootleg
racket in a big city. He rules his domain with an iron hand. After
a time, however, he turns the racket over to a lieutenant (Cagney)
and gets married. Later his wife betrays him, and then his brother
is killed by a rival hoodlum. As his attempt to go straight becomes
thwarted, Louis Ricarno decides to return to avenge his brother's
death. Instead, he meets his own end at the hands of his former
gang.

DOWN THREE DARK STREETS   (United Artists, 1954)   85 min.

   Producer, Arthur Gardner; associate producer, Jules V.
Levy; director, Arthur Laven; based on the novel Case File F.B.I.
by the Gordons; screenplay, The Gordons, Bernard C. Schoenfeld;

Claude Akins, Broderick Crawford, Gene Reynolds and Harlan Warde
in Down Three Dark Streets (1954).

music, Paul Sawtell; assistant director, Milton Carter; camera,
Joseph Biroc; editor, Grant Whytock.
      Broderick Crawford (Ripley); Ruth Roman (Kate Martel); Mar-
tha Hyer (Connie Anderson); Marisa Pavan (Julie Angelino); Casey
Adams (Dave Milson); Kenneth Tobey (Zack Stewart); Gene Reynolds
(Vince Angelino).

      In 1949 Broderick Crawford won an Academy Award for his
sterling performance in All the King's Men.   Yet, within five years,
Columbia let his career sink into a morass of "B" films like Down
Three Dark Streets.
      This cheapie was made merely to exploit Crawford's name.
He appeared not to have taken the affair very seriously, since he
left the better emoting to Ruth Roman as the victim of an extortionist, and to Marisa Pavan as the blind wife of an alleged car thief.
      F. B. I. agent Ripley (Crawford) inherits his partner's case
load when the latter is murdered.   In particular, there are three
unsolved crimes, hence the film's title.   The bulk of this potentially
fine film was then given over to the tracking down and killing of a
bank robber, the break-up of an interstate auto theft ring, and the
capturing of an extortionist who had murdered the law agent in the
first place.
      More astute filmgoers could note with scorn that the scripters
did not bother to instill Crawford's Ripley with much brains.   At
no time during the film's eighty-five minute playing time does he

bother to check into the Bureau's files to see if the alleged killer
might have had a criminal record!

THE DRAGNET   (Paramount, 1928)   7,866'

    Director, Josef von Sternberg; story, Oliver H. P. Garrett;
adaptor, Jules Furthman; screenplay, Jules Furthman, Charles
Furthman; titles, Herman J. Mankiewicz; set designer, Hans Dreier;
camera, Harold Rosson; editor, Helen Lewis.
    George Bancroft (Two-Gun Nolan); Evelyn Brent (The Magpie);
William Powell (Dapper Frank Trent); Fred Kohler ("Gabby" Steve);
Francis McDonald (Sniper Dawson); Leslie Fenton (Shakespeare).

    Following the huge success of Underworld, q. v. , the previous
year, Paramount reteamed with director Josef von Sternberg for The
Dragnet which was issued in May, 1928.   Today no print of the movie is known to exist and, therefore, no comparison between these
two silent features can be made.   Most cinema historians tend to
regulate The Dragnet to a place far below its predecessor.
    Adapted for the screen by Jules Furthman from Oliver H. P.
Garrett's Night Stick, the film tells of a detective (Bancroft) who
turns to the bottle after resigning from the police force following
the death of his buddy (Fenton) when the two were chasing bootleg
hijackers.   Nolan thinks that he had been the cause of the homicide.
Later the girlfriend (Brent) of the gang leader (Powell) squeals to
Nolan about underworld deals.   This information leads Two-Gun to
abandon his life in the gutter.   Later he is forced to kill Dapper
Frank Trent after that hood has shot his moll for talking.   The girl
lives, however, and she and Two-Gun are married.   To make the
ending even better, he rejoins the police force.
    David Robinson in Hollywood in the Twenties (1968) would
report, "... as in Underworld, Sternberg's pictorialism proved an
entirely dynamic and in no way static element: the story and its
characters are developed through well-observed visual detail. "

DRAGNET   (Warner Bros. , 1954)   C-89 min.

    Producer, Stanley Meyer; director, Jack Webb; screenplay,
Richard L. Breen; music, Walter Schumann; assistant director,
Oren Haglund; camera, Edward Colman; editor, Robert M. Leeds.
    Jack Webb (Sergeant Joe Friday); Ben Alexander (Officer
Frank Smith); Richard Boone (Captain Hamilton); Ann Robinson (Grace
Downey); Stacy Harris (Max Troy); Virginia Gregg (Ethel Marie
Starkie); Victor Perrin (Adolph Alexander); Georgia Ellis (Belle Da-
vitt); James Griffith (Jesse Quinn); Dick Cathcart (Roy Cleaver);
Malcolm Atterbury (Lee Reinhard); Willard Sage (Chester Davitt);
Olan Soule (Ray Pinker); Dennis Weaver (Captain Lohrman); James
Anderson (Fred Kemp); Monte Masters (Fabian Gerard); Herb Vigran
(Mr. Archer); Virginia Christine (Mrs. Caldwell); Guy Hamilton
(Walker Scott); Ramsey Williams (Wesley Cannon); Harry Bartell
(Lieutenant Stevens); Herb Ellis (Booking Sergeant); Harlan Warde
(Interne); Cliff Arquette (Charlie Weaver).

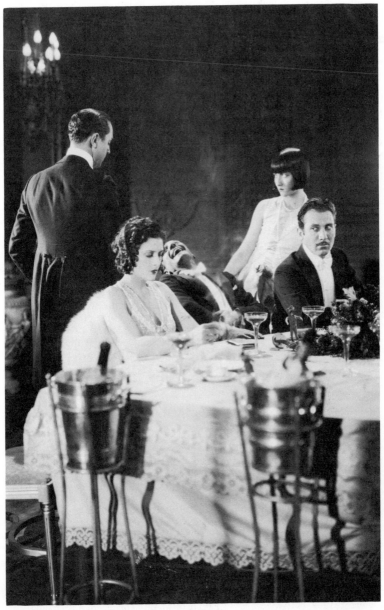

William Powell, Evelyn Brent and Francis McDonald in <u>The Drag-net</u> (1928).

Jack Webb's popular crime series "Dragnet" ("dum-du-dum-dum") had spectacular runs on radio and television. The producer-director brought the heavily documentary (based on actual L.A. case histories "with the names changed to protect the innocent") concept to movie theatres. This spinoff was entitled simply Dragnet. The film, like the original teleseries which ran until 1959, proved to be exceedingly popular and a large moneymaker. In retrospect, however, much of Webb's deadpan style, both as director and star Sergeant Joe Friday, seems supercilious.

The low-keyed tale revolves around the attempt by tough Sergeant Joe Friday (Webb) and pal Officer Frank Smith (Alexander) to find the killer of a hoodlum. This law-enforcement team dogs suspects, and demonstrates that cops can be as steadfast and imaginative as crooks. During the film's course, today's alert viewer can note strong evidence of the pre-Civil Rights era, as Friday et al. browbeat suspects, decry the use of the Fifth Amendment, and vocally favor wiretapping.

Concerning Dragnet the New York Times observed, "the atmosphere is hard and real." Virginia Gregg as the murdered man's grieving wife and Richard Boone as the head of the intelligence division were especially effective.

In 1966 "Dragnet" returned to the small screen with Webb in the lead and Harry Morgan as his partner, Officer Bill Gannon. The pilot for the series' return had been a two-hour telefeature shot in 1966 but not aired until early in 1969 due to the highly rated success of the new video series. The long awaited feature, again entitled Dragnet, scored a 38 per cent share of the TV viewing audience. It detailed Friday and Gannon's attempts to discover the reasons for the murders of several young models. Like the TV series, the film contained a number of cameos, including one by Virginia Gregg. The telefeature emphasized the long, tedious toil of very thorough police methods. This aspect, so much a part of Webb's show, was also the principal flaw of the property.

DRESSED TO KILL   (Fox, 1928) 6,566'

Presenter, William Fox; director, Irving Cummings; story, William Conselman, Cummings; screenplay, Howard Estabrook; titles, Malcolm Stuart Boylan; assistant director, Charles Woolstenhulme; camera, Conrad Wells; editor, Frank Hull.

Edmund Lowe ("Mile-Away" Barry); Mary Astor (Jeanne); Ben Bard (Nick); Robert Perry (Ritzy Hogan); Joe Brown (Himself); Tom Dugan (Silky Levine); John Kelly (Biff Simpson); Robert E. O'Connor (Detective Gilroy); R. O. Pennell ("Professor"); Ed Brady ("Singing Walter"); Charles Morton (Jeanne's Beau).

A minor but popular entry from Fox into the crime sweepstakes of 1928. Howard Estabrook, who later worked in Westerns, wrote the screenplay from a story co-authored by Irving Cummings, who also served as director of the piece. Its slight premise had gang leader "Mile-Away" Barry (Lowe) fall for hard-boiled Jeanne (Astor). She is really a nice girl who has joined the gang in order to recover stolen bonds that will prove her bank officer boyfriend

guiltless of their theft.   This proof will free him from his prison
term.   The rather austere finale finds Jeanne and her beau reunited, but Barry is gunned down by his own gang for helping the
girl.

DU RIFIFI A PANAME (RIFIFI IN PANAMA) (Comacico, 1966)
C-100 min.
      Executive producer, Raymond Danon; producer, Maurice Jac-
quin; director, Denys de la Patelliere; based on the novel by
Auguste Le Breton; screenplay, Alphonse Boudard, de la Patelliere;
music, Georges Garvarentz; art director, Robert Clavel; assistant
director, Robert Bodega; costumes, Jacques Fontenay; camera,
Walter Wollitz; editor, Claude Durand.
      Jean Gabin (Paulo Berger); George Raft (Charles Binnaggio);
Gert Frobe (Walter); Nadja Tiller (Irene); Mireille Darc (Lili Prin-
cesse); Claudio Brook (Mike Coppolano); Marcel Bozzuffi (Marque
Mal); Jean-Claude Bercq (Jo le Pale); Dany Dauberson (Lea); Claude
Brasseur (Giulio); Daniel Ceccaldi (Commissaire Noel); Yves Bar-
sacq (Fifty Year Old Man); Claude Cerval (Rene); Philippe Clair
(Wounded Man); Carlo Nell (Sergio). Christa Lang (Mario's Daughter).
      U.S. release: Upper Hand (Paramount, 1967) C-86 min. -
Dubbed.

      This international crime melodrama was produced in France
by the Copernic Company owned by Jean Gabin and Fernandel.   For
added box-office attraction, veteran Gabin was teamed with George
Raft and Gert Frobe, the latter having had global success as the
villain of Goldfinger.
      The leisurely-paced feature presented the account of an aging
hoodlum (Gabin) and his antique dealer partner (Frobe) who operate
a gold smuggling ring amongst the world's largest cities.   A subplot
has the syndicate taking on a new agent, a newspaper man (Brook)
who is really a U.S. Treasury agent looking for connections between
the Mafia and the sale of weapons to Cuba.   The Mafia tries to
pressure its way into Berger's operations and, in the process, kills
Walter.   In revenge, Berger meets with the U.S. Mafia leader
(Raft!) and plants a bomb.   As it prepares to explode, he leaves
the building.   However, he walks right into the custody of the police.
      Although the New York Times panned the entry as "dull gang-
ster melodrama, " it did have internal excitement.   Especially forceful was the tense scene in which Gabin coolly walks into the meeting
with Raft, while the latter coyly flips a coin.   The pacing during
this scene, which includes a long conversation between the two stars,
is well done.
      The film was issued in the U.S., with fourteen minutes cut
from the final product, as The Upper Hand.

DU RIFIFI A TOKYO (Cipra, 1961) 89 min.

      Producer, Jacques Bar; director, Jacques Deray; screenplay,

Aguste Lebreton; script adaptors, Jose Giovanni, R. M. Arlaud,
Deray; music, Georges Delerue; camera, Tadashi Aramaki; editor,
Albert Jurgenson.

Karl Boehm (Carl Mersen); Michel Vitold (Merigne); Charles
Vanel (Van Hekkin); Eric Okada (Danny Riquet); Keiko Kishi (Assmi);
Barbara Lass (Francoise Merigne); Yanagi (Ishimoto).

U. S. release: Rififi in Tokyo (MGM, 1963).

"... little more than a routine and shopworn study of the
campaign of a ring of jewel thieves. The only noteworthy plot variation is a technical one designed to illustrate that bank protection of
valuables has moved into the electronic age... " (Variety).

Set in the Tokyo back alleys, this uninspired caper revolves
around the plot to remove a large, flawless diamond from the vault
of the Bank of Tokyo. By now such heist gambits had become so
commonplace, that the only way to insure audience interest was to
envelop the robot-like robbers with engaging characterizations. Du
Rififi a Tokyo committed the grave error of delaying too long before
investing the array of characters with any motivation.

DU RIFIFI CHEZ LES FEMMES (RIFIFI AMONG THE WOMEN)
(Cinedis, 1958) 105 min.

Director, Alex Joffe; screenplay, Auguste Le Breton, Gabriel
Arout, Joffe; camera, Pierre Montazel; editor, Leonide Azar.

Nadja Tiller (Vicky); Robert Hossein (Marcel); Silva Montfort
(Yoko); Roger Hanin (Bug); Pierre Blanchar (Le Pirate); Francoise
Rosay (Bertha); Jean Gaven (James).

Unlike its predecessor, this follow-up production coasts on
the reputation of its originator. It lacked the erotic little touches
which, joined with the proper suspense values, made Du Rififi Chez
Les Hommes, q. v. , so worthy.

Here there is a supposedly foolproof scheme to rob the Bank
of Belgium. The operation is carried out, but gangland feuds liquidate everyone involved. Once again, the old adage that "crime does
not pay" emerges victorious.

Du Rififi a Tokyo (1961), q. v. , and Du Rififi a Paname (1966),
q. v. , would wind up the series.

DU RIFIFI CHEZ DES HOMMES (RIFIFI) (Miracle, 1955) 113 min.

Director, Jules Dassin; based on the novel by Auguste le
Breton; screenplay, Rene Wheeler, Dassin, le Breton; art director,
Auguste Capelier; music, Georges Auric; sound, J. Lebreton; cam-
era, Philippe Agostini; editor, Roger Dwyre.

Jean Servais (Tony le Stephanois); Carl Mohner (Jo le Suedois);
Robert Manuel (Mario); Perlo Vita (Cesar); Magali Noel (Viviane);
Marie Subouret (Mado); Janine Darcy (Louise); Pierre Grasset (Louis);
Robert Hossein (Remi); Marcel Lupovici (Pierre); Dominique Maurin
(Tonio); Claude Sylvain (Ida).

Jean Servais and Carl Mohner (right) in <u>Du Rififi</u> (1955).

"This is perhaps the keenest crime film that ever came out
of France," according to critic Bosley Crowther (<u>New York Times</u>).
Or, as <u>Cue</u> magazine analyzed, "... the movie-makers make certain there's enough action to keep the hoods hopping and the audience
interested." This well-staged robbery film began a gangster film
cycle in France and Europe in the mid-1950s. The feature was co-
written and directed by Jules Dassin, who also played a traitor in
the movie under the acting name of Perlo Vita.
    As most people know, or should know, the storyline concerns
the planning and execution of a nighttime robbery of a posh English
jewelry shop in the Rue de Rivoli of Paris. After the grab is made,
a rival gang attempts to acquire the loot by kidnapping the small son
of one of the robbers. They plan to hold him as ransom for the
loot. At the same time the film delves into the French underworld
life, as well as into the particular happenstances of the individual
lawbreakers and their women. The highlight of this motion picture
is its well staged robbery sequence. It runs for thirty-five minutes
and requires <u>no</u> dialog to underline its successful suspense.
    <u>Variety</u> alerted its readers, "Compared to the Hollywood type
of gangster movie, <u>Rififi</u> is more sophisticated and, if anything,
more socially irresponsible." Less enthusiastic was the British
<u>Monthly Film Bulletin</u>: "In its creation of a world where all the

actions and reactions appear normal except for the fact that they in-
form a pattern of criminal life, Rififi invites an inevitable comparison to The Asphalt Jungle. And in this Rififi must come off worst,
for its relationships are not so densely textured and it lacks the
formal economy of the Huston picture. But it is still an intensely
exciting film. "

Perhaps John Gabree in Gangsters (1973) best pinpointed the
reason for the feature's success. He noted it "... had the interesting effect of making its audience feel like accomplices to the
crime before visiting retribution on the criminals.... "

EACH DAWN I DIE   (Warner Bros. , 1939)   92 min.

Associate producer, David Lewis; director, William Keighley; based on the novel by Jerome Odlum; screenplay, Norman Reilly Raine, Warren Duff, Charles Perry; assistant director, Frank
Heath; technical adviser, William Buckley; art director, Max Parker;
music, Max Steiner; music director, Leo F. Forbstein; costumes,
Howard Shoup; makeup, Perc Westmore; sound, E. A. Brown; camera, Arthur Edeson; editor, Thomas Richards.

James Cagney (Frank Ross); George Raft ("Hood" Stacey);
Jane Bryan (Joyce Conover); George Bancroft (Warden John Arm-
strong); Maxie Rosenbloom (Fargo Red); Stanley Ridges (Muller);
Alan Baxter (Polecat Carlisle); Victor Jory (W. J. Grayce); Willard
Robertson (Lang); Paul Hurst (Garsky); John Wray (Peter Kassock);
Louis Jean Heydt (Joe Lassiter); Ed Pawley (Dale); Joe Downing
(Limpy Julien); Emma Dunn (Mrs. Ross); Thurston Hall (District
Attorney Jesse Hanley); Clay Clement (Attorney Lockhart); William
Davidson (Bill Mason); John Ridgely (Jerry Poague the Reporter);
John Harron (Lew Keller the Reporter); Selmer Jackson (Patterson);
Robert Homans (Mac the Guard); Harry Cording (Temple); Abner
Biberman (Shake Edwards); Napoleon Simpson (Mose); Maris Wrixon
(Girl in Car); Charles Trowbridge (Judge); Eddy Chandler (Deputy);
Walter Miller (Turnkey); Frank Mayo (Telegraph Editor); Mack Gray
(Joe); Bob Perry (Bud); Fred Graham (Cell Guard).

One of the box-office blockbusters of 1939 was this screen
teaming of Warner Bros.' two top gangster stars, James Cagney
and George Raft. Time complimented the "crackling screenplay"
that was "made memorable by the easy mastery of its two principals, " and the New York Daily Mirror called the film "lusty ...
Messrs. Raft and Cagney never have been better. "

When reporter Frank Ross uncovers the fact that the district
attorney has been concealing vital information about a crooked con-
struction company, he prints the account. Thereafter, the district
attorney arranges for Frank to be framed on a drunken driving-man-
slaughter charge. Frank is sent to prison and is prevented from
getting a parole by outside influences. While behind bars, flinty
Frank becomes the buddy of notorious underworld figure "Hood"
Stacey (Raft). When the daring courtroom escape Frank has planned
for "Hood" goes slighty awry, Stacey and company think Ross has
squealed on them. But eventually "Hood" finds the real culprit

Paul Hurst, Bob Perry, George Raft, Al Hill and Mack Gray in
Each Dawn I Die (1939).

(Wray).   The taut feature climaxes with a bloody battle behind bars
between prisoners trying to escape and the police.   Stacey is killed
in the uprising, but Frank survives to help bring reform to the
prison system.

With feisty Cagney and Raft as the focal figures and ex-mov-
ie tough guy George Bancroft as the hard-but-understanding prison
warden, Each Dawn I Die emerged as a very solid production.   However, there were a great many subplot moments which smacked of
prior Warners' movies, and the soundstage prison seemed peopled
with the same performers who had appeared in countless cellblock
entries (did they have life sentences?).   But, unlike the typical
John Garfield prison drama, there was very little overt preaching
here, either against the ills of the Depression or the pressures of
jail life.   In a far more subtle manner, the filmmakers just let the
viewer draw his own conclusions from the rugged scenes of confinement.   The monotonous daily existence, and the hopeless ambience
that surrounded a convict's every waking moment were all very real.

THE EARL OF CHICAGO   (MGM, 1940)   85 min.

Producer, Victor Saville; director, Richard Thorpe; story,
Brock Williams, Charles de Grandcourt, Gene Fowler; screenplay,

Lesser Samuels; art director, Cedric Gibbons; music, Werner R.
Heymann; camera, Ray June; editor, Fred Sullivan.

Robert Montgomery (Silky Kilmount); Edward Arnold (Don
Ramsey); Edmund Gwenn (Muncie); Reginald Owen (Gervase Gonwell);
Ronald Sinclair (Gerald Kilmount); E. E. Clive (Redwood); Frederic
Worlock (Lord Elfie); Miles Mander (Attorney General); William
Stack (Coroner); Norma Varden (Maureen Kilmount); Kenneth Hunter
(Lord Tyrmanell); Ian Wolfe (Reading Clerk); Peter Godfrey (Judson);
Charles Coleman (Bishop); Rex Evans (Vicar); John Burton (Clerk);
Art Berry, Sr. (Seedman); David Dunbar (Plowman); Harold Howard,
Bob Corey (Fishermen); Henry Flynn (Villager); Vangie Beilby (Old
Maid); Radford Allen (Boy); Craufurd Kent (Specialist); Nora Perry
(Receptionist); William Haade (Crapshooter); Gladys Blake (Silken
Legs); Alec Craig (Son); Billy Bevan (Guide); Temple Pigott (Mrs.
Oakes); Halliwell Hobbes (Lord High Chancellor); Zeffie Tilbury (Old
Lady); Robert Warwick (Parliament Clerk); Holmes Herbert (Sergeant
at Arms).

This glossy but decidedly minor gangster film had the unusual
plot gimmick of an American gangster (Montgomery) finding out that
he is actually a part of British nobility. He journeys to London to
collect his inheritance and begins to enjoy the British way of life.
However, a lawbreaker will always be a lawbreaker. He eventually
ends up being tried for murder before the House of Lords, and ex-
claims, "He ratted on me!"

Debonair Montgomery did very nicely with this offbeat role
while Edward Arnold offered his usual professional rendering of a
sinister character, this time as the hoodlum's duplistic lawyer.
Edmund Gwenn gave a very nice balance to the proceedings as Muncie, the soft-spoken servant who has much good advice for his un-
tutored employer (Montgomery).

With tongue-in-cheek, the New York Times noted the film
was "... a jape, an opulent and Britishly learned jape."

THE ENFORCER   (Warner Bros., 1951)   87 min.

Producer, Milton Sperling; director (credited), Bretaigne
Windust, (actually), Raoul Walsh; screenplay, Martin Rackin; music,
David Buttolph; orchestrator, Maurice de Packh; assistant director,
Chuck Hansen; art director, Charles H. Clarke; set decorator, Wil-
liam Kuehl; sound, Dolph Thomas; camera, Robert Burks; editor,
Fred Allen.

Humphrey Bogart (Martin Ferguson); Zero Mostel (Big Babe
Lazich); Ted De Corsia (Albert Mendoza); Everett Sloane (Albert
Mendoza); Roy Roberts (Captain Frank Nelson); Lawrence Tolan
(Duke Malloy); King Donovan (Sergeant Whitlow); Bob Steele (Herman);
Adelaide Klein (Olga Kirshen); Don Beddoe (Thomas O'Hara); Tito
Vuolo (Tony Vetto); John Kellogg (Vince); Jack Lambert (Philadelphia
Tom Zaca); Patricia Joiner (Angela Vetto); Susan Cabot (Nina Lom-
bardo); Mario Siletti (Louis the Barber); Alan Foster (Shorty); Harry
Wilson (B. J.); Pete Kellett, Barry Reagan (Internes); Dan Riss

Humphrey Bogart and Roy Roberts in The Enforcer (1951).

(Mayor); Art Dupuis (Keeper); Bud Wolfe (Fireman); Creighton Hale (Clerk); Patricia Hayes (Teenager).

The Enforcer was made in the "Dragnet" documentary style that was so popular in the 1950s. The film tells of the efforts of a District Attorney (Bogart) to jail the head of Murder, Inc. After a star witness "accidentally" dies while the leader (Sloane) is awaiting trial, the hunt for more evidence begins. After the confession of one hired killer, many others are found and the whole complex organization of hired assassins is laid bare. Later public prosecutor Ferguson finds a witness to the murder of a victim of the organization, but another hired killer (Steele) is set on her trail. At the climax, Ferguson guns down Herman. The rescued girl testifies against Albert Mendoza and the latter is convicted. He is sentenced to the electric chair. The power of the organization is smashed--for a time, at least.

Straight from the headlines, this film was one of the first efforts by Hollywood to expose the Murder, Inc., rings operating in America. Unfortunately this melodrama relied too heavily on a non-fictional ambience and there were long dull stretches with little entertainment value.

It was star Bogart who asked specifically that Bob Steele portray a hired assassin, being impressed by his work in a similar role in The Big Sleep (1946).

ESCAPE IN THE DESERT   see   THE PETRIFIED FOREST

EVERY LITTLE CROOK AND NANNY   (MGM, 1972)   C-92 min.

Producer, Leonard J. Ackerman; associate producer, Nicky Blair; director, Cy Howard; based on the novel by Ed McBain (Evan Hunter); screenplay, Howard, Jonathan Axelrod, Robert Klane; music, Fred Karlin; song, Karlin, Tylwyth Kymry; production designer, Philip Jefferies; set decorator, James I. Berkey; wardrobe, Margo Baxley, Buckey Rous; makeup, William P. Turner; assistant director, Ted Schilz; sound, Bruce Wright, Harry W. Tetrick; camera, Philip Lathrop; editor, Henry Berman.

Lynn Redgrave (Nanny [Miss Poole]); Victor Mature (Carmine Ganucci); Paul Sand (Benny Napkins); Maggie Blye (Stella Ganucci); Austin Pendleton (Luther); John Astin (Garbugli); Dom DeLuise (Azzecca); Louise Sorel (Marie); Phillip Graves (Lewis Ganucci); Lou Cutell (Landruncola); Leopoldo Trieste (Truffatore); Pat Morita (Nonaka); Phil Foster (Lieutenant Bozzaris); Pat Harrington (Willie Shakespeare); Severn Darden (Dominick); Katharine Victory (Jeanette Kay); Mina Kolb (Ida); Bebe Louie (Sarah); Lee Kafafian (Bobby); Sally Marr (Ida's Mother).

This semi-amusing gangster spoof, taken from an Evan Hunter

Maggie Blye and Victor Mature in Every Little Crook and Nanny (1972).

novel, never lived up to its possibilities. Film Digest recorded
that "... a crew of good comics liven up the lumbering script" for
this PG-rated comedy.
        Underworld czar Carmine Ganucci (Mature) becomes a soft-
drink manufacturer.   When he and his wife (Blye) go on a Naples
vacation, they leave their son (Graves) in the charge of an English
nanny (Redgrave).   The boy is kidnapped and a $50,000 ransom is
demanded.   Miss Poole has no idea where to obtain the money to
earn the child's release.   So she draws a low-class hoodlum (Sand)
and two Italian lawyers (Astin, Deluise) into the plot, hoping to retrieve her charge before Ganucci and his wife return to America.
        Despite the good premise, nothing much worked in this re-
lease.   The fact that once dour-faced Mature turned in a surprisingly adept comic performance went largely unnoticed.   A pity.

THE FALCON IN SAN FRANCISCO (RKO, 1945) 65 min.

        Producer, Maurice Geraghty; director, Joseph H. Lewis;
based on the character created by Michael Arlen; story, Robert
Kent; screenplay, Kent, Ben Markson; music, Paul Sawtell; music
director, C. Bakaleinikoff; art directors, Albert S. D'Agostino,
Charles Pyke; set decorators, Darrell Silvera, Victor Gangelin;
assistant director, Harry Mancke; sound, William Fox; special ef-
fects, Vernon L. Walker; camera, Virgil Miller, William Sickner;
editor, Ernie Leadlay.
        Tom Conway (Falcon); Rita Corday (Joan Marshall); Edward
S. Brophy (Goldie); Sharyn Moffett (Annie Marshall); Faye Helm
(Doreen Temple); Robert Armstrong (De Forrest); Carl Kent (Rickey);
George Holmes (Dalman); John Mylong (Peter Vantine); Edmund Cobb
(Cop); Myrna Dell (Beautiful Girl); Esther Howard (Mrs. Peabody).

THE FALCON STRIKES BACK (RKO, 1943) 66 min.

        Producer, Maurice Geraghty; director, Edward Dymtryk;
based on the character created by Michael Arlen; story, Stuart Palmer; screenplay, Edward Dein, Gerald Geraghty; music, Roy Webb;
music director, C. Bakaleinikoff; art directors, Albert S. D'Agostino,
Walter E. Keller; set decorators, Darrell Silvera, William Stevens;
assistant director, James Casey; sound, Terry Kellum, James Stewart; camera, Jack MacKenzie; editor, George Crone.
        Tom Conway (Falcon); Harriet Hilliard (Gwynne Gregory);
Jane Randolph (Marcia Brooks); Edgar Kennedy (Smiley Dugan); Cliff
Edwards (Goldy); Rita Corday (Mia Bruger); Erford Gage (Mickey
Davis); Wynne Gibson (Mrs. Lipton); Richard Loo (Jerry); Andre
Charlot (Bruno Steffen); Cliff Clark (Inspector Donovan); Ed Gargan
(Bates); Velma Dawson Puppets (Specialty); Byron Foulger (Argyle
the Motel Clerk); Joan Barclay, Ann Summers (Bits); Patti Brill,
Margaret Landry, Margie Stewart (Girl Bellhops); Frank Faylen
(Cecil the Hobo); Jack Norton (Hobo); Lorna Dunn (Taxi Driver);
Perc Launders (Bartender); Jean Brooks (Spanish Girl); Eddie Dunn
(Grimes).

Tom Conway, Wynne Gibson and Harriet Hilliard in The Falcon Strikes Back (1943).

Michael Arlen's sleuth "The Falcon" was conceived as a hard-boiled Sam Spade type, but when RKO Radio brought the character to the screen he was presented as an offshoot of The Saint, even to the point of having George Sanders, who had appeared in that film series, in the new title role. Later, when high-class Sanders grew weary of the programmer part, his brother Tom Conway took over as The Falcon's brother and continued the movie series with even more success.

In the Edward Dmytryk-directed The Falcon Strikes Back, Tom Lawrence, The Falcon (Conway), is led by a pretty girl (Corday) into the midst of a war bond racket. After being tricked by Mia Bruger and knocked out, he awakens to discover he is being accused of murdering a bank messenger and of stealing war bonds. He escapes from the police to a roadhouse and finds Mia has been murdered. But the intrepid Falcon eventually uncovers the racket.

Later, in The Falcon in San Francisco (the man certainly did get around: The Falcon out West, ... in Hollywood, ... in Mexico, etc.), the sleuth (Conway) subdues a gang of silk smugglers. In this entry he must cope with average type hoods. Although he and his valet Goldie Locke (usually played by Brophy) did have criminal pasts, they were always presented in direct contrast to their opponents. Most of The Falcon's energies in this installment

were devoted to chatting with an ingratiating little girl (Moffett) and
to clearing her father's (Armstrong) name.

Few filmgoers ever seemed to complain that these movie
sleuths (The Saint, the Falcon, the Lone Wolf, the Thin Man, etc.)
were so sophisticated--no matter what their pedigrees--that they
hardly seemed capable of combating criminal brawn and violence with
no more than charm and wit.

THE FAMILY RICO (CBS-TV, 1972) C-90 min.

Producer, George LeMaire; director, Paul Wendkos; based
on the novel by Georges Simenon; teleplay, David Karp; art director, Al Herschong; set decorator, Harry Gordon; music, Dave Grusin; camera, Bob Hauser; editor, Carroll Sax.

Ben Gazzara (Eddie Rico); Jack Carter (McGee); Dane Clark
(Boston Phil); Leif Erickson (Mike Lamont); James Farentino (Gino
Rico); John Marley (Sid Kubik); Sal Mineo (Nick Rico); John Ran-
dolph (Malaks); Jo Van Fleet (Mama Rico); Sian Barbara Allen (Nora);
Michael Anderson Jr. (Georgie Lamont); Alan Vint (John Ryan); Tom
Pedi (Angelo); Richard Gittings (Accountant); Alberto Morin (Chauf-
feur).

"Few themes have gotten shopworn so quickly as the one
about troubles in The Family (crime syndicate). Among its other
accomplishments, The Godfather has just about preempted the formula for all intents and purposes" (Variety).

Nick Rico (Mineo) has had enough of the mob way of life.
He wants to drop out of the family "business" and become a dirt
farmer in California with his hippie bride. But the don of the house-
hold, Eddie Rico (Gazzara), must maintain tradition and order. Before the ninety minutes are concluded, Nick is dead, and one learns
again that there are all kinds of gangsters, some better than others.
Plying the old gambit that really, after all, a Mafia family is much
like any ordinary domestic unit, the teleplay offered no new insights
into the genre. However, it did boast a cast of high class players,
many of whom had become identified with films of violence.

THE FBI STORY (Warner Bros., 1959) C-149 min.

Producer-director, Mervyn LeRoy; based on the book by Don
Whitehead; screenplay, Richard L. Breen, John Twist; art director,
John Beckman; set decorator, Ralph S. Hurst; music, Max Steiner;
orchestrator, Murray Cutter; makeup, Gordon Bau; costumes, Adele
Palmer; assistant directors, David Silver, Gil Kissell; sound, M. A.
Merrick; camera, Joseph Biroc; editor, Philip W. Anderson.

James Stewart (Chip Hardesty); Vera Miles (Lucy Hardesty);
Murray Hamilton (Sam Crandall); Larry Pennell (George Crandall);
Nick Adams (Jack Graham); Diane Jergens (Jennie as an Adult);
Jean Willes (Anna Sage); Joyce Taylor (Anne as an Adult); Victor
Millan (Mario); Parley Baer (Harry Dakins); Fay Roope (McCutcheon);
Ed Prentiss (U.S. Marshal); Robert Gist (Medicine Salesman); Buzz

Martin (Mike as an Adult); Kenneth Mayer (Casket Salesman); Paul Genge (Suspect); Ann Doran (Mrs. Ballard); Forrest Taylor (Wedding Minister).

Overblown, overly cautious, and too prefabricated, and completely false to the book it was "based" upon: these were the ingredients which detracted from this saga of the history of the Federal Bureau of Investigation. To spruce up the chronicle of the bureau, which had its start in 1924, James Stewart and Vera Miles were cast in the leads. Hopefully, they were to give the episodic account a personalized focus.

Chip Hardesty's girl (Miles) wants him to quit the newly-formed law enforcement agency and become a lawyer. But after meeting the new bureau chief, J. Edgar Hoover, Chip is convinced he should remain with the federal organization. He and Lucy wed and later have three children. In the ensuing years, Chip fights the Ku Klux Klan in the 1920s, the murderer of oil rich Osage Indians in Oklahoma, and joins in the capture and the obliteration of the notorious criminals of the 1930s, one of whom, Baby Face Nelson, kills his partner (Hamilton). During World War II Chip opposes the Axis in South America and his son (Martin) is killed in action. After the Armistice, Hardesty combats the Communist infiltrators in New York City and ends his illustrious career by becoming a Bureau instructor for new cadets.

Too frequent scenes of the trials and tribulations of Chip's family life detracted from the action. At one point in the narrative, Lucy leaves him, but soon returns. She has become accustomed to the fact that Chip is also married to his job. How trite and unimaginative an intrusion upon the plotline can one possibly imagine?

Comparing The F. B. I. Story to, say, The Roaring Twenties (1939), q. v. , proved that Hollywood had not come a long way in two decades.

THE FBI STORY: ALVIN KARPIS, PUBLIC ENEMY NUMBER ONE (CBS-TV, 1974) C-100 min.

Executive producer, Quinn Martin; producer, Philip Saltzman; director, Marvin Chomsky; teleplay, Calvin Clements; music, Duane Tatro; camera, Jacques Marquette; editor, Jerry Young.

Robert Foxworth (Alvin Karpis); Harris Yulin (J. Edgar Hoover); Kay Lenz (Shirley); Eileen Heckart (Ma Barker); David Wayne (Maynard Richards); Chris Robinson (Man); Gary Lockwood (Fred Barker); Anne Francis (Colette); James Gammon (Alex Denton); Charles Cyphers (Arthur); Alexandra Hay (Vicky Clinton); Mark Miller (F. B. I. Agent); Robert Emhardt (Dr. Williams); Whit Bissell (Senator); Queenie Smith (Flora).

More melodramatic than truthful, this was one of six to nine telefeatures based on famous F. B. I. cases to be telecast through 1976. This particular outing, the first of these specials, dealt with Alvin Karpis (Foxworth), a Canadian youth who, through a series of robberies, becomes the F.B.I.'s most wanted man in the period of the Thirties. The telefeature details his outlaw activities after joining the "Ma" Barker gang, which includes Ma (Heckart), her drunken lover (Wayne), and her vicious son Fred (Lockwood). When the police get too close to the gang, they feel that Richards has informed on them and the boys eliminate the old man. A series of robberies of banks and, later, trains keeps the gang in funds although Karpis is torn between a life of crime and the girl (Letz) he comes to love. Later she joins him as he teams up with Alex Denton (Gammon) and his wife (Hay) on a new crime spree. Interspersed with the action are semi-documentary style scenes of the F.B.I. in action, showing Hoover (Yulin) and his agents as they build the reputation of the organization by capturing the top criminals of the day. Hoover promises that Karpis is next and that he will make the arrest himself. Eventually, Karpis, who has been forced to desert Shirley and their child, is captured--peacefully-- in New Orleans by the F.B.I. True to his word, Hoover makes the arrest. (In real life, Karpis was sentenced to a prison term where he remained until 1960. Then he was paroled and deported to Canada.)

"The principal crime committed in this two-hour special about Alvin Karpis, desperado of the Depression Era, was that it failed to realize what potentially could and should have been a highly dramatic show.... The major miscalculation was use of the semidocumentary approach, which holds suspense to a minimum and robs it of reality" (Daily Variety). The New York Times was even less impressed with this relatively expensive offering. It thought "boredom" was the "sole survivor" of the show.

FEDERAL OPERATOR 99   (Republic, 1945)   twelve chapters

Associate producer, Ronald Davidson; directors, Spencer Gordon Bennet, Wallace Grissell, Yakima Canutt; screenplay, Albert DeMond, Basil Dickey, Jesse Duffy, Joseph Poland; music director, Richard Cherwin; camera, Bud Thackery; editors, Cliff Bell, Harold Minter.

Marten Lamont (Jerry Blake); Helen Talbot (Joyce Kingston); George J. Lewis (Jim Belmont); Lorna Gray (Rita Parker); Hal Taliaferro (Matt Farrell); LeRoy Mason (Morton); Bill Stevens (Martin); Maurice Cass (Morello); Kernan Cripps (Jeffries); Elaine Lange (The Countess); Frank Jaquet (Hunter); Forrest Taylor (Wolfe); Jay Novello (Heinrick); Rom London (Crawford); Jack Ingram (Riggs).

Chapters: 1) The Case of the Crown Jewels; 2) The Case of the Stolen Ransom; 3) The Case of the Lawful Counterfeit; 4) The Case of the Telegraph Code; 5) The Case of the Missing Expert; 6) The Case of the Double Trap; 7) The Case of the Golden Car; 8) The Case of the Invulnerable Criminal; 9) The Case of the Torn Blueprint; 10) The Case of the Hidden Witness; 11) The Case of the Stradivarious; 12) The Case of the Musical Clue.

This cliffhanger was a fast but complicated entry on the serial scene and proved to be one of the better productions on the fading chapterplay market.

After being rescued from a prison-bound train, a gang leader (Lewis) conspires to steal crown jewels located in a local bank vault. Later, Operator 99, alias Jerry Blake (Lamont), arrives on the scene. However, the gang, including adventuress Rita Parker (Gray), steals the vault key and kidnaps a countess (Lange), the latter slated to escort the jewels to her country. Some time later, the hoodlums steal the actual gems. Belmont demands a huge ransom for the jewels. The countess agrees to pay the sum, with Blake as her emissary and secretary Joyce Kingston (Talbot) as the actual go-between. Belmont's men take the money from her but refuse to provide her with the stones. However, suspecting foul play, Blake has trailed them. He arrives on the scene via parachute, and captures the henchmen. Menwhile, Belmont kidnaps Joyce and offers to trade her for Matt Farrell. Some time later, Jerry discovers a wiretapping device in his office. He traces the installation wires to Belmont's hideout, and in the final fight Belmont is killed and Joyce is rescued.

As in most serials, the good guys versus the bad guys merely provided an easy excuse for plenty of action, whether fist fights, shootouts, or chases by land and air. The kiddie matinee audiences loved it. Those adults who thrived on such enterprises were generally satisfied that the performers offered colorful, if empty, characterizations.

THE FIEND WHO WALKED THE WEST see KISS OF DEATH

THE FINGER POINTS (First National, 1931)   88 min.

        Director, John Francis Dillon; based on a story by John Monk Saunders, W. R. Burnett, inspired by the murder of Chicago reporter Jake Lingle; screenplay, Robert Lord; dialog, Saunders; technical advisers, Jim Mitchell, Speed Kendall, George Beale, Frank Butler, John Barrymore; sound, Dolph Thomas; camera, Ernest Haller; editor, Leroy Stone.

        Richard Barthelmess (Breckenridge Lee); Fay Wray (Marcia Collins); Regis Toomey (Breezy Russell); Clark Gable (Louis Blanco); Robert Elliott (City Editor); Oscar Apfel (Managing Editor); Robert Gleckler (Larry Hayes); Mickey Bennett (Office Boy); Herman Krumpfel (Tailor); J. Carrol Naish (Voice).

        With each succeeding year of the talkies, the career of Richard Barthelmess, once a silent screen idol, declined further. The Finger Points, released in the spring of 1931, did little to stem the tide.

        Playing a southern boy (as he would in the later Cabin in the Cotton), Barthelmess appears as Breckenridge Lee who goes to work for a big city newspaper. He learns soon thereafter that taking graft from hoodlums for hushing up bad publicity is an easy way to make a nice living. A girl reporter (Wray) is attracted to him. When she uncovers his unscrupulous activities she attempts to stop

him from taking further "blood money. " But he is too deeply in
the rackets' pay to get out.   Finally a gang leader (Gable, borrowed from MGM to play yet another underworld figure) has two
men killed.   The story is accidentally published.   Believing he has
been double-crossed, Louis Blanco has Breckenridge murdered.

Despite the impressive array of principals, Film Daily was
correct when it summed up the movie by saying "it doesn't hold
much. "

FOG OVER FRISCO   (First National, 1934) 68 min.

Production supervisor, Robert Lord; director, William Dieterle; story, George Dyer; screenplay, Robert N. Lee, Eugene So-
low; camera, Tony Gaudio; editor, Hal McLernon.

Bette Davis (Arlene Bradford); Donald Woods (Tony Stirling);
Margaret Lindsay (Valkyr Bradford); Lyle Talbot (Spencer Carleton);
Arthur Byron (Everett Bradford); Hugh Herbert (Izzy Wright); Robert
Barrat (Thorne); Douglass Dumbrille (Joshua Mayard); Irving Pichel
(Jane Bellow); Gordon Westcott (Joe Bellow); Henry O'Neill (Oren
Porter); Charles C. Wilson (Sergeant O'Hagen); Alan Hale (Chief
C. B. O'Malley); William B. Davidson (Joe Hague); Douglas Cos-
grove (Lieutenant Davis); George Chandler (Taxi Driver); Harold
Minnauer (Archie Van Ness); William Demarest (Spike Smith); Harry
Seymour (Bill the Messenger); Ralph Brooks (Musician); Dick French
(Dick the Orchestra Leader); Dennis O'Keefe (Van Brugh); Selmer
Jackson (Radio Announcer); Hal Price (Bartender); Robert Walker
(Hood); Lester Door (Reporter).

This film was way above the average double-bill entry of
its day, due to a sterling cast and the zest that director William
Dieterle imparted to the highly melodramatic story.   Although
Variety commented that a "veneer of theatricalism prevails throughout, " the New York Times said "... what [it] lacks in the matter
of credibility, it atones for partly by its breathtaking suspense and
abundance of action. "

Valkyr Bradford (Lindsay) becomes concerned when she
learns that her step-sister Arlene (Davis) is cavorting with underworld characters.   Meanwhile her stepfather (Byron) believes Arlene has persuaded her fiancee (Talbot), his employee, to sell
stolen securities through his brokerage firm.   Because Carleton
may be found out, Everett Bradford persuades Arlene to reform
and she promises to do so.   Arlene, however, is under the power
of a gang leader (Pichel).   She does give Valkyr enough evidence
to convict Bellow and then foolishly admits her act to Bellow.   The
enraged gangster orders her killed and the evidence recovered.
Meanwhile, friends of Val (Woods and Herbert) try to find Arlene.
At this point Val is kidnapped and Carleton is murdered.   The gang
demands the sought-after evidence in exchange for Val, but Stirling
leads the police to the gang's waterfront hideout.   After a gun battle, Val is saved.   The mastermind of the bond thieves is then dis-
covered to be an employee of Bradford's firm.

    If the plot seems suspiciously familiar, it was used again,
shortly after, for Spy Ship (1942).

FORTUNE AND MEN'S EYES (MGM, 1971) C-102 min.

    Producers, Lester Persky, Lewis M. Allen; co-producer,
Donald Ginsberg; director, Harvey Hart; based on the play by John
Herbert; screenplay, Herbert; music, Galt MacDermot; songs, Mac-
Dermot; MacDermot and William Dumareso; Michael Greet; choreog-
raphy, Jill Courtney; production designer, Earl G. Preston; cos-
tumes, Marcel Carpenter; makeup, Jacques Lafleur; assistant direc-
tor, Arthur Voronka; sound, Joseph Champagne, Alban Streeter;
camera, George Dufaux; editor, Douglas Robertson.
    Wendell Burton (Smith); Michael Greet (Queenie); Zooey Hall
(Rocky); Danny Freedman (Mona); Larry Perkins (Screwdriver);
James Barron (Holy Face Peters); Lazaro Perez (Catso); Jon Granik
(Sergeant Gritt); Tom Harvey (Warden Gasher); Hugh Webster (Rabbit);
Kirk McColl (Guard Sullivan); Vance Davis (Sailor); Robert Goodier
(Doctor); Cathy Wiele (Cathy); Georges Allard (Fiddler); Modesto (One
Eye); Robert Saab (Drummer); Michel Gilbert (Young Prisoner).

    Public tastes, as reflected by censor boards, for many years
decreed that the subject of sexual perversion within prison be deleted
from scenarios. Occasionally, a cagey script writer would work
subtle inferences about the subject's unusual sexual inclinations into
the storyline, legitimately pointing out that often there was and is
a strong link between criminal behavior, gangland camaraderie, prison isolation-segregation, and sexual makeup.
    By the sexually-"liberated" Sixties, off-Broadway was ready
to explore the subject with Fortune and Men's Eyes, which had a
382-performance run in 1967. Two years later, Sal Mineo directed
a highly-touted and controversial revival of the drama, his production being noted for its use of onstage nudity.
    The film version, shot in Canada, was overly cautious in its
presentation of the subject of prison homosexuality. Although R-
rated, it was very tame and hardly lived up to its advertising campaign: "It's a crime what goes on in prison. "
    The narrative focused on Smitty (Burton), a young college
student sent to prison for six months on a marijuana possession
charge. His cellmates include the flagrant drag queen named Queenie (Greer), a tough hustler (Hall), and a sensitive gay type (Freedman). Paralleling Smitty's toughening under the rigors of prison
life is his capitulation and then aggressive behavior as a circum-
stantially-induced homosexual.
    Granted that both the play original (especially in the Mineo
version) and the film edition were nothing better than mild soap
opera, there was more to Fortune and Men's Eyes than merely tagging it "The Boys in the Band Go to Jail. " It was a pathfinding
film venture that unfortunately has not been followed up with well-
intentioned variations (there have been other exploitive pornographic
features dealing with sex life in men and women's prisons).
    "Like so many other pictures that tackle controversial topics,

this release exploits rather then explores its material. As a result, sensationalism obscures a multitude of serious issues.... Undoubtedly, the tortured, jealous relationships, the gang rapes, the tacit sanction of every sort of depravity and degradation by guards, the indifference of top-level authorities depicted in this intensely theatrical film take place in prisons the world over. But ... [here it] remains unconvincing because it invariably aims for shock rather than credibility or enlightenment" (Los Angeles Times).

FOUR WALLS (MGM, 1928) 6,620'

     Director, William Nigh; based on the play by Dand Burnet, George Abbott; continuity, Alice D. G. Miller; titles, Joe Farnham; sets, Cedric Gibbons; wardrobe, David Dox; camera, James Howe; editor, Harry Reynolds.
     John Gilbert (Benny); Joan Crawford (Frieda); Vera Gordon (Mrs. Horowitz); Carmel Myers (Bertha); Robert Emmett O'Connor (Sullivan); Louis Natheaux (Monk); Jack Byron (Duke Roma).

     Stars John Gilbert and Joan Crawford gave Four Walls whatever life it had and, due to Gilbert's extreme popularity, the movie enjoyed considerable box-office success.
     Neighborhood gang leader Benny (Gilbert) is convicted of murdering his rival and is sent to prison. While behind bars he decides to go straight with the help of his mother (Gordon) and a good girl (Myers) who befriends him. While he is away, Benny's gang is taken over by an underling (Natheaux) who also inherits his moll (Crawford). After four years Benny is released from prison. Now reformed, he will have nothing to do with his old pals. One night, however, after his girlfriend rejects him, he goes to a party where a rival gang attacks his former buddies. Drawn into action, he takes command again. Later he escapes with Frieda. Monk pursues them, but he falls to his death from a rooftop, and the film concludes with Benny being acquitted of his rival's murder.
     Variety labeled the picture as "well done" and especially like Nigh's direction "... for its reality, restraint and knowledge of his element. " Like many films made in the late silent period, Four Walls had no dialog but it did have a theme song of the same title which was co-written by Al Jolson. Jolson recorded the tune for Brunswick Records, which may well be the only real memorable result of the film. The recording was reissued in 1973 by Pelican Records on an LP called The Vintage Jolson.

A FREE SOUL (MGM, 1931) 91 min.

     Director, Clarence Brown; based on the book by Adela Rogers St. John; screenplay, John Meehan; sound, Anstruther MacDonald; camera, William Daniels; editor, Hugh Wynn.
     Norma Shearer (Jan Ashe); Lionel Barrymore (Steve Ashe); Clark Gable (Ace Wilfong); Leslie Howard (Dwight Winthrop); James Gleason (Eddie); Lucy Beaumont (Grandmother Ashe); Claire Whitney

Clark Gable and Norma Shearer in A Free Soul (1931).

(Aunt Helen); Frank Sheridan (Prosecuting Attorney); E. Alyn Warren
(Bottomley--Ace's Chinese Boy); George Irving (Johnson--Defense At-
torney); Edward Brophy (Slouch); William Stacy (Dick); James Donlin
(Reporter); Sam McDaniel (Valet); Lee Phelps (Court Clerk); Roscoe
Ates (Men's Room Patron Who Is Shot At); Larry Steers (Casino
Proprietor); Francis Ford (Skidrow Drunk); Henry Hall (Detective).

     Adapted from Adela Rogers St. John's novel, this film was
based somewhat on the author's early life and that of her famous
father, Los Angeles attorney Earl Rogers. It proved to be one of
the projects which launched the movie career of Clark Gable. In addition, for his work in A Free Soul, Lionel Barrymore received the
1931 Academy Award for Best Actor.
     Steve Ashe is a hard-drinking, rebellious attorney who is not
well liked by his strait-laced family, especially after he brings a
gangster figure (Gable) to his mother's (Beaumont) birthday gathering. Ashe and Wilfong are asked to leave the celebration and they
do so with the lawyer's motherless daughter (Shearer). Infatuated
by the handsome if disreputable Ace, the spoiled Jan soon shows a
preference for him over her former beau, Dwight Winthrop. Later
she becomes his mistress, but Ashe refuses to allow her to marry

him.   Thereafter Ashe and Jan make a pact.   She agrees to stop seeing Ace, if Ashe will stop drinking.   However, he is too addicted to his alcoholic ways.   She returns to Wilfong, and, in one of the early 1930s most memorable movie moments, he slugs her.   Instead of being offended, she is thrilled.   When the hoodlum tries to rape Jan, Dwight appears on the scene.   He saves her "honor, " kills Ace, and is himself arrested.   Jan locates her near-derelict father and urges him to help Dwight.   To save the day, Ashe makes a courtroom confession to the crime, saying that his association with underworld figures led his impressionable daughter to this unpleasant situation.   Steve is later gunned by Ace's mob.

Some called A Free Soul overly melodramatic and sordid. But most viewers were intrigued by the anything-goes air about the production.   Moreover, the chemistry between the Queen of the MGM lot, Shearer, and newcomer Gable was electric, and was heightened further by Barrymore's dynamic presence.   Shearer's noteworthy performance as a girl burning with animal sexuality was the type of characterization which was to disappear after the formation of the Legion of Decency and the takeover by the Hays office.   But the theme of the society girl intrigued with the sordid world of criminals would recur over and over again in forthcoming screen dramas.

A Free Soul had a lacklustre updating when it served as the Elizabeth Taylor-Fernando Lamas picture, The Girl Who Had Everything.   By 1953 most of the subject matter within A Free Soul had become tiresome clichés.

THE FRENCH CONNECTION   (Twentieth Century-Fox, 1971)   C-104 min.

Executive producer, G. David Schine; producer, Philip D'Antoni; associate producer, Kenneth Utt; director, William Friedkin; based on the book by Robin Moore; screenplay, Ernest Tidyman; art director, Ben Kazaskow; set decorator, Ed Garzero; music-music director, Don Ellis; technical consultants, Eddie Egan, Sonny Grosso; stunt co-ordinator, Bill Hickman; sound, Chris Newman, Theodore Soderberg; special effects, Sass Bedig; camera, Owen Roizman; editor, Jerry Greenberg.

Gene Hackman (Jimmy "Popeye" Doyle); Fernando Rey (Alain Charnier); Roy Scheider (Buddy Russo); Tony Lo Bianco (Sal Boca); Marcel Bozzuffi (Pierre Nicoli); Frederic de Pasquale (Devereaux); Bill Hickman (Mulderig); Ann Rebbot (Marie Charnier); Harold Gary (Weinstock); Arlene Farber (Angie Boca); Eddie Egan (Simonson); Andre Ernotte (La Valle); Sonny Grosso (Klein); Pat McDermott (Chemist); Alan Weeks (Drug Pusher); Al Fann (Informant); Irving Abrahams (Police Mechanic); Randy Jurgenson (Police Sergeant); William Coke (Motorman); The Three Degrees (Themselves).

One of the all-time top-grossing thrillers ($27.5 million), The French Connection collected a bundle of Academy Awards, including Best Film and Best Actor (Gene Hackman) for 1971.   Shot on location in New York City and based on Robin Moore's bestseller, the movie set a pattern for many cop confession stories that

Roy Scheider (on ground), Eddie Egan (with hat) and Gene Hackman
in The French Connection (1971).

were to follow.   None to date has had the action or entertainment
value of this film.   (French Connection II was released in
1975).
          Centered on two NYC cops, Popeye (Hackman) and his part-
ner (Scheider), the motion picture relates how, while sometimes vi-
olating the law themselves, the two track down heroin smuggled into
this country from Marseilles by two high class dope pushers (Boz-
zulfi and Rey).
          Besides highlighting a rugged cop's desperate fight to get his
man, the film contained one of the best chase scenes in film history.
The memorable sequence finds Doyle driving a stolen car pell mell
down a Queens freeway attempting to catch up with one of the smugglers who is trapped aboard a subway above.
          Hackman offered an interesting, if a little hammy, perform-
ance as Popeye, who eventually fails to corner the mastermind of

the dope operation. Ironically, Doyle and Russo are rewarded for
their efforts by being transferred to another department. They are
now the black sheep of the police bureau.

"This thriller was made to grab your insides, and it does....
Made with razor skills and a good sardonic sense of the film tradition it comes out of, it jets off from the beginning and, since in a
way it's open-ended, it may still be going.... No bad guys against
good guys, just black against gray. It's a script about cool modern
professionals, each one good at his trade: pushing drugs, murdering people or hunting people who push drugs. Without a lot of psy-
chologizing about it, the script tells us that people have their pride:
the pusher likes his cleverness, the chaser likes the chase" (New
Republic).

Eddie Egan and Sonny Grosso, the real-life cop figures on
whose exploits the film was based, were hired for this film as technical advisers and also undertook featured roles in the picture.

FRIC FRAC   (Distributeurs Français, 1949) 95 min.

Producer-director, Maurice Lehmann; based on the play by
Edouard Bourdet; adaptor, Michel Duran; music, Oberfeld; camera,
Thirard, Nee.

Fernandel (Marcel); Michel Simon (Jo); Arletty (Loulou);
Helene Robert (Renee).

Often foreign language comedies, more than any other type
of films, lose the bulk of their meaning in dubbing or subtitles.
The intricate style of French comic Fernandel was almost completely lost in this entry released in the U. S. by Oxford Films.

The title, in French, refers to the underworld term for
"burglary" or "house breaking."

Provincial and naive Marcel (Fernandel) ignores his fiancée
(Robert), preferring Loulou (Arletty), the moll pal of underworld
character Jo (Simon). The one-time jeweler's assistant Marcel is
so entranced by his new milieu and friends that he is easily drawn
into a robbery caper, in which his boss' store is to be hit.

The New York Times termed this entry "obvious and dreary,"
but The National Legion of Decency condemned the feature with a
C rating, claiming it "glorifies crime and criminals. Moreover,
it is indecent in treatment."

THE FRIENDS OF EDDIE COYLE   (Paramount, 1973) C-102 min.

Producer, Paul Monash; associate producer, Charles Maguire; director, Peter Yates; based on the novel by George V. Higgins; screenplay, Monash; production designer, Gene Callahan; set
decorator, Don Galvin; music, Dave Grusin; titles, Everett Aison;
sound, Dick Raguse; camera, Victor J. Kemper; editor, Pat Jaffe.

Robert Mitchum (Eddie Coyle); Peter Boyle (Dillon); Richard
Jordan (Dave Foley); Steven Keats (Jackie); Alex Rocco (Scalise);
Joe Santos (Artie Van); Mitchell Ryan (Waters); Peter MacLean

(Patridge); Kevin O'Morrison (Manager of Second Bank); Marvin
Lichterman (Vernon); Carolyn Pickman (Nancy); James Tolkan (The
Man's Contact Man); Margaret Ladd (Andrea); Matthew Cowles (Pete);
Helena Carroll (Sheila Coyle); Jane House (Wanda); Michael McCleery
(The Kid); Alan Koss (Phil); Dennis McMullen (Webber); Judith Og-
den Cabot (Mrs. Partridge); Jan Egleson (Pale Kid); Jack Kehoe (The
Beard); Robert Anthony (Moran); Gus Johnson (Ames); Ted Maynard
(Sauter); Sheldon Feldner (Ferris).

What happens to aging hoodlums, especially those who were
never big shots in their heyday? Peter "Bullitt" Yates explored
this intriguing aspect of the underworld milieu in his Boston-shot
The Friends of Eddie Coyle.
        Concerned about his family's well-being, middle-aged Eddie
Coyle (Mitchum) agrees to act as informant for Dave Foley (Jordan)
of the Boston Treasury Bureau. In exchange, Foley will give the
needed good word to the court which is planning to sentence Eddie
after his second conviction.
        Eddie functions as a go-between, buying guns from a young
thug and selling them to the head (Rocco) of a bank robbery gang.
Thinking he has performed his share of the bargain, Coyle is informed that life will go better for him, if he cooperates further.
His mission is to betray Scalise and his gang. Before he can really act, Eddie is advised that Scalise has been captured. The underworld thinks Eddie did the deed and he is ordered killed. It develops that his assassin, Dillon (Boyle), was actually the informant.
Foley is happy to have his crook caught and seems, on the surface
at least, unmindful that Eddie has been sacrificed.
        "... [O]nce the mechanism is set in motion, and the system
defined in which Eddie and company manage to be both exploiters
and victims, the film moves with neatly plotted intricacy to its final elimination round. The eventual disappointment is that it does
remain very much a mechanism, with Yates unwilling or unable to
see his characters, even briefly, removed from the system ... or
to deal closely enough with the predicament of the broken ex-con,
who is grieved to think that his family will have to go on welfare
if he returns to prison, and is treacherously manoeuvred into the
no-man's land of becoming 'permanent goddamned fink'. "

G-MEN   (Warner Bros., 1935)   85 min.

        Director, William Keighley; based on the book Public Enemy
No. 1 by Gregory Rogers; screenplay, Seton I. Miller; art director,
John J. Hughes; costumes, Orry-Kelly; makeup, Perc Westmore;
assistant director, Chuck Hansen; choreography, Bobby Connolly;
music director, Leo F. Forbstein; song, Sammy Fain and Irving
Kahal; technical adviser, Frank Gompert; camera, Sol Polito; editor, Jack Killifer.

        James Cagney (James "Brick" Davis); Ann Dvorak (Jean Mor-
gan); Margaret Lindsay (Kay McCord); Robert Armstrong (Jeff Mc-
Cord); Barton MacLane (Brad Collins); Lloyd Nolan (Hugh Farrell);

Russell Hopton, James Cagney, Edward Pawley and Barton MacLane in G-Men (1935).

William Harrigan (McKay); Edward Pawley (Danny Leggett); Russell Hopton (Gerard); Noel Madison (Durfee); Fegis Toomey (Eddie Buchanan); Addison Richards (Bruce J. Gregory); Harold Huber (Venke); Raymond Hatton (The Man); Monte Blue (Analyst); Mary Treen (Gregory's Secretary); Adrian Morris (Accomplice); Emmett Vogan (Bill the Ballistics Expert); James Flavin (Agent); Stanley Blystone, Pat Flaherty (Cops); James T. Mack (Agent); Jonathan Hale (Congressman); Charles Sherlock (Short Man); Wheeler Oakman (Henchman at Lodge); Gordon "Bill" Elliott (Interne); Perry Ivins (Doctor at Store); Frank Marlowe (Hood Shot at Lodge); Gertrude Short (Collins' Moll); Florence Dudley (Durfee's Moll); Monte Vandergrift (Deputy Sheriff); Lee Phelps (McCord's Aide); Marc Lawrence (Hood at Lodge); Brooks Benedict (Man); David Brian (The Chief--Prologue of 1949 reissue of the film).

      Taken from Gregory Rogers' informative novel, Public Enemy No. One, this was the first time the term "G-Men" was ever used in a film title, and it resulted in the general acceptance of the word to describe those who worked for the federal government in combating crime. More importantly, it was the first of a new series of

gangster pictures. Instead of the Public Enemy/Little Caesar/Scar-
face syndrome in which the arch criminal was glorified, here the
movie star was playing a good guy hero.
        Shot in six weeks on a big $450,000 budget, the slick fea-
ture told of a big time racketeer who educates a boy (Cagney).
The latter becomes a lawyer and later a G-Man out to avenge the
murder of a buddy. Due to his unique background, James "Brick"
Davis has many underworld contacts and many on the force think
he is a spy. An old girlfriend (Dvorak) married to a hoodlum, informs Brick of the gang's hideout. He discovers that the spot is
owned by the man who raised him, and is forced to shoot the gang.
Thereafter he almost resigns, but when his boss' (Armstrong) sister (Lindsay) is in danger, he rescues her from another mob and
remains a dedicated law enforcer.
        As the New York Sun jubilantly reported, "The gangster is
back, racing madly through one of the fastest melodramas ever
made, scattering death and destruction over the screen. G-Men
has started something." The London Times added, "It is not violence alone which is in the air; there are also a skillfully contrived
and well maintained suspense, and throughout a feeling of respect
for the men who are prepared to die in the execution of necessary
work."
        Variety cautioned, "One thing that G-Men demonstrates is
that the new cycle which is causing so much chatter is not likely to
last very long. This picture has about all the elements the type
can be endowed with. It is red hot off the front page. But beyond
that it has nothing but a weak scenario along hackneyed lines. The
others in this line can't grab very much from the front page that
isn't here, and can't, if playing the same or a similar line, get in
any better story background."
        G-Men was reissued in 1949 as part of the celebration of the
twenty-fifth anniversary of the F.B.I. A special prologue, starring
David Brian as The Chief, was tacked onto the feature.

G-MEN NEVER FORGET (Republic, 1948) 12 chapters

        Associate producer Mike Frankovich; directors, Fred Bran-
non, Yakima Canutt; screenplay, Franklin Adreon, Basil Dickey,
Jesse Duffy; music, Mort Glickman; special effects, How-
ard and Theodore Lydecker; camera, John MacBurnie.
        Clayton Moore (Ted O'Hara); Roy Barcroft (Murkland/Cam-
eron); Ramsay Ames (Frances Blake); Drew Allen (Duke); Tom
Steele (Parker); Dale Van Sickel (Brent); Edmund Cobb (Cook); Stan-
ley Price (Benson); Jack O'Shea (Slater); Barry Brooks (George);
Doug Aylesworth (Hayden); Frank O'Connor (District Attorney); Dian
Fauntelle (Miss Stewart); Eddie Acuff (Fiddler); George Magrill
(Staley); Ken Terrell (Kelsey); Bud Wolfe (Foy); David Sharpe (Vance);
James Linn (Bailey); Arvon Dale (Moore); Charles Sullivan (Motor
Cop); Tom Monroe (Joe the Pilot); Russ Whiteman (Baxter); Charles
Regan (Hinky).
        Chapters: 1) Death Rides the Torrent; 2) The Flaming Doll
House; 3) Code Six-Four-Five; 4) Shipyard Saboteurs; 5) The Dead

Man Speaks; 6) Marked Money; 7) Hot Cargo; 8) The Fatal Letter; 9) The Death Wind; 10) The Innocent Victim; 11) Counter-Plot; 12) Exposed.

A gangster (Barcroft) who runs a protection insurance racket is busted out of jail and his henchman (Price), a plastic surgeon, makes him look like the police commissioner (Barcroft). The latter is kidnapped and held at Benson's sanitarium. The criminal, in his new guise, then uses the police headquarters to run his sinister operations. Meanwhile, two detectives (Moore and Ames) are called into the case and prevent the gang from completing a "shake down" on a local contractor. The mastermind tries to get rid of the duo by assorted violent means, including poison gas, bombs, and flaming gasoline. However, at the big battle finale, the hoodlum's true identity is made known, and he is put away forever. The true police chief is rescued and the crimes stop.

Definitely made at the end of the Republic cycle of top notch serials, this twelve-part cliffhanger had mediocre production values (it was filled with stock footage), although its relatively fast-paced action satisfied some of the juvenile trade. The case included Moore in his pre-"Lone Ranger" days, all-time top serial villain Barcroft (in a dual role), and the delightful presence of luscious Ramsay Ames. It is a pity that she never received her rightful cinema treatment.

GAMBLING SHIP   see   MR. LUCKY

THE GANG BUSTER   (Paramount, 1931)   68 min.

Director, A. Edward Sutherland; story-screenplay, Percy Heath; dialog, Joseph L. Mankiewicz; sound, Harold McNiff; camera, Harry Fischbeck; editor, Jane Loring.

Jack Oakie (Charlie [Cyclone Case]); Jean Arthur (Sylvia Martine); William (Stage) Boyd (Sudden Mike Slade); Wynne Gibson (Zella Cameron); William Morris (Andrew Martine); Francis McDonald (Pete Caltek); Albert Conti (Carlo); Tom Kennedy (Gopher Brant); Harry Stubbs (Faulkner); Ernie Adams (Sammy); Constantine Romanoff (Otto); Pat Harmon (McGintey); Eddie Dunn (Taxi Driver); Arthur Hoyt (Phone Caller).

This early talkie was an attempt to kid the gangster movie cycle at its outset. Critic Mordaunt Hall (New York Times) declared it to be "cheery entertainment."

The rather complicated but jovial plot concerned a half-baked insurance salesman (Oakie) who is highly superstitious. He sells a large policy to a man after saving him from a bad wreck. The individual, a lawyer for hoodlum Sudden Mike Slade (Boyd), buys a $100,000 policy. Cyclone's joy over the sale soon turns sour, for his company refuses to back the agreement. The firm has learned that the lawyer has broken his dealings with Slade, and the hoodlum has promised retribution. Sudden Mike is true to his word,

Jack Oakie and Jean Arthur in The Gang Buster (1931).

and he kidnaps Andrew Martine's daughter Sylvia (Arthur).   Cyclone
decides to find the hoodlum and demand that he let the girl go.
Meanwhile Sudden Mike and his moll (Gibson) have a falling out and,
seeing Cyclone in a bad situation, she calls in an insurance agent.
All ends well with Cyclone rescuing Sylvia and the police rounding
up Sudden Mike and his pals.

GANG BUSTERS (Universal, 1942) 13 chapters

         Associate producer, Ford Beebe; directors, Ray Taylor,
Noel Smith; based on the radio serial by Phillips H. Lord; screenplay, Morgan Cox, Al Martin, Vic McLeod, George Plympton; camera, William Sickner, John Boyle.
         Kent Taylor (Detective Lieutenant Bill Bannister); Irene Her-
vey (Vicki Logan); Ralph Morgan (Professor Mortis); Robert Armstrong (Detective Tim Nolan); Richard Davies (Happy Haskins); Joseph Crehan (Chief Martin O'Brien); George Watts (Mayor Hansen);
Ralf Harolde (Halliger); John Gallaudet (Wilkinson); William Haade
(Mike Taboni); Victor Zimmerman (Barnard); George Lewis (Mason);

Opposite: Irene Hervey and Richard Davies in Gang Busters (1942).

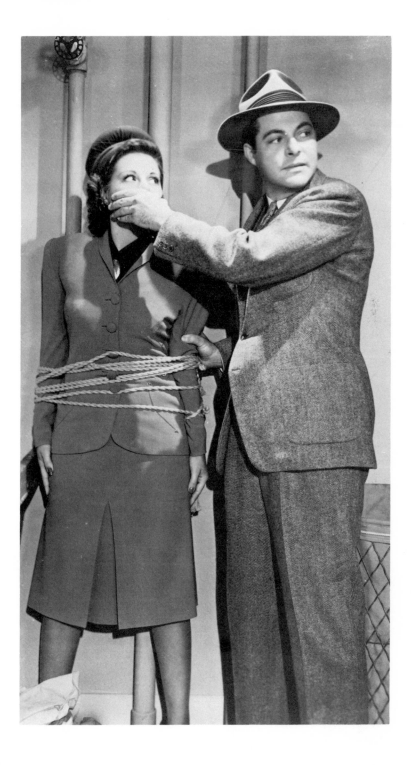

Johnnie Berkes (Mr. Grub); Pat O'Malley (Police Chemist Randall);
Grace Cunard (Mrs. Megg the Landlady); Edward Emerson (Frenchy
Ludoc); Stanley Blystone (Doctor); Jack Gardner (Police Broadcast-
er); Ed Fetherston (Ground Radioman); Edward Peil (Police Guard);
Frank Marlowe (Garageman); Eddie Foster (Jerry Rogan); William
Desmond (Extra at Ragan's Death Scene); Stanley Price (Corky
Watts); Ethan Laidlaw (Bartender); Jack Mulhall (Lab Technician);
Beatrice Roberts (O'Brien's Secretary); Milton Kibbee (Station Mas-
ter).

Chapters: 1) The League of Murdered Men; 2) The Death
Plunge; 3) Murder Blockade; 4) Hangman's Noose; 5) Man under
Cover; 6) Under Crumbling Walls; 7) The Water Trap; 8) Murder
by Proxy; 9) Gang Bait; 10) Mob Vengeance; 11) Wanted at Headquarters; 12) The Long Chance; 13) Law and Order.

Universal may not have been up to Republic in the serial
sweepstakes, but this production, taken from the long-running radio
serial, had its enthusiasts.

Bill Bannister (Taylor) is ordered by his police superiors to
track down a gang of terrorists who have taken hold of power in
the city.   Others involved in the case are Bill's partner Tim Nolan
(Armstrong), a news photographer (Hervey), and the latter's reporter pal (Davies).   Before long Bill deduces that the mysterious
Professor Mortis (Morgan) is the head of the gang and his headquarters are under the subway tracks.   Bill also unearths the fact
that Mortis' henchmen are composed of criminals whom the police
files list as dead.   It is through this "League of Murdered Men"
that Mortis carries out his reign of crime.   Eventually, through
dogged efforts, Bill corrals the professor in a subway tunnel.   A
train roars into view, killing Mortis.   When the gang is taken into
custody, Bill is promoted to captain of detectives.

THE GANG THAT COULDN'T SHOOT STRAIGHT   (MGM, 1971)
C-96 min.

Producers, Irwin Winkler, Robert Chartoff; director, James
Goldstone; based on the novel by Jimmy Breslin; screenplay, Waldo
Salt; art director, Robert Gundiach; set decorator, George Dititta;
music, Dave Grusin; assistant director, William Gerrity; costumes,
Joseph Garibaldi Aulisi; sound, Jack Jacobsen, Harry W. Tetrick;
camera, Owen Rotzman; editor, Edward A. Biery.

Jerry Orbach (Salvatore "Kid Sally" Palumbo); Leigh Taylor-
Young (Angela Palumbo); Jo Van Fleet (Big Momma); Lionel Stander
(Baccala); Robert De Niro (Mario); Irving Selbst (Big Jelly); Herve
Villechaize (Beppo); Joe Santos (Ezmo); Carmine Caridi (Tony the
Indian); Frank Campanella (Water Buffalo); Harry Basch (De Lauria);
Sander Vanocur (TV Commentator); Phil Bruns (Gallagher); Philip
Sterling (District Attorney Goodman); Roy Shuman (The Mayor); Alice
Hirson (Mayor's Wife); Jack Kehoe (Scuderi); Despo (Mourner); Sam
J. Coppola (Julie); James J. Sloyan (Joey); Paul Benedict (Shots
O'Toole); Louis Criscuolo (Junior); George Loros (Jerry); Harry
Davis (Dominic Laviano); Burt Young (Willie Quarequio); Jackie

Jerry Orbach (third from left), Jo Van Fleet and Irving Selbst in
The Gang That Couldn't Shoot Straight (1971).

Vernon (Herman); Ted Beniades, Fat Thomas Rand and Michael Gazzo (Black Suits); Robert Gerringer (Commissioner McGrady); Walter
Flanagan (The Super); Dan Morgan (Muldoon); Dorothi Fox (Meter
Maid); Florence Tarlow (Police Matron); Tom Lacy (Religious Salesman); George Stefans (Greek Captain); Gloria Leroy (Ida the Waitress).

    Damon Runyon aside, rarely has anyone been able to make
the gangster milieu amusing. People, it seems, would much rather
have a dose of blood and gore than chuckles when the celluloid underworld is involved.
    In a very heavy-handed treatment, the jubilant qualities of
Jimmy Breslin's amusing novel were spoiled in the cinema adaptation. Kid Sally Palumbo (Orbach), urged on by Big Momma (Van
Fleet), decides to cut into the territory of Mafia boss Baccala (Stander). The latter is soon fearing for his very life (he even has his
obedient wife start his car each day to see if it will blow up). His
fears are well-founded, for the Kid is continually planning various
schemes (murders, heists, kidnappings) to eliminate Baccala and
make himself the gang leader.   But all his machinations fail.
Tossed into the storyline was a six-day marathon bike race, the
physically oddball membership of Kid Sally's underlings, and the
romance between Kid's sister Angela (Taylor-Young) and a Southern

Italian cyclist (De Niro).

"You don't have to be Italian to hate The Gang That Couldn't Shoot Straight, although that gives you a distinct edge. The movie's febrile witlessness easily transcends all ethnic boundaries and comes guaranteed to outrage virtually everybody.... The actors, who were apparently given their heads, perform in an assortment of styles that range from self-parody to self-abuse" (Time).

GANG WAR   (Twentieth Century-Fox, 1958)   74 min.

Producer, Harold E. Knox; director, Gene Fowler, Jr.; based on the novel The Hoods Take Over by Ovid Demaris; screenplay, Louis Vittes; music-music conductor, Paul Dunlap; assistant director, Frank Parmenter; art director, John Mansbridge; set decorators, Walter M. Scott, Bertram Granger; wardrobe, James Taylor; makeup, Jack Obringer; sound, Eugene Irvine; camera, John M. Nikolaus, Jr.; editor, Frank Baldridge.

Charles Bronson (Alan Avery); Kent Taylor (Bryce Barker); Jennifer Holden (Marie); John Doucette (Maxie Matthews); Gloria Henry (Edie Avery); Gloria Grey (Marsha Brown); Barney Phillips (Sam Johnson); Ralph Maza (Axe Duncan); George Eldredge (Sergeant Ernie Tucker); Billy Snyder (Mr. Tomkins); Jack Reynolds (Joe Reno); Dan Simmons (Bob Cross); Shirle Haven (Nicki); Don Giovanni (Mike Scipio); Stacey Marshall (Millie); Whit Bissell (Mark); Marion Sherman (Agner).

Long before he became a superstar of the 1970s, Charles Bronson was plying his craft in small-time programmers. Here he has a Death Wish (1974) type role as a school teacher who has witnessed a gangland murder. Because he testifies to the crime, the hoodlum head (Doucette) orders that Avery's pregnant wife be killed. Thereafter Avery is bent on revenge. Before he can accomplish his goal, he finds that Matthews, deep in the throes of losing his underworld power, has gone mad. Avery decides that law and nature should take their course, and he leaves Matthews to his fate.

"Holds up as a bang-bang opus with more than enough excitement for a second-feature...." (Variety).

GANGBUSTERS   (Visual Drama, Inc.-States Right, 1955)   78 min.

Producers, William J. Faris, William H. Clothier; director, Bill Karn; screenplay, Phillips H. Lord; music director, Richard Aurandt; camera, Clothier; editor, Faris.

Myron Healey (John Omar Pinson); D. C. Harvey (Detective Walsh); Frank Gerstle (Detective Fuller); Sam Edwards (Long); Kate MacKenna (Aunt Jenny); Rusty Wescoatt (Mike); William Justine (Louie); Allan Ray (Slick Harry); William Fawcett (Truck Driver); Ed Colbrook (Pool Hall Operator); Charles Victor (Officer Rondeau); Bob Carson (Doctor); Joyce Jameson (Girl in Car); Mike Ragan (Police Officer); Robert Bice, Ed Hinton (Guards).

Standing: Don C. Harvey and Frank Gerstle in Gangbusters (1955).

     This seventy-eight-minute melodrama had the dubious distinction of being the first theatrical release to be composed of segments of a television series. The film derived from the short-running program "Convicted," and its trio of stories were edited together and issued to theatres by Visual Drama.

     Gangbusters, shot partially in Oregon and in a semi-documentary style, told of the various prison escapes of John Omar Pinson (Healey), at one time listed as Public Enemy #4. Although Variety pegged it as a "dull, repetitive affair," the film made money and in 1957 Visual Drama issued Guns Don't Argue, composed of additional episodes of the "Convicted" teleseries. This outing, co-directed by Bill Karn and Richard C. Kahn, dealt with the lives of various hoodlums like Bonnie Parker (Jean Harvey) and Ma Barker (Lurene Tuttle).

GANGS OF CHICAGO (Republic, 1940) 66 min.

     Associate producer, Robert North; director, Arthur Lubin; screenplay, Karl Brown; art director, John Victor Mackay; music director, Cy Feuer; wardrobe, Adele Palmer; camera, Elwood

Bredell; editors, Murray Seldeen, Lester Orlebeck.

Lloyd Nolan (Matty Burns); Barton MacLane (Ramsey); Lola
Lane (June); Ray Middleton (Bill Whitaker); Astrid Allwyn (Virginia);
Horace McMahon (Cry-Baby); Howard Hickman (Judge); Leona Roberts
(Mrs. Whitaker); Charles Halton (Bromo); Addison Richards (Blake);
John Harmon (Rabbit); Dwight Frye (Pinky).

By the 1940s it was a commonplace practice for the movies
to depict crooked law enforcers, and even shady attorneys. Gangs
of Chicago, a modestly conceived programmer, used resolute Lloyd
Nolan as Matty Burns, who as a youth saw his dad, a minor crook,
killed by the police. He was so embittered by the experience that
when he grew up, he determined to become a criminal lawyer and
use his position to subvert the proper functioning of law and order!

In law school Matty ties up with gang leader Ramsey (Mac-
Lane), and offers him advice on how to circumvent the law. Upon
graduation from law school, Burns is actually in charge of recruiting and supervising Ramsey's gang. The F.B.I. urge Bill Whitaker
(Middleton), Matty's former friend and fellow attorney, to use his
relationship to get the goods on Burns. Later Matty realizes the
error of his ways, and in a tussle with Ramsey kills him. His
future, however, is bleak: he will either be given life imprisonment or death for his act of homicide.

"If gangster pictures must go on--and apparently they must
as long as action houses continue to do business with them--Repub-
lic can fake a moderate bow on this one" (Variety). The New York
Daily News gave the film 2 1/2 stars.

THE GANGSTER (Allied Artists, 1947) 84 min.

Producers, Maurice King, Frank King; director, Gordon
Wiles; based on the novel Low Company by Daniel Fuchs; screen-
play, Fuchs; art director, F. Paul Sylos; set director, Sidney
Moore; music, Louis Gruenberg; music director, Irvin Talbot; song,
Gordon Clifford and Nacio Herb Brown; assistant director, Frank S.
Heath; sound, William Randall; special camera effects, Roy W. Sea-
wright; camera, Paul Ivano; editor, Walter Thompson.

Barry Sullivan (Shubunka); Belita (Nancy Starr); Joan Lorring
(Dorothy); Akim Tamiroff (Nick Jammey); Henry "Harry" Morgan
(Shorty); John Ireland (Karty); Fifi D'Orsay (Mrs. Ostroleng); Vir-
ginia Christine (Mrs. Karty); Sheldon Leonard (Cornell); Charles
McGraw (Dugas); John Kellogg (Sterling); Elisha Cook, Jr. (Oval);
Ted Hecht (Swain); Jeff Corey, Peter Whitney, Clancy Cooper
(Brothers-in-Law); Murray Alper (Eddie); Shelley Winters (Hazel);
Norma Jean Nilsson (Little Girl); Billy Gray (Little Boy); Greta
Grandstedt (Woman). Maxine Semon (Hotel Maid); Parker Gee (Man
in Corridor); Dolores Castle (Cigarette Girl).

After the box-office bonanza of Dillinger in 1945, producers
Frank and Maurice King returned to the genre for The Gangster
but the result was for "... some, a shoddy example of picture
making" (New York Times).

Barry Sullivan starred as Shubunka, who had been the victim of his slum childhood environment.   Later he became a hoodlum. However, when he becomes crime boss he desires respectability. Now that he has attained wealth he wants to forget that it was obtained by extorting protection loot from illicit enterprises.   But he finds no happiness at the top of the ladder, and eventually his moll fingers him for a murder and he is eliminated by a rival gang.

The underlying theme of <u>The Gangster</u> was definitely worthy of close scrutiny.   So many gangster films had focused merely on the kingpin's rise to power and left the "hero" at this point.   But success, in any field, has its bag of trouble, as this film attempted to elucidate.

GANGSTER'S BOY   (Monogram, 1938)   80 min.

Associate producer, William T. Lackey; director, William Nigh; story, Karl Brown; screenplay, Robert D. Andrews; song, Edward Kay and Ned Washington; choreography, Tommy Wonder; camera, Harry Neumann.

Jackie Cooper (Larry Kelly); Lucy Gilman (Julie Davis); Robert Warwick (Tim "Knuckles" Kelly); Louise Lorimer (Molly Kelly); Tommy Wonder (Bill Davis); Selmer Jackson (Judge Roger Davis); Bobby Stone (Salvatore); Betty Blythe (Mrs. Davis); Bradley

Jackie Cooper, Lucy Gilman, Tommy Wonder and Jack Kennedy in <u>Gangster's Boy</u> (1938).

Metcalfe (Arthur); Huntley Gordon (Principal Benson); William Gould (District Attorney Edward Jameson); Jack Kennedy (Sergeant); Herbert Evans (Stevens the Butler); Buddy Pepper (Boy); Hooper Atchley (Sammy Trip the Gangster); Byron Foulger (District Attorney's Secretary); Joe Devlin (Jim, a Cop); Edward Piel (Editor); Jack Gardner (Photographer); Harry Harvey (Reporter).

This minor melodrama was one of a series of "specials" young Jackie Cooper made for Monogram in his post-MGM stardom days.   In this entry he was a Millsville High School boy with good grades who served as drummer in the school band.   He hopes to win an appointment to West Point, and is in love with Julie Davis (Gilman), the daughter of the town's snobbish judge.
Then along comes Tim "Knuckles" Kelly (Warwick), Larry's dad, who has decided now to settle down and enjoy life with his family.   He acquires a big mansion in Millsville, but soon rumors are spreading about the source of his money.   His past has caught up with him!   Through the ensuing crisis, Larry sticks by his father, and, eventually, all ends satisfactorily.
"No matter how improbable the cases may be, pictures about youngsters who have to answer to society for parental mistakes are always touching" (New York Daily News).

GANGSTERS: LONDON   see   DAS RATSEL DER ROTEN ORCHIDEE

THE GANGSTERS OF NEW YORK   (Reliance-Mutual, 1914)   four reels

Director, James Kirkwood.
Henry B. Walthall (Porkey Dugan); Jack Dillon (Biff Dugan); Master O. Child (Jimmie Dugan); A. Horine (Jessie Dugan); Fred Herzog (Hennessy the District Attorney); Consuelo Bailey (Cora Drew); R. Riely (Billy Drew); C. Lambert (Henry Davis the Reformer); Ralph Lewis (Spike Golden); B. Craig (Mrs. Murphy); Jack Pickford (Spot the Spy).

This early example of the underworld melodrama adopted for the screen the naturalism approach so prevalent in the novels of Stephen Crane and Theodore Dreiser.
The Dugan family live in a crowded tenement on the lower East Side of New York.   Bill (Dillon), the older brother, heads the gang of which Porkey (Walthall) is a member.   Jessie (Horine), who works in a sweatshop, disapproves of her brothers' activities. Meanwhile Billy (Riley) and Cora Drew (Bailey) come to New York with a letter of introduction to reformer Henry Davis (Lambert). While at Davis' mission, the Dugan boys rough up the charity home, but Davis refuses to press charges.   Later Cora and Porkey, who are neighbors in the same building, fall in love.   However, not until he reforms will Cora marry him.   Eventually, they move to the country and start a farm.

THE GEORGE RAFT STORY   (Allied Artists, 1961)   105 min.

Producer, Ben Schwalb; director, Joseph M. Newman; based upon the life of George Raft; screenplay, Crane Wilbur; art director, David Milton; set decorator, Joseph Kish; music, Jeff Alexander; assistant director, Lindsley Parsons, Jr.; wardrobe, Roger W. Weinberg, Norah Sharpe; makeup, Norman Pringle; sound, Monty Pearce, Ralph Butler; camera, Carl Guthrie; editor, George White.

Ray Danton (George Raft); Jayne Mansfield (Lisa Lang); Julie London (Sheila Patton); Barrie Chase (June); Barbara Nichols (Texas Guinan); Frank Gorshin (Moxie Cusack); Margo Moore (Ruth Harris); Brad Dexter (Benny Siegel); Neville Brand (Al Capone); Robert Strauss (Frenchie); Herschel Bernardi (Sam); Joe De Santis (Frankie Donatella); Jack Lambert (Jerry Fitzpatrick); Argentina Brunetti (Mrs. Raft); Robert H. Harris (Harvey); Jack Albertson (Milton); Pepper Davis and Tony Reese (Comedy Team); Cecile Rogers (Charleston Dancer); Murvyn Vye (Johnny); Tol Avery (Mizner the Wit).

For years, rumors of George Raft's connections with the underworld were bandied about and in the early 1950s the star himself detailed a few such minor incidents in his Saturday Evening Post memoirs. (In 1974, two biographies of the gangster movie star would appear in the marketplace.) This exploitation feature, however, tended to play down the more sordid side of the actor's

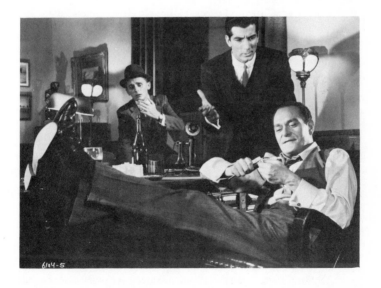

Frank Gorshin, Ray Danton and Joe DeSantis in The George Raft Story (1961).

offscreen life. At the same time it was unsuccessful in creating with any credibility the excitement he had engendered as a movie star.

A quickie production based on a largely fictional story, the motion picture had short, squat Raft played by tall, lanky Danton, rising from the status of a poor boy in Hell's Kitchen to a top dancer in the Twenties, and his subsequent brush with hoodlums. In the Thirties he becomes a movie star, but personal troubles and changing times aid in the decline of his career. The film concludes with his comeback in Some Like It Hot, after his unsuccessful venture with a gambling casino in Cuba.

Only the performances gave any interest to this flaccid biography. Danton as Raft did as much as he could with his ill-conceived part while Jayne Mansfield as a pseudo-Betty Grable (one of Raft's romantic interests in private life) was poor. Julie London as Sheila Patton, the songstress who adores Raft, was sound. Also effective were Barbara Nichols as Texas Guinan, the hotcha club hostess who first brought George to Hollywood, and Herschel Bernardi as his kindly agent. Also on hand was Neville Brand, recreating his Al Capone role from "The Untouchables" teleseries. In real life, Raft was said to be Capone's favorite dancer and on celluloid the hoodlum leader comments on the actor's screen work in Scarface.

THE GETAWAY   (Cinerama, 1972)   C-122 min.

     Producers, David Foster, Mitchell Brower; associate producer, Gordon T. Dawson; director, Sam Peckinpah; based on the novel by Jim Thompson; screenplay, Walter Hill; art directors, Ted Haworth, Angelo Graham; set decorator, George R. Nelson; music, Quincy Jones; sound, Charles M. Wilborn; camera, Lucien Ballard; editor, Robert Wolfe.
     Steve McQueen (Doc McCoy); Ali MacGraw (Carol McCoy); Ben Johnson (Jack Benyon); Sally Struthers (Fran Clinton); Al Lettieri (Rudy Butler); Slim Pickens (Cowboy); Richard Bright (Thief); Jack Dodson (Harold Clinton); Dub Taylor (Laughlin); Bo Hopkins (Frank Jackson); Roy Jenson (Cully); John Bryson (Accountant); Tom Runyon (Swain); Whitney Jones (Soldier); Raymond King, Ivan Thomas (Boys on Train); Brenda W. King, C. W. White (Boys' Mothers); W. Dee Kutach (Parole Board Chairman); Brick Lowry (Parole Board Commissioner); Martin Colley (McCoy's Lawyer); O. S. Savage (Field Captain); Bruce Bissonette (Sporting Goods Salesman); Tom Bush (Cowboy's Helper).

     With distributors' domestic rentals of over $17.5 million, The Getaway gave renewed life to the thriller. It may have been just another variation on the old theme used in High Sierra (1941), q.v., but with the combination of star Steve McQueen and violent action director Sam Peckinpah, the picture was very representative of the blood-and-guts-alienation film syndrome of the 1970s.
     "It does something to you, in there," says Doc McCoy of

Opposite: Steve McQueen in Getaway (1972).

his prison stretch.   His wife Carol (MacGraw) has arranged for his jail release through the aid of Jack Benyon (Johnson), a nefarious businessman.   Benyon wants Doc to supervise a bank robbery which has been set to occur in a small Texas town.   The money raid is successful, although a bank guard is shot.   Doc and Carol escape with the money, and are forced to kill one of the henchmen who would like to double-cross them.   Thereafter, Doc is told by Benyon that he wants not only the loot but Carol.   Suddenly she appears and shoots Benyon.   Doc and his wife make a quick exit, but he is furious that she did not reveal Benyon's plans.   Joined by the other robbery participant, the wounded Rudy Butler (Lettieri), as well as by a captured veterinarian (Dodson) and his trampish wife (Struthers), the group heads for El Paso and hopes to escape over the Mexican border.   Troubles soon multiply, but Doc and Carol, with the help of an agreeable cowboy (Pickens) and his rusty pick-up truck, make their way into Mexico.

Within this tightly-knit, closely confined film, characterization is held to a minimum; determination and survival seem to be the principals' chief attributes.   In the true Peckinpah tradition, there are ample scenes of bloody encounters, fast-paced action, and a strong anti-feminine attitude.   Offcamera, McQueen and MacGraw engaged in a romance that led to marriage.   But on camera, their intricate, often unspoken character relationship denied the film any richness of thought.   It seemed nearly everything could be blamed on the environment surrounding them, whether Doc's lessons in toughness learned in prison, or Carol's complicity with Benyon, ostensibly to earn her husband quick jail release.   True to most gangster melodramas, greed for money, more than lust for sexual fulfillment, was the keynote guiding the plotline.

The fourth estate had a field day debating in print the pros and cons of this gratuitously violent screen exercise.   Peckinpah was content to continue onward, making more such films, although his later exercises have yet to be as successful as this caper-escape production.

When The Getaway is finally shown on CBS-TV during the 1975-1976 season, viewers will not see the original ending as filmed for theatrical audiences (i. e., McQueen-MacGraw driving into Mexico free).   Instead, the "revised" climax will have the lead characters receiving just retribution for their lawless careers.

GIRL ON THE RUN   (Warner Bros., 1958)   77 min.

Executive producer, William T. Orr; producer, Roy Huggins; director, Richard L. Bare; story, Huggins; screenplay, Marion Hargrove; art director, William Campbell; set decorator, Ben Bone; music director, Howard Jackson; assistant director, Rusty Meek; sound, Frank McWhorter; camera, Harold Stine; editor, Harold Minter.

Efrem Zimbalist, Jr. (Stuart Bailey); Erin O'Brien (Kathy Allen/Karen Shay); Shepperd Strudwick (McCullough); Edward (Edd) Byrnes (Smiley); Barton MacLane (Brannigan); Ray Teal (Lieutenant

Harper); Vince Barnett (Janitor); Harry Lauter (Drunk); Charles
Cane (Webster); Jeanne Evans (Dorothy).

This obscure feature was issued to television in the late
1960s, although it was actually filmed in 1958 and served as the
pilot (October 10th) for the successful ABC-TV series, "77 Sunset
Strip. " Directed by Richard L. Bare, this seventy-seven-minute
entry told of a young lady on the lam from hoodlums and the involvement of the Los Angeles detectives (Zimbalist, Jr. , Smith and
Byrnes) who starred in the program. The resultant film was a
compact motion picture which might have had some success in theatres had it not been for its TV origins and the fact that it was not
issued, even to the Late Show, until a decade after it was made.

THE GIRL WHO HAD EVERYTHING   see FREE SOUL

THE GLASS KEY (Paramount, 1935) 80 min.

Producer, E. Lloyd Sheldon; director, Frank Tuttle; based
on the novel by Dashiell Hammett; screenplay, Kathryn Scola, Kubec
Glasmon, Harry Ruskin; camera, Henry Sharp; editor, Hugh Bennett.

George Raft, Edward Arnold and Tammany Young in The Glass Key
(1935).

George Raft (Ed Beaumont); Edward Arnold (Paul Madvig); Claire Dodd (Janet Henry); Rosalind Keith (Opal Madvig); Charles Richman (Senator Henry); Robert Gleckler (Shad O'Rory); Guinn Williams (Jeff); Ray Milland (Taylor Henry); Tammany Young (Clarkie); Harry Tyler (Henry Sloss); Charles C. Wilson (Farr); Emma Dunn (Mom); Matt McHugh (Puggy); Patrick Moriarity (Mulrooney); Mack Gray (Duke); Frank Marlowe (Walter Ivans); Herbert Evans (Senator's Butler); George H. Reed (Black Serving Man); Percy Morris (Bartender); Irving Bacon (Waiter); Ann Sheridan (Nurse); Henry Roquemore (Rinkle); Frank O'Connor (McLaughlin); Michael Mark (Swartz); Del Cambre (Reporter); Veda Buckland (Landlady); George Ernest (Boy).

THE GLASS KEY (Paramount, 1942) 85 min.

Producer, Fred Kohlmar; director, Stuart Heisler; based on the novel by Dashiell Hammett; screenplay, Jonathan Latimer; art directors, Hans Dreier, Haldane Douglas; music, Victor Young; camera, Theodor Sparkuhl; editor, Archie Marshek.

Brian Donlevy (Paul Madvig); Veronica Lake (Janet Henry); Alan Ladd (Ed Beaumont); Bonita Granville (Opal Madvig); Richard Denning (Taylor Henry); Joseph Calleia (Nick Varna); William

Brian Donlevy, Alan Ladd and Veronica Lake in a pose for The Glass Key (1942).

Bendix (Jeff); Frances Gifford (Nurse); Donald MacBride (Farr);
Margaret Hayes (Elosie Matthews); Moroni Olsen (Ralph Henry); Ed-
die Marr (Rusty); Arthur Loft (Clyde Matthews); George Meader
(Claude Tuttle); Pat O'Malley, Ed Peil, Sr., James Millican (Poli-
ticians); Edmund Cobb, Frank Bruno, Jack Luden, Jack Gardner,
Joe McGuinn, Frank Hagney (Reporters); John W. DeNoria (Grog-
gins); Jack Mulhall (Lynch); Joseph King (Fisher); Al Hill (Bum);
Freddie Walburn (Kid); Conrad Binyon (Stubby); Vernon Dent (Bar-
tender); Stanley Price, Kenneth Christy (Men in Barroom); Dane
Clark (Henry Sloss); William Wagner (Butler); Charles Sullivan
(Taxi Driver); Lillian Randolph (Entertainer at Basement Club).

While not as well known as the remake, the 1935 edition
does capture much of the flair of the Hammett book.

George Raft, in a solid, cold, and calculating performance,
is the henchman to a political boss (Arnold). His Ed Beaumont sets
out to prove Paul Madvig is innocent of a charge of murdering the
son (Milland) of a political ally (Richman). Taylor Henry had been
dating Madvig's daughter Opal. In the course of his investigation,
Ed Beaumont is beaten up, but he eventually discovers that the culprit is gambling czar Shad O'Rory (Gleckler), an underworld figure
Madvig had tried to prosecute.

Besides good camera work, a flowing script, and Raft's
more-than-usually sturdy performance, the feature was highlighted
by memorable individual, roughneck scenes; two in particular concern Jeff (Williams), who has a fierce way with his fists.

Seven years later Paramount decided to reteam Alan Ladd
and Veronica Lake of This Gun for Hire in a remake of The Glass
Key.

The Forties' edition followed the original screenplay quite
closely. Ladd was cast as Ed Beaumont, with Brian Donlevy as
the political boss Paul Madvig, and Bonita Granville as the latter's
daughter Opal. Peek-a-boo blonde Lake made her appearance as
Janet Henry, the calculating, sexy daughter of Madvig's gubernatorial
rival, Ralph Henry (Olsen). While the pint-sized Ladd-Lake duo
made an engaging, smoldering love team, it was burly William Bendix as thick-skinned but quick-to-anger Jeff who provided the movie's
best performance. He was the thug working for ruthless gambling
syndicate leader Nick Varna (Calleia).

In a more glamorous way than other such films, The Glass
Key would provide filmgoers with a few insights into the relationship
between the underworld and the political arena. As suggested by
Hammett in his book, and in the film adaptations, the alliance was
often closer and more usual than most people in a democracy would
care to realize.

GLI INTOCCABILI (Euroatlantica, 1968)   C-115 min.

Producers, Marco Vicario, Bruno Cicogna; associate producer, Ascanio Cicogna; director, Giuliano Montaedo; story, Mino Roli;
screenplay, Roli, Montaldo; assistant director, Gianni Fabrizio; art
director, Flavio Mogherini; set decorator, Ennio Michettoni; set

designer, Roberto Veloccia; music, Ennio Morricone; sound, Luciano
Welisch; camera, Erico Menczer; editor, Franco Fraticelli.

John Cassavetes (Hank McCain); Britt Ekland (Irene Tucker);
Peter Falk (Charlie Adamo); Gabriele Ferzetti (Don Francesco De
Marco); Salvo Randone (Don Salvatore); Pierluigi Apra (Jack McCain);
Gena Rowlands (Rosemary Scott); Florinda Bolkan (Joni Adamo);
Margherita Guzzinati (Margaret De Marco); Stephen Zacharias (Abe
Stilberman); Luigi Pistilli (Duke Mazzanga); Jim Morrison (Joby
Cuda); Claudio Biava (Barclay); Tony Kendall [Luciano Stella] (Pete
Zacari); Ermanno Consolazione (Gennarino Esposito); Dennis Sallas
(Fred Tecosky); Jack Ackerman (Britten); Billy Lee (Pepe).

U.S. release: Machine Gun McCain (Columbia, 1970) C-96
min.

Tough thug Hank McCain (Cassavetes) is sprung from prison
by Charlie Adamo (Falk), the West Coast head of the Cosa Nostra.
Hank agrees to assist his son Jack (Apra) rob a well-appointed Las
Vegas hotel. Although they learn that their backer, Adamo, has
been frightened off the job by the East Coast mob, Hank and Jack
plan to go through with the heist. Jack is later killed, but Hank,
according to plan, lifts two million dollars from the hotel safe.
However, Hank and his new girl (Ekland) are hunted down by the
syndicate and killed in a spray of machine-gun bullets.

Regarding this Italian-made entry which had better than average playdates in the U.S. and elsewhere, the British Monthly Film
Bulletin reported, "There are some familiar faces--John Cassavetes,
with his manic smile/smirk and seven o'clock shadow that neatly
epitomises the gangster life-style; and Peter Falk, ventriloquist's
gravel voice, slight squint, Big Time. But apart from an over-use
of the Techniscope zoom lens, there's no style to speak of."

THE GODFATHER (Paramount, 1972) C-175 min.

Producer, Albert S. Ruddy; director, Francis Ford Coppola;
based on the novel by Mario Puzo; screenplay, Puzo, Coppola; production designer, Dean Tavoularis; art director, Warren Clymer;
set decorator, Philip Smith; music, Nino Rota; music conductor,
Carlo Savina; costumes, Anna Hill Johnstone; makeup, Dick Smith,
Philip Rhodes; assistant directors, Fred Gallo, Steve Skloot, Tony
Brandt; sound, Bud Grenzbach, Richard Portman, Christopher Newman; special effects, A. D. Flowers, Joe Lombardi, Sass Bedig;
camera, Gordon Willis; editors, William Reynolds, Peter Zinner,
Marc Laub, Murray Solomon.

Marlon Brando (Don Vito Corleone); Al Pacino (Michael Corleone); James Caan (Sonny Corleone); Richard Castellano (Clemenza);
Robert Duvall (Tom Hagen); Sterling Hayden (McCluskey); John Marley (Jack Woltz); Richard Conte (Barzini); Diane Keaton (Kay Adams);
Al Lettieri (Sollozzo); Abe Vigoda (Tessio); Talia Shire (Connie

Opposite: Robert Duvall, Tere Livrano, John Cazale, Gianni Ruso,
Talia Shire, Morgana King, Marlon Brando, James Caan, Julie
Gregg and Jeannie Linero in The Godfather (1972).

Rizzi); Gianni Russo (Carlo Rizzi); John Cazale (Fredo Corleone);
Rudy Bond (Cuneo); Al Martino (Johnny Fontane); Morgana King
(Mama Corleone); John Martino (Paulie Gatto); Lenny Montana (Luca
Brasi); Alex Rocco (Moe Greene); Tony Giorgio (Bruno Tattaglia);
Vito Scotti (Nazorine); Victor Livrano (Phillip Tattaglia); Jeannie
Linero (Lucy Mancini); Julie Gregg (Sandra Corleone); Ardell Sheri-
dan (Mrs. Clemenza); Corrado Gaipa (Don Tommasino); Angelo In-
fanti (Fabrizio); Saro Urzi (Vitelli); Franco Citti (Calo).

  With a distributors' domestic gross of over $85 million, this
Mafia* film is the most financially successful gangster movie in
history. Running close to three hours, The Godfather, taken from
Mario Puzo's best seller, is for today's generation of moviegoers
what The Public Enemy, q. v. , and Little Caesar, q. v. , were to
1930s film audiences. Interestingly enough, the gangster theme is
becoming less the concept of an individual hoodlum against the
world than a family theme, with "the Family" against other Families as well as the law.
  Mario Puzo co-authored the screenplay with director Francis
Ford Coppola and the result is a fine study of a family (from the
1940s onward) knee-deep in ancient rivalries and the big business
world, part of which the film claims these Mafia families control.
Despite its length, the feature is well-paced, easily jumping from
family life to a shoot-out, shown in all its blood and gore.
  What makes The Godfather so memorable, however, are individual scenes, not the over-all production. Outstanding are the
wedding sequences detailing the gaiety and festivity of an Italian
family marriage; the gunning-down of Don Vito Corleone in a fruit
market and his slow disintegration and death; the rise of one son
(Pacino) who never wanted to be a part of the Mafia but eventually
becomes its head; and the murder of another son (Caan) who wants
more than anything to avenge his father's shooting and to succeed
him.
  Producer Albert S. Ruddy was apparently aware that any
good gangster film must be loaded with familiar faces and a number
of fine cameos are presented: Richard Conte--originally signed for
Brando's part--as a rival mobster head, John Marley as a Harry
Cohn-type, Al Martino as a thinly-disguised Frank Sinatra, Sterling
Hayden as a crooked cop, Morgana King as the Godmother, and
Richard Castellano as Clemenza, a local family employee.
  Marlon Brando won his second Academy Award for his part
as the title character, although time may very well take away the
edge from his performance. Pacino's fine emoting certainly car-
ried the major portion and the footage involving his business and
personal relationships gave the latter half of the film needed focus.
  Perhaps, the great success of The Godfather is due to its

---

*A few days before shooting of The Godfather commenced in March,
1971, producer Ruddy met with members of the Italian American
Civil Rights League. This summit meeting led to some compro-
mises in the scenario, such as the elimination of any direct use of
the words "Mafia" or "Cosa Nostra. "

epic theme.   More than any other gangster film, it ties together
all the myths, realities, and harshnesses of underworld life.   It
shows the gangster milieu to be a dog-eat-dog existence, with none
of the slickness of such pictures of the past.   The Corleones were
gangsters because of tradition, not because of want or need.   In
the past, the gangster was depicted as an individual or a member
of a small clique, not part of a whole family with roots dating back
hundreds of years.

Moreover, The Godfather openly suggested that gangsterism
hovers over every family in the land, not just the Corleones.   For
as the tentacles of the Mafia reach out into business (as this movie
ends, Pacino's Michael takes over a Las Vegas club), so does the
violence, greed, and rivalry portrayed in the film reach into the
suburbs of American life.

THE GODFATHER, PART II   (Paramount, 1974)   C-200 min.

Producer, Francis Ford Coppola; co-producers, Gray Gred-
erickson, Fred Roos; associate producer, Mona Skager; director,
Coppola; based on the novel The Godfather by Mario Puzo; screenplay, Coppola, Puzo; production designer, Dean Tavoularis; art
director, Angelo Graham; set decorator, George R. Nelson; assistant directors, Newton Arnold, Henry J. Lange, Jr., Chuck Myers,
Mike Kusley, Alan Hopkins, Burt Bluestein; music, Nino Rota; music conductor, Carmine Coppola; costumes, Theadora Van Runkle;
sound, Walter Murch; special effects, A. D. Flowers, Joe Lombardi; camera, Gordon Willis; editors, Peter Zinner, Barry Malkin,
Richard Marks.

Al Pacino (Michael Corleone); Robert Duvall (Tom Hagen);
Diane Keaton (Kay); Robert De Niro (Vito Corleone); John Cazale
(Fredo Corleone); Talia Shire (Connie Corleone); Lee Strasberg (Hy-
man Roth); Michael V. Gazzo Frankie Pentangeli); G. D. Spradlin
(Senator Pat Geary); Richard Bright (Al Neri); Gaston Moschin (Fa-
nutti); Tom Rosqui (Rocco Lampone); B. Kirby, Jr. (Young Clemen-
za); Frank Svero (Genco); Francesca deSapio (Young Mama Corleone);
Morgana King (Mama Corleone); Mariana Hill (Deanna Corleone);
Leopoldo Trieste (Signor Roberto); Dominic Chianese (Johnny Ola);
Amerigo Tot (Michael's Bodyguard); Troy Donahue (Merle Johnson);
John Aprea (Young Tessio); Abe Vigoda (Tessio); Tere Livrano
(Theresa Hagen); Gianni Russo (Carlo); Joe Spinell (Willi Cicci);
Maria Carta (Vito's Mother); Oreste Baldini (Victor Andolini as a
Boy); Guiseppe Sillato (Don Francesco); Mario Cotone (Don Tomma-
sino); James Gounaris (Anthony Corleone); Fay Spain (Marcia Roth);
Harry Dean Stanton, David Baker (F.B.I. Men); Ezio Flagello (Im-
presario); Peter Donat (Questadt); Roger Corman (Senator); James
Caan (Sonny).

Rarely, if ever, has Hollywood turned out a sequel that was
equal to or superior to the original.   Francis Ford Coppola did the
"impossible" with the massive Godfather, Part II, which in two
hundred minutes is far more than a companion piece to the 1972
edition.   As the Hollywood Reporter indicated, it is "... an

admirable, responsible production, less emotionally disturbing than
its predecessor, but a grand historical epic studying the nature of
power in the United States' heritage. "
    Of this $15.5 million production (about two-and-a-half times
the cost of the original), Variety pointed out, "There should be
very few criticisms that the latest film glorifies criminality since
the script never lets one forget for very long that [Al] Pacino as
well as Robert De Niro, excellent as the immigrant Sicilian who
became the crime family chief as played by Marlon Brando in the
first pic, and all their aides are callous, selfish and undeserving
of either pity or adulation. Yet, at the same time, there's enough
superficial glory in the panoramic story structure to satisfy the demands of less discriminating filmgoers. " Women's Wear Daily
summed it up, "The high points of the first film were moments of
violence and suspense; here they are moments of intensely deep and
difficult human emotions. Taken together, the films are the equivalent of those great, panoramic 19th-Century novels that relate the
progress of a family and a society. "
    Via flashbacks and flashforwards (from the time point of
Godfather, Part I) the viewer learns of the personal circumstances
surrounding the background of Don Vito (Brando in the original, De
Niro in the sequel) in Sicily and of his early years in New York's
tenements. Balancing this nostalgia turn are the sections of the
epic dealing with Michael's career in the Nevada gambling rackets
from about 1958 onward, as well as the tie-ins with Florida-Cuba
underworld czar Hyman Roth (Strasberg).
    If The Godfather pointed up the parallels between the Mafia
and big business, this production furthers the analogy, depicting
Pacino's Michael as an unswerving dictator who will accept no way
as right except his own.
    Coppola-Puzo emphasize the inhumanity of the organized
crime leaders by displaying the humanity of their underlings, women,
and relatives. Michael's wife (Keaton) finally cannot bear the type
of life forced on her and the children by her unrelenting spouse;
Michael's older brother (Cazale) is a weakling who betrays the new
Godfather; long-time pal and legal counsel Tom Hagen (Duvall) vac-
illates between loyalty and breaking free of his power-hungry com-
rade and step-brother; and ailing Jewish kingpin Hyman Roth (Strasberg) admires, fears, and detests his young competitor Michael.
    For those who insist that gangster films are merely displays of
tommy-guns, foul language, and violence, The Godfather, Part II amply
disputes that theory. In many categories, this carefully conceived picture is of Oscar-winning calibre. And it did win several Oscars at the
annual ceremony. In-mid-1975, both Godfather films were sold to NBC
TV in an unique $15 million dollar deal. The pictures will be re-edited
and reassembled, adding material originally cut from the film. The new
version will run nine or ten hours to be shown over several nights in
1976. (NBC paid Paramount nearly $10 million in 1974 for a one-time
TV showing of The Godfather Part I.)

THE GODFATHER OF HARLEM see BLACK CAESAR

THE GODSON (1972) see LE SAMOURAI

GREAT GUY (Grand National, 1936) 75 min.

    Presenter, Edward L. Alperson; producer, Douglas MacLean; director, John G. Blystone; based on The Johnny Cave Stories by James Edward Grant; screenplay, Grant, Harry Ruskin; additional dialog, Horace McCoy; art director, Ben Carre; music director, Merlin Skiles; assistant director, John Sherwood; costumes, Dorothy Beal; sound, Harold Bumbaugh; camera, Jack McKenzie; editor, Russell Schoengarth.
    James Cagney (Johnny Cave); Mae Clarke (Janet Henry); James Burke (Pat Haley); Edward Brophy (Pete Reilly); Henry Kolker (Conning); Bernadene Hayes (Hazel Scott); Edward J. McNamara (Captain Pat Hanlon); Robert Gleckler (Cavanaugh); Joe Sawyer (Joe Burton); Matty Fain (Tim); Ed Gargan (Al); Mary Gordon (Mrs. Ogilvie); Wallis Clark (Joel Green); Douglas Wood (The Mayor); Jeffrey Sayre (Clerk); Eddy Chandler (Meat Clerk); Murdock MacQuarrie (Client); Kate Price (Woman at Accident); Frank O'Connor (Detective); Henry Roquemore (Store Manager); Jack Pennick (Truck Driver); Bud Geary, Dennis O'Keefe (Guests); Robert Lowery (Parker); Gertrude Green (Nurse); Kernan Cripps (Deputy); Lee Shumway (Mike the Cop); John Dilson (City Editor); Bobby Barber (Grocery Clerk).

    After a series of epic contractual battles with Warner Bros., James Cagney left the studio and appeared in Douglas MacLean's production of Great Guy for the independent studio, Grand National. Not only did Grand National obtain the services of big star Cagney for its first independent outing, but the company wisely reunited him with Mae Clarke from The Public Enemy, and the duo again worked well together.
    Pugnacious Cagney was cast as Johnny Cave, an ex-fighter, now a chief deputy in the Department of Weights and Measures of a large city. He combats the racketeers who are trying to cheat the public in the food marketplace. Clarke plays Janet Henry, employed as a secretary for Conning, who, unknown to her, is one of the racketeer leaders of the district.
    When the racketeers try to bribe Cave and he refuses their offer, they beat him up and then try to pin a robbery rap on him. None of these intimidations works, and with the help of an ex-fighter pal (Brophy), now in politics, and the local police, Johnny obtains the needed evidence to prove Conning guilty.
    Shot on a small budget, Great Guy simply lacked the plot motivation and action to make it more than a good "B" film, with Cagney's name the marquee crutch needed to get it playdates. The film did well financially. However, Great Guy did have a few assets above and beyond Cagney's standard high-pressure performance. There was a stout supporting cast, especially Brophy as Cagney's former ring foe, James Burke as the star's Irish assistant, Joe Sawyer as a thug, and that wonderful Irish type, Mary Gordon, as the orphanage supervisor.

GRISBI   see   PARIS TOUCHEZ PAS AU GRISBI

THE GREAT ST. LOUIS BANK ROBBERY   (United Artists, 1959)
86 min.

        Producer, Charles Guggenheim; associate producer, Richard
T. Heffron; directors, Guggenheim, John Stix; based upon an actual
incident; screenplay, Richard T. Heffron; music, Bernardo Segall;
song, Segall and Peter Ude; music conductor, Hershy Kay; guitar
ballads, Jim Symington; sound, Frank Lewin, Arthur Stotter, Edward Johnston; camera, Victor Duncan; editor, Warren Adams.
        Steve McQueen (George Fowler); David Clarke (Gino); Crahan
Denton (John Egan); Molly McCarthy (Ann); James Dukas (Willie);
The St. Louis Police Department (Themselves).

        Well before his genre work in The Getaway (1972), q.v.,
Steve McQueen worked in this small thriller shot on location in St.
Louis and Springfield, Massachusetts. The film, although minor,
did obtain audience attention, since it was issued as the bottom half
of a dual bill with the popular The Rise and Fall of Legs Diamond.
        Unfortunately, too much of this little film was a rehash of
the usual heist plan and execution, with tempers clashing between the

Steve McQueen in The Great St. Louis Bank Robbery (1959).

four hoodlums involved.   The semi-documentary flavor helped to disguise the low-budget aspects of production.

THE GRISSOM GANG   (Cinerama, 1971)   C-127 min.

Producer, Robert Aldrich; associate producer, Walter Blake; director, Aldrich; based on the novel <u>No Orchids for Miss Blandish</u> by James Hadley Chase; screenplay, Leon Griffiths; music, Gerald Fried; song, Jimmy McHugh and Dorothy Fields; title theme song by Rudy Vallee; choreography, Alex Romero; costumes, Norma Koch; makeup, William Turner; assistant directors, Malcolm Harding, William Morrison; sound, Harry W. Tetrick, Richard Church; special effects, Henry Millar; camera, Joseph Birco; editor, Michael Luciano.

Kim Darby (Barbara Blandish); Scott Wilson (Slim Grissom); Tony Musante (Eddie Hagan); Robert Lansing (Dave Fenner); Irene Dailey (Ma Grissom); Connie Stevens (Anna Borg); Wesley Addy (John P. Blandish); Joey Faye (Woppy); Don Keefer (Doc); Dotts Johnson (Johnny Hutchins); Mort Marshall (Heinie); Michael Baseleon (Connor); Ralph Waite (Mace); Hal Baylor (Chief McLaine); Matt Clark((Bailey); Alvin Hammer (Sam); Dave Willock (Rocky); Alex

Dotts Johnson and Robert Lansing in <u>The Grissom Gang</u> (1971).

Wilson (Jerry McGowan); Elliott Street (Gas Station Boy); John Steadman (Old Man); Raymond Guth (Farmer).

This "R"-rated remake of James Hadley Chase's novel No
Orchids for Miss Blandish, had been predated by another version
filmed in England. This version took place in the 1930s in rural
Missouri and told of a country girl (Darby) who is kidnapped by an
outlaw gang which includes a ruthless woman (Dailey) and her dimwit, murderous son (Wilson). In the course of the labored story
line, Barbara and Slim fall in love, but their romance hardly com-
pensates for the long, boorish stretches of unsubtle violence. In
this overly violent film there was a good flavor of the Thirties,
even including Rudy Vallee singing the film's theme song, "I Can't
Give You Anything but Love, Baby."
        Critic Vincent Canby (New York Times) called the picture
"... offensive, immoral and perhaps even lascivious ... carrier
lurid melodrama and violence to outrageous limits."
        From a historical point of view, it is intriguing to compare
The Grissom Gang not only with the British-made No Orchids for
Miss Blandish, q.v., but also with the two American films made
from William Faulkner's Sanctuary, the book from which Chase
"borrowed" his plotline. These two Hollywood entries, The Story
of Temple Drake, q.v., and Sanctuary, had personalities all their
own.

GUN CRAZY   see   DEADLY IS THE FEMALE

GUNS DON'T ARGUE   see   GANG BUSTERS (1955)

GUYS AND DOLLS   (MGM, 1955)   C-158 min.

        Producer, Samuel Goldwyn; director, Joseph L. Mankiewicz;
based on the musical by Jo Swerling, Abe Burrows; from a story
by Damon Runyon; screenplay, Mankiewicz; costumes, Irene Sharaff;
songs, Frank Loesser; choreography-musical numbers staged by
Michael Kidd; camera, Harry Stradling; editor, Daniel Mandell.
        Marlon Brando (Sky Masterson); Jean Simmons (Sarah Brown);
Frank Sinatra (Nathan Detroit); Vivian Blaine (Adelaide); Robert
Keith (Lieutenant Brannigan); Stubby Kaye (Nicely-Nicely Johnson);
B. S. Pully (Big Jule); Johnny Silver (Benny Southstreet); Sheldon
Leonard (Harry the Horse); Dan Dayton (Rusty Charlie); George E.
Stone (Society Max); Regis Toomey (Arvide Abernathy); Kathryn
Givney (General Cartwright); Veda Ann Borg (Laverne); Mary Alan
Hokanson (Agatha); Joe McTurk (Angie the Ox); Kay Kuter (Calvin);
Stapleton Kent (Mission Member); Renee Renoir (Cuban Singer);
Earle Hodgins (Pitchman); Larri Thomas, Jann Darlyn, June Kirby,
Madelyn Darrow, Barbara Brent (The 1955 Goldwyn Girls).

        Even the most minor of Damon Runyon's stories have been
successfully translated to the screen. However, the verve of the

smash Broadway musical which preceded this film was not successfully transported to celluloid. For a motion picture that cost $5.5
million, the results seemed peculiarly amateurish and certainly not
much fun.

Taken from the story "The Idyll of Miss Sarah Brown," the
warmth, pacing, and structure of the stage vehicle was somehow
askew oncamera. Perhaps part of the trouble was the film's tam-
pering with Frank Loesser's stage musical score, with three new
songs* added to the film and five of the Broadway tunes deleted.

Another major difficulty in this overblown rendering of a
charming original was the miscasting of Marlon Brando in the pivotal role of Sky Masterson, an experienced gambler. Also in evidence was a mediocre performance by Frank Sinatra as Nathan Detroit, which helped to bog down the film's progress. On the asset
side, however, was Jean Simmons' radiant performance in an ill-
conceived role (she even danced well). Vivian Blaine, repeating
her Broadway role as Nathan's long-time fiancee, shone in her vulgar quaintness. Also from the original show was Stubby Kaye, as
that roly-poly bundle of humor, Nicely-Nicely Johnson.

Films in Review pinpointed the problem: "... the film lacks
one of the basic elements of the stage version's charm--a feeling
of New York."

To its credit, the screen Guys and Dolls came at a time
when the American cinema was satiated with crime exposé features,
depicting even the most innocent businessman as a ganglord's underling. The lawbreakers within Guys and Dolls were basically nice
guys. Granted that they liked to play craps, to place illegal bets
on the horses (this was in the pre-Offtrack Betting days), and to
have their molls dress in frilly finery, but was that so bad? After
all, who else would have helped the Salvation Army cause as much
as Nathan, Sky, and the boys?

THE HAPPENING (Columbia, 1967) C-92 min.

Producer, Jud Kinberg; associate producers, Robert Manchel,
David Wolfson, Howard Jaffe; director, Elliot Silverstein; based on
a story by James D. Buchanan, Ronald Austin; screenplay, Frank
R. Pierson, Buchanan, Austin; music, De Vol; song, De Vol and
William Roy; production designer, Richard Day; art director, Al
Brenner; set decorator, Don Ivey; costumes, Eugene Coffin, Jason
Silverstein; makeup, George Fields; assistant director, Ray Gosnell;
sound, Howard Warren, Jack Haynes; special effects, Willis Cook;
camera, Philip Lathrop; second unit camera, Howard Winner; editor,
Philip Anderson.

Anthony Quinn (Roc Delmonico); George Maharis (Taurus);
Michael Parks (Sureshot); Robert Walker (Herby); Martha Hyer
(Monica); Faye Dunaway (Sandy); Milton Berle (Fred); Oscar Homol-
ka (Sam); Jack Kruschen (Inspector); Clifton James (O'Reilly);

---

*One of the songs, "A Woman in Love," would become a best-selling
record for Frankie Laine in 1956, and, of course, "Love and Marriage" became a standard of sorts.

Eugene Roche, Luke Askew (Motorcycle Officers); James Randolph
Kuhl (Arnold).

This Elliot Silverstein-directed farce was "a wacky comedy
a la mode, oddly mixed and only spasmodically effective" (Variety).
Basically a misfire, still the feature is not to be ignored. Not only does it contain a most unusual group of co-players, but it has a
very reflective concept at heart, concerning itself with the relationships among gangland procedures, the hippie movement, and the
Mafia, all of which is tied together in a plot thread of a kidnapping.
    In the film Anthony Quinn appears as Roc Delmonico, a big-
time hoodlum who is spirited away by a group of daffy hippies (Dunaway, Maharis, Parks and Walker, Jr.) who hold him for ransom.
Their ingenious plan goes astray when Roc's wife (Hyer) and pal
(Berle) refuse to pay the sum demanded. A disgusted Roc takes
over the scheme to double cross his wife and his own gang. Martha Hyer as Monica offers an infatuating performance as the coldly-
calculating wife.

THE HARDER THEY FALL   (Columbia, 1956)   109 min.

    Producer, Philip Yordan; director, Mark Robson; based on
the novel by Budd Schulberg; screenplay, Yordan; music, Hugo
Friedhofer; orchestrator, Arthur Morton; music director, Lionel
Newman; art director, William Flannery; set decorators, William
Kiernan, Alfred E. Spencer; technical adviser, John Indrisano;
makeup, Clay Campbell; sound, Lambert Day; camera, Burnett Guf-
fey; editor, Jerome Thoms.
    Humphrey Bogart (Eddie Willis); Rod Steiger (Nick Benko);
Jan Sterling (Beth Willis); Mike Lane (Toro Moreno); Max Baer
(Buddy Brannen); Jersey Joe Walcott (George); Edward Andrews
(Jim Weyerhause); Harold J. Stone (Art Leavitt); Carlos Montalban
(Luis Agrandi); Nehemiah Persoff (Leo); Felice Orlandi (Vince Faw-
cett); Herbie Faye (Max); Rusty Lane (Danny McKeogh); Jack Albert-
son (Pop); Val Avery (Frank); Tommy Herman (Tommy); Vinnie De-
Carlo (Joey); Pat Comiskey (Gus Dundee); Matt Murphy (Sailor
Rigazzo); Abel Fernandez (Chief Firebird); Marion Carr (Alice).

    This is the most anti-boxing film ever made. It literally
calls for the abolition of the sport. Humphrey Bogart, in his final
film, is a public relations man working for a South American fighter (Lane). Through publicity and fixed matches, Toro Moreno is
built into a top attraction, a status which is not matched by his
ability. The incidents were broadly based on the career of heavy-
weight champion Primo Carnera, whose ring career occurred during
the Thirties.
    As Nick Benko, Rod Steiger charges through the picture,
playing the head of a fight promotion syndicate who pushes his new
freak attraction into a top boxing spot. The unknowing boxer becomes a useful tool to Benko for a spell, but then he decides to
ditch him, selling the contract to Jim Weyerhause (Andrews). Eddie
is the only one in the operation with scruples. To salve his

Rod Steiger, Humphrey Bogart and Mike Lane in The Harder They
Fall (1956).

conscience, he gives Toro his own share of the loot, sends him
back to Argentina, and then begins a campaign to have prize fighting banned in the U. S.

    A depressingly realistic feature, The Harder They Fall
delves deeply into the relationship between organized crime and boxing. What holds the film together, even more than its topical theme,
are the picture's performances. The leads were commendable, but
the supporting players were outstanding, especially Andrews as the
second-rate manager who thought "fighters ain't human." Also memorable was Max Baer as Buddy Brannen, the sadistic champion who
batters Toro in their title contest.

HARRY IN YOUR POCKET (United Artists, 1973) C-103 min.

    Executive producer, Alden Schwimmer; producer, Bruce Gel-
ler; associate producer, Alan Godfrey; director, Geller; screenplay,
Ron Austin, James Buchanan; art director-set decorator, William
Bates; music, Lalo Schifrin; song, Schifrin and Geller; technical
adviser, Tony Giorgio; sound, Les Freshcoltz; camera, Fred

Koenekamp; editor, Arthur Hilton.
        James Coburn (Harry); Michael Sarrazin (Ray Houlihan);
Trish Van Devere (Sandy Coletto); Walter Pidgeon (Casey); Michael
C. Gwynne (Fence); Tony Giorgio, Michael Stearns (Detectives); Sue
Mullen (Francine); Duane Bennett (Salesman); Stanley Bolt (Mr.
Bates); Barry Grimshaw (Bellboy).

        "Like so many films purporting to explore the mysteries of
some outlandish skill or profession, Harry in Your Pocket develops
cold feet along the way and begins to fall back increasingly on a
conventional triangle subplot.... Geller is content to remain on
the surface, endlessly repeating the gang's external strategy (se-
lecting, setting up, confusing the victim, then the disposal of the
take), but hurriedly changing the subject when it comes to showing
hands at work" (British Monthly Film Bulletin).
        With too much emphasis on the how-it-is-done aspect and
not enough on contrasting the various group members, the story
tells of divorcee Sandy Coletto (Van Devere) who takes up with Ray
Houlihan (Sarrazin) after he tries to lift her watch. He tries to
make amends (while she was pursuing him, her baggage was stolen)
by selling his day's take. This in turn leads them to Harry (Coburn)
who is collecting a new squad of pickpockets. Sandy and Ray are
taken into the gang, and participate in several hauls from the unsuspecting public (the montage sequences of these events become
taxing to even the indulgent viewer). Eventually the elder group
member, Casey (Pidgeon), is caught. Ray tries to steal enough
money for his defense. By this time Harry realizes that Sandy
loves Ray and he stops his pursuit of the level-headed, if over-
romantic young woman.
        With such a talented, diverse cast, it is a pity the film lived
up to none of its potential. In its minor way, it might have been
a gem of a study of nonchalant lawbreakers at work and play, 1970s-
style.

HEAT LIGHTNING (Warner Bros. , 1934) 63 min.

        Director, Mervyn LeRoy; based on the play by Leon Abrams,
George Abbott; screenplay, Brown Holmes, Warren Duff; camera,
Sid Hickox; editor, Howard Bretherton.
        Aline MacMahon (Olga); Ann Dvorak (Myra); Preston Foster
(George); Lyle Talbot (Jeff); Glenda Farrell (Mrs. Rifton [Feathers]);
Frank McHugh (Chauffeur [Frank]); Ruth Donnelly (Mrs. Ashton-
Ansley [Tinkle]); Theodore Newton (Steve); Willard Robertson (Eve-
rett); Edgar Kennedy (Husband); Muriel Evans (Blonde); Jane Darwell
(Wife); Harry C. Bradley (Man); Jill Bennett (Black Bangs); James
Durkins (Sheriff); Chris-Pin Martin (Mexican); Margareta Montez
(Wife); Eddie Shubert (Man).

        Predating the film version of The Petrified Forest (1936),
q. v. , this melodrama presented the account of two thugs (Foster and
Talbot) on the run to the Mexican border. They stop at a Southwest
filling-station cum restaurant, run by George's ex-love (MacMahon).

Also working at the cafe is Olga's pretty young sister, Myra (Dvorak), whom Jeff seduces. For comedy relief--and Warner Bros.' scripters were good about this--there were two divorcees (Farrell and Donnelly) from Reno and their chauffeur (McHugh) who also have stopped at the roadhouse.

To keep the plotline moving, it develops that the two wealthy gals have put their diamonds in the house safe and now George plans to steal the gems. Olga, however, learns of his plan and also about Myra's seduction. She obtains her retribution by killing the hoodlums before the G-Men arrive on the scene.

At the time of its issuance, the New York Times found the film "... a drab melodrama with occasional flashes of forced comedy." Today, however, this Mervyn LeRoy-directed feature stands up very well, especially in the acting department. The scenes between Farrell and Donnelly, as two bitchy divorcees, are delightful, especially in tandem with McHugh's milquetoast performance as their harried driver.

Warner Bros. intended this film to be the first of a number of starring vehicles for Aline MacMahon, but the studio decided soon thereafter that she was more forceful in character roles.

HELL ON FRISCO BAY (Warner Bros., 1956)   C-98 min.

Associate producer, George Bertholon; director, Frank Tuttle; based on the novel by William P. McGivern; screenplay, Sydney Boehm, Martin Rackin; art director, John Beckman; music, Max Steiner; sound, Charles B. Lang; camera, John Seitz; editor, Folmar Blangsted.

Alan Ladd (Steve Rollins) Edward G. Robinson (Victor Amato); Joanne Dru (Marcia Rollins); William Demarest (Dan Bianco); Paul Stewart (Joe Lye); Fay Wray (Kay Stanley); Perry Lopez (Mario Amato); Renata Vanni (Anna Amato); Nestor Paiva (Lou Fiaschetti); Stanley Adams (Hammy); Willis Bouchey (Lieutenant Neville); Peter Hanson (Detective Connors); Tina Carver (Bessie); Rodney Taylor (Brody Evans); Anthony Caruso (Sebastian Pasmonick); Peter Votrian (George Pasmonick); George J. Lewis (Father Larocca); Jayne Mansfield (Blonde).

Teaming stars of a particular genre together in one film has usually resulted in good box-office. In 1956 Warners teamed Alan Ladd, Edward G. Robinson, and lesser light Paul Stewart in this rugged melodrama. The result was "... two or three cuts above the quality of the run of pictures in this hackneyed genre" (New York Times).

Ex-cop Steve Rollins (Ladd), framed on manslaughter charges, is released from prison after five years. He is now determined to find those responsible for framing him. He rejects the help of his faithless wife (Dru) and ex-chief (Demarest). Instead, he seeks underworld connections and from them learns that Frisco docks racketeer Victor Amato (Robinson) made the frame. Rollins is invited to join Victor's gang, and when he refuses, he is pursued and has to shoot his way to freedom. Later, Steve locates Kay Stanley

Alan Ladd and Rod Taylor in Hell on Frisco Bay (1956).

(Wray), the lover of a hood done in by Victor. She knows enough
to clear Steve's name, and agrees to do so. Rollins corners Victor, but the latter escapes--temporarily--in a motor boat. It later
cracks up and the crime lord is arrested. At the finale, resolute
Steve returns to Marcia.

An acceptable plot, a good cast of stars, and the 1950s'
hard-as-nails approach to the genre made this a popular film. One
might wish that the feature had further explored the practical relationship between opposite sides of the law working together for various motives. As On the Waterfront (1954), q.v., had definitively
proved, the waterfront was literally a haven for undesirable characters and shady dealings. In Hell on Frisco Bay this fact of life is
accepted and exploited to an acceptable degree.

HELL UP IN HARLEM (American International, 1973) C-96 min.

Executive producer, Peter Sabiston; co-producer-director-
screenplay, Janelle Cohen; music, Freddie Perren, Fonce Mizell;

Fred Williamson in <u>Hell up in Harlem</u> (1974).

production designer, Larry Lurin; sound, A. Vanderkar; camera,
Fenton Hamilton; editor, Peter Honess.

Fred Williamson (Tommy Gibbs); Jules W. Harris (Papa
Gibbs); Gloria Hendry (Helen Bradley); Margaret Avery (Sister Jen-
nifer); D'Urville Martin (Reverend Rufus); Tony King (Zach); Gerald
Gordon (Mr. D'Angelo).

Whatever the color of the heavies' skin, this black exploitation feature was just another excuse for showing violence at its
goriest.   By the 1970s, this genre had reached its peak of blood-
and-guts-and-sex; there seemed to be no new variations of the format to titillate audiences.   As the <u>New York Times</u> summed it up,
it "... has the right title for a slaughter pile-up...."
The simplistic plot had a black underworld czar (Williamson)
wiping out all those in his path, including a fictional New York City
district attorney.   This "R"-rated entry was filled with illogical
sequences of on-the-street gun battles, bedroom toss-abouts, and
gangland meeting room arguments.

HELL'S KITCHEN   (Warner Bors. , 1939)   81 min.

Producers, Mark Hellinger, Bryan Foy; directors, Lewis
Seiler, E. A. Dupont; story, Crane Wilbur; screenplay, Wilbur,
Fred Niblo, Jr. ; camera, Charles Rosher.

Billy Halop (Tony); Bobby Jordan (Joey); Leo Gorcey (Gyp);
Huntz Hall (Ace); Gabriel Dell (Bingo); Bernard Punsley (Ouch);
Frankie Burke (Soap); Margaret Lindsay (Beth); Ronald Reagan (Jim);
Stanley Fields (Buck); Grant Mitchell (Crispin); Fred Tozere (Steve
Garvy); Arthur Loft (Jed Crispin); Vera Lewis (Sarah Grispin); Char-
les Foy (Flugue); Robert Homans (Hardy); Robert Strange (Callahan);
Raymond Bailey (Whitey); Clem Bevans (Mr. Quill); George Irving
(Judge Chandler); Lee Phelps (Bailiff); Cliff Saum (Guard); Charles
Sullivan, Jack Gardner (Henchmen); Jimmy O'Gatty (Mug); Jack
Mower (Detective); Ruth Robinson (Mrs. Chandler); George Offerman
Jury Foreman).

This remake of The Mayor of Hell (1933) was a continuation
of the Dead End Kids' saga.   It had the boys being graduated from
reform school and sent to the Hudson Shelter where a vicious superintendent (Mitchell) treats them harshly and eventually tortures one
youth to death.   A one-time hoodlum, now a humanitarian (Fields),
tries to get paroled by assisting in the management of the shelter.
However, he is forced to go in hiding and temporarily to ignore the
institution's internal problems.   Before the "happy" finale, the Kids
attempt an in-house revolt and even threaten to murder the sadistic
Crispin.
"Production starts off auspiciously and then gets tangled in
the final reels when devious and absurd counter-plots assert themselves.   It never completely untracks itself" (Variety).   The New
York World-Telegram warned, "The number of tears shed in Hell's
Kitchen ... would more than fill the Boulder Dam, since this is
just about the weepiest film of the year. "
Although the social injustice theme is not geographically
structured around the real Hell's Kitchen area of New York (10th
Avenue in the Forties), it does present a frightening picture of the
supposedly benevolent adolescent welfare home.   With its Oliver
Twist-like theme, one can appreciate why most observers were distracted from commenting that one of the film's heroes was actually
a long-standing underworld figure (Fields).
Margaret Lindsay and Ronald Reagan as the Home co-workers
supplied the "love" interest.

HICKEY AND BOGGS   (United Artists, 1972)   C-111 min.

Executive producer, Richard L. O'Connor; producer, Fouad
Said; director, Robert Culp; screenplay, Walter Hill; assistant direc-
tor, Edward Teets; music-music director, Ted Ashford; sound, Gene
Cantamessa; camera, Wilmer Butler; second unit camera, Rexford
Metz, Rex Hosea; editor, David Berlatsky.

Bill Cosby (Al Hickey); Robert Culp (Frank Boggs); Rosalind
Cash (Nyona); Carmen (Mary Jane); Louis Moreno (Quemando); Ron

Robert Culp in <u>Hickey and Boggs</u> (1972).

Henrique (Quemando's Brother the Florist); Robert Mandan (Mr.
Brill); Michael Moriarty (Ballard); Lester Fletcher (Rice); Sil Words
(Leroy); Bernie Schwartz (Bernie); Vincent Gardenia (Papadakis); Bill
Hickman (Monte); Matt Bennett (Fatboy); Jack Colvin (Shaw); James
Woods (Lieutenant Wyatt); Gil Stuart (Farrow); Sheila Sullivan (Edith
Boggs); Jason Culp (Mary Jane's Son); Gary Sanchez (Mary Jane's
Daughter); Isabel Sanford (Nyona's Mother); Ta-Ronce Allen (Nyona's
Daughter); Lou Frizzell (Lawyer); Tommy Signorelli (Nick); Gerald
Peters (Jack); Nancy Howard (Apartment Manager's Wife); Bernard
Nedell (Used Car Salesman); Ed Lauter (Ted); Wanda Spell, Winston
Spell (Playground Kids).

        For several seasons, Robert Culp and Bill Cosby starred on
the teleseries "I Spy" and the duo re-teamed for Culp's theatrical
film directorial debut.   The <u>New York Times</u> noted that it had the
"... swift pace necessary for the genre. "
        In the story by Walter Hill, director Culp utilized good Los
Angeles locations to advantage, especially the sleazy areas of the
sprawling city.   There was good cross-cutting and a plethora of
violence, including numerous murders and shootouts in the Los Angeles Coliseum and Dodger Stadium.

Culp and Cosby starred as detectives Al Hickey and Frank
Boggs who are after a cache of $400,000 taken in a heist from a
Pittsburgh bank.   Also after the precious loot are gangsters, the
police, gunmen, fences, and other detectives.   The money is in the
hands of a group of nervous Chicanos, confederates who are beginning to wish they had never seen the funds.   Human interest plot in-
terpolations include the detectives' private problems: Hickey's ex-
wife (Cash) is murdered by hoodlums and Boggs' ex-spouse is a
stripper (Carmen) driven to drink.

Integration had come a long way by the Seventies, but it was
no longer a sufficient gimmick to give "personality" to the two lead
detective figures.   Thankfully, both Culp and Cosby have their own
distinctive brand of projection.

HIDE-OUT   (MGM, 1934)   82 min.

Director, W. S. Van Dyke II; story, Mauri Grashin; screenplay, Frances Goodrich, Albert Hackett; camera, Ray June, Sidney
Wagner; editor, Basil Wrangell.

Robert Montgomery (Lucky Wilson); Maureen O'Sullivan
(Pauline); Edward Arnold (MacCarthy); Elizabeth Patterson (Mrs.
Miller); Whitford Kane (Mr. Miller); Mickey Rooney (Willie); C.
Henry Gordon (Tony Berrelli); Muriel Evans (Babe); Edward Brophy
(Britt); Henry Armetta (Louis Shuman); Herman Bing (Jake Lillie);
Louise Henry (Millie); Harold Huber (Dr. Warner); Roberta Gale
(Hat Check Girl); Arthur Belasco, Billy Arnold, Louis Natheaux
(Henchmen); Dick Kipling (Clerk); Frank Leighton (Head Waiter);
Lucille Browne, Jeanette Loff, Herta Lind (Girls); Frank Marlowe
(Laundry Driver); Bobby Watson (Master of Ceremonies); Frank
O'Connor (Policeman); Douglass Dumbrille (Nightclub Owner).

Sometimes a hackneyed plot (such as the heavy being transformed into a good guy through the influence of a rural setting, a
good girl, or both) can turn out well.   Such is the case with Hide-
Out, which boasted a well-polished MGM cast and fine technicians
behind the cameras.

Amorous racketeer Lucky Wilson (Montgomery) works as an
underling in an extortionist protection racket run by Tony Berrelli
(Gordon).   When a police detective (Arnold) gets on his trail, Lucky
is shot in the hand and takes refuge on a farm where he tells the
family he was a victim of hoodlum gunplay.   In the country, Lucky's
life takes a better turn as nature and the farmer's comely daughter
(O'Sullivan) have their effect.   Several good scenes detail Lucky's
acclimation to farm life; eventually he is forced to tell Pauline of
his unsavory background.   Among the supporting cast, Mickey
Rooney was effective as the pint-sized, irritating brother.

Metro would remake the story as I'll Wait for You (1941)
with Robert Sterling in the lead.

HIGH SCHOOL CONFIDENTIAL   (MGM, 1958)   85 min.

Producer, Albert Zugsmith; director, Jack Arnold; story,
Robert Blees; screenplay, Lewis Meltzer, Blees; art directors,
William A. Horning, Hans Peters; set decorators, Henry Grace,
Arthur Krams; assistant director, Joseph E. Kenny; makeup, Wil-
liam Tuttle; song, Jerry Lee Lewis, Ron Hargraves; special ma-
terial, Mel Welles; sound, Dr. Wesley C. Miller; camera, Harold
J. Marzorati; editor, Ben Lewis.

Russ Tamblyn (Tony Baker [Mike Wilson]); Jan Sterling (Ar-
lene Williams); John Drew Barrymore (J. I. Coleridge); Mamie Van
Doren (Gwen Dulaine); Diane Jergens (Joan Staples); Jerry Lee
Lewis (Himself); Ray Anthony (Bix); Jackie Coogan (Mr. A.); Char-
les Chaplin, Jr. (Quinn); Burt Douglas (Jukey Judlow); Jody Fair
(Doris); Phillipa Fallon (Poetess); Robin Raymond (Kitty); James
Todd (Jack Staples); Lyle Talbot (William Remington Kane); William
Wellman, Jr. (Wheeler-Dealer); Kim Chance (Waitress); Michael
Landon (Steve Bentley); Della Malzahn (Woman at Race); Gil Perkins
(Police Sergeant); Pierre Watkin (David Wingate).
A. k. a. Young Hellions.

The problem of drug traffic in the public schools has been
a serious one for some time, but this tawdry thriller provided little insight on the problem.
Tony Baker (Tamblyn) is an F.B.I. undercover agent who
masquerades as a high school student in order to infiltrate a drug
running gang in a large California high school. Also embroiled in
the caper are Marlene Williams (Sterling), an understanding teacher,
J. I. Coleridge (Barrymore), a drug pusher, and Gwen Dulaine (Van
Doren), who is Tony's amorous aunt. For added box-office attraction, producer Zugsmith even included rock 'n roll performer Jerry
Lee Lewis, big bank leader Ray Anthony, and ex-child star Jackie
Coogan (as the nefarious Mr. A).
"There is no surer way to keep people away from the movies
than the production, distribution and exhibition of venalities such as
this...." (Films in Review). Zugsmith had the poor taste to do a
follow-up in 1960 called College Confidential, which was a conventional murder-mystery with a totally silly plotline.

HIGH SIERRA   (Warner Bros. , 1941)   100 min.

Executive producer, Hal B. Wallis; associate producer, Mark
Hellinger; director, Raoul Walsh; based on the novel by W. R. Burnett; screenplay, John Huston, Burnett; music, Adolph Deutsch;
orchestrator, Arthur Lange; art director, Ted Smith; gowns, Milo
Anderson; makeup, Perc Westmore; sound, Dolph Thomas; special
effects, Byron Haskin, H. F. Koenekamp; camera, Tony Gaudio;
editor, Jack Killifer.

Humphrey Bogart (Roy Earle); Ida Lupino (Marie Garson);
Alan Curtis (Babe Kozak); Arthur Kennedy (Red Hattery); Joan Leslie (Velma); Henry Hull ("Doc" Banton); Barton MacLane (Jake Kranmer); Henry Travers (Pa); Elisabeth Risdon (Ma); Cornel Wilde

Humphrey Bogart and Ida Lupino in High Sierra (1941).

(Louis Mendoza); Minna Gombell (Mrs. Gaughman); Paul Harvey
(Mr. Baughman); Donald MacBride (Big Mac); Jerome Cowan (Healy);
John Eldredge (Lou Preiser); Isabel Jewell (Blonde); Willie Best
(Algeron); Arthur Aylesworth (Auto Court Owner); Robert Strange
(Art); Wade Boteler (Sheriff); Sam Hayes (Radio Commentator); Er-
ville Alderson (Farmer); Spencer Charters (Ed); Cliff Saum (Shaw);
Eddy Chandler (Policeman); Richard Clayton (Bellboy); Louis Jean
Heydt, William Hopper, Robert Emmett Keane (Men); Maris Wrixon
(Blonde); Lucia Carroll (Brunette); Ralph Sanford (Fat Man); Frank
Moran, Lee Phelps (Officers); Frank Cordell (Marksman); Zero the
Dog (Pard the Dog).

        When George Raft declined the role of Roy "Mad Dog" Earle
in High Sierra, Humphrey Bogart was chosen for the part.   The
Raoul Walsh-directed thriller was a huge success, a classic of the
gangster genre, and it began Bogie on his road to superstardom.
        Derived from a W. R. Burnett novel, the plotline was basic
enough: the old hood being broken out of the penitentiary for one
last big heist.   In this case it was robbery of a resort hotel and
the film traces the activity of Roy Earle (Bogart), an aging toughie,

as he works with younger men (Kennedy and Curtis) on the stick-up and becomes attracted by their moll (Lupino). Along the way he meets a poor family (Travers and Risdon) and tries to help their crippled granddaughter (Leslie).

When planning this job, bed-ridden Big Mac (MacBride) sighs to Roy, "All the A-1 guys are gone--dead or in Alcatraz. "

Earle responds, "Sometimes I feel I don't know what this [racket] is about anymore. "

Big Mac: 'I'm going to die. Anyhow, so are you. So are we all. To your health, Roy. "

This interlude provides the key to High Sierra, revealing the thrust of the John Huston/W. R. Burnett scenario. It is almost as if the scripters, with the help of an already famous screen racketeer (Bogart), are kissing goodbye to a bygone era, while pointing the way to the thrust of Forties' gangster yarns.

Set against the splendor of the High Sierra, this adventure tale was untypical of director Walsh in that it mainly focused on the individual characters rather than on just lots of action.

Allegedly, the character of Roy Earle was based on John Dillinger, so much so that Bogart was made-up to resemble that famous wanted man. Earle was humanized, however, and killed others only because he had to. Although the censors demanded the character die at the end (the reason Raft rejected the film), Bogart very humanly portrayed the inner feelings of a hunted man, who knows he has but one destiny: to be gunned down by the law. As presented here, death for Earle is almost a pardon, a release from the pressures of life. In the closing moments, moll Marie (Lupino) picks up Pard the dog, and as she goes off with the police, looks mistily upward, remarking, almost to herself, that now Roy is finally free .... free.

With less effect, High Sierra would be remade as I Died a Thousand Times (1955), q. v.

HIGHWAY 301 (Warner Bros. , 1950) 83 min.

Producer, Bryan Foy; director-screenplay, Andrew Stone; camera, Carl Guthrie; editor, Owen Marks.

Steve Cochran (George Legenza); Virginia Grey (Mary Simms); Gaby Andre (Lee Fontaine); Edmon Ryan (Truscott); Robert Webber (William B. Phillips); Wally Cassell (Robert Mais); Aline Towne (Madeline Welton); Richard Evan (Herbie Brooks); Edward Norris (Noyes).

After a tedious introduction featuring the governors of Virginia, Maryland, and North Carolina delivering an anti-crime sermon, the story gets off to its tough plotline about the exploits, successes, and eventual demise of a tri-state gang. Most gory is the finish meted out to George Legenza (Cochran), the gang's leader. When his getaway car is put out of commission, he escapes on foot, is wounded, and then falls beneath a speeding train.

For diversion and sex appeal, three group members' dolls are portrayed. One, Mary Simms, as the spouse of Robert Mais

(Cassell) has some comedy relief moments; she is the type who is so addicted to her radio soap operas that she even carries a portable radio with her on the job.

HIS KIND OF WOMAN (RKO, 1951) 120 min.

Executive producer, Howard Hughes; associate producer, Robert Sparks; director, John Farrow; story, Frank Fenton, Jack Leonard; screenplay, Fenton; art director, Albert S. D'Agostino; music director, C. Bakaleinikoff; songs, Sam Coslow; Harold Adamson and Jimmy McHugh; camera, Harry J. Wild; editor, Eda Warren.

Robert Mitchum (Dan Milner); Jane Russell (Lenore Brent); Vincent Price (Mark Cardigan); Tim Holt (Bill Lusk); Charles McGraw (Thompson); Marjorie Reynolds (Helen Cardigan); Raymond Burr (Nick Ferraro); Leslye Banning (Jennie Stone); Jim Backus (Myron Winton); Philip Van Zandt (Jose Morro); John Mylong (Martin Krafft); Carleton G. Young (Hobson); Erno Verebes (Estaban); Dan White (Tex Kearns); Richard Berggren (Milton Stone); Stacy Harris (Harry); Robert Cornthwaite (Hernandez); Jim Burke (Barkeep); Paul Frees (Corle); Joe Granby (Arnold); Daniel De Laurentis (Mexican Boy); John Sheehan (Husband); Sally Yarnell (Wife); Anthony Caruso (Tony); Robert Rose (Corle's Servant); Tol Avery (The Fat One); Paul Fierro, Mickey Simpson (Hoodlums); Ed Rand, Jerry James (Cops); Joel Fluellen (Sam); Joey Ray, Barry Brooks (Card Players); Barbara Freking, Mamie Van Doren, Joy Windsor, Jerri Jordan, Mary Brewer (Girls); Saul Gorss (Viscount); Mariette Elliott (Redhead).

When this offbeat melodrama-comedy was issued, Louella O. Parsons gave it plenty of attention, hoping to launch her daughter Harriet's return to RKO as a producer. Apparently, RKO boss Howard Hughes did not share Parsons' enthusiasm for the project: the film looked as though it has been shot on the cheap. Nevertheless, due to Jane Russell's bosomy appearance and the high camping of Vincent Price as a hammy movie star, the feature has gained its own following.

Hard-luck gambler Dan Miller (Mitchum) is paid $500 to go to a small Mexican resort village. Only later does he find out that deported hoodlum Nick Ferraro (Burr) intends to have him killed and to assume his identity in order to re-enter the U.S. Also at the resort is man hunter-vocalist Lenore Brent (Russell), who pretends to be well-heeled; egocentric matinee idol Mark Cardigan (Price) and federal agent Bill Lusk (Holt). Of all things it is adventure-seeking Cardigan who leads a rescue squad of Mexican police to save Miller from an unpleasant end.

The New York Times sneered, "In addition to being one of the worst Hollywood pictures in years, it is probably the only one since the advent of Vitaphone that needs sub-titles [referring to the cast's diction, or lack thereof]. "

However, one should not discount Russell's animalistic performance, nor her singing of "Five Little Miles from San Berdoo. "

Also to be savored are the sexual tensions in the pull-and-tug relationship of Russell's and Mitchum's characters, as well as the
then standard (but now archaic) stereotype of the foreign-born, U.S.-
based lawbreaker.

HIT! (Paramount, 1973) C-134 min.

     Executive producer, Gray Frederickson; producer, Harry
Korshak; director, Sidney J. Furie; screenplay, Alan R. Trustman,
David M. Wolf; assistant directors, Robin Clark, Louis Pitzele;
art director, George Petitot; set decorator, Leonard Maizola; music, Lalo Schifrin; sound, David Ronne; sound effects, Keith Stafford; special effects, Joe Lombardi; camera, John A. Alonzo; editor, Argyle Nelson.
     Billy Dee Williams (Nick Allen); Richard Pryor (Mike Will-
mer); Paul Hampton (Barry Strong); Gwen Welles (Sherry Nielson);
Warren Kemmerling (Dutch Schiller); Janet Brandt (Ida); Sid Melton
(Herman); David Hall (Carlin); Todd Martin (Crosby); Norman Burton (Director); Jenny Astruc (Madame Frelou); Yves Barsacq (Ro-
main); Jean-Claude Bercq (Jean-Baptiste); Henri Cogan (Bornou);
Pierre Collet (Zero); Jerry Jones (The Weasel); Don McGovern
(Roger); Janear Hines (Esther).

     When his daughter dies from drug addiction, federal agent
Nick Allen (Williams) vows to corral the French-based drug ring
responsible for supplying the heroin. Because his superiors will
not aid in the manhunt, Allen is forced to gather his own investigating team. Some of his inducement methods are unorthodox, as
when he promises prostitute Sherry Nielson (Welles) a lifetime supply of heroin for her aid. The trail leads to British Columbia
where Allen trains his commando group, and then to Marseilles
where the nine-man drug syndicate is based. They hit their targets, and Allen is later informed by his superiors that the matter
can be easily justified on the books.
     The British Monthly Film Bulletin credited director Sidney
J. Furie with an attempt to "... invest thriller formulas with im-
provised dialogue and doodling bits of comic business," but there
was not enough to lift this entry out of the black exploitation film
fold. Using the co-star (Williams) of his well-received Lady Sings
the Blues (1972), director Furie went astray in his attempt to be
different. Said the New York Times, "... the kicks are so implausible, so humorless, so without redeeming style and wit that to
sit through it is to give oneself a false low." But did not this criticism apply to most of the 1970s' black action features?

HIT LADY (ABC-TV, 1974) C-90 min.

     Producers, Aaron Spelling, Leonard Goldberg; associate pro-
ducer, Shelley Hull; director, Tracy Keenan Wynn; teleplay, Yvette
Mimieux; music, George Tipton; art director, Tracy Bousman; Miss
Mimieux's wardrobe, Nolen Miller; camera, Tim Southcott; editor,
Sid Levin.

Yvette Mimieux (Angela de Vries); Joseph Campanella (Jeffrey Baine); Clu Gulager (Roarke); Dack Rambo (Doug Reynolds); Keenan Wynn (Buddy McCormack); Roy Jensen (Eddie); Paul Genge (Webb); Del Monroe (Hansen); Mitzi Hoag (Woman at Airport).

Hard-pressed for decent roles for herself, star Yvette Mimieux wrote the teleplay for this entry. Emmy Award winning writer Tracy Keenan Wynn made his directorial debut on this ABC-TV "Tuesday Movie of the Week. "

Yvette was showcased as Angela de Vries, a professional artist who works on the side as a paid assassin for the syndicate. (How timely for woman's lib!) After she falls in love with a photographer (Reynolds) she wants out of the racket. But there is the proverbial one more job. She lures a wealthy cattleman (Keenan Wynn) to a lonely spot where she shoots him. But this is hardly the end for Angela. Her superior (Gulager) says she must first murder a labor leader (Campanella) before she can be released from her obligations. Learning that the man cannot swim, she induces him to take her to a lonely resort spot and there she attempts to drown him. Failing in her mission, she runs away to Mexico, hoping to elude the mob. But the once hired female killer now becomes the stalked prey of a hit man.

THE HOLE IN THE WALL (Paramount, 1929) 73 min.

Director, Robert Florey; based on the play by Fred Jackson; screenplay, Pierre Collings; camera, George Folsey; editor, Morton Blumenstock.

Claudette Colbert (Jean Oliver); Edward G. Robinson ("The Fox"); David Newell (Gordon Grant); Nelly Savage (Madame Mystera); Donald Meek (Goofy); Alan Brooks (Jim); Louise Closser Hale (Mrs. Ramsey); Katherine Emmet (Mrs. Carslake); Marcia Kagno (Marcia); Barry Macollum (Dogface); George McQuarrie (Inspector); Helen Crane (Mrs. Lyons).

The one distinguishing note of this feature is that it was Robinson's first gangster film.

Cast as "The Fox", Robinson becomes enamored of Jean Oliver (Colbert), a bitter young woman who is driven to seek revenge on Mrs. Ramsey (Hale), the lady who was responsible for sending Jean to jail on a false charge. Reporter Gordon Grant (Newell) also is enamored of Jean, but she is hell-bent to win her eye for an eye. Later, The Fox kidnaps the granddaughter of Mrs. Ramsay and then uses the child as a wedge to force the police to allow the wrong-thinking Jean to go her way. Cleared of her past, Jean finds happiness with her newspaperman beau.

HONOR THY FATHER (CBS-TV, 1973) C-90 min.

Executive producer, Charles W. Fries; producer, Harold D. Cohen; director, Paul Wendkos; based on the novel by Gay Talese;

Richard Castellano in <u>Honor Thy Father</u> (1973).

teleplay, Lewis John Carlino; music, George Dunning; editor, Richard Halsey.

Raf Vallone (Joseph "Joe Bananas" Bonanno); Joseph Bologna (Salvatore "Bill" Bonanno); Brenda Vaccaro (Rosalie Bonanno); Richard Castellano (Frank Labruzzo); Joe De Santis (Joe Magliocco); Marc Lawrence (Stephane Magaddino); Louis Zorich (Joe Notaro); James J. Sloyan (Pete Notaro); Gilbert Green (Di Gregorio); Henry Ferrentino, Frank Albanese (Gangsters); Joseph Campanella (Narrator).

'It's our father's war. We're their sons. We've got no choice. It's a question of honor. " So Frank Labruzzo (Castellano) explains to Bill Bonanno (Bologna) why two hundred year old vendettas started in Sicily are still being fought in the U.S. today between the key Mafia families.

Close on the heels of the extravagantly successful The God-father (1972), q.v., CBS-TV contracted to film Gay Talese's best seller as a TV film with theatrical release abroad. It was also an inside view of an underworld family and their feudal wars, centering on the actual story of the alleged kidnapping of Joe Bonanno (Vallone) in 1964 and the slow disintegration of the Bonanno empire after Joe's alienation with "The Committee" made up of the heads of the various Mafia families. The teleplay, like the novel, concludes with the 1971 imprisonment of Joe's son Bill (Bologna) on charges of fraudulent use of a credit card.

Shot mainly in New York City's West Greenwich Village, Honor Thy Father provided good entertainment without the violence (this was, after all, for TV audiences) associated with The God-father. The movie offered a conscientious study of a modern day Mafia family, the fears and pressures of their everyday lives based on venerated traditions. The more lurid aspects of Mafia operations were toned down and the fighting between the families became the main theme of the chronicle.

HOODLUM EMPIRE   (Republic, 1952)   98 min.

Producer, Herbert J. Yates; associate producer-director, Joseph Kane; story, Bob Considine; screenplay, Bruce Manning, Considine; art director, Frank Arrigo; music, Nathan Scott; camera, Reggie Lanning; editor, Richard L. Van Enger.

Brian Donlevy (Senator Bill Stephens); Claire Trevor (Connie Williams); Forrest Tucker (Charley Fignatalli); Vera Ralston (Marte Dufour); Luther Adler (Nicky Mancani); John Russell (Joe Gray); Gene Lockhart (Senator Tower); Grant Withers (Reverend Andrews); Taylor Holmes (Benjamin Lawton); Roy Barcroft (Louie Draper); William Murphy (Pete Dailey); Richard Jaeckel (Ted Dawson); Don Beddoe (Senator Blake); Roy Roberts (Chief Tayls); Richard Benedict (Tanner); Phillip Pine (Louis Barretti); Damian O'Flynn (Foster); Pat Flaherty (Mikkelson); Ric Roman (Fergus); Douglas Kennedy (Brinkley); Don Haggerty (Mark Flynn); Francis Pierlot (Uncle Jean); Sarah Spencer (Mrs. Stephens); Thomas Browne Henry (Commodore Mermant); Jack Pennick (Tracey); Fred Kohler, Jr. (German

Roy Barcroft, Luther Adler and Forrest Tucker in a pose for Hoodlum Empire (1952).

Soldier); William Schallert (Inquiry Clerk); Charles Trowbridge
(Commander Garrison); Whit Bissell (Filby); Andy Brennan (Taxi
Driver).

When Herbert J. Yates' playland, Republic Studios, decided
to film the life of gangster Frank Costello (1893-1973), George Raft
was offered the lead role. Raft rather smartly rejected the part of
his old friend and the job went to beefy Luther Adler. Despite sensible direction by Joseph Kane and a fair-sized name cast, including Vera Ralston, the film never rose to any dramatic heights.

When Raft turned down the project, the emphasis of the storyline was switched from the gang leader to the methods used to get
back at mob deserter Joe Gray (Russell). The latter decides to
make a clean break with the syndicate after becoming patriotic during World War II. Paralleling the hoodlum's dragnet are the in-
vestigatory procedures of federal operators, headed by Senator Bill
Stephens (Donlevy), in their tracking of organized crime. The main
gist of the story was that the gang was using Joe Gray's name as
the leader of their payoff operations, despite the fact that he was now
the legitimate operator of a service station and had no knowledge of
their underhanded doings.

With the holier-than-thou attitude of Washington officials in this film, <u>Hoodlum Empire</u> dates badly, especially in light of Watergate and other recent activities of public officials.

THE HOODLUM SAINT   (MGM, 1946)   93 min.

    Producer, Cliff Reid; director, Norman Taurog; screenplay, Frank Wead, James Hill; art directors, Cedric Gibbons, Harry McAfee; set decorator, Edwin B. Willis; assistant director, Horace Hough; music, Nathaniel Shilkret; sound, Douglas Shearer; special effects, Warren Newcombe; camera, Ray June; editor, Ferris Webster.
    William Powell (Terry Ellerton O'Neill); Esther Williams (May Lorrison); Angela Lansbury (Dusty Millard); James Gleason (Snarp); Lewis Stone (Father Nolan); Rags Ragland (Fishface); Frank McHugh (Three-Fingers); Slim Summerville (Eel); Roman Bohnen (Father O'Doul); Charles Arnt (Cy Nolan); Louis Jean Heydt (Mike Flaherty); Charles Trowbridge (Uncle Joe Lorrison); Henry O'Neill (Lewis J. Malbery); Matt Moore (Father Duffy); Trevor Bardette (Rabbi Meyerberg); Addison Richards (Reverend Miller); Tom Dugan (Buggsy); Emma Dunn (Maggie); Mary Gordon (Trina); Ernest Anderson (Sam); Charles D. Brown (Ed Collner); Paul Langton (Burton Kinston); Al Murphy (Benny); Will Wright (Allan Smith); Byron Foulger (J. Cornwall Travers); Charles Judels (Waiter Captain); William B. Davidson (Annoyed Man); Stanley Blystone (Cop at Employment Office); Eddie Dunn (Gateman); Frank Orth (<u>Chronicle</u> Editor); Stanley Andrews (<u>Chronicle</u> Publisher).

    Big studios could go astray, even with a big-name cast, as in The Hoodlum Saint. "Thin Man" star William Powell and aquatic beauty Esther Williams were teamed in this rather preposterous yarn which attempted to trace the recovery of a con artist's soul.
    Disillusioned after World War I., ex-doughboy Terry O'Neill (Powell) determines to make a fortune any way he can. Meanwhile he brushes off several hoodlum friends bent on handouts. He sells them on devotion to St. Dismas, the Good Thief on the Cross. Eventually his own salesmanship inspires him to a new way of life.
    "There's no feeling of struggle in the development of the plot, everything coming too easily to the characters.... " (Variety). Cast as a club warbler, Angela Lansbury offered the most vivid performance. For some strange reason, her singing of "If I Had You" and "How Am I to Know?" (the only lyrics Dorothy Parker ever wrote) was dubbed.

THE HOT ROCK   (Twentieth Century-Fox, 1972)   C-110 min.

    Producers, Hal Landers, Bobby Roberts; director, Peter Yates; based on the novel by Donald E. Westlake; screenplay, William Goldman; music, Quincy Jones; song, Bill Rinehart; production designer, John Robert Lloyd; art director, Bob Wrightman; set decorator, Robert Drumheller; costumes, Ruth Morley; makeup, Irving Buchman; assistant director, Ted Zachary; stunt coordinator, Carey

Ron Leibman, George Segal, Robert Redford and Paul Sand in a
publicity shot for <u>The Hot Rock</u> (1972).

Loftin; sound, James Sabata, Theodore Soderberg; camera, Ed
Brown; editors, Frank P. Keller, Fred W. Berger.

Robert Redford (John Dortmunder); George Segal (Andrew
Kelp); Zero Mostel (Abe Greenberg); Ron Leibman (Murch); Paul
Sand (Alan Greenberg); Moses Gunn (Dr. Amusa); William Redfield
(Lieutenant Hoover); Topo Swope (Sis); Charlotte Rae (Ma Murch);
Graham P. Jarvis (Warden); Harry Bellaver (Rollo the Bartender);
Seth Allen (Happy Hippie); Robert Levine (Cop at Police Station);
Lee Wallace (Dr. Strauss); Robert Weil (Albert); Lynne Gordon
(Miasmo); Fred Cook (Otto); Grania O'Malley (Bird Lady); Mark
Dawson (Big Museum Guard); Ed Bernard, Charles White, Christo-
pher Guest (Cops); Gilbert Lewis, George Vartenieff (Museum
Guards).

With distributors' domestic grosses of over $3.5 million,
The Hot Rock proved a favorite with theatre audiences, boosted no
little by its engaging cast of rogues.

This pleasantly complicated feature had an African United Na-
tions diplomat (Gunn) hire Andrew Kelp (Segal) to steal a priceless
diamond, "The Saber Stone," from the Brooklyn Museum.   Dr.
Amusa reasons that the gem originally belonged to his country, and
he now wants it back.   Kelp hires an ex-convict, John Dortmunder
(Redford), who in turn contracts Alan Greenberg (Sand) and Murch
(Leibman), two alleged heist experts.   After casing the museum, the
hapless hoods stage a diversionary tactic raid and one of their number takes the gem.   The latter is surrounded by police detectives
and before capture, he swallows the stone.   The diplomat, however,
is not dissuaded.   He still wants the stone.   The gang breaks into
prison to bust out Greenberg, hoping to make him confess where
his crooked lawyer father (Mostel) has hidden the valuable loot.   As
a last resort, the feckless group must break into a police station
where the gem is stashed.

On an academic level, the critics were less enthused about
this well-bungled heist thriller.   Judith Crist of New York magazine
complained, "... we wind up remembering chuckles rather than guffaws, bits and pieces rather than a total delight." Possibly Time's
Jay Cocks was closest to the point when he noted, "... the trouble
with such yarns is that they tend to be about mechanics, not people."

The Donald Westlake novel, from which The Hot Rock derived,
was also the basis for the George C. Scott-starring feature, The
Bank Shot, which misfired at the 1974 boxoffice.   Topkapi (1964),
q.v., remains the definitive study in this species.

THE HOUSTON STORY (Columbia, 1956) 79 min.

Producer, Sam Katzman; director, William Castle; story-
screenplay, James B. Gordon; art director, Paul Palmentola; assistant director, Gene Anderson, Jr.; camera, Henry Freulich; editor,
Edwin Bryant.

Gene Barry (Frank Duncan); Barbara Hale (Zoe Crane); Edward Arnold (Paul Atlas); Paul Richards (Gordie Shay); Jeanne
Cooper (Madge); Frank Jenks (Louie); John Zaremba (Emile Constant);

Barbara Hale, Gene Barry, Paul Richards and Edward Arnold in
The Houston Story (1956).

Chris Alcaide (Chris Barker); Paul Levitt (Duke); Pete Kellett (Kalo);
Leslie Hunt (Inspector Gregg); Claudia Bryar (Clara); Charles Gray
(Stokes); Larry W. Fultz (Talbot).

If one believed everything he saw in the cinema, it seemed
there was not a city in America in the Fifties which did not have an
exposé story tucked away in the files of its local chamber of commerce. Most of these films turned to standard plots, using the special locales of the rural area in question to make one film different
from another.

Dark-haired, attractive Barbara Hale turned blonde for this
entry, and was directed by later horror film expert, William Castle.
According to this programmer, there was a lot of unpleasantness in
this Texas city. Alas, the feature was merely dreary.

HUSH MONEY (Fox, 1931) 68 min.

Director, Sidney Lanfield; story-screenplay, Philip Klein,
Courtney Terrett; dialog, Dudley Nichols; camera, John Seitz.

Owen Moore, Myrna Loy and C. Henry Gordon in <u>Hush Money</u> (1931).

Joan Bennett (Janet Gordon); Hardie Albright (Stuart Elliott); Owen Moore (Steve Pelton); Myrna Loy (Flo Curtis); C. Henry Gordon (Jack Curtis); Douglas Cosgrove (Dan Emmett); George Raft (Maxie); Hugh White (Puggie).

This film is one of the tough but very refined gangster entries that so typified the early 1930s. Minor in almost all categories, <u>Hush Money</u> is only remembered today because George Raft had a brief role as one of Owen Moore's gang members.

This confession story told of Janet Gordon (Bennett) who becomes mixed up with a hoodlum (Moore). His gang plans a murder but they are caught and Janet is sentenced to a year in prison. After her release, she is befriended by a thoughtful policeman (Cosgrove) and she later weds a millionaire (Albright). When Felton is released from jail he tries to blackmail Janet about her past, but Emmett is on hand to help her once again. Using a rather unusual way of producing the desired results, he lets Felton's old gang know that it was Felton who squealed on all of them. As a result, Felton meets a rather dire end.

I AM THE LAW   (Columbia, 1938)   83 min.

Producer, Everett Riskin; director, Alexander Hall; based on magazine articles by Fred Allhoff; screenplay, Jo Swerling; music director, Morris Stoloff; camera, Henry Freulich; editor, Viola Lawrence.

Edward G. Robinson (John Lindsay); Barbara O'Neil (Jerry Lindsay); John Beal (Paul Ferguson); Wendy Barrie (Frankie Ballou); Otto Kruger (Eugene Ferguson); Arthur Loft (Tom Ross); Marc Lawrence (Eddie Girard); Douglas Wood (Berry); Robert Middlemass (Moss Kitchell); Ivan Miller (Inspector Gleason); Charles Halton (Leander); Louis Jean Heydt (J. W. Butler); Emory Parnell (Brophy); Joseph Downing (Cronin); Theodore Von Eltz (Martin); Horace McMahon (Prisoner); Frederick Burton (Governor); Lucien Littlefield (Roberts); Ed Keane, Robert Cummings, Sr., Harvey Clark, James Flavin (Witnesses); Fay Helm (Mrs. Butler); Kane Richmond, James Bush, Anthony Nace (Students); Bud Jamison (Bartender); Bess Flowers (Secretary); Bud Wiser, Lane Chandler (Policemen); Reginald Simpson, Cyril Ring (Photographers).

Alexander Hall, who was making a distinguished name for himself in the field of light comedy at Columbia, directed Edward G. Robinson in this good-humored gangster feature.

Professor John Lindsay (Robinson) is an expert in the arena of law. He is hired by a town to clean out racketeers. On the urging of Eugene Ferguson (Kruger), a civic leader, the earnest law enforcer hires the man's son (Beal), a former student, to aid him. It develops that the real culprit is none other than Eugene Ferguson. Among the latter's accomplices is Frankie Ballou (Barrie), a newspaperwoman. It is not long before the townfolk become impatient with Lindsay's inability to find sufficient evidence to have the gang prosecuted. He is fired, but the good man continues on the job on his own. Pitting gang members against each other, he and Paul Ferguson eventually find out about Fersugon, Sr. With the aid of the police, Lindsay herds the criminals into a tent and shows them a film of electrocution. He also proves a point with Paul Ferguson, who later makes a will leaving his fortune to crime control and then commits suicide.

Although the New York Times rated this "the liveliest melodrama in town," the movie, with its hokey sequence showing the end result of crime, seemed more than it actually was.

I AM NOT AFRAID   see   THE STAR WITNESS

I DIED A THOUSAND TIMES   (Warner Bros., 1955)   C-100 min.

Producer, Willis Goldbeck; director, Stuart Heisler; screenplay, W. R. Burnett; art director, Edward Carrere; music, David Buttolph; orchestrator, Maurice de Packh; assistant director, Chuck Hansen; wardrobe, Moss Mabry; camera, Ted McCord; editor, Clarence Kolster.

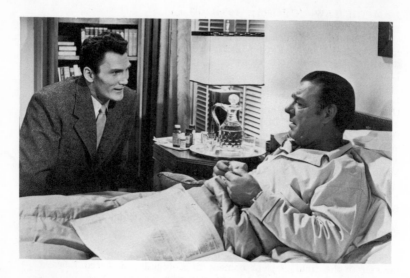

Jack Palance and Lon Chaney, Jr. in I Died a Thousand Times
(1955).

Jack Palance (Roy Earle); Shelley Winters (Marie Garson);
Lori Nelson (Velma); Lee Marvin (Babe); Earl Holliman (Red); Perry
Lopez (Louis Mendoza); Lon Chaney, Jr. (Big Mac); Howard St.
John (Doc Banton); Ralph Moody (Pa); Olive Carey (Ma); Joseph
Millikin (Kranmer); Dick Davalos (Lon Breisser); Bill Kennedy
(Sheriff); Peggy Maley (Kranmer's Girl); Dub Taylor (Ed); Dick
Reeves (Deputy); Ed Fury, Larve Farlow, Hubie Kerns (Bits); Mae
Clarke (Mabel Baughman); Hugh Sanders (Mr. Baughman); Nick Ad-
ams, Darren Dublin (Bell Boys); Dennis Hopper (Joe); Myra Fahey
(Margie); Herb Vigran (Art); Dennis Moore, Mickey Simpson (Offi-
cers); John Pickard (Sheriff's Deputy); James Seay (Man in Tropico
Lobby).

Hollywood, like many another, just cannot seem to leave a
good thing alone. Despite a most successful earlier version (High
Sierra) which had become a cinema classic, W. R. Burnett agreed
to re-adapt his novel for this remake. It turned out to be no more
than a "frippery remake" (New York Times) of the Humphrey Bogart
classic of 1941, q.v. Only beautiful photography and on-location shooting
at Mount Whitney and in the California desert region saved this
melodrama from being boredom incarnate.
    As before the story focused on a dying big time hoodlum
(Chaney) who plans a big job at the Frontier Hotel in Palm Springs.
He arranges for famous hoodlum Roy Earle (Palance) to get out of
prison to aid in the heist. Roy arrives at the mountain retreat and
joins the assembled gang (Marvin, Holliman and Lopez) in the job.

He trades glances with moll Marie Garson (Winters) but he is really attracted to a crippled girl (Nelson) whom he helps to have a
needed operation.   Finally the robbery is accomplished, the criminals fall out, and Earle is hunted down and murdered by the law in
the High Sierras.
       Although following closely the plotline of the film original,
this edition lacked the frank, crisp direction of Raoul Walsh.   Good
as Palance was as "Mad Dog" Earle, his did not compare with the
Bogart interpretation.
       Earlier, in 1949, Warner Bros. had used the plotline of
High Sierra for the Western, Colorado Territory, a Joel McCrea-
Virginia Mayo vehicle.

I, MOBSTER   (Twentieth Century-Fox, 1959)   82 min.

       Producers, Roger and Gene Corman; director, Roger Corman;
based on the novel by Joseph Hilton Smyth; screenplay, Steve Fisher;
assistant director, Donald Daves; music, Gerald Fried, Edward L.
Alperson, Jr.; songs, Alperson and Jerry Winn; art director, Daniel
Haller; set decorator, Harry Reif; sound, Philip N. Mitchell; camera,
Floyd Crosby; editor, William B. Murphy.
       Steve Cochran (Joe Sante); Lita Milan (Teresa Porter); Robert
Strauss (Black Frankie); Celia Lovsky (Mrs. Sante); Lili St. Cyr

Grant Withers and Steve Cochran in I, Mobster (1959).

(Herself); John Brinkley (Ernie Porter); Yvette Vickers (The Blonde); Jeri Southern (Herself); Grant Withers (Paul Moran); John Mylong (Mr. Sante); Wally Cassell (Cherry-Nose); Robert Shayne (Senator); Frank Gerstle (District Attorney).

The prolific Roger Corman not only produced-directed science fiction and horror films, but he also turned his hand to the crime genre. Variety rated this low budget entry a "Well-turned-out gangster film.... [He] manages to capture the gangster feeling...."

At the Senate Rackets Hearing, Joe Sante (Cochran) is on the witness stand. During his testimony he recalls, mentally, his early life in crime. Through flashbacks his rise in the mobster world is traced, culminating with his murder of Paul Moran (Withers), the crime boss of the nation. Back in the present, Joe realizes he is pegged by the syndicate to be eradicated. As irony would have it, it is Black Frankie (Strauss), the man who taught Joe everything he knows about the rackets, who is the trigger man.

Back in the Forties, Cochran seemed to be the most likely candidate to win pre-eminence in playing gangsters. Here, near the end of his career rope, the semi-dissipated Cochran was still at the old stereotype. Fortunately for the sake of this economy feature, his personality was well suited to such roles, even when he was hardly trying.

I STOLE A MILLION   (Universal, 1939)   80 min.

Associate producer, Burt Kelly; director, Frank Tuttle; story, Lester Cole; screenplay, Nathaniel West; dialog director, Harold Erikson; camera, Milton Krasner; editor, Edward Curtiss.

George Raft (Joe Laurik [Harris]); Claire Trevor (Laura Benson); Dick Foran (Paul Carver); Henry Armetta (Nick Respino); Victor Jory (Pation); Joseph Sawyer (Billings); Robert Elliott (Paterson); Stanley Ridges (George Downs); Irving Bacon (Simpson); Jerry Marlowe (Photographer); Edmund MacDonald, Dick Wessel, Emory Parnell (Cops); Ben Taggart (Police Captain); Tom Fadden (Verne); John Hamilton (District Attorney Wilson); Wallis Clark (Jenkins); Hobart Cavanaugh, Billy Engle (Bookkeepers); Sarah Padden (Lady in Post Office); Arthur Q. Bryan, Henry Roquimore (Managers); Emmett Vogan, Charles Irwin (Theatre Managers); Dick Elliott (Small Town Doctor); Mack Gray, Harry B. Stafford, J. Anthony Hughes, Hal K. Dawson, Ed Fliegel (Men); George Chandler (Clothing Store Clerk); Mira McKinney (Mrs. Loomis); Phil Tead (Charlie); Eddie Dunn (Superintendent); Ernie Adams (The Mouch); Sammy Finn, Raymond Bailey (Cabbies); Russ Powell (Watchman); Jason Robards, Sr. (Bank Teller); Tom Steele (Cop); Frances Robinson (Elise the Movie Cashier); Constantine Romanoff (Wrestler).

Despite its rather listless pacing, this Universal release did illustrate how a victim of circumstances can fall into a life of crime and how crime itself can snowball into a grim finale.

Joe Laurik, alias Harris (Raft), is a cab driver who is cheated legally by a finance company. Due to the protection of the

firm by the law, Joe decides to become a criminal, and he gradual-
ly works his way up to being a front man in a bank robbery. After the big caper he travels to California where Laura Benson
(Trevor) gives up her law-abiding beau (Foran) to wed Joe. Under
her good influence, Joe becomes a garage owner and agrees to clear
his name. But he goes on one last job to get money to support his
wife and unborn child while he will be serving time in the penitentiary.

Both Raft and Trevor managed to breathe life into the film.
Raft continued to portray the gangster who is a criminal not for the
thrills, but because fate has decreed it.

I WALK ALONE   (Paramount, 1948)   97 min.

Producer, Hal B. Wallis; director, Byron Haskins; based on
the play Beggars Are Coming to Town by Theodore Reeves; screenplay, Charles Schnee; adaptors, Robert Smith, John Bright; dialog
director, Joan Hathaway; assistant director, Richard McWhorter;
art directors, Hans Dreier, Franz Bachelin; set decorators, Sam
Comer, Patrick Delany; music, Victor Young; song, Ned Washington and Allie Wrubel; sound, Harry Lindgren, Walter Oberst; process camera, Farciot Edouart; camera, Leo Tover; editor, Arthur
Schmidt.

Burt Lancaster (Frankie Madison); Lizabeth Scott (Kay Law-
rence); Kirk Douglas (Noll Turner); Wendell Corey (Dave); Kristine
Miller (Mrs. Richardson); George Rigaud (Maurice); Marc Lawrence
(Nick Palestro); Mike Mazurki (Dan); Mickey Knox (Skinner); Roger
Neury (Felix); John Bishop (Ben the Bartender); Bruce Lester
(Charles); Gino Corrado (George the Assistant Chef); Jean Del Val
(Henri the Chef); Dewey Robinson (Heinz); Jack Perrin (Policeman);
Bobby Barber (Newsboy); James Davies (Masseur); Olin Howlin
(Watchman); Walter Anthony Merrill (Schreiber); Freddie Steele (Ti-
ger).

Following the success of The Killers (1946), q. v. , moody
crime thrillers were the vogue in the late Forties. This Hal B.
Wallis production was a minor league attempt to cash in on this popular type of gangster feature. For one of the first times oncamera,
it delineated crime, like big business, as operating on assorted
corporate levels. Instead of promoting this novel aspect of the film,
Paramount followed the tried and true route, exploiting the sex angle. Thus the publicity campaign read, "He fell for the oldest trick
in the world.... If you want to pump a guy--send a dame!"

Ex-rum runner Frankie Madison (Lancaster) has spent fourteen years in prison. When he is released, he cannot adjust to outside life and becomes bitter. He wants revenge against Noll Turner
(Douglas), who framed him on the rap in the first place. He becomes attracted to Noll's club singer Kay Lawrence (Scott), who happens to be Turner's property. This rouses Noll's ire and sets the
stage for the final bloody showdown.

The picture's stars repeated their roles on "Lux Radio Theatre" on May 24, 1948.

Susan Hayward in <u>I Want to Live</u> (1958).

I WANT TO LIVE   (United Artists, 1958)   120 min.

Producer, Walter Wanger; director, Robert Wise; based on newspaper articles of Ed Montgomery and the letters of Barbara Graham; screenplay, Nelson Gidding, Don Mankiewicz; music-music conductor, John Mandel; art director, Edward Haworth; set decorator, Victor Gangelin; assistant director, George Vieira; sound, Fred Lau; camera, Lionel Lindon; editor, William Hornbeck.

Susan Hayward (Barbara Graham); Simon Oakland (Ed Montgomery); Virginia Vincent (Peg); Theodore Bikel (Carl Palmberg); Wesley Lau (Henry Graham); Philip Coolidge (Emmett Perkins); Lou Krugman (Jack Santo); James Philbrook (Bruce King); Bartlett Robinson (District Attorney); Gage Clark (Richard G. Tibrow); Joe De Santis (Al Matthews); John Marley (Father Devers); Raymond Bailey (San Quentin Warden); Alice Backes (San Quentin Nurse); Russell Thorson (San Quentin Sergeant); Dabbs Greer (San Quentin Captain); Stafford Repp (Sergeant); Gavin MacLeod (Lieutenant).

On June 3, 1955, thirty-two year old Barbara Graham died in the gas chamber at San Quentin prison.   The four-time wed woman, who was the mother of three, had been found guilty of the 1953 murder of Mrs. Mabel Monohan.   Some twenty years later, legal authorities and some of the public (those who remember) are not sure whether Barbara Graham was guilty or just a victim of circumstantial evidence.

Guilty of dope addiction, prostitution, shilling, and what have you, Barbara Graham (Hayward) insists to the very end that she is innocent of the murder of the elderly widow.   But one of her gangland associates turns state's evidence and pins the rap on her, and she foolishly tries to buy an alibi from a cellmate's friend (who turns out to be a law enforcer).   In the course of her hell on earth, Barbara wins one stay of execution after another.   Finally, her appeals for leniency and a fresh trial are denied.   She is led to the gas chamber and executed.

Anyone who has seen Susan Hayward's Academy Award-winning performance as the ill-fated Barbara Graham cannot forget her vibrant interpretation of a woman fighting for her life.   "Why do they torture me?" she screams at one point, distraught by the legal system which tantalizes, and terrorizes the hapless prisoner.

Regarding this shocking feature, Time said, "... what is the meaning of the painful lesson.... Is it a sermon on the wages of sin? Not really.   The heroine, according to the script, is not punished for something she did, but for something she did not do. Is it an attack on capital punishment? Possibly.   But the script spends no sympathy on the two men convicted as the heroine's accomplices, who meet the same fate as she does.   Well then, what is it?   To judge from the far-out photography, real desperate sound track, and dragsville dialogue that Krylon-spray the whole film with a cheap glaze of don't-care-if-I-do-die juvenility, Producer Walter Wanger seems less concerned to assist the triumph of justice than to provide the morbid market with a sure-enough gasser. "

No matter what one's reaction to the script, the performances, or the thrust of the feature, it does make one very salient point.

People are judged by who their friends are, and having underworld associates is no recommendation in a tight spot.

ILLEGAL   (Warner Bros. , 1955)   88 min.

   Producer, Frank P. Rosenberg; director, Lewis Allen; based on the play The Mouthpiece by Frank J. Collins; screenplay, W. R. Burnett, James R. Webb; art director, Stanley Fleischer; music, Max Steiner; assistant director, Phil Quinn; wardrobe, Moss Mabry; camera, Peverell Marley; editor, Thomas Reilly.
   Edward G. Robinson (Victor Scott); Nina Foch (Ellen Miles); Hugh Marlowe (Ray Borden); Robert Ellenstein (Joe Knight); De Forrest Kelly (Edward Clary); Jay Adler (Joseph Carter); James McCallion (Allen Parker); Edward Platt (Ralph Ford); Albert Dekker (Frank Garland); Jan Merlin (Andy Garth); Ellen Corby (Miss Hinkel); Jayne Mansfield (Angel O'Hara); Clark Howat (George Graves); Henry Kulky (Taylor); Addison Richards (Steve Harper); Howard St. John (E. A. Smith); Lawrence Dobkin (Al Carol); George Ross (Policeman); John McKee, Barry Hudson (Detectives); Kathy Marlowe (Blonde Girl); Ted Stanhope (Bailiff); Charles Evans (Judge); Jonathan Hale (Doctor); Marjorie Stapp (Night Orderly); Fred Coby (Guard); Julie Bennett (Miss Worth); Archie Twitchell (Mr. Manning); Herb Vigran (Policeman).

   Warner Bros. ' remake of The Mouthpiece (1933), q. v. , and The Man Who Talked Too Much (1940) looked to many viewers like an imitation of The Asphalt Jungle, q. v.
   Edward G. Robinson plays a district attorney who quits his post after sending the wrong man to the electric chair.   Later he pulls himself together and becomes a defense lawyer.   One of his new clients is a racketeer (Dekker) who has an outlet in the D. A. 's office.   The man (Marlowe) is Victor Scott's pal and former investigator.   When Ellen (Foch), Borden's wife, learns of her husband's underhanded dealings she kills him in self-defense.   However, the D. A. thinks she is really the informer and that she killed Ray to hide her crimes.   Frank Garland, on the other hand, wants her in jail and tries to kill Scott, her attorney.   Although injured, Victor comes to court with Garland's ex-mistress (Mansfield).   She implicates her ex-lover and helps to set Ellen free.
   Beefed up with a lot of action, Illegal is historically interesting today largely because of fledgling Mansfield's screen appearance.

IN NOMME DELLA LAGGE   (Lux, 1949)   100 min.

   Producer, Luigi Rovere; director, Pietro Germi; based on the novel Piccola Pretura by G. E. Losciavo; screenplay, Federico Fellini, Giuseppe Mangioni; sets, Gino Mirici; music, Carlo Rustichelli; camera, Leonida Barboni.
   Massimo Girotti (The Judge); Charles Vanel (Farmer Turi); Jone Salinas (The Baroness); Camillo Mastrocinque (The Baron);

Peppino Spadero (Counselor-at-Law); Saro Urzi (The Sergeant); Ignazio Balsamo (Messana); Nanda de Santis (Lorenzina).

U. S. release: <u>Mafia</u> (1950).

A young judge (Girotti) is sent to a small Sicilian village to untangle its legal problems. Once there, he finds the town is under the thumb of the Mafia and the mine owned by a man is temporarily closed. Despite opposition, the fearless judge orders the arrest of Mafia leaders and demands the mine to be reopened. His actions bring the townspeople to his side. When a young boy who has befriended the judge is killed, the lawyer vows to rid the town of the organized crime. The villagers join him, and the murderer is captured.

Despite its excellent photography and its importance as one of Fellini's early cinematic presentations, the <u>New York Times</u> complained, that it "... is no definite study of a feared organization," although the paper admitted the feature was "robust." The film industry, whether abroad or in America, was still too diplomatic (or too afraid?) to deal dispassionately, yet truthfully, with the subject of the Mafioso influence.

INSIDE THE MAFIA   (United Artists, 1959) 72 min.

Producer, Robert E. Kent; director, Edward L. Cahn; screenplay, Orville H. Hampton; art director, Bill Glasgow; set decorator, Morris Hoffman; costumes, Einar Bourman; sound, Al Overton; camera, Maury Gertsman; editor, Grant Whytock.

Cameron Mitchell (Tony Ledo); Elaine Edwards (Anne Balcom); Robert Strauss (Sam Galey); Jim L. Brown (Doug Blair); Ted De Corsia (Augie Martello); Grant Richards (Johnny Lucero); Richard Karlan (Chins Dayton); Frank Gerstle (Julie Otranto); Sid Clute (Beery); Louis Jean Heydt (Rod Balcon); Steve Roberts (Raycheck); Hal Torey (Molina); Carl Milletaire (Dave Alto); Carol Nugent (Sandy Balcon); Edward Platt (Dan Regent); Michael Monroe (Buzz); Jack Daley (Joe the Barber); Raymond Guth (Morgan); Jim Bannon (Corino); John Hart (Police Sergeant); Donna Dale (Manicurist); Jack Kenny (Vince DeMao); Anthony Carbone (Kronis).

Behind the guise of fiction, this exposé-style feature utilized real life events in building up its plotline. Filled with the usual run-of-the-mill brutality, it maintained a sharp pace throughout.

Johnny Lucero (Richards) is about to return incognito to the U.S. after ten years of deportation. He plans to meet with the Mafia gang leaders in an inconspicuous upstate New York retreat. Meanwhile, Tony Ledo (Mitchell) is scheming to place his ailing boss, Augie Martello (De Corsia), on the underworld throne. His plan is to murder Lucero when he lands at the local airport. However, Martello dies at the crucial moment. Switching to an alternate plan, Tony agrees to let Lucero live if he makes Tony the successor to Martello. However, at the council meeting, Lucero shoots the Mafia heads, including Tony, and Lucero is arrested by waiting police.

INTOLERANCE   (Wark Distributing, 1916) 210 min.

Director-screenplay, D. W. Griffith; assistant directors,
Erich von Stroheim, W. S. Van Dyke II, Tod Browning, George
Siegman, Joseph Henaberry, Elmer Clifton, Edward Dillon; music
arranged by Joseph Carl Breil, Griffith; camera, G. W. Bitzer,
Karl Brown.
Lillian Gish (The Woman Who Rocks the Cradle).
The Modern Story:
Mae Marsh (The Girl); Fred Turner (Her Father); Robert
Harron (The Boy); Sam de Grasse (Jenkins); Vera Lewis (Mary T.
Jenkins); Mary Alden, Pearl Elmore, Lucille Brown, Luray Huntley,
Mrs. Arthur Mackley (Uplifters); Tom Wilson (The Policeman); Wal-
ter Long (Musketeer of the Slums); Lloyd Ingraham (The Judge);
Ralph Lewis (The Governor); Monte Blue (Striker); Max Davidson
(Friendly Neighbor); Reverend A. W. McClure (Father Farley); Mar-
guerite Marsh (Debutante); Tod Browning (Owner of Car); Edward
Dillon (Chief Detective); Clyde Hopkins (Jenkins' Secretary); William
Brown (The Warden); Alberta Lee (Wife of the Neighbor).
The Judean Story:
Howard Gaye (The Nazarene); Lillian Langdon (Mary the Moth-
er); Olga Grey (Mary Magdalene); Erich von Stroheim, Gunther von
Ritzau (Pharisees); Bessie Love (Bride of Cana); George Walsh
(Bridegroom).
Medieval French Story:
Margery Wilson (Brown Eyes); Eugene Pallette (Prosper La-
tour); Spottiswoode Aiken (Her Father); Ruth Handforth (Her Mother);
Frank Bennett (King Charles IX); A. D. Sears (The Mercenary);
Maxfield Stanley (Duc d'Anjou); Josephine Crowell (Catherine de Medi-
ci); Constance Talmadge (Marguerite de Valois); W. E. Lawrence
(Henry of Navarre); Joseph Henaberry (Admiral Coligny); Douglas
Fairbanks (Man on White Horse--Huguenot).
Babylonian Story:
Constance Talmadge (The Mountain Girl); Elmer Clifton (The
Rhapsode); Alfred Paget (Belshazzar); Seena Owen (Princes Beloved);
Carl Stockdale (King Nabonidas); Tully Marshall (High Priest of Bel);
George Seigmann (Cyrus the Persian); Elmo Lincoln (The Mighty
Man of Valor); Goerge Fawcett (Judge); Kate Bruce (Old Woman);
Loyolo O'Connor (Slave); James Curley (Charioteer); Howard Scott
(Babylonian Dandy); Alma Rubens, Ruth Darling, Margaret Mooney
(Girls of the Marriage Market); Mildred Harris, Pauline Starke,
Winifred Westover (Favorites of the Harem); Eve Southern, Carmel
Myers, Jewel Carmen, Colleen Moore, Natalie Talmadge, Carol
Dempster, Ethel Terry, Daisy Robinson, Anna Mae Walthall, The
Denishawn Dancers (Entertainers at Belshazzar's Feast); William
Dark Cloud (Ethiopian Chieftain); Charles Eagle Eye (Barbarian
Chieftain).

The modern story of Intolerance, "The Mother and the Law,"
was filmed prior to the issuance of The Birth of a Nation (1915).
Director D. W. Griffith then decided to weave three other stories
around "The Mother and the Law," and make a gigantic film detailing man's inhumanity to man. The resultant film was so spectacular

that audiences still marvel at it today.   Technically, the film quali-
fies in the gangster genre only in its modern story segment, and
then just barely.
     This highly melodramatic portion of the film told of a factory
owner who inflicts many injustices on his workers, even to the point
of using violence against them.   The main plot finds a young man
(Harron) going to the gallows on a false murder charge.   This scene
was made intensely exciting by Griffith's cross-cutting into the story
the other three episodes of the film at their climaxes, thus heighten-
ing the tension to an orchestrated pitch.
     There is less of a gangster motif in "The Mother and the
Law" than in the director's earlier short, The Musketeers of Pig
Alley (1912), q. v.   However, this portion of Intolerance does depict
the dishonesty, evil and corruption of big business, and its exploitation of workers.   Such attitudes provided the breeding ground that
would spawn the gangsters and hoodlums of the next decade.

INVISIBLE STRIPES   (Warner Bros. , 1939) 82 min.

     Executive producer, Hal B. Wallis; associate producer, Louis
F. Edelman; director, Lloyd Bacon; based on the book by Warden
Lewis E. Lawes; story, Jonathan Finn; screenplay, Warren Duff;
music, Heinz Roehmheld; orchestrator, Ray Heindorf; assistant di-
rector, Elmer Decker; dialog director, Irving Rapper; art director,
Max Parker; gowns, Milo Anderson; makeup, Perc Westmore; sound,
Dolph Thomas; special effects, Byron Haskin; camera, Ernest Haller;
editor, James Gibbons.
     George Raft (Cliff Taylor); Jane Bryan (Peggy); William Hol-
den (Tim Taylor); Humphrey Bogart (Chuck Martin); Flora Robson
(Mrs. Taylor); Paul Kelly (Ed Kruger); Lee Patrick (Molly Daniels);
Henry O'Neill (Parole Officer Masters); Frankie Thomas (Tommy);
Moroni Olsen (Warden); Margot Stevenson (Sue); Marc Lawrence (Lef-
ty); Joseph Downing (Johnny); Leo Gorcey (Jimmy); William Haade
(Shrank); Tully Marshall (Old Peter); Chester Clute (Mr. Butler);
Jack Mower (Guard in Charge); Frank Mayo (Guard at Gate); Frank
Bruno (Smitty, a Prisoner); John Irwin (Prisoner); G. Pat Collins
(Alex, a Prisoner); Mack Gray, Joe Devlin, Mike Lally, Al Hill
(Henchmen); John Ridgely (Employment Clerk); Victor Kilian (Fore-
man); William Davidson (Chief Foreman); Irving Bacon (Personnel
Director); Maude Allen (Woman); Charles Wilson, Robert Elliott,
Lane Chandler (Detectives); Emory Parnell, Cliff Clark (Policemen);
John Hamilton (Captain Johnson); Bruce Bennett (Rich Man).

     Under Lloyd Bacon's direction, Warner Bros. again utilized
Warden Lewis Lawes' work about prison life and developed a film
project, this time Invisible Stripes, starring George Raft.   It retold the classic plot of two men (Raft and Bogart) who are released
from prison; one tries to go on the right course, the other returns
to the world of crime.
     After gaining his freedom, Cliff Taylor finds he wears invisi-
ble stripes due to his prison record.   He discovers it is difficult to
keep a job and when he does get work (menial at that), he is soon

picked up on suspicion. Meanwhile, his kid brother (Holden) is
desperate to earn enough money to support his girl (Bryan) and decides that crime may be the only course available. To avoid Tim
falling into the underworld syndrome, Cliff joins Chuck Martin's
gang. After a series of robberies he has enough money to buy himself and Tim a filling station. He quits the gang, but later the
hoods use his business as a getaway point after a job. An injured
Chuck seeks Cliff's help. Later, Martin's boys believe he has
squealed on them to the cops and they gun him down.

Variety rated the film a "... top grade underworld melodrama. " It certainly was one of Raft's better gangster pictures at
Warner Bros. His scenes with Flora Robson, as his mother, were
really touching. As in most Warner underworld dramas, there were
many sequences depicting just how hopeless it was to be poor and
what the plight of the impoverished was really like in the hell of
urban tenements.

JIMMY THE GENT   (Warner Bros. , 1934)   67 min.

     Executive producer, Jack L. Warner; director, Michael
Curtiz; story, Laird Doyle, Ray Nazarro; dialog director, Daniel
Reed; music conductor, Leo F. Forbstein; costumes, Orry-Kelly;
makeup, Perc Westmore; art director, Esdras Hartley; camera, Ira
Morgan; editor, Thomas Richards.
     James Cagney (Jimmy Corrigan); Bette Davis (Joan Martin);
Alice White (Mabel); Allen Jenkins (Louis); Alan Dinehart (Charles
Wallingham); Mayo Methot (Gladys Farrell); Hobart Cavanaugh
(Worthington the Imposter); Philip Faversham (Interne); Phillip Reed
(Ronnie Gatson); Arthur Hohl (Joe Rector [Monty Barton]); Ralf Har-
olde (Hendrickson); Renee Whitney (Bessie the Phone Girl); Merna
Kennedy (Jitters the Typist); Camile Rovelle (File Clerk); Joe Saw-
yer (Mike the Heir Chaser); Stanley Mack (Pete); Tom Costello
(Grant); Ben Hendricks (Ferris); Billy West (Halley); Lee Moran
(Stew); Harry Wallace (Eddie); Robert Homans (Irish Cop); Milton
Kibbee (Ambulance Driver); Howard Hickman (Doctor); Eula Guy
(Nurse); Juliet Ware (Viola); Rickey Newell (Blonde); Lorena Layson
(Brunette); Dennis O'Keefe (Chester Coots); Dick French, Jay Eaton
(Young Men); Robert Warwick (Civil Judge); Nora Lane (Posy Barton);
Pat Wing (Secretary); Monica Bannister (Tea Assistant); Leonard
Mudie (Steamship Ticket Clerk).

     This Michael Curtiz-directed yarn, with its emphasis on
comedy, is the first screen teaming of James Cagney and Bette
Davis. Time termed the result as "hard and amusing" while the
New York American thought the movie was "... fast and flip, rough
and rowdy, peppered with a running fire of slang-spiced dialogue. "
The New York Times lauded it as "a swift-paced comedy, " while
Variety said it "... is good fun and moves at a breakneck speed
throughout. " Not bad recommendations for an assembly-line feature.
     Opportunist con artist Jimmy Corrigan has a neat racket.
He locates the heirs to fortunes lying unclaimed by next of kin who
are not aware of their legacy. Joan Martin (Davis), although she

loves Jimmy, is aghast at his sharp business practices and goes to work for his competitor Charles Wallingham (Dinehart) who she believes, runs a legitimate operation. To seek his own brand of revenge, Jimmy not only restyles his wardrobe and manner to approximate that of dandy Wallingham, but sets out to expose the latter as the fraud he really is. His plan succeeds and he rewins the loyalty of Joan.

In this nifty entry, it seems that crime, of a sort, does pay.

JINSEI GEKIJO (THEATRE OF LIFE) (Shochiku, 1958) 166 min.

Producer, Yoshiji Mishima, Yoshiro Nomura; director, Tai Kato; story, Shiro Ozaki; screenplay, Nomura, Haruhiko Mimura, Kato; camera, Kejii Maruyama; editor, Shizu Ohsawa.

Muga Takawaki (Hyokici Aonari); Jiro Tamiya (Kira Tsune); Hideki Takahashi (Hisahakaku); Tetsuya Watari (Miyasawa); Hisaya Morishige (Hyotaro Aonari); Keiko Tsushima (Omine); Yoshiko Kayama (Osode); Mitsuko Baisho (Otoyo).

With the marked contrast of each culture's traditions and customs, it is always fascinating to observe how others deal with the gangster film genre. This yakuza (gangster) picture was directed by Tai Kato who has helmed over thirty-five features ranging from samurai to yakuza dramas.

Opening in 1916, this story traces a decade in the lives of fighting clans, focusing on two generations of a yakuza family as observed through the eyes of the father's underling (Takewaki). Its primary concern is to show how difficult it is for any member of the yakuza way of life to leave this ambiance and to start out a fresh. The gory shootouts led many film followers to compare this feature to the Sergio Leone Italian Westerns.

JOE MACBETH (Columbia, 1955) 90 min.

Producer, Mike Frankovich; associate producer, George Maynard; director, Ken Hughes; screenplay, Philip Yordan; art director, Alan Harris; music director, Richard Taylor; assistant director, Phil Shipway; wardrobe, Jean Fairlie; camera, Basil Emmett; editor, Peter Rolfe Johnson.

Paul Douglas (Joe Macbeth); Ruth Roman (Lily Macbeth); Bonar Colleano (Lennie); Gregoire Aslan (Duncan); Sidney James (Banky); Harry Green (Big Dutch); Teresa Thorne (Ruth); Minerva Pious (Rosie); Nicholas Stuart (Duffy); Robert Arden (Ross); Bill Nagy (Marty); Kay Callard (Ruth); Walter Crisham (Angus); Mark Baher (Benny); Alfred Mulock, George Margo (Assassins); Philip Vickers (Tommy).

Shakespeare has been dead for more than three centuries, but his enduring plays have been serving modern dramatists and scenarists well, even in the mid-twentieth century. It seems that, when in need of a plot, it is the practice to borrow from the Bard and deck out the result in modern dress.   Thus this British-made melo-drama takes <u>Macbeth</u> and transfers it into modern gangland terms. However, the result "... paraphrased the plot of the Scottish in-trigue into sophomoric precosity" (<u>New York Times</u>).   With a small budget and a short production schedule, the American co-stars rushed through their paces.

Through the urgings of his ruthless, ambitious wife (Roman), Joe Macbeth (Douglas) changes from a confident henchman to a brag-gart-bully.   Paralleling the Shakespearian drama, Joe Macbeth is led by a fortune teller into killing one gangland rival after another, as his wife pushes him on to larger goals.   Finally one mobster's son (Colleano) learns of his father's killer and seeks revenge.   The finale evolves into an underworld tug of war.

JOHNNY ALLEGRO   (Columbia, 1949)   81 min.

Producer, Irving Starr; director, Ted Tetzlaff; story, James Edward Grant; screenplay, Karen DeWolf, Guy Endore; art director, Perry Smith; set decorator, Frank Tuttle; music, George Duning; music director, Morris Stoloff; costumes, Jean Louis; assistant di-rector, Earl Bellamy; makeup, Irving Berns; sound, Jack Goodrich; camera, Joseph Biroc; editor, Jerome Thoms.

Nina Foch, George Macready and George Raft in <u>Johnny Allegro</u> (1949).

George Raft (Johnny Allegro); Nina Foch (Glenda Chapman); George Macready (Morgan Vallin); Will Geer (Shultzy); Gloria Henry (Addie); Ivan Triesault (Pelham Vetch); Harry Antrim (Pudgy); William "Bill" Phillips (Roy); Walter Rode (Grote); Thomas Browne Henry (Detective); Paul E. Burns (Gray); Matilda Caldwell (Servant); Joe Palma, Charles Hamilton, Brick Sullivan (Guards); George Offerman (Elevator Boy); Fred Sears (Desk Clerk); Eddie Acuff (Maintenance Man); Saul Gorss (Jeffrey); Cosmo Sardo (Waiter); Larry Thompson (Operator); Frank Dae (Dr. Jaynes); Mary Bear (Nurse); Gaylor "Steve" Pendleton (Young Man); Harlan Warde (Coast Guard Officer).

This film predates the themes of many Sixties' spy pictures in that it has as its hero a former hoodlum, now on the side of the law. In this case George Raft is cast as an ex-hood, now working for the Treasury Department. He is sent to a Caribbean Isle to get sufficient evidence against a neo-Fascist (Macready) who is trying to overthrow the U.S. government by flooding the market with bogus money. Once there, Johnny Allegro comes face to face with Morgan Vallin, a sadistic soul who disposes of his victims by hunting them down in the woods (as in The Most Dangerous Game). The self-sufficient Johnny also runs into an assortment of other troubles, including seductive Glenda Chapman (Foch).

Although the New York Herald-Tribune found this offering "run of the mill," star Raft had quite an athletic workout as the hero who engages in various fight scenes, sometimes using judo. The producers wisely filled the footage with action, good scenic shots, and plenty of focus on both Macready and Foch.

JOHNNY APOLLO (Twentieth Century-Fox, 1940) 93 min.

Producer, Darryl F. Zanuck; associate producer, Harry Joe Brown; director, Henry Hathaway; story, Samuel G. Engel, Hal Long; screenplay, Philip Dunne, Rowland Brown; songs, Frank Loesser and Lionel Newman; camera, Arthur Miller; editor, Robert Bischoff.

Tyrone Power (Bob Cain); Dorothy Lamour ("Lucky" Dubarry); Edward Arnold (Robert Cain, Sr.); Lloyd Nolan (Nickey Dwyer); Charles Grapewin (Judge Emmett F. Brennan); Lionel Atwill (Jim McLaughlin); Marc Lawrence (Bates); Jonathan Hale (Dr. Brown); Russell Hicks (District Attorney); Fuzzy Knight (Cellmate); Charles Lane (Assistant District Attorney); Selmer Jackson (Warden); Charles Trowbridge (Judge); George Irving (Mr. Ives); Eddie Marr, Anthony Caruso (Henchmen); Harry Rosenthal (Piano Player); William Pawley (Paul); Eric Wilton (Butler); Stanley Andrews (Welfare Secretary); Wally Albright (Office Boy); Charles Williams (Photographer); Bess Flowers (Secretary); Milburn Stone, Phil Tead, Charles Tannen (Reporters); Tom Dugan (Prisoner); Jim Pierce, Walter Miller, William Haade, Louis Jean Heydt, Stanley Blystone, James Flavin, Don Rowan, James Blain (Guards).

In this stoutly directed production, Tyrone Power, the darling

Charley Grapewin and Dorothy Lamour in Johnny Apollo (1940).

of 20th Century-Fox, was appropriately cast as a gentleman gangster.   He is the son of a Wall Street broker (Arnold) who is in the
process of being convicted of fraudulent manipulations of funds.
When the so-called friends of Robert Cain, Sr. turn their backs on
their one-time associate, Bob Cain turns his back on society and
his social class.   He finds more likable friends among the gangster
set, even becoming the right-hand man of hoodlum chief Nickey
Dwyer (Nolan).   Bob makes the near-fatal mistake of becoming infatuated with Nickey's empty-headed moll (Lamour) and she recipro-
cates his interest.   The situation changes again when Bob is sent to
prison and is reunited with his father.   Cain, Sr. risks his life to
save his son when the young man tries a prison break.   The harrow-
ing experience brings Bob back to his senses.
        While not an essentially important film, Johnny Apollo served
to perpetrate the myth (reality?) of the attraction between society and
gangland members.   The relatively slow-moving story was not helped
by the lack of general background music.
        On February 17, 1941, the drama was offered on "Lux Radio
Theatre," with Arnold and Lamour repeating their key roles, and
Burgess Meredith playing the title part.

JOHNNY EAGER   (MGM, 1942)   107 min.

Producer, John W. Considine, Jr.; director, Mervyn LeRoy; story, James Edward Grant; screenplay, John Lee Mahin, Grant; camera, Harold Rosson; editor, Albert Akst.

Robert Taylor (Johnny Eager); Lana Turner (Lisbeth Bard); Edward Arnold (John Benson Farrell); Van Heflin (Jeff Hartnett); Robert Sterling (Jimmy Lanthrop); Patricia Dane (Garnet); Glenda Farrell (Mae Blythe); Barry Nelson (Lew Rankin); Henry O'Neill (A. J. Verne); Charles Dingle (A. Frazier Marco); Cy Kendall (Bill Halligan); Don Costello (Billiken); Paul Stewart (Julio); Diana Lewis (Judy Sanford); Lou Lubin (Benjy); Connie Gilchrist (Peg Fowler); Robin Raymond (Matilda Fowler); Cliff Danielson (Floyd Markham); Leona Maricle (Miss Mines); Byron Shores (Joe Agridowski); Edward Earle, Alonzo Price (Men); Sheldon Bennett (Headwaiter); Art Miles (Lieutenant Allen); Alice Keating (Maid); Alex Pollard (Butler); Jack Carr (Cupid); Gohr Van Vleck (French); Joe Whitehead (Ruffing).

Delving into the psychology of the criminal was a frequent plot device in features of the Thirties and Forties (The Amazing Dr. Clitterhouse, Blind Alibi, etc.), but the theme did not become really popular until the Fifties. MGM in 1942, however, again tried the formula in Johnny Eager in which a sociology student (Turner) tries to find out what makes a gang leader (Taylor) tick. She ends up by falling in love with him.

The expensively mounted film reveals that Eager might not have been a criminal had it not been for his unfeeling childhood (the lad did not even have a dog!). As he matures, Johnny uses his raw luck to push onward and upward in the world. Sometimes he resorts to fraud and murder to accomplish his ends. Finally the D.A. tries to stop him, but Johnny frames the man's adopted daughter (Turner). Later he cannot convince the young lady that she is actually not guilty in the frame-up. Eager meets his "just" end in a torrent of bullets.

"At times Johnny Eager is a little too mawkish and sacrificial for either comfort or conviction. But, as gangster films go these days, it is hard-boiled and exciting enough" (Newsweek).

For once, insipid pretty boy Taylor performed well as the toughened heavy who does mind shooting other gangsters and burying them in cement. Interestingly enough, the Production Code demanded that this outlaw-hero be redeemed, morally that is, before he dies.

Van Heflin, as Johnny Eager's heavy drinking but brainy assistant, won an Oscar as Best Supporting Actor.

JOHNNY STOOL PIGEON   (Universal, 1949)   76 min.

Producer, Aaron Rosenberg; director, William Castle; story, Henry Jordan; screenplay, Robert L. Richards; art directors, Bernard Herzbrun, Emrich Nicholson; set decorators, Russell A. Gausman, John Austin; music-music director, Milton Schwartzwald; assistant director, Jesse Hibbs; makeup, Bud Westmore; costumes,

Dan Duryea and Howard Duff in <u>Johnny Stool Pigeon</u> (1949).

Orry-Kelly; sound, Leslie I. Carey, Richard DeWeese; special effects, David S. Horsley; camera, Maury Gertsman; editor, Ted J. Kent.

Howard Duff (George Morton); Shelley Winters (Terry); Dan Duryea (Johnny Evans); Tony Curtis (Joey Hyatt); John McIntire (Avery); Gar Moore (Sam Harrison); Leif Erickson (Pringle); Barry Kelley (McCandles); Hugh Reilly (Charlie); Wally Maher (Benson); Nacho Galindo (Martinez); Gregg Barton (Treasury Man); Charles Drake (Hotel Clerk); Duke York (Body Guard); William H. McLean (Taxi Driver); Don Hayden (Whelan); Watson Downs (Watchman); Al Ferguson, Colin Kenny (Porters); Harry H. Evans (Federal Judge); Robert Kimball (Bartender).

Director William Castle usually had the knack of taking a low budget property and transforming it into an interesting, exciting, profitable venture. <u>Johnny Stool Pigeon</u> is a good example of his success.

In simplistic terms the film told of narcotics agents out to smash a dope ring and of an agent (Duff) who works out a deal with an imprisoned hoodlum (Duryea) whose wife was a victim of the dope market. With Johnny Evans' help, Morton infiltrates the gang and travels with them to San Francisco, Vancouver, Tucson, and Mexico.

They all return to Tucson where the gang and the dope cache are
corraled. Feisty Shelley Winters stormed on camera as Terry,
the moll who comes to Morton's aid at the appropriate right moment.
     Said the New York Times, "Despite a serious attempt at au-
thenticity it is merely a brisk cops-and-smugglers melodrama, which
follows an obvious pattern and is fairly strong on suspense but short
on originality and impressive histrionics. "

THE JOKER IS WILD (Paramount, 1957) 123 min.

     Producer, Samuel J. Briskin; director, Charles Vidor; based
on the book by Art Cohn; screenplay, Oscar Saul; music-music director, Walter Scharf; orchestrators, Leo Shuken, Jack Hayes; or-
chestral arranger, Nelson Riddle; specialty songs, parodies, Harry
Harris; choreography, Josephine Earl; art directors, Hal Pereira,
Roland Anderson; set decorators, Sam Comer, Grace Gregory; costumes, Edith Head; makeup, Wally Westmore; assistant director,
C. C. Coleman, Jr., sound, Harold Lewis, Charles Grenzbach; spe-
cial camera effects, John P. Fulton; camera, Daniel L. Fapp; edi-
tor, Everett Douglas; songs, James Van Heusen and Sammy Cahn;
Jimmy Johnson and Henry Creamer; Fred Fisher; Arthur Freed,
Gus Arnheim, and Abe Lyman.
     Frank Sinatra (Joe E. Lewis); Mitzi Gaynor (Martha Stewart);
Jeanne Crain (Letty Page); Eddie Albert (Austin Mack); Beverly Gar-
land (Cassie Mack); Jackie Coogan (Swifty Morgan); Barry Kelley
(Captain Hugh McCarthy); Ted De Corsia (Georgie Parker); Leonard
Graves (Tim Coogan); Valerie Allen (Flora); Hank Henry (Burlesque
Comedian); Harold Huber (Harry Bliss); Ned Glass (Johnson); Ned
Wever (Dr. Pierson); Walter Woolf King (Mr. Page); John Harding
(Allen); Sid Melton (Runner); Wally Brown, Don Beddoe, Mary Treen
(Hecklers); Sophie Tucker (Herself); Maurice Hart (Squawk Box Voice);
Paul Gary, Billy Snyder, Joseph Dante, Ralph Montgomery (Men in
Hotel Suite); Bill Hickman, Paul T. Salata (Mugs); Frank Mills
(Florist Truck Driver); Eric Alden (Doorman at Copacabana); Eric
Wilton (Butler); Ruby Fleming (Girl); Mabel Rea (Chorus Girl).
     A. k. a. All the Way.

     This film is a colorful but rather empty biography picture of
the life of nightclub comic, Joe E. Lewis (Sinatra). It offers a
rather tinseled picture of the Roaring Twenties when Lewis worked
as a club singer. The crooner, however, lost his career when
hoodlums damaged his throat and the picture follows his return to
show business as a nightclub comic who eventually becomes legendary. Also interlaced into the proceedings are the three women
(Garland, Gaynor and Crain) in his life.
     The Joker Is Wild benefited from good dialog, a fitting re-
creation of the Twenties and Thirties, and a flinty performance
from cocky Sinatra. Strangely, the black-and-white feature only did
moderate box-office business until its theme song, "All the Way, "
won an Academy Award. Thereafter the movie was reissued under
the song's title and turned a tidy profit.

Jackie Coogan and Frank Sinatra in <u>The Joker Is Wild</u> (1957).

KEY LARGO   (Warner Bros. , 1948)   101 min.

     Producer, Jerry Wald; director, John Huston; based on the play by Maxwell Anderson; screenplay, Richard Brooks; art director, Leo K. Kuter; set decorator, Fred M. MacLean; music, Max Steiner; orchestrator, Murray Cutter; song, Ralph Rainger and Howard Dietz; assistant director, Art Lueker; sound, Dolph Thomas; special effects, William McGann, Robert Burks; camera, Karl Freund; editor, Rudi Fehr.

     Humphrey Bogart (Frank McCloud); Edward G. Robinson (Johnny Rocco [Howard Brown]); Lauren Bacall (Nora Temple); Lionel Barrymore (James Temple); Claire Trevor (Gaye Dawn [Maggie Mooney]); Thomas Gomez (Curley [Richard Hoff]); Harry Lewis (Toots [Ed Bass]); John Rodney (Deputy Clyde Sawyer); Marc Lawrence (Ziggy); Dan Seymour (Angel Garcia); Monte Blue (Sheriff Ben Wade); Jay Silverheels (John Osceola); Rodric Redwing (Tom Osceola); William Haade (Ralph Feeney); Joe P. Smith (Bus Driver); Alberto Morin (Skipper); Pat Flaherty, Jerry Jerome, John Phillips, Lute Crockett (Ziggy's Henchmen); Felipa Gomez (Old Indian Woman).

     Set off the coast of Florida, this reworking of Maxwell Anderson's stage play became a fitting vehicle to reteam the husband-and-wife team of Humphrey Bogart and Lauren Bacall, as well as

providing an acting ground for Edward G. Robinson, Lionel Barrymore (on loan from MGM) and assorted others, including poignant
Claire Trevor.

James Temple (Barrymore) and his widowed daughter-in-law
(Bacall) run the island's hotel. They are visited by her late husband's wartime friend, Frank McCloud (Bogart). Upon arrival the
pacifist, alienated Frank finds the hotel inhabited by a deported
racketeer (Robinson) and his gang of stooges. Temple and Nora
ask Frank to stay. Meanwhile another hoodlum is scheduled to arrive with a bundle of counterfeit money. When a deputy is murdered by the hoodlums, local Indians are blamed. In order to get
the racketeer and his cohorts off the island, Frank agrees to pilot
the hoods to Cuba and on the trip he engages in a shootout with
Rocco and his underlings. The victorious Frank returns to the island and to the waiting Nora.

The film was reminiscent of The Petrified Forest (1936),
q. v. , but Variety found it to be ". . . too full of words and highly
cross-purpose implications to give the action full chance. " However,
the New York Herald-Tribune, more in accord with the actuality,
found it to be ". . . a bowstring-tight humdinger of movie make-believe. "

Usually soundstage filming gave a restrictive quality to most
productions set in the outdoors, but in the case of Key Largo, the
constructed hotel sets and the dockside all benefited from the fabricated set design. These sets gave the picture the proper claustrophobic ambience, and created a unity among the diverse players.

Individual scenes within Key Largo are vividly memorable.
There is the bit where Robinson's Johnny Rocco, one of the old-
style gangster big shots, comments on how he "hopes" prohibition
will come back "in a coupla years. " There is the sequence where
he holds a drink as bait in front of his ex-mistress (Trevor), now
a lush, as he makes her sing "Moanin' Low. " There is a fascinating moment where sparkling-eyed Johnny Rocco whispers obsceni-
ties into Nora's ear, while Frank stands by impotently. Such celluloid moments give this study of antiquated gangland leaders much
more urgency and conviction than is to be found in most other films
about gangsters.

KID GALAHAD (Warner Bros. , 1937) 101 min.

Associate producer, Samuel Bischoff; director, Michael Curtiz; based on the novel by Francis Wallace; screenplay, Seton I.
Miller; assistant director, Jack Sullivan; dialog director, Irving
Rapper; art director, Carl Jules Weyl; music, Heinz Roemheld,
Max Steiner; orchestrator, Hugo Friedhofer; song, M. K. Jerome
and Jack Scholl; gowns, Orry-Kelly; sound, Charles Lang; special
effects, James Gibbons, Edwin B. DuPar; camera, Tony Gaudio;
editor, George Amy.

Edward G. Robinson (Nick Donati); Bette Davis (Louise "Fluff"
Phillips); Humphrey Bogart (Turkey Morgan); Wayne Morris (Ward
Guisenberry [Kid Galahad]); Jane Bryan (Marie Donati); Ben Welden
(Buzz Stevens); Harry Carey (Silver Jackson); William Haade (Chuck
McGraw); Joe Cunningham (Joe Taylor); Soledad Jimenez (Mrs.

Donati); Veda Ann Borg (The Redhead); Harland Tucker (Gunman);
Frank Faylen (Barney); Bob Nestell (Tim O'Brian); George Blake
(Referee); George Humbert (Barber); Mary Doran (Operator); Billy
Wayne (Bell Captain); Virginia Dabney (Girl at Party); Joyce Compton (Drunken Girl on Phone); Emmett Vogan (Ring Announcer);
Carlyle Moore, Jr. (Bellhop); Horace McMahon, Milton Kibbee,
Max Hoffman, Jr., Harry Harvey, Edward Price, Billy Arnold (Reporters); L Stanford Jolley (Ringsider); Kenneth Harlan, Eddie
Fetherstone (Reporters at Ring); John Ridgley (Photographer); John
Shelton (Reporter at Press Conference); Don DeFore (Ringsider-Extra).
        TV title: Battling Bellhop.

KID GALAHAD   (United Artists, 1962)   C-95 min.

        Producer, David Weisbart; director, Phil Karlson; story,
Francis Wallace; screenplay, William Fay; art director, Cary Odell;
set decorator, Edward G. Boyle; wardrobe, Bert Henrikson, Irene
Caine; makeup, Lynn Reynolds; assistant director, Jerome M. Siegel; music, Jeff Alexander; songs, Ruth Batchelor and Bob Roberts;
Fred Wise and Ben Wiseman; Sherman Edwards and Hal David, Dee
Fuller, Fred Wise, and Wiseman; Batchelor and Sharon Silbert;
sound, Lambert Day; special effects, Milt Rice; camera, Burnett
Guffey; editor, Stuart Gilmore.
        Elvis Presley (Walter Gulick); Gig Young (Willy Grogan);
Lola Albright (Dolly Fletcher); Joan Blackman (Rose Grogan);
Charles Bronson (Lew Nyack); Ned Glass (Lieberman); Robert Emhardt (Maynard); David Lewis (Otto Danzig); Michael Dante (Joie
Shakes); Judson Pratt (Zimmerman); George Mitchell (Sperling);
Richard Devon (Marvin); Jeffrey Morris (Ralphie); Liam Redmond
(Father Higgins).

        The fight game has always been tinged with underworld activity and Kid Galahad convincingly outlined the development of a
fighter from pugnacious bellhop to top contender. Along the way,
he experiences many hard knocks and is surrounded by corruption.
        When Ward Guisenberry (Morris) Kayos the world champion
boxer (Haade) in a hotel fracas, down-and-out fight manager Nick
Donati is convinced he has a new champion. Nick's mistress (Davis) dubs the boy "Kid Galahad" and the name sticks. During his
training and climb in the fight world, the Kid meets Nick's young
sister (Bryan) and they quickly fall in love. Fluff also is romantically attracted to the Kid. However, when Nick learns of both
girls' affection for the Kid he decides to get even with his client.
He signs the Kid to fight the champion, although Ward is too green
for a title shot. Nick also arranges a fix with gangster-manager
Turkey Morgan (Bogart). During the important bout, the Kid takes
a terrific beating until Nick, persuaded by the two girls, softens
and gives the Kid the proper instructions and faith by which he can
win the match. Double-crossed Turkey thereafter wants revenge.
In an ensuing gun battle, both Nick and Turkey die. Although he
has won the precious boxing title, the Kid vacates the throne to

wed Marie.

The critics were rightly enthusiastic about this hard-hitting film. The New York Times judged it "... a good little picture, lively and positively echoing...." Film Daily insisted that it is "... easily one of the best fight pictures ever screened"; and the New York Journal-American thought the movie offered Robinson his "best role since Little Caesar."

Wayne Morris later starred in a "B" follow-up, The Kid Comes Back (1938) and the studio remade the original film with a circus background as The Wagons Roll at Night (1941).

In general, the less said about Elvis Presley's run of feature films the better. However, the singer did make movies in a number of genres, including the gangster motif. This 1963 remake of the 1930s' original was souped up with music, while the gangster element was subjugated to rhythm and some ring action. As Bosley Crowther (New York Times) confessed, "for a film about a singing prize fighter (which is silly enough), it will do."

Amateur boxer Walter Gulick (Presley) is mercilessly exploited by Willy Grogan (Young), a Catskills hotel owner who prefers drink to his fighter's welfare. Also in the cast were Lola Albright as Grogan's unhappy girl; Joan Blackman as Rose, who falls for Walter; and Charles Bronson as Walter's well-muscled trainer.

THE KILLERS (Universal, 1946) 105 min.

Producer, Mark Hellinger; director, Robert Siodmak; based on the story by Ernest Hemingway; screenplay, Anthony Veiller; art directors, Jack Otterson, Martin Obzina; set decorators, Russell A. Gausman, E. R. Robinson; music, Miklos Rosza; assistant director, Melville Shyer; sound, Bernard B. Brown, William Hedgcock; special camera, D. S. Horsley; camera, Woody Bredell; editor, Arthur Hilton.

Edmond O'Brien (Riordan); Ave Gardner (Kitty Collins); Burt Lancaster (Swede); Albert Dekker (Colfax); Sam Levene (Lubinsky); John Miljan (Jake); Virginia Christine (Lilly); Vince Barnett (Charleston); Charles D. Brown (Packy); Donald MacBride (Kenyon); Phil Brown (Nick); Charles McGraw (Al); William Conrad (Max); Queenie Smith (Queenie); Garry Owen (Joe); Harry Hayden (George); Bill Walker (Sam); Jack Lambert (Dum Dum); Jeff Corey (Blinky); Wally Scott (Charlie); Gabrielle Windsor (Ginny); Rex Dale (Man); Harry Brown (Paymaster); Beatrice Roberts (Nurse); Howard Freeman (Police Chief); John Berkes (Plunther); John Sheehan (Doctor); Al Hill (Customer); Noel Cravat (Lou Tingle); Reverend Neal Dodd (Minister); Vera Lewis (Mrs. Hirsch); Wally Ross (Bartender); Mike Donovan (Timekeeper).

THE KILLERS (Universal, 1964) C-93 min.

Producer-director, Donald Siegel; based on the story by Ernest Hemingway; screenplay, Gene L. Coon; art directors, Frank

John Cassavetes in The Killers (1964).

Arrigo, George Chan; set decorators, John McCarthy, James S.
Redd; music, Johnny Williams; music supervisor, Stanley Wilson;
song, Henry Mancini and Don Raye; technical adviser, Hall Brock;
sound, David H. Moriarty; camera, Richard L. Rawlings; editor,
Richard Belding.
      Lee Marvin (Charlie); Angie Dickinson (Sheila Farr); John
Cassavetes (Johnny North); Ronald Reagan (Browning); Clu Gulager
(Lee); Claude Akins (Earl Sylvester); Norman Fell (Mickey); Virginia
Christine (Miss Watson); Don Haggerty (Mail Truck Driver); Robert
Phillips (George); Kathleen O'Malley (Receptionist); Ted Jacques
(Gym Assistant); Irvin Mosley (Mail Truck Guard); Jimmy Joyce
(Salesman); Seymour Cassel (Desk Clerk).

      Broadway columnist Mark Hellinger made his big league
producing debut in this film version of Ernest Hemingway's story.
In the fleshed-out form it bore little relation to the literary original, but critic James Agee said, "[such] energy combined with attention to form and detail doesn't turn up every day; neither does
good entertainment."
      Told via flashbacks, this sizzling, violent story tells of un-
derworld hoodlums and the fight racket.   Former fighter Swede

(Lancaster) has been double-crossed by hoodlums and his no-good girl (Gardner). The story is focused around two hired assassins (McGraw and Conrad) who await their victim (Lancaster) in a lunch-room-bar, while the marked man lies in bed and relives the situa-tions which led up to his now precarious spot.

Among the cast enhancing the production were Lancaster as the youngish, but worn-out boxer, Gardner as a Hollywood version of a corrupted/corruptible siren, Edmond O'Brien as a tight-lipped insurance investigator, Sam Levene as a cop, and Albert Dekker as a slimey thug.

"... It makes a diverting picture--diverting, that is, if you enjoy the unraveling of crime enigmas involving pernicious folks" (New York Times). Variety was even more enthusiastic: "Seldom does a melodrama consistently maintain the high tension that dis-tinguishes this one."

If the storyline was good enough in 1946, it was still service-able in 1964. Universal made the remake as a telefeature, but the resultant footage proved too violent for the small screen and its initial showings were in movie theatres. This new version was produced and directed by Don Siegel, the craftsman Hellinger had wanted to handle the 1946 edition.

The plotline was updated; now the plot revolves around auto racing in California and a million dollar post office truck robbery. How did the critics react to this unsubtle follow-up? It is "... 93 minutes of sock-em-in-the-mouth rough stuff that beats the original story to a bloody pulp" (Newsweek).

The Killers, 1964-type, finds Johnny North (Cassavetes), the ex-auto racing driver, now a teacher in a school for the blind. Charlie (Marvin) and Lee (Gulager) are on their way to kill him, and shoot a blind secretary who crosses their path. Johnny got in-to this predicament through a woman, no less. Leggy Sheila Farr (Dickinson) had persuaded him to participate in a mail truck rob-bery devised by businessman Browning (Reagan). In a double-cross, Browning and Sheila plan to keep the loot and let the rest of the gang believe Johnny is at fault. When North discovers the ploy, he traces Browning and Sheila to a motel, where Browning shoots him. Barely surviving, and with little interest left in life, Johnny begins teaching and waits for the time when he will be killed. Before "The End" flashes on the screen, there is enough gunplay to keep any action fan happy, as members of the original gang kill each other one by one.

As Stuart M. Kaminsky said in retrospect in his Don Siegel: Director (1974), "The Killers is Siegel at his best, creating a chill-ing, urban world in which anyone could find himself the next victim of sudden violence."

THE KILLING (United Artists, 1956) 83 min.

Producer, James B. Harris; director, Stanley Kubrick; based on the novel Clean Break by Lionel White; screenplay, Kubrick; ad-ditional dialog, Jim Thompson; art director, Ruth Sobotka Kubrick;

camera, Lucien Ballard; editor, Betty Steinberg.
      Sterling Hayden (Johnny Clay); Coleen Gray (Fay); Vince Ed-
wards (Bal Cannon); Jay C. Flippen (Marvin Unger); Marie Windsor
(Sherry Peatty); Ted De Corsia (Randy Kennan); Elisha Cook, Jr.
(George Peatty); Joe Sawyer (Mike O'Reilly); Tim Carey (Nikki
Arane); Jay Adler (Leo); Joseph Turkel (Tiny); Maurice Oboukhoff
(Kola Kwarian); James Edwards (Black Man).

      This was director Stanley Kubrick's first important feature,
one which he co-scripted. It dealt with a gang planning a $2 mil-
lion robbery during a crucial horse race. Like most heist films
it closely followed the preparations for the job as well as highlight-
ing some of the motivations of those principally involved. The difference between this "engrossing little adventure" (New York Times)
and other such films was that Kubrick emphasized an arty approach
to the story rather than a matter-of-fact manner. (Like Citizen
Kane, the film showed the same events through different characters'
viewpoints.)
      With on-location shooting at Bay Meadows, the film was pho-
tographically satisfying. It contained several fascinating subplots
and performances, especially Sterling Hayden as the ex-con planning
the caper. Among the cast were Timothy Carey as a cool killer,
and pint-sized Elisha Cook, Jr. as a race-track cashier involved in
the lawlessness in order to buy his mercenary wife's (Marie Windsor) attention. As is typical with Cook's screen roles, his character's fate is doomed without his being aware of the dire consequen-
ces. Joe Sawyer as the track bartender, Jay C. Flippen as a reformed drunk, and Ted De Corsia as a racketeering cop added
dimension to the proceedings.
      As in many robbery stories, the ending has an ironic twist.
One often wonders whether this gimmick is to appease the "crime
does not pay" censors, or to provide the plotline with an easy out.
In this case, it blended in well with the prior happenings. As
Variety opined of The Killing, it is done in a "... tense and suspenseful vein which carries through to an unexpected and ironic windup. "

KING OF ALCATRAZ (Paramount, 1938) 56 min.

      Associate producer, William C. Thomas; director, Robert Florey;
story-screenplay, Irving Reis; art directors, Hans Dreier, Earl Hedrick;
music, Boris Morros; camera, Harry Fischbeck; editor, Eda Warren.
      Gail Patrick (Dale Borden); Lloyd Nolan (Raymond Grayson);
Harry Carey (Captain Glennan); J. Carrol Naish (Steve Murkil);
Robert Preston (Robert MacArthur); Anthony Quinn (Lou Gedney);
Dennis Morgan (First Mate Rogers); Virginia Dabney (Bonnie Lar-
kin); Nora Cecil (Nora Kane); Emory Parnell (Olaf); Dorothy Howe
(Dixie); John Hart, Phillip Warren (Radio Operators); Porter Hall
(Matthew Talbot); Richard Denning (Harry Vay); Tom Tyler (Gus
Banshek); Konstantin Shayne (Murok); Harry Worth (Pietr Mozda);
Edward Marr (Dave Carter); Clay Clement (Fred Cateny); Monte
Blue (Officer); Gustav von Seyffertitz (Bill Lustig); Paul Fix ("Nails"
Miller); Eddie Acuff (Steward); Buddy Roosevelt (Purser); Charles
McAvoy (Quartermaster); Ruth Rogers (Girl).

Despite its misleading title, this nifty little "B" opus is still exceedingly popular on the late, late show. Due to its solid story-line, compact direction, and a cast of outstanding personality play-ers (from the leads to bit parts), the picture is a zinger. Film buffs often view it today simply to pick out all the two dozen famil-iar faces in its line-up.

Steve Murkil (Naish) and ten other hoodlums make a getaway on a cruise freighter, but one of the men becomes ill and requires surgery. The boat's nurse (Patrick) performs the operation via in-structions given to her on a ship-to-ship wireless. The captivating finale has the nominal heroes being defeated in battle by the gang-sters. But the latter are nonetheless captured through a quirk of fate.

KING OF GAMBLERS (Paramount, 1937) 79 min.

Director, Robert Florey; story, Tiffany Thayer; screenplay, Doris Anderson; art directors, Hans Dreier, Robert Odell; music director, Boris Morros; songs, Ralph Rainger, Richard A. Whiting and Leo Robin; Burton Lane and Ralph Freed; camera, Harry Fisch-beck; editor, Harvey Johnstone.

Claire Trevor (Dixie); Lloyd Nolan (Jim); Akim Tamiroff (Steve Kalkas); Larry "Buster" Crabbe (Eddie); Helen Burgess (Jackie Nolan); Porter Hall (George Kramer); Harvey Stephens (J. G.

Akim Tamiroff in <u>King of Gamblers</u> (1937).

Temple); Barlowe Borland (Mr. Parker); Purnell Pratt (Strohm); Colin Tapley (Joe); Paul Fix (Charlie); Cecil Cunningham (Big Edna); Robert Gleckler (Ed Murkil); Nick Lukats (Taxi Driver); Fay Holden (Nurse); John Patterson (Freddie); Evelyn Brent (Cora); Estelle Etterre (Laura); Priscilla Lawson (Grace); Louise Brooks (Joyce Beaton); Harry Worth (Chris); Connie Tom (Tika); Richard Terry (Solly); Alphonse Martell (Headwaiter); Natalie Moorhead (Woman at Table); Ethel Clayton, Gloria Williams (Women); Gertrude Messinger (Telephone Operator); Frank Puglia (Barber); Russell Hicks (Man at Temple's Table).
    TV title: Czar of the Slot Machines.

    Prolific Robert Florey directed this production for the Paramount economy division. This was one of the series of Akim Tamiroff gangster pictures turned out for the studio. However, since the Doris Anderson screenplay made little sense, the inventive director was forced to use various mechanical tricks to hold the footage into some semblance of entertainment. The result was a visually satisfying but heavily contrived picture.
    Slick murderer Steve Kalkas is involved with a club singer (Trevor), as well as being mixed up in her sister's (Burgess) death. He finds he must compete with newspaper reporter Jim (Nolan) who really cares for the thrush.

KING OF THE ROARING TWENTIES: The Story of Arnold Rothstein (Allied Artists, 1961) 106 min.

    Producers, Samuel Bischoff, David Diamond; director, Joseph M. Newman; based on the book The Big Bankroll by Leo Katcher; screenplay, Jo Swerling; music-music conductor, Franz Waxman; art director, David Milton; set decorator, Joseph Kish; assistant director, Lindsley Parsons, Jr.; wardrobe, Roger Weinberg, Norah Sharpe; makeup, Allan Snyder; sound, Charles Schelling, Marty Greco, Ralph Butler; special effects, Milt Olsen; camera, Carl Guthrie; editor, George White.
    David Janssen (Arnold Rothstein); Dianne Foster (Carolyn Green); Mickey Rooney (Johnny Burke); Jack Carson ("Big Tim" O'Brien); Diana Dors (Madge); Dan O'Herlihy (Phil Butler); Mickey Shaughnessy (Jim Kelly); Keenan Wynn (Tom Fowler); Joseph Schildkraut (Abraham Rothstein); William Demarest (Hecht); Murvyn Vye (Williams); Regis Toomey (Bill Baird); Robert Ellenstein (Lenny); Teri Janssen (Joanie); Jim Baird (Arnold as a Boy).
    British title: The Big Bankroll.

    Considering that this film came from lower case Allied Artists, it was a very slick production and featured a powerhouse cast. It was one more production in the series of celluloid gangland biographies inspired by "The Untouchables" success on television.
    The life of Arnold Rothstein (1882-1928) was so filled with amazing complexities and intriguing aspects that no one film seemed able to do justice to his unique existence. Although he is brought up in good, moral surroundings, Rothstein (Janssen) seems fated for

a life of lawlessness. A mathematical whiz with a fascination for gambling, he is always seeking the sure thing, the easy dollar. With a minimum of efforts, he contrives to become the gambling czar of the lower East Side. No one and nothing is sacred in his rise, including actress Carolyn Green (Foster), whom he weds but fails to retain. His duplicity and double dealings eventually lead to his downfall; he is gunned down in a hotel room as he is playing poker. Ironically, his dying hand was a royal flush!

There were two camps of critical thought on this picture. "Choppy and superficial," said Variety, while Time praised it as "... a B that doesn't stumble--thanks to a tight script, sharp direction, and neat performances." Particularly praised for his screen work here was pint-sized Mickey Rooney as Johnny Burke, Rothstein's childhood pal. He is the one who supplies the gambler with information on Phil Butler (O'Herlihy), Rothstein's arch enemy. For his efforts, Burke is gunned down by paid assassins.

KING OF THE UNDERWORLD (Warner Bros., 1939) 69 min.

Associate producer, Bryan Foy; director, Lewis Seiler; based on the story Dr. Socrates by W. R. Burnett; screenplay, George Bricker, Vincent Sherman; music, Heinz Roemheld; dialog director, Sherman; assistant director, Frank Heath; art director, Charles Novi; gowns, Orry-Kelly; technical adviser, Dr. Leo Schulman; sound, Everett A. Brown; camera, Sid Hickox; editor, Frank Dewar.

Humphrey Bogart (Joe Gurney); Kay Francis (Carole Nelson); James Stephenson (Bill Forrest); John Eldredge (Niles Nelson); Jessie Busley (Aunt Margaret); Arthur Aylesworth (Dr. Sanders); Raymond Brown (Sheriff); Harland Tucker (Mr. Ames); Ralph Remley (Mr. Roberts); Charles Foy (Eddie); Murray Alper (Mugsy); Joe Devlin (Porky); Elliott Sullivan (Butch); Alan Davis (Slick); John Harmon (Slats); Ed Stanley (Dr. Jacobs); Richard Bond (Interne); Pierre Watkin (District Attorney); John Ridgely (Jerry the Interne); Charles Trowbridge (Dr. Ryan); Herbert Heywood (Clem); Paul MacWilliams (Anaesthetist); Richard Quine (Student); Ralph Dunn (Fat Policeman); Janet Shaw, Ann Robinson (Nurses); Edgar Dearing (Detective); Carl Stockdale, Nat Carr, Clem Bevans (Villagers); Tom Wilson, Glen Cavender (Deputies); Jimmy O'Gatty, Frank Bruno, Paul Panzer, Cliff Saum, Doc Stone (Gangsters); Jack Mower, John Harron (G-Men --Assistants to Ames).

Warner Bros.'s former glamour queen Kay Francis was near the end of her studio run when this feature was made, shelved, and later released. By the time of its issuance Humphrey Bogart was a "hot" property by anyone's standards and he received top billing in this revamping of Dr. Socrates (1935), q.v., an earlier Paul Muni movie.

This alleged remake had a distaff physician (Francis) out for revenge against a hood (Bogart) who had manipulated her husband (Eldredge) into his gang after he aided an injured gang member. The husband was killed when police raided the gang headquarters. Carole

Nelson helps a writer (Stephenson) infiltrate the gang. Later, to save herself and Bill Forrest, Carole is forced to treat Joe Gurney who had been injured during a jailbreak. As part of her revenge scheme, she infects his wounds and blinds him with an eyedrop solution. (What would the AMA's ethics committee think of this?) In the climax, a blinded, dying Joe chases the couple through the gang's hideout, but he is gunned down by the on-the-spot police.

After viewing this film, Noël Coward is supposed to have asked Bogart, "Have you and Jack Warner no shame?"

KISS OF DEATH (Twentieth Century-Fox, 1947) 98 min.

Producer, Fred Kohlmar; director, Henry Hathaway; story, Eleazar Lipsky; screenplay, Ben Hecht, Charles Lederer; art directors, Lyle Wheeler, Leland Fuller; set decorator, Thomas Little; music, David Buttolph; music arranger-orchestrator, Earle Hagen; assistant director, Abe Steinberg; sound, W. D. Flick, Roger Heman; camera, Norbert Brodine; editor, J. Watson Webb, Jr.

Victor Mature (Nick Bianco); Brian Donlevy (D'Angelo); Colleen Gray (Nettie); Richard Widmark (Tom Udo); Taylor Holmes (Earl Howser); Howard Smith (Warden); Karl Malden (Sergeant William Cullen); Anthony Ross (Williams); Mildred Dunnock (Ma Rizzo); Millard Mitchell (Max Schulte); Temple Texas (Blondie); J. Scott Smart (Skeets); Wendell Phillips (Pep Mangone); Lew Herbert, Harry Kadison (Policemen); John Kullers (Prisoner); Victor Thorley (Sing Sing Guard); Iris Mann (Congetta at Age Seven); Marilee Grassini (Rosaria at Age Six); Norman McKay (Captain Dolan); Harry Cooke (Taxi Driver); Robert Karnes (Hoodlum); Harry Carter, Robert Adler (Detectives); Harold Crane (Mr. Morgemann); Greg Martell (Turnkey); Tito Vuolo (Luigi); Mary Morrison (Mother Superior); Eva Condon (Sister); Eda Heinemann (Mrs. Keller).

With its on-location filming in New York City, excellent camerawork by Norbert Brodine, and top flight direction by Henry Hathaway from the Ben Hecht-Charles Lederer scenario, this feature has since become a classic of its kind.

In what the New York Times labeled "a pip of melodrama ... most satisfying entertainment," Victor Mature appeared as Nick Bianco, a complete malfeasant. His father had been killed in a hold-up and Nick himself went to prison at an early age for petty thievery. After release, he attempts to go straight, marries, and has two children. But after his wife's untimely death, he returns to a life of crime to support his children. Wanting to get out of jail again, he turns informant on his own gang. Once released, he now lives in mortal fear of the men's retribution.

Kiss of Death contained a well-modulated performance by beefcake king Mature, and other good ones by Colleen Gray as the gal who helps him, and by Brian Donlevy as the resolute district attorney. However, it was Richard Widmark, in his screen debut, who won most notice. He played the psychopathic, vicious punk gang leader who vows revenge. Widmark's hyena-style laughter became his trademark and stepping-stone to fame.

In 1958 a loose remake of the film, The Fiend Who Walked the West, was issued, but proved to be minor league stuff.

KISS TOMORROW GOODBYE (Warner Bros. , 1950) 102 min.

Producer, William Cagney; director, Gordon Douglas; based on the novel by Horace McCoy; screenplay, Harry Brown; art director, Wiard Ihnen; set decorator, Joe Kish; music, Carmen Dragon; assistant director, William Kissell; sound, William Lynch; camera, Peverell Marley; editors, Truman K. Wood, Walter Hannemann.

James Cagney (Ralph Cotter); Barbara Payton (Holiday Carleton); Helena Carter (Margaret Dobson); Ward Bond (Inspector Weber); Luther Adler (Cherokee Mandon); Barton MacLane (Reece); Steve Brodie (Jinx Raynor); Rhys Williams (Vic Mason); Herbert Heyes (Ezra Dobson); John Litel (Chief of Police Tolgate); William Frawley (Byers); Robert Karnes (Gray); Kenneth Tobey (Fowler); Dan Riss (District Attorney); Frank Reicher (Doc Green); John Halloran (Cobbett); Neville Brand (Carleton); George Spaulding (Judge); Mark Strong (Bailiff); Jack Gargan (Clerk of Court); Frank Marlowe (Joe the Milkman); Ann Tyrrell (Miss Staines); Clark Howat (Interne); John Day, William Murphy (Motorcycle Cops); Charles Meredith (Mr. Golightly); Gordon Richards (Butler); Frank Wilcox (Doctor); William Cagney (Ralph's Brother).

Following the fine reception to White Heat (1949), q. v. , Warners cast James Cagney in Kiss Tomorrow Goodbye, which was produced by his actor brother, William. The result was an overly violent feature which was barred from showings in the state of Ohio.

Brutal killer Ralph Cotter (Cagney) breaks out of jail, kills his ex-partner (Brand) and forcefully takes the man's wife (Payton). Later he stages a market robbery. Two crooked cops try to blackmail him, but he frames them with the use of a hidden tape recorder (the technology age, so much a part of serials, was catching up with the world of features). At the finale, however, the law catches up with the insane killer.

"A sorry throwback, Kiss Tomorrow Goodbye is a stone-age gangster film with none of the psychological trimmings" (Andrew Bergman, James Cagney, (1973).

LADIES LOVE BRUTES (Paramount, 1930) 83 min.

Director, Rowland V. Lee; based on the play Pardon My Glove by Zoë Akins; adaptors-dialog, Waldemar Young, Herman J. Mankiewicz; sound, J. A. Goodrich; camera, Harry Fischbeck; editor, Eda Warren.

George Bancroft (Joe Froziati); Mary Astor (Mimi Howell); Fredric March (Dwight Howell); Margaret Quimby (Lucille Gates); Stanley Fields (Mike Mendino); Ben Hendricks, Jr. (Slattery); Lawford Davidson (George Wyndham); Ferike Boros (Mrs. Forziati); David Durand (Joey Forziati); Freddie Burke Frederick (Jackie Howell); Paul Fix (Slip); Claude Allister (The Tailor); Craufurd Kent, E. H. Calvert (Committeemen); Henry Armetta (Headwaiter).

Mary Astor, George Bancroft, Stanley Fields, Ben Hendricks, Jr.
and Henry Armetta in Ladies Love Brutes (1930).

From Zöe Akins' play, this minor Paramount picture served
as a showcase for George Bancroft, who had been enjoying a vogue
as a rough, tough gangster since working with Josef von Sternberg
in the Twenties. Here he played a shady building contractor in love
with a married society girl (Astor) whose marriage to Dwight Howell
(March) is on the rocks. Much footage is devoted to Joe Froziati's
humorous attempts to dandify himself in order to win Mimi's heart.
She finally informs him that she cannot marry beneath her station.
After all, she must think of her child's future.

For revenge, Joe plans to kidnap the kid, but a rival gangster finds out the plan and kidnaps both Mimi's and Joe's offsprings.
Joe eventually rescues the youngsters, but he does not win the heroine's heart.

LADIES THEY TALK ABOUT   (Warner Bros. , 1933)   69 min.

Directors, Howard Bretherton, William Keighley; based on
the play Women in Prison by Dorothy Mackaye, Carlton Miles;
screenplay, Sidney Sutherland, Brown Holmes; art director, Esdras
Hartley; costumes, Orry-Kelly; camera, John Seitz; editor, Basil
Wrangel.

Barbara Stanwyck (Nan Taylor); Preston Foster (David Salde);
Lyle Talbot (Don); Dorothy Burgess (Susie); Lillian Roth (Linda);
Maude Eburne (Aunt Maggie); Harold Huber (Lefty); Ruth Donnelly
(Noonan); Robert Warwick (The Warden); Helen Ware (Miss Johnson);
DeWitt Jennings (Tracy); Robert McWade (District Attorney); Cecil
Cunningham (Mrs. Arlington); Helen Mann (Blondie); Grace Cunard
(Marie); Mme. Sul-te-Wan (Mustard); Harold Healy (Dutch); Harry
Gribbon (Bank Guard).

Over the years there would be several features detailing the
experiences of women in prison, such as Ladies of the Big House
(1933) with Sylvia Sidney, Prison without Bars (1939) with Edna Best,
Girls Behind Bars (1950), The Weak and the Wicked (1953) with
Glynis Johns, Women's Prison (1955) with Ida Lupino, Yield to the
Night (1956) with Diana Dors, Girls' Prison (1956) with Joan Taylor,
and Women in Chains (telefeature, 1971) with Ida Lupino, as well as
the very famous studies, Caged (1949), q.v., with Eleanor Parker,
and I Want to Live (1958), q.v., starring Susan Hayward.
    Ladies They Talk About was one of the earliest, most casual,
more campy (in retrospect), and most entertaining of the lot.
    Most of the storyline is focused on life in the women's sec-
tion of San Quentin. Nan Taylor (Stanwyck) is sentenced to the big
house for her participation in some bank stick-ups. The man who
sends her to jail is reformer David Slade (Foster), a childhood
friend. Just as on the outside, within the prison Nan is a natural-
born leader. She is so tough and sneery that the other "ladies" incarcerated there soon allow her to take over as their unofficial boss.
Unlike such later films as the Jean Harlow-Clark Gable vehicle Hold
Your Man (1933), which depicts a women's prison as sort of a
church charity ward, there is nothing very pleasant about this place
where Nan and her comrades reside. If it were not for the plotline's demands, there would certainly be nothing in the jailhouse air
to arouse any notions of rehabilitation among the women. Isolated
from the world, these ladies hungered for two things: freedom and
male companionship. These twin desires were enough to drive some
of the occupants crazy, and this is what the movie depicted in its
own very theatrical manner.
    As the New York Times reported, the film "... is effective
when it is describing the behavior of the prisoners, the variety of
their misdemeanors, their positions in the social whirl outside, their
ingenuity in giving an intimate domestic touch to the prison, and their
frequently picturesque way of exhibiting pride, jealousy, vanity and
other untrammeled feminine emotions."

THE LADY AND THE MOB (Columbia, 1939) 65 min.

    Producer, Fred Kohlmar; director, Ben Stoloff; based on a
story by George Bradshaw, Price Day; screenplay, Richard Maibaum,
Gertrude Purcell; camera, John Stumar; editor, Otto Meyer.
    Fay Bainter (Hattie Leonard); Ida Lupino (Lila Thorne); Lee
Bowman (Fred Leonard); Henry Armetta (Zambrogio); Warren Hymer
(Frankie O'Fallon); Harold Huber (Harry the Lug); Forbes Murray

(District Attorney); Joseph Sawyer (Blinky Mack); Tom Dugan (Brains Logan); Joseph Caits (Bert the Beetle); Jim Toney (Big Time Tim); Tommy Mack (The Canary); George Meeker (George Watson).

Long before woman's lib became the order of the day, Hollywood was turning to the gimmick of having a distaff gang leader in order to spice up the tired underworld film genre.

Mid-Victorian grande dame Hattie Leonard (Bainter), who is head of a bank, becomes involved with a gang engaged in the protection racket. When she has difficulty in combating the mob by orderly methods, she fights fire with fire and forms her own gang with the help of ex-thug Frankie O'Fallen (Hymer). The results proved nonsensical, but funny, and exploited the charms of Best Supporting Actress Oscar winner (for Jezebel) Bainter. For romantic interest, there were Fred Leonard (Bowman) and Lila Thorne (Lupino).

One distracting element of the feature had Bainter's white-haired Hattie Leonard launching into an overly patriotic speech ("... since when has any good American been afraid to die?... ")

LADY FOR A DAY   (Columbia, 1933)   95 min.

Director, Frank Capra; based on the story Madam La Gimp by Damon Runyon; adaptor, Robert Riskin; sound, E. L. Bernds; camera, Joseph Walker; editor, Gene Havlick.

Warren William (Dave the Dude); May Robson (Apple Annie); Guy Kibbee (Judge Blake); Glenda Farrell (Missouri Martin); Ned Sparks (Happy); Jean Parker (Louise); Walter Connolly (Count Romero); Nat Pendleton (Shakespeare); Robert Emmet O'Connor (Inspector); Wallis Clark (Commissioner); Hobart Bosworth (Governor); Barry Norton (Young Man); Blind Dad Mills (Blind Man); "Shorty" (Panhandler).

Who else but Damon Runyon would have dreamed up a lovable old scamp like Apple Annie, a ragpicker with as colorful a tongue as her bizarre outfits? Her story, brought to the screen by director Frank Capra, was nominated for four Academy Awards: best picture, best writing, best directing, best actress. Although it won no Oscars, its popularity inspired Columbia Pictures to make a semi-follow-up, Lady By Choice (1934), with May Robson again starring. Then, nearly 30 years later, Runyon's story, Madam La Gimp, was again used by Capra when he remade Lady for a Day as Pocketful of Miracles (1961), q. v.

While some of the technical qualities of Lady for a Day are clumsy, this annoyance should hardly stand in the way of enjoying a film which the New York Times termed "... a merry tale with touches of sentiment. "

This Cinderella tale had big time gambler, Dave the Dude (William), putting street peddler Apple Annie (Robson) in a huge mansion for a week. He helps her to masquerade as the wealthy Mrs. E. Worthington Manville. Her ploy is to convince her daughter (Parker) that mama has not been fibbing all these years when she wrote little Louise about her stately position in life. (Louise, who spent most of her time at private schools, is now returning home with her Spanish nobleman fiancé.) Also wrangled into the hoax are a drunken judge (Kibbee) and nightclub hostess Missouri Martin (Farrell). The scheme almost falls apart when Count Romero (Connolly), Louise's future father-in-law, arrives in town and suspects something funny is going on.

As with other screen adaptations of Runyon's flavorful stories, Lady for a Day was a refreshing antidote to the rash of films showing gangsters as psychopathic fiends (which most were not). Mainly, they were rogues who wanted an easy way to earn a buck, but they often had their own charm and humor.

LADY GANGSTER (Warner Bros., 1942) 62 min.

Director, Florian Roberts (Robert Florey); based on the play by Dorothy Mackaye, Carlton Miles; screenplay, Anthony Coldewey; art director, Ted Smith; camera, Arthur Todd; editor, Harold McLernon.

Faye Emerson (Dot Barton); Frank Wilcos (Kenneth Phillips); Julie Bishop (Myrtle Reed); Roland Drew (Candy Wells); Jackie Gleason (Wilson); Ruth Ford (Lucy Fenton); Virginia Brissac (Mrs. Stoner); Dorothy Vaughn (Jenkins); Dorothy Adams (Deaf Annie); Vera Lewis (Ma Silsby); Bill Hopper (John); Herbert Rawlinson (Lewis Sinton); Charles Wilson (Detective); Peggy Diggins (Mary); Bill Phillips (Stew); Frank Mayo (Walker); Ken Christy (Bank Guard); Sol Gorss, Fred Kelsey (Cops); Daisy Bufford (Black Girl); Leah Baird (Matron); Joan Winfield (Nurse); Jack Mower (Sergeant).

"... One of those low budgeters which surprises by being entertaining" (New York Daily Mirror.)

Small town girl Dot Barton (Emerson) arrives in the big city and promptly becomes involved with the wrong crowd. For her participation in a bank robbery she is sent to jail. Among the prison crowd is Myrtle Reed (Bishop) who becomes her close friend; while Lucy Fenton (Ford) is the local troublemaker. Upon her release, Dot wants revenge on Kenneth Phillips (Wilcox), a radio commentator whom she had known from her childhood days. He had been the one who innocently put the police on her trail. However, Dot discovers eventually that she loves Kenneth.

LADY IN CEMENT (Twentieth Century-Fox, 1968) C-93 min.

Producer, Aaron Rosenberg; director, Gordon Douglas; based on the novel by Marvin H. Albert; screenplay, Albert, Jack Guss; underwater sequences staged by Ricou Browning; music-music conductor, Hugo Montenegro; orchestrator, Billy May; costumes, Moss Mabry; art director, Leroy Deane; set decorators, Walter M. Scott, Jerry Wunderlich; assistant director, Richard Lang; makeup, Dan Striepke, Layne Britton; sound, Howard Warren, David Dockendorf; special effects, L. B. Abbott, Art Cruickshank; camera, Joseph

Biroc; editor, Robert Simpson.

Frank Sinatra (Tony Rome); Raquel Welch (Kit Forrest); Dan
Blocker (Gronsky); Richard Conte (Lieutenant Santini); Martin Gabel
(Al Mungar); Lainie Kazan (Maria Baretto); Pat Henry (Hal Rubin);
Steve Peck (Paul Mungar); Virginia Wood (Audrey); Richard Deacon
(Arnie Sherwin); Frank Raiter (Danny Yale); Peter Hock (Frenchy);
Alex Stevens (Shev); Christine Todd (Sandra Lomax); Mac Robbins
(Sidney the Organizer); Tommy Uhlar (The Kid); Ray Baumel (Paco);
Pauly Dash (McComb); Andy Jarrell (Pool Boy); Joe E. Lewis (Him-
self).

Frank Sinatra returned to his previous role as the Miami
Beach shamus, Tony Rome, in Lady in Cement, a sequel to Tony
Rome (1967), q. v.   Although more violent and vulgar than its flashy
predecessor, the film was not as popular and Sinatra thereafter made
no more Tony Rome films.   (For a time, Fox considered a teleseries of the property to star Tony Scotti.)
        In the midst of diving for sunken treasure, flippant private
eye Tony Rome (Sinatra) comes across the nude corpse of a blonde
whose feet have been set in cement.   Meanwhile, burly ex-convict
Gronsky (Blocker) hires Tony to find out if the victim might be his
go-go-dancer friend Sandra Lomax (Todd), who has been missing
for some time.   The trail leads to heiress Kit Forrest (Welch).
While pursuing this clue, Tony is warned by Kit's neighbor, ex-
Mafia overlord Al Mungar (Gabel), to stop pestering Kit.   Thereafter, Mungar is killed, but, unperturbed, Tony continues with his investigation, which points toward Mungar's son Paul (Peck).   With
the case closed, Tony hands over the evidence to Lieutenant Santini
(Conte), and Tony and Kit go out to sea searching for treasure, adventure, and....
        Although primarily in the detective genre, Lady in Cement
leaned heavily on the action-violence gambits which were so much a
part of the revived gangster cycle.   Judith Crist (New York magazine) ripped apart the film as "A cheap and tawdry stinker" which
was nothing more than "smutty nonsense. "   Even granting the daz-
zling, slick production values and the southern geography so nicely
lensed, the New York Times had to admit the film was "consistently crude. "   However, added Vincent Canby of the Times, it "...
turns its fakery and garishness into negative virtues that can be ap-
preciated, if not particularly admired. "
        The acting level was on a par with the plotline continuity;
rip-off à la mode.

LADY SCARFACE (RKO, 1941) 69 min.

Producer, Cliff Reid; director, Frank Woodruff; screenplay,
Arnaud D'Usseau, Richard Collins; camera, Nicholas Musuraca; edi-
tor, Harry Marker.
        Dennis O'Keefe (Lieutenant Mason); Judith Anderson (Slade);
Frances Neal (Ann Rogers); Mildred Coles (Mary Powell); Eric
Blore (Mr. Hartford); Marc Lawrence (Lefty Landers); Damian
O'Flynn (Onslow); Marion Martin (Ruby); Rand Brooks (Jimmy Powell);

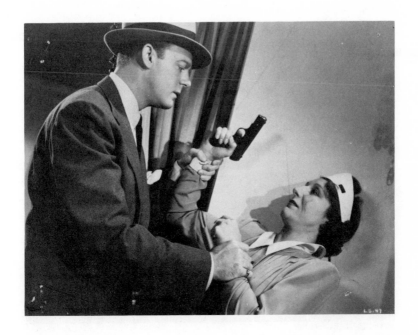

Dennis O'Keefe and Judith Anderson in <u>Lady Scarface</u> (1941).

Andrew Tombes (Seidel); Arthur Shields (Matt); Lee Bonnell (George);
Harry Burns (Semeneff); Horace McMahon (Mullen); Eddy Conrad
(Hotel Waiter); Joey Ray (Mr. Barlowe); Charles Halton (Mr. Pinch-
beck); Ruth Dietrich (Pinchbeck's Secretary); Robert Middlemass
(Captain Lovell--New York); Harry Humphrey (Watchman); Bert
Howard (Mr. Tuckerman); Claire McDowell (Mrs. Tuckerman).

     Distinguished Broadway actress Judith Anderson, who rarely
had a good screen outing (<u>Rebecca</u>, 1940, and a few others excepted),
dug deep into her role as a sadistic criminal in <u>Lady Scarface</u>. It
is unfortunate that RKO relegated the project to a quickie budget,
and that the focus was on police lieutenant Mason (O'Keefe) and the
girl photographer (Neal) whom he loves. Since the latter two engage in extended lovers' spats, the film evolves into more of a
domestic drama than a study of crime.

THE LADYKILLERS (J. Arthur Rank, 1955) C-94 min.

     Producer, Michael Balcon; associate producer, Seth Holt;
director, Alexander Mackendrick; story-screenplay, William Rose;

Danny Green, Alec Guinness and Herbert Lom in The Ladykillers
(1955).

art director, Jim Morahan; music, Tristram Cary; camera, Otto
Heller.
    Alec Guinness (The Professor); Cecil Parker (The Major);
Herbert Lom (Louis); Peter Sellers (Harry); Danny Green (One-
Round); Datie Johnson (Mrs. Wilberforce); Jack Warner (Police Su-
perintendent); Frankie Howerd (Barrow Boy); Philip Stainton (Police
Sergeant); Fred Griffiths (The Junkman); Kenneth Connor (The Cab
Driver).

    The British are always at their best with tongue-in-cheek
criminal capers. This marvelous feature detailed the basically simple plot of a notorious gang being foiled in their intricate robbery
scheme by a sweet old lady (Johnson). It all evolved into a delightful crime spoof.
    A motley group of robbers rent a room in Mrs. Wilberforce's
(Johnson) boarding house. Ostensibly they are a classical music
quarter requiring a place to practice. Actually they are planning an
elaborate robbery, and eventually a murder. The luckless culprits
are constantly being bothered by the good-natured old lady who eventually brings about their downfall.

Arch scene-stealer Alec Guinness as the Professor met his
match in Miss Johnson, who grabbed front and center attention as
the benign house owner. Also amusing was Peter Sellers, in his
pre-ego trip days, as Barry, one of the accomplices. The film
benefited from especially fitting atmosphere, particularly the old
lady's Victorian abode.

LARCENY, INC. (Warner Bros., 1942) 95 min.

Producer, Hal B. Wallis; associate producers, Jack Saper,
Jerry Wald; director, Lloyd Bacon; based on the play The Night
Before Christmas by Laura and S. J. Perelman; screenplay,
Everett Freeman, Edwin Gilbert; camera, Tony Gaudio; editor,
Ralph Dawson.
Edward G. Robinson (Pressure Maxwell); Jane Wyman (Den-
ny Costello); Broderick Crawford (Jug Martin); Jack Carson (Jeff
Randolph); Anthony Quinn (Leo Dexter); Edward Brophy (Weepy Da-
vis); Harry Davenport (Homer Bigelow); John Qualen (Sam Bachrach);
Barbara Jo Allen [Vera Vague], (Mademoiselle Gloris); Grant Mit-
chell (Aspinwall); Jackie Gleason (Hobart); Andrew Tombes (Oscar

Broderick Crawford and Edward G. Robinson in Larceny, Inc. (1942).

Engelhart); Joseph Downing (Smitty); George Meeker (Mr. Jackson);
Fortunio Bonanova (Anton Copolulos); Joseph Crehan (Warden); Jean
Ames (Florence); William Davidson (McCarthy); Chester Clute (Bu-
chanan); Creighton Hale (Mr. Carmichael); Emory Parnell (Officer
O'Casey); Joe Devlin (Umpire); Jimmy O'Gatty, Jack Kenney (Con-
victs); John Kelly (Batter); Eddy Chandler, James Flavin (Guards);
Bill Phillips (Muggsy); Hank Mann, Eddie Foster, Cliff Saum,
Charles Sullivan (Players); Lucien Littlefield, William Hopper (Cus-
tomers); Ray Montgomery (Young Man); Grace Stafford (Secretary);
Charles Drake (Auto Driver).

During World War II, dynamic Edward G. Robinson returned
to Warner Bros. to star in the comedy-drama gangster film, Larceny, Inc. While the antics proved to be somewhat forced, even a
pseudo-laugh was good in the tense war years. By this point in
time, it had become standard form for Robinson to burlesque his
once serious portrayals of gangland figures.

Pressure Maxwell (Robinson) and Jug Martin (Crawford) are
released from jail and are asked to participate in a bank robbery.
They refuse but set up their own caper by purchasing a luggage
store which just happens to be next door to a bank. Denny Costello
(Wyman), Pressure's daughter, is put in charge. She promptly falls
in love with salesman Jeff Randolph (Carson). Meanwhile, the hoods,
pretending to be respected citizens, plan to tunnel into the neighbor-
ing bank vault. But then they have a change of heart. However, an
old pal, Leo Dexter (Quinn), is released from the penitentiary and
he determines to go through with the robbery. He bungles the job,
using too much dynamite, and blows up the luggage shop. The police lead him off to jail, leaving Pressure and Jug to take another
crack at being above-reproach city dwellers.

THE LAST EXPLOITS OF THE OLSEN GANG see OLSEN-BANDENS
SIDSTE BEDRIFTER

THE LAST GANGSTER (MGM, 1937) 81 min.

Director, Edward Ludwing; story, William A. Wellman,
Robert Carson; screenplay, John Lee Mahin; art directors, Cedric
Gibbons, Daniel Cathcart; set decorator, Edwin Willis; montages,
Slavko Vorkapich; camera, William Daniels; editor, Ben Lewis.
Edward G. Robinson (Joe Krozac); James Stewart (Paul
North); Rose Stradner (Talya Krozac); Lionel Stander (Curly); Doug-
las Scott (Paul North, Jr.); John Carradine (Casper); Sidney Black-
mer (San Francisco Editor); Edward Brophy (Fats Garvey); Alan
Baxter ("Acey" Kile); Edward Marr (Frankie Kile); Grant Mitchell
(Warden); Frank Conroy (Sid Gorman); Moroni Olson (Shea); Ivan
Miller (Wilson); Willard Robertson (Broderick); Louise Beavers
(Gloria); Donald Barry (Billy Ernst); Ben Welden (Bottles Bailey);
Horace McMahon (Limpy); Edward Pawley (Brockett); John Kelly
(Red); David Leo Tillotson, Jim Kaehner, Billy Smith, Reggie
Streeter (Boys); Pierre Watkin (Editor); William Benedict (Office

Boy); Walter Miller (Mike Kile); Wade Boteler (Turnkey); Larry
Simms (Jo Krozac); Lee Phelps (Train Guard); Frederick Burton
(Boston Editor); Phillip Terry (First Reporter); Douglas McPhail,
Ernest Wood (Reporters).

Even before the Thirties expired, moviemakers were pre-
dicting the final end of the gangster craze with such titles as The
Last Gangster.   Elitist studio Metro-Goldwyn-Mayer borrowed Edward G. Robinson from Warner Bros. for this melodrama and
teamed him with the studio's new find, James Stewart.   The result
was a rather overlong attempt at a genre classic.   It lacked the
excitement, pacing, and flavor that Warners' would have given the
project.
    Big time hoodlum Joe Krozac (Robinson) returns from his
European honeymoon to find that another has taken over his gang.
He arranges a reprisal, and is sent to prison for his efforts.   His
bride (Stradner) eventually divorces him and weds a newsman (Stewart) who adopts the gangster's son as his own.   A decade later, Joe
is released and heads East to find his wife and son.   Part of the intriguing focus of the film revolves around his adjusting to the
changes time has wrought in all walks of life.   Members of Joe's
old gang kidnap him and force Joe to tell them the location of long
hidden loot.   Krozac eventually confesses to them, then goes to kill
Talya and North.   However, upon observing that the boy (Scott) is
better off with his stepfather, Joe leaves, and later is killed by a
rival hoodlum (Baxter).
    Had Metro produced the feature with more guts and realism
than lustrous gloss, this portrait of a man (Robinson) outliving his
usefulness both professionally and personally would have packed a
far greater wallop.

THE LAST MILE   (World Wide, 1932)   84 min.

    Presenter, E. W. Hammons; director, Sam Bischoff; based
on the play by John Wexley; screenplay, Seton I. Miller; music di-
rector, Val Burton; settings, Ralph DeLacy; camera, Arthur Ede-
son; editors, Martin G. Cohn, Rose Loewinger.
    Preston S. Foster (Killer Mears); Howard Phillips (Richard
Walters); George E. Stone (Berg); Noel Madison (D'Amoro); Alan
Roscoe (Kirby); Paul Fix (Eddie Werner); Al Hill (Fred Mayer);
Daniel L. Haynes (Sonny Jackson); Frank Sheridan (Warden Frank
Lewis); Alec B. Francis (Father O'Connors); Edward Van Sloan
(Rabbi); Louise Carter (Mrs. Walters); Ralph Theodore (Pat Calla-
han the Principal Keeper); Albert J. Smith (Drake); Kenneth Mac-
Donald (Harris); Walter Walker (Governor Blaine); Francis Mc-
Donald (Holdup Man); William Scott (Peddie); Jack Kennedy (O'Flaher-
ty).

THE LAST MILE   (United Artists, 1959)   81 min.

    Producers, Max J. Rosenberg, Milton Subotsky; director,

Howard W. Koch; based on the play by John Wexley; screenplay,
Subotsky, Seton I. Miller; music-music conductor, Van Alexander;
assistant director, Charles Maguire; scenic design, Paul Barnes;
set decorator, Jack Wright, Jr.; makeup, Robert Jiras; costumes,
Frank Thompson; sound, Dick Gramaglia; special effects, Milton
Olson, Vincent Brady; camera, Joseph Brun; editors, Robert Brockman, Patricia Jaffe.

Mickey Rooney ("Killer" John Mears); Alan Bunce (The Ward-
en); Frank Conroy (O'Flaherty the Guard); Leon Janney (Callahan the
Guard); Frank Overton (Father O'Connors); Clifford David (Convict
Richard Walters); Harry Millard (Convict Fred Mayer);John McCur-
ry (Convict Vince Jackson); Ford Rainey (Convict Red Kirby); John
Seven (Convict Tom D'Amoro); Michael Constantine (Convict Ed
Werner); John Vari (Convict Jimmy Martin); Donald Barry (Drake
the Guard); Clifton James (Harris the Guard);(Milton Selzer (Peddie
the Guard); George Marcy (Convict Pete Rodrigues).

Based on true life events, John Wexler's exciting play had
been done on Broadway by Spencer Tracy and on the road by Clark
Gable, bringing eventual stardom to each actor. In 1932, Samuel
Bischoff, in his only sound-directed film, helmed the project for
World Wide Pictures. Preston Foster starred as Killer Mears, a
hardened condemned criminal on death row who must cope with the
taunting of sadistic guards and the reactions of the several other
prisoners in the cellblock. Eventually he is driven to leading an
escape attempt, a scheme which is hopeless from the start. Extremely violent in its presentation, The Last Mile was an effective
screen vehicle. Looking back on this semi-landmark feature, Don
Miller in B Movies (1973) reflects, "The film may have been too
strong for the feminine matinee trade, but it was raw meat for action devotees and coming as it did in the midst of the gangster prison cycle, it proved popular."

A quarter of a century later, The Last Mile was hauled off
the shelf as a starring project for Mickey Rooney. As Killer Mears,
he enjoyed one of his most effective adult roles. Again it was the
taut story of men awaiting execution on death row. The monotony
and fears of their existence is interrupted only by the men being
taken, one by one, to the death house. The taunting of the unfeeling prison guards add to their agony. Eventually the situation
reaches the boiling point and the men lead a bloody revolt that results in tragedy.

Of this effective remake, the New York Herald-Tribune complimented, "A fast, savage drama of a deathhouse.... Although it
hints at some doubts about the form of capital punishment, it doesn't
come to grips with it but only approaches it. If anything it seems
in favor only of abolishing the long deathhouse wait, presumably by
doing in a convicted man promptly to avoid the mental torment of
hoping for stays of execution...." Variety said of the 1959 rendition, "Packs quite a wallop.... Inevitably, the audience must iden-
tify with the men waiting for the hour of execution, and it's a fairly
sickening sensation that produces both tension and terror."

THE LAVENDER HILL MOB   (J. Arthur Rank, 1951)   82 min.

Producer, Michael Balcon; director, Charles Crichton; screenplay, T. E. B. Clarke; art director, William Kellner; music,
Georges Auric; music director, Ernest Irving; sound, Stephen Dalby;
camera, Douglas Slocombe; editor, Seth Holt.

Alec Guinness (Holland); Stanley Holloway (Pendlebury); Sid-
ney James (Lackery); Alfie Bass (Shorty); Marjorie Fielding (Mrs.
Chalk); Edie Martin (Miss Evesham); John Salew (Parkin); Ronald
Adam (Turner); Arthur Hambling (Wallis); Gibb McLaughlin (Godwin);
John Gregson (Farrow); Clive Morton (Station Sergeant); Sidney Taf-
ler (Clayton); Frederick Piper (Cafe Proprietor); Peter Bull (Joe the
Gab); Patric Doonan (Craggs); Audrey Hepburn (Girl).

This film is one of the best of the Ealing Studio's comedies,
and it still holds up well today.   The Lavender Hill Mob was a
splendid tongue-in-cheek jibe at the typical heist film.

Alec Guinness starred as a timid clerk who masterminds a
plot to steal gold bullion and smuggle it out of England to France.
Since it is his regular job to transfer the precious metal to desig-
nated banks, clerk Holland has easy access to the loot.   He obtains
the services of a local loudmouthed scamp (Holloway) to aid him in
having the bullion melted down.   With the help of a maker of sou-
venir models, he has the gold transformed into small likenesses of
the Eiffel Tower, thus allowing for an easy means of exporting the
loot.   Any wise filmgoer could tell you that something would go
astray, and it does.   One particularly hilarious scene finds the two
crooks in a chase sequence with six schoolgirls, the latter having
purchased the expensive models.   Another joyous bit has the thieves
mixing up police messages and sending the cop cars into total confusion.

Above and beyond the comic elements of The Lavender Hill
Mob, the film did succeed in throwing some celluloid myths to the
wind.   The mastermind of a criminal plot did not have to be a
gruff tough hardened criminal or even an oily smooth swindler.
Even such a meek-looking, mild-living man as Holland could perpetrate such fraud.   (In late years, James Mason would carry this
concept further in several heist features.)   Most intriguing of all
was the stated fact that Guinness' Holland is unrepentant about his
deed.   He may have moments of doubt and apprehension, but he
pushes onward with his lawless scheme, determined to have his moment of monetary glory.

LEAGUE OF GENTLEMEN   (J. Arthur Rank, 1960)   116 min.

Producers, Michael Relph, Basil Dearden; director, Deardon;
based on the novel by John Boland; screenplay, Bryan Forbes; music, Phil Green; camera, Arthur Ibbotson; editor, John Guthridge.

Jack Hawkins (Hyde); Nigel Patrick (Race); Roger Livesey
(Mycroft); Richard Attenborough (Lexy); Bryan Forbes (Porthill);
Kieron Moore (Stevens); Robert Coote (Bunny Warren); Terence Al-
exander (Rupert); Melissa Stribling (Peggy); Norman Bird (Weaver);

Patrick Wymark (Wylie); Nanette Newman (Elizabeth); David Lodge
(C. S. M.); Doris Hare (Molly Weaver); Gerald Harper (Captain
Saunders); Bryan Murray (Grogan).

"The only snag is that according to film law, crime mustn't
be allowed to pay off, so that audiences will know that the gang will
slip up and the main problem at the end is how.   Rarely have audiences wished more fervently for the criminals to get away with it"
(Variety).
This well-strung thriller was one of the most enticing films
ever to detail a bank robbery.   Each intricate portion of the heist
plan is presented to the filmgoer in minute detail.
With sturdy dialog and fitting character delineation, the
British-made feature details a plot by eight ex-army officers who
use military strategy to pull off a complicated bank robbery.   Prior
to the big event, the characters of the men are laid bare as they
endure a rigorous training program in preparation for the crime.
Since each participant is to receive 100,000 pounds for his share
of the booty, they all are very anxious to make this the perfect
snatch.
As Time jocularly observed, "It demonstrates, more im-
pressively than most recruiting pictures, the advantages of military
training in subsequent civilian life. "

THE LEGEND OF MACHINE GUN KELLY   see MELVIN PURVIS,
G-MAN

LET 'EM HAVE IT   (United Artists, 1935) 90 min.

Producer, Edward Small; director, Sam Wood; story-screen-
play, Joseph Moncure March, Elmer Harris; camera, J. Peverell
Marley, Robert Planck; editor, Grant Whytock.
Richard Arlen (Mal Stevens); Virginia Bruce (Eleanor Spen-
cer); Alice Brady (Aunt Ethel); Bruce Cabot (Joe Keefer); Harvey
Stephens (Van Rensseler); Eric Linden (Buddy Spencer); Joyce Comp-
ton (Barbara); Gordon Jones (Tex Logan); J. Farrell MacDonald
(Mr. Keefer); Bodil Rosing (Mrs. Keefer); Paul Stanton (Department
Chief); Robert Emmet O'Connor (Police Captain); Hale Hamilton (Ex-
Senator Reilly); Dorothy Appleby (Lola); Barbara Pepper (Milly);
Mathew Betz (Thompson); Harry Woods (Big Bill); Clyde Dillson
(Pete); Matty Fain (Brooklyn); Paul Fix (Sam); Donald Kirke (Curley);
Eugene Strong (Dude); Christian Rub (Henkel); Eleanor Wesselhoeff
(Mrs. Henkel); Wesley Barry (Walton); Ian MacLaren (Reconstruction-
ist); George Pauncefort (Dr. Hoffman); Landers Stevens (Parole
Chairman); Katharine Clare Ward (Ma Harrison); Sidney Bracy (But-
ler); Dennis O'Keefe (Trainee); Tom London (Guard); Jed Prouty,
Joseph Crehan, Hooper Atchley (Bits).

Basically a follow-up to Warner Bros. ' G-Men (1935), q. v. ,
this entry provided arduous detail on F. B. I. methods used to detect
and capture criminals at large.   Woven around the documentation

was a flimsy story held together by a willing cast and plenty of
hard-nosed action.

Society girl Eleanor Spencer (Bruce) is warned that her
chauffeur (Cabot) is a punk who plans to kidnap her.   However, she
ignores the possibility.   When Joe Keefer is sent to jail, she arranges for him to be paroled.   He promptly returned to his bad
ways, staging a breakout of his gang.   Together with his men, he
embarks on a terror spree throughout the midwest.   When Eleanor's
younger brother Buddy joins the G-Men, he comes into contact with
Keefer's mob.   Buddy is killed and confederate Mal Stevens and the
other law enforcers vow not to rest easy until Keefer's gang is captured.

Savage and terroristic in several spots, Let 'Em Have It
has its own cult of followers.   Cabot once again proved what an effective heavy he could be.

Few who have seen the film will forget the scene in which
the bandages are removed from Joe Keefer's face after a plastic
surgery operation.   It is revealed that the doctor has carved Keefer's initials into his face, branding him as the criminal he is.

LIGHTS OF NEW YORK (Warner Bros., 1928) 5,267'

Director, Bryan Foy; story-screenplay-dialog, Hugh Herbert,
Murray Roth; camera, Ed Du Par; editor, Jack Killifer.

Helene Costello (Kitty Lewis); Cullen Landis (Eddie Morgan);
Gladys Brockwell (Molly Thompson); Mary Carr (Mrs. Morgan);
Wheeler Oakman (Hawk Miller); Eugene Pallette (Gene); Robert El-
liott (Detective Crosby); Tom Dugan (Sam); Tom McGuire (Collins);
Guy Dennery (Tommy); Walter Percival (Mr. Jackson); Jere Delaney
(Mr. Dickson).

Billed as "... the first 100 per cent all-talking picture,"
Variety called Lights of New York "100 per cent crude." Even for
its time, this stodgy little effort had no primary enticement for audiences other than the novelty of sound (and non-stop talking).   But
the novelty worked, and Warner Bros. enjoyed a tremendous monetary return from the production.

Eddie Morgan (Landis) and Gene (Pallette) move downstate to
Manhattan to open a barbershop.   Before long they find their business is being used as a front for a bootleg operation.   Later Eddie
is framed for the murder of a nightclub owner (Oakman) when he is
found with the murder weapon which belongs to his girl (Costello),
a club dancer.   The police naturally arrest Eddie, Gene, and Kitty,
but Miller's mistress (Brockwell) finally confesses to the crime.
Lights of New York does have a special claim to fame.
Within the storyline, Hawk Miller tells a henchman concerning a
victim at hand, "Take him for a ride."

LITTLE CAESAR (First National, 1931) 77 min.

Director, Mervyn LeRoy; based on the novel by W. R.

Edward G. Robinson in <u>Little Caesar</u> (1931).

Burnett; screenplay, Francis Faragoh; camera, Tony Gaudio.
Edward G. Robinson (Cesare Enrico Bandello [Rico--Little
Caesar]); Douglas Fairbanks, Jr. (Joe Massara); Glenda Farrell
(Olga Strassoff); William Collier, Jr. (Tony Passa); Ralph Ince
(Diamond Pete Montana); George E. Stone (Otero); Thomas Jackson
(Lieutenant Tom Flaherty); Stanley Fields (Sam Vettori); Armand
Kaliz (DeVoss); Sidney Blackmer (The Big Boy); Landers Stevens
(Commissioner McClure); Maurice Black (Little Arnie Lorch); Noel
Madison (Peppi); Nick Bela (Ritz Colonna); Lucille La Verne (Ma
Magdalena); Ben Hendricks, Jr. (Kid Bean); George Daly (Machine
Gunner); Ernie Adams (Cashier); Larry Steers (Cafe Guest); Louis
Natheaux (A Hood); Kernan Cripps (Detective).

More so than any other American film, Little Caesar should
be credited with initiating the gangster movie popularity of the
1930s. Followed by such strong entries as The Public Enemy
(1931), q.v., and Scarface (1932), q.v., the gangster picture took
a firm grip on Depression audiences. Edward G. Robinson's over-
powering portrayal of hoodlum Cesare "Rico" Bandello, who rose
from the gutter and returned to the gutter, made a tremendous impact on moviegoers and filmmakers alike. It is a true milestone in
the history of the gangster picture.
At the time of its release, the New York Times criticized
the film as "ordinary" despite a praiseworthy script and some excellent performances. It is true that the picture is slow and sometimes plodding, but in its eighty minutes it methodically delineates
the rise and fall of an underworld figure.
Small town crooks Bandello (Robinson) and Joe Massara
(Fairbanks, Jr.) head for the big city to seek fame and fortune.
Joe, who would rather dance, falls for classy hoofer Olga Strassoff
(Farrell), and together they perform a dance act at a top club which
is backed by crook "Little Arnie" Lorch (Black). Bandello, on the
other hand, obtains a post with mobster Sam Vettori (Fields) and is
told by a bigger hood (Ince) to play down violence due to a crime
commission investigation then proceeding. At a New Year's Eve
party at the club where Joe works, the gang uses Joe as a front
man and rob the place. Bandello caps the episode by murdering
the crime commissioner who is on the premises.
After the robbery, Bandello takes over the gang, making
Vettori his underling and Otero (Stone) his right-hand man. Later
he is forced to shoot a co-worker (Collier, Jr.) who turns yellow.
But in true gangland tradition, the late and now lamented Tony Passa is given a big funeral send-off. The same day the criminals
give their new leader a testimonial dinner and a gold watch "from
the boys." (The timepiece turns out to be stolen merchandise).
"Little Arnie" thereafter tries to kill competitor Bandello, but Joe
overhears the plot and tips off "Little Caesar."
Little Caesar suggests to "Little Arnie" that he leave town.
The latter does and "Big Boy" (Blackmer), who runs the town,
hands over all of Arnie's territory, along with that of "Bull" Montana (Ince) to Little Caesar.
Now near the top of the underworld heap, Little Caesar plots
to get rid of "Big Boy." He asks Joe to return as his henchman,

but Joe declines, saying he wants to keep on dancing and to wed
Olga. Little Caesar threatens to kill the girl and later attempts
to rub out Joe, who is planning to turn states' evidence. However,
Rico, the crime bigshot, cannot murder his long-standing friend.

Circumstances soon change Little Caesar's status: Otero is
killed, Rico's gang is captured, and Sam Vettori is sent to the
electric chair. For a time the once-mighty Rico hides out with an
old woman (La Verne), but she fleeces him of his bankroll, and he
ends up in a flophouse. Reading in the newspapers that the police
have termed him "yellow," the irate Rico phones the police and
they trace the call. While walking down the street, the law men
spot him and take sanctuary behind a billboard (advertising Joe and
Olga's act). Rico is shot. As he falls down, near death, he asks
aloud, "Mother of Mercy ... is this the end of Rico?"

Obviously the most important facet of Little Caesar is the
character. He was, for all practical purposes, the first important
screen hood with psychological problems presented for audience
analysis. John Gabree, in his survey book Gangsters (1973), goes
so far as to suggest that Rico was homosexual. More probably,
Robinson's Rico was asexual, in love only with power, for in the
early part of the feature he informs Fairbanks' Joe that money and
women are not everything, but "being somebody" and "having your
own way or nothin'" is what's important. Friends, "having somebody you can trust," were only important as safeguards and as
stepping stones to reaching and staying on top. As far as Rico's
interest in Joe's dancing goes, he thought the profession was for a
"sissy."

Several scenes within Little Caesar stand out vividly. Robinson's Little Caesar is seen strutting down the street after buying
several newspapers which contain his pictures, and then almost
being killed by members of Little Arnie's gang. Another scene
finds the hoodlums laughing over a column item which Rico has had
planted, detailing that Little Arnie has left for Detroit--permanently.
One of the most stark scenes in the feature was, of course, Rico's
gunning down of Tony Passa on the steps of a church (it was a
camera step-up used later in the decade in The Roaring Twenties).

Most of all, Little Caesar brilliantly unfolded the ironic tale
of two men, both on the wrong path, with one taking the road
toward redemption and the other the "easy" way to fame and fortune,
and eventual violent death.

THE LITTLE GIANT   (First National, 1933)   74 min.

Director, Roy Del Ruth; story, Robert Lord; screenplay,
Lord and Wilson Mizner; music conductor, Leo F. Forbstein; art
director, Robert Haas; camera, Sid Hickox; editor, George Marks.

Edward G. Robinson (James Francis "Bugs" Ahearn); Helen
Vinson (Polly Cass); Mary Astor (Ruth Wayburn); Kenneth Thomson
(John Stanley); Russell Hopton (Al Daniels); Shirley Grey (Edith
Merriam); Donald Dillaway (Gordon Cass); Louise Mackintosh (Mrs.
Cass); Berton Churchill (Donald Hadley Cass); Helen Mann (Frankie);
Selmer Jackson (Voice of Radio Announcer); Dewey Robinson (Butch

Mary Astor and Edward G. Robinson in <u>The Little Giant</u> (1933).

Zanqutoski); John Kelly (Ed [Tim]); Rolfe Sedan (Waiter); Bob Perry,
Adrian Morris (Joe Milano's Hoods); Charles Coleman (Charteris);
Bill Elliott (Guest); Leonard Carey (Ingleby); Nora Cecil (Maid);
Lester Dorr, Lorin Raker (Investment Clerks); Joan Barclay, Lo-
retta Layson, Maxine Cantway, Jayne Shadduck, Loretta Andrews,
Ann Hovey, Lynn Browning, Renee Whitney, Margaret LaMarr,
Alice Jans, Barbara Rogers, Bonny Bannon, Toby Wing, Pat Wing,
(Society Girls); Guy Usher (Detective); John Marston (D. A.); Harry
Tenbrook (Pulido).

     Predating Warners' A Slight Case of Murder (1938), q. v. by
several years, this Roy Del Ruth-directed feature, was a successful
attempt to poke fun at the gangster film and the already typed gangster character. Who better than Edward G. Robinson could sass
his own celluloid stereotype?
     James Francis "Bugs" Ahearn (Robinson) is financially on
the brink of disaster with the coming of the end of the Prohibition
Era. But ever resourceful, he decides it is time to expand his
horizons, in particular to break into polite society and become part
of the polo set of southern California. His initial enthusiasm proves
insufficient and he is snubbed by the rich folk. However, Polly
Cass (Vinson) takes him home to her family, and her supposedly
proper relatives promptly defraud him by selling him bogus stock.
When the gambit is uncovered, Bugs persuades the local district attorney not to prosecute. Instead, he brings in his boys to help him
retrieve the lost funds. Successful in this venture, he dumps snooty,
calculating Polly and takes up with Ruth Wayburn (Astor), a very
good girl.
     Although Variety said the film was "... not intelligent enough
to entertain intelligent fans, " the New York Herald-Tribune found it
"an amusing bit of fluff" and the New York World-Telegram rated
it "fast moving and [a] thoroughly entertaining picture. "

LITTLE MISS MARKER (Paramount, 1934) 80 min.

     Producer, B. P. Schulberg; director, Alexander Hall; based
on the story by Damon Runyon; screenplay, William R. Lipman,
Sam Hellman, Gladys Lehman; songs, Leo Robin and Ralph Rainger;
camera, Alfred Gilks; editor, William Shea.
     Adolphe Menjou (Sorrowful Jones); Dorothy Dell (Bangles Car-
son); Charles Bickford (Big Steve); Shirley Temple (Miss Marker);
Lynne Overman (Regret); Frank McGlynn, Sr. (Doc Chesley); Jack
Sheehan (Sun Rise); Garry Owen (Grinder); Willie Best (Dizzy Mem-
phis); Puggy White (Eddie); Tammany Young (Buggs); Sam Hardy
(Bennie the Gouge); Edward Earle (Marky's Father); Warren Hymer
(Sore Toe); John Kelly (Canvas Back); Frank Conroy (Dr. Ingalls);
James Burke (Detective Reardon); Ernie Adams, Don Brodie (Bet-
ters); Stanley Price (Bookie).

     Ingratiating little Shirley Temple took another giant step
forward to moppet stardom when she was featured in the title role
of Little Miss Marker. The production beautifully blended comedy

Adolphe Menjou and Shirley Temple in <u>Little Miss Marker</u> (1934).

and pathos without too much sugar, resulting in a most palatable
dessert for cinema goers.

A little girl (Temple) is left with Sorrowful Jones (Menjou),
a bookmaker, to cover a $20 bet. It is soon assumed that the
man who left "Miss Marker" has been killed. Through a rash of
circumstances, Sorrowful finds himself forced to care for the child.
The fanciful little girl soon believes that Sorrowful and his race-
track cronies are none other than embodiments of King Arthur's
Knights of the Round Table. The child so influences Jones that he
turns to religion, and the reformed hoods hold a costume party for
the tyke. To please her, they all dress in medieval regalia, with
a racehorse brought in as the child's charger. Later Miss Marker
becomes ill. Sorrowful's bitter enemy, Big Steve (Bickford), proves
to be the only person with the proper blood type to save her life,
which he does. Before the wrap-up, Sorrowful decides to wed his
tough girl friend Bangles Carsons (Dell) and to settle down to a
domestic life with wife and adopted daughter (Temple).

"This picture is a delight in many respects, for it has been
produced so pleasingly and with such efficient portrayals that only
a dyed-in-the-wool cynic could fail to be affected by its sterling
humor and pathos" (New York Times).

In one of the film's musical interludes, Shirley and Dell duet "Laugh You Son-of-a-Gun," just another reason for this ingratiating feature being so endearing. The remake, Sorrowful Jones (1949), q. v. , with Bob Hope and Lucille Ball, was far less resourceful, and the spinoff, 40 Pounds of Trouble, (1962) with Tony Curtis and Suzanne Pleshette was embarrassingly trite.

LOVE ME OR LEAVE ME   (MGM, 1955)   C-122 min.

Producer, Joe Pasternak; director, Charles Vidor; story, Daniel Fuchs; screenplay, Fuchs, Isobel Lennart; art directors, Cedric Gibbons, Urie McCleary; music director, George Stoll; Miss Day's music, Percy Faith; music adviser, Irving Aaronson; choreography, Alex Romero; songs, Ted Koehler and Rube Bloom; Joe McCarthy and James Monaco; Jack Palmer and Spencer Williams; Walter Donaldson; B. G. DeSylva, Lew Brown, and Ray Henderson; Gus Kahn and Donaldson; Roy Turk and Fred Ahlert; Richard Rodgers and Lorenz Hart; Irving Berlin; Chilton Price; Nicholas Brodzky and Sammy Cahn; costumes, Helen Rose; sound, Wesley C. Miller; special effects, Warren Newcombe; camera, Arthur E. Arling; editor, Ralph E. Winters.

Doris Day (Ruth Etting); James Cagney (Martin "The Gimp" Snyder); Cameron Mitchell (Johnny Alderman); Robert Keith (Bernard V. Loomis); Tom Tully (Frobisher); Harry Bellaver (Georgie); Richard Gaines (Paul Hunter); Peter Leeds (Fred Taylor); Claude Stroud (Eddie Fulton); Audrey Young (Jingle Girl); John Harding (Greg Trent); Dorothy Abbott (Dancer); Phil Schumacher, Otto Reichow, Henry Kulky (Bouncers); Jay Adler (Orry); Mauritz Hugo (Irate Customer); Veda Ann Borg (Hostess); Claire Carleton (Claire); Larri Thomas, Patti Nestor, Winona Smith, Shirley Wilson (Chorus Girls); Benny Burt (Stage Manager); Robert B. Carson (Mr. Brelston the Radio Station Manager); James Drury (Assistant Director); Robert Malcolm (Doorman); Robert Stephenson (Waiter); Richard Simmons (Dance Director); Michael Kostrick (Assistant Director); Paul McGuire (Drapery Man); Dale Van Sickel, Johnny Day (Stagehands); Genevieve Aumont (Woman); Henry Randolph, Jimmy Cross (Photographer).

One of the first, and most popular, of screen bio-pics of singing stars of the Twenties and Thirties was Love Me or Leave Me. The film chronicles the "story" of Nebraska farm girl Ruth Etting (Day), who became one of the top singers of the Jazz Age and became involved with racketeer laundryman, Martin "The Gimp" Snyder (Cagney). Snyder makes the girl a big Ziegfeld star, forces her to marry him, and then drives her to drink with his boorish ways. After a dozen years she leaves the hoodlum and he takes revenge by shooting her accompanist (Mitchell).

A very colorful musical-gangster epic, the film received six Academy Award nominations, the sole winner being Daniel Fuchs' for his original story. Time said the film "... has the bite of authenticity. "

Containing many Twenties' tunes, including most of Miss Ettings' best-selling records, the film predated The Helen Morgan

Robert Keith, James Cagney and Doris Day in <u>Love Me or Leave Me</u> (1955).

<u>Story</u> (1957), which was quite similar in context.   Despite the fabrications within the scenario and the gossamer treatment of many aspects of the storyline, MGM had to be complimented for having met a part of the plotline with head-on reality.

Although second-billed to songbird Day (making a dramatic stand here as the harrowed heroine), Cagney again created a definitive portrayal of a hoodlum.   It was entirely different from his previous screen gangster and has remained memorable for its lively and realistic dimensions.   As the dime-a-dance dancer/vocalist involved with both the underworld and the show business life, Day gave one of her best screen performances.   The movie's soundtrack album, long out of print and a collector's item, has been reissued recently by Columbia Records.   When the film was released in 1955, Columbia Records re-issued an LP album of Miss Etting's old platters, an album that has never been discontinued.

LUCKY JORDAN   (Paramount, 1942)   84 min.

Associate producer, Fred Kohlmar; director, Frank Tuttle; story, Charles Leonard; screenplay, Darrell Ware, Karl Tunberg; art directors, Hans Dreier, Ernst Fegte; camera, John Seitz; editor, Archie Marshek.

Alan Ladd (Lucky Jordan); Helen Walker (Jill Evans); Sheldon

Alan Ladd and Helen Walker in Lucky Jordan (1942).

Leonard (Slip Moran); Mabel Paige (Annie); Marie McDonald (Pearl);
Lloyd Corrigan (Ernest Higgins); Russell Hoyt (Eddie); Dave Willock
(Angelo Palacio); Miles Mander (Kilpatrick); John Wengraf (Kessel-
man); Charles Cane (Sergeant); George F. Meader (Little Man); Vir-
ginia Brissac (Woman with Little Man); Al M. Hill, Fred Kohler,
Jr. (Killers); Jack Roberts (Johnny); Clem Bevans (Gas Station At-
tendant); Olaf Hytten (Charles the Servant); William Halligan (Miller
the Gateman); Kitty Kelly (Mrs. Maggotti); George Humbert (Joe
Maggotti); Dorothy Dandridge (Maid at Hollyhock School); Paul Phil-
lips, Joseph Downing (Stick-Up Men); Danny Duncan (Clerk in Cigar
Store); Carol Hughes (Girl in Back Room); Ralph Dunn (Army Guard);
Kenneth Christy (Sergeant); Edward Earle, Jack Baxley (Men);
Edythe Elliott (Secretary); Albert Ferris, Crane Whitley (Gardeners);
Kirk Alyn (Pearl's Boy Friend); Terry Ray (Sentry); Bud McTaggart,
Keith Richards (Soldiers); Virginia Farmer (Lady); Ethel Clayton
(Woman); Harold Minjir (Clerk in Flower Shop); Ralph Peters (Brig
Sergeant); Yvonne De Carlo (Girl on the Street).

During World War II, even gangsters joined the Allied cause,
as exemplified by Alan Ladd in Lucky Jordan. Trenchcoated Ladd
was cast as a poolroom racketeer who is drafted, goes A. W. O. L.,
and takes pretty Jill Evans (Walker) as a hostage. After a long
chase by the military police, Lucky becomes involved with an international spy ring which uses a botanical garden as a front for its
nefarious activities. Eventually, Jordan, with Jill's help, rounds
up the clan of fifth columnists and proves that even a hoodlum, albeit a petty one, puts his country's welfare above foreign powers.
(This was also the gist of Humphrey Bogart's All Through the Night,
1942.) More often than not, and contrary to the theme of Lucky
Jordan, heartless thugs were usually presented by Hollywood as aid-
ing the Axis.

Regarding Lucky Jordan, Time said, "As a sociological trea-
tise, Lucky Jordan shows that U. S. gangsters are infinitely nicer
than Nazis because 1) they are Americans, 2) they do not like to go
around beating up old women." The latter incident, when Annie
(Mabel Paige) gives Lucky shelter, helps turn the lawbreaker toward
his patriotic actions.

LUCKY LUCIANO (Avco Embassy, 1974) C-116 min.

Presenter, Joseph E. Levine; producer, Franco Cristaldi;
director-story, Francesco Rosi; screenplay, Rosi, Lino Jannuzzi,
Tonino Guerra; music, Piero Piccioni; technical consultant, Charles
Siragusa; camera, Pasqualino De Santis; editor, Ruggero Mastroian-
ni.

Gian-Maria Volonte (Lucky Luciano); Rod Steiger (Gene Giannini); Charles Siragusa (Himself); Edmond O'Brien (Harry J. An-
slinger); Vincent Gardenia (American Colonel); Silverio Blasi (Italian
Captain); Charles Cioffi (Vito Genovese); Magda Konopka (The Con-
tessa); Larry Gates (Herlands); Jacques Monod (French Commissioner); Dino Curcio (Don Ciccio); Karin Petersen (Igea).

Rod Steiger in Lucky Luciano (1974).

     The California film industry of the 1970s would not have dared to turn out a specious film like Lucky Luciano. But leave it to exploitation-oriented producer Joseph E. Levine to purchase this Italian-made picture, hoping to take advantage of the current film craze swamping America.

     If schoolboys ever use this film as a visual source, they will have little idea of the actuality of the life and times of Charles "Lucky" Luciano (Volonte). As displayed on screen, the vicious Mafia figure, who pushed his way to a top spot in the organization before deportation proceedings in 1946, was a very gentle man indeed. According to director Francesco Rosi, once the crime lord figure returns to Naples he becomes an almost saintly figure. He converses with local clergyman, donates to worthy charities, and samples the pasta at waterside cafes. There are occasional references to his unlawful activities, and to the far-reaching ramifications of his still criminal occupations in the late Forties and throughout the Fifties.

     What vitiates the film's entertainment, the glorification of the subject matter aside, is the unsubtle acting. Except for Volonte, who mimes appropriately enough through the tableau of events in Lucky's very active life, the other name cast members are

embarrassingly flagrant in their performances. It is hard to decide
who is least effective: O'Brien as a raspy-voiced Narcotics Bureau
chief (who talks like a schoolteacher addressing five year olds),
Steiger as a minor organization figure who is rubbed out, or Gardenia as a corrupt American general in Occupation Italy.

    Unlike The Valachi Papers (1972), q.v., or The Stone Killers
(1973), q.v., other Rome-New York co-produced affairs, Lucky
Luciano offers little credibility, excitement, or information.

LUCKY NICK CAIN (Twentieth Century-Fox, 1951) 87 min.

    Producer, Joseph Kaufman; director, Joseph M. Newman;
based on the novel I'll Get You for This by James Hadley Chase,
screenplay, George Callahan, William Rose; art director, Ralph
Brinton; music, Walter Goehr; sound, John Mitchell; camera, Otto
Heller; editor, Russell Lloyd.

    George Raft (Nick Cain); Coleen Gray (Kay Wonderly); Enzio
Staiola (Toni); Charles Goldner (Massini); Walter Rilla (Mueller);
Martin Benson (Sperazza); Peter Illing (Ceralde); Hugh French
(Travers); Peter Bull (Hans); Elwyn Brook-Jones (The Fence); Con-
stance Smith (Nina); Greta Gynt (Claudette); Margot Grahame (Mrs.
Langley); Donald Stewart (Kennedy).

George Raft and Colleen Gray in Lucky Nick Cain (1951).

In the early 1950s, down-on-his-luck George Raft accepted an offer from Italian producers to star in an international gangster film. The resultant melodrama was a rather slow-moving vehicle, but one that was attractively lensed along the Italian Riviera. For those moviegoers brought up on the tommy gun entries of the Thirties, seeing a film of this nature was a bit of nostalgia, especially with Raft in the lead.

Nick Cain (Raft) is a vacationing gambler who is framed for the Riviera murder of a U.S. Treasury Agent. The hoodlums, it seems, make bogus U.S. currency with old Nazi plates and are disseminating the bills. Nick sets out to capture the gang and clear his name. In the course of his activities, he falls in love with American Kay Wonderly (Gray), and the trail takes him along the Italian coast.

Perhaps the highlight of the film was a cabaret sequence in which Nick and Kay begin to dance and the music stops. When a tango starts to play, Kay asks Nick, "Do you tango?" "I used to," he says with a twinkle in his eye, and they begin to dance.

For box-office assurance, the producers added the presence of three British leading ladies (Gynt, Smith and Grahame) with whom Raft's Nick was allowed to have brief romantic entanglements.

MA BARKER'S KILLER BROOD   (Film Service, 1960)   82 min.

Producer, William J. Faris; director, Bill Karan; screenplay, F. Paul Hall; music, Gene Kauer; music conductor, William Hinshaw; song, Ama Lou Barnes; art director, Paul E. Mullen; set decorator, Harry Reif; sound, John Kean; camera, Clark Ramsey.

Lurene Tuttle (Ma Barker); Tris Coffin (Arthur Dunlop); Paul Dubov (Alvin Karpis); Nelson Leigh (George Barker); Myrna Dell (Lou); Vic Lundin (Machine Gun Kelly); Donald Spruance (Herman Barker); Don Grady (Herman as a Boy); Ronald Foster (Doc Barker); Gary Ammann (Doc as a Boy); Roye Baker (Lloyd Barker); Donald Towers (Lloyd as a Boy); Eric Morris (Fred Barker); Michael Smith (Fred as a Boy); Byron Foulger (Dr. Guelffe); Eric Sinclair (John Dillinger); Robert Kendall (Baby Face Nelson); Irene Windust (Mrs. Khortney); John McNamara (Mr. Khortney); Dan Riss (Baxter); David Carlile (Avery); Charles Tannen, Daniel White (Sheriffs); Riley Hill (Deputy).

Derived from a teleseries, with episodes strung together, this low budget entry got a ten-year jump on Shelley Winters' Bloody Mama, q. v.

Enduring character actress Lurene Tuttle appeared as Ma Barker (1872-1935), the grandmotherly lady whose four sons participated in a bloody reign of terror organized by her. According to this rather tacky version, she joins in capers with such notorious wanted fugitives as Baby Face Nelson (Kendall), John Dillinger (Sinclair), and Machine Gun Kelly (Lundin).

Charles Bronson, Susan Cabot and Richard Devon in <u>Machine Gun Kelly</u> (1958).

MACHINE GUN KELLY   (American International, 1958)   84 min.

Executive producers, James H. Nicholson, Samuel Z. Arkoff; producer-director, Roger Corman; screenplay, R. Wright Campbell; music-music conductor, Gerald Fried; assistant director, Jack Bohrer; art director, Dan Haller; set decorator, Harry Reif; wardrobe, Margo Corso; makeup, Dave Newell; sound, Philip Mitchell; camera, Floyd Crosby; editor, Ronald Sinclair.

Charles Bronson (Machine Gun Kelly); Susan Cabot (Flo); Morey Amsterdam (Fandango); Jack Lambert (Howard); Wally Campo (Maize); Bob Griffin (Vito); Barboura Morris (Lynn); Richard Devon (Apple); Ted Thorp (Teddy); Mitzi McCall (Harriet); Frank De Kova (Harry); Shirley Falls (Martha); Connie Gilchrist (Ma); Mike Fox (Clinton); Larry Thor (Drummond); George Archambeault (Frank); Jay Sayer (Philip Ashton).

Distortion of facts is nothing new to the cinema, and this rat-a-tat-tat version of a segment of the life of George R. "Machine Gun" Kelly" (1897-1954) left a lot to be desired historically. However, as an action entry it was "A first-rate little picture" (<u>Variety</u>). The same trade paper lauded producer-director Roger Corman for taking "... the trouble to sketch briefly but effectively, minor characters and incidents that give weight and meaning to the otherwise

sordid story. "
     Ex-bootlegger Machine Gun Kelly (Bronson) in the Thirties
has become one of the country's most infamous gunmen-bank robbers.   As a change of professional pace, he turns to kidnapping,
making a steel executive's daughter his first expensive prey.   However, Fandango (Amsterdam), a former underling, squeals to the
police and Kelly's success turns to failure and capture (he turns
cowardly at the end).
     Rugged Bronson was in his proper element as the physical,
brooding killer, a type of role that would earn him a fortune in the
1970s.

MACHINE GUN McCAIN   see   GLI INTOCCABILI

McQ   (Warner Bros. , 1974)   C-111 min.

     Executive producer, Michael A. Wayne; producers, Jules
Levy, Arthur Gardner, Michael A. Wayne; director, John Sturges;
screenplay, Lawrence Roman; assistant director, Ric Rondell; sec-
ond unit director, Ron R. Rondell; production designer, Walter
Simonds; set decorator Tony Montenaro; music, Elmer Bernstein;
titles, Wayne Fitzgerald; sound, Charles M. Wilborn; special effects,
Howard Jensen; camera, Harry Stradling, Jr. ; editor, William Zieg-
ler.
     John Wayne (Lon McQ); Eddie Albert (Captain Ed Kosterman);
Diana Muldaur (Lois Boyle); Colleen Dewhurst (Myra); Clu Gulager
(Franklin Toms); David Huddleston (Pinky Farrow); Jim Watkins
(J. C.); Al Lettieri (Manny Santiago); Julie Adams (Elaine Forrester);
Roger E. Mosley (Rosey); William Bryant (Sergeant Stan Boyle); Joe
Tornatore (LaSalle); Kim Sanford (Ginger); Richard Kelton (Radical);
Richard Eastham (Walter Forrester); Dick Friel (Bob Mahoney); Fred
Waugh (Bodyguard).

     John Wayne, typed in the saddle for more than three decades,
temporarily vacated the range for a small sports car and romped
through Seattle as an older generation Serpico, trying to clean out
corruption in the area's police department.   Although obviously an
imitation of Dirty Harry (1971), q. v. , Bullitt (1968), q. v. , and
others of like ilk, the film did quite well in release.
     Combining all the action of a typical Wayne film with a lit-
erate script about drug pushers within the police department, the
story has old-time cop rebel Lon McQ (Wayne) quitting the police,
his life's occupation, in order to track down the bunch responsible
for his best buddy's death.   Throughout the 111-minute feature, those
involved with McQ all seem to meet a bad end, including an aging
hooker (Dewhurst).
     Also at odds with the hero is the police department itself,
helmed by Captain Ed Kosterman (Albert).   As the film demonstrated, the red tape of supposed law and order can be its own worst
enemy in the battle against organized crime.

John Wayne and James Watkins in McQ (1974).

MADAME RACKETEER (Paramount, 1932) 72 min.

    Directors, Alexander Hall, Harry Wagstaff Gribble; story-
screenplay, Malcolm Stuart Boylan, Harvey Gates; camera, Henry
Sharp.
    Alison Skipworth (Countess von Claudwig [Martha Hicks]);
Richard Bennett (Elmer Hicks); George Raft (Jack Houston); John
Breeden (David Butterworth); Evalyn Knapp (Alice Hicks); Gertrude
Messinger (Patsy Hicks); Robert McWade (James Butterworth); J.
Farrell MacDonald (John Adams); Walter Walker (Arthur Gregory);
George Barbier (Warden Waddell); Cora Shumway (Matron); Jessie
Arnold (Frankie); Anna Chandler (Stella); Kate Morgan (Maxine);
Robert Homans (Chief of Police); Arthur Hill (Shanks); Eleanor
Wesselhoeft (Mrs. Donkenspeil); Ed Brady (Taxi Driver); Irving
Bacon (Gus the Desk Clerk); Frank Beal, Edgar Lewis, Scott Seat-
on, William Humphrey, Alf James (Bank Directors).

    Four years before she was cast as a female Kaspar Gutman
in Satan Met a Lady (1936), q.v., Paramount had salty Alison Skipworth playing a thief known as "the Countess" in this offbeat feature.
This lawbreaker earned her distinctive title while she was

Alison Skipworth in <u>Madame Racketeer</u> (1932).

incarcerated in England (she always stayed in the best British jails).
Back in America, when she is released, she becomes determined to
con her hotel owner husband (Bennett) out of as much money as is
necessary to insure future happiness of her two daughters (Knapp and
Messinger).

With her dishonest methods the Countess does her best to wed
Alice to a rich banker's son. Her scheme is to produce a phony
will in which she lists huge assets to be left to the girl. Next she
breaks up Patsy's romance with Chicago hoodlum Jack Houston (Raft)
by joining forces with him and showing him up for the crook he is.
Working with Houston, however, earns the Countess a return trip to
jail. But she does not mind, for she is reunited with her old comrades in crime, and over tea, she has plenty of new tales to tell
them.

The entire thing sounds a bit too cute, but it worked exceedingly well.

Richard Widmark and Harry Guardino in Madigan (1968).

MADIGAN (Universal, 1968) C-101 min.

Producer, Frank P. Rosenberg; director, Don Siegel; based on the novel The Commissioner by Richard Dougherty; screenplay, Henri Simoun, Abraham Polonsky; music, Don Costa; music supervisor, Joseph Gershenson; art directors, Alexander Golitzen, George C. Webb; set decorators, John McCarthy, John Austin; makeup, Bud Westmore; assistant director, Joe Cavalier; sound, Waldon O. Watson, Lyle Cain; camera, Russell Metty; editor, Milton Shifman.

Richard Widmark (Detective Daniel Madigan); Henry Fonda (Commissioner Anthony X. Russell); Inger Stevens (Julia Madigan); Harry Guardino (Detective Rocco Bonaro); James Whitmore (Chief Inspector Charles Kane); Susan Clark (Tricia Bentley); Steve Ihnat (Barney Benesch); Michael Dunn (Midget Castiglione); Don Stroud (Hughie); Sheree North (Jonesy); Warren Stevens (Ben Williams); Raymond St. Jacques (Dr. Taylor); Bert Freed (Chief Detective Hap Lynch); Harry Bellaver (Mickey Dunn); Frank Marth (Lieutenant James Price); Lloyd Gough (Chief Inspector Earl Griffin); Virginia Gregg (Esther Newman); Toian Machinga (Rosita); Rita Lynn (Rita Bonaro); Robert Granere (Buster); Henry Beckman (Patrolman Philip Downes); Woodrow Parfrey (Marvin); Dallas Mitchell (Detective Tom Gavin); Diane Sayer (Doreen).

This rough, tough melodrama, directed by cult favorite Don
Siegel, slickly detailed the efforts of two New York City detectives,
Madigan (Widmark) and his partner (Guardino) to corral a wanted
killer (Ihnat) who always has escaped their clutches. Police Commissioner Russell (Fonda), occupied with a series of departmental
and personal problems, gives the two veteran cops 72 hours to
bring in the murderer.   Through a lead supplied by Midget Castiglione (Dunn), a bookie, the duo confront Benesch at an East 102nd
Street hold-out.   In the ensuing gunbattle, Madigan is mortally
wounded.   His widow (Stevens) insists that Russell is a cold, calculating administrator who regarded her husband as "just another
lousy cop. "
This rugged actioner was one of the first major features to
show the drabness in the life of big city policement.   Corruption
and bribery are a part of their daily life, and Russell's attitude of
coping with Chief Inspector Kane's (Whitmore) infractions of the
rules, such as covering up a pimps' hangout for money, is strictly
realistic, rather than a Hollywood gimmick. Abraham Polonsky, a
"victim" of the McCarthy Anti-Red hearing, co-authored the screenplay, which pointed a sharp finger at the so-called high ethics of
the police bureaucracy.
As _Time_ viewed it, "Madigan is a good movie about some
bads at New York City's police department.... From the commissioner on down, everybody is up to his badge in problems. " _Vari-_
ety analyzed, "Psychological problems that affect leading cops do
not detract from the fact that it is primarily an actioner with punch. "
Although the title character dies at the end of the film, a
television series called "Madigan" starring Widmark appeared for one
season.   It was not successful.

MAFIA   (American International, 1969)   C-90 min.

Producers, Ermanno Donait, Luigi Carpentieri; director,
Damiano Domiani; based on the novel _Day of the Owl_ by Leonardo
Sciascia; screenplay, Ugo Pirro, Domiani.
Claudia Cardinale (Rosa); Franco Nero (Captain Bellodi); Lee
J. Cobb (Don Mariano); Nehemiah Persoff (Pizzuco).

A busload of passengers deny seeing or knowing anything about
the body of a man which has caused the halt of their trip.   The
body has been found in the middle of the road.   This strange silence
on the part of all the known witnesses leads the police to delve deeper into the case.   It is revealed that a Sicilian crime syndicate is
blocking the murder investigation.   Thereafter, the Mafia uses assorted pressures to keep the witnesses silent.

MAFIA   see   IN NOMME DELLA LAGGE

MAFIA MOB   see   VIVA L'AMERICA

MAFIOSO (C. C. C. , 1962) 105 min.

Producer, Dino DeLaurentiis; director, Alberto Lattuada; story, Bruno Caruso; screenplay, Marco Ferreri, Rafael Azcona, A. Scarpelli; music, Piero Piccioni; camera, Armando Nannuzzi; editor, Nino Baragli.

Alberto Sordi (Antonio Badalamenti); Norma Bengell (Marta); Ugo Attanasio (Don Vincenzo); Carmelo Oliviero (Don Liborio); Gabriella Conti (Rosalie).

This 1962 Italian-made entry did not have American distribution until 1964, although it won the 1963 Golden Shell Award for Best Film at the San Sebastian Film Festival. In hard-punching fashion, it told of the terrors of a family mixed up in Mafia affairs.

Alberto Sordi, more noted for his comedy roles, gave a strong performance in the lead as a Sicilian factory foreman working in Milan. Later he returns home with his northern wife and kids and becomes involved with the Mafia. He is sent to New York by the organization to kill one of the society's enemy. (His family is led to believe that he is going away on a hunting trip.)

The stark impression left by this realistic study is haunting. "... [it] comes about as close to an actual picture of what that underground organization is like as anything that has ever been put on the screen" (New York Morning Telegraph).

MAGNUM FORCE see DIRTY HARRY

THE MALTESE FALCON (Warner Bros. , 1931) 75 min.

Director, Roy Del Ruth; based on the novel by Dashiell Hammett; screenplay, Hammett (uncredited), Maude Fulton, Lucien Hubbard, Brown Holmes; camera, William Rees; editor, George Marks.

Bebe Daniels (Ruth Wonderly); Ricardo Cortez (Sam Spade); Dudley Digges (Gutman); Una Merkel (Effie); Robert Elliott (Detective Dundy); J. Farrell MacDonald (Polhouse); Otto Matiesen (Cairo); Morgan Wallace (District Attorney); Walter Long (Archer); Dwight Frye (Wilmer); Thelma Todd (Iva Archer); Augostino Borgato (Captain Jacobi).

TV title: Dangerous Female.

THE MALTESE FALCON (Warner Bros. , 1941) 100 min.

Executive producer, Hal B. Wallis; associate producer, Henry Blanke; director, John Huston; based on the novel by Dashiell Hammett; screenplay, Huston; music, Adolph Deutsch; orchestrator, Arthur Lange; dialog director, Robert Foulk; assistant director, Claude Archer; art director, Robert Haas; gowns, Orry-Kelly; make-up, Perc Westmore; sound, Oliver S. Garretson; camera, Arthur Edeson; editor, Thomas Richards.

Humphrey Bogart (Sam Spade); Mary Astor (Brigid

Peter Lorre, Mary Astor and Sydney Greenstreet in The Maltese
Falcon (1941).

O'Shaughnessy); Gladys George (Iva Archer); Peter Lorre (Joel Cai-
ro); Barton MacLane (Lieutenant Dundy); Lee Patrick (Effie Perine);
Sydney Greenstreet (Casper Gutman); Ward Bond (Detective Tom
Polhaus); Jerome Cowan (Miles Archer); Elisha Cook, Jr. (Wilmer
Cook); James Burke (Luke); Murray Alper (Frank); John Hamilton
(District Attorney Bryan); Emory Parnell (Mate of the La Paloma);
Walter Huston (Captain Jacobi); Jack Mower (Announcer); Hank Mann,
William Hopper, Charles Drake (Reporters); Creighton Hale (Stenog-
rapher).

      Many critics claim that the most definitive of detective novels
is Dashiell Hammett's The Maltese Falcon and that the 1941 film
version of that book is the all-time best detective film.   Certainly
the character of Sam Spade, the hard-boiled detective, was the pre-
cursor of many such book/film/TV sleuths that were to follow.
The John Huston-directed film must rank as one of the best examples of the successful transference of literature to celluloid, as well
as being a classic in the detective film genre.   Quite naturally, this
story overlaps the distinct detective genre with that of the gangster
tale.   (While the emphasis is most definitely on the private eye, the
very colorful underworld characters present in this chronicle make

it a must inclusion within this volume.)

In 1931 Warner Bros. first brought The Maltese Falcon to the screen with Latin idol, Ricardo Cortez (actually Jake Krantz of Brooklyn) as Sam Spade. The screenplay closely followed the novel, and, in fact, Hammett (uncredited), along with Lucien Hubbard and Brown Holmes, worked on the screen adaptation. With Roy Del Ruth directing, the seventy-five minute vehicle told of a group of people searching for the priceless bird of the title, and object encrusted with gems and made of ebony.

In the case were Bebe Daniels, the one-time silent star comedienne and more recently talking film singing lead, as Ruth Wonderly, alias Brigid O'Shaughnessy. She proves to be a cold-blooded murderess. In addition, the film sported Dudley Diggs as Gutman, the fat man, Una Merkel as Effie, Spade's broad-minded, loyal secretary, Robert Elliott as the not-too honest policeman Dundy, Thelma Todd as the two-timing wife of Spade's partner (Long), Otto Matieson as Joel Cairo, the effeminate partner of Gutman, and Dwight Frye as Wilmer, Gutman's gunman.

The Maltese Falcon was well-received when released, although it would never then or later be considered a classic. The New York Times recorded, "Played with disarming ease and warmth by Ricardo Cortez, the character of Sam Spade is enormously unique and attractive.... The film is Mr. Cortez' and Mr. Ruth's. " To avoid mix-up with the 1941 version, the film now plays on TV as Dangerous Female.

In 1936, Warner Bros. , like other studios eager to re-use a property it had already purchased, decided to re-film the Hammett book. But the Brown Holmes scenario had mutilated the original work, to the point of changing the characters' names and adding a tongue-in-cheek attitude to the plot. William Dieterle directed this assembly-line mess which found ingenue-ish Bette Davis as Valerie Purvis, alias Brigid O'Shaughnessy, Warren William as Ted Shayne, alias Sam Spade, Marie Wilson, as Miss Murgatroyd, alias Effie Perrine (the only good casting in the film). Strangest of all, the pivotal Gutman character was switched to that of a woman, Madame Barabbas, played by Alison Skipworth. The whole melage was best summed up by one of the lines Miss Davis spits out in the film, 'I've got a cousin who specializes in brain diseases. Maybe we'd better turn the case over to him. " Titled Satan Met a Lady, the film was (and is) an excellent example of how a major studio could take a fine work of literature and turn it into an unredeemably bad "B" movie.

Five years later, scripter John Huston was seeking a vehicle with which to make his directorial debut. His resultant directing-scripting of this well-worn property pushed him into the front ranks of Hollywood talent. The film itself became a genre classic.

While The Maltese Falcon did much for the careers of Humphrey Bogart (Sam Spade), Mary Astor (Brigid O'Shaughnessy), Peter Lorre (Joel Cairo) and Elisha Cook, Jr. (Wilmer Cook), by far the best casting in the feature was that of Sydney Greenstreet. The sixty-one year old, 285-pound stage actor made his film debut as Casper Gutman, the pseudo gentleman, whose sole purpose in life seemed to be gaining possession of the valuable objet d'art, the falcon. Greenstreet's appearance and performance gave new dimension to the typical screen gangster. With his great bulk and beady eyes, the actor turned the Fat Man into a menacing figure, very much at odds with the uncouth, virile, fast-moving types made famous by Edward G. Robinson, Paul Muni, James Cagney, or Humphrey Bogart. But like these heavies, Greenstreet's Gutman had one strong trait: ruthlessness. For his characterization of the glib, determined Casper, Greenstreet earned an Academy Award nomination for Best Supporting Actor.

Within The Maltese Falcon, the scene where Spade meets the Fat man is a classic. Gutman greets tough Sam Spade with a handshake and leads him into the main room, while offering him a spiked drink. "By gad, sir, " says devious Gutman, "you are a character. I like talking to a man who likes to talk. " It is an indication that this law-versus-disorder plot will be more a battle of wits and words than a contest of brute strength. Yet, like most gangsters, Gutman is quick to turn to physical violence. When he cannot get Spade to talk, and the drugged drink has taken effect, Casper orders Wilmen to kick Spade in the head. The latter does so with great relish, while Gutman looms over the scene with great satisfaction, a great mound of fat.

So popular was the new The Maltese Falcon that Warners planned a sequel, The Further Adventures of the Maltese Falcon, reuniting the principal cast members. But nothing came of these plans. Finally in 1975 the studio produced a sort of follow-up starring George Segal and featuring Elisha Cook, Jr. and Lee Patrick (both from the 1941 edition). It was called The Black Bird and turned out to be more of a spoof than a follow-up to the original masterpiece.

THE MAN WHO DARED see THE STAR WITNESS

MANHATTAN MELODRAMA (MGM, 1934) 98 min.

Producer, David O. Selznick; director, W. S. Van Dyke, II; story, Arthur Caesar; screenplay, Oliver H. P. Garrett, Joseph L. Mankiewicz; song, Richard Rodgers and Lorenz Hart; camera, James Wong Howe; editor, Ben Lewis.

Clark Gable (Blackie Gallagher); William Powell (Jim Wade); Myrna Loy (Eleanor Packer); Leo Carrillo (Father Pat); Nat Pendleton (Spud); George Sidney (Poppa Rosen); Isabel Jewell (Annabelle); Muriel Evans (Tootsie Malone); Claudelle Kaye (Miss Adams); Frank Conroy (Blackie's Attorney); Jimmy Butler (Jim as a Boy); Mickey Rooney (Blackie as a Boy); Landers Stevens (Inspector of Police); Harry Seymour (Piano Player); William N. Bailey, King Mojave, W. R. Walsh (Croupiers); Charles R. Moore (Black Boy in Speakeasy); John Marston (Coates); Lew Harvey (Crap Dealer); Billy Arnold (Black Jack Dealer); Jim James (Chemin De Fer Dealer); Stanley Taylor (Police Interne); James Curtis (Party Leader); Herman Bing (German Proprietor); Edward Van Sloan (Yacht Skipper); Jay Eaton (Drunk); Harrison Greene (Eleanor's Dance Partner); Leslie

William Powell and Myrna Loy in <u>Manhattan Melodrama</u> (1934).

Preston (Jim's Dance Partner); William Stack (Judge); Emmett Vogan, Sherry Hall (Assistant District Attornies); Lee Phelps (Bailiff); Charles Dunbar (Panhandler); John M. Bleifer (Chauffeur); Allen Thompson (Spectator on Street); Wade Boteler (Guard in Prison); Sam McDaniel (Black Man in Prison); James C. Eagles (Boy in Prison); Samuel S. Hinds (Warden); Don Brodie, Ralph McCullough, Eddie Hart (Reporters); Lee Shumway, Carl Stockdale, Jack Kenny (Policemen); Alexander Melesh (Master of Ceremonies); Vernon Dent (Old German Man); Henry Roquemore (Band Leader); Stanley Blystone, William Augustin (Detectives); Oscar Apfel (Assembly Speaker); Shirley Ross (Black Singer); Leonid Kinsky (Trotsky Aide); Leo Lane (Trotsky); Noel Madison (Nannie Arnold); Thomas Jackson (Richard Snow).

The old story of three youths growing up together, with one turning out good, one successful, and the other bad, was transferred to the gangster motif in this film. Directed by W. S. Van Dyke II, Manhattan Melodrama was issued in the spring of 1934. The film quickly became a classic, and Arthur Caesar won an Academy Award for his original story. It set a formula trend that would continue throughout the following decades.

The three pals were up and coming politician Jim Wade (Powell), gangster Blackie Gallagher (Gable) and priest Father Pat (Carrillo). Most of the action centered about the first two characters.

Blackie's chic mistress Eleanor (Loy) wants him to quit the rackets,
and when he refuses, she falls for Jim Wade.   Later they are wed.
When Wade becomes district attorney he fires a crooked assistant
(Jackson), and the latter tries to ruin him.   Eleanor tells Blackie
of Wade's plight and he is driven to murdering the blackmailer.
When Gallagher is arrested for the homicide, Jim is forced to prosecute and Blackie is convicted and sentenced to death.   The head-
lined case wins Jim the governor's race, but when Eleanor tells him
the truth about why Blackie killed the man, Jim goes to the prison.
He tells Blackie he wants to have the sentence commuted.   But Gallagher refuses the offer, which would ruin Jim's career.   Instead,
he walks off to meet his fate with Father Pat at his side.

Six years after this threshold-crossing feature was issued,
Powell and Loy (by then well famous as Mr. and Mrs. Nick Charles
of The Thin Man series) joined with Don Ameche in recreating the
scenario from Manhattan Melodrama for "Lux Radio Theatre."

MANO NERA, LA   see   THE BLACK HAND

MARKED WOMAN   (Warner Bros., 1937)   96 min.

Executive producers, Jack L. Warner, Hal B. Wallis; producer, Lou Edelman; director, Lloyd Bacon; screenplay, Robert
Rosson, Abem Finkel; additional dialog, Seton I. Miller; music,
Bernard Kaum, Heinz Roemheld; music director, Leo F. Forbstein;
songs, Harry Warren and Al Dubin; gowns, Orry-Kelly; art director, Max Parker; camera, George Barnes; editor, Jack Killifer.

Bette Davis (Mary Dwight [Strauber]); Humphrey Bogart (Spe-
cial Prosecutor David Graham); Jane Bryan (Betty Strauber); Eduardo
Ciannelli (Johnny Vanning); Isabel Jewell (Emmy Lou Egan); Allen
Jenkins (Louis); Mayo Methot (Estelle Porter); Lola Lane (Gabby
Marvin); Ben Welden (Charley Delaney); Henry O'Neill (District At-
torney Arthur Sheldon); Rosalind Marquis (Florrie Liggett); John Li-
tel (Gordon); Damian O'Flynn (Ralph Krawford); Robert Strange
(George Beler); James Robbins (Bell Captain); William B. Davidson
(Bob Crandall); John Sheehan (Vincent--a Sugar Daddy); Sam Wren
(Mac); Kenneth Harlan (Eddie--a Sugar Daddy); Raymond Hatton (Law-
yer at Jail); Alan Davis, Allen Matthews (Henchmen); John Harron,
Frank Faylen (Taxi Drivers); Alphonse Martel (Doorman); Carlos San
Martin (Headwaiter); Harlan Briggs (Man in Phone Booth); Philip G.
Sleeman (Crap Table Attendant); Guy Usher (Ferguson the Detective);
Ed Stanley (Casey the Detective); Milton Kibbee (Male Secretary at
D.A.'s Office); Mark Strong (Bartender); Emmett Vogan (Court
Clerk); Jack Mower (Foreman); Herman Marks (Little Joe); Wendell
Niles (News Commentator).

All too often the role of women in gangster films has been
regulated to that of molls, temptresses, or sweet heroines innocently caught up in the web of violence.   Marked Woman, "a strong and
well made underworld drama" (Variety), crisply told the tale of a
clip joint hostess (Davis) who knowingly works in the underworld and

Ralph Dunn (clerk), Humphrey Bogart, Gordon Hart and Bette Davis in <u>Marked Woman</u> (1937).

lives to regret her sordid activities.

As Mary Strauber (alias Dwight), Davis gave a strong performance as a young woman employed by hood Johnny Vanning (Ciannelli). He kills one of his customers when the man cannot make good on his gambling losses. A crusading District Attorney (Bogart) brings the accused killer to trial, but Mary, a witness to the homicide, is threatened and gives conflicting evidence which sets Vanning free. Later, the gangster is responsible for the death of Mary's sister, Betty (Bryan), when she resists one of his henchmen. As for Mary, her face is scarred by one of Vanning's thugs as a warning. She rebels, however, and turns state's evidence. Her testimony convicts Vanning and makes a hero of David Graham. Mary is left to cope with her past, her unsavory reputation, and her marked face; but at least she has some sort of future.

MARY BURNS, FUGITIVE (Paramount, 1935) 84 min.

Producer, Walter Wanger; director, William K. Howard; story, Gene Towne, Graham Baker; screenplay, Towne, Baker, Louis Stevens; camera, Leon Shamroy; editor, Pete Fritsch.

Sylvia Sidney (Mary Burns); Melvyn Douglas (Barton Powell); Alan Baxter ("Babe" Wilson); Pert Kelton (Goldie Gordon); Wallace Ford (Harper); Brian Donlevy (Spike); Esther Dale (Kate); Frank Sully (Steve); Boothe Howard (Red Martin); Norman Willis (Joe); Frances Gregg (Matron); Charles Waldron (District Attorney); William

Ingersoll (Judge); Rita Stanwood Warner (Nurse Agnes); Grace Hayle
(Nurse Jennie); Daniel Haynes (Jeremiah); Joe Twerp (Willie);
James Mack (Farmer); William Pawley (Mike); Isabel Carlisle (Wom-
an Tourist); Dorothy Vaughn (Irish Matron); Esther Howard (Land-
lady); Morgan Wallace (Managing Editor); Phil Tead (Reporter); Ann
Doran (Newspaper Girl); Fuzzy Knight (Dance Hall Attendant);
Charles Wilson (G-Man in Dance Hall); Kernan Cripps (G-Man);
George Chandler (Cashier); Cora Sue Collins (Little Girl).

After viewing this effort, the New York Times reported,
"The cinema continues to discover variations on the outmoded gangster cycle.... " The British Daily Film Renter observed, "There
is plenty of strong meat in this film.... "

Actually this Walter Wanger production was little more than
a potboiler, exploiting the weepy, put-upon screen image of star
Sylvia Sidney. It was another case of an innocent girl being hounded
by both the law and a member of the underworld.

Mary Burns (Sidney) owns a rural coffee shop and happens to
love "Babe" Wilson (Baxter), not knowing that he is a gangster.
Due to him she becomes implicated in a crime, and though protest-
ing her innocence, she is convicted by a jury. (Why she is, on no
real evidence, is the major loophole in the storyline). Sent to
prison, she is permitted to escape, along with her tough cellmate
Goldie Gordon (Kelton). The police hope Mary will lead them to
Wilson. On the lam, Mary encounters explorer Powell (Douglas)
who is hospitalized with temporary blindness. They develop a romantic rapport. Later, after kidnapping Mary, Babe is caught by
the police in a bloody shootout. With her name now cleared, Mary
is free to romance Powell, he having recovered his sight.

On April 11, 1938, a version of Mary Burns, Fugitive was
presented on "Lux Radio Theatre" with Miriam Hopkins and Henry
Fonda in the leads.

ME, GANGSTER (Fox, 1928) 6,042'

Presenter, William Fox; director, Raoul Walsh; based on the
book by Charles Francis Coe; screenplay, Charles Francis Coe,
Walsh; titles, William Kernell; assistant director, Archibald Buchanan; camera, Arthur Edeson; editor, Louis Loeffler.

June Collyer (Mary Regan); Don Terry (Jimmy Williams);
Anders Randolf (Russ Williams); Stella Adams (Lizzie Williams);
Burt McIntosh (Bill Lane); Walter James (Captain Dodds); Gustav
von Seyffertitz (Factory Owner); Al Hill (Danny); Herbert Ashton
(Sucker); Bob Perry (Tuxedo George); Harry Castle (Philly Kid);
Carol(e) Lombard (Blonde Rosie); Joe Brown (Himself); Nigel De
Brulier (Danish Looie); Arthur Stone (Dan the Dude).

While this silent feature based on Charles Francis Coe's
bestseller of 1927 would seem to be strictly a gang-cops-and-robbers
type film, it actually dealt with the attempt by a young hood (Terry)
to go straight after falling in love with the right girl (Collyer).

Me, Gangster told of a slum boy (Terry) always on the wrong

side of the law, who makes it into big-time crime by stealing and
hiding $50,000. For his trouble he goes to jail. Meanwhile, he
has an opportunity to appreciate his affection for Mary Regan (Collyer). When he is later paroled he decides to return the loot. His
former gang, however, has other ideas and try to thwart his plans.
But in the end right triumphs over wrong.

For director Raoul Walsh this film is just one of the "forgotten" titles in his impressive filmography. But for leads Terry
and Collyer it may well be the apex of their careers, both of which
dwindled into "B" pictures, serials, and poverty row productions in
the Thirties. Miss Collyer did enjoy a revival in the Fifties when
she co-starred with her husband, Stuart Erwin, in the long-running
teleseries, "Trouble with Father."

THE MECHANIC (United Artists, 1972) C-100 min.

Producers, Irwin Winkler, Robert Chartoff; assistant producer, Henry Gellis; director, Michael Winner; screenplay, Lewis John
Carlino; assistant directors, Jerome M. Siegel, Peter Price, Francesco Cinieri; second unit director, Antonio Tarruella; music-music
conductor, Jerry Fielding; art directors, Roger E. Maus, Herbert
Westbrook; stunt coordinator, Alan R. Gibbs; makeup, Phillip Rhodes;
costumes, Lambert Marks; sound, Burdick S. Trask, Terence Rawlings; camera, Richard Kline, Robert Paynter; editor, Freddie Wilson.

Charles Bronson (Arthur Bishop); Jan-Michael Vincent (Steve
McKenna); Keenan Wynn (Harry McKenna); Jill Ireland (Prostitute);
Linda Ridgeway (Louise); Frank De Kova (The Man); Lindsay H.
Crosby (Policeman); Takayuki Kubota (Karate Master); Martin Gordon
(American Tourist); James Davidson (Intern); Steve Cory (Messenger);
Patrick O'Moore (Old Man); Celeste Yarnall (The Mark's Girl); Athe-
na Lorde Howard Morton (Car Polish Man); Gerald Peters (Butler);
Alison Rose (Young Girl); Ken Wolger, Stephen Vinovich, Trina
Mitchum (Hippies); Kevin O'Neal, Linda Grant, Hank Hamilton, Sara
Taft, John Barclay (Bits).

"... cold, calculating, efficient, flashy, and ... vacuous."
That is how the British Monthly Film Bulletin described this largely
European-lensed feature which starred box-office favorite Charles
Bronson. On the surface it was an allegedly serious study of a
"mechanic," a professional assassin who is a full-time employee of
the Organization. However, as delineated on camera, it became a
plotline excuse for violence and bloodshed. Viewers got little insight
into the rationale of the paid killer, of his ethics or his emotions.

Arthur Bishop (Bronson) is an expert in his field of hired
killing, making each of his assignments look like an accident. Steve
McKenna (Vincent) convinces Bishop to make him his assistant, giving no indication that he knows Arthur was the murderer of his father (Wynn). Only later does Bishop perceive that the Organization
has hired Steve to eliminate him. After the two complete a mission
successfully, McKenna poisons Arthur and returns to the States, only to become a victim of Bishop's booby-trapped car. It seems that
Arthur had foreseen such an outcome, and guaranteed his revenge.

MELODIE EN SOUS-SOL   (MGM, 1963)   118 min.

Producer, Jacques Bar; director, Henri Verneuil; based on
the novel by John Trinlan; screenplay, Albert Simonin, Michel
Audiard, Verneiul; music, Michel Magne; assistant directors, Claude
Pinoteau, Christian De Chalonge; art director, Robert Clavel; sound,
Jean Rieul; camera, Louis Page; editor, Francoise Verneiul.

Jean Gabin (Charles); Alain Delon (Francis); Viviane Romance
(Ginette); Maurice Biraud (Louis); Carla Marlier (Brigitte); Jose de
Vilallonga (Grimp); Germaine Montero (Francis' Mother); Jean Car-
met (Barman); Dora Doll (Countess); Henri Virlojeux (Marie); Rita
Cadillac (Lillane); Anne Marie Coffinet (Marcelle); Jimmy David
(Sam); Dominque Davray (Leone); Ben Tyber Ballet Troupe (Them-
selves).

U. S. release: Any Number Can Win (MGM, 1963) 110 min.

The French have always had a special way with gangster
thrillers, especially those dealing with planned heists.   This film,
although reminiscent of the earlier Rififi series   q. v. , was solid entertainment and big box-office in Europe.   Adding to its allure was
the teaming of France's two biggest box-office names, Jean Gabin
and Alain Delon, who would later co-star in an even bigger moneymaker, Le Clan Des Siciliens (1970), q. v.

This effort finds Gabin as Charles, an aging crook just released from jail, who confides to his wife (Romance) that he must
undertake one last, big job.   To aid in the effort he enlists his
former cellmate, Francis (Delon).   Together they plan the robbery
of a gambling casino at Cannes.   With measured on-location photography on the Riviera, the well-paced feature traces the planning of
the heist through the robbery, and to its ironic climax.   "... the
scheme is a dilly and its development both nerve-tingling and grown-
up. ...   The minutiae of the arrangements are fascinating even before the splitting of seconds begin.   By the time zero hour approaches you're with these ex-cons all the way" (New York Herald-Tribune).
Perhaps Bosley Crowther (New York Times) said it all when he reflected that the film "... has the captivating air of professional ar-
rangement and performance. "

MELVIN PURVIS, G-MAN   (ABC-TV, 1974)   C-90 min.

Executive producer, Paul R. Picard; producer-director, Dan
Curtis; story, John Milius; teleplay, Milius, William F. Nolan; art
director, Trevor Williams; music, Robert Cobert; camera, Jacques
Marquette; editor, Richard Harris.

Dale Robertson (Melvin Purvis); Harris Yulin (George "Ma-
chine Gun" Kelly); Margaret Blye (Katherine Kelly); Matt Clark
(Charles Parlmetter); Elliott Street (Thomas "Buckwheat" Longaker);
John Karlen (Tony Redecci); David Canary (Eugene Farber); Steve
Kanaly (Sam Crowley); Woodrow Parfrey (Nash Covington); Dick
Sargent (Thatcher Covington).

Continental release title: The Legend of Machine Gun Kelly.

One of J. Edgar Hoover's most famous F.B.I. associates
was Melvin Purvis, who is credited with popularizing the term G-
Man in the Thirties.   Throughout that decade Purvis led the fight
against numerous hoodlums, the most famous being John Dillinger.
[See Ben Johnson's sturdy portrayal of the lawman in Dillinger
(1973), q.v.]   American International, the same company which made
the former film, decided to turn Purvis' exploits into a telefeature,
which would be released theatrically abroad.   It was almost forty
years after Republic Pictures had toyed with the idea of featuring
Purvis as the lead character in a serial.

Made as an obvious series pilot, this entry had the Midwest
F.B.I. Bureau Chief (Robertson) on the trail of "Machine Gun" Kelly
(Yulin) and his gang in 1933 after the wanted men have staged the
daring kidnap of a millionaire playboy (Sargent).   The gang demands
$500,000 ransom.   When the money-hostage exchange is made,
Covington lies to Purvis because he has fallen in love with Kelly's
girl (Blythe).   Eventually the G-Man official sees through Covington's deception, the gang is hunted down, and Kelly is killed.   The
money is repossessed.

This production stayed close to the Bonnie and Clyde-type
recreation of the Depression era, including nostalgia music (unfortunately the songs selected were from the Twenties, not the Thirties).
Despite an overly flamboyant performance by Robertson and a very
sensual one by Blythe, the overall effect was empty.

Variety observed, "In view of the recent Pastore sub-commit-
tee hearings on TV violence and the networks' stance on the curtail-
ment of same, ABC-TV's airing of its Melvin Purvis, G-Man pilot-
feature seemed extremely untimely."

MENS SAGFØREREN SOVER (WHILE THE ATTORNEY IS ASLEEP)
(A/S Palladium, 1945) 80 min.

Director, Johan Jacobsen; based on a story by Gunnar Robert
Hansen; screenplay, Arvid Müller; art director, Erik Aaes; music,
Kai Møller; camera, Einar Olsen; editor, Edith Schlüssel.

Gunnar Lauring (Erik Jessen the Attorney); Beatrice Bon-
nesen (Else Jessen--His Daughter); Christian Arhoff (Magnus Stripp);
Elith Pio (Robert Jensen); Gerda Neumann (Lilian Berner); Sam
Besekow (Takituki the Butler); Poul Reichardt (Charlie); Freddy Al-
bech (Joe); Gunnar Lemvigh (Mike); Per Gundmann (Sam); Valdemar
Skjerning (Mr. Jorgensen); Knud Heglund (Tardini).

Wanted by the U.S. police, four Danish-American hoodlums
(Reichardt, Albeck, Lemvigh and Gundmann) head back to the old
country where they plan a big heist.   Their plot is to steal the famous Crown jewels in the Rosenborg castle.   Since they require an
alibi, they make an appointment with an attorney in their hotel room
for an alleged real estate deal.   They drug the lawyer and rob the
jewels while he sleeps.   Later, when the attorney awakes, all he
can tell the police (who suspect the four hoods) is that they were
with him in the hotel during the time of the crime.   Previously the
quartet had met another Danish-American for business.   Their

behavior had aroused the suspicion of the man's secretary and of her young admirer (Arhoff). Stripp and his girl eventually manage to foil the gangsters and help the Danish police wrap up the case.

This film was merely a Danish rendition of the seemingly parochial American gangster-heist yarn. For the record, Christian Arhoff has been termed Denmark's top comedian.

THE MIAMI STORY (Columbia, 1954) 75 min.

Producer, Sam Katzman; director, Fred F. Sears; story-screenplay, Robert E. Kent; art director, Paul Palmentola; camera, Henry Freulich; editor, Viola Lawrence.

Barry Sullivan (Mick Flagg); Luther Adler (Tony Brill); John Baer (Ted Delacorte); Adele Jergens (Gwen Abbott); Beverly Garland (Holly Abbott); Dan Riss (Frank Alton); Damian O'Flynn (Chief Martin Belman); Christopher Alcaide (Robert Bishop); Gene D'Arcy (Johnny Loker); George E. Stone (Louie Mott); David Kasday (Gil Flagg); Tom Greenway (Charles Earnshaw).

A stout, "neat" little "B" film, this thriller told of a syndicate based in Florida and how a former toughie (Sullivan) teams with the law to stop the group which is led by Tony Brill (Adler).

Beverly Garland and Barry Sullivan in The Miami Story (1954).

Unfolded in a semi-documentary style, the feature was well-handled by Fred F. Sears, an expert at making the most out of a small budget. Flavorful Adele Jergens and Beverly Garland were on hand to add some bite to the storyline.

MR. LUCKY (RKO, 1943) 100 min.

Producer, David Hempstead; director, H. C. Potter; based on the story Bundles for Freedom by Milton Holmes; screenplay, Holmes, Adrian Scott; music, Roy Webb; music director, C. Bakaleinikoff; production designer, William Cameron Menzies; art directors, Albert S. D'Agostino, Mark-Lee Kirk; set decorators, Darrell Silvera, Claude Carpenter; assistant director, Harry Scott; sound, Richard Van Hessen, James G. Stewart; special effects, Vernon L. Walker; camera, George Barnes; editor, Theron Warth.

Cary Grant (Joe Adams); Laraine Day (Dorothy Bryant); Charles Bickford (Hard Swede); Gladys Cooper (Captain Steadman); Alan Carney (Crunk); Henry Stephenson (Mr. Bryant); Paul Stewart (Zepp); Kay Johnson (Mrs. Ostrander); Erford Gage (The Gaffer); Walter Kingsford (Commissioner Hargraves); J. M. Kerrigan (McDougal); Edward Fielding (Foster); Vladimir Sokoloff (Greek Priest); Florence Bates (Mrs. Van Every); Al Rhein, Sammy Finn, Al

Laraine Day, Cary Grant and Paul Stewart in Mr. Lucky (1943).

Murphy, Fred Rapport (Gamblers); John Bleifer (Siga); Juan Varro (Bascopolus); Frank Mills (Workman at Slot Machine); Mary Forbes (Dowager); Rita Corday, Ariel Heath, Mary Stuart (Bits); Don Brodie (Dealer); Joe Crehan, Kernan Cripps (Plainclothesmen); Art Yeoman, Jack Gargan (Reporters); Major Sam Harris (Gambling Extra); Hal Dawson (Draft Board Director).

This film was a half screwball, half-sophisticated take-off on the gangster motion picture. Joe Adams (Grant), appearing as a gambling boat owner, is roped into managing a charity affair on Park Avenue the $100,000 proceeds of which will be used to finance a relief ship's trip to Europe. Joe plans to abscond with the cash, but several roadblocks materialize, including his falling in love with a society girl (Day) and a double-cross by members of his own mob.
    The storyline would be reused for RKO's Gambling House (1950) starring Victor Mature (no Cary Grant, but he had his own brand of screen charm), and would also provide the basis and title for an adventure teleseries in the late Fifties.

MR. MOTO'S GAMBLE (Twentieth Century-Fox, 1938) 71 min.

    Director, James Tinling; based on the character created by John P. Marquand; screenplay, Charles Belden, Jerry Cady; camera, Lucien Andriot.
    Peter Lorre (Mr. Moto); Keye Luke (Lee Chan); Dick Baldwin (Bill Steele); Lynn Bari (Penny Kendall); Douglas Fowley (Nick Crowder); Jayne Regan (Linda Benton); Harold Huber (Lieutenant Riggs); Maxie Rosenbloom (Knockout Wellington); John Hamilton (Phillip Benton); George E. Stone (Connors); Bernard Nedell (Clipper McCoy); Charles Williams (Gabby Marden); Ward Bond (Biff Moran); Cliff Clark (McGuire); Edward Marr (Sammy); Russ Clark (Frankie Stanton); Lon Chaney, Jr. (Joey); Pierre Watkin (District Attorney); Charles D. Brown (Editor "Scotty"); Paul Fix (Gangster); Fred Kelsey (Mahoney); Frank McGlynn, Jr., Ralph Dunn, David Newell (Detectives); George Magrill, Adrian Morris, Bob Ryan (Policemen); Jack Stoney (Kid Grant); Frank Fanning (Turnkey); Edward Earle (Medical Examiner); Emmett Vogan (Fingerprint Man); Irving Bacon (Sheriff); Olin Howland (Deputy Sheriff).

    Originally this film was conceived as a part of the Charlie Chan series and was to be called Charlie Chan at the Fights or Charlie Chan at the Arena. After filming began, however, series star Warner Oland died and the project was quickly rewritten for Twentieth Century-Fox's second Oriental sleuth, the Japanese Mr. Moto (Lorre), a property derived from John P. Marquand's books. Footage already shot with Keye Luke as Lee Chan was interpolated into the film, with Lee now a student in Moto's school of criminology.
    The plot has Moto assign his students the task of solving the murder of a boxer who died in the ring as a result of poison on his opponent's (Baldwin) gloves. Believing Bill Steele innocent, Moto eventually proves that a betting syndicate was behind the crime and

he rousts out the guilty ones by placing a huge bet on a champion-
ship bout.

It might well be worth investigating why Hollywood scenarists
of the Thirties always insisted upon pitting law enforcers' brains
against crooks' brawn.   Surely there were sufficient numbers of the
latter who had high I.Q.'s!

THE MOB   (Columbia, 1951)   87 min.

Producer, Jerry Bresler; director, Robert Parrish; based on
the story Waterfront by Ferguson Findley; screenplay, William Bowers; art director, Cary Odell; music director, Morris Stoloff; camera, Joseph Walker; editor, Charles Nelson.

Broderick Crawford (Johnny Damico); Betty Buehler (Mary
Kiernan); Richard Kiley (Thomas Clancy); Otto Hulett (Lieutenant
Banks); Matt Crowley (Smoothie); Neville Brand (Gunner); Ernest
Borgnine (Joe Castro); Walter Klavun (Sergeant Bennion); Lynne Bag-
gett (Peggy); Jean Alexander (Doris); Ralph Dumke (Police Commis-
sioner); John Marley (Tony); Frank de Kova (Culio); Jay Adler (Rus-
sell); Duke Watson (Radford); Emile Meyer (Gas Station Attendant);
Carleton Young (District Attorney); Fred Coby (Plainclothesman);
Ric Roman (Police Officer); Michael McHale (Talbert); Kenneth

Broderick Crawford and Don Megowan in The Mob (1951).

Harvey (Paul); Don Megowan (Bruiser); Robert Foulk (Gunman); Al
Mellon (Joe); Don De Leo (Cigar Store Owner); Ernie Venneri (Crew
Member); Robert Anderson (Mate); Charles Bronson (Jack); Mary
Alan Hokanson, Virginia Chapman (Nurses); Harry Lauter (Daniels).

Lots of violence, sensible pacing, and fitting performances
combined to give this Columbia product a lift.   Burly Broderick
Crawford starred as Johnny Damico, an undercover agent.   When he
fails to capture Smoothie (Crowley), a top waterfront mobster, he is
sent back to finish the job.   During the process he is nearly killed
by the wanted man's gang.   After much action, however, Damico
eventually causes the hoodlum to be killed in a hospital.
    "A bland melodrama, it makes no attempt to be pretty and
its violence is as exciting and as fast paced as you could ask for... "
(New York Times).
    It is amazing that movie audiences could ever believe that
law enforcers, fighting a single-handed battle against overwhelming
odds, might ever be frightened (or, heaven forbid, ever turn cowardly).   Films such as these, certainly, gave no perspective as to the
psyche of the crusading, public-spirited good guy.

THE MOUTHPIECE (Warner Bros. , 1932) 90 min.

    Directors, James Flood, Elliott Nugent; based on the story
by Frank Collins; screenplay, Earl Baldwin; camera, Barney Mc-
Gill; editor, George Amy.
    Warren William (Vincent Day); Sidney Fox (Celia); Aline Mac-
Mahon (Miss Hickey); William Janney (John); John Wray (Barton);
Polly Walters (Gladys); Ralph Ince (J. B.); Mae Madison (Elaine);
Noel Francis (Miss DeVere); Morgan Wallace (Smith); Guy Kibbee
(Bartender); J. Carrol Naish (Tony); Walter Walker (Forbes); Jack
LaRue (Garland); Stanley Fields (Pondapoint); Murray Kinnell (Jarvis);
Emerson Treacey (Wilson); Selmer Jackson (Prison Clerk); Charles
Lane (Desk Clerk); Willie Fung, Murray Kinnell (Waiters); Paulette
Goddard (Girl at Party).

    Voted one of the ten best films of 1932 by the New York
Times, this feature turned out to be one of the most interesting
gangster films of its period.
    Based on the famed, late New York City attorney William J.
Fallon, * the film cast dapper Warren William as Vincent Day, a
lawyer who had once been an assistant district attorney.   In that
capacity he had been responsible for sending an innocent man to his
death.   After this tragedy he turns to defending hoodlums and to
using grand theatrics in the courtroom to win his cases.   Also he

---

*When the film played in Syracuse, New York, Ruth Fallon, the
eighteen year old daughter of the late underworld defender, brought
an injunction against the theatre manager.   He was fined $100 or
100 days in jail for criminal libel.   (Thereafter, the case between
Miss Fallon and Warner Bros. was settled out of court.)

Warren William and Sidney Fox in The Mouthpiece (1932).

is not above being a bit dishonest himself; the film contains numerous scenes in which he is engaged in illegal activities.   In one situation, a client comes to him after stealing $90,000 from his em-
ployer and gets him to agree to accept the "remaining" $40,000.
He pockets the rest for himself.   When the client learns of the deception, he goes to the D.A., but the latter advises him that he
has taken part in compounding a felony and that, if he presses
charges against the lawyer, he will be in trouble also.

The lawyer's downfall comes through a girl (Fox).   She is
the pretty typist whom he desires, but who spurns him.   He is
eventually killed for her sake after sending a gang leader to jail.
The arrested man's underlings do in the lawyer.   Aline MacMahon
was featured as Day's level-headed secretary, Miss Hickey.

Of this fast-moving story, the New York World-Telegram
judged, "A thrilling and exciting melodrama. "

The film would be remade as The Man Who Talks Too Much
(1940) with George Brent, and Illegal (1955), q.v., with Edward G.
Robinson.

MURDER, INC.   (Twentieth Century-Fox, 1960)   103 min.

Producer, Burt Balaban; directors, Balaban, Stuart Rosen-
berg; based on the book by Burton Turkus, Sid Feder; screenplay,
Irv Tunick, Mel Barr; art director, Dick Sylbert; set decorator,
Charles Bailey; assistant director, Tony LeMarca; costumes, Bill
Walstrom; makeup, Bill Herman; sound, Emil Kolisch; camera,
Gaine Rescher; editor, Ralph Rosenblum.
Stuart Whitman (Joey Collins); May Britt (Eadie Collins);
Henry Morgan (Burton Turkus); Peter Falk (Abe Reles); David J.
Stewart (Louis "Lepke" Bucholter); Simon Oakland (Detective Tobin);
Morey Amsterdam (Walter Sage); Sarah Vaughan (Nightclub Singer);
Warren Fennerty (The Bug); Joseph Bernard (Mendy Weiss); Eli
Mintz (Joe Rosen); Vincent Gardenia (Lawyer Laslo); Howard I.
Smith (Albert Anastasia); Joseph Campanella (Panto); Seymour Cas-
sell, Paul Porter (Teenagers).

Using a semi-documentary style with the names and places
drawn from history, this recreation of the violence of the Thirties
starred TV personality Henry Morgan as assistant D.A. Burton
Turkus (co-author of the book from which the film was taken), who
fought to stop Murder, Inc.   Chief among the assassins was Abe
Reles (Falk), a psychotic killer who was eventually pushed out of a
window at Coney Island's Half Moon Hotel (a crime never solved).
Also caught up in the two-hour foray, largely filmed in New York,
were Joey Collins (Whitman), a captive of the organization, and
Eadie (Britt), his worried spouse.
Films in Review pointed out that this "superior, modestly-
budgeted, 103 minute, black-&-white programmer ... tells no more
than did the witnesses at the public hearings and trials, and the
newspapers of the time.   Which is to say, it does not tell who murdered Reles, nor who the corrupt police and politicians were who
allowed Lepke to operate, and would have continued to allow him to
operate had he not been too demanding. "

THE MUSKETEERS OF PIG ALLEY   (Biograph, 1912)   1000'

Director, D. W. Griffith.
With: Lillian Gish, Walter Miller, Harry Carey, Elmer
Booth, Lionel Barrymore, Jack Dillon, Alfred Paget, W. C. Robin-
son, Robert Harron.

Most film historians tend to list this Biograph one-reeler as
the first gangster film made.   Shot on the streets of New York City
by D. W. Griffith, the movie actually contains some material previously used by the director.   Nevertheless, it is certainly the pre-
cursor of the Warner Bros. underworld epics of the Thirties.   In
D. W. Griffith: American Film Master (1965), Iris Barry states,
"Whether as a study in realism, as an ancestor of the gangster
film of later decades or as an exercise in motion picture composi-
tion, this is a remarkable piece. "
The rather interesting plot of the film finds Lillian Gish as

the young wife of a musician who is attracted by a local hooligan (Booth) but is loyal to her husband (Miller).   Booth later helps save Miller from a run-in with the law.

Advertised as "a depiction of the gangster evil, " the film contained typical Griffith sequence themes that would be expanded upon in Intolerance (1916), q.v.   It is also worthwhile to note the similarity between Booth's performance and the type of character interpretation offered by James Cagney in gangster dramas two decades later.

Said Robert M. Henderson in D. W. Griffith: The Years at Biograph (1970), "... [it] projects a documentary reality with considerable force.   The cinematography is crisp and well defined, and the exterior scenes depict an excellent cross section of New York tenement life during the period. "

MY SIX CONVICTS (Columbia, 1952) 104 min.

Producer, Stanley Kramer; director, Hugo Fregonese; story, Donald Powell Wilson; screenplay, Michael Blankfort; music, Dimitri Tiomkin; art director, Edward Ilou; camera, Guy Roe; editor, Gene Havlick.

Millard Mitchell (James Connie); Gilbert Roland (Punch

Alf Kjellin, Gilbert Roland and Millard Mitchell in My Six Convicts (1952).

Pinero); John Beal (Doc); Marshall Thompson (Blivens Scott); Alf
Kjellin (Clem Randall); Henry Morgan (Dawson); Jay Adler (Steve
Kopac); Regis Toomey (Doctor Gordon); Fay Roope (Warden Potter);
Carlton Young (Captain Haggerty); John Marley (Knotty Johnson);
Russ Conway (Doctor Hughes); Byron Foulger (Doc Brint); Charles
Bronson, Peter Virgo, George Eldredge, Paul Hoffman, Dick Cogan,
Allen Mathews, H. George Stern (Convicts); Jack Carr (Higgins);
Carol Savage (Mrs. Randall); Danny Jackson (Convict #1538); Joe
Haworth (Convict #9670); Chester Jones (Convict #7546); Vincent
Renno (Convict #9919); Frank Mitchell (Convict #3007); Joe McTurk
(Big Benny); Harry Stanton (Banker); Fred Kelsey (Store Detective);
Edwin Parker (Guard on Dump Truck); Joe Palma (Convict Driver).

"... penology, psychology and crime have been blended into
a compassionate, thoughtful, incisive and, above all, genuinely humorous account of life behind prison walls" (New York Times).

A young psychologist, Doc (Beal), recounts his experiences
with prisoners at the fictional Harbor State Prison in this well-made
account of prison life and rehabilitation. The film focused on the
physician and the half-dozen trustees who composed his staff of
psychological testers.

James Connie (Mitchell) was the safe-cracker who knew most
everything that went on inside the walls and who was even allowed
on the outside to open an accidentally locked safe. It was he who
helped to ingratiate the doctor with the other prisoners. Among the
latter were: Punch Pinero (Roland), a hoodlum with a high I.Q.;
Dawson (Morgan), a bright but cold killer whose escape attempts almost costs Doc his life; Clem Randall (Kjellin), a robber who longs
for his wife; and Blivens Scott (Thompson), a boozing ballplayer who
has taken a rap for a girl.

Unlike many of the standard, exploitational prison dramas
such as Riot in Cell Block 11 (1954), q.v., Unchained (1955), q.v.,
or Cell 2455, Death Row (1955), q.v., this entry gave some humanity and dimension to the prisoners, who were not just cons in striped
outfits, but real persons (granted a little too humorous and cute for
their own good).

THE NAKED CITY (Universal, 1948) 96 min.

Producer, Mark Hellinger; associate producer, Jules Buck;
director, Jules Dassin; story, Malvin Wald; screenplay, Albert
Maltz, Wald; art director, John F. DeCuir; set decorators, Russell
A. Gausman, Oliver Emert; music, Miklos Rozsa, Frank Skinner;
music director, Milton Schwartzwald; assistant director, Fred Frank;
makeup, Bud Westmore; costumes, Grace Houston; sound, Leslie I.
Carey, Vernon W. Kramer; camera, William Daniels; editor, Paul
Weatherwax.

Barry Fitzgerald (Lieutenant Dan Muldoon); Howard Duff
(Frank Niles); Dorothy Hart (Ruth Morrison); Don Taylor (Jimmy
Halloren); Ted DeCorsia (Willie Garzah); Jean Adair (Little Old
Lady); Nicholas Joy (McCormick); House Jameson (Dr. Lawrence
Stoneman); Anne Sargent (Mrs. Halloran); Adelaide Klein (Mrs.

Batory); Grover Burgess (Mr. Batory); Tom Pedi (Detective Perelli);
Enid Markey (Mrs. Hylton); Frank Conroy (Captain Sam Donahue);
Mark Hellinger (Narrator); Walter Burke (Peter Backalis); David
Opatoshu (Ben Miller); John McQuade (Constentino); Hester Sonder-
gaard (Nurse); Paul Ford (Henry Fowler); Ralph Bunker (Dr. Hoff-
man); Curt Conway (Nick); Arthur O'Connell (Shaeffer); Beverly
Bayne (Mrs. Stoneman); James Gregory (Officer Hicks); Elliott Sul-
livan (Trainer); John Marley (Managing Editor); Ray Greenleaf (City
Editor); Kathleen Freeman (Stout Girl); Lee Shumway (Patrolman);
Henri D. Foster (Jeweler); Mildred E. Stronger (Little Girl); Nehemiah Persoff (Extra); Harold Crane (Prosperous Man); Retta Coleman (Crippled Girl); Richard W. Shankland (Blind Man); Joseph
Karney (Wrestler).

Shot almost entirely in Manhattan by cunning photographer
William Daniels, this feature is a companion piece to Mark Hellinger's* previous Brute Force (1947), q. v. As that prison film had
relentlessly pursued and explored facets of confined urban life, so
The Naked City revealed aspects of big city existence that were
reprehensible, frightening, and almost unsurmountable. Focusing
on the daily lives of cops as they hunt for a bathtub murderer, the
picture realistically captured the New York scene (a near novelty
for Hollywood at this time). It was no accident that director Jules
Dassin, who found so much to complain about in American politics
(and suffered accordingly via the McCarthy Anti-Red purge of Hollywood), should have tackled this pioneering exploration of urban bu-
reacracy (i. e. the police) combating violent anti-establishment (i. e.
the killer) forces.
    James Agee lauded The Naked City for "a visually majestic
finish. Otherwise mawkish and naive," while Bosley Crowther (New
York Times) pegged it, peculiarly, as a "rambling, romantic picture." In retrospect, Charles Higham and Joel Greenberg in Hollywood in the Forties (1968) rightfully recognized the production for
raising "... the realistic crime thriller to new levels of craftsman-
ship. "
    Barry Fitzgerald, too often type cast as a Blarney sort, was
wonderfully wry as Lieutenant Dan Muldoon who supervises the manhunt through East Side Manhattan and over the Williamsburg Bridge.
As well as reflecting the slangy ambience of unsophisticated sections
of New York, director Dassin handled his chase tautly and well.
    A long-running TV series used the film's title when telecast
over ABC-TV in the early Sixties. To what extent many subsequent
films owe their substance and style to The Naked City is hard to
assess, but its influence is likely.

NEVER STEAL ANYTHING SMALL (Universal, 1959) C-94 min.

    Producer, Aaron Rosenberg; director, Charles Lederer;

---

*Hellinger, a former New York columnist, served as the narrator
of The Naked City. He died shortly after the picture's completion.

James Cagney and Shirley Jones in <u>Never Steal Anything Small</u>
(1959).

based on the play <u>Devil's Hornpipe</u> by Maxwell Anderson, Rouben
Mamoulian; screenplay, Lederer; art director, Alexander Golitzen;
set decorators, Russell A. Gausman, Ollie Emert; music, Allie
Wrubel; songs, Wrubel and Anderson; shoreography, Hermes Pan;
costumes, Bill Thomas; makeup, Bud Westmore; assistant directors,
Dave Silver, Ray De Camp; sound, Leslie L. Carey, Robert Prit-
chard; camera, Harold Lipstein; editor, Russ Schoengarth.
        James Cagney (Jake MacIllaney); Shirley Jones (Linda Cabot);
Roger Smith (Dan Cabot); Cara Williams (Winnipeg Simmons); Ne-
hemiah Persoff (Finelli); Horace McMahon (Merritt); Virginia Vin-
cent (Ginger); Jack Albertson (Sleep-Out Charlie); Royal Dano (Words
Cannon); Robert J. Wilke (Lennie); Herbie Faye (Hymie); Billy M.
Greene (Ed); John Duke (Ward); Jack Orrison (Caborne); Ingrid Goude
(Model); Sanford Seegar (Fats Ranney); Gregg Barton (Deputy Ward-
en); Ed "Skipper" McNally (Thomas); Herman Belmonte (Salesman--
Dance Number); Roy Fitzell, Joseph Paz, Jerry Rush, Todd Miller
(Specialty Dancers--Singers); Anthony Caruso (Lieutenant Tevis);
Roland Winters (Doctor); Hugh Sanders (Spokesman); John Halloran,

Harvey Parry (Detectives); Bill Meader (Secretary); Eugene Dorian (Cameraman); Phyllis Kennedy (Waitress); Rebecca Sand (Coffee Vendor); Pat Patterson (Stevedore).

Every decade or so, James Cagney would return nostalgically to his song and dance forte. Never Steal Anything Small would be his swansong in this film forte, as well as in the gangster milieu. For such a landmark happening, the resultant picture was unfortunately trite and unmemorable.

Based on a 1952 play, Never Steal Anything Small was merely a satire on union politics, gussied up with undistinguished songs.

Jake MacIllaney (Cagney), a tough stevedore, has designs on the wife (Jones) of another man (Smith), and tries to have a false corruption charge placed on the man. Jake later becomes president of a local union and rises to the presidency of the worker's group through perjury, bribery, crooked elections, grand larceny, and murder. Justice triumphs, or so the theme is here, with Jake losing out on everything by the closeout.

A poor man's sugary On the Waterfront (1954), q.v., this entry was unconvincing all the way down the line, including Cagney's lead role. He was too old to play a character who rises from nothing to "success," even through corruption. It was a sad way for the movie gangster great to say goodbye to the genre that had made him globally famous.

NEW YORK CONFIDENTIAL   (Warner Bros., 1955)   87 min.

Producer, Clarence Greene; director, Russell Rouse; suggested by the book by Jack Lait, Lee Mortimer; screenplay, Greene, Rouse; music, Joseph Mullendore; assistant director, James W. Lane; costumes, Ernest Newman; camera, Edward Fitzgerald; editor, Grant Whytock.

Broderick Crawford (Charles Lupo); Richard Conte (Nick Magellan); Marilyn Maxwell (Iris Palmer); Anne Bancroft (Katherine Lupo); J. Carrol Naish (Ben Dagajanian); Onslow Stevens (Johnny Achilles); Barry Kelley (Frawley); Celia Lovsky (Mama Lupo); Herbert Heyes (James Marshall); Steven Geray (Morris Franklin); William "Bill" Phillips (Whitey); Henry Kulky (Gino); Nester Paiva (Martinelli); Joe Vitale (Batista); Carl Milletaire (Sumak); William Forrest (Paul Williamson); Ian Keith (Waluska); Charles Evans (Judge Kincaid); Mickey Simpson (Hartmann); Tom Powers (District Attorney Rossi); Lee Trent (Ferrari); Lennie Bremen (Larry); John Doucette (Shorty); Frank Ferguson (Dr. Ludlow); Hope Landin (Mrs. Wesley); Fortunio Bonanova (Senor).

Two of the screen's most over-exposed hood types (Crawford and Conte) joined forces here. Allegedly, the New York City Anti-Crime Committee vouched for the overall authenticity of this melodrama.

Within eighty-seven minutes, there is presented the rise and fall of an organized crime syndicate headed by Charles Lupo (Crawford). His association is involved in all the rackets, including

Broderick Crawford and Anne Bancroft in New York Confidential
(1955).

killings.   But Lupo worries more about his elderly mother (Lovsky)
and his terrified daughter (Bancroft) than he does about his mob.
When Lupo attempts to marry off daughter Katherine to his cold-
blooded henchman (Conte), she commits suicide. It is the beginning
of the end for him.   Later a traitor threatens to turn state's evidence on the gang. Since Lupo is now considered a security risk
to the overall crime ring, he is eliminated.
        The New York Times reported of this feature, it "... lacks
only one thing--real power.... in addition to fast pacing and trim
dialogue, the performances are generally vigorous and believable."

NEW YORK NIGHTS   (United Artists, 1929) 7,447'

        Presenter, Joseph M. Schenck; supervisor, John W. Consi-
dine, Jr.; director, Lewis Milestone; based on the play Tin Pan
Alley by Hugh Stanislaus Stange; adaptor, Jules Furthman; song, Al
Jolson and Ballard MacDonald; sound, Oscar Lagerstrom; camera,
Ray June; editor, Hal Kern.
        Norma Talmadge (Jill Deverne); Gilbert Roland (Fred De-
berne); John Wray (Joe Prividi); Lilyan Tashman (Peggy); Mary
Doran (Ruthie Day); Roscoe Karns (Johnny Dolan).

This film holds a spot in cinema history because it was the talking picture debut of fading silent screen star Norma Talmadge. However, the production was complicated but trivial in its presentation.

Jill Deverne (Talmadge) is a chorus girl who supports her alcoholic, songwriter husband (Roland). In order to help him out she takes Fred's songs to producer Joe Prividi (Wray), who soon reveals his yen for her. He purchases the song but when Fred finds out why, he walks away in disgust. Later, the club where Jill works is raided, and Fred is found with another chorine. Jill leaves him for Prividi. The plot thickens when Prividi frames Fred for a killing in order to remove him permanently from the scene. Eventually, Prividi is exposed as the true killer, and Jill and Fred are reunited.

The film may have ended happily for Miss Talmadge on camera, but career-wise it nearly did her in, and after one more film she wisely called it quits. New York Nights was produced by the star's husband, Joseph M. Schenck, and featured her romantic interest of the moment, Roland.

NEWMAN'S LAW (Universal, 1974)   C-98 min.

Producer, Richard Irving; director, Richard Heffron; screenplay, Anthony Wilson; music, Robert Prince; art director, Alexander A. Mayer; assistant director, John Gaudioso; sound, Richard J. Stumph, John Kean; camera, Vilis Lapenieks; editor, John Dumas.

George Peppard (Vince Newman); Roger Robinson (Garry); Eugene Roche (Reardon); Gordon Pinsent (Eastman); Abe Vigoda (Dellanzia); Louis Zorich (Falcone); Michael Lerner (Frank Acker); Victor Campos (Jimenez); Mel Stewart (Quist); Jack Murdock (Beutel); David Spielberg (Hinney); Theodore Wilson (Jaycee); Marlene Clark (Edie); Kip Niven (Assistant Coroner); Penelope Gilette (Matron); Don Hammer (Real Estate Agent).

This underrated entry is a cross-breed between the (police) detective and the gangster genre. Obviously one cannot have one species without character members from the other as the antogonists. Usually, however, one side or the other is more clearly emphasized. But with Peppard as the understated hero-cop, the colorful gangsters come just as sharply into focus.

Vince Newman (Peppard) and his black police partner (Robinson) break into a dope pusher's hideout. The seemingly small-time operation leads the two law enforcers onto the trail of an international dope syndicate. Meanwhile, Vince is framed on a dope possession charge and is suspended from the force. He hunts for the crooked cop responsible for his plight, all of which leads to the breakdown of the drug ring.

There are the usual open air shootouts, the tough talk, the domestic scenes between cops and their spouses, and the inevitable shop talk down at police headquarters. By the mid-1970s, the racial integration scene, the Mafia angle, and the tough life of a cop (in contrast to the easy situation of the big boys of the underworld)

George Peppard, Theodore Wilson and Roger Robinson in <u>Newman's Law</u> (1974).

had become such commonplace plot elements that it was hard for this film to find a new angle.

As <u>Variety</u> acknowledged, the film is "... highlighted by suspenseful movement and physical action. " But, said the unusually severe <u>Hollywood Reporter</u>, it "... is virtually indistinguishable from television fare, save for some rough language. " Perhaps this double-bill item was reflecting the early signs of the demise of the present gangster-cops-violence cycle.

NIGHT AFTER NIGHT   (Paramount, 1932)   70 min.

Producer, William LeBaron; director, Archie Mayo; based on the novel <u>Single Night</u> by Louis Bromfield; adaptor-screenplay, Vincent Lawrence; continuity, Kathryn Scola; additional dialog, Mae West; camera, Ernest Haller.

George Raft (Joe Anton); Constance Cummings (Jerry Healy); Wynne Gibson (Iris Dawn); Mae West (Maudie Triplett); Alison Skipworth (Mrs. Mabel Jellyman); Roscoe Karns (Leo); Al Hill (Blainey);

George Raft and Roscoe Karns in <u>Night After Night</u> (1932).

Louis Calhern (Dick Madden); Harry Wallace (Jerky); Dink Templeton (Patsy); Bradley Page (Frankie Guard); Marty Martyn (Malloy); Tom Kennedy (Tom); Gordon "Bill" Elliott (Escort).

Remembered more as Mae West's introduction to talkies than as George Raft's first starring vehicle at Paramount, <u>Night After Night</u> managed to toss into the ring all the growing clichés of the gambling/gangster/society field.

Ex-fighter Joe Anton (Raft) owns a nightclub which he operates with his valet (Karns). After a series of bad affairs, culminating with drunk Iris Dawn (Gibson), he decides to become cultivated and hires a teacher, Mrs. Mabel Jellyman (Skipworth). Feeling more refined and confident, he can better handle his budding relationship with disillusioned society girl Jerry Healy (Cummings). A rival gangster (Page) demands to buy out Joe's interest in the club. When Joe refuses, Frankie Guard orders that he be taught a lesson. But Anton still has himself, if not the club, and he discovers that Jerry really would prefer marrying him than golddigging a millionaire.

La West, as the one-time flame of Raft's Joe Anton, literally stole the show as the wise-cracking dame who had the right answer to anyone's comment or flick of an eyebrow.

NIGHT AND THE CITY (Twentieth Century-Fox, 1950) 95 min.

Producer, Samuel G. Engel; director, Jules Dassin; based on

the novel by Gerald Kersh; screenplay, Jo Eisinger; art director,
C. P. Norman; camera, Mac Greene; editors, Nick DeMaggio, Sidney Stone.

Richard Widmark (Harry Fabian); Gene Tierney (Mary Bristol); Googie Withers (Helen Nosseross); Hugh Marlowe (Adam Dunn);
Francis L. Sullivan (Phil Nosseross); Herbert Lom (Kristo); Stanislaus Zbyszko (Gregorius); Mike Mazurki (Strangler); Charles Farrell (Beer); Ada Reeve (Molly); Ken Richmond (Nikolas); Eliot Make-
ham (Pinkney); Betty Shale (Mrs. Pinkney); Russell Westwood (Yosh);
James Hayter (Figler); Tommy Simpson (Cozen); Maureen Delaney
(Anna Siberia); Tomas Gallagher (Bagrag).

A tawdry tale of a low-life club tout (Widmark) who tries to
corner the crooked wrestling trade in London. Also involved in his
seamy scheme are disreputable club owner Phil Nosseross (Sullivan),
the club owner's wife (Withers), the woman (Tierney) who cares for
Harry Fabian, a slimy wrestling impresario (Lom), and a vicious
wrestler (Mazurki). Also in the cast is old-time wrestling champion Stanislaus Zbysyko, who opposes Harry Fabian's activities and
dies brutally after a match with the Strangler.

The New York Times ranked this as "moody, morbid ...
pointless," but on the plus side were good atmosphere and a remind-
er that other countries besides the U.S. had sleazy underworld pockets.

THE NIGHT ROSE see VOICES OF THE CITY

NIGHT WORLD (Universal, 1932) 59 min.

Director, Hobart Henley; story, P. J. Wolfson, Allen Rivkin;
screenplay, Richard Schayer; dances staged by Busby Berkeley; camera, Merritt Gerstad; editor, Maurice Pivar.

Lew Ayres (Michael Rand); Mae Clarke (Ruth Taylor); Boris
Karloff (Happy MacDonald); Dorothy Revier (Mrs. MacDonald); Rus-
sell Hopton (Klauss); Bert Roach (Tommy); Dorothy Peterson (Edith
Blair); Florence Lake (Miss Smith); Gene Morgan (Joe); Paisley
Noon (Clarence); Hedda Hopper (Mrs. Rand); Greta Grandstedt
(Blonde); Louise Beavers (Maid); Sammy Blum (Salesman); Harry
Woods (Gang Leader); Eddie Phillips (Vaudevillian); Tom Tamarez
(Gigolo); Clarence Muse (Tim the Doorman); Huntley Gordon (Jim);
George Raft (Ed Powell); Robert Emmett O'Connor (Policeman);
Geneva Mitchell (Florabelle); Arletta Duncan (Cigarette Girl); Pat
Somerset (Guest); Joe Wallace, Charles Giblyn, Dorothy Granger,
Frank Beale, John K. Wells (Bits); Hal Grayson's Recording Or-
chestra (Themselves); Frankie Farr (Trick Waiter); Amo Ingraham,
Alice Adair (Chorines).

Opposite: Mae Clarke and Lew Ayres in a publicity shot for Night
World (1932).

This minor Grand Hotel-type story set in the club entertainment sphere had two points of interest: the appearance of Boris Karloff as the club owner and the dance routines staged by Busby Berkeley.

Between midnight and early morning, a good deal happens at Happy MacDonald's (Karloff) night spot. His whoring wife (Revier) aids in his murder by a gang of hoodlums, and society drunk Michael Rand (Ayres), whose mother (Hopper) has killed Mr. Rand, falls in love with dancer Ruth Taylor (Clarke). Powell (Raft) makes a play for Ruth, but she rejects him. While many of the club staff and guests do not fare well, Michael and Ruth have found one another and have hopes for the future.

NIGHTFALL   (Columbia, 1957) 78 min.

Producer, Ted Richmond; director, Jacques Tourneur; based on the novel by David Goodis; screenplay, Stirling Silliphant; music, George Duning; music conductor, Morris Stoloff; orchestrator, Arthur Morton; song, Sam M. Lewis, Peter DeRose, and Charles Harold; assistant director, Irving Moore; gowns, Jean Louis; camera, Burnett Guffey; editor, William A. Lyon.

Aldo Ray (James Vanning); Brian Keith (John); Anne Bancroft (Marie Gardner); Jocelyn Brando (Laura Fraser); James Gregory (Ben Fraser); Frank Albertson (Dr. Edward Gurston); Rudy Bond (Red); George Cisar (Bus Driver); Eddie McLean (Taxi Driver); Lillian Culver, Maya Van Horn (Women); Orlando Beltran, Maria Delmar (Spanish Couple); Arline Anderson (Hostess); Gene Roth (Bartender); Robert Cherry (Bit); Winifred Waring (Fashion M. C.); Jane Lyon, Betty Koch, Lillian Kassan, Joan Fotre, Pat Jones, Annabelle George (Models).

This entry is greatly admired by the Jacques Tourneur cult. Told in flashback sequences, the story has James Vanning (Ray) hunted by both hoodlums and the law for a robbery-murder which he did not commit. A non-violent man, Vanning and his best friend (Albertson) were actually on a hunting trip in the Wyoming mountains when they were accosted by two robbers (Keith and Bond) who had just pulled a murderous robbery. On the run, the desperate men shoot both Vanning and Gurston. Vanning survives, but now both sides of the law want him and the money (which everyone thinks he knows about). Along the way he meets Marie Gardner (Bancroft) who believes in him. Eventually, Vanning finds himself back at the same Wyoming locale and forced to kill the robbers to save himself and Marie, as well as to prove his innocence.

Highly suspenseful, the best segment of this feature was, of course, the climax, with Vanning using an oversized vehicle to chase the calculating killers.

This premise, in the hands of Alfred Hitchcock, and given the production values of MGM's North by Northwest (1959), would be far more entertaining to the general moviegoers.

James Gregory and Jocelyn Brando in <u>Nightfall</u> (1957).

NO ORCHIDS FOR MISS BLANDISH   (Renown, 1948)   104 min.

Producers, A. R. Shipman, Oswald Mitchell; director, St. John L. Clowes; based on the novel by James Hadley Chase; screenplay, Clowes; camera, Gerald Gibbs; editor, Manuel del Campo.
Jack LaRue (Slim Grissom); Hugh McDermott (Fenner); Linden Travers (Miss Blandish); Watler Grisham (Eddie); Leslie Bradley (Bailey); Zoe Gail (Margo); Charles Goldner (Louis); Macdonald Parke (Doc); Lily Molnar (Ma Grissom); Danny Green (Flyn); Percy Marmont (Mr. Blandish); Michael Balfour (Barney); Frances Marsden (Ann Borg); Irene Prador (Olga).

Since the Twenties and the popularity of the Edgar Wallace thrillers, the British have been turning out gangster films. Many of them are first-rate, but too many are parochial in their style and outlook. St. John L. Clowes adapted and directed this version of James Hadley Chase's novel (which borrowed heavily from William Faulkner's Sanctuary). * The result was one of the most unintentionally laughable films ever made with a British cast--except for star Jack LaRue--playing it seriously as Americans. The players' emulation of American slang and accents could almost be termed a comedy, except for the fact that the film was filled with tremendous brutality.
Set in New York City (the same locale that banned those under sixteen from seeing the film when it debuted in the U. S.), two petty crooks kidnap an heiress (Travers), but lose her to a big time operator (LaRue). Miss Blandish and Slim Grissom fall in love and go into hiding. Eventually Grissom's gang decide to do away with him before he leaves the country with the girl and they lose out on the juicy ransom.
Reporting from London, Variety noted, "As a supposed American gangster thriller this film touches bottom in sadism, morbidity and taste. " The London Evening Standard called the picture, "A disgrace to British films ... vicious display of sadism, brutality and suggestiveness. " The Public Control Committee of the London County Council in April, 1948 ordered the film, which was billed as the first American picture, British-made, "cleaned up. " (Some scenes were cut.) Calling the film "As fragrant as a cesspool" (London Daily Mirror) only served to whet the public's appetite. The movie cleaned up in its London release, but in America it came and went rather quickly.
A more definitive remake of the Chase novel would be made by Robert Aldrich as The Grissom Gang (1971), q. v.

OCEAN'S 11   (Warner Bros. , 1960)   C-127 min.

Producer, Lewis Milestone; associate producers, Henry W. Sanicola, Milton Ebbins; director, Milestone; story, George Clayton Johnson, Jack Golden Russell; screenplay, Harry Brown, Charles

---

*Filmed twice, in 1933 as The Story of Temple Drake, q. v. , and in 1961 as Sanctuary.

Dean Martin in <u>Ocean's Eleven</u> (1960).

Lederer; art director, Nicholai Remisoff; set decorator, Howard
Bristol; music-music director, Nelson Riddle; songs, Sammy Cahn
and James Van Heusen; costumes, Howard Shoup; assistant director,
Ray Gosnell, Jr. ; titles, Saul Bass; makeup, Gordon Bau; sound,
M. A. Merrick; camera, William A. Daniels; editor, Philip W. An-
derson.

 Frank Sinatra (Danny Ocean); Dean Martin (Sam Harmon);
Sammy Davis, Jr. (Josh Howard); Peter Lawford (Jimmy Foster);
Angie Dickinson (Beatrice Ocean); Richard Conte (Anthony Bergdorf);
Cesar Romero (Duke Santos); Patrice Wymore (Adele Ekstrom); Joey
Bishop ("Mushy" O'Conners); Akim Tamiroff (Spyros Acebos); Shirley
MacLaine (Drunk); Red Skelton (Client); George Raft (Jack Strager);
Henry Silva (Roger Corneal); Ilka Chase (Mrs. Restes); Buddy Lester
(Vincent Massler); Richard Benedict ("Curly" Steffens); Jean Willes
(Mrs. Bergdorf); Clem Harvey (Louis Jackson); Norman Fell (Peter
Rheimer); Hank Henry (Mr. Kelly); Lew Gallo (Young Man); Hoot
Gibson (Deputy Sheriff); George E. Stone (Shopkeeper); Laura Cor-
nell, Shiva (Dancers); Donald Barry (Nightclub Owner); Red Norvo
(Orchestra Leader); Marjorie Bennett (Miss Allenby).

 Filmed on location, this was one of many productions to detail a robbery caper in glittery, tempting Las Vegas. Separating
the film from other similar entries, however, was the starring cast
of Frank Sinatra's Rat Pack (Martin, Davis, Jr. , Lawford, Bishop,
et al), some of whom would later join together in <u>Robin and the
Seven Hoods</u> (1964), q. v. The other attraction of this catch-as-
catch-can feature was the use of cinema veterans like Conte,

Tamiroff, Silva, Raft, Lester, Barry, Stone, and Gibson in supporting and cameo roles.
    Five wartime buddies reunite for the purpose of robbing a
Las Vegas gambling casino on New Year's Eve. The plan calls for
the breaking of the casino's safe after blanketing the power lines in
the vicinity. The loot is to be placed in a trash can and collected
later. The plan goes amuck (of course!). It seems that Duke
Santos (Romero), a hoodlum, wants half the action, which leads the
two factions to engage in a gun battle.
    As flippant, specious, and flashy as some of its cast mem-
bers, Ocean's 11 was a slick, impromptu film. When not performing on camera, money earners Sinatra, Martin, and Davis, Jr. were
performing onstage at Las Vegas casinos. The only ones who lost
anything on this venture were moviegoers who expected the cast to
try to put on a sincere show.

OLSEN BANDENS SIDSTE BEDRIFTER (THE LAST EXPLOITS OF
THE OLSEN GANG) (Nordisk, 1974) C-99 min.

    Director, Erik Balling; story-screenplay, Henning Bahs, Ball-
ing; music, Bent Fabriclus-Bjerre; special effects, Bahs; camera,
Henning Kristansen; editor, Ole Steen Nietsen.
    Ove Sprogoe (Egon Olsen); Morten Grunwald (Benny); Poul
Bundgaard (Kjeld).

    This film was the sixth, and probably not the last, of the wild
adventures of three petty crooks who are always hoping to hit the big
time. The first entry, Olsen-Banden (The Olsen Gang) appeared in
1970, followed by: Olsen-Banden Pa Spanden (The Olsen Gang in
Trouble (1970), Olsen-Banden I Jylland (The Olsen Gang in Jutland)
(1971), Olsen-Banden's Store Kup (Olsen Gang's Big Heist) (1972),
and Olsen-Banden Gar Amok (The Olsen Gang Goes Wild) (1973).
    Said Variety's stringer from Copenhagen of this newest addi-
tion to the series, it is "... every bit as funny as its predecessors....
By now ... [the trio] are as familiar to local (and to some in East-
ern Europe where sales have been good) audiences as ever Laurel &
Hardy were. And they are every inch as sharply drawn by inventors
and actors alike. "
    This time around the safecracker and his pals are out to get
some diamonds and become involved with black money transactions.

ON THE WATERFRONT (Columbia, 1954) 108 min.

    Producer, Sam Spiegel; director, Elia Kazan; based on arti-
cles by Malcolm Johnson; screenplay, Budd Schulberg; art director,
Richard Day; music, Leonard Bernstein; camera, Boris Kaufmann;
editor, Gene Milford.
    Marlon Brando (Terry Malloy); Karl Malden (Father Barry);
Lee J. Cobb (Johnny Friendly); Rod Steiger (Charley Malloy); Pat
Henning (Kayo Dugan); Eva Marie Saint (Edie Doyle); Leif Erickson
(Glover); James Westerfield (Big Mac); Tony Galento (Truck); Tami

Mauriello (Tillio); John Hamilton (Pop Doyle); Heldabrand (Mott); Rudy Bond (Moose); Don Blackman (Luke); Arthur Keegan (Jimmy); Martin Balsam (Gilette); Fred Gwynne (Slim); Anne Hegira (Mrs. Collins); Thomas Handley (Tommy).

As Robert Montgomery and several other concerned individuals tried to tell Hollywood and the country at large, Hollywood was, had been, and would be, for some time to come, filled with organized crime. No union in the industry was safe from underworld syndication. Little wonder then that, until On the Waterfront, very little had been done onscreen about the exploitation of the public and of union members by gangs at all levels. It was an explosive subject then, and is still so now. The fact that On the Waterfront had an intelligent script, a very able cast (mostly from the Actor's Studio), a brilliant director (Elia Kazan) not only turned it into a multi-Oscar winner, but made it a must-see film with the public. It set new trends for the "gangster" film of the Fifties and thereafter.

Dock worker Terry Malloy (Brando) has ambitions to be a big shot boxer, but fate treats him unkindly. Not too bright, he does possess a tender quality (demonstrated in his care of domesticated pigeons caged on the tenement roof). His older brother, Charley Malloy (Steiger) is a conniving lawyer in the employ of the dockers' union. The latter organization is controlled by racketeer Johnny Friendly (Cobb). Friendly takes a paternalistic interest in Terry, but does not hesitate to involve him in the set-up for the murder of a too free-talking dock worker. Later, Terry meets the dead man's sister (Saint) and through her he slowly begins to comprehend just how devastating a hold the racketeers have on the people they are supposed to be benefitting. Both she and Father Barry (Malden), a waterfront priest, urge him to help expose the criminals.

Paralleling Terry's romance with Edie is his decision to break up the syndicate. His brother tries to warn him, but to no avail. When Charley is later killed by Friendly's boys, Terry is convinced he must testify at the Crime Commission hearing. At a final showdown, Friendly and Terry engage in a brawl on the waterfront. Battered but not beaten, Terry has finally earned the respect of his fellow workers. The power of the syndicate is smashed, at least for the time being.

The semi-documentary style used by Kazan made this powerful film all the more effective, conveying to the public at large a little of what actually was going on in America. With a minimum of celluloid gore, Kazan was able to reflect the tension, terror, and trauma of the underworld's domination of poor people's lives and livelihood.

ONE DANGEROUS NIGHT (Columbia, 1943) 77 min.

Producer, David Chatkin; director, Michael Gordon; based upon characters by Louis Joseph Vance; story, Arnold Phillips, Max Nosseck; screenplay, Donald Davis; art directors, Lionel Banks, Robert Peterson; music, Morris W. Stoloff; assistant director, Rex Bailey; sound, Ed Bernds; camera, L. W. O'Connell; editor, Viola

Lawrence.
     Warren William (Michael Lanyard); Marguerite Chapman (Eve
Andrews); Eric Blore (Jameson); Mona Barrie (Jane Merrick); Tala
Birell (Sonia); Margaret Hayes (Patricia); Ann Savage (Vivian);
Thurston Hall (Inspector Crane); Warren Ashe (Sidney); Fred Kelsey
(Dickens); Frank Sully (Hartzog); Eddie Marr (Mac); Gerald Mohr
(Harry Cooper); Louis Jean Heydt (Arthur); Roger Clark (John Shel-
don); Gregory Gaye (Dr. Eric); Dick Rush (Doorman); Symona Boni-
face (Woman); John Tyrrell (Attendant); Ed Laughton (Drunk); Joe
McGuinn (Motor Cop); Chuck Hamilton, Bill Lally, Pat Lane (Cops);
George Calliga (Headwaiter); George Ghermanoff (Waiter); Ann Hunt-
er (Coatroom Girl); Hal Price (Doorman); Ralph Peters (House Detective); Wedgwood Nowell (Attendant).

     The foxy Lone Wolf, better known as Michael Lanyard (Wil-
liam), was up to his smooth old tricks in this series' entry.
     Here the ex-jewel thief is again a gentleman detective aided
by his rather snobbish valet Jameson (Blore). Like most celluloid
detectives during World War II, Lanyard was usually involved with
murder or Nazis or both, but rarely with gangsters. One Dangerous Night was an exception.
     In this enjoyable, although simple and predictable story, Lan-
yard is blamed for the death of a gangster. The man was shot in
the presence of three women whom he had been blackmailing. Poor
Michael Lanyard must dodge both the police and the late man's punks
in order to clear himself by solving the case.

OUT OF THE PAST (RKO, 1947) 97 min.

     Executive producer, Robert Sparks; producer, Warren Duff;
director, Jacques Tourneur; based on the novel Build My Gallows
High by Geoffrey Homes; screenplay, Homes; art directors, Albert
S. d'Agostino, Jack Okey; set decorator, Darrell Silvera; music,
Roy Webb; music director, C. Bakaleinikoff; assistant director, Har-
ry Mancoke; sound, Francis M. Sarver, Clem Portman; special ef-
fects, Russell A. Cully; camera, Nicholas Musuraca; editor, Samuel
E. Beetley.
     Robert Mitchum (Jeff Bailey); Jane Greer (Kathie Moffatt);
Kirk Douglas (Whit Sterling); Rhonda Fleming (Meta Carson); Richard
Webb (Jim); Steve Brodie (Fisher); Virginia Huston (Ann Miller);
Paul Valentine (Joe Stefanos); Dickie Moore (The Kid); Ken Niles
(Lloyd Eels); Lee Elson (Cop); Frank Wilcox (Sheriff Douglas); Mary
Field (Marney); Jose Portugal (Mexican Waiter); Jess Escobar (Mex-
ican Doorman); Hubert Brill (Car Manipulator); Primo Lopez (Mexi-
can Bellhop); Mildred Boy, Ted Collins (Couple at Harlem Club);
Sam Warren (Waiter at Harlem Club); Wesley Bly (Headwaiter);
Theresa Harris (Eunice); James Bush (Doorman); Harry Hayden
(Canby Miller); Archie Twitchell (Rafferty).

     Following the success of The Killers (1946), q.v., the char-
acter of the wicked female who leads the unsuspecting hero down the
road to ruin was again popular and Jane Greer gave one of her best

performances as the alluring golddigger in Out of the Past. It is a gem of the 1940s' cinema.

The complex story was related mostly in flashback. It concerned a small desert town gas station owner (Mitchum) who is called to Lake Tahoe by hoodlum kingpin Whit Sterling (Douglas). He leaves behind the girl (Huston) and goes to his appointment. It seems Jeff Bailey was once a New York detective hired by Sterling to find an ex-mistress (Greer) who had tried to kill him and who had stolen $40,000 from him.

In those bygone days, Jeff had accepted the case and trailed the girl to Mexico City. There he finds Kathie Moffatt and falls under her spell. The hot romance, however, cools after the team travel to San Francisco where Jeff's partner (Brodie) tries to close the case. Kathie shoots Fisher. In disgust, Jeff leaves her.

Back in the present, Jeff arrives at Tahoe to find that Kathie is back with Whit. "What else could I do?" she asks him. She plans to use Jeff again, claiming she must get away from Sterling. Before long, Kathie shoots suspecting Sterling and then informs Jeff that unless he does just what she says, she will put the blame on him. Sensing that he will doublecross her, she shoots him in the getaway car, and, thereafter, she is killed in a police ambush.

The New York Daily Mirror pegged this quasi-private eye entry as a "honey of a thriller."

THE OUTFIT (MGM, 1973) C-102 min.

Producer, Carter De Haven; director, John Flynn; based on the novel by Richard Stark; screenplay, Flynn; music, Jerry Fielding; art director, Tambi Larsen; set decorator, James L. Berkey; assistant director, William McGarry; sound, Richard Raguse, Jall Watkins; camera, Bruce Surtees; editor, Ralph E. Winters.

Robert Duvall (Macklin); Karen Black (Bett Harrow); Joe Don Baker (Cody); Robert Ryan (Mailer); Timothy Carey (Menner); Richard Jaeckel (Chemey); Sheree North (Buck's Wife); Felice Orlandi (Frank Orlandi); Marie Windsor (Madge Coyle); Jane Greer (Alma); Henry Jones (Doctor); Joanna Cassidy (Rita); Tom Reese (Man); Elisha Cook, Jr. (Carl); Anita O'Day (Herself); Archie Moore (Packard); Roy Roberts (Bob Caswell); Tony Trabel (Himself); Army Archerd (Butler); James Bacon (Bookie).

Filmed on location in Southern California, this suspense yarn was a throwback to the gangster melodramas of the Forties. A goodly number of the cast had played in such films in those World War II years.

Macklin (Duvall) and Cody (Baker) are two criminals marked for death by the syndicate for robbing a bank owned by the group. Meanwhile, Macklin is hunting for the man who murdered his brother. Eventually the trail leads to the head of the syndicate (Ryan), and they are forced to storm his heavily guarded home.

"It's rough, tough and violent--but that is what gangster movies are all about," said Judith Crist in New York magazine.

Robert Duvall and Karen Black in <u>The Outfit</u> (1973).

OUTSIDE THE LAW (Universal, 1921) 8,000'

    Presenter, Carl Laemmle; director-story, Tod Browning;
screenplay, Lucien Hubbard, Browning; camera, William Fildew.
    Priscilla Dean (Molly Madden [Silky Moll]); Ralph Lewis
("Silent" Madden); Lon Chaney ("Black Mike" Sylva [Ah Wing]);
Wheeler Oakman ("Dapper Bill" Ballard); E. A. Warren (Chang Lo);
Stanley Goethals ("That Kid"); Melbourne MacDowell (Morgan Spen-
cer); Wilton Taylor (Inspector).

OUTSIDE THE LAW (Universal, 1930) 70 min.

    Director, Tod Browning; screenplay, Browning, Garrett Fort;
sound, C. Roy Hunter; camera, Roy Overbaugh; editor, Milton Car-
ruth.
    Edward G. Robinson (Cobra Collins); Mary Nolan (Connie);
Owen Moore ("Fingers" O'Dell); Edwin Sturgis (Jake); John George
(Humpy); Delmar Watson (The Kid); DeWitt Jennings (Police Chief);
Rockliffe Fellowes (Police Captain); Frank Burke, Sydney Bracey
(Bits).

An early gangster movie, this was directed by the

bizarre-oriented Tod Browning from his own story and co-screen-
play. The film also marked the first occasion on which Lon Chaney
portrayed an Oriental for the big screen.

A Confucian (Warren) persuades a hoodlum (Lewis) and his
daughter (Dean) to go legitimate. However, a frameup by another
gang leader (Chaney) leads Madden to jail. Molly then joins Black
Mike's gang and learns of a plan for a jewel robbery. After the
heist she takes the gems to Chang Lo. In a gang battle that follows,
Black Mike is killed. The police capture Molly and her beau (Oakman). After Chang Lo returns the jewels, the duo are released.

Besides playing the gang leader, Chaney was also cast as
Oriental Joe, but was billed on screen as "Guess Who. "

The film was re-issued in 1926.

Although sharing the same title, and same director-co-scripter, the 1930 Outside the Law had a rather different plot from its
predecessor.

Crook "Fingers" O'Dell plans a big heist but is up against a
local force (Robinson) who wants a portion of the loot. Fingers'
moll, Connie (Nolan), tells Cobra Collins the wrong date for the
robbery and Fingers is able to get the booty without Cobra's knowledge. Later, Cobra arrives at the bank for the holdup, at the "assigned" time, and in a shootout is killed by the police. The film
fades with Fingers and Connie going to jail.

Rather primitive in its execution, the Thirties' Outside the
Law is only valuable cinematically as an early example of Robinson's
casting as a crook.

PALE FLOWER (Shoiku, 1964) 96 min.

Director, Mashairo Shinoda; based on the novel by Sintaro
Ishihara; screenplay, Ataru Baba, Shinoda; music, Toru Takemitsu;
camera, Masao Kosugi.

Ryo Ikebe (Muraki); Mariko Kaga (Saeko).

Many critics compare this feature to Jean-Luc Godard's
A Bout de Souffle (Breathless) (1959), q. v. , with its study of a
gangster (Ikebe) released from prison who becomes involved with a
high-living woman (Kaga). The latter observes the homicide which
leads to Muraki's return to jail.

Although not strictly a part of the Yakuza crime world series
so popular in Japan, this feature has an underworld flavor all its
own. "One comes away with the memory of a well-defined pictorial
style, moody, black and white, given to depicting people in the
shadowy perimeters around cores of light" (New York Times).

PARIS TOUCHEZ PAS AU GRISBI (GRISBI) (Corona, 1953) 88 min.

Producer, Robert Dorfmann; director, Jacques Becker; based
on the novel by Albert Aimonin; screenplay, Becker, Simonin,
Maurice Griffe.

Jean Gabin (Max); Dery (Riton); Paul Frankeur (Pierrot);

Advertisement for <u>Paris Touchez Pas Au Grisbi</u> (1953).

Lino Ventura (Angelo); Vittorio Sangoli (Ramon); Jeanne Moreau (Joay).

Deciding he is close to "retirement," gangster Max (Gabin) wants to leave the trade on the proceeds from a heist of gold bullion he and Riton (Dary), his partner, have taken from the Orly Airport. But a rival gang leader (Ventura) learns of the haul, kidnaps Riton and, in exchange for his freedom, Max agrees to turn over the precious metal. Before the final encounter is concluded, both Angelo and Riton have been killed and the gold has come into police possession. Max, at least is free.

"Here is an odd number indeed--odd, even exasperating, yet curiously fascinating to watch, with an impact all its own" (<u>New York Times</u>). The <u>New York Herald-Tribune</u> noted of this well-acted venture, "One only wonders at the point of view, which is that of the underworld, in sympathizing with the devotion and loyalty of 'honest' gangsters without any suggestion that their ultimate downfall may derive from the fundamental error of their ways."

PARTY GIRL (MGM, 1958) C-99 min.

Producer, Joe Pasternak; director, Nicholas Ray; story, Leo Katcher; screenplay, George Wells; music, Jeff Alexander; song, Nicholas Brodszky and Sammy Cahn; choreography, Robert Sidney; title theme sung by Tony Martin; art directors, William A. Horning, Randall Duell; set decorators, Henry Grace, Richard Pefferle; assistant director, Erich Von Stroheim, Jr. ; makeup, William Tuttle; costumes, Helen Rose; sound, Dr. Wesley C. Miller; special effects, Lee LeBlanc; camera, Robert Bronner; editor, John McSweeney, Jr.

Robert Taylor (Thomas Farrell); Cyd Charisse (Vicki Gaye); Lee J. Cobb (Rico Angelo); John Ireland (Louis Canetto); Kent Smith (Prosecutor Jeffrey Stewart); Claire Kelly (Genevieve Farrell); Corey Allen (Cookie); Lewis Charles (Danny Rimett); David Opatoshu (Lou Forbes); Kem Dibbs (Joey Vulner); Patrick McVey (O'Malley); Barbara Lang (Tall Blonde); Myrna Hansen (Joy Hampton); Betty Utey (Showgirl); Jack Lambert (Nick); Sam McDaniel (Jesse); Barrie Chase (Showgirl); Erich Von Stroheim, Jr. (Police Lieutenant); Carmen Phillips (Rico's Secretary); Carl Thayler, Mike Pierce, John Franco, Ken Perry (Cookie's Henchmen); Irving Greenberg, Richard Devine, Georges Saurel (Rico's Hoods).

This antidiluvian entry is worthy of note only because it was even made--and at such a late date. Time called it "A caricature of an old-fashioned gangster picture, done in a clever but vulgar style. All the usual features are there, but all are comically exaggerated.... The violence is parodied too, but in a sly way that permits the moviegoer to lick his lips over the horror just before he sees the humor of a situation--or vise versa. " The public was not impressed.

As directed by Nicholas Ray, this glossy programmer was set in the Chicago underworld of the Thirties. Crippled but ambitious criminal lawyer Thomas Farrell (Taylor) serves as the "mouthpiece" for a gang run by Rico Angelo (Cobb). Farrell is enchanted with dancer Vicki Gaye (Charisse). When Rico's men want to do away with her, Farrell turns state's evidence which launches a gang war and leads to the downfall of Angelo.

PAY OR DIE (Allied Artists, 1960) 111 min.

Producer-director, Richard Wilson; based on the life of Lieutenant Joseph Petrosino; screenplay, Richard Collins, Bertram Millhauser; music-music conductor, David Raksin; production designer, Fernando Carrere; set decorator, Darrell Silvera; assistant director, Clark L. Paylow; makeup, Lou Lacava, Bob Mark; wardrobe, Roger J. Weinberg; sound, Ralph Butler; special effects, Milt Olsen; camera, Lucien Ballard; editor, Walter Hannemann.

Ernest Borgnine (Lieutenant Joseph Petrosino); Zohra Lampert (Adelina Saulino); Alan Austin (Johnny Viscardi); Renata Vanni (Mama Saulino); Bruno Della Santina (Papa Saulino); Franco Corsaro (Vito Zarillo); Robert F. Simon (Commissioner); Robert Ellenstein (Luigi Di Sarno); Howard Caine (Enrico Caruso); John Duke (Lupo

Miano); John Marley (Caputo); Mario Siletti (Loria); Mimi Doyle
(Nun); Mary Carver (Mrs. Rossi); Paul Birch (Mayor); Vito Scotti
(Simonetti); Nick Pawl (Palumbo); Sherry Alberoni (Guilia De Sarno);
Sal Armetta (Dotti); Leslie Glenn (Girl at Bombing); Carlo Tricoli
(Don Cesare); Bart Bradley (Nicolo); Sam Capuano (Rossi); Judy
Strangis (Marisa Rossi); David Poleri (Voice of Caruso).

Following the success of Al Capone (1959), q. v. , Allied Artists and producer-director Richard Wilson returned to the crime
field for Pay or Die. It was all very reminiscent of MGM's The
Black Hand (1950), q. v. Both pictures told of detectives' efforts
to quell the tyranny of the Mafia in New York's Little Italy at the
turn of the century.
        In the story based on true incidents surrounding the life of
the late Joseph Petrosino, Ernest Borgnine was cast as the crusading detective. Within the storyline, Petrosino and his small band of
loyal officers reduce Mafia crimes in Little Italy. The film traces
his career as he pleads with his superiors for more help in putting
down the reign of terror (bombings, beatings, muggings, extortion,
murder, etc). As a commercial ploy, the movie also highlights
Petrosino's romance with young Adelina Saulino (Lampert). The
film then proceeds to detail his eventual death at the hands of his
arch enemy, the Mafia, and the subsequent capture of a Mafia chief-
tan.

THE PENALTY (Goldwyn, 1920) 7 reels

        Director, Wallace Worsley; based on the novel by Gouverneur
Morris.
        Lon Chaney (Blizzard); Claire Adams (Barbara Ferris); Ken-
neth Harlan (Dr. Wilmot Allen); Charles Clary (Dr. Ferris); Ethel
Grey Terry (Rose); Edouard Treboel (Bubbles); Milton Ross (Lich-
tenstein); James Mason (Frisco Pete); Doris Pawn (Barbary Nell);
Lee Phelps (Cop).

THE PENALTY (MGM, 1941) 81 min.

        Producer, Jack Chertok; director, Harold S. Bucquet; story,
Martin Berkeley; screenplay, Harry Ruskin, John C. Higgins; cam-
era, Harold Rosson; editor, Ralph Winters.
        Edward Arnold (Martin "Stuff" Nelson); Lionel Barrymore
(Grandpap Logan); Gene Reynolds (Roosty/Russell Nelson); Robert
Sterling (Ed McCormick); Marsha Hunt (Katherine Logan); Veda Ann
Borg (Julie); Emma Dunn (Ma McCormick); Richard Lane (Craig);
Gloria DeHaven (Anne Logan); Grant Mitchell (Judge); Phil Silvers
(Hobo); Warren Ashe (Jay); William Haade (Van); Ralph Byrd (Detec-
tive Brock); Edgar Barrier (Burns); Al Hill (Coney); Byron Foulger
(Bank Manager); Mimi Doyle (Salesgirl); Tim Ryan (Police Sergeant);
Alonzo Price (Captain Harbridge).

        "... an altogether incredible melodrama that, by its excesses,

Gus Schilling and Edward Arnold in The Penalty (1941).

mocks even the friendliest spectator's love of life as it is often fic-
titiously created on the screen" (New York Times).
        Once again Lon Chaney picked a very offbeat vehicle to high-
light his talents as a silent screen pantomimist and contortionist.
        By error Dr. Ferris (Clary) amputates the legs of a boy in-
jured in a traffic accident.   Twenty-seven years later, legless Blizzard (Chaney) heads the underworld of San Francisco's Barbary
Coast.   He falls for a girl (Adams)--actually the doctor's daughter
--who uses him to pose for a bust of Satan, and he plans an operation in which her fiancé's (Harlan) legs will be grafted onto his own,
so that he will be normal and can have the girl.   During the operation, however, a tumor is removed from Blizzard's brain.   His
mental balance is restored.   However, Pete (Mason), fearing that
Blizzard will turn in all the members of his former gang, shoots
him.
        Chaney gave a vivid performance in this physically taxing
role.   The film's ending, however, was changed from the actual
story, for in the book the cured criminal married the girl and became a community leader.

In 1941, MGM used the title, The Penalty, for a "B" film, but the material was taken from a play by Martin Berkeley. It told of a lad (Sterling) the son of a killer, who gets into trouble with the law. He is caught, but is given over to the custody of a crusty old farmer (Barrymore). The country influences the boy positively and he is regenerated. When his blustering father (Arnold) comes for him, the boy rebels and orders him away at gunpoint. For action devotees, the film also encompassed a battle between G-Men and gangsters. Some of the storyline made it seem evident that this was a partial remake of Metro's Hide-Out (1934), q.v.

PEPE LE MOKO (Paris Films, 1937) 90 min.

Director, Julien Duvivier; based on the book by M. Ashelbe; screenplay, Duvivier; camera, Marc Frossard, Kreuger.
Jean Gabin (Pepe Le Moko); Mirelle Balin (Gaby); Line Noro (Ines); Lucas Girdoux (Slimane); Gabriel Gabrio (Carlos); Saturnin Fabre (The Grandfather); Charpin (Regis).

This is the granddaddy of the romantic gangster film, responsible for spawning renewed interest in the charming underworld type-character. As depicted in Pepe Le Moko, the lawbreaker lives by a stricter code than the average man, his sense of ethics always a part of his every action. He may be reckless with his or others' lives and/or property, but he is exceedingly careful when dealing with the subject of honor.
Long ago, hardened criminal Pepe Le Moko (Gabin) had to flee from Paris, the city he loves so dearly. He seeks refuge in Casablanca in the Casbah. In this confining quarter he is free from interference by the law authorities who control the city, but he is also a prisoner within the sector. Respected by his fellow thieves and crooks, Pepe carries on a liaison with Inez, a member of the underworld coterie. However, when he encounters Parisian traveler Gaby (Balin) his sense of propriety goes awry. He is enamored of this woman who reminds him so much of his lost love, Paris. At first she is annoyed by him, then amused by his attentions, and, later, she is seemingly respectful of his status within his peer group. But she has a life of her own and when she leaves the city, not caring about his fate, he no longer has the will to live. By this point, he has ventured out of the protected Casbah and, through an informer, has been turned over to the police. As her ship sails out of sight, he stabs himself and dies.
"It is a simple plot, in summary, but it is tremendously honest and fascinating" (New York Herald-Tribune).
This feature, highly popular in Europe, has had a strange history. Upon its release in France, Erich von Stroheim wired MGM in Hollywood, suggesting that they purchase the rights. The studio did so, for $38,000, and also decided to bring over the director (Duvivier) and co-star Balin. (Gabin refused to make the journey, claiming that like French wine, he "did not travel well.") Once in California, Duvivier was put to work on another project, and Balin sat about till she became bored and returned to France. MGM lost

interest in the property and sold it to Walter Wanger. That producer intended starring Sylvia Sidney in the property, but the star
and Wanger had a contractual dispute. Instead, Wanger borrowed
MGM's newest European import, Hedy Lamarr, who, along with
Charles Boyer and Sigrid Gurie, formed the triumvirate for Algiers
(1938), q. v. Although softened up for American consumption it
maintained a good deal of the mystique, charm, mystery, and tension of the stark original.

It was not until 1942 that Pepe Le Moko had any American
distribution, since Wanger, who controlled the rights, did not want
it to compete with his version. In 1948 Universal made Casbah,
q. v. , a musical edition of the story, starring Tony Martin and
Yvonne De Carlo. Three years later, the French did their own
unstarry remake of Pepe Le Moko.

PETE KELLY'S BLUES   (Warner Bros. , 1955)   C-95 min.

Producer-director, Jack Webb; screenplay, Richard L.
Breen; art director, Feild Gray; production designer, Harper Goff;
set decorator, John Sturtevant; assistant director, Harry D'Arcy;
costume designer, Howard Shoup; wardrobe, Gene Martin; songs,
Ray Heindorf and Sammy Cahn; Arthur Hamilton; arranger, Matty
Matlock; makeup, Gordon Bau; sound, Leslie G. Hewitt, Dolph
Thomas; camera, Hal Rosson; editor, Robert M. Leeds.

Jack Webb (Pete Kelly); Janet Leigh (Ivy Conrad); Edmond
O'Brien (Fran McCarg); Peggy Lee (Rose Hopkins); Andy Devine
(George Tenell); Lee Marvin (Al Gannaway); Ella Fitzgerald (Maggie
Jackson); Martin Milner (Joey); Than Wyenn (Rudy); Herb Ellis (Be-
dido); John Dennis (Bettenhauser); Jayne Mansfield (Cigarette Girl);
Mort Marshall (Cootie); Dick Cathcart, Matty Matlock, Moe Schnei-
der, Eddie Miller, George Van Eps, Nick Fatool, Ray Sherman,
Jud De Naut (Pete Kelly's Group); Joe Venuti, Harper Goff, Perry
Bodkin (Featured Members of the Tuxedo Band).

The story of a musician involved with Kansas City mobsters
in the Prohibition era would hardly seem to be Jack "Dragnet"
Webb's cup of tea. But he produced, directed and starred in this
mood-provoking bit of nostalgia-musical delight in the same matter-
of-fact style that made his teleseries, "Dragnet" so enormously
popular. Jazz enthusiasts have found, and still find, special delight
in the musical numbers, while general film goers were impressed
by the recreation of life in a 1927 midwestern speakeasy [the ambience can be contrasted to that of Broadway (1929, 1942) q. v.].

The plotline deals with Fran McCarg's (O'Brien) efforts to
move his bootlegging activities into new arenas, by muscling into
the band field. Cornet player Pete Kelly (Webb) opposes this drive,
with the climax ending in a shootout.

Peggy Lee was Oscar-nominated for her performance as the
drink-happy flapper vocalist who, in the course of the feature, sings
"Sugar" and "Somebody Loves Me" among other songs, while Ella
Fitzgerald vocalized "Hard-Hearted Hannah" and the title tune. Janet
Leigh was along for decorative appeal as a Roaring Twenties' disciple.

Humphrey Bogart, Leslie Howard and Bette Davis in The Petrified
Forest (1936).

THE PETRIFIED FOREST   (Warner Bros. , 1936)   83 min.

        Associate producer, Henry Blanke; director, Archie Mayo;
based on the play by Robert E. Sherwood; screenplay, Charles Ken-
yon, Delmer Daves; art director, John Hughes; assistant director,
Dick Mayberry; music, Bernhard Kaun; gowns, Orry-Kelly; sound,
Charles Lang; special effects, Warren E. Lynch, Fred Jackman,
Willard Van Enger; camera, Sol Polito; editor, Owen Marks.
        Leslie Howard (Alan Squire); Bette Davis (Gabrielle Maple);
Genevieve Tobin (Mrs. Chisholm); Dick Foran (Boze Hertzlinger);
Humphrey Bogart (Duke Mantee); Joe Sawyer (Jackie); Porter Hall
(Jason Maple); Charley Grapewin (Gramp Maple); Paul Harvey (Mr.
Chisholm); Eddie Acuff (Lineman); Adrian Morris (Ruby); Nina Cam-
pana (Paula); Slim Thompson (Slim); John Alexander (Joseph); Arthur
Aylesworth (Commander of Black Horse Troopers); George Guhl
(Trooper); James Farley (Sheriff); Jack Cheatham (Deputy); Addison
Richards (Radio Announcer).

        Each decade sees so many fresh topical problems occurring
that often the basic struggle of brute force versus intellectualism is
overlooked.   In the mid-1930s, Robert E. Sherwood's The Petrified

Forest delineated just this complex tug-of-war. On the surface it
may seem "just" a gangster story, but its mind-provoking rationale
goes much deeper. As one of the parable's characters says, "...
we've been fighting nature and nature can't be beaten." But is nature on the side of the desperate, brutal outlaw, or of the deep
thinker?

Leslie Howard repeats his Broadway role of writer-gigolo
Alan Squire, who has more verbal than writing ability. Humphrey
Bogart appears as Duke Mantee, "the world famous killer," whose
gang holes up at the Black Mesa Barbecue Cafe and Gas Station
near the arid desert and the Petrified Forest. The run-down water-
ing hole is owned by a patriotic zealot (Hall) operated by his lonely
but beautiful and intelligent daughter (Davis), and overseen by Gramp
Maple (Grapewin), a man who knew Samuel Clemens and Billy the
Kid. Also thrown into the situation are ex-footballer (now gas station attendant) Boze Hertzlinger (Foran), the wealthy travelers (Tobin
and Harvey), and members of Mantee's group (Sawyer, Morris and
Thompson).

The early part of the story centers on Squire's exposition of
his philosophy. He believes nature is fighting back at man and
causing chaos. One of the prime examples of his theory is gangster
Duke Mantee, who storms the cafe and holds everyone there prisoner. Mantee turns out to be more of a victim of society than a born
killer. He is stalling for time at the restaurant, waiting for his
girl to arrive, so that he and his gang can make a dash for the
Mexican border and freedom. Meanwhile, Squire, who can find no
good reason to stay alive, begs the Duke to shoot him* before he
leaves, so that Alan's insurance policy can buy Gabrielle that long-
desired trip to France and a chance for cultural expression.

Although basically actionless, except for one good shoot-out
scene with the law at the cafe, The Petrified Forest is one of those
talky films which concretely holds audience attention. With interesting, offbeat characters and the background of the desert, the film
exemplifies the best of Warner Bros.' picturemaking of the decade.
While a very stagey production, it is still widely popular today.

Within The Petrified Forest, there are some thought-provok-
ing observations made on the gangster figure. Gramps says at one
point about Mantee, that he is not a gangster. "Gangsters are foreigners, he's an American." At another point in time, Squire observes, "Cowardice isn't the cause of crime, is it? ... it has
something to do with glands." Later on, Alan, who has great ad-
miration for this Neanderthal type of throwback, says to the Duke,
"You're a man of imagination. You're not afraid to do outlandish
things." In contrast, Squire, in a self-deprecating moment, says
of himself, "I doubt if you could find a more likely candidate for
extinction." (Obviously, playwright Sherwood had a very pessimis-
tic outlook on the future of the intellectual in contemporary society.)

Edward G. Robinson, the studio's original choice for Duke

---

*Unconvinced whether or not to follow the morbid, downbeat ending
of the stage play, Warners filmed two endings for The Petrified Forest, one with Squire dying, the other with him surviving. After pre-
views, the former version was selected for the release prints.

Mantee (until Howard demanded that his pal Bogart be allowed to recreate his own stage role), finally got a chance to do the Mantee role on "Lux Radio Theatre" on February 8, 1943, with Gail Patrick and Laird Cregar co-featured.

In 1945, Warners would remake The Petrified Forest as Escape in the Desert, turning it into a tale about an escaped Nazi flyer (Helmut Dantine) caught in the desert. For "Producer's Showcase," Bogart, Lauren Bacall, and Henry Fonda would star in a television version of The Petrified Forest in 1955, directed by Delbert Mann.

THE PHENIX CITY STORY   (Allied Artists, 1955) 100 min.

Producers, Samuel Bischoff, David Daimond; director, Phil Karlson; screenplay, Crane Wilbur, Daniel Mainwaring; music-music conductor, Harry Sukman; song, Harold Spina; camera, Harry Neumann; editor, George White.

John McIntire (Albert Patterson); Richard Kiley (John Patterson); Kathryn Grant (Ellie Rhodes); Edward Andrews (Rhett Tanner); Lenka Paterson (Mary Jo Patterson); Biff McGuire (Fred Gage); Truman Smith (Ed Gage); Jean Carson (Cassie); John Larch (Clem Wilson); James Edwards (Zeke Ward); Otto Hulett (Hugh Bentley); Ma Beachie, James Ed Seymour (Themselves).

For a while Phenix City, Alabama, was known as "the wickedest city in the U.S.," and this film wanted to show why.

To heighten the screen drama, a few incidents have been reshifted for story flow, but otherwise, the feature follows the facts. When his father, a political candidate, is murdered, returning G. I. John Patterson (Kiley) agrees to accept the post of attorney general to bring about the downfall of "sin" in this southern city. Rhett Tanner (Andrews) proves to be the crime boss of the area, and the particular target of Patterson's clean-up campaign.

A thirteen-minute prologue features on-the-spot interviews with townsfolk who were involved with the 1954 slaying of Albert Patterson. (The exhibitor had the option whether or not to utilize the extra footage.)

As Life observed of this dramatic recreation, "The outrageous violence that took place last year in Phenix City, Ala. was so melodramatic that any movie version of it seemed bound to be tame by comparison."

POCKETFUL OF MIRACLES   (United Artists, 1961) C-136 min.

Producer, Frank Capra; associate producers, Glenn Ford, Joseph Sistrom; director, Capra; based on the story Madame La Gimp by Damon Runyon and a screenplay by Robert Riskin; new screenplay, Hal Kantor, Harry Tugend, (uncredited) Jimmy Cannon; music-music conductor, Walter Scharf; orchestrator, Gil Grau; choreography, Nick Castle; songs, James Van Heusen and Sammy Cahn, Tom Blackburn and George Bruns; art directors, Hal Pereira,

Ann-Margret, Bette Davis, Glenn Ford and Thomas Mitchell in
Pocketful of Miracles (1961).

Roland Anderson; set decorators, Sam Comer, Ray Moyer; women's
costumes, Edith Head; men's costumes, Walter Plunkett; assistant
director, Arthur S. Black, Jr.; makeup, Wally Westmore; sound,
Hugo Grenzbach, Charles Grenzbach; process camera, Farciot
Edouart; camera, Robert Bronner; editor, Frank P. Keller.
    Glenn Ford (Dave the Dude Conway); Bette Davis (Apple An-
nie [Mrs. E. Worthington Manville]); Hope Lange (Elizabeth "Queen-
ie" Martin); Arthur O'Connell (Count Alfonso Romero); Peter Falk
(Joy Boy); Thomas Mitchell (Judge Henry G. Blake); Edward Everett
Horton (Hutchins the Butler); Mickey Shaughnessy (Junior); David
Brian (Governor); Sheldon Leonard (Steve Darcey); Peter Mann (Car-
los Romero); Ann-Margret (Louise); Barton MacLane (Police Com-
missioner); John Litel (Inspector McCrary); Jerome Cowan (Mayor);
Jay Novello (Cortega the Spanish Consul); Fritz Feld (Pierre); Ellen
Corby (Soho Sal); Frank Ferguson, Willis Bouchey (Newspaper Edi-
tors); Gavin Gordon (Mr. Cole the Hotel Manager); Mike Mazurki
(Big Mike); Jack Alam (Cheesecake); Benny Rubin (Flyaway); Snub
Pollard (Knuckles); George E. Stone (Shimkey); Betty Bronson (The
Mayor's Wife); Stuart Holmes (Ringsider).

    Frank Capra's expansive, if indulgent, remake of his 1933
hit, Lady for a Day, q.v., was a colorful, glittering comedy about
Depression era gangsters and one hood, Dave the Dude (Ford) with
a heart of gold. Despite adequate critical reviews and a star-jammed

cast, the feature was not a financial success. However, as an oddball entry it remains a favorite of late show audiences. The film
marked the end of Capra's career as a producer-director.

Robert Riskin's screenplay for the original film along with
Damon Runyon's story "Madame La Gimp" were used by scenarists
Hal Kantor and Harry Tugend (and uncredited Jimmy Cannon) to
fashion Pocketful of Miracles. So much of the first film appears in
the second that, as Donald C. Willis states in The Films of Frank
Capra (1974), "the similarities cheapen the remake.... Capra
might have justified his remake with variant routines and sequences,
as Hitchcock justified his remake of The Man Who Knew Too Much,
but most of the additional material is weak."

Once again there is the story of Dave the Dude making an
old apple peddler, Apple Annie (Davis), a respectable lady. He has
heard she plans to commit suicide because her European-educated
daughter (Ann-Margret) is returning home with a highbrow fiancé
(Mann) and wants to meet her alleged "high"-society mama. Since
Annie's apples are the Dude's good luck charm, he feels obligated
to help her in this time of need. He sets her up in a fashionable
apartment with a butler (Horton), and a drunken judge (Mitchell) as
her escort. Despite the snowballing problems, the hoax works well
enough for a time. Just when everything seems to be falling apart,
though, the governor (Brian) and the major (Cowan) show up at a
testimonial dinner for Annie and the young couple leave believing
Annie is what she claims to be. As a topper, the judge proposes
to Annie and even voices a hope that he can give up booze.

Sentiment is a dirty word in recent years, but it does have
its place. Pocketful of Miracles is dripping with it, and it's not all
correctly placed or handled. Like most any work derived from a
Damon Runyon original, such as Bob Hope's The Lemon Drop Kid
(1951), the guys and dolls from the underworld who populate the
narrative have wonderful hearts of gold buried close to the surface
of their eccentric personalities. One could never believe that these
lawbreakers would ever knowingly hurt a fly.

POINT BLANK (MGM, 1967) C-92 min.

Producers, Judd Bernard, Robert Chartoff; director, John
Boorman; based on the novel The Hunter by Richard Stark; screen-
play, Alexander Jacobs, David Newhouse, Rafe Newhouse; music,
Johnny Mandel; song, Stu Gardner; art directors, George W. Davis,
Albert Brenner; set decorators, Henry Grace, Keogh Gleason; assis-
tant director, Al Jennings; sound, Franklin Milton; special camera
effects, J. McMillan Johnson; camera, Philip H. Lathrop; editor,
Henry Berman.

Lee Marvin (Walker); Angie Dickinson (Chris); Keenan Wynn
(Yost/Fairfax); Carroll O'Connor (Brewster); Lloyd Bochner (Fred-
erick Carter); Michael Strong (Stegman); John Vernon (Mal Reese);
Sharon Acker (Lynne); James Sikking (Hired Gun); Sandra Warner
(Waitress); Kathleen Freeman (Citizen); Sid Haig, Michael Bell

(Penthouse Lobby Guards); Ron Walters, George Stratton (Young
Man in Apartment); Rico Cattani, Roland Lastarza (Reese's
Guards).

This was the film that amazed some viewers, astounded others, annoyed another segment, and led to a loud call for non-violent
films.   "There are shootings galore, karate chops and tortures and
torments and more concentrated brutality than you have yet seen on
a screen. . . .   The performances are stereotypes of the sadism
genre--and the point of Point Blank is indeed a very blank and nasty
one" (Judith Crist, NBC-TV "Today Show").
    Some time after he has participated in the snatching of a huge
shipment of cash being relayed to others at deserted Alcatraz, Walker (Marvin) is confronted by a stranger (Wynn) who offers to help
him recover the lost loot.   Yost leads Walker to Lynne (Acker), the
latter's duplistic wife.   Lynne, who has betrayed Walker, kills herself.   The trail then leads to Lynne's sister Chris (Dickinson) who
takes Walker to Male Reese's (Vernon) penthouse headquarters.   In
a scuffle, Reese plunges to his death.   But Walker is not satisfied
with the mere death of his ex-partner; he wants the money.   Before
long, he learns that Yost, alias Fairfax, has been using him to
eliminate troublesome organization men.   At the finale, Walker walks
off into the darkness rather than risk tagging along further with the
treacherous Fairfax.
    Said Variety of this trend-setting venture, "Point Blank is a
violent, dynamic, thinly-scripted film. . . .   The real star of the
film is the film itself--the uptight assemblage of footage, meticulous
over-recording of sound. "

PORTRAIT OF A MOBSTER   (Warner Bros. , 1961)   108 min.

    Director, Joseph Pevney; based on the book by Harry Grey;
screenplay, Howard Browne; art director, Jack Poplin; set decora-
tor, George James Hopkins; music, Max Steiner; costumes, Howard
Shoup; makeup, Gordon Bau; assistant director, Charles Hansen;
sound, M. A. Merrick; camera, Eugene Polito; editor, Leo H.
Shreve.
    Vic Morrow (Dutch Schultz); Leslie Parrish (Iris Murphy);
Peter Breck (Frank Brennan); Ray Danton (Legs Diamond); Norman
Alden (Bo Wetzel); Robert McQueeney (Michael Ferris); Ken Lynch
(Lieutenant D. Corbin); Frank de Kova (Anthony Parazzo); Stephen
Roberts (James Guthrie); Evan McCord (Vincent "Mad Dog" Coll);
Arthur Tenen (Steve Matryck); Frances Morris (Louise Murphy);
Larry Blake (John Murphy); Joseph Turkel (Joe Noe); Eddie Hanley
(Matty Krause); John Kowal (Lou Rhodes); Harry Holcombe, Jr.
(Captain Bayridge); Anthony Eisley (Legal Adviser); Poncie Ponce
(Master of Ceremonies); Gil Perkins (Joe Murdoch); Roy Renard
(Bartender).

    Whether one cares to admit or remember it, the teleseries
"The Untouchables" had a profound affect on the entertainment industry and, in turn, on the filmwatching public.   A plethora of gangster

Vic Morrow and Norman Alden (right) in Portrait of a Mobster
(1961).

biography pictures flooded the screen following that program's success. This entry, based on Harry Grey's book, digs into the story
of Dutch Schultz (Morrow). The career of Arthur "Dutch" Flegen-
heimer (1902-1935), the Bronx-born son of a saloon and stable owner,
is a fascinating one. It would be Dutch who would instigate Manhattan's first full-fledged gang war--no novelty to Chicago, but not a
part of New York's underworld procedure--when a former lieutenant,
Legs Diamond (Danton), began hijacking the liquid refreshment destined for Dutch's speakeasies.

Like many other such screen chronicles, Portrait of a Mobster disguised its paltry budget behind a smoke-screen of violence.
One critic, offering an offhand compliment to the feature, said, "...
it seems to have been lifted intact from previous Warner epics. "
A favorite gimmick of movies like this was to include a line-up of
famous badmen, allowing audience association with these rogues to
carry over to the film (at no cost to the producers).

PRETTY BOY FLOYD   (Continental, 1960) 96 min.

Producer, Monroe Sachson; director-screenplay, Herbert J.
Leder; music, Del Sirino, William Sanford; assistant directors,
Tony LeMarca, Dominic D'Antonio; costumes, Bill Walstrom; sound,
Dick Gramaglia; camera, Chuck Austin; editor, Ralph Rosenblum.
John Ericson (Pretty Boy Floyd); Barry Newman (Al Riccar-
do); Joan Harvey (Lil Courtney); Herbert Evers (Blackie Faulkner);
Carl York (Curly); Roy Fant (Jed Watkins); Shirley Smith (Ann Court-
ney); Phil Kenneally (Baker); Norman Burton (Bill Courtney); Charles
Bradswell (Neil Trane); Truman Smith (Mr. Whitney); Ted Chapman
(Grindon, Jr.); Leo Bloom (Ed Courtney); Casey Peyson (Gail); Effie
Afton (Ma Parks); Peter Falk (Shorty Walters); Paul Lipson (Mike
Clouder); Jim Dukas (Big Dutch); Dina Paisner (Lonely Woman).

The character of "Pretty Boy" Floyd has always proved good
fodder for films and TV. This dual bill entry, written and directed by Eugene J. Lederer, rather convincingly presented John
Ericson (the ex-MGM pretty boy) as the Oklahoma youth (1901-1934)
who started in petty crime and liked the monetary rewards so much
that he continued onward as a full-fledged criminal.
As many a gangster film would demonstrate--more so in the
1930s than after--often an ex-punk tries to go straight, but his past
catches up with him and he has no alternative but to fall back into
a life of crime. This is the case, so the scenario would have us
believe, with Charles Arthur "Pretty Boy" Floyd. Rejected for an
honest job, he returns to Oklahoma to avenge the murder of his father. He then robs the nearby bank and gives some of the loot to
needy farmers in the area. (For a time he was known as the "Sagebrush Robin Hood. ") In Kansas City, Floyd takes up with Lil Courtney (Harvey), the wife of a stool pigeon that Pretty Boy has silenced.
(Women were rarely presented as thinking, feeling individuals in
these types of dramas.) Backed up by Curly (York), Pretty Boy goes

on a rampage of crime, culminating in the Kansas City Massacre in
which five law enforcement officers are shot down. For this action
he is labeled Public Enemy Number One. On the lam, he seeks
refuge on a farm near East Liverpool, Ohio, where, on October 22,
1934, he is killed by F.B.I. officials.

The New York Herald-Tribune observed, "Early in the film,
an effort is made to explore the causes of Floyd's behavior. Commendable as this may be, the attempt at social analysis and authenticity is not sustained. Soon the screenplay descends into stereotyped violence. "

PRIME CUT (National General, 1972) C-86 min.

Executive producer, Kenneth Evans; producer, Joe Wizan;
associate producer, Mickey Borofsky; director, Michael Ritchie;
screenplay, Robert Dillon; assistant director, Michael Daves; art
director, Bill Malley; set decorator, James Payne; music, Lalo
Schifrin; titles, Don Record; sound, Barry Thomas; special effects,
Logan Frazee; camera, Gene Polito; editor, Carl Pingatore.

Lee Marvin (Nick Devlin); Gene Hackman (Mary Ann); Angel
Thompkins (Clarabelle); Gregory Walcott (Weenie); Sissy Spacek
(Poppy); Janit Baldwin (Violet); William Morey (Shay); Clint Ellison
(Delaney); Howard Platt (Shaughnessy); Les Lannom (O'Brien); Eddie
Egan (Jake); Therese Reinsch (Jake's Girl); Bob Wilson (Reaper
Driver); Gordon Signer (Brockman); Gladys Watson (Milk Lady);
Hugh Gillin, Jr. (Desk Clerk); P. Lund (Mrs. O'Brien); David Sav-
age (Ox-Eye); Craig Chapman (Farmer Bob); Jim Taksas (Big Jim);
Wayne Savage (Freckle Face).

The main reason for this rather unimportant Michael Ritchie-
directed thriller seemed to be the box-office teaming of Gene Hackman and Lee Marvin for a violent film. However, except for the
shocking opening scene in which a man is murdered and run through
a sausage factory production line, coming out as hot dog lengths,
the violence was relatively restrained so that the film could retain
a PG rating and better box-office returns.

In a rather cavalier style, the narrative unfolded a story of
the rivalry between a Chicago mob led by Nick Devlin (Marvin) and
a Kansas City gang headed by Mary Ann (Hackman). There were
the predictable shootouts and chases and even such ingenuities as a
gun-fest in a field of sunflowers. The on-location sequences in
Kansas were the most worthwhile element of this all too casual feature.

PRISON TRAIN (Equity, 1938) 66 min.

Director, Gordon Wiles; story, Mathew Borden; screenplay,
Spencer Towne; camera, Marcel Le Picard.

Fred Keating (Frankie Terris); Linda Winters (Louise Terris);

Clarence Muse (George); Faith Bacon (Maxine); Alexander Leftwich
(Manny Robbins); James Blakely (Joe Robbins); Sam Bernard (Steward); John Pearson (Red); Nestor Paiva (Sullen); Val Stanton (Morose);
Peter Potter (Bill Adams); Kit Guard (Guard); Franklyn Farnum (District Attorney); George Lloyd (Bull); Harry Anderson (Hardface).

Released on the states' rights market, this low budget item
combined two recurring themes effectively. It took the formula train
film (Shanghai Express, Bombay Mail, etc.) and added the gangster
motif. The result was original and at least somewhat entertaining.
Gangster Frankie Terris (Keating), head of a numbers racket,
is captured and sentenced to a stay at Alcatraz. Aboard the cross
country prison train, many unexpected events occur. A rival mobster plans his own revenge, hoping to hold up the train in Kansas
and knock off Terris. The big plot question was whether the convicted hoodlum would make it to the prison alive.

PUBLIC ENEMY (Warner Bros., 1931) 83 min.

Director, William A. Wellman; based on the story Beer and
Blood by John Bright; adaptor-dialog, Harvey Thew; screenplay,
Kubec Glasmon, Bright; art director, Max Parker; music director,
David Mendoza; costumes, Earl Luick; makeup, Perc Westmore;
camera, Dev Jennings; editor, Ed McCormick.
James Cagney (Tom Powers); Jean Harlow (Gwen Allen);
Edward Woods (Matt Doyle); Joan Blondell (Mamie); Beryl Mercer
(Ma Powers); Donald Cook (Mike Powers); Mae Clarke (Kitty); Mia
Marvin (Jane); Leslie Fenton (Nails Nathan); Robert Emmet O'Con-
nor (Paddy Ryan); Rita Flynn (Molly Doyle); Murray Kinnell (Putty
Nose); Ben Hendricks, Jr. (Bugs Moran); Adele Watson (Mrs. Doyle);
Frank Coghlan, Jr. (Tommy as a Boy); Frankie Darro (Matt as a
Boy); Robert E. Homans (Pat Burke); Dorothy Gee (Nails' Girl);
Purnell Pratt (Officer Powers); Lee Phelps (Steve the Bartender);
Nanci Price, Helen Parrish, Dorothy Gray (Little Girls); Ben Hen-
dricks, III (Bugs as a Boy); Eddie Kane (Joe the Headwaiter); Doug-
las Gerrard (Assistant Tailor); Sam McDaniel (Black Headwaiter);
William H. Strauss (Pawnbroker); Snitz Edwards (Hack); Landers
Stevens (Doctor); Russ Powell (Bartender).

One of the all time great gangster films, this classic production tells of two Chicago ghetto pals who grow up in the environment
of petty crime. When they are adults they are handed a gun by their
piano player-fence pal (Kinnell). The men (Cagney and Woods) pull
a robbery and kill a cop. Thus begin their lives of crime.
They go to work as truck drivers for bootleggers. With
their sudden affluence they try to obtain class. Tom Powers tells
his widowed mother (Mercer) that he now has contacts, but his war
veteran brother (Cook) will not be a part of the rackets. Therefter-
ter, thanks to his money, Tom can afford a series of mistresses,
including Kitty (Clarke) whom he later drops. After planting a

grapefruit in Kitty's face, he tumbles for siren-ish Gwen Allen (Harlow). Later he kills Putty Nose to settle an old score, and even shoots a horse which throws and kills a pal (Fenton). By now Tom and Matt have graduated to working as front men who threaten barroom owners to use their supply of liquor or else. A rival gang, however, retaliates by killing Matt and wounding Tom. Later the mobsters yank Tom from his hospital bed, call his mother to say he is coming home, and when his brother goes to the door to let him in, Tom's bullet-ridden body wrapped like a mummy, falls to the floor.

Unlike many early Thirties gangster features, The Public Enemy does not date badly. Many scenes are memorable, even in today's violence-glutted marketplace. One cannot easily forget the finale where Tom Powers, wrapped like a mummy, falls wide-eyed and face down into his own home after being murdered. Just as shocking as Clark Gable's slap of Norma Shearer in A Free Soul (1931), q.v., is the moment when pugnacious Powers pushes the grapefruit into Kitty's surprised face. On a less artistic but catchy level, is Gwen's seduction section, where she taunts Tom to the strains of "I Surrender Dear" coming from a radio.

Beyond the charismatic power of Cagney in the title role, The Public Enemy offered its own brand of moralizing, and convincingly told how a normal person could be changed by his environment into a heartless, brutal criminal.

PUBLIC HERO #1 (MGM, 1935) 89 min.

Producer, Lucien Hubbard; director, J. Walter Ruben; story, Ruben, Wells Root; screenplay, Root; camera, Gregg Toland; editor, Frank Sullivan.

Chester Morris (Jeff Crane); Jean Arthur (Theresa O'Reilly); Lionel Barrymore (Doctor Josiah Glass); Paul Kelly (Duff); Lewis Stone (Warden Alcott); Joseph Calleia (Sonny Black); Sam Baker (Mose); Paul Hurst (Rufe Parker); John Kelly (Truck Driver); Selmer Jackson (Simpson); Larry Wheat (Andrews); Cora Sue Collins (Little Girl); Lillian Harmer (Mrs. Higgins); George E. Stone (Butch); Frank McGlynn, Jr., James Flavin, Gladden James, Pat O'Malley (Federal Agents); Frank Moran (Prison Guard); Walter Brennan (Farmer); Zeffie Tilbury (Deaf Woman); Helene Costello (Girl); Carl Stockdale (Train Conductor); Greta Meyer (Housekeeper); Tammany Young (Bartender); Bert Roach (Masher); Jonathan Hale (Prison Board Member).

Opposite: Selmer Jackson, Chester Morris and Joseph Calleia (right) in Public Hero #1 (1935).

Balancing violence with humor, this narrative presents the story of a Dillinger-like hoodlum (Calleia) whose life is one hectic mess from the time he escapes from prison until he is gunned down by F.B.I. men.

While Sonny (Calleia) is in jail, a government agent (Morris) is assigned as his cellmate, in the hope that the criminal will lead him to the notorious Purple Gang, of which Sonny is the leader. Theresa (Arthur), Sonny's sister, however, wrecks the plot after the two men break jail. When she flirts with Jeff, Sonny becomes quite upset. Later on, Sonny and his boys get involved with a drunken doctor (Barrymore), who hates criminals. The F.B.I. gets Sonny coming out of a movie theatre, thus ending his life of crime.

In 1941, MGM would revamp the film's plot and remake it as The Get-Away with Dan Dailey (Jr.) in the Calleia part and with Donna Reed as his sister. Stock footage from the original was interpolated with new scenes directed by Edward Buzzell.

PULP   (United Artists, 1972)   C-95 min.

Producer, Michael Klinger; director-screenplay, Mike Hodges; assistant director, Michael Dryhurst; production designer, Patrick Downing; art director, Darrell Lass; music-music director, George Martin; sound, Christian Wangler; camera, Ousama Rawi; editor, John Glenn.

Michael Caine (Mickey King); Mickey Rooney (Preston Gilbert); Lionel Stander (Ben Dinuccio); Lizabeth Scott (Princess Betty Cippola); Nadia Cassini (Liz Adams); Al Lettieri (Miller); Dennis Price (Mysterious Englishman); Amerigo Tot (Stogio); Leopoldo Trieste (Marcovic); Joe Zammit Cordina (Santana); Ave Nichi (Chambermaid); Werner Hasselman, Louise Lambert (American Tourists in Restaurant); Luciano Pigozzi (Del Duce); Iver Gilborn, Elaine Olcott (Tourists in Coach); Maria Quasimodo (Senora Pavone); Janet Agren (Silvana); Cristina Gaioni (Blonde Typist); Cyrus Elias (Guide); Mary Caruana (Mae West); Jeanne Lass (Marlene Dietrich); Kate Sullivan (Joan Crawford); Anna Pace Donnela (Jean Harlow); Jennifer Gauci (Shirley Temple); Tondi Barr (Gloria Swanson).

With an eye on nostalgia, this unusual, little-noticed feature told of a pornography hack writer (Caine) who travels to Malta to write a biography of a retired Mafia leader (Rooney), and of the attempts of other Mafiosa to insure that the book project is not completed. With good location work, this Michael Hodges production nearly becomes a satire on the gangster-detective film, with some scenes appearing to be parodies of former film classics.

The cast included movie racketeer favorite Lionel Stander, and the film also saw the screen return of Forties' tough girl, Lizabeth Scott.

THE PUZZLE OF THE RED ORCHID   see   DAS RATSEL DER ROTEN ORCHIDEE

QUEEN OF THE MOB   (Paramount, 1940)   61 min.

Director, James Hogan; based on the book Persons in Hiding
by J. Edgar Hoover; screenplay, Horace McCoy, William R. Lipman; art directors, Hans Dreier, Ernst Fegte; camera, Theodor
Sparkuhl; editor, Arthur Schmidt.

Ralph Bellamy (Scott Langham); Jack Carson (Ross Waring);
Blanche Yurka (Ma Webster); Richard Denning (Charlie Webster);
James Seay (Eddie Webster); Paul Kelly (Tom Webster); William
Henry (Bert Webster); Jeanne Cagney (Ethel Webster); J. Carrol
Naish (George Frost); Hedda Hopper (Mrs. Emily Sturgis); Pierre
Watkin (Stitch Torey); Billy Gilbert (Caterer); John Harmon (Pinky);
Raymond Hatton (Auto Camp Proprietor); Betty McLaughlin (Girl);
Charlotte Wynters (Mrs. Grimley); Neil Hamilton (Murdock); Robert
Ryan (Jim); Paul Stanton (Mr. Edmonds the Banker); Donald Douglas
(F. B. I. Director); James Flavin (F.B.I. Chief); Mary Gordon (Jani-
tress); Paul Fix (Man); Ethan Laidlaw (Court Officer).

Very loosely based on the exploits of murderous Ma Barker
and her emotionally disturbed sons, this fast-paced budget film had
Blanche Yurka play the title role.   "... told factually, without any
sentimental trimmings, the film is packed with action and suspense
and shows crime as it is in real life, not as it is cooked up in fiction" (New York World-Telegram).

Ma and her three homicidal sons (Kelly, Denning and Carson)
go on a robbery and murder spree which nets them $400,000.   Al-
so involved is the woman's one good son (Henry), his wife (Cagney)
and child, another hoodlum (Naish) and an F.B.I. agent (Bellamy).
The film derived from J. Edgar Hoover's 1939 book, Persons in
Hiding, and was one of a quartet of features Paramount created from
the work.

In The Bad Guys (1964), William K. Everson comments,
"Blanche Yurka made every bit as ruthless a gang leader as Robinson or Cagney had done. "   It is a picture to be seen, as few punches are pulled.

QUICK MILLIONS   (Fox, 1931)   72 min.

Director, Rowland Brown; story, Courtney Terrett, Brown;
screenplay, Terrett, Brown; art director, Duncan Cramer; costumes,
Sophie Wachner; sound, W. W. Lindsay, Jr. ; camera, Joseph August.

Spencer Tracy (Bugs Raymond); Marguerite Churchill (Dorothy
Stone); Sally Eilers (Daisy de Lisle); Robert Burns (Arkansas Smith);
John Wray (Kenneth Stone); Warner Richmond (Nails Markey); George
Raft (Jimmy Kirk); John Swor (Contractor).

A young Spencer Tracy was featured as a hood who was "...
too lazy to work and too nervous to steal. "   Starting as a truck
driver, Bugs Raymond works his way into the rackets and forms a
protection syndicate.   He then becomes very powerful and wants to
wed a society girl (Churchill), but she rejects him.   To get revenge,
he decides to kidnap her on her wedding day, but his gang turns on

Jeanne Cagney and William Henry in a publicity pose for Queen of
the Mob (1940).

him and takes him for a one-way ride.

Despite its rather simplistic plot, this Fox release was quite entertaining. The National Board of Review magazine termed it "the most intelligent of the gangster films." One of the best remembered scenes in the picture has Bugs coldly murdering his bodyguard (Raft) when he thinks the man has betrayed him.

As countless other films would attempt to do over the years, Quick Millions both exploited and moralized against the concept of making an easy buck the crooked way.

RACE STREET (RKO, 1948) 79 min.

Executive producer, Jack J. Gross; producer, Nat Holt; director, Edwin L. Marin; suggested by the story The Twisted Road by Maurice Davis; screenplay, Martin Rackin; art director, Abert S. D'Agostino, Walter E. Keller; set decorators, Darrell Silvera, William Stevens; music, Roy Webb; music director, C. Bakaleinikoff; songs, Don Raye and Gene DePaul; Ray Heindorf; Ted Koehler and M. K. Jerome; choreography, Charles O'Curran; assistant director, Grayson Rogers; costumes, Edward Stevenson; sound, Jean L. Speak, Terry Kellum; special effects, Russell A. Cully; camera, J. Roy Hunt; editor, Sam E. Beetley.

George Raft (Dan Gannin); William Bendix (Runson); Marilyn Maxwell (Robbie); Frank Faylen (Phil Dickson); Henry "Harry" Morgan (Hal Towers); Gale Robbins (Elaine Gannin); Cully Richards (Mike Hadley); Mack Gray (Stringy); Russell Hicks (Easy Mason); Tom Keene (Al); William Forrest (Nick Waters); Jim Nolan (Herbie); George Turner (Dixie); Richard Benedict (Sam); Dean White (Big Jack); Freddie Steele (Monty); Mike Lally, Eddie Arden, Franklyn Farnum, George Murray (Men); Sam McDaniel (Garage Attendant); June Pickrell (Woman); Charles Lane (Desk Clerk at Robbie's Apartment Building); Jason Robards, Sr. (Desk Clerk).

When intriguing or even mildly interesting parts are lacking in gangster pictures, writers tend to bolster the proceedings with an excessive amount of violence. Such was the case with Race Street.

Bookie Dan Gannin (Raft) decides to go straight when he becomes involved romantically with the widow (Maxwell) of a war hero. However, when his buddy (Morgan) is killed by an extortionist gang, Dan vows revenge. In doing so, he learns that Robbie is actually wed to the leader of the gang (Faylen). Dan's boyhood pal, Runson, a plainclothes cop, is the one who finally comes to Gannin's rescue.

THE RACKET (Paramount, 1928) 7,646'

Presenter, Howard Hughes; director, Lewis Milestone; based on the play by Bartlett Cormack; screenplay, Harry Behn, Del Andrews; adaptor, Cormack; titles, Eddie Adams; camera, Tony Gaudio; editor, Tom Miranda.

Lizabeth Scott and Brett King in The Racket (1951).

Thomas Meighan (Captain McQuigg); Marie Prevost (Helen Hayes); Louis Wolheim (Nick Scarsi); George E. Stone (Joe Scarsi); John Darrow (Ames the Reporter); Skeets Gallagher (Miller the Reporter); Lee Moran (Pratt the Reporter); Lucien Prival (Chick); Tony Marlo (Chick's Chauffeur); Henry Sedley (Corcan); Sam De Grasse (District Attorney); Burr McIntosh ("The Old Man"); G. Pat Collins (Johnson the Patrolman).

THE RACKET   (RKO, 1951)   89 min.

Executive producer, Howard Hughes; producer, Edmund Grainger; director, John Cromwell; based on the play by Bartlett Cormack; screenplay, William Wister Haines, W. R. Burnett; art directors, Albert S. D'Agostino, Jack Ikey; music director, Mischa Bakaleinikoff; song, Jimmy McHugh and Harold Adamson; camera, George E. Diskant; editor, Sherman Todd.

Robert Mitchum (Captain Thomas McQuigg); Lizabeth Scott (Irene Hayes); Robert Ryan (Nick Scanlon); William Talman (Johnson); Ray Collins (Welch); Joyce MacKenzie (Mary McQuigg); Robert Hutton (Dave Ames); Virginia Huston (Lucy Johnson); William Conrad (Turck); Walter Sande (Delaney); Les Tremayne (Chief Henry Craig); Don Porter (Connolly); Walter Baldwin (Sullivan); Brett King (Joe Scanlon);   Richard Karlan (Enright); Tito Vuolo (Tony); Howard Petrie (Governor); William Forrest (Governor's Aide); Iris Adrian

(Sadie); Mike Lally (Duty Sergeant); Milburn Stone (Foster the Assistant); Don Beddoe (Mitchell); Ed Parker (Hodd); Art DuPuis, Harry Lavter (Radio Cops).

Howard Hughes' dabbling in films brought forth two versions of The Racket, each based on Bartlett Cormack's 1927 play which was a sensational exposé of big city racketeering.

The silent version, with its adept use of lighting and focusing, created an ambience of crime visually. It was all very arty yet commercial. The 1951 update produced by bashful billionaire Hughes for his RKO studios was much more pedestrian in concept and execution. It brought back Robert Mitchum and Robert Ryan, who had appeared together in the successful Crossfire (1947).

In the Fifties' version, Captain Thomas McQuigg (Mitchum) is a honest cop who refuses to take bribes from a corrupt politician (Collins) and hoodlums led by Nick Scanlon (Ryan). The tough but vapid film is centered around a club where thrush Irene Hayes (Scott) is employed. She is romantically allied with reporter Dave Ames (Hutton). One of the more rewarding performances was provided by William Talman as an honest policeman.

Regarding this remake, the New York Times sighed, "... as for the film's observations on crooks and politics, they are so generalized and familiar that this is just a case of one more time around. "

RACKET BUSTERS (Warner Bros. , 1938) 71 min.

Associate producer, Samuel Bischoff; director, Lloyd Bacon; screenplay, Robert Rossen, Leonardo Bercovici; assistant director, Dick Mayberry; art director, Esdras Hartley; gowns, Howard Shoup; music, Adolph Deutsch; orchestrator, Hugo Friedhofer; sound, Robert B. Lee; camera, Arthur Edeson; editor, James Gibbon.

George Brent (Denny Jordan); Humphrey Bogart (John "Czar" Martin); Gloria Dickson (Nora Jordan); Allen Jenkins (Skeets Wilson); Walter Abel (Hugh Allison); Penny Singleton (Gladys Christie); Henry O'Neill (Governor); Oscar O'Shea (Pop); Elliott Sullivan (Charlie Smith); Fay Helm (Mrs. Smith); Joe Downing (Joe); Norman Willis (Gus); Don Rowan (Cliff Kimball); Anthony Averill (Dave Crane); Mary Currier (Mrs. Allison); Ferris Taylor (Man); Jack Goodrich (Clerk); James Nolan (Jim Smith--Allison's Secretary); Jim Pierce, Ethan Laidlaw (Martin's Henchmen); Herbert Heywood (Gas Station Owner); Irving Bacon (Counterman); Dale Van Sickel (Special Officer); Jan Holm (Nurse at Sanitarium); Monte Vandergrift (Detective); Charles Trowbridge (Judge); William B. Davidson (Union Chairman).

This film is one of those mindless, delightful diversions that were such a standard way of life in the Thirties. At the time of its release it was regarded as "... a hard-grained and generally exciting film" (New York Times), but today it is one of the lesser known of the Warners' gangster epics.

Gang leader John Martin (Bogart) tries to take over a trucking enterprise, but he is opposed by special prosecutor Hugh Allison

(Abel) and a loner truck driver, Denny Jordan (Brent), whose vehicle had been burned by the mob. Later, in order to support his pregnant wife (Dickson), Denny robs the trucking office and is caught. However, the law allows him to go free if he will join the hoodlums and uncover information for the D.A. While Denny is involved with the organization, Martin tries to take over the food market. He calls a strike and when Skeets Wilson (Jenkins) opposes him, he is murdered. In revenge for this act, Denny leads the truckers in revolt against the racketeers. Denny beats up Martin, and the latter is arrested.

Infiltrating a particular industry would be a favorite theme of gangster films, allowing for fresh locales and situations to distract from a tired formula.

THE RACKETEER (Pathé, 1929) 5,119'

Associate producer, Ralph Block; director, Howard Higgin; story-screenplay, Paul Gangelin; dialog, A. A. Kline; dialog director, Rollo Lloyd; art director, Edward Jewell; set dresser, T. E. Dickson; assistant director, George Webster; costumes, Gwen Wakeling; sound, D. A. Cutler, Clarence M. Wickes; camera, David Abel; editor, Doane Harrison.

Robert Armstrong (Keene); Carol(e) Lombard (Rhoda); Roland Drew (Tony); Jeanette Loff (Millie); John Loder (Jack); Paul Hurst (Mehaffy); Winter Hall (Mr. Simpson); Winifred Harris (Mrs. Simpson); Kit Guard (Gus); Al Hill (Squid); Bobby Dunn (The Rat); Hedda Hopper (Mrs. Lee); Bud Fine (Weber).

As in later decades, for every one decent gangster film, there would be a score of mediocre ones. Often the only redeeming facet of the run-of-the-mill efforts would be performances by stars-in-the-making. Such was The Racketeer which featured Robert Armstrong and Carol(e) Lombard, both of whom would be served much better by Hollywood in later years.

The film's rather weird plot found gangster Keene (Armstrong) reforming a violinist (Drew) who had gone astray, because Keene is attracted to the musician's girl (Lombard). Rhoda, in turn, has left her husband to reform the same hard-drinking fiddle player. When Tony is sober enough to give a concert, Keene postpones a robbery so he can attend the event. Later he kills a rival gangster (Fine) who threatens Tony and Rhoda. For his troubles, the love-struck hood is liquidated by the rival's gang. And, of course, the now-successful violinist and Rhoda walk off into the sunset to a life of happiness.

DAS RATSEL DER ROTEN ORCHIDEE (Rialto, 1961) 84 min.

Director, Helmut Ashley; based on the novel When the Gangs Came to London by Edgar Wallace; screenplay, Trygve Larsen; music, Peter Thomas; camera, Franz Lederle.

With: Christopher Lee, Marisa Mell, Klaus Kinski, Adrian

Carole Lombard and Robert Armstrong in The Racketeer (1929).

Hoven, Fritz Rasp, Christiane Nielsen, Walter Gotell.
      U.S. TV title: The Puzzle of the Red Orchid.
      A.k.a. Gangsters: London.

        Filmed in both German and English language versions, this
Edgar Wallace thriller detailed the rather complicated story of rival
U.S. and British hoodlums having a disagreement after the London
syndicate, which blackmails rich Britishers, holds out on their
American counterparts. To add to the confusion, both the F.B.I.
and Scotland Yard converge on London to round up both gangs. For
box-office "appeal" a series of brutal crimes is performed by the
hoodlums in the course of their extortionist attempts.
        What usually made the Wallace-derived thrillers so intriguing
was the bizarre quality of the underworld characters. It was this
particular ambience that was so contrary to any concept filmgoers
(via American movies) had of criminal types.

RAW DEAL (Eagle Lion, 1948) 79 min.

        Producer, Edward Small; director, Anthony Mann; story,

Arnold B. Armstrong, Audrey Ashley; screenplay, Leopold Atlas,
John C. Higgins; music, Paul Sawtelle; camera, John Alton; editor,
Alfred De Gaetano.
     Dennis O'Keefe (Joe Sullivan); Claire Trevor (Pat); Marsha
Hunt (Ann Martin); John Ireland (Fantail); Raymond Burr (Rick
Coyle); Curt Conway (Spider); Chill Williams (Marey).

     This well-engineered, unpretentious production proved to be
an expensive mounting, which was not necessary for a nicely-paced
venture.   As Variety weighed it, it "... is a fast-rolling gangster
melodrama with a strong undercurrent of romance.... "
     Convict Joe Sullivan (O'Keefe) smashes out of prison with the
help of tough Pat (Trevor).   Along the way to a rendezvous with a
gang chief (Burr), they pick up a social worker (Hunt) as a hostage
for added protection.   Before long, Joe is more attracted to Ann
than to faithful Pat.   The climax finds Rick Coyle trying to pull a
deadly double-cross, with fatal results to himself and Joe.   The
problems of being an unglamourous gun moll were sharply etched
by the very proficient Miss Trevor.

RIFIFI   see   DU RIFIFI CHEZ DES HOMMES

RIFIFI AMONG THE WOMEN   see   DU RIFIFI CHEZ LES FEMMES

RIFIFI IN PANAMA   see   DU RIFIFI A PANAME

RIFIFI IN TOKYO   see   DU RIFIFI A TOKYO

THE RIOT   see   RIOT IN CELL BLOCK 11

RIOT IN CELL BLOCK 11   (Allied Artists, 1954)   80 min.

     Producer, Walter Wanger; director, Don Siegel; screenplay,
Richard Collins; art director, David Milton; set decorator, Robert
Priestley; music, Herschell Gilbert; camera, Russell Harlan; editor,
Bruce Pierce.
     Neville Brand (Dunn); Emile Meyer (The Warden); Frank Fay-
len (Haskel); Leo Gordon (Carnie); Robert Osterloh (The Colonel);
Paul Frees (Monroe); Don Keefer (Newsman); Alvy Moore (Gator);
Dabbs Greer (Schuyler); Whit Bissell (Snader); James Acton (Acton);
Carleton Young (Captain Barrett); Harold J. Kennedy (Graphic Re-
porter); William Schallert (Reporter); Joe Kerr (Mac); Roy Glenn
(Delmar).

     The Thirties had The Big House, The Last Mile, 20,000
Years in Sing Sing, and Each Dawn I Die; the Forties turned out
Brute Force.   In the Fifties this modestly but cagily produced

feature proved to be the prison study most remembered.

"The grim business of melodrama behind prison walls, so often depicted in standard, banal fashion in films, is given both tension and dignity...[here]. Although it is explosive enough to satisfy the most rabid of the cons versus 'screws' school of moviegoer, it also makes a sincere and adult plea for a captive male society revolting against penal injustice. [Producer Walter Wanger had served some time in prison in the 1950s.]... [it] is a realistic and effective combination of brawn, brains and heart" (New York Times).

As Stuart M. Kaminsky in Don Siegel: Director (1974) points out, this film "... broke two cardinal Hollywood rules: the good guys lost and there were no women in the picture. Furthermore, the picture clearly had something to say about a serious subject, prison reform, and it spoke seriously, soberly and, above all, realistically. "

Filmed at Folsom Prison but, unlike Inside the Walls of Folsom Prison (1951), a truly graphic study of conditions in incarceration, this well-respected feature finds Dunn (Brand), a multiple-sentence prisoner, heading the group which seizes some guards as hostages and bargains for better living conditions, food, etc. Despite the efforts of the understanding warden (Meyer), Carnie (Gordon) and other prisoners go berserk. Not until the governor signs the prisoners' petition, does the havoc stop.

Newsweek judged this grim study "a model of movie realism" and praised it as a film "full of criminological insights. " It was a far cry from such trash as The Riot (1969) which exploited black ex-football player Jim Brown and the violence ambience

THE RISE AND FALL OF LEGS DIAMOND (Warner Bros. , 1960) 103 min.

Producer, Milton Sperling; associate producer, Leon Chooluck; director, Budd Boetticher; screenplay, Joseph Landon; music, Leonard Rosenman; assistant director, Gene Anderson, Jr. ; makeup, Gordon Bau; costumes, Howard Shoup; art director, Jack Poplin; set decorator, Clarence I. Steensen; sound, Samuel F. Goode; camera, Lucien Ballard; editor, Folmar Blangsted.

Ray Danton (Jack "Legs" Diamond); Karen Steele (Alice Shiffer); Elaine Stewart (Monica Drake); Jesse White (Leo Bremer); Simon Oakland (Lieutenant Moody); Robert Lowery (Arnold Rothstein); Judson Pratt (Fats Walsh); Warren Oates (Eddie Diamond); Frank De Kova (Chairman); Gordon Jones (Sergeant Cassidy); Joseph Ruskin (Matt Moren); Dyan Cannon (Dixie); Richard Gardner (Vince Coll); Sid Melton (Little Augie); Nesdon Booth (Fence); Buzz Henry, Dyke Johnson, Roy Jenson (Bodyguards); Joe Marr, Jim Drum (Officers); Dorothy Neumann, Frances Mercer (Women); Judd Holdren (Haberdashery Clerk); Geroge Taylor (Switchboard Operator); Robert Herron, Carey Loftin (Thugs); Norman Dupont (Maitre D' Louis).

Following a series of excellent Westerns with Randolph Scott, director Budd Boetticher turned to the gangster genre for The Rise and Fall of Legs Diamond.

Ray Danton and Karen Steele in <u>The Rise and Fall of Legs Diamond</u> (1960).

Although not very accurate historically, the film did present a most entertaining picture of Jack "Legs" Diamond (Danton), a petty crook who rose from being a small-time dancer at the Hotsy Totsy Club to become the bodyguard of Arnold Rothstein (Lowery), the gangland king. Also detailed were Legs' affairs with two gals (Steele and Stewart) whom he uses to rise to the top. Escaping an assassination attempt, he takes a European jaunt. When he returns, his former flame (Stewart) plots his downfall. She lifts his hotel keys, and, thereafter, one night as he lies in a drunken daze, he is killed by mobsters.

An interesting bit of casting had future gangster film star Warren "Dillinger" Oates as Eddie Diamond, Legs' drunken brother whom the latter lets die so that he will not contaminate his rise to fame.

Said the <u>New York Herald-Tribune</u>, "Its biographical form fosters an illusion of factualness but restricts the drama to brief episodes of violence. On the other hand, its somewhat standoffish, neutralized viewpoint keeps the spectator from any very close personal involvement and lessens the immediacy."

ROADHOUSE NIGHTS (Paramount, 1930) 71 min.

Director, Hobart Henley; story, Ben Hecht; screenplay-dialog,

Garrett Fort; songs, E. Y. Harburg and Jay Gorney; Eddie Jackson, Lou Clayton, and Jimmy Durante; camera, William Steiner; editor, Helene Turner.

Helen Morgan (Lola Fagan); Charles Ruggles (Willie Bindbugel); Fred Kohler (Sam Horner); Jimmy Durante (Daffy); Fuller Mellish, Jr. (Hogan); Leo Donnelly (City Editor); Tammany Young (Jerry); Joe King (Hanson); Lou Clayton (Joe); Eddie Jackson (Moe).

For her starring debut in films, Helen Morgan was cast as Lola Fagan, second-rate club singer. Jimmy Durante, in his film debut, appeared as Daffy, a club comedian.

Bootlegger Sam Horner (Kohler) controls a small town and a big city newspaper sends a reporter to expose the situation. Horner finds out and kills the writer. The paper sends another newsman (Ruggles) to find out just what happened to the first. At the gang's headquarters, a roadhouse, Willie meets Lola, his old sweetheart. He is aghast to learn she is the mistress of Horner and the songstress in his place. However, their romance is renewed and to save Willie from Horner's vengeance, she later tries to lead him away from the gangster's presence. But thanks to the help of Daffy (Durante) and the timely arrival of the Coast Guard (!), Lola and Willie are saved.

Highly melodramatic, but effective, Roadhouse Nights was an early example of the special flavor that gangster films would exhibit throughout the following decades. Filmmakers took it as an accepted practice that to mingle society with racketeers and toss in the nightclub environment made for a very sophisticated, adult, daring film. Besides, this combined ambience would intrigue the ticket buyer no matter how tawdry the plotline or acting. It did not always work that way.

THE ROARING TWENTIES (Warner Bros., 1939) 106 min.

Executive producer, Hal B. Wallis; associate producer, Samuel Bischoff; directors, Raoul Walsh, Anatole Litvak; story-foreword, Mark Hellinger; screenplay, Jerry Wald, Richard Macaulay, Robert Rossen; music, Heinz Roemheld, Ray Heindorf; orchestrator, Ray Heindorf; songs, Ernie Burnett and George A. Norton, Eubie Blake and Noble Sissle; Isham Jones and Gus Kahn; Jack Little, Joseph Young, and John Siras; dialog director, Hugh Cummings; assistant director, Dick Mayberry; art director, Max Parker; makeup, Perc Westmore; wardrobe, Milo Anderson; sound, Everett A. Brown; special effects, Byron Haskin, Edwin B. DuPar; camera, Ernest Haller; editor, Jack Killifer.

James Cagney (Eddie Bartlett); Priscilla Lane (Jean Sherman); Humphrey Bogart (George Hally); Jeffrey Lynn (Lloyd Hart); Gladys George (Panama Smith); Frank McHugh (Danny Green); Paul Kelly (Nick Brown); Elisabeth Risdon (Mrs. Sherman); Ed Keane (Pete Henderson); Joseph Sawyer (Sergeant Pete Jones); Abner Biberman (Lefty); John Deering (Commentator); Ray Cooke (Orderly); Robert Dobson (Lieutenant); John Harron (Soldier); Vera Lewis (Mrs. Gray); Murray Alper, Dick Wessel (Mechanics); Joseph Crehan (Fletcher the

Humphrey Bogart and James Cagney in The Roaring Twenties (1939).

Foreman); Norman Willis (Bootlegger); Robert Elliott, Eddy Chand-
ler (Officers); John Hamilton (Judge); Pat O'Malley (Jailer); Wade
Boteler (Policeman); Arthur Loft (Proprietor of Still); Al Hill, Ray-
mond Bailey, Lew Harvey (Ex-Convicts); Creighton Hale (Customer);
Major Sam Harris (Man in Club); Cyril Ring (Charlie the Clerk);
Stuart Holmes (Man for Turkish Bath).

        A decade before he created the definitive White Heat (1949),
q. v. , director Raoul Walsh, replacing Anatole Litvak, directed this
sparkling feature. It ended the decade of the '30s with one of the
best action gangster films ever made. Starring James Cagney, it
told of how the Prohibition era spawned and supported a new breed
of hoodlums.
        Made in a semi-documentary fashion (the forte of story writ-
er Mark Hellinger), it tells of three World War I veterans: Lloyd
Hart (Lynn) who becomes a lawyer, George Hally (Bogart) who becomes a bootlegger and Eddie Bartlett (Cagney) who drives a cab.
Eddie later joins a middle-aged prostitute (George) in the bootleg
business and they establish a fleet of cabs which are used to carry
the liquor to customers. Lloyd is hired as Eddie's lawyer, and
maturing Jean Sherman (Lane) begins to fall for the attorney. Later,

a gang war erupts when Eddie hijacks booze from a rival (Kelly) who is in league with Hally. Hally then joins Eddie and sends the F.B.I. after Nick Brown. Brown is eventually eliminated, but by then Eddie and Hally have become fierce rivals, and their gang splits apart. In the 1929 crash and the ending of Prohibition in the early Thirties, Eddie loses all his money except for one cab. Jean, who has wed Lloyd, finds it necessary to come to Eddie for help, while her husband is threatened by Hally. Eddie kills Hally, but is later gunned down in front of a church.

Using a lot of contemporary music rather than a specially composed soundtrack, The Roaring Twenties admirably recaptured the fun and fiercely fluctuating moods and types of the hectic decade. Eddie's on-camera decline and his demise at the finale ("he used to be a somebody" says loyal Panama Smith), were symbolic of the end of the glorious era of gangster films. What came thereafter would never match the robust, full-bodied underworld adventures of the 1930s, where a snarling Cagney, a lisping Bogart, a chipper Frank McHugh, or a sneering Joe Sawyer would together pepper a film with their bigger-than-life personalities.

ROBBERY (Embassy, 1967) C-114 min.

Executive producer, Joseph E. Levine; producers, Michael Deeley, Stanley Baker; associate producers, Jonathan Clowes, Alec Natas; director, Peter Yates; screenplay, Edward Boyd, Yates, George Markstein; music, Johnny Keating; assistant director, Derek Cracknell; art director, Michael Seymour; wardrobe, Brian Owen-Smith; makeup, Wally Schneiderman; sound, Dudley Plummer; camera, Douglas Slocombe; editor, Reginald Beck.

Stanley Baker (Paul Clifton); Joanna Pettet (Kate Clifton); James Booth (Inspector Langdon); Frank Finlay (Robinson); Barry Foster (Frank); William Marlowe (Dave); Clinton Greyn (Jack); George Sewell (Ben); Michael McStay (Don); Patrick Jordan (Freddy); Ken Farrington (Robber); Glyn Edwards (Squad Chief); Anthony Sweeney (Detective Inspector); David Pinner (Constable--Information Room); Rachel Herbert (School Teacher); Martin Wyldeck (Chief Constable on Track); Roger Booth (Detective); Malcolm Taylor (Delta 1 Observer); Linda Marlowe (Debutante at Nightclub).

After the famous train heist in Britain in the mid-1960s, a number of films were made on similar subjects, one of the best being Robbery. Stanley Baker, who produced and starred in this film, also financed and fought the legal battles necessary to reproduce on celluloid England's "great train robbery."

Big-time hoodlum Paul Clifton (Baker) rounds up a large group of accomplices to rob a Glasgow-to-London mail express of a three million dollar cargo. As the grab is planned, however, a Scotland Yard inspector (Booth) begins to suspect such a heist is afoot.

The writing team of Edward Boyd, director Yates, and George Markstein received the Team Plaque for Best British original screenplay for the year. The New York Times approved:

Stanley Baker (center) in Robbery (1967).

"This sure footed cops-and-robbers case is a dandy of its kind, right up to the home stretch. "

ROBIN AND THE 7 HOODS (Warner Bros. , 1964) C-123 min.

Executive producer, Howard W. Koch; producer, Frank Sinatra; associate producer, William H. Daniels; director, Gordon Douglas; screenplay, David R. Schwartz; music-music conductor, Nelson Riddle; songs, Sammy Cahn and James Van Heusen; orchestrator, Gil C. Grau; assistant directors, David Salven, Lee White; art director, Leroy Deane; set decorator, Ralph Bretton; makeup, Gordon Bau; dialog supervisor, Thom Conroy; costumes, Don Feld; sound, Everett Hughes, Vinton Vernon; camera, William H. Daniels; editor, Sam O'Steen.

Frank Sinatra (Robbo); Dean Martin (John); Sammy Davis, Jr. (Will); Bing Crosby (Allen A. Dale); Edward G. Robinson (Big Jim); Peter Falk (Guy Gisborne); Barbara Rush (Marian); Victor Buono (Sheriff Potts); Hank Henry (Six Seconds); Allen Jenkins (Vermin); Jack LaRue (Tomatoes); Robert Foulk (Sheriff Glick); Robert Carricart (Blue Jaw); Phil Arnold (Hatrack); Harry Swoger (Sonny King); Phil Crosby, Sonny King, Harry Wilson, Richard Bakalyan (Hoods); Joseph Ruskin (Twitch); Bernard Fein (Bananas); Carol Hill (Waitress); Hans Conried (Mr. Ricks); Linda Brent (Derelict); Larry Mann (Workman); Sig Ruman (Hammacher); Diane Sayer (Booze Number Witness); Ron Dayton (Man).

Hank Henry, Dean Martin, Sammy Davis, Jr., Frank Sinatra,
Richard Barkalayan, Bing Crosby and Phil Crosby in Robin and the
7 Hoods (1964).

     Frank Sinatra produced and pal Gordon Douglas directed this
glittery but hollow effort to satirize the gangster melodrama.   Instead of being a delightful escape into fun, it was "strained and archaic ... artless and obvious" (New York Times).   Despite such a
splashy cast of "in" and old-time names, Robin and the 7 Hoods was
not a legitimate moneymaker on the film marketplace.
     The best bit in the film occurs at the outset.   In 1928, a
party is thrown for Big Jim (Robinson), a Little Caesar-style hood.
At this birthday party he is gunned down, à la George Raft in Some
Like It Hot.   Several ambitious followers then attempt to take over
his North Chicago territory.   Warfare follows, with one hood (Sinatra) getting away with $50,000 and becoming a hero of sorts.   He
is then beset by Big Jim's daughter (Rush) and a con artist (Crosby),
the latter claiming to be from an orphanage in need of financial support.   The punks almost cancel each other out, but at least they
survive to hit the streets as beggars.   Who gets the girl?   Allen A.
Dale.
     Self-indulgent films like this did little for anyone, except may-
be the cast's ego.

(In cab) Victor McLaglen and Preston Foster; (on truck) Frank
Jenks, George E. Stone, John Harmon, Ivan Miller, Horace McMahon and Dick Rich in Roger Touhy, Gangster! (1944).

ROGER TOUHY, GANGSTER!   (Twentieth Century-Fox, 1944)
65 min.

> Producer, Lee Marcus; director, Robert Florey; story, Crane
Wilbur; screenplay, Wilbur, Jerry Cady; art directors, James Basevi,
Lewis Creber; set decorators, Thomas Little, Al Orenbach; music,
Hugo W. Friedhofer; music director, Emil Newman; assistant direc-
tor, Jasper Blystone; sound, Bernard Freericks; special camera ef-
fects, Fred Sersen; camera, Glen MacWilliams; editor, Harry Rey-
nolds.
> Preston Foster (Roger Touhy); Victor McLaglen (Owl Bang-
hart); Lois Andrews (Daisy); Kent Taylor (Steve Warren); Anthony
Quinn (George Carroll); William Post, Jr. (Joe Sutton); Henry "Harry" Morgan (Smoke Reardon); Matt Briggs (Cameron); Moroni Olsen
(Riley); Reed Hadley (Boyden the F.B.I. Agent); Trudy Marshall
(Gloria); John Archer (Kerrigan the F.B.I. Agent); Frank Jenks
(Troubles Connors); George E. Stone (Ice Box Hamilton); Charles
Lang (F.B.I. Agent); Kane Richmond (Mason); Frank Orth (Comic
in Theatre); George Holmes (McNair); Horace McMahon (Max Shar-
key); Edmund MacDonald (Barnes); Murray Alper (Ralph Burke); By-
ron Foulger (Court Clerk); Joseph Crehan (Warden); Addison Richards
(Priest); Jim Farley (Bailiff); Charles Wilson (Police Captain).

Although the title seems to promise a combination of a gangster epic and a biography, this film came up with little of the former and hardly any factual information for the latter. The film's
foreword warns that only the real names of close co-workers of
Touhy are used, and that all others are fictional to protect the "innocent" from identification.

Set in Chicago, the film tells of Touhy (Foster), a bootlegger
in opposition to Al Capone (the latter's name is never mentioned in
the film). Using the Ajax Novelty Company as a front for their operations, Touhy and the boys are framed on a kidnapping rap. Later, one of the gang's members (Morgan) turns state's evidence and
promises to tell the true story of how Touhy was framed by a
crooked investment broker. It was this man, Touhy's former partner, who was allegedly kidnapped. However, Smoke Reardon is
killed before he can spill the beans. Meanwhile, Touhy's group escapes, although they are soon recaptured by the F.B.I. At the
film's end, the warden of the Illinois State Penitentiary at Stateville,
where Touhy had been sent, makes a plea for citizens to obey the
law and to avoid the life of crime.

In real life, Roger Touhy was sentenced to a 99-year prison
term. In 1954, the judgment which sent him to jail was overruled,
but he remained in custody until 1959. Twenty-three days after his
release, he was gunned down, apparently a victim of the remnants
of the Capone mob. It was a case of reality being more vivid and
dramatic than fiction.

ROGUE COP (MGM, 1954) 92 min.

Producer, Nicholas Nayfack; director, Roy Rowland; based on
the novel by William P. McGivern; screenplay, Sydney Boehm; assistant director, Ridgeway Callow; music, Jeff Alexander; art director, Cedric Gibbons; set decorators, Edwin B. Willis, Keogh Gleason; makeup, William Tuttle; women's costumes, Helen Rose; sound,
Wesley C. Miller; special effects, A. Arnold Gillespie; camera,
John Seitz.

Robert Taylor (Christopher Kelvaney); Janet Leigh (Karen
Stephanson); George Raft (Dan Beaumonte); Steve Forrest (Eddie Kel-
vaney); Anne Francis (Nancy Corlane); Robert Ellenstein (Sidney Y.
Myers); Robert F. Simon (Ackerman); Anthony Ross (Father Ahern);
Alan Hale, Jr. (Johnny Stark); Peter Brocco (Wrinkles Fallon);
Vince Edwards (Langley); Olive Carey (Selma); Roy Barcroft (Lieu-
tenant Vince D. Bardeman); Dale Van Sickel (Manny); Ray Teal
(Patrolman Mullens); Guy Prescott (Detective Ferrari); Dick Sim-
mons (Detective Ralston); Phil Chambers (Detective Dirksen); Nicky
Blair (Marsh); Richard Deacon (Stacey); Gilda Oliva (Italian Girl);
Milton Parsons (Tucker); Carl Victor (Orderly).

Flashy but also rough and tough as it was, this film, wrote
the New York Herald-Tribune, was "... a simple, streamlined
movie about crookedness."

Graft-oriented law enforcer Christopher Kelvaney (Taylor)
accepts bribes from underworld figure Dan Beaumonte (Raft). When

Robert Taylor and Vince Edwards in <u>Rogue Cop</u> (1954).

Kelvaney's young cop brother (Forrest) arrests one of Beaumonte's
hoods (Brocco), he is offered a gift to forget the incident, but refuses. Beaumonte has another hood (Edwards) kill him. Angered,
Kelvaney informs on Beaumonte and builds a case against him. In
a shootout he kills his former benefactor, but then must go to prison
because of his past shady activities.

  Basically another excuse to have Robert Taylor appear as a
good-bad type, the film veered toward the over-violent. Raft, however, had an exceedingly meaty role and played it to the hilt, giving
him the film's best notices. Perhaps his best scene as the cold-
blooded gangster was in beating up his drunken young mistress
(Francis) whom he later has killed when she gets in his way.

ST. BENNY THE DIP (United Artists, 1951) 80 min.

  Producers, Edward J. Danziger, Harry Lee Danziger; director, Edgar Ulmer; story, George Auerbach; screenplay, John Roe-
burt; music, Robert Stringer; camera, Don Malkames.
  Dick Haymes (Benny); Nina Foch (Linda Kovacs); Roland

Lionel Stander in <u>St. Benny the Dip</u> (1951).

Young (Matthew); Lionel Stander (Monk); Freddie Bartholomew (Reverend Wilbur); Oscar Karlweis (Mr. Kovacs); Dort Clark (Lieutenant Saunders); Will Lee (Sergeant Monahan); Verne Colette (Walter); Richard Gordon (Reverend Miles).

George Auerbach's original story for this film was cut heavily by the producers, the Danziger brothers. The resultant film, which originally was to have starred Marlon Brando, Louis Calhern, Roland Young, and Meg Mundy (or Hildegarde Knef), was shot on the cheap in New York City. Critic Arthur Knight would report that the film "... will prove offensive to many, painful to some and satisfactory diversion to none at all."

Still, this Edgar G. Ulmer-directed film had some charm in its tale of three con men on the lam who disguise themselves as priests, running a Bowery mission as a front. Dick Haymes starred as a singing "clergyman" who is reformed through the love of Linda Kovacs (Foch), a pert East Side commercial artist. Roland Young as Matthew and Lionel Stander as Monk were the other members of the lawbreaking trio, with Freddie Bartholomew as a real Reverend. The Hollywood conception of a lower East Side mission was not up to Damon Runyon standards, nor was the alleged comedy anywhere near as funny as anticipated.

THE ST. VALENTINE'S DAY MASSACRE (Twentieth Century-Fox, 1967) C-100 min.

Producer, Roger Corman; associate producer, Paul Rapp; director, Corman; screenplay, Howard Browne; art directors, Jack Martin Smith, Philip Jefferies; set decorators, Walter M. Scott, Steven Potter; makeup, Ben Nye; music, Fred Steiner; music conductor, Lionel Newman; sound, Herman Lewis, David Dockendorf; special camera effects, L. B. Abbott, Art Cruickshank, Emil Kosa, Jr.; camera, Milton Krasner; editor, William B. Murphy.

Jason Robards (Al Capone); George Segal (Peter Gusenberg); Ralph Meeker (George "Bugs" Moran); Jean Hale (Myrtle Nelson [Koppelman]); Clint Ritchie (Machine Gun Jack McGurn [Vincenzo Di Mora]); Frank Silvera (Nicholas Sorello); Joseph Campanella (Al Wienshank); Richard Bakalyan (John Scalisi); David Canary (Frank Gusenberg); Bruce Dern (Johnny May); Harold J. Stone (Frank Nitti); Kurt Kreuger (James Clark); Paul Richards (Charles Fischetti); Joseph Turkel (Jake Guzik); Milton Frome (Adam Heyer); Mickey Deems (Reinhart Schwimmer); John Agar (Dion O'Banion); Celia Lovsky (Josephine Schwimmer); Tom Reese (Ted Newberry); Jan Merlin (Willie Marks); Alex D'Arcy (Hymie Weiss); Gus Trikonis (Rio); Charles Dierkop (Salvanti); Tom Signorelli (Bobo Borotto); Rico Cattani (Albert Anselmi); Alex Rocco (Diamond); Leo Gordon (James Morton); Paul Frees (Narrator); Barboura Morris (Jeanette Landsman); Mary Grace Canfield (Mrs. Doody); Ron Gans (Chapman); Jack Del Rio, Phil Haran, Bob Brandin, Ernesto Moralli, Nick Borgani (Capone's Board Members); Ken Scott (Policeman); Joan Shawlee (Edna--Frank's Girlfriend); Dale Van Sickel (Stunt Double); Jack Nicholson (Gino).

Filmdom has told and retold the events of February 14, 1929 on Chicago's North Clark Street when Al Capone's men mowed down several of Bug Moran's boys in an attempt to end the latter's power on the northside of the city. Exactly why producer-director Roger Corman decided to detail the massacre again is not sure. What is certain, however, is that the semi-documentary effect of the film was interesting, but the overall production was badly hampered by the miscasting of Jason Robards as the infamous, intriguing Al Capone.

The feature methodically details the assorted side stories leading up to the shootout, including the lives of those involved in the event.

While Robards was physically most unconvincing as Capone, George Segal as Peter Gusenberg and Ralph Meeker as Bugs Moran were quite good, as were the rest of the cast.

Reactions to the film were mixed. Variety went overboard in labeling it a "socko production, direction, scripting." The New York Times, on the other hand, found "it is not a good gangster picture in any sense of the word. It isn't well constructed, well directed or well played. It is sloppily overwritten and quite excessively performed, so it artificializes and confuses the tawdry history it is supposed to relate."

Despite everything--or because of everything--it grossed $1.7 million in distributors' domestic rentals. Today it remains a stable for television late show viewers.

LE SAMOURAI (C.I.C.C.-Fida Cinematografica, 1967) C-103 min.

Producer, Eugene Lepicier; director, Jean-Pierre Melville; based on the novel The Ronin by Joan McLeod; screenplay, Melville; music, Francois De Roubaix; art director, Francois De Lamothe; assistant director, Georges Pellegrin; sound, Rene Longuet; camera, Henri Decae; editors, Monique Bonnot, Yolande Maurette.

Alain Delon (Jef Costello); Nathalie Delon (Jane Lagrange); Francois Perier (The Inspector); Cathy Rosier (Valerie); Jacques Leroy (The Gunman); Jean-Pierre Posier (Olivier Rey); Catherine Jourdan (Hatcheck Girl); Michel Boisrond (Wiener); Robert Favart (Barman); Andre Salgues (Garage Man).

U.S. release: The Godson (Artists International, 1972) C-103 min.

A worker for the gangster syndicate in Paris, Jef Costello (Alain Delon) is a professional killer with a very strong code of ethics. His every business activity is accompanied by ritualistic action. He is ordered to kill the owner of a nightclub, which he does, counting on prostitute Jane Lagrange to provide him with an alibi. While at the club for the killing, he is spotted by black songstress Valerie (Rosier). However, the latter later refuses to pick out Jef in a police-lineup. Jef decides from subsequent happenings that his employer has fingered him for death. Instead, he learns the man's (Posier) identity and kills him. But the wheels of annihilation are in motion, and Jef knows it is only a matter of

time before his demise is a reality.   Instead of waiting further, he
walks into a police trap and allows himself to be gunned down by
the law enforcers.

The box-office mystique of Alain Delon (with or without his
wife on camera) had dwindled in the U.S. by the 1970s.   To bolster
potential grosses, the title was altered to The Godson in an attempt
to take advantage of The Godfather spell.   Despite this gimmick,
the feature, which was poorly dubbed, did little business in the U.S.
market.

Said Newsweek, "If The Godfather went down like a plateful
of spicy meatballs, The Godson goes down like a single, chilled
radish--without salt."   But Newsweek was quick to add, "... it is
nonetheless a first-rate thriller of uncompromising simplicity, time-
bomb pacing--and an acuteness about the world of a professional
criminal that puts The Godfather near to Cheaper by the Dozen....
In Melville's vision, prison is no answer to the criminal; he is already there."

In some critical quarters it was felt that by adapting an
American novel to a French cast and technical crew, a lot of the
original flavor was lost, and that the parallels the director drew between the hoodlum's hired assassin and the Japanese samurai were
too heavy-handed.   Nevertheless, the film remains an interesting
adjunct to the gangster canon.

SAN QUENTIN   (Warner Bros., 1937)   70 min.

Associate producer, Samuel Bischoff; director, Lloyd Bacon;
story, Robert Tasker, John Bright; screenplay, Peter Milne, Humphrey Cobb; music, Heinz Roemheld, Charles Maxwell, David Raksin;
orchestrators, Joseph Nussbaum, Ray Heindorf; song, Harry Warren
and Al Dubin; assistant director, Dick Mayberry; art director, Esdras Hartley; gowns, Howard Shoup; sound, Everett A. Brown; special effects, James Gibbons, H. F. Koenekamp; camera, Sid Hickox;
editor, William Holmes.

Pat O'Brien (Captain Steve Jamiesson); Humphrey Bogart (Joe
"Red" Kennedy); Ann Sheridan (May Kennedy); Barton MacLane (Lieu-
tenant Druggin); Joseph Sawyer (Sailor Boy Hansen); Veda Ann Borg
(Helen); James Robbins (Mickey Callahan); Joseph King (Warden Tay-
lor); Gordon Oliver (Captain); Garry Owen (Dopey); Marc Lawrence
(Venetti); Emmett Vogan (Lieutenant); William Pawley, George Lloyd,
Al Hill (Convicts); Max Wagner (Prison Runner); Ernie Adams (Fink);
Raymond Hatton (Pawnbroker); Hal Neiman (Convict #38216); Glen
Cavender (Hastings); William Williams (Conklin); George Offenman,
Jr. (Young Convict); Lane Chandler (Guard); Edward Peil, Sr. (Dep-
uty); Dennis Moore (Simpson); John Ince (Old Convict); Ralph Byrd
(Policeman on Phone); Ray Flynn (Police Officer); Claire White,
Jack Mower (Couple in Car); Douglas Wood (Chairman of Prison
Board); Ernest Wood (Attorney); Saul Gorss (Clerk); Jerry Fletcher
(Hoffman).

The epitome of the "B" gangster film of the Thirties could be
found in San Quentin.   It had all the formulas of the genre: a

Pat O'Brien, Weldon Heyburn and Humphrey Bogart in San Quentin
(1937).

good-bad guy crook, his sweet sister, an honest policeman, a
crooked cop, an evil gangster, his moll, a prison background, and
a bevy of jailbird characters. Combined with a classic cast (from
the Warner Bros. stock company), San Quentin mirrors all the expected aspects of the true gangster feature.

Its plot concerns a prison yard captain (O'Brien), an ex-
officer, who wants to help the inmates at San Quentin. He falls for
cafe singer May Kennedy (Sheridan), the sister of Joe (Bogart), one
of the prisoners. Jamiesson tries reform methods by separating
newcomers from hardened criminals, but he is thwarted by his superior (MacLane) who plants an informer (Sawyer) in the rehabilitation
camp to cause trouble. Hansen plants suspicion about May in Jamiesson's mind and he talks Joe into an escape attempt with the help
of his moll (Borg), who will drive the getaway car. Making a successful break, Joe goes to his sister's apartment where he is confronted by Jamiesson. When the latter tries to convince him to return to prison, Joe shoots him. Undaunted, May explains the Captain's good intentions and persuades Joe to return to the penitentiary.
He is mortally wounded by the police, but Joe survives long enough to
tell the other prisoners to go along with Jamiesson's reforms.

Although the New York Times passed the feature off as "another of those Warner Brothers screen parables of prison life, " the film is loaded with good, old-fashioned action and plot. As an added treat, the cast, even down to the bit players, is superb. Besides, there is Ernie Adams, the perennial "fink, " who gets his in the boiler room for squealing on the other prisoners.

SATAN MET A LADY (Warner Bros., 1936) 66 min.

Producer, Henry Blanke; director, William Dieterle; based on the novel The Maltese Falcon by Dashiell Hammett; screenplay, Brown Holmes; music director, Leo F. Forbstein; gowns, Orry-Kelly; camera, Arthur Edeson; editors, Max Parker, Warren Low.

Bette Davis (Valerie Purvis); Warren William (Ted Shayne); Alison Skipworth (Madame Barabbas); Arthur Treacher (Anthony Travers); Winifred Shaw (Astrid Ames); Marie Wilson (Murgetroyd); Porter Hall (Mr. Ames); Maynard Holmes (Kenneth); Charles Wilson (Pollock); Olin Howland (Dunhill); Joseph King (McElroy); Barbara Blane (Babe); Eddie Shubert, James P. Burtis, Francis Sayles (Detectives); Billy Bletcher, Alice La Mont (Parents of Sextuplets); May Beatty (Mrs. Arden); John Alexander (Black Porter); Alphonse Martell (Headwaiter); Huey White (Taxi Driver); John Elliott (City Father); Saul Gorss (Farrow); Cliff Saum (Night Watchman); Douglas Williams (Dock Walloper); Kid Herman, J. H. Allen (Bootblacks). See THE MALTESE FALCON (1931).

THE SCARFACE MOB (Cari Releasing, 1962) 105 min.

In charge of production, Desi Arnaz; executive producer, Bert Granet; producer, Quinn Martin; associate producer, Jack Aldworth; director, Phil Karlson; based on the novel The Untouchables by Eliot Ness, Oscar Fraley; teleplay, Paul Monash; music, Wilbur Hatch; choreography, Jack Baker; assistant director, Vincent McEveety; art directors, Ralph Berger, Frank T. Smith; set decorator, Sandy Grace; makeup, Edwin Butterworth; wardrobe, Jerry Bos, Maria Donovan; sound, Cam McCullouch; camera, Charles Straumer; editor, Robert L. Swanson.

Robert Stack (Eliot Ness); Keenan Wynn (Joe Fuselli); Barbara Nichols (Brandy La France); Walter Winchell (Narrator); Pat Crowley (Betty Anderson); Neville Brand (Al Capone); Bill Williams (Martin Flaherty); Joe Mantell (George Ritchie); Bruce Gordon (Frank Nitti); Peter Leeds (Lamarr Kane); Eddie Firestone (Eric Hansen); Robert Osterloh (Tom Kopkac); Abel Fernandez (William Youngfellow); John Beradino (Johnny Giannini); Wolfe Barzell (Picco); Frank Wilcox (Beecher Asbury); Herman Rudin (Mops Volpe); Richard Benedict (Furs Sammons); James Westerfield (Ed Marriatt).

Issued in England and Europe as a feature, The Scarface Mob had served originally as the pilot for the successful Desilu teleseries, "The Untouchables. " The Phil Karlson-directed melodrama contained two segments of the program which told of the F.B.I.

fight led by Eliot Ness (Stack) against organized crime in Chicago of
the Twenties. The segments were initially telecast on April 20 and
27, 1958 and saw theatrical release in 1962. Said Jack E.
Nolan in Films in Review, "Not a few critics thought [it] one of filmdom's
best recreations of the gang-ridden Chicago of the 20s. " The "feature" was released in France as Tueur de Chicago.

SCARFACE: SHAME OF A NATION   (United Artists, 1932)   99 min.

Producer-supervisor, Howard Hughes; director, Howard
Hawks; based on the novel by Armitage Trail; screenplay, Ben Hecht,
Seton I. Miller, John Lee Mahin, W. R. Burnett, Fred Palsey; mu-
sic, Adolph Tandler, Gus Arnheim; assistant director, Richard Ros-
son; sound, William Snyder; camera, Lee Garmes, L. William
O'Connell; editor, Edward D. Curtiss.

Paul Muni (Tony Camonte); Ann Dvorak (Cesca Camonte);
Karen Morley (Poppy); Osgood Perkins (Johnny Lovo); Boris Karloff
(Gaffney); C. Henry Gordon (Guarino); George Raft (Guido Rinaldo);
Purnell Pratt (Publisher); Vince Barnett (Angelo); Inez Palange (Mrs.
Camonte); Harry J. Vejar (Costillo); Edwin Maxwell (Chief of Detec-
tives); Tully Marshall (Managing Editor); Henry Armetta (Pietro);
Charles Sullivan, Harry Tenbrook (Bootleggers); Hank Mann (Worker);
Paul Fix (Gaffney Hood); Maurice Black (Hood); Bert Starkey (Ep-
stein); Howard Hawks (Man on Bed); Dennis O'Keefe (Dance extra).

This release rounded out the trilogy of gangster film classics
produced in the first three years of the decade, being preceded by
Little Caesar (1931), q. v. and The Public Enemy (1931), q. v. Both
previous features told of the rise and fall of small time hoodlums
while this Howard Hughes-produced melodrama was a thinly disguised
version of the life of Al Capone (1899-1947). Howard Hawks directed Scarface from a screenplay concocted by several writers,
including Ben Hecht and William R. Burnett (who had written Little
Caesar). Harrison's Reports termed the movie "the most vicious
and demoralizing gangster pic produced. "
As Tony Camonte, Paul Muni gives a definitive portrayal of
the Capone-like figure. He plays the immigrant who gets into the
bootleg business as a bodyguard but soon takes over the small outfit. Later he goes to other territory, liquidates the big boss (Perkins) and a chief rival (Karloff), and wins Lovo's girl (Morley).
Thereafter the plot takes on a deeply psychological nature as an incest theme is developed with Camonte's feelings for his sister (Dvorak). He is deeply jealous of Casca, and when she begins dating
his henchman (Raft) he kills the man after finding him in a hotel
room with the girl, not realizing they have just been married. Casca, however, forgives her brother and at the finale she dies with
him in a shootout. At the end he pleads for mercy, but to no avail.
Three versions of the film's ending were shot, but the most
widely used one was the stereotyped climax set by Little Caesar,
with the once fearless gang leader begging for mercy.
Not only did Scarface cause a sensation (it was the bane of
the censors throughout the U.S.), but it consolidated Muni's screen

George Raft and C. Henry Gordon in Scarface (1932).

reputation and made a star of George Raft.   As the henchman Guido
Renaldo, Raft was the underling with slick hair who cut out paper
dolls and flipped a coin.   Ironically, Raft, a real life dancing favorite of Capone's, had been hired to give technical assistance to the
filmmakers.   In return, his part had been beefed up by the producers.   Boris Karloff, who would remain much better known for his
horror film output, had a memorable sequence in Scarface.   As he
makes a strike in a bowling alley, he is killed by gangland rivals.
         In retrospect, it is hard to do full justice to Scarface (or
Little Caesar or The Public Enemy).   So many innovative or smooth-
ly-working facets of the trio of films were duplicated or imitated
time and time again that today the originals seem occasionally to be
rip-offs of later movies.   But they were the real McCoy!

THE SECRET SIX   (MGM, 1931)   83 min.

         Director, George Hill; story-screenplay, Frances Marion;
sound, Robert Shirley; camera, Harold Wenstrom; editor, Blanche
Sewell.

Jean Harlow, John Mack Brown and Wallace Beery in The Secret Six
(1931).

Wallace Beery (Louis Scorpio); Lewis Stone (Newton); John
Mack Brown (Hank Rogers); Jean Harlow (Anne Courtland); Marjorie
Rambeau (Peaches); Paul Hurst (Nick Mizoski the Gouger); Clark Ga-
ble (Carl Luckner); Ralph Bellamy (Johnny Franks); John Miljan (Joe
Colimo); DeWitt Jennings (Chief Donlin); Murray Kinnell (Dummy
Metz); Fletcher Norton (Jimmy Delano); Louis Natheaux (Eddie); Frank
McGlynn (Judge); Theodore Von Eltz (District Attorney); Tom London
(Hood).

The title of this film, written by upper-case scripter Frances
Marion, refers to a group of leading businessmen who hire two reporters (Gable and Brown) to obtain evidence on a gang run by
Scorpio (Beery) and his amoral lawyer (Stone). In a war over bootleg liquor, the gang has already rubbed out some of its own double-
crossing members and rival gang leaders. When burly Scorpio discovers what the reporters are investigating, he has his hat-check
girl (Harlow) distract them. She, however, falls for Hank Rogers,
so Scorpio has him murdered. Anne goes to the law and is ready
to testify, but Scorpio is acquitted by a fixed jury. Later, out for
revenge, Scorpio kidnaps the girl but Carl comes to her rescue.
As the police surround the gang, Scorpio and Newton kill one another in an argument over some stashed loot.
Photoplay magazine exclaimed of this well-produced vehicle,
'No, gangster pictures are not dead--not as long as they produce

them like this. " The New York Post added, "... [it is] another
neat gang melodrama, genuinely thrilling" while the New York
Times noted, "... the picture moves along swiftly and the dialog is
quite well written. "

With MGM usually sticking to sophisticated drawing room
dramas or musicals, it was unusual for the studio to turn out this
almost-serial-like entry, with the masked group of vigilantes out to
break up the crime ring. From the standpoint of the careers of
its cast, this film showed Beery on the upswing in the talkies, John
Mack Brown on the decline at Metro, and Gable, already a staple
as a cinema tough guy, on the fast rise.

SERPICO (Paramount, 1973) C-130 min.

Executive producer, Dino De Laurentiis; producer, Martin
Bregman; associate producer, Roger M. Rothstein; director, Sidney
Lumet; based on the novel by Peter Maas; screenplay, Waldo Salt,
Norman Wexler; art director, Douglas Higgins; set decorator,
Thomas H. Wright; scenic artists, Jack Hughes; music, Mikis The-
odorakis; music director, Bob James; sound, James J. Sabat; cam-
era, Arthur J. Ornitz; editors, Dede Allen, Richard Marks.

Al Pacino (Frank Serpico); John Randolph (Sidney Green);
Jack Kehoe (Tom Keough); Biff McGuire (Inspector McClain); Barbara Eda-Young (Laurie); Cornelia Sharpe (Leslie Lane); Tony Roberts (Bob Blair); John Medici (Pasquale); Allan Rich (District Attorney Tauber); Norman Ornellas (Rubello); Ed Grover (Lombardo);
Al Henderson (Peluce); Hank Garrett (Malone); Joe Bova (Potts);
Gus Fleming (Dr. Metz); Charles White (Commissioner Delaney).

It is bad enough that the public is brainwashed with the notion that crime and corruption are everywhere, but lately the moviemakers have been making financial hay by force-feeding us with
the unpleasant realization that many law-enforcers are on the take,
or, worse yet, are direct participants in organized crime. The
film on the subject is Serpico, dealing with one honest cop's battle
to convince his teammates to join him in cleansing the force of
grafting public servants.

Set in New York City, the film details the career of Frank
Serpico (Pacino), a one-man army against bribery and collusion
among the city's cops. As he rises from rookie to experienced law
enforcer, he hopes to become a detective, but his continual rebuk-
ing of unethical practices by his superiors leads to his being marked
a "troublemaker. " Switched from precinct to precinct, he is followed by his honest reputation and is ostracized by many fellow police officers. Undaunted, he demands that his investigation of lawman corruption be brought to the attention of Commissioner Delaney
(White). No official action is forthcoming, so eventually Serpico,
supported by a friend (Roberts) on the mayor's investigating committee and by a compassionate police Inspector (Grover), spills his
story to the New York Times. Thereafter an inquiry is opened in
earnest. Meanwhile Serpico is transferred to Brooklyn's Narcotics
Division and on a raid he is seriously wounded (because his "fellow"

officers have abandoned him). Rejecting the detective's badge now
offered him as a peace bribe, he gives his Commission testimony and
then quits the force.

Without the fine, focal performance of Pacino, Serpico could
not have passed muster at the box-office. He gave continuity to the
jumble of scenes and episodes, balancing his on-duty attitudes with
his "relaxed" manner when away from the job (but still brooding
about it) and romancing one girl or another.

As is well known, the film was loosely based on a real-life
character in the New York police department whose revelations began an anti-corruption campaign in the New York City force.

711 OCEAN DRIVE (Columbia, 1950) 102 min.

Producer, Frank N. Seltzer; director, Joseph H. Newman;
story-screenplay, Richard English, Francis Swan; camera, Franz
Planer; editor, Bert Jordan.

Sammy White, Dorothy Patrick and Edmond O'Brien in 711 Ocean
Drive (1950).

Edmond O'Brien (Mal Granger); Joanne Dru (Gail Mason);
Donald Porter (Larry Mason); Sammy White (Chippie Evans); Doro-
thy Pattrick (Trudy Maxwell); Barry Kelley (Vince Walters); Otto
Kruger (Carl Stephans); Howard St. John (Lieutenant Pete Wright);
Robert Osterloh (Gizzi); Bert Freed (Marshak); Carl Milletaire (Joe
Gish); Charles La Torre (Rocco); Fred Aldrich (Peterson); Charles
Jordan (Tim); Sidney Dubin (Mendel Weiss).

Telephone man Mal Granger (O'Brien) becomes entangled in
the set-up of a bookmaker's wire room and rises to become a kingpin in the bookmaking and gambling syndicate. His goals are simple, however. They include acquiring the wife (Dru) of a big boss
(Kruger). Meanwhile, Carl Stephans decides he wants a piece of the
action in Granger's sphere of influence and with the aid of his deadly henchman (Porter), he instigates a gang war. Granger is nearly
done in over the Boulder Dam.
A documentary-style thriller which was too meek for its own
good, this film somehow won the endorsement of Senator Alexander
Wilex of Wisconsin, a member of the special Senate committee investigating crime. The Congressman lauded the film for its "importance" in revealing aspects of crime sweeping the nation. About
the only thing this entry showed effectively was the workings of a
bookmaker's wireroom.

SEVEN THIEVES (Twentieth Century-Fox, 1960) 100 min.

Producer, Sydney Boehm; director, Henry Hathaway; based
on the novel Lions at the Kill by Max Catto; screenplay, Boehm;
music, Dominic Frontiere; assistant director, Ad Schaumer; art di-
rector, Lyle R. Wheeler, John De Cuir; set decorators, Walter M.
Scott, Stuart A. Reiss; costumes, Bill Thomas; makeup, Ben Nye;
sound, Charles Peck, Harry M. Leonard; camera, Sam Leavitt; editor, Dorothy Spencer.
Edward G. Robinson (Theo Wilkins); Rod Steiger (Paul Mason);
Joan Collins (Melanie); Eli Wallach (Pancho); Alexander Scourby
(Raymond Le May); Michael Dante (Louis); Berry Kroeger (Hugo
Baumer); Sebastian Cabot (Monte Carlo Director); Marcel Hillaire
(Duc di Salins); John Berardino (Chief of Detectives); Alphonse Mar-
tell (Governor); Jonathan Kidd (Seymour); Marga Ann Deighton (Gov-
ernor's Wife).

Beginning his fourth decade as a gangster movie star, Edward G. Robinson appeared in Seven Thieves.
The ploy of the old gangster pulling the final big job is a
dated one in the genre, although it never seems to lose its popularity. "Clever and almost believable" stated the Saturday Review of
this variation of the heist caper. "... [It] won't show you how to
break the bank at Monte Carlo, but it will entertain you as the bank
is being robbed" (Films in Review).
American criminal Theo Wilkins (Robinson) arranges a daring
plan to steal four million dollars from a Monte Carlo gaming palace.
The elaborate set-up, which involves six others, has Theo pretending

to be the physician to an elderly baron who "dies" of a heart attack at the gambling table. The getaway requires the stashing of the loot in the ambulance which takes the gang away from the casino. Of course, there has to be an unexpected catch which blows the scheme to smitherens. But why spoil it; see the film for yourself.

SHADOW OF THE THIN MAN   (MGM, 1941)   97 min.

Producer, Hunt Stromberg; director, W. S. Van Dyke II; story, Harry Kurnitz; screenplay, Irving Brecher, Kurnitz; camera, William Daniels; editor, Robert J. Kern.

William Powell (Nick Charles); Myrna Loy (Nora Charles); Barry Nelson (Paul Clarke); Donna Reed (Molly Ford); Sam Levene (Lieutenant Abrams); Alan Baxter (Whitey Barrow); Dickie Hall (Nick Charles, Jr.); Loring Smith (Link Stephens); Joseph Anthony (Fred Macy); Henry O'Neill (Major Jason I. Sculley); Stella Adler (Claire Porter); Lou Lubin ("Rainbow" Benny Loomis); Louise Beavers (Stella); Will Wright (Maguire); Edgar Dearing (Motor Cop);

William Powell and Myrna Loy in Shadow of the Thin Man (1941).

Noel Cravat (Baku); Tito Vuolo (Luis); Oliver Blake (Penster); John
Dilson (Coroner); Cliff Danielson, J. Louis Smith, Buddy Roosevelt,
Jerry Jerome, Roger Moore (Reporters); Frankie Burke (Buddy
Burns); Inez Cooper (Girl in Cab); Robert Kellard (Policeman); Pat
McGee (Handler); Arch Hendricks (Photographer); Harry Burns
(Greek Janitor).

Poor gangsters. Why couldn't they ever be as bright or enterprising as a movie series' detective hero? The Thin Man property ran for more than a decade, encompassing six films. This was
number four in the adventures of Nick and Nora Charles (Powell and
Loy).

Nick is maneuvered into investigating a racetrack murder,
and he finds there is an impressive list of red herrings. Involved
in the case are a big shot gangster (Smith) and his henchmen, his
girlfriend (Adler), two reporters (Baxter and Nelson) out to break
up the syndicate, the chairman (O'Neill) of the state athletic commission, and a police lieutenant (Levene). In the usual finale for
this particular series (which was produced generally on a class
budget), Nick and Nora round up all the suspects, and slowly eliminate each, until only the real killer is left.

Nick and Nora, meanwhile, were still battling domestically,
were involved with bringing up Nick, Jr. (Hall), and still had a
fondness for liquid refreshment and chic talk.

SHERLOCK HOLMES (Fox, 1932) 68 min.
Director, William K. Howard; based on the stories by Sir
Arthur Conan Doyle and the play by William Gillette; screenplay,
Bertram Milhauser; art director, John Hughes; assistant director,
Philip Ford; camera, George Barnes.
Clive Brook (Sherlock Holmes); Ernest Torrence (Professor
Moriarity); Reginald Owen (Dr. Watson); Miriam Jordan (Alice Faulk-
ner); Howard Leeds (Little Billy); Alan Mowbray (Gore-King); Her-
bert Mundin (Pub Keeper); Montague Shaw (Judge); Arnold Lucy
(Chaplain); Lucien Prival (Hans the Hun); Roy D'Arcy (Manuel Lopez);
Stanley Fields (Tony Ardetti); Eddie Dillon (Ardetti's Henchman);
Robert Graves, Jr. (Gaston Roux); Brandon Hurst (Secretary to Ers-
kine); Claude King (Sir Albert Hastings).

Almost all literary detectives, once they have been trans-
mitted to the screen a few times, have had run-ins with organized
crime. Even Sir Arthur Conan Doyle's Sherlock Holmes had a
round with hoodlums in the 1932 Fox seven-reeler, Sherlock Holmes,
which presented Clive Brook as Holmes for the third* and last time.
This William K. Howard-directed melodrama, which Bertram
Milhauser (who later wrote some of the Universal-Holmes entries)
adapted from William Gillette's play, had a nice plot set-up. The
intrepid Holmes (Brook) is at odds with Professor Moriarity (Tor-
rance) who is using Chicago strong-arm men to force London pub

*Brook portrayed Holmes in The Return of Sherlock Holmes (1929)
and in a skit for Paramount on Parade (1930).

Clive Brook and Miriam Jordan in <u>Sherlock Holmes</u> (1932).

owners to pay protection money. At times Holmes disguises himself as an old aunt or a workman, and the ingenious detective finally apprehends Moriarity and ends (for the time being) his nefarious activities. At the film's end, Holmes weds Alice Faulkner (Jordan), a Gillette-created character, and they take up chicken farming.

It is interesting to note that Reginald Owen, who played Dr. Watson in this production, would later portray Holmes in A Study in Scarlet (1933), making him the only screen actor to play both parts.

SHOW THEM NO MERCY (Twentieth Century-Fox, 1935) 76 min.

Producer, Raymond Griffith; director, George Marshall; story, Kubec Glasmon; screenplay, Glasmon, Henry Lehrman; camera, Bert Glennon; editor, Jack Murray.

Rochelle Hudson (Loretta Martin); Cesar Romero (Tobey); Bruce Cabot (Pitch); Edward Norris (Joe Martin); Edward Brophy (Buzz); Warren Hymer (Gimp); Herbert Rawlinson (Kurt Hansen);

Cesar Romero and Bruce Cabot in Show Them No Mercy (1935).

Robert Gleckler (Gus Hansen); Charles C. Wilson (Clifford); William Davidson (Chief Haggerty); Frank Conroy (Reed); Edythe Elliott (Mrs. Hansen); William Benedict (Willie); Orrin Burke (Judge Fry); Boothe Howard (Lester Mills); Paul McVey (Dr. Peterson); Lester Dorr (Milkman); Georgie Cooper, Grace Goodall (Women); Stanley E. King, Larry Wheat, Philip Morris, Lee Shumway (G-Men); Gregg O'Brien, Stanley Blystone (Announcers); Wilfred Lucas (Druggist); Edward Keane (Doctor); Otto Hoffman (Hick).

Kubec Glasmon, the co-author of The Public Enemy, wrote this turgid gangster feature based on the Weyerhaeuser kidnapping. It relates the dirty deeds of a gaggle of criminals who pull a "snatch" and is concerned with their jealousies and psychological problems and their hunting down and rounding up by G-Men.

The hoodlums (Cabot, Brophy and Hymer), led by Tobey (Romero), obtain the ransom money for their kidnapping, but their hideout is invaded by a young couple (Hudson and Norris) and their sick baby. Madman Pitch (Cabot) wants to kill the intruders but the gang decides to send Joe Martin to pick up the loot from safekeeping; Loretta and the baby will be held as hostages. Meanwhile, the FBI traces the serial numbers of the bills and finds the gang's hideout.

This taut film proved to be ". . . a frightening experience in the cinema" (New York Times) as it zoomed into the lives of the punks: cunning and corrupt Tobey; Pitch, a killer made worse by excessive drinking; Buzz, a dumb hood and the butt of Pitch's vicious jokes (at one point Pitch sets fire to a newspaper which is being used as a blanket by the sleeping Buzz); and Gimp, a mental deficient.

The terrifying climax has the gang surrounded by G-Men. During the shootout, to save herself and the baby, Loretta, in an unforgettable scene, grabs a tommygun and riddles Pitch's chest with bullets.

THE SICILIAN CLAN see LE CLAN DES SICILIENS

SIDE STREET (MGM, 1949) 83 min.

Producer, Sam Zimbalist; director, Anthony Mann; story-screenplay, Sydney Boehm; art directors, Cedric Gibbons, Daniel B. Ruttenberg; music, Lennie Hayton; camera, Joseh Ruttenberg; editor, Conrad A. Nervig.

Farley Granger (Joe Norson); Cathy O'Donnell (Ellen Norson); James Craig (Georgie Garsell); Paul Kelly (Captain Walter Anderson); Jean Hagen (Harriet Sinton); Paul Harvey (Emil Lorrison); Edmon Ryan (Victor Backett); Charles McGraw (Stanley Simon); Ed Max (Nick Drumman); Adele Jergens (Lucille "Lucky" Colner); Harry Bellaver (Larry Giff); Whit Bissell (Harold Simpsen); John Gallaudet (Gus Heldon); Esther Somers (Mrs. Malby); Harry Antrim (Mr. Malby).

This well-conceived account presented the story of a New

York City mailman (Granger) who steals money which turns out to
be "hot" and how he is terrorized by the tough cops and hoodlums
before a big chase finale.

Shot in the popular semi-documentary style, the production
preached loudly that crime does not pay, but it also told of how an
unusually honest person can be dragged into crime and then, through
innate goodness, live to regret the action. Granger and O'Donnell,
who had appeared together in the earlier-filmed They Live by Night
(1949), q. v., were still being groomed as a new screen love team.

SIN STREET CONFIDENTIAL see WHITE HEAT

SIX BRIDGES TO CROSS (Universal, 1955) 96 min.

Producer, Aaron Rosenberg; director, Joseph Pevney; based
on the story They Stole $2,500,000--and Got Away with It by Joseph
Dineen; screenplay, Sydney Boehm; art directors, Alexander Golit-
zen, Robert Clatworthy; music director, Joseph Gershenson; assis-
tant directors, Ronnie Rondell, Marsh Green; camera, William
Daniels; editors, Russell Schoengarth, Verna MacCurran.
Tony Curtis (Jerry Florea); Julie Adams (Ellen Gallagher);
George Nader (Edward Gallagher); J. C. Flippen (Vincent Concannon);
Sal Mineo (Jerry--as a Boy); Jan Merlin (Andy Morris); William
Murphy (Red Flanagan); Kenny Roberts (Res--as a Boy); Richard
Castle (Skids Radzievich); Harry Bartel (Father Bonelli); Kendall
Clark (Sanborn); Claudia Hall (Maggie); Anabel Shaw (Virginia Stew-
art); Ken Patterson (Inspector Walsh); Peter Avramo (Hymie--as a
Boy); Hal Conklin (Jerry's Attorney); Don Keefer (Special Prosecu-
tor).

Projecting "a good bit of pictorial muscularity" (New York
Times), this unpretentious feature was based on the $2.5-million
Brinks truck robbery in Boston and told of the rise, fall, and re-
generation of a slick punk (Curtis).
Shot largely on location in Massachusetts, the film had the
added advantage of a contrasting cast, with Curtis offering a convincing performance as the wrongdoer, along with George Nader's
work as his cop friend and Julie Adams as the lawman's spouse.
Like most crime thrillers, the film detailed the array of
events leading up to and including the famous haul.

SKIDOO (Paramount, 1968) C-98 min.

Producer-director, Otto Preminger; screenplay, Doran William Cannon; music-songs, Harry Nilsson; music arranger-conductor,
George Tipton; choreography, Tom Hansen; art director, Robert E.
Smith; set decorator, Fred Price; visual consultant, Sandy Dvore;
assistant directors, Erich von Stroheim, Jr., Wally Jones, Al Murphy, Steven Smith; costumes, Rudi Gernreich; makeup, Web Over-
lander; sound, Glenn Anderson, Franklin Milton, Lloyd Hanks;

special effects, Charles Spurderson; camera, Leon Shamroy; editor, George Rohrs.
Jackie Gleason (Tony Banks); Carol Channing (Flo Banks); Groucho Marx ("God"); Frankie Avalon (Angie); Fred Clark (A Tower Guard); Michael Constantine (Leech); Frank Gorshin (The Man); John Phillip Law (Stash); Peter Lawford (The Senator); Burgess Meredith (The Warden); George Raft (Captain Garbaldo); Cesar Romero (Hechy); Mickey Rooney ("Blue Chips" Packard); Alexandra Hay (Darlene Banks); Austin Pendleton (Fred the Professor); Luna ("God's" Mistress); Doro Merande (The Mayor); Arnold Stang (Harry); Slim Pickens, Robert Donner (Switchboard Operators); Harry Nilsson (Tower Guard); Orange County Ramblers (Green Bay Ramblers).

Just how low the gangster genre had sunk by the late Sixties was exemplified sadly in Skidoo, an alleged spoof produced and directed in heavy-handed style by Otto Preminger.
The story was about a San Francisco mobster (Gleason) who is told by "God" (Marx), a Mafia chief, to kill a stoolie (Rooney), an informer now serving time in prison. Tony, however, gets mixed up with the hippie culture and becomes a love (!) freak.
Variety said of the lacklustre venture: it was a "... dreary, unfunny attempt at contemporary comedy ... overproduced, underdirected and lifelessly acted."

SKIN DEEP (Warner Bros. , 1929) 5,964'

Director, Ray Enright; based on the novel Lucky Damage by Marc Edmund Jones; screenplay, Gordon Rigby; titles, De Leon Anthony; song, Sidney Mitchell, Archie Gottler, and Con Conrad; sound, Cal Applegate; camera, Barney McGill; editor, George Marks.
Monte Blue (Joe Daley); Davey Lee (District Attorney Carlson's Son); Betty Compson (Sadie Rogers); Alice Day (Elsa Langdon); John Davidson (Blackie Culver); John Bowers (District Attorney Carlson); Georgie Stone (Dippy); Tully Marshall (Dr. Bruce Landon); Robert Perry (Tim).

A remake of the 1922 Associated First National film (with Milton Sills and Florence Vidor), the new Skin Deep was also a crime melodrama concerning a big city underworld head (Blue) who decides to go straight after wedding a golddigger (Compson). The bride, however, loves Joe's rival (Davidson) and the two frame Joe on a robbery charge. He is railroaded to prison. Hoping that Joe will be killed, Sadie tells him that the D.A. is desirous of her. However, this knowledge leads Joe to escape from prison. During the breakout he gets hurt badly. He encounters a girl (Day) whose plastic surgeon father remakes Joe's face. With his new identity he learns just how and why Sadie has betrayed him. When Sadie is killed, accidentally, Joe returns to Elsa and a new life.
Released in both silent and sound versions, this Ray Enright-directed melodrama contains plot elements used in the Humphrey Bogart thriller, Dark Passage (1947), q.v.

Betty Compson and Monte Blue in Skin Deep (1929).

SLAUGHTER (American International, 1972) C-90 min.

Producer, Monroe Sachson; associate producer, Don Williams; director, Jack Starrett; screenplay, Mark Hanna, Don Williams; assistant director, Ricci Rondell; set decorator, Carlos Grandjean; music-music director, Luchi de Jesus; songs, Billy Preston; de Jesus and Ric Marlow; stunt co-ordinator, Paul Knuckles; sound, Manuel Topete; camera, Rosalio Solano; editor, Clarence C. Reynolds.

Jim Brown (Slaughter); Stella Stevens (Ann Cooper); Rip Torn (Dominick Hoffo); Don Gordon (Harry Bastoli); Cameron Mitchell (A. W. Price); Marlene Clark (Kim Walker); Robert Phillips (Frank Morelli); Marion Brash (Jenny); Norman Alfe (Mario Felice); Eddie LoRusso (Little Al); Buddy Garion (Eddie); Ronald C. Ross, Ricardo Adalid, B. Gerardo Zepeda (Hoods); Roger Cudney (Gio); Lance Winston (Interne); Juan Jose Laboriel (Uncle); Francisca Lopes de Laboriel (Aunt).

Jim Brown in <u>Slaughter</u> (1972).

If you can't beat 'em, join 'em; and so the 1970s saw a rash
of black action films, most of them so short on convincing plotline
or acting that it was difficult to distinguish one from another. Ironically (?), most of them made money at the box-office. To find an
excuse for the carnage that saturated these features, a revenge
theme was frequently brought into play. For "heroes" such films
relied on black detectives like Shaft or black lawbreakers like Superfly, or ex-Vietnam War officers like Slaughter (Brown). Their
sworn enemies were usually the underworld, or more frequently,
gangster rivals.

Slaughter is determined to find the mobsters responsible for
his parents' death. When he kills two underlings at the airport, the
F.B.I. offers him the choice of going to jail or pursuing the syndicate to its Mexican headquarters and finding its computerized records. Once south of the border, Slaughter finds that syndicate lieutenant Dominick Hoffo (Torn) is his worst adversary. The latter is
not only attempting to take over the operations but is fiercely jealous over the attentions that his white girlfriend (Stevens) is paying
to Slaughter. The 90 minutes of hot and heavy action concludes
with a fiery finish for Hoffo.

For many critics the highlights of this black action thriller
were the numerous nude scenes of blonde Miss Stevens.

Any self-respecting film that makes any money, deserves a
return match: thus, Slaughter's Big Rip-Off, which boasts the presence of Johnny Carson's sidekick, Ed McMahon.

SLAUGHTER'S BIG RIP-OFF   (American International, 1973)   C-93
min.

Executive producer, Samuel Z. Arkoff; producer, Monroe
Sachson; associate producer, Don Williams; director, Gordon Douglas; based on the character created by Don Williams; screenplay,
Charles Johnson; assistant directors, Ray Taylor, Robert Della Santina; art director, Alfeo Bocchicchio; set decorator, Tony Montenaro; music, James Brown, Fred Wesley; songs, Brown, Wesley,
and Charles Bobbit; sound, John V. Speak; special effects, Logan
Franzee; camera, Charles Wheeler; editor, Christopher Holmes.

Jim Brown (Slaughter); Ed McMahon (Duncan); Brock Peters
(Reynolds); Don Stroud (Kird); Gloria Hendry (Marcia); Richard Williams (Joe Creole); Art Metrano (Burtoli); Judy Brown (Norja); Eddie
Lo Russo (Arnie); Jackie Giroux (Mrs. Duncan); Russ Marin (Crow-
der); Tony Brubaker (Ed Pratt); Gene LeBell (Leo); Fuji (Chin);
Russ McGinn (Harvey); and: Hoke Howell, Chuck Hicks, Leu Cama-
cho, Piper Alvez, Lisa Moore, Chuck G. Niles, Reg Parton.

Again, ex-football star Jim Brown was Slaughter, who finds
that the gangsters are still on his trail after the Mexico episode.
In Los Angeles, Slaughter's best friend is killed and the ex-G.I.
determines to get those responsible. Black detective Reynolds
(Peters) offers his aid, but Slaughter rejects it. Where else to find
the racketeers but at the neighborhood nightclub? After numerous
assaults and batteries, murders, and assorted mayhem, Slaughter

gets his people (but does anyone ever deplete the underground? ...
they seem to keep multiplying like rabbits).

If undiscriminating Americans accepted the nonsence of
Slaughter, Europeans were a little more discerning in their entertainment tastes. The British Monthly Film Bulletin wrote, "Los
Angeles, the screenplay suggests, is as deep in high-life perversion
as in smog: but no amount of random glimpses of people at swim-
ming pools piling powder up their nostrils can transform the suggestion into anything tangible. Slaughter is patently a new broom
sweeping as dirty as the old ones; yet we are expected to award
him a halo for his studied imperviousness to the vice and vermin
around."

SLAUGHTER ON TENTH AVENUE (Universal, 1957) 103 min.

Producer, Albert Zugsmith; director, Arnold Laven; based
on the book The Man Who Rocked the Boat by William J. Keating,
Richard Carter; screenplay, Lawrence Roman; assistant director,
Phil Bowles; songs, Richard Rodgers; music director, Joseph
Gershenson; music arranger, Herschel Gilbert; art directors, Alex-
ander Golitzen, Robert E. Smith; camera, Fred Jackman; editor,
Russell F. Schoengarth.

Richard Egan (William Keating); Jan Sterling (Madge Pitts);
Dan Duryea (John Jacob Masters); Julie Adams (Dee); Walter Mat-
thau (Al Dahlke); Charles McGraw (Lieutenant Anthony Vosnick);
Sam Levene (Howard Rysdale); Mickey Shaughnessy (Solly Pitts);
Harry Bellaver (Benjy Karp); Nick Dennis (Midget); Ned Weaver (Ed-
die "Cockeye" Cook); Billy M. Greene ("Monk" Mohler); Johnny
McNamara (Judge); Amzie Strickland (Mrs. Cavanagh); Mickey Hargi-
tay (Big John).

The New York waterfront was in for another dissection in
this sturdy exploitation feature. Deputy District Attorney Keating
(Egan) is assigned to investigate the murder of a boss longshoreman
(Shaughnessy) and uncovers labor racketeering on the Manhattan
docks (what else is new?). Trying to follow up the case, Keating
finds that the murdered man's wife (Sterling) and family are unwilling to talk and soon a suspect is being heavily guarded by a local
labor leader. Keating thinks it funny that his own boss (Levene) is
not keen on pressing the case, since the defense attorney (Duryea)
is a pal and former staff member.

The film climaxes in a courtroom battle, while the drama
itself terminates with an actionful battle between stevedores.

The film is accompanied by a fine music score.

THE SLEEPING CITY (Universal, 1950) 83 1/3 min.

Producer, Leonard Goldstein; director, George Sherman;
story-screenplay, Joe Eisinger; art directors, Bernard Herzbrun,
Emrich Nicholson; music, Frank Skinner; camera, William Miller;
editor, Frank Gross.

Richard Conte in The Sleeping City (1950).

Richard Conte (Fred Rowan); Coleen Gray (Ann Sebastian); Peggy Dow (Kathy Hall); John Alexander (Inspector Gordon); Alex Nicol (Dr. Bob Anderson); Richard Taber (Pop Ware); James J. Van Dyk (Dr. Sharpley); Hugh Reilly (Dr. Foster); Michael Strong (Dr. Connell); Frank M. Thomas (Lieutenant Lally); Richard Kendrick (Dr. Dutra); Henry Hart (Dr. Nester); Robert Strauss (Lieutenant Marty Miller); Herbert Ratner (Detective Reese); Mickey Cochran (Detective Diamond); Ernest Sarracino (Detective Abate); Russell Collins (Medical Examiner); Mrs. Priestly Morrison (Miss Wardly); Frank Tweddell (Kingdon); Tom Hoirer (Gay the Proprietor of Toy Store); Frank Baxter, James Daly, Dort Clark (Internes); Rod McLennan (Detective).

Another "Naked City"-style drama, this one focuses on the dope smuggling racket at a big city hospital. What might have been a breakthrough, both in presentation and information, was cast aside to turn out a conventional product.

Conte was Fred Rowan, the thoughtful police detective

assigned to Bellevue where he poses as an interne, hoping to corner the drug thief amid the corridors, wards, and operating rooms of the big city hospital. Sadly, "It is not the fine cosmopolitan drama of medical practice and human life that it had every chance to be" (New York Times).

A SLIGHT CASE OF MURDER (Warner Bros., 1938) 85 min.

Producer, Hal B. Wallis; associate producer, Sam Bischoff; director, Lloyd Bacon; based on the play by Damon Runyon, Howard Lindsay; screenplay, Earl Baldwin, Joseph Schrank; songs, M. K. Jerome and Jack Scholl; art director, Max Parker; camera, Sid Hickox; editor, James Gibbons.

Edward G. Robinson (Remy Marco); Jane Bryan (Mary Marco); Willard Parker (Dick Whitewood); Ruth Donnelly (Mora Marco); Allen Jenkins (Mike); John Litel (Post); Eric Stanley (Ritter); Harold Huber (Giuseppe); Edward Brophy (Lefty); Paul Harvey (Mr. Whitewood); Margaret Hamilton (Mrs. Cagle); George E. Stone (Ex-Jockey Kirk); Bert Hanlon (Sad Sam); Jean Benedict (Remy's Secretary); Betty Compson (Loretta); Harry Seymour (The Singer); George Lloyd (Little Butch); John Harmon (Blackhead Gallagher); Duke York (Champ); Bert Roach (Speakeasy Proprietor); Ben Hendricks, Ralph Dunn, Wade Boteler (Cops).

In the gangster films of the Thirties there was hardly any "comedy" relief, an aspect not true of most other genre films. Occasionally there were lighthearted attempts like Stolen Harmony (1935), q.v. and The Whole Town's Talking (1935), q.v., but even these films contained more melodrama than laughs. In 1938, however, Warner Bros., who created most of the gangster classics of the decade, offered the first, and still the best, hilarious satire on the gangster film, A Slight Case of Murder.

The primary actor who is credited with promulgating the gangster craze, Edward G. ("Little Caesar") Robinson, here most expertly kidded his bread and butter genre as Remy Marco, a beer baron who decides to go straight with the end of Prohibition and to crash society. [The plot is reminiscent of Robinson's The Little Giant (1933), q.v.] After he and his wife (Donnelly) find a country place, their daughter (Bryan) falls for a rich young man (Parker) whom she will not marry until he gets a job. He does find one-- as a cop! Thereafter, a rival gang decides to murder Remy in his home but they end up shooting each other. The boyfriend shoots them again, thinking he has captured them. How does Remy come out of the situation? Much better. He lifts $500,000 from the dead gangsters and uses the money to make an improved brand of beer (he has finally tasted his own wicked brew).

The New York Herald-Tribune correctly labeled the film "... one of the funniest and most satisfying farces which has come out of Hollywood in some time."

Warners would remake the successful venture as Stop, You're Killing Me (1952), q.v. with Broderick Crawford in the lead.

366   Smart Money

SMART MONEY   (Warner Bros. , 1931)   90 min.

        Director, Alfred E. Green; based on the story The Idol by
Lucien Hubbard, Joseph Jackson; screenplay, Kubec Glasmon, John
Bright, Hubbard, Jackson; camera, Robert Kurrle; editor, Jack
Killifer.
        Edward G. Robinson (Nick "The Barber" Venizelos); James
Cagney (Jack); Evalyn Knapp (Irene Graham); Ralf Harolde (Sleepy
Sam); Noel Francis (Marie); Margaret Livingston (District Attorney's
Girl); Maurice Black (The Greek Barber); Boris Karloff (Sport Wil-
liams); Morgan Wallace (District Attorney Black); Billy House (Sales-
man-Gambler); Paul Porcasi (Alexander Amenoppopolus); Polly Wal-
ters (Lola); Gladys Lloyd (Cigar Stand Clerk); Clark Burroughs
(Back-to-Back Schultz); Edwin Argus (Two-Time Phil); John Larkin
(Snake Eyes); Mae Madison (Small Town Girl); Eddie Kane (Tom, a
Customer); Clinton Rosemond (George the Porter); John George
(Dwarf on Train).

        After the overwhelming success of Little Caesar and The
Public Enemy, both in 1931, Warner Bros. wisely teamed Edward
G. Robinson and James Cagney for a genre lark. Cagney had a
decidedly small part in the duo's only joint film. Lucien Hubbard
and Joseph Jackson's original story, The Idol, was nominated for
an Academy Award.
        Small town barber Nick Venizelos (Robinson) operates a
small gambling room in the rear. Some of his friends, including
fellow worker Jack (Cagney), raise $10,000 for him to go to the
big city to bet against the syndicate. A girl (Francis) cons him
into a big game and he loses the bundle. He vows revenge. Nick
and Jack set up a shop in the city and Nick begins betting successfully on the horses. He outmaneuvers the man (Harolde) who had
beaten him in the crooked game and he forces Marie to live with
him. When Nick becomes the operator of a big gambling house,
the District Attorney (Wallace) marks Nick for investigation. The
law enforcer uses a blonde (Knapp) to frame Nick for a six-month
sentence. Jack knows Irene framed Nick and after a quarrel over
the girl, Jack is accidentally killed by Nick. Nick goes to jail, but
Irene agrees to wait for him.
        As many studio productions would delineate it in the Thirties,
the city here was a hotbed of vice and temptation, just overflowing
with crime. And generally, pity the poor rube who tries to make
good in these urban surroundings! Organized crime just will not
let him. Pretty soon the filmgoing public was (almost) convinced
that this often heard-about but seldom seen criminal syndicate was
a bigger enemy to Everyman than the Depression.

SOME LIKE IT HOT   (United Artists, 1959)   120 min.

        Producer, Billy Wilder; associate producer, Doane Harrison,
I.A.L. Diamond; director, Wilder; based on an unpublished story
by R. Thoeren, M. Logan; screenplay, Wilder, Diamond; art director, Ted Haworth; set decorator, Edward G. Boyle; music, Adolph

Deutsch; songs, A. H. Gibbs and Leo Wood; Herbert Stothart and
Bert Kalmar; Matty Malneck and Gus Kahn; costumes, Orry-Kelly;
sound, Fred Lau; camera, Charles Lang, Jr.; editor, Arthur
Schmidt.
  Marilyn Monroe (Sugar Kane [Kumulchek]); Tony Curtis (Joe
[Josephine]); Jack Lemmon (Jerry [Daphne]); George Raft (Spats
Columbo); Pat O'Brien (Mulligan); Joe E. Brown (Osgood Fielding
III); Nehemiah Persoff (Little Bonaparte); Joan Shawlee (Sweet Sue);
Billy Gray (Sig Poliakoff); George E. Stone (Toothpick); Dave Barry
(Beinstock); Mike Mazurki, Harry Wilson (Spats' Henchmen); Bever-
ly Wills (Dolores); Barbara Drew (Nellie); Edward G. Robinson, Jr.
(Paradise); Tom Kennedy (Bouncer); John Indrisano (Waiter).

  Billy Wilder's colorful satire on the Roaring Twenties and the
gangster milieu was a delightful concoction of song, action, and
comedy in a pleasant twist of history. The nostalgic comedy grossed
more than $8.3 million in distributors' domestic rentals.
  The film begins with the St. Valentine's Day Massacre, after
a stoolie (Stone) has squealed to a federal agent (O'Brien). Two
second-rate musicians (Curtis and Lemmon) witness the massacre
and head for Miami with an all-girl band to avoid being caught by
the guilty hoods. In the retreat, Jerry, dressed like a showgirl
named Daphne, and Joe, gussied up as Josephine, cavort with the
resort crowd. Both musicians are entranced with Sugar Kane (Monroe), the band vocalist. Sugar, who likes Jerry as an understanding "girl," is really out to land a Florida millionaire. Thus, while
really wealthy Osgood Fielding III (Brown) is pursuing Jerry, Sugar
sets her mark on Joe, who has donned a second disguise as a playboy bachelor. Breaking up the jovial proceedings is Spats Columbo
(Raft) and his gang, who have come for a gangland meeting. Spats
and his pals recognize Joe and Jerry as the two wanted witnesses,
but before they can rub them out, Spats is done in by rivals at a
party given in his honor.
  Again, there was veteran George Raft, flipping a coin and
kidding his own gangster image. And, of course, there were the
Monroe-sung songs, and the finale which has the cinema classic
line, "Nobody's perfect" as uttered by big-mouthed Brown to Lem-
mon-in-drag.
  The property would become the 1970s Broadway musical,
Sugar.

SORROWFUL JONES (Paramount, 1949) 88 min.

  Producer, Robert L. Welch; director, Sidney Lanfield; based
on the story Little Miss Marker by Damon Runyon; screenplay
adaptors, William R. Lipman, Sam Hellman, Gladys Lehman; screenplay, Melville Shavelson, Edmund Hartmann, Jack Rose; art directors, Hans Dreier, Albert Nozaki; set decorators, Sam Comer,
Bertram Granger; music, Robert Emmett Dolan; songs, Jay Livingston and Ray Evans; assistant director, Oscar Rudolph; makeup,
Wally Westmore; costumes, Mary Kay Dodson; sound, Harold Lewis,
John Cope; special effects, Gordon Jennings; process camera,

Farciot Edouart; camera, Daniel L. Fapp; editor, Arthur Schmidt.
Bob Hope (Sorrowful Jones); Lucille Ball (Gladys O'Neill);
William Demarest (Regret); Bruce Cabot (Big Steve Holloway);
Thomas Gomez (Reardon); Tom Pedi (Once-Over Sam); Paul Lees
(Orville Smith); Houseley Stevenson (Doc Chesley); Mary Jayne
Saunders (Martha Jane Smith); Claire Carleton (Agnes "Happy Hips"
Noonan); Ben Welden (Big Steve's Bodyguard); Harry Tyler (Blinky);
John "Skins" Miller (Head Phone Man); Charley Cooley (Shorty);
Marc Krah (Barber); Sid Tomack (Waiter at Steve's Place); Patsy
O'Byrne (Charwoman); Ralph Peters (Cab Driver); Ed Dearing (Po-
lice Lieutenant Mitchell); Arthur Space (Plainclothesman); Emmett
Vogan, Maurice Cass (Psychiatrists); John Shay, Selmer Jackson
(Doctors); William Yip, George Chan (Chinamen); Sally Rawlinson,
Louise Lorimer (Nurses).

For their first of three screen teamings, Lucille Ball and
Bob Hope joined together in a remake of Little Miss Marker (1934),
q. v. This version, however, subjugated the lead role of the little
waif (Saunders) who is adopted by Sorrowful Jones (Hope), a race-
track hack, to the character played by the ski-nosed comic. He
mugged mercilessly with his seedy gags, lessening the value of the
original Damon Runyon story. As Gladys O'Neill, the wisecracking
girlfriend of Sorrowful, Ball is also reformed when she too falls
under the charm of the innocent tyke.

Hope and Ball repeated their roles on "Lux Radio Theatre"
on November 21, 1954.

SPIN OF THE COIN   see   THE GEORGE RAFT STORY

THE SPLIT   (MGM, 1968)   C-90 min.

Producers, Irwin Winkler, Robert Chartoff; director, Gordon
Flemyng; based on the novel The Seventh by Richard Stark; screen-
play, Robert Sabaroff; art directors, George W. Davis, Urie Mc-
Cleary; set decorators, Henry Grace, Keogh Gleason; music, Quincy
Jones; songs, Jones and Ernie Shelby; Jones and Sheb Wooley; as-
sistant director, Al Jennings; makeup, William Tuttle; sound, Larry
Jost; camera, Burnett Guffey; editor, Rita Roland.
Jim Brown (McClain); Diahann Carroll (Ellie McClain); Julie
Harris (Gladys); Ernest Borgnine (Bert Clinger); Gene Hackman
(Lieutenant Walter Brill); Jack Klugman (Harry Kifka); Warren Oates
(Marty Gough); James Whitmore (Herb Sutro); Donald Sutherland
(Dave Negli); Jackie Joseph (Jackie); Harry Hickox (Detective); Joyce
Jameson (Jenifer); Warren Vanders (Mason); George Cisar (Door-
man); Karen Norris (Proprietress); Duane Grey (Guard); Howard
Curtis, Chuck Hicks, Bill Couch, Gene LeBell, George Robotham
(Physical Instructors); Thordis Brandt (Airline Clerk); Priscilla Ann
(Spanish Girl).

Back in 1968, it was considered somewhat daring to have
two black performers (Brown and Carroll) as a major film's stars,

but MGM was in a financial plight and anything that might earn some
coins for the beleaguered studio was okay.

Successful thief McClain (Brown) returns to Los Angeles and
teams with Gladys (Harris) in a plot to rob half a million dollars in
receipts from the L.A. Coliseum during a big football game.   In
gathering his accomplices, McClain maintains very strict standards.
He comes up with four acceptable recruits, including driver Harry
Kifka (Klugman), safe robber Marty Gough (Oates), a full-time killer Dave Negli (Sutherland), and gym instructor Bert Clinger (Borgnine).   The robbery is carried off as planned and the loot is hidden,
but everything starts to go wrong, particularly when disreputable
police lieutenant Walter Brill (Hackman) enters the case.   At the
finish, McClain has the option of "splitting" with the money to Mexico or keeping his promise to his ex-wife Ellie (Carroll) that he
would go straight.

With its mixture of genre--thriller and race relations--The
Split was far more than just a heist adventure.   The higher brow
critics were repulsed, however, by the presentation.   Said Judith
Crist in New York magazine, "... race relations are furthered by
Brown's demonstrating that a noble black crook can mastermind a
half-million dollar caper for a bunch of nasty white crooks and come
out with clean hands once he's bumped them all off.   New twist?"

SPY SHIP   see   FOG OVER FRISCO

THE SQUEALER   (Columbia, 1930)   6,358'

Producer, Harry Cohn; director, Harry J. Brown; based on
the play by Mark Linder; screenplay, Dorothy Howell; continuity,
Casey Robinson; dialog, Jo Swerling; art director, Edward Jewell;
technical director, Edward Shulter; sound, Edward Bernds; camera,
Ted Tetzlaff; editor, Leonard Wheeler.

Jack Holt (Charles Hart); Dorothy Revier (Margaret Hart);
Davey Lee (Bunny Hart); Matt Moore (John Sheridan); Zasu Pitts
(Bella); Robert Ellis (Valletti); Mathew Betz (Red Majors); Arthur
Housman (Mitter Davis); Louis Natheaux (Edwards); Eddie Kane
(Whisper); Eddie Sturgis (The Killer); Elmer Ballard (Pimply-Face).

This quickie gangster melodrama, from Mark Linder's 1928
novel, starred tough guy Jack Holt as a bootleg baron who uses a
real estate enterprise as a front.   A ruthless individual, he has a
rival killed, but on the domestic scene he is plagued by family
problems, because his wife (Revier) secretly loves his lawyer-best
friend (Moore).   After the murder of a rival (Ellis), Hart is sentenced to jail but he breaks out to take revenge on his wife and
Sheridan, only to find his son is better off with Margaret and Sheridan.   He then falls into a police trap (knowingly) set by the lawyer,
and he is killed.

A portion of the plot element of this film was later used in
MGM's The Last Gangster (1937), q.v.   Perhaps the most imaginative element of this production was the use of unique character

names for the minor villains: Ratface Edwards, Mitter Davis, and
Pimply-Face.

THE STAR WITNESS   (Warner Bros. , 1931) 68 min.

      Director, William Wellman; story-screenplay, Lucien Hub-
bard; camera, James Van Trees; editor, Hal McLernon.
      Walter Huston (D. A. Whitlock); Charles "Chic" Sale (Gran'pa
Summerill); Frances Starr (Ma Leeds); Sally Blane (Sue Leeds); Tom
Dugan (Brown); Ralph Ince (Maxey Campo); Russell Hopton (Thorpe);
Robert Elliott (Williams); Fletcher Norton (Dopey); Guy d'Ennery
(Jack Short); Noel Madison (Horan); Mike Donlin (Mickey); Ed Dear-
ing (Sackett); Nat Pendleton (Big Jack); George Ernest (Ned Leeds);
Dickie Moore (Donny Leeds); Grant Mitchell (Pa Leeds); Edward J.
Nugent (Jackie Leeds); George Irving (Judge); Allan Lane (Clerk);
William A. Wellman (Company Workman).

      Old man impersonator Charles "Chic" Sale had a popular
career on the stage before the coming of sound films. His portrayal of crotchety but lovable elderly gentlemen became even more
successful in films, where, during the Thirties, he starred in both
features and short subjects and occasionally did characters roles.
      One of his best assignments was in this William Wellman-
supervised production. As Gran'pa Summerill, on leave from a
soldier's home, he visits his family. While there, he observes a
gang war in progress in front of the house. One of the hoodlum
groups, escaping from a car, invades the house. While passing
through, they give the family an excellent look at their faces. The
relatives even recognize the pack leader (Ince). Shortly thereafter,
the district attorney (Huston) appears on the scene and Pa Leeds
(Mitchell) agrees to testify. Pa, however, is later kidnapped and
beaten up by the hoodlums when he refuses to accept a bribe for
not testifying. To insure that he will remain silent, the group kidnaps Donny Leeds (Moore). Gran'pa, bless him, has no fear of the
criminals and goes before the jury. Later he rescues the little boy
from captivity.
      This combination of melodrama and sentiment was remade as
The Man Who Dared (a. k. a. I Am Not Afraid) (1939) with Charley
Grapewin and Henry O'Neill in the Sale-Mitchell parts respectively.
      In retrospect, one can only wonder at the film's philosophy,
which seems to equate foreigners with criminals.

THE STEEL JUNGLE   (Warner Bros. , 1956) 86 min.

      Producer, David Weisbart; director-screenplay, Walter Doni-
ger; art director, Leo K. Kuter; music, David Buttolph; orchestra-
tor, Maurice de Packh; camera, J. Peverell Marley; editor, Folmar
Blangsted.
      Perry Lopez (Ed Novak); Beverly Garland (Frances Novak);
Walter Abel (Warden Keller); Ted de Corsia (Steve Madden); Ken
Tobey (Dr. Lewy); Allison Hayes (Mrs. Archer); Leo Gordon (Lupo);

Stafford Repp (Beakeley); Kay Kuter (Stringbean); Ralph Moody (Andy Macklin); Bob Steele (Dan Bucci); Gregory Walcott (Guard Weaver); Charles Cane, Fred Graham (Detectives); Carey Loftin (Truck Driver); Jack Kruschen (Helper); Edward Platt (Judge Wahller); Lyle Latell (Bailiff); Richard Karlan (C.O.D.); Frank Gerstle (Kadinski); Tom McKee (Sergeant Hayes); Eddie Baker (Schiller); Joel Smith (Newspaperman); Lane Bradford (Guard); Malcolm Atterbury (Mailman); Mack Williams (Lieutenant Bryant); Robert Bray (Lieutenant Soberman); Peter Gray (Lieutenant Murray).

Just as people's (morbid) curiosity seems unsatiable about the goings-on in mental institutions, so filmgoers can usually be counted on to find a behind-the-scenes prison study of interest.

Here prison warden Keller (Abel) and psychologist (Tobey) attempt to persuade a young syndicate member (Lopez) to reveal who murdered a guard. The prisoner, however, will not talk, being determined to protect his boss. The latter, syndicate king Steve Madden (de Corsia), is serving time with his henchmen (Gordon, Kuter and Karlan) but is still running the rackets on the outside. In time, however, Ed Novak realizes Madden has no use for him and he agrees to implicate Madden in the murder plot.

THE STING (Universal, 1973) C-129 min.

Producers, Tony Bill, Michael S. Phillips, Julia Phillips; associate producer, Robert L. Crawford; director, George Roy Hill; screenplay, David S. Ward; art director, Henry Bumstead; set decorator, James Payne; music (piano rags) by Scott Jopkin; music adaptor, Marvin Hamlisch; costumes, Edith Head; sound, Robert Bertrand, Ronald Pierce; special camera effects, Albert Whitlock; special effects, Bob Warner; camera, Robert Surtees; editor, William Reynolds.

Paul Newman (Henry Gondorff); Robert Redford (Johnny Hooker); Robert Shaw (Doyle Lonnegan); Charles Durning (Lieutenant William Snyder); Ray Walston (J. J. Singleton); Eileen Brennan (Billie); Harold Gould (Kid Twist); John Heffernan (Eddie Niles); Dana Elcar (F.B.I. Agent Polk); Jack Kehoe (Erie Kid); Dimitra Arliss (Loretta); Robert Earl Jones (Luther Coleman); James J. Sloyan (Mottola); Charles Dierkop (Floyd); Sally Kirkland (Crystal); John Quade (Riley); Paulene Myers (Alva Coleman); William Benedict (Roulette Dealer).

Set in the Thirties, this enormously popular (both as an Oscar winner and box-office success) shaggy dog tale is perhaps the most expansive heist film yet made in America. It plies the gimmick of male camaraderie (Paul Newman and Robert Redford repeating their 1969 Butch Cassidy and the Sundance Kid gambit) and gives it a Damon Runyonesque flavor. Audiences were captivated by the visuals, the dialogue, and the revival of the Scott Joplin piano ragtime music.

When his confidence-game partner Luther Coleman (Jones) is killed, Johnny Hooker (Redford) goes to Chicago to locate Henry Gondorff (Newman). Johnny wants a crash course in how to get

revenge on Doyle Lonnegan (Shaw), the racketeer responsible for
Luther's death. With great dispatch, imagination, and verve the
two build up an enormous ruse to trap Doyle into being the fall guy
for a large sum of money. There are twists, doublecrosses, and
almost unspotted red herrings, but the ruse works. Johnny and
Henry join their success celebration. Grossed to date: $68,450,000.

STOLEN HARMONY (Paramount, 1935) 74 min.

Producer, Albert Lewis; director, Alfred Werker; story,
Leon Gordon; screenplay, Gordon, Harry Ruskin, Claude Binyon,
Lewis Foster; songs, Harry Revel and Mack Gordon; choreography,
LeRoy J. Prinz; art directors, Hans Dreier, Bernard Herzbrun;
camera, Harry Fischbeck; editor, Otho Lovering.

George Raft (Ray Angelo--alias Ray Ferraro); Ben Bernie
(Jack Conrad); Grace Bradley (Jean Loring); Goodee Montgomery
(Lil Davis); Lloyd Nolan (Chesty Burrage); Ralf Harolde (Dude Williams); William Cagney (Schoolboy Howe); William Pawley (Turk
Connors); Charles E. Arnt (Clem Walters); Cully Richards (Pete
the Cabby); Jack Norton (Dick Phillips); Christian Rub (Mathew Hux-
ley); Leslie Fenton (Joe Harris); Fred "Snowflake" Toones (Henry
the Bartender on the Bus); Ruth Clifford (Nurse); Jack Judge (Photographer); Robert Emmet O'Connor (Warden Clark); Eddie McGill,
Jack Perry, Jack Herrick (Prison Trio); Constantine Romanoff (Pic-
colo Player); Stanley Andrews (Patrol Chief); Lois January, Ada
Ince, Margaret Nearing, Adele Jerome (Girls in Sextette); Ben Taggart (Sergeant--Hotel Cop); Harry Bernard (Peanut Vendor); Colonel
Manny Prager (Nell's Father); Purv Pullen (Little Nell); Billy Wilson (Sheriff); John King (Fagin).

The mixture of music and gangsters has never been particularly exciting or popular. One of the earlier efforts to use this
blended motif, Stolen Harmony featured bandleader Ben Bernie, whom
Paramount was prepping for screen stardom.
Bandleader Jack Conrad (Bernie) hears jailbird Ray Angelo
(Raft) playing the saxophone on a radio broadcast. After the convict's release he is hired by Conrad for a one night stand tour.
On the road Ray falls for dancer Jean Loring (Bradley). When her
partner is unable to go on with the show, Ray proves he is adept on
the dancing floor. Later, ex-con Joe Harris (Fentor) arrives on the
scene and tries to draw Ray into his plot to fleece Conrad's tour
receipts. Ray refuses. After Harris pulls the heist, Ray gives
chase. He wins back the money but when the police find him with
the funds no one will believe his story and he is dismissed from the
band. Another hoodlum (Nolan) later kidnaps the band for a personal show. But plucky Ray saves the captured group, rejoins the
band, and wins Jean's love.
The best things in the film are not the musical interludes
nor even the overly elaborate club bus, but the scene where Chesty
Burrage's boys discuss their favorite alma maters, in their cases,
prisons.

THE STONE KILLER   (Columbia, 1973)   C-95 min.

Producer-director, Michael Winner; based on the book A
Complete State of Death by John Gardner; screenplay, Gerald Wil-
son; art director, Ward Preston; assistant directors, Joe Ellis,
Mel Effros; music, Roy Budd; stunt co-ordinator, Alan Gibbs; cam-
era, Richard Moore; editor.
Charles Bronson (Torrey); Martin Balsam (Vescari); David
Sheiner (Lorenz); Norman Fell (Daniels); Ralph Waite (Mathews);
Eddie Firestone (Armitage); Walter Burke (J. D.); David Moody
(Lipper); Charles Tyner (Psychiatrist); Paul Koslo (Langley); Stuart
Margolin (Lawrence); John Ritter (Hart); Byron Morrow (Police
Chief); Jack Colvin (Jumper); Frank Campanella (Calabriese); Alfred
Ryder (Champion); Gene Woodbury (Paul Long); Harry Basch (Moss-
man); Lisabeth Hush (Helen); Kelly Miles (Gerry Wexton); Robert
Emhardt (Fussy Man).

Charles Bronson, who wavers back and forth on celluloid between the law and disorder, was here cast as an unconventional
New York police member, who is suspended from the police force
for shooting a fleeing seventeen year old suspect.   He is promptly
hired by the L.A. cop force and there learns of pending problems
within the Manhattan-based Mafia organization.   Before the grand
finale, there is a rash of killings, kidnappings, and of course,
chases.
Casting very New York-like Martin Balsam as the vengeful
Mafia chief was a strange choice (like Eli Wallach in The Don Is
Dead), since his attempts at an Italian dialect and mannerism are
laughable.   Anyhow, Vescari is the one who hires an especially
trained group of Vietnam veterans to assassinate those responsible
for a Mafia purge in 1931.   Why Vescari waited forty-two years to
get his eye for an eye is never clearly explained, but the ninety-five
minute caper moves along very briskly and surely.   It does point
out once again, that, as usual, the underworld's worst enemies are
their fellow workers.

STOP, YOU'RE KILLING ME   (Warner Bros. , 1952)   C-86 min.

Producer, Louis F. Edelman; director, Roy Del Ruth; based
on the play by Damon Runyon, Howard Lindsay; screenplay, James
O'Hanlon; art director, Charles H. Clarke; choreography, LeRoy
Prinz; music director, Ray Heindorf; camera, Ted McCord; editor,
Owen Marks.
Broderick Crawford (Remy Marko); Claire Trevor (Nora
Marko); Virginia Gibson (Mary Marko); Bill Hayes (Chance Whitelaw);
Margaret Dumont (Mrs. Whitelaw); Howard St. John (Mahoney);
Charles Cantor (Mike); Sheldon Leonard (Lefty); Joe Vitale (Guiseppe);
Louis Lettieri (Donnie Reynolds); Henry (Harry) Morgan (Innocence);
Stephen Chase (Cal Ritter); Don Beddoe (Clyde Post); Henry Slate
(Ryan); Ned Glass (Sad Sam); Jack Pepper (The Singer); Joe McTurk
Ex-Jockey Kirk); Ralph Sanford (Cop); John Crawford (State Trooper);
Phil Arnold (Little Dutch); Frank Richards (Black Hat); Mushy

Claire Trevor and Broderick Crawford in <u>Stop, You're Killing Me</u>
(1952).

Callahan (No Nose); Phyllis Kirk (Nurse); Sherry Moreland, Joann Arnold (Party Girls); Dolly Jarvis (Secretary).

A watered-down rehash of A Slight Case of Murder (1938), q. v. , with the added "bonus" of musical interludes. It retold poorly the tale of an ex-beer baron (Crawford) who attempts to go legitimate, despite a country house full of hoodlums, some murders, and stolen money.

"... a mixture of Technicolored musical and broad-beamed burlesque, thrown together with little inspiration ... should afford some low entertainment in a strictly burlesque vein" (New York Times).

THE STORY OF PRETTY BOY FLOYD (ABC-TV, 1974) C-90 min.

Executive producer, Roy Huggins; producer, Jo Swerling, Jr. ; director-teleplay, Clyde Ware; art director, Alfeo Bocchicchio; set decorator, Jerry Adams; costumes, Charles Waldo; camera, J. J. Jones; editors, Charles K. McClelland, Gioryette Clark.

Martin Sheen (Charley Arthur Floyd); Kim Darby (Ruby Hardgraves); Michael Parks (Bradley Floyd); Ellen Corby (Ma Floyd); Steven Keats (Eddie Richetti); Abe Vigoda (Dominic Morell); Joseph Estevez (E. W. Floyd); Ford Rainey (Mr. Suggs); Frank Christi (Phil Donnati); Bill Vint (Bill Miller); Ted Gehring (Decker); Ann Doran (Secretary); Roy Applegate (Deputy); Mills Watson (Shine Rush); Arlene Farber (Juanita).

After all the previous cinema attempts to dissect the personality of Charles Arthur "Pretty Boy" Floyd, one would think there was little left to be said. But here was another attempt to present the true and definitive study of the life of the handsome hood.

For authenticity, writer-director Clyde Ware, a native of Floyd's home state of Oklahoma, visited the legendary criminal's home town and spoke with his remaining relatives, including his sister. Following the completion of the main body of the telefeature, Ware and star Martin Sheen returned to Sallisaw, Oklahoma to make a prologue for the film which utilized still photos of the Floyd family, whose comments and recollections were heard on the film's soundtrack.

Sheen offered another of his James Dean-like portrayals as the title character in this obviously low-budget rendition. The narrative begins in 1922 in Oklahoma's Cookson Hills with farmboy Floyd deserting his family truck bootleg whiskey. With money in his pocket he returns home and weds his girl (Darby). Then an old associate draws him back into a life of crime. It leads to his eventual death after being hunted by the F. B. I. under the leadership of G-Man Melvin Purvis (Binney).

The drama's best performance came from Ellen Corby as Floyd's mother. Daily Variety analyzed, "Film fails to flesh out real relationship between Floyd and his wife (Kim Darby), ticks off his associates with no sense of mutuality except for one weak link (Mills Watson). Gaps among segments require mental readjustments and acceptances. "

Kim Darby and Martin Sheen in The Story of Pretty Boy Floyd (1974).

THE STORY OF TEMPLE DRAKE   (Paramount, 1933)   70 min.

    Director, Stephen Roberts; based on the novel Sanctuary by
William Faulkner; screenplay, Oliver H. P. Garrett; camera, Karl
Struss.
    Miriam Hopkins (Temple Drake); Jack LaRue (Trigger); Wil-
liam Gargan (Stephen Benbow); William Collier, Jr. (Toddy Gowan);
Irving Pichel (Lee Goodwin); Sir Guy Standing (Judge Drake); Eliza-
beth Patterson (Aunt Jennie); Florence Eldridge (Ruby Lemar);
James Eagles (Tommy); Harlan E. Knight (Pap); James Mason (Van);
Jobyna Howland (Miss Reba); Henry Hall (Judge); John Carradine
(Courtroom Extra); Frank Darien (Gas Station Proprietor); Clarence
Sherwood (Lunch Wagon Proprietor); Oscar Apfel (District Attorney);
Kent Taylor (Jellybeans).

    Derived from William Faulkner's Sanctuary, this sordid
melodrama was a shocker in its day, disconcerting censors and the
public alike.   A refined girl like Temple Drake (Hopkins) becoming
involved with thugs, being raped, and liking it, was not the usual
formula for a movie in 1933.
    Temple Drake is the wild, self-willed granddaughter of a
southern judge (Standing).   She goes on a spree with drinker Toddy
Gowan (Collier, Jr.).   The duo have a minor car accident and are
forced to seek refuge in a house controlled by ruthless, silent

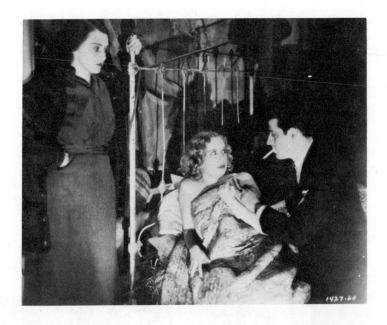

Florence Eldridge, Miriam Hopkins and Jack LaRue in The Story of
Temple Drake (1933).

bootlegger (La Rue).   Under the hoodlum's influence are weak-willed
Tommy (Eagles), a white trash slavey (Eldridge), and a physically
powerful dimwit (Pichel) who fears Trigger's pistol.   Later Trigger,
who has raped Temple, kills Tommy and intends to put the blame
on Lee Goodwin.   Trigger takes Temple to the "city," she too
numb by her array of experiences to protest.   Thereafter, in the
urban setting, she and Trigger have a run-in, and she kills him.
When Lee Goodwin is placed on trial for Tommy's murder, Temple
cannot keep silent.   She insists upon going on the witness stand,
and in front of her one-time beau, attorney Stephen Benhow (Gargan),
she reveals her tawdry episodes of recent date.

"It is grim and sordid, but at the same time a picture which
is enormously helped by its definite dramatic value" (New York
Times).

The lascivious, decadent ambience considered so much a part
of the criminal's daily life was at the heart of this adult drama.
Twenty-eight years later, Twentieth Century-Fox would turn out
Sanctuary, this time basing its scenario on Sanctuary and Requiem
for a Nun, and the stage adaptation of Requiem for a Nun.   The
new conglomerate proved to be "Melodrama of the most mechanical
and meretricious sort..." (New York Times).   Or, as Time

magazine aptly labeled it, "Another jugful of Hollywood's Southern Discomfort."

Meantime, James Hadley Chase had written No Orchids for Miss Blandish, which was an "adaptation" of the Temple Drake-Trigger alliance from Sanctuary. It was twice-filmed, once in England as No Orchids for Miss Blandish (1948), q.v., and then in the U.S. under the title The Grissom Gang (1971), q.v.

THE STREET WITH NO NAME   (Twentieth Century-Fox, 1948)   91 min.

Producer, Samuel C. Engel; director, William Keighley; screenplay, Harry Kleiner; assistant director, Henry Weinberger; art directors, Lyle Wheeler, Chester Gore; set decorator, Thomas Little; music director, Lionel Newman; makeup, Ben Nye, Tommy Tuttle; costumes, Kay Nelson; sound, W. D. Flick, Roger Heman; special effects, Fred Sersen; camera, Joe MacDonald; editor, William Reynolds.

Mark Stevens (Cordell); Richard Widmark (Alec Stiles); Lloyd Nolan (Inspector Briggs); Barbara Lawrence (Judy); Ed Begley (Chief Harmatz); Donald Buka (Shivvy); Joseph Pevney (Matty); John McIntire

Richard Widmark, Donald Buka and Mark Stevens in The Street with No Name (1948).

(Cy Gordon); Walter Greaza (Lieutenant Staller); Howard Smith (Commissioner Demory); Joan Chandler (Joan Mitchell); Bill Mauch (Mutt); Sam Edwards (Whitey); Don Kohler (F. B. I. Agent Atkins); Roger McGee (Joe); Vincent Donahue (Cholly); Phillip Pine (Monk); Buddy Wright (Giveno); Larry Anzalone (Sparring Partner); Robert Karnes (Dave); Robert Patten (Danker); Joan Blair (Valentine Leval); Edmund Cobb (Desk Sergeant); Philip Van Zandt (Manager of Bonding Company); Kid Wagner (Old Pug); Charles Tannen (Cab Driver).

Following his fine reception in Kiss of Death (1947), q. v., Twentieth Century-Fox cast screen tough Richard Widmark as a criminal again in The Street with No Name. This stark feature was lensed mostly on Los Angeles' skid row in a semi-documentary style. For this production, William Keighley won the Photoplay magazine Award for Best Director of the Year.

In a low-keyed style, the narrative traces the methods employed by the F. B. I. to break up a criminal gang, in this case, an association formed by hoodlum Alec Stiles "along scientific lines." The crook, it seems, has a dislike for window drafts, a mania that highlights his mentally-distorted manner. Cordell (Stevens) is the government agent from Washington who infiltrates the youthful gang and smashes its force.

With sinister, hyena-like emoting from Widmark, the film gained sufficient momentum to win popularity at the box-office. With Japanese settings, the story was remade as House of Bamboo (1955) and directed by Samuel Fuller.

T-MEN (Eagle Lion, 1947)   96 min.

Producer, Aubrey Schenck; associate producer, Turner Shelton; director, Anthony Mann; suggested by a story by Virginia Kellogg; screenplay, John C. Higgins; art director, Edward C. Jewell; set decorator, Armor Marlowe; music, Paul Sawtell; orchestrator, Emil Cadin; music director, Irving Friedman; assistant director, Howard W. Koch; sound, Leon Becker, Frank McWhorter; special effects, George J. Teague; camera, John Alton; editor, Fred Allen.

Dennis O'Keefe (Dennis O'Brien); Alfred Ryder (Tony Genaro); Mary Meade (Evangeline); Wally (Wallace) Ford (Schemer); June Lockhart (Mary Genaro); Charles McGraw (Moxie); Jane Randolph (Diana); Art Smith (Gregg); Herbert Heyes (Chief Carson); Jack Overman (Brownie); John Wengraf (Shiv); Jim Bannon (Lindsay); William Malten (Paul Miller); Gayne Whitman (Narrator); Vivian Austin (Genevieve); James Seay (Hardy); Lyle Latell (Isgreg); John Newland (Jackson Lee); Victor Cutler (Snapbrim); Tito Vuolo (Pasquale); John Parrish (Harry); Curt Conway (Shorty); Ricki Van Dusen (Girl on Plane); Keefe Brasselle (Cigar Attendant); Salvadore Barroga (Filipino Houseboy); George Carleton (Morgue Attendant).

This excellent quasi-documentary feature was given a big publicity campaign by small studio Eagle Lion, and the results paid off in good box-office.

With some location shooting in Detroit and Los Angeles, and

Alfred Ryder in T-Men (1947).

a filmed introduction by Elmer L. Irey, the former head of the
Treasury Department's law enforcement agencies, the film concerned
two T-Men (O'Keefe and Ryder). These government workers have a
tough time making a living, dogging the trail of counterfeiters. Detailed examples of government crime detection played a big role in
the celluloid footage here.

Even at this point in the history of the talkies, such manhunt
studies were becoming quite trite. In addition, it was becoming difficult for the average movie patron to discern the difference among
T-Men, G-Men, and other alphabet-oriented law enforcers.

TAXI! (Warner Bros., 1932) 68 min.

Director, Roy Del Ruth; based on the play The Bind Spot by
Kenyon Nicholson; screenplay, Kubec Glasmon, John Bright; art di-
rector, Esdras Hartley; music director, Leo F. Forbstein; makeup,
Perc Westmore; assistant director, William Cannon; camera, James
Van Trees; editor, James Gibbons.

James Cagney (Matt Nolan); Loretta Young (Sue Riley); George
E. Stone (Skeets); Guy Kibbee (Pop Riley); David Landau (Buck

Gerard); Ray Cooke (Danny Nolan); Leila Bennett (Ruby); Dorothy
Burgess (Marie Costa); Matt McHugh (Joe Silva); George MacFar-
lane (Father Nulty); Polly Walters (Polly); Nat Pendleton (Truckdriv-
er); Berton Churchill (Judge); Lee Phelps (Onlooker); George Raft
(Willie); Harry Tenbrook (Cabby); Robert Emmet O'Connor (Cop with
Jewish Man); Eddie Fetherstone (Judge); Ben Taggart (Cop); The
Cotton Club Orchestra (Themselves); Hector V. Sarno (Monument
Maker); Aggie Herring (Cleaning woman); Donald Cook, Evalyn Knapp
(Movie Stars).

    After his huge success in The Public Enemy (1931), q. v. ,
Warner Bros. contract player James Cagney found himself in constant demand for hard-hitting features on the studio lot. In Taxi!
he is on the right side of the law, this time as the leader of a
group of cabbies who fight against an organized taxi trust. While
his wife (Young) tries to tear down his ambitions, a racketeer kills
his younger brother (Cooke) and Matt Nolan vows revenge. Eventually he catches and eliminates the killer and breaks up the underworld's hold on the taxi business.
    Time said of the breezy, sixty-eight minute entry, that it was
a "... sordid but amusing observation on minor metropolitan en-
deavors. "
    Today Taxi! is best remembered for two aspects: it marked
the first time Cagney danced on screen (at a dance contest with
Young as his partner) and it was the first teaming of the star with
George Raft, the latter having a minor part in the feature. Seven
years later the duo would make the immensely popular, Each Dawn
I Die, q. v. , also for Warners.
    Taxi! would be reissued in 1936.

TEN MILLION DOLLAR GRAB (PRC/RKO, 1966) C-100 min.

    Producer-director-story-screenplay, Bitto Albertini; art di-
rector, Franco Sohioppa; music, Nico Modenco; camera, Ennio Rar-
riano.
    Brad Harris (Robert Coleman); Elaine de Witt (Gaby); Dana
Andrews (George); Franco Andrei (Max Hunter); Arrigo Peri (Lucas).
    A. k. a. Thousand Carat Diamond

    This film was a complicated thriller about a quartet of thieves
who lift the world's largest uncut diamond, belonging to a billionaire
(Andrews), from the hull of an ocean liner. The rich man recovers
the diamond and plans to keep it concealed, thus holding on to the
gem and collecting the ten million dollar insurance. But, as it
turns out, the would-be snatchers happen to work for the same insurance firm, and now they must repossess the stone in order to
get the goods on him.
    Although the feature received no U. S. release, it has been
shown on television in a dubbed version. One of the film's better
moments occurs when the crooks bust a diamond cutter (Peri) out of
prison so that he can cut the gem. There was also a wry flavor to
the plotline. For instance, at the finale, the seeming beaten George

is sitting down to plan a new con scheme, this time at the Vatican.

THEATRE OF LIFE   see   JINSEI GEKIJO

THEY CAME TO ROB LAS VEGAS   (Warner Bros. , 1969)   C-129 min.

     Executive producer, Nat Wachsberger; director, Antonio Isasi; based on the novel by Andre Lay; screenplay, Isasi, Jo Eisinger, Luis Comeron, Jorge Illa; dialog, Eisinger; art directors, Tony Cortes, Juan Alberto Soler; assistant directors, Luis Garcia, Marcelino Riba, U. Volz; music, Georges Garvarentz; special effects, Antonio Baquero; camera, Juan Gelpi; editors, Elena Jaumandreu, Emilio Rodriguez.
     Gary Lockwood (Tony Vincenzo); Elke Sommer (Anne); Lee

Jack Palance and Lee J. Cobb in They Came to Rob Las Vegas (1969).

J. Cobb (Skorsky); Jack Palance (Douglas); George Geret (Leroy); Gustavo Re (Salvatore); Daniel Martin (Merino); Jean Servais (Gino Vincenzo); Roger Hanin (The Boss); Maurizio Arena (Clark); Armand Mestral (Mass); Fabrizio Capucci (Cooper); Enrique Avila (Baxter).

Greed for the box-office coin leads producers to manufacture storylines about characters greedy for the easy buck ... and so goes the vicious circle.

This Spanish-American co-production (whose title is a misnomer) proceeds along safe lines with a big robbery being planned: the goal is to gain possession of a van carrying gold in the desert outside Las Vegas. Precious metal smuggler Skorsky (Cobb), his mistress (Sommer), and her boyfriend (Lockwood) and their gang, comprise the focal attention. The desired theft is accomplished, the robbers hide out in the desert and set about cutting through the van's casing with a blowtorch to obtain the loot. By this time an insurance investigator (Palance), really with the F.B.I., shows up on the scene. Before long, the shooting starts.

THEY LIVE BY NIGHT (RKO, 1948)

Executive producer, Dore Schary; producer, John Houseman; director, Nicholas Ray; based on the novel by Edward Anderson; adaptor, Ray; screenplay, Charles Schnee; art directors, Albert S. D'Agostino, Al Herman; set decorators, Darrell Silvera, Maurice Yates; music, Leigh Harline; music director, C. Bakaleinikoff; assistant director, James Lane; costumes, Adele Balkin; sound, John Cass, Clem Portman; special effects, Russell A. Cully; camera, George E. Diskant; editor, Sherman Todd.

Cathy O'Donnell (Keechie); Farley Granger (Bowie); Howard da Silva (Chicamaw); Jay C. Flippen (T-Dub); Helen Craig (Mattie); Will Wrifht (Mobley); Marie Bryant (Singer); Ian Wolfe (Hawkins); William Phipps (Young Farmer); Harry Harvey (Hagenheimer).

Nicholas Ray has long had a special ranking with cultists, and this screen exercise is a good demonstration why. Recently remade as Thieves Like Us (1974), q.v., the original holds up quite well.

Bowie (Granger) escapes from a southwest prison farm with two older, rougher criminals (da Silva and Flippen). While avoiding the law, the group becomes enmeshed in further criminal acts. But fate is against Bowie, and his end is not far away. As an interlude along the course, he has a romance with a sensitive farm girl (O'Donnell) who respects him as a human being, leaving the judgment of his moral standards to others.

"... has the failing of waxing sentimental over crime, but it manages to generate interest with its crisp dramatic movement and clear-cut types" (New York Times). Not since the Thirties and John Garfield's celluloid heyday had the screen presented such a touching rendition of the unlucky hounded man, who, given half a chance, might have gone legitimate. That the tender young "hero" has such a capacity for gentleness (and not of the psychopathic sort)

made the account all the more sympathetic, and the strain of his
plight more convincing. It was all a refreshing antidote to the
stereotype of the braggart, tough-guy hood who has a big mouth, a
loud gun, and a smacking paw.

This film was held up on the shelf for nearly two years because Howard Hughes, when he took over RKO, wanted little or
nothing to do with product made by the previous regime.

THIEVES LIKE US (United Artists, 1974) C-121 min.

Executive producer, George Litto; producer, Jerry Bick; director, Robert Altman; based on the novel by Edward Anderson;
screenplay, Calder Willingham, Joan Tewkesbury, Altman; assistant
director, Tommy Thompson; sound, Richard Vorisek; camera, Jean
Boffety; editor, Lou Lombardo.

Keith Carradine (Bowie); Shelley Duvall (Keechie); John
Schuck (Chicamaw); Bert Remsem (T-Dub); Louise Fletcher (Mattie);
Ann Latham (Lula); Tom Skerritt (Dee Mobley); Al Scott (Captain
Stammers); John Roper (Jasbo).

Acerbic John Simon (Esquire) insisted: "Robert Altman's
latest film Thieves Like Us, which has been garnering solid raves,
is, characteristically, a new filmization of Edward Anderson's 1937
novel on which Nicholas Ray's 1948 They Live by Night [q. v.] was
based. More importantly, it is almost servilely derived from Arthur Penn's Bonnie and Clyde. Still more importantly, the people
in the film are barely on the fringes of the middle class, the period
is the already-remote Thirties, and the characters are criminals
and their womenfolk. And this is how close we have come to a
serious adult film thus far in 1974."

On the other hand, sources such as Daily Variety praised
this entry as "... an exceptional film, one mostly devoid of clutter,
auteurist mannerism, and other cinema chic.... A far better film
than Nicholas Ray's first jab at the story in 1948, the mid-'30s tale
of lower-class young love and Dixie bank-robbing is a classic tragedy for all ages and for all seasons."

As in They Live by Night the story focuses on the escape
from the Mississippi penitentiary of the young, impressionable convict Bowie (Carradine) and two older, hardened criminals (Schuck
and Remsen) their flight from the law, and their falling back on old
ways--robbing, and other lawlessness.

The R rating came from the bits of nudity occurring in the
country idyll sequences between Bowie and Keechie (Duvall), the latter the simple girl who is attracted to this sensitive loner. The
tragedy, and such it is geared to be, ends with a crunch of bloodshed as Bowie is mowed down by unfeeling law enforcers.

Altman captures a great deal of the flavor of the time, not
only among his leads but among the supporting players as well, the
latter reacting with general nonchalance to the professions of the
trio of wanted men.

Clearly there is still far more to be explored in the gangster
milieu than has been up to this time. Thieves Like Us pointed the
way to such new approaches.

THE THIRD MAN   (British Lion, 1949)   104 min.

Producer, Carol Reed; associate producer, Hugh Perceval; director, Reed; screenplay, Graham Greene; art director, Vincent Korda; sets, Dario Simoni; continuity, Peggie McLafferty; zither music, Anton Karas; camera, Robert Krasker; editor, Oswald Hafenrichter.

Joseph Cotten (Holly Martins); Valli (Anna Schmidt); Orson Welles (Harry Lime); Trevor Howard (Major Calloway); Bernard Lee (Sergeant Paine); Ernst Deutsch (Baron Kurtz); Erich Ponto (Dr. Winkel); Wilfrid Hyde-White (Crabbin); Siegfried Breuer (Popesco); Paul Hoerbiger (Harry's Porter); Hedwig Bleibtreu (Anna's Old Woman); Frederick Schreicker (Hansel's Father); Herbert Halbik (Hansel); Jenny Werner (Winkel's Maid); Nelly Arno (Kurtz's Mother); Alexis Chesnakov (Brodsky); Leo Bieber (Barman); Paul Smith (M. P.).

This well-remembered thriller won the Grand Prix for best feature film at the 1949 Cannes Film Festival. Photographer Robert Krashe won an Academy Award for his cinematography on the picture. The Third Man also launched producer-director Carol Reed onto international success. Zither player Anton Karas' score has become an enduringly popular piece.

A bleak, sombre film, The Third Man presented a different type of gangster, one who did not rob banks for hire or for money, but a cold, ruthless man who sold black market medicine (the adulterated, cut and rancid sort that led to buyers' agony and pain). Although seen only a few times in the footage, Harry Lime's (Welles) character engulfs the whole picture.

Set in post-war Vienna, the film has pulp writer Holly Martins (Cotten) come to find his friend Harry Lime, who has offered him a job. There he learns that Harry has been killed in a traffic accident and he reaches the cemetery in time to see his friend's coffin being lowered into the grave. At the funeral Holly spots Anna Schmidt (Valli), Harry's girl. He meets a British military officer (Howard) who informs him that Harry was nothing more than a hoodlum and murderer.

Later Holly begins to question Lime's neighbors about the accident and tries to find Anna, the actress. When a porter (Hoerbiger) who witnessed the accident is found dead after being questioned by Holly, the latter suspects something is wrong. Later, two hoodlums try to beat up Holly, who subsequently gets drunk and goes to Anna, with whom he has fallen in love. That night he actually sees Harry Lime.

The finale is set in the sewers of Vienna where the climactic manhunt is carried out. It presents Lime in his new environment, sunk to the level of a sewer rat.

Interestingly, the character of Harry Lime would be revived for television in the late 1950s, but this time he was a crime fighter in "The Third Man" series starring Michael Rennie.

THIS DAY AND AGE   (Paramount, 1933)   85 min.

Producer-director, Cecil B. DeMille; screenplay, Bartlett Cormack; music, Howard Jackson, L. W. Gilbert, Abel Baer; camera, J. Peverell Marley; editor, Anne Bauchens.

Charles Bickford (Garrett); Judith Allen (Gay Merrick); Richard Cromwell (Steve Smith); Harry Green (Herman); Eddie Nugent (Don Merrick); Ben Alexander (Morry Dover); Oscar Rudolph (Gus); Billy Gilbert (Manager of Nightclub); Lester Arnold (Sam Weber); Fuzzy Knight (Max); Wade Boteler (Sheriff); Bradley Page (Toledo); Harry C. Bradley (Mr. Smith); Louise Carter (Mrs. Smith); Guy Usher (Chief of Police); Charles Middleton (District Attorney); Warner Richmond (Defense Attorney); Arthur Vinton (Little Fellow); Nella Walker (Little Fellow's Mother); Mickey Daniels (Mosher); Samuel S. Hinds (Mayor); Donald Barry (Young Man).

During the silent era Cecil B. DeMille rarely worked with the gangster theme and his only sound excursion into the genre was this nine-reeler.

A group of school boys take over the reins of municipal government for one day and during that time a gangster (Bickford) kills one of their friends.   The boys, led by Steve Smith (Cromwell), find

Ben Alexander, Judith Allen and Richard Cromwell in This Day and Age (1933).

out about the murder but corrupt city officials allow Garrett to go
free.   Trying to prove he committed the homicide, the youths kidnap the hood and take him to an abandoned brickyard where they
apply torture to extract a confession from him (a confession that
really wouldn't stand up in court).   A local girl (Allen) tells the police where the boys are, just as Garrett's gang is about to slaughter them.   Justice triumphs over evil once again.

      "A sensational and courageous picture" and "starkly realis-
tic" (Motion Picture Herald).   In many respects, this picture her-
alded the type of product that Frank Capra would soon turn out for
family audiences.   The passionate study, however, does go overboard in its plotlines and histrionics.   Today the film's major interest is that it is one of DeMille's few contemporary-set talkie
features.

THIS GUN FOR HIRE   (Paramount, 1942)   80 min.

      Producer, Richard M. Blumenthal; director, Frank Tuttle;
based on the novel by Graham Greene; screenplay, Albert Maltz,
W. R. Burnett; art director, Hans Dreier; songs, Frank Loesser
and Jacques Press; camera, John Seitz; editor, Archie Marshek.
      Veronica Lake (Ellen Graham); Robert Preston (Michael
Crane); Laird Cregar (Willard Gates); Alan Ladd (Philip Raven);
Tully Marshall (Alvin Brewster); Mikhail Rasumny (Slukey); Marc
Lawrence (Tommy); Pamela Blake (Annie); Harry Shannon (Finnerty);
Frank Ferguson (Albert Baker); Bernadene Hayes (Baker's Secre-
tary); James Farley (Night Watchman); Virita Campbell (Crippled
Girl); Roger Imhof (Senator Burnett); Victor Kilian (Brewster's Sec-
retary); Olin Howland (Fletcher); Emmett Vogan (Charlie); Chester
Clute (Mr. Stewart); Charles Arnt (Will Gates); Virginia Farmer
(Woman in Shop); Clem Bevans (Old Timer); Harry Hayden (Restau-
rant Manager); Tim Ryan (Guard); Yvonne De Carlo (Show Girl); Ed
Stanley (Police Captain); Eddy Chandler (Foreman); Louise La
Planche (Dancer); Richard Webb (Young Man); Lora Lee (Girl in Car);
Cyril Ring (Waiter); William Cabanne (Laundry Truck Driver).

      Due to this feature, Alan Ladd became a top star.   Here he
was featured as a soulless gunman named Philip Raven.   Taken from
Graham Greene's novel, with W. R. Burnett co-scripting, the motion
picture was a very popular wartime item, both as a thriller and as
the initiation of one of the hottest screen love teams of the Forties,
Ladd and equally pint-sized Veronica Lake.
      The plotline (distilled and distorted from the book original)
found Los Angeles policeman Michael Crane (Preston) and his singer
girlfriend Ellen Graham (Lake) attempting to find out who was behind
a conspiracy to sell poison gas to Japan.   Ellen becomes a singer
in Willard Gates' (Cregar) posh club and starts working undercover
when gunman Raven arrives on the scene to find the men who have
double-crossed him on a prior deal.   Eventually it turns out that
Ellen and Raven are seeking the same people, for fat Willard is
mixed up with invalid industrialist Alvin Brewster (Marshall).
Rugged Raven later kidnaps petite Ellen and confronts the villains.

Veronica Lake and Alan Ladd in <u>This Gun for Hire</u> (1942).

He murders them, but he is eventually gunned down. At the finale
Philip dies with his face in Ellen's lap. Variety noted jocularly,
"Better men have died with their heads in less pleasant places. "
It had been a long time since the cinema had witnessed such
a conscienceless, pathological crazed killer as Ladd's Philip Raven.
It was a portrait of a criminal one could not easily forget, of a
man who was cruel, cold-blooded, and very resourceful.

Paramount would remake the film sixteen years later as a
Western, Short Cut to Hell, with James Cagney directing and appearing in the film's prologue. It was merely a "B" entry.

THOSE WHO DANCE (Warner Bros. , 1930) 6,876'

Director, William Beaudine; story, George Kibbe Turner;
screenplay-dialog, Joseph Jackson; sound, Clare A. Riggs; camera,
Sid Hickox; editor, George Amy.

Monte Blue (Dan Hogan); Lila Lee (Nora Brady); William
Boyd ("Diamond Joe" Jennings); Betty Compson (Kitty); William
Janney (Tim Brady); Wilfred Lucas ("Big Ben" Benson); Cornelius
Keefe (Pat Hogan); DeWitt Jennings (Captain O'Brien); Gino Corrado
(Tony); Bob Perry (Bartender); Charles McAvoy (Prison Guard);
Kernan Cripps (Detective); Richard Cramer (Steve Daley); Harry
Semels, Nick Thompson, Frank Mills, Lew Meehan (Hoods).

After her brother (Janney) is framed for a killing by a group
of thieves, Nora Brady (Lee) asks the murder victim's brother
(Blue), a detective, to join the gang secretly and obtain the needed
evidence to clear her brother. Dan Hogan does that, but in the
climactic scene he is forced to shoot the group's leader (Boyd).
Tim is saved, and Dan and Nora decide to wed.

This was a remake of the 1924 Associated First National
film of the same name. The earlier rendition, produced by Thomas
H. Ince and directed by Lambert Hillyer (who adapted the work to
the screen), was filmed in two formats with more emphasis on the
bootlegging angle. The stars of the 1924 production were Blanche
Sweet, Bessie Love, and Warner Baxter.

THOUSAND CARAT HEIST see TEN MILLION DOLLAR GRAB

THREE ON A MATCH (First National, 1932) 64 min.

Associate producer, Samuel Bischoff; director, Mervyn Le-
Roy; story, Kubec Glasmon, John Bright; screenplay, Lucien Hub-
bard; art director, Robert Haas; camera, Sol Polito; editor, Ray
Curtis.

Joan Blondell (Mary Keaton); Warren William (Robert Kirkwood); Ann Dvorak (Vivian Revere); Bette Davis (Ruth Westcoff);
Lyle Talbot (Mike); Humphrey Bogart (Harve); Shelia Terry (Naomi
--Bob's Secretary); Grant Mitchell (Principal Gilmore); Glenda Farrell (Reformatory Girl); Frankie Darro (Bobby); Clara Blandick

(Mrs. Keaton); Anne Shirley (Vivian as a Child); Virginia Davis
(Mary as a Child); Betty Carse (Ruth as a Child); Buster Phelps
(Junior); John Marston (Randall); Edward Arnold (Ace); Allen Jenk-
ins (Dick); Sidney Miller (Willie Goldberg); Herman Bing (Professor
Irving Finklestein); Ann Brody (Mrs. Goldberg); Mary Doran (Prison-
er); Blanche Frederici (Miss Blazer); Hardie Albright (Lawyer);
Selmer Jackson (Voice of Radio Announcer); Harry Seymour (Jerry
Carter).

   This was perhaps the beginning of the streamlined gangster
yarn. The picture was built on the old adage about bad luck befall-
ing the last person to employ a match used to light more than one
cigarette. In this case it was a triangle involving three old school
chums, meeting a decade after graduation. Mary (Blondell) is a
stage actress who had been in reform school; Vivian (Dvorak) is a
society woman who has wed a lawyer (William); and Ruth (Davis) is
in business.
   Vivian is the one who seems destined for trouble. It all
starts when she runs off with Mike (Talbot), Mary's beau. Kirkwood asks Mary for help in locating Vivian, and he finds her with
Mike. He sues for divorce and obtains custody of their small son.
Vivian hits the skids with drink and dope. In order to pay off
gambling debts, her "friend" Mike kidnaps her son. Knowing the
boy will be killed, Vivian commits suicide by jumping out of a window with a message giving the boy's whereabouts pinned to her
dress. The boy's life is saved.
   In a concise sixty-four minutes, director Mervyn LeRoy
pushes through a lot of storyline, keeping an effective, breezy pacing. The gangsters who course through the plot are taken very
much for granted by the onscreen characters: opposition to be
coped with, but not regarded as distasteful freaks. America had
come a long way.
   The film would be remade as Broadway Musketeers (1938).

THREE TOUGH GUYS (Paramount, 1974) C-92 min.

   Producer, Dino De Laurentiis; director, Duccio Tessari;
screenplay, Luciano Vincenzoni, Nicola Badalucco; art director,
Francesco Bronzi; assistant director, Gianni Cozzo; music, Isaac
Hayes; camera, Aldo Tonti; editors, Mario Morra, Richard Marks.
   Lino Ventura (Father Charlie); Isaac Hayes (Lee Stevens);
Fred Williamson (Joe Snake); Paula Kelly (Fay Collins); William
Berger (Captain Ryan); Luciano Salce (Bishop); Vitterio Sanipoli
(Mike Petralia); Jacques Herlin (Tequila); Jess Hahn (Bartender);
Loretta De Luca (Anne Lombardo); Thurman E. Scott (Tony Red).

   In what was aimed as a successor (of sorts) to Serpico, q. v.
Paramount presented Three Tough Guys which had multiple box-
office draw with its three stars. Isaac Hayes made his screen debut along with writing the film's musical score. Duccio Tessari,
who helmed the picture, was a veteran of gangster opuses.
   With interior filming in Italy and exteriors lensed in Chicago,

the feature told of a Chicago gun-toting priest (Ventura) who joins
forces with an ex-cop (Hayes) to solve a million dollar bank robbery,
an event which had led to Lee Stevens' dismissal from the police
force. Also caught up in the search are hoodlum Joe Snake (Williamson), a Mafia good guy (Sanipoli), a dishonest policeman (Berger), and Joe's girl (Kelly).

During the course of the action there are multiple killings by
Stevens, with Father Charlie saying last rites over the victims as
the police, mobsters and the Mafia all vie for the stolen loot.

Despite its satisfactory playoff dates on the action film market, Daily Variety could justifiably complain that it "... would be
a moderately effective parody of the Mafia and blaxploitation genres
if even some small portion of its ludicrous dialog, absurd plotting
or broad acting was intentionally risible. "

THUNDER ROAD (United Artists, 1958) 94 min.

Producer, Robert Mitchum; director, Arthur Ripley; story,
Mitchum; screenplay, James Atlee Phillips, Walter Wise; assistant
directors, James Casey, Jack Doran; songs, Mitchum and Don Raye;
makeup, Carly Taylor; sound, Frank Webster; special effects, Jack
Lannan, Lester Swartz; camera, Alan Stensvold, David Ettinson;
editor, Harry Marker.

Robert Mitchum (Lucas "Luke" Doolin); Gene Barry (Troy
Barrett); Jacques Aubuchon (Carl Kogan); Keely Smith (Francie
Wymore); Trevor Bardette (Vernon Doolin); Sandra Knight (Roxanna
Ledbetter); Jim Mitchum (Robin Doolin); Betsy Holt (Mary Barrett);
Frances Koon (Sarah Doolin); Randy Sparks (Singer-Guitarist); Mitch
Ryan (Jed Moultrie); Peter Breck (Stacey Gouge); Peter Hornsby
(Lucky); Jerry Hardin (Niles Penland); Robert Porterfield (Preacher).

Lawbreakers do not always operate in urban areas, as was
demonstrated in Thunder Road. This actionful tale dealt with the
moonshine trade in the deep South and portrayed "... a man [who]
has a right to do anything, including making whiskey, as long as he
makes it on his own land. " In this case, Lucas Doolin's (Robert
Mitchum) dad (Bardette) makes the hootch and his well-muscled son
totes the load through the Tennessee hills in a spare gas tank in
his souped-up jalopy. The chronicle has the Doolin family at odds
with revenue agents from the Treasury Department who are out to
stop the illegal liquor transportation and sale, and with big city
hoodlums who are trying to organize the moonshiners. Tied into
the plot were Lucas' younger brother (Jim Mitchum) and Luke's
romance with nightclub singer Francis Wymore (Smith).

Particularly good were the film's chase scenes between Mitchum and the revenue officers through the Tennessee hills before
the "... devil sent the moonshine and the boy straight to hell. "

Besides writing the scenario, Robert Mitchum also composed
two songs for the film, "The Ballad of Thunder Road" and "Poor
Whippoorwill. "

"It's just this Jim--I want to be decent---again."   1197-30

Fay Wray and George Bancroft in <u>Thunderbolt</u> (1929).

THUNDERBOLT (Paramount, 1929) 95 min.

    Director, Josef von Sternberg; story, Jules Furthman, Charles Furthman; screenplay, Charles Furthman; dialog, Herman Mankiewicz; art director, Hans Dreier; songs, Sam Coslow; camera, Henry Gerrard; editor, Helen Lewis.

    George Bancroft (Jim Lang--Thunderbolt); Richard Arlen (Bob Moran); Fay Wray (Mary--Ritzy); Tully Marshall (Warden); Eugene Besserer (Mrs. Moran); James Spottswood (Snapper O'Shea); Fred Kohler (Bad Al Frieberg); Mike Donlin (Kentucky Sampson); S. S. Stewart (Black Convict); George Irving (Bank Officer); Robert Elliott (Priest); William Thorne (Police Inspector); E. P. Calvert (District Attorney).

    When Mary (Wray), mistress to bank robber Thunderbolt (Bancroft), falls in love with young banker Bob Moran (Arlen) she wants to quit the underworld. Not knowing that the police are following her, she goes with Thunderbolt to a nightclub where she hopes to persuade him to set her free. He refuses, swearing he will kill any man who tries to take her from him. Meanwhile, Bob is fired from his bank post because of his association with Mary.

Thunderbolt later calls Mary to say he is coming to get her and to even the score with Bob. However, Thunderbolt is caught and sentenced to death. He is joined on death row by Bob who has been framed by Thunderbolt's pals. The hardened criminal plans to kill Bob, but when he learns from the intended victim that Bob and Mary were childhood sweethearts and it was Thunderbolt who stole away another's girl, the gangster relents. He goes to the electric chair "cheerfully."

Completing his trilogy of 1920s gangster films at Paramount, director von Sternberg again starred the bulky, but effective George Bancroft (the screen's first real genre star). A mixture of fantasy and realism about the underworld milieu, it ably captured the milieu of the criminal life, whether it be a Harlem nightspot or Death Row.

This was von Sternberg's first sound film, and he used no musical background.

THUNDERBOLT AND LIGHTFOOT (United Artists, 1974) C-115 min.

Producer, Robert Daley; director-screenplay, Michael Cimino; art director, Tambi Larsen; set decorator, James Berkey; music, Dee Barton; song, Paul Williams; titles, Wayne Fitzgerald; stunt coordinator, Buddy Van Horn; special action sequences, Carey Loftin; sound, Bert Hallberg, Norman Webster; special effects, Sam Bedig; camera, Frank Stanley; editor, Ferris Webster.

Clint Eastwood (John "Thunderbolt" Doherty); Jeff Bridges (Lightfoot); George Kennedy (Red Leary); Geoffrey Lewis (Goody); Catherine Bach (Melody); Gary Busey (Curly); Jack Dodson (Vault Manager); Gene Elman, Lila Teigh (Tourists); Burton Gilliam (Welder); Roy Jenson (Dunlop); Claudia Lennear (Secretary); Bill McKinney (Crazy Driver); Vic Tayback (Mario); Dub Taylor (Gas Station Attendant); Gregory Walcot (Used Car Salesman); Erica Hagen (Waitress); Virginia Baker, Stuart Nisbet (Couple at Gas Station); Alvin Childress (Janitor); Irene K. Cooper (Cashier); Cliff Emmich (Fat Man); June Fairchild (Gloria); Ted Foulkes (Little Boy); Karen Lamm (Girl on Motorcycle); Leslie Oliver, Mark Montgomery (Teenagers); Luanne Roberts (Suburban Housewife); Tito Vandis (Counterman).

This relatively minor adventure melodrama was boosted by the marquee lustre attached to the Clint Eastwood name.

Ex-soldier John "Thunderbolt" Doherty is masquerading as a preacher, hiding out from former co-crooks. It seems both Red Leary (Kennedy) and Goody (Lewis) were part of Thunderbolt's federal reserve bank robbery squad. Thunderbolt made his escape, but the others had been captured. Everyone now wants to know where the loot is hidden. At this dangerous juncture Thunderbolt is saved by Lightfoot (Bridges), a young drifter with vast resources as a con artist. The two develop a rapport and decide to remain together as a non-official team.

To appease the angered Red and Goody, Thunderbolt and Lightfoot join in a plan to rob the same federal reserve bank again.

The robbery is executed, but thereafter the men turn on each other.
Meanwhile, Thunderbolt and Lightfoot find the old school house
(which has been moved) where the original loot has been stored.
But success is not to be Lightfoot's future. He has been severely
beaten up by Leary and as a result dies of brain injuries. Thunderbolt, who has purchased a new Cadillac with some of the loot,
is left to drive off alone. (Red has met a gruesome end at the
teeth and paws of vicious department store guard dogs.)

The British Monthly Film Bulletin noted of this camaraderie-
style thriller, "As it progresses the film darkens, Bonnie and Clyde
fashion, from broad and sometimes knockabout comedy to the more
immediate violence of later scenes.... On the way, the movie de-
votes a good deal of attention to minor details and incidental characters who range from the quirky to the sheer lunatic...."

TIGHT SPOT (Columbia, 1955) 97 min.

Producer, Lewis J. Rachmil; director, Phil Karlson; based
on the novel Dead Pigeon by Lenard Kantor; screenplay, William

Brian Keith and Lorne Greene in Tight Spot (1955).

Bowers; art director, Carl Anderson; music director, Morris Stoloff;
camera, Burnett Guffey; editor, Viola Lawrence.

Ginger Rogers (Sherry Conley); Edward G. Robinson (Lloyd
Hallett); Brian Keith (Vince Striker); Lucy Marlow (Prison Girl);
Lorne Greene (Benjamin Costain); Katherine Anderson (Mrs. Wil-
loughby); Allen Nourse (Marvin Rickles); Peter Leeds (Fred Packer);
Doye O'Dell (Mississippi Mac); Eve McVeagh (Clara Moran); Helen
Wallace (Warden); Frank Gerstle (Jim Hornsby); Gloria Ann Simpson
(Miss Masters); Robert Shield (Carlyle); Norman Keats (Arny); Kath-
ryn Grant (Girl Honeymooner); Ed "Skipper" McNally (Harris); Erik
Paige (Man); John Marshall (Detective); Tom de Graffenried (Doctor);
Bob Hopkins (TV Salesman).

The plight of the stool pigeon/informer is not easy, for he
or she (in this case) is a marked prey for both the law and the lawless.

U. S. attorney Lloyd Hallett obtains custody of model Sherry
Conley (Rogers) who had been sent to prison on a bum rap. The
government wants her to testify on a big-time racketeer (Green)
with whom she was formerly associated. Wise in the ways of the
world, Sherry refuses to aid the cause. But when a female law
agent (Anderson) is killed by one of Costain's henchmen, Sherry begins to change her mind. She falls in love with cop Vince Striker
(Keith) who is guarding her in the hotel room. Later Vince turns
out to be working for Costain and a cat-and-mouse game develops
when Sherry realizes just how hazardous her situation really is.
Finally, Sherry agrees to go to court. Her new profession is as
a "racket buster."

TONY ROME (Twentieth Century-Fox, 1967) C-110 min.

Producer, Aaron Rosenberg; director, Gordon Douglas; based
on the novel Miami Mayhem by Marvin H. Albert; screenplay, Richard
L. Breen; assistant director, Richard Lang; action sequences director,
Buzz Henry; music-music conductor, Billy May; songs, May and Ran-
dy Newman; Lee Hazelwood; art directors, Jack Martin Smith, James
Roth; set decorators, Walter M. Scott, Warren Welch; costumes,
Moss Mabry; makeup, Ben Nye; sound, Howard Warren; David
Dockendorf; camera, Joseph Biroc; editor, Robert Simpson.

Frank Sinatra (Tony Rome); Jill St. John (Ann Archer);
Richard Conte (Lieutenant Santini); Sue Lyon (Diana Pines); Gena
Rowlands (Rita Kosterman); Simon Oakland (Rudolph Kosterman);
Jeffrey Lynn (Adam Boyd); Lloyd Bochner (Vic Rood); Robert J.
Wilke (Ralph Turpin); Richard Krisher (Donald Pines); Virginia Vin-
cent (Sally Bullock); Lloyd Gough (Langley); Rocky Graziano (Packy);
Elizabeth Fraser (Irma); Buzz Henry (Nimmo); Shecky Greene (Cat-
leg); Mike Romanoff (Maitre d'Hotel).

His cinema career faltering, middle-aged Frank Sinatra attempted a Philip Marlowe-like detective portrayal in this thriller,
which did sufficiently well at the box-office to merit a sequel, Lady
in Cement (1968), q. v. The first film, however, was the better of

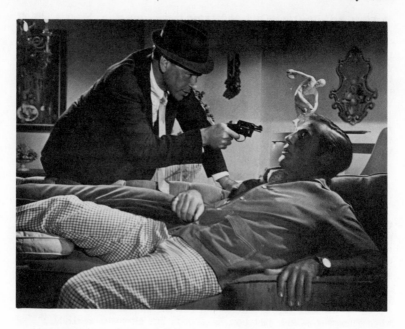

Frank Sinatra and Lloyd Bochner in <u>Tony Rome</u> (1967).

the two outings.   It even featured daughter Nancy warbling the title
theme tune written by Lee Hazelwood.

It seems crime and crooks are not only part of big northern
city life, but can and do exist way down south--in sunny Florida,
no less.

Living on a yacht harbored at Biscayne Bay, amorous Tony
Rome (Sinatra) spends much of his time getting into trouble and romancing the ladies, not to mention his fondness for horse racing.
At the present time, he is hired to investigate the facts behind the
tragedy of a newlywed socialite (Lyon) who is enslaved by alcohol.
He also becomes involved with a stolen piece of valuable jewelry and
ends up at odds with a stripteaser, her lover, a drug addict, her
pusher, and two assassins.   To add fuel to the plotline flame, he
angers a corrupt building contractor (Oakland) and his wife (Rowlands), a divorcee (St. John), and the police, although at times he
is helped out by police pal Lieutenant Santini (Conte).

Along the way in these adventures, Tony covers the more
seamy life of Miami Beach, where the feature was shot on location.

<u>Variety</u> summed it up best when it labeled the proceedings
"a very commercial blend of tasteful and tasteless vulgarity. "

TOPKAPI (United Artists, 1964) C-120 min.

Producer-director, Jules Dassin; based upon the novel The Light of Day by Eric Ambler; screenplay, Monja Danischewsky; costumes, Denny Vachlioti; assistant directors, Tom Pevesner, Joseph Dassin; assistant art director, Jacques Douy; sets, Max Douy; sound, William Sivel; camera, Henri Alekan; editor, Roger Dwyre.

Melina Mercouri (Elizabeth Lipp); Peter Ustinov (Arthur Simpson); Maximilian Schell (William Walter); Robert Morley (Cedric Page); Akim Tamiroff (Geven); Gilles Segal (Guilio); Jess Hahn (Fischer); Titos Wandis (Harback); Ege Ernart (Major Tufan); Senih Orkan, Ahmet Danyal Topatan (Shadows); Amy Dalby (Nanny); Joseph Dassin (Josef); Despo Diamantidou (Voula).

"Topkapi is a tongue twister. But don't waste time pronouncing it. Go see it. It happens to be one of the moviest movies around, a lush and lovely confection of things cinematic that add up to one of the best comedy adventure films in years. It has a plot to fascinate you, a cast to captivate you, a 40-minute suspense sequence to knock you for a loop, a script to satisfy you on both the sophisticated and simple-minded pleasure-levels, and simply beautiful color" (New York Herald-Tribune).

A decade after his Rififi, q.v., producer-director Jules Dassin returned to the heist genre that had won him an international reputation. For many critics, this cosmopolitan, tongue-in-cheek exercise remains the epitome of the robbery caper. The fact that the picture, like most of the species, has a downbeat ending in essence (i.e., the crooks, being captured) does not spoil the bouncy verve of the production.

Enterprising Elizabeth Lipp (Mercouri) and her lover (Schell) plot to steal the invaluable emerald-laden dagger from Istanbul's Topkapi Museum. Among those recruited to assist on the foray are: Cedric Page (Morley), a bizarre British inventor; Giulio (Segal), a silent muscleman; and Fischer (Hahn) another muscled man. The group also ensnarls low-life con artist Arthur Simpson (Ustinov) to participate in the adventure, but without alerting him to their actual plans. Later, Major Tufan (Ernart) of the Turkish police believes the group is up to terrorist activities, while Geven (Tamiroff), at the home the gang rents, thinks they are all Russian spies. Eventually the museum robbery is executed, but a quirk of fate leads to the group's capture. Undaunted, the imprisoned Elizabeth is already planning her next caper, this time the theft of the Romanoff gems from the Kremlin.

"It is another adroitly plotted crime film, played this time for guffaws, and if you don't split something, either laughing or squirming in suspense, we'll be surprised. We'll also be surprised if you're not dazzled by the extravagantly colorful decor and the brilliantly atmospheric setting, which happens to be Istanbul" (New York Times).

TUER DE CHICAGO see THE SCARFACE MOB

Arthur Byron, Bette Davis and Spencer Tracy in 20,000 Years in
Sing Sing (1933).

20,000 YEARS IN SING SING   (First National, 1933)   77 min.

     Associate producer, Robert Lord; director, Michael Curtiz;
based on the book by Warden Lewis E. Lawes; adaptors, Courtney
Terrett, Lord; screenplay, Wilson Mizner, Brown Holmes; music,
Bernhard Kaun; camera, Barney McGill; editor, George Amy.
     Spencer Tracy (Tom Connors); Bette Davis (Fay); Lyle Tal-
bot (Bud); Arthur Byron (Warden Long); Grant Mitchell (Dr. Ames);
Warren Hymer (Hype); Louis Calhern (Joe Finn); Sheila Terry (Bil-
lie); Edward McNamara (Chief of Guard); Spencer Charters (Daniels);
Nella Walker (Mrs. Long); Harold Huber (Tony); William Le Maire
(Black Jack); Arthur Hoyt (Dr. Meeker); George Pat Collins (Mike).

     This production was the first of several screen adaptations
of Warden Lewis E. Lawes' book. In it, Tom Connors (Tracy) is

sent to prison and fails to conform to the system. For the love of
his girl (Davis), however, he tries to go straight. When she is
seriously hurt in a car crash, he is given a twenty-four-hour leave
from jail. When Fay dies, Tom kills the man (Calhern) responsible for her death, the same person who railroaded him to prison.
Tom then returns to jail to die for his crime.

With its low-keyed presentation, 20,000 Years in Sing Sing
was a starkly effective melodrama. The New York Times noted it
had "... some extraordinary interesting glimpses of prison routine"
while Variety maintained, "... of pictures having the inside of penal
institutions as their locale, this is one of the best."

One of the most interesting dialog exchanges in the film occurs when Fay comes to visit a morally beaten Tom in prison. He
begins a lament about Tuesdays. He tells her he was born on Tuesday, caught on a Tuesday, sentenced on a Tuesday, and sent to jail
on a Tuesday. "And you met me on a Tuesday," she replies. [In
the remake, Castle on the Hudson (1940), q.v., John Garfield and
Ann Sheridan would have the leads, and the fateful day for the "hero" would be Saturday not Tuesday.]

It is interesting to note that, despite features such as these
which showed what drab, dismal fates awaited lawbreakers in prison, the filmgoing public still remained entranced with the "glamor"
and excitement of the criminal life.

UNCHAINED (Warner Bros., 1955) 75 min.

Producer-director, Hall Bartlett; based on the book Prisoners
Are People by Kenyon J. Scudder; screenplay, Bartlett; music, Alex
North; song, North and Hy Zaret; orchestrator, Maurice de Packh;
assistant director, Bob Farfan; sound, Hal Bumbaugh; camera,
Virgil E. Miller; editor, Cotton Warburton.

Elroy Hirsh (Steve Davitt); Barbara Hale (Mary Davitt);
Chester Morris (Kenyon J. Scudder); Todd Duncan (Bill Howard);
Johnny Johnston (Eddie Garrity); Peggy Knudsen (Elaine); Jerry Paris
(Joe Ravens); Bill Kennedy (Leonard Haskins); Henry Nakamura (Jer-
ry Hakara); Kathryn Grant (Sally Haskins); Bob Patten (Swanson);
Don Kennedy (Gladstone); Mack Williams (Mr. Johnson); Tim Consi-
dine (Win Davitt); Saul Gorss (Police Captain).

Producer-director Hall Bartlett made a laudable attempt to offer some insight into the unusual unwalled prison farm at Chino,
California, where the prisoners are treated as human beings. While
Chester Morris gave a restrained performance as the understanding
warden, Elroy "Crazylegs" Hirsh, the ex-football player, was not
up to handling the focal role, and vitiated a good deal of the story's
impact (the reformation of a decent man who had gone temporarily
dishonest).

As with many another film, the most memorable item of the
production turned out to be its theme song, "Unchained Melody,"
which has remained a standard over the decades.

THE UNDERCOVER MAN   (Columbia, 1949)   85 min.

Producer, Robert Rossen; director, Joseph H. Lewis; based upon an article by Frank J. Wilson and a story outline by Jack Rubin; screenplay, Sidney Boehm; additional dialog, Malvin Wald; music director, Morris Stoloff; art director, Walter Holscher; camera, Burnett Guffey; editor, Al Clark.

Glenn Ford (Frank Warren); Nina Foch (Judith Warren); James Whitmore (George Pappas); Barry Kelley (Edward O'Rourke); David Wolfe (Stanley Weinberg); Frank Tweddell (Inspector Herzog); Howard St. John (Joseph S. Horan); John F. Hamilton (Sergeant Shannon); Leo Penn (Sidney Gordon); Joan Lazer (Ross Rocco); Anthony Caruso (Salvatore Rocco); Robert Osterloh (Manny Zanger); Kay Medford (Gladys LaVerne); Patricia White (Muriel Gordon); Peter Brocco (Johnny); Everett Glass (Judge Parker); Michael Cisney (Fred Ferguson); Joe Mantell (Newsboy); Sidney Dubin (Harris); Marcella Cisney (Alice Ferguson); Tom Coffey (Gunman); Harlan Warde (Hood); Franklin Farnum (Federal Judge); Ken Harvey (Big Fellow); Wheaton Chambers (Male Secretary).

This workmanlike account tells the story of a unit of the Treasury Department, the tax detectives, who try to uncover those gentleman thieves, the income tax evaders. In this assignment, agent Frank Warren (Ford) is after a syndicate operator (an Al Capone type) who owes over three million dollars in back taxes. The crime boss, however, is very powerful and has men killed, threatens government officials, intimidates the police, and has T-Men roughed up. But persistent Warren gets the goods on him.

UNDERWORLD   (Paramount, 1927)   7,643'

Presenters, Adolph Zukor, Jesse L. Lasky; producer, Hector Turnbull; director, Josef von Sternberg; story, Ben Hecht; adaptor, Charles Furthman; screenplay, Robert N. Lee; titles, George Marion, Jr.; set designs, Hans Dreier; camera, Bert Glennon.

George Bancroft (Bull Weed); Clive Brook (Rolls Royce); Evelyn Brent (Feathers); Larry Semon (Slippy Lewis); Fred Kohler (Buck Mulligan); Helen Lynch (Mulligan's Girl); Jerry Mandy (Paloma); Karl Morse (High Collar Sam).

Director Josef von Sternberg first established his reputation as a director in the gangster genre with a group of films beginning with Underworld, followed by The Docks of New York (1928), q.v., The Dragnet (1928), q.v., and Thunderbolt (1929), q.v. It was Underworld, however, which had the greatest lasting impact. Herman G. Weinberg said in Josef von Sternberg (1967) that the film "started a vogue that lasted an entire generation" and that it "set the pattern for the whole cycle of American gangster films to come." Other plaudits from cinema historians include the evaluation of Kevin Brownlow in The Parade's Gone By (1968) that it is "the masterpiece of the genre."

Based on a Ben Hecht story that won him an Academy Award

Evelyn Brent, George Bancroft and Clive Brook in a publicity pose
for Underworld (1927).

for Best Original Story, Underworld detailed the plight of gang leader Bull Weed (Bancroft) who, through one of his few acts of kind-
ness, befriends a derelict (Brook) and dubs him Rolls Royce because
of his gentlemanly ways. He makes Rolls a gang member and the
latter quickly rises to become the brains of the operation. Bull's
girl, Feathers (Brent), takes a liking to Rolls. Then, at a dance
a rival hood (Kohler) makes a pass at her and Bull kills him. As
a result Bull is tried and sentenced to die. A scheme to break
him out, masterminded by Rolls, fails. Bull thinks he has been
double-crossed so he escapes by himself to take revenge on his ex-
pal. The police find the duo and during a gun battle, Rolls is killed.
Bull now realizes that Rolls was his true pal. Remorseful over the
turn of events, he surrenders peacefully to the law.
        The impact of Underworld has not dimmed through the years.
Today it is still well received. For the record, Underworld is
credited with being the first film which had midnight showings to
accommodate the crowds (at the New York Palace Theatre).

UNDERWORLD U.S.A.   (Columbia, 1961)   98 min.

        Producer-director-screenplay, Samuel Fuller; art director,
Robert Peterson; set decorator, Bill Calvert; assistant director,

Robert Emhardt, Richard Rust and Cliff Robertson in <u>Underworld</u>,
<u>U.S.A.</u> (1961).

Floyd Joyer; costumes, Bernice Pontrell; music, Harry Sukman;
orchestrators, Leo Shuken, Jack Hayes; camera, Hal Mohr; editor,
Jerome Thoms.
        Cliff Robertson (Tolly Devlin); Dolores Dorn (Cuddles); Bea-
trice Kay (Sandy); Paul Dubov (Gela); Robert Emhardt (Connors);
Larry Gates (Driscoll); Richard Rust (Gus); Gerald Milton (Gunther);
Allan Gruener (Smith); David Kent (Tolly at Age Twelve); Tina Rome
(Woman); Sally Mills (Connie); Robert P. Lieb (Officer); Neyle Mor-
row (Barney); Henry Norell (Prison Doctor).

        "A slick gangster melodrama made to order for filmgoers
who prefer screen fare explosive and uncomplicated.... As in most
gangster films, it is the tone of the acting and the tautness of the
direction that count, and it is here that Samuel Fuller's production
tallies its winning points" (Variety).
        As a child Tolly Devlin (Robertson) had witnessed the under-
world murder of his father. As an adult, he becomes a minor crook,
determined to revenge his father's death and kill the four men responsible. He learns that three of them are involved with a local
crime ring. He infiltrates the organization, at the same time co-
operating with the Federal Crime Commission. His romance with

Cuddles (Dorn) is what brings about his downfall, although he succeeds in engineering the deaths of his intended victims.

In a supporting role Robert Emhardt as Driscoll, the roly-
poly syndicate leader, was very effective.

THE UNHOLY THREE   (MGM, 1925)   6,948'

Presenter, Louis B. Mayer; director, Tod Browning; based
on the novel by Clarence Aaron Robbins; screenplay, Waldemar
Young; sets, Cedric Gibbons, Joseph Wright; camera, David Kesson;
editor, Daniel J. Gray.

Lon Chaney (Echo); Mae Busch (Rosie O'Grady); Matt Moore
(Hector McDonald); Victor McLaglen (Hercules); Harry Earles (Tweedledee); Harry Betz (Regan); Edward Connelly (Judge); William Hum-
phreys (Attorney); A. E. Warren (Prosecuting Attorney); John Mer-
kyl (Jeweler); Charles Wellesley (John Arlington).

THE UNHOLY THREE   (MGM, 1930)   75 min.

Director, Jack Conway; based on the novel by Clarence Aaron
Robbins; screenplay, J. C. Nugent, Elliott Nugent; art director, Ce-
dric Gibbons; wardrobe, David Cox; sound, Douglas Shearer; camera,
Percy Hilburn; editor, Frank Sullivan.

Lon Chaney (Echo); Lila Lee (Rosie); Elliott Nugent (Hector);
Harry Earles (Midget); John Miljan (Prosecuting Attorney); Ivan
Linow (Hercules); Clarence Burton (Regan); Craufurd Kent (Defense
Attorney).

Clarence Aaron Robbins' 1917 novel, The Unholy Three, was
the basis of two films starring Lon Chaney. Because the latter version was the star's one and only talkie (he died of throat cancer
soon thereafter), the work is still remembered today.

Both versions of the novel follow the same essential plotline.
In the silent edition, Chaney appears as Echo, a ventriloquist, who
works with two other sideshow freaks, Hercules (McLaglen), a
strongman, and Tweedledee (Earles), a dwarf. The trio work with
Rosie (Busch) who runs a sideshow shakedown and later, they set up
a parrot shop with Echo disguised as an old woman. The store is
used as a front to rob customers' homes, until a hired clerk (Moore)
falls for Rosie. When Hercules and Tweedledee kill a man, Hector
is blamed and in court Echo, dressed as the old woman, throws his
voice to the young man in the witness box with testimony that sets
him free. Later, Hercules kills Tweedledee and is, in turn, done
in by Echo's pet gorilla.

The climax of the 1930 talkie, directed by Jack Conway, who
also co-adapted the book, was somewhat different. Here, Chaney,
as Echo, takes the witness stand to provide evidence against the
young man (Nugent). He accidentally lowers his voice, giving away
his true identity while under cross examination by the prosecuting
attorney (Miljan). Echo goes to prison. Harry Earles repeated his
role of Tweedledee in the remake, but McLaglen was replaced by

Harry Earles, Victor McLaglen and Lon Chaney in The Unholy Three (1930).

Ivan Linow.
   The 1925 version of The Unholy Three, which was more atmospheric in its presentation of the bizarre criminal alliance,
grossed over two million dollars.

UPPER HAND   see   DU RIFIFI A PANAME

UP THE RIVER   (Fox, 1930)   92 min.

   Presenter, William Fox; director, John Ford; stager, Wil-
liam Collier, Jr.; story-screenplay-dialog, Maurine Watkins; songs,
Joseph McCarthy and James F. Hanley; assistant directors, Edward
O'Fearna, Wingate Smith; wardrobe, Sophie Wachner; set designer,
Duncan Cramer; sound, W. W. Lindsay; camera, Joseph August;
editor, Frank E. Hull.
   Spencer Tracy (St. Louis); Warren Hymer (Dannemora Dan);
Humphrey Bogart (Steve); Claire Luce (Judy); Joan Lawes (Jean);
Sharon Lynn (Edith La Verne); George MacFarlane, (Jessup); Gay-
lord Pendleton (Morris); William Collier, Sr., Robert E. O'Connor
(Guards); Louise MacIntosh (Mrs. Massey); Edythe Chapman (Mrs.
Jordan); Johnny Walker (Happy); Noel Francis (Sophie); Mildred Vin-
cnet (Annie); Wilbur Mack (Whitelay); Goodee Montgomery (Kit); Al-
thea Henly (Cynthia); Carol Wines (Daisy Elmore); Adele Windsor
(Minnie); Richard Keene (Dick); Elizabeth Keating (May); Helen Keat-
ing (June); Robert Burns (Slim); John Swor (Clem); Pat Somerset
(Beauchamp); Joe Brown (Deputy Warden); Harvey Clark (Nash);
Black and Blue (Slim and Clem); Morgan Wallace (Frosby); Robert
Parrish (Bit).

UP THE RIVER   (Twentieth Century-Fox, 1938)   75 min.

   Producer, Sol M. Wurtzel; director, Alfred Werker; story,
Maurine Watkins; screenplay, Lou Breslow, John Patrick; art direc-
tors, Bernard Herzbrun, Chester Gore; music director, Samuel
Kaylin; choreography, Nicholas Castle, Geneva Sawyer; camera,
Peverell Marley; editor, Nick DeMaggio.
   Preston Foster (Chipper Morgan); Tony Martin (Tommy
Grant); Phyllis Brooks (Helen); Slim Summerville (Slim Nelson);
Arthur Treacher (Darby Randall); Alan Dinehart (Warden Willis); Ed-
die Collins (Fisheye Conroy); Jane Darwell (Mrs. Graham); Sidney
Toler (Jeffrey Mitchell); Bill Robinson (Memphis Jones); Edward
Gargan (Tiny); Robert Allen (Ray Douglas); Dorothy Dearing (Martha
Graham); Charles D. Brown (Warden Harris).

   Director John Ford is said to have regarded Up the River as
"one of his mortal sins. "
   The hokey story dealt with two convicts (Tracy and Hymer)
who escape from prison, have a falling out, are caught, and then
are returned to the penitentiary.   Also in jail is Steve (Bogart),
there for accidental manslaughter.   Steve meets Judy (Luce), a

Warren Hymer, Humphrey Bogart, William Collier, Sr., and
Spencer Tracy in Up the River (1930).

prisoner in the women's section, who is incarcerated on a trumped-
up charge of stealing. When Judy is paroled, she promises to wait
for him, and she and Steve plan to marry in the future. But the
man (Wallace) on the outside who framed Judy hears of Judy's romance and threatens to ruin Steve's future release unless he plans
to cooperate. Judy asks St. Louis and Dan to help. They escape
from jail, stop Frosby and return to prison in time to help the team
win a basketball game.

Eight years later, Twentieth Century-Fox had the audacity to
remake Up the River and inflict it on the public with Preston Foster,
Tony Martin, and Arthur Treacher wasted in the programmer.

THE VALACHI PAPERS (Columbia, 1972) C-127 min.

Executive producer, Nino E. Krisman; producer, Dino De
Laurentiis; director, Terence Young; based on the book by Peter
Maas; screenplay, Stephen Geller; art director, Mario Carbuglia;

set decorator, John Godfrey; music, Riz Ortolani; sound, Roy Mangano; special effects, Eros Baciucchi; camera, Aldo Tonti; editor, John Dwyre.

Mario Pilar (Salerno); Charles Bronson (Joseph [Joey Cago] Valachi); Fred Valleca (Johnny Beck); Giacomino De Michelis (Little Augie); Arny Freeman (Warden at Atlanta Penitentiary); Gerald S. O'Loughlin (F. B. I. Special Agent Ryan); Lino Ventura (Vito Genovese); Sylvester Lamont (Commander at Fort Monmouth); Guido Leontini (Tony Bender); Walter Chiari (Dominick "The Gap" Petrilli); Amedeo Nazzari (Gaetano Reina); Joseph Wiseman (Salvatore Maranzano); Franco Corelli (Buster from Chicago); Alessandro Sperli (Giuseppe "Joe the Boss" Masseria); Angelo Infatni (Charles "Lucky" Luciano); John Alarimo (Ferrigno); Jill Ireland (Maria Valachi); Pupella Maggio (Rosanna Reina); Imelde Marani (Donna's Girlfriend); Anthony Dawson (Federal Investigator).

Perhaps Columbia Pictures should have taken a lesson from The Godfather (1972), q. v. when it made The Valachi Papers. The producers of the former film certainly made a violent essay into the gangster genre, but violence was hardly its total substance.

With a $20,000 contract offered for his death, convict Joseph Valachi (Bronson) talks about his Mafia life to F. B. I. agent Ryan (O'Loughlin). Via flashback, the film is a blueprint of underworld activities: inter-gang wars, murder, beatings, torture, doublecrosses, and even castration.

Released after The Godfather, the Italian-produced feature did a respectable $2.4 million business in the U.S. and helped to launch Bronson on his way to the top ten in male film players of the 1970s.

VIOLENT SATURDAY (Twentieth Century-Fox, 1955) C-91 min.

Producer, Buddy Adler; director, Richard Fleischer; based on the novel by William I. Heath; screenplay, Sydney Boehm; art directors, Lyle Wheeler, George W. Davis; music director, Lionel Newman; orchestrator, Edward B. Powell; camera, Charles G. Clarke; editor, Louis Loeffler.

Victor Mature (Shelley Martin); Richard Egan (Boyd Fairchild); Stephen McNally (Harper); Virginia Leith (Linda); Tommy Noonan (Harry Reeves); Lee Marvin (Bill); Margaret Hayes (Emily); J. Carrol Naish (Chapman); Sylvia Sidney (Elsie); Ernest Borgnine (Stadt); Dorothy Patrick (Helen); Billy Chapin (Steve Martin); Brad Dexter (Gil Clayton); Donald Gamble (Bobby); Raymond Greenleaf (Mr. Fairchild); Richey Murray (Georgie); Robert Adler (Stan); Harry Carter (Bart); Ann Morrison (Mrs. Stadt); Kevin Corcoran (David Stadt); Noreen Corcoran (Mary Stadt); Boyd "Red" Morgan (Slick); Florence Ravenel (Miss Shirley); Dorothy Phillips (Bank Customer); Virignia Carroll (Marion the Secretary); Harry Seymour (Conductor); Sammy Ogg (Bit).

Every decade has its run of the big caper entries. This all-star fare lived up to its title as a turgid melodrama detailing the robbery of an Arizona mining town bank.

Three hoodlums (Marvin, Naish and McNally) plan a bank robbery that will set them on easy street for life. Among those caught in the web of terror are Shelley Martin (Mature) as a mining executive fearful of his bravery, Elsie (Sidney) as a kleptomaniac librarian, Boyd Fairchild (Egan) as a man turned drunkard due to his wife's infidelity, and, among others, a group of Amish farmers. Most outstanding among the cast were Ernest Borgnine as a peace-loving farmer who turns pugnacious and Marvin as the benzedrine-sniffing sadist.

VIVA L'AMERICA (Copercines, 1969) C-93 min.

Director, Javier Seto.
With: Jeffrey Hunter, Margaret Lee, William Bogart, Gogo Rouo, Anna Maria Pierangeli, Eduardo Fajardo, Beni Deus, Miguel Del Castillo.
A. k. a. Mafia Mob.

This film was given an X certificate when issued in England in 1970. More importantly, it was a firm pictorial recreation of the Prohibition era in Chicago.
Made in Spain, it was an Italian-Spanish co-production. Former MGM star Pier Angeli had by this time reverted to her real name for billing.

VOICES OF THE CITY (Goldwyn, 1921) 5,630'

Producer, Samuel Goldwyn; director, Wallace Worsley; story, Leroy Scott; screenplay, Arthur F. Statter.
Leatrice Joy (Georgia Rodman); Lon Chaney (O'Rourke); John Bowers (Graham); Cullen Landis (Jimmy); Richard Tucker (Clancy); Mary Warren (Mrs. Rodman); Edythe Chapman (Mrs. Rodman); Betty Schade (Sally); Maurice B. Flynn (Pierson); H. Milton Ross (Courey); John Cossar (Garrison).
Original title: The Night Rose

This Goldwyn feature had difficulty in obtaining national release, being banned by the New York censors. After a title change from The Night Rose to Voices of the City and with some cuts in the original print, it received national release.
In a San Francisco cafe a young couple (Joy and Landis) witness a gangland murder of a policeman and are held for questioning. As a result, Georgia is tossed out of her home. Gangleader O'Rourke comes on the scene and offers to get her a room. Meanwhile, D. A. Graham (Bowers) plans to use Georgia and Jimmy as star witnesses in his case against O'Rourke. The latter is already trying to bribe Graham and to kill Jimmy. At this crucial time, O'Rourke's mistress (Schade) finds out about his feeling for Georgia and she shoots the gangland big shot. Georgia and Jimmy now can find happiness together.
This early gangster epic contained many subplots which were

later used in better-known genre films: the gang leader falling for
a girl and trying to kill her lover; the jealous-vengeful mistress;
the industrious D. S. who wants to use the hero and heroine to capture the villain.

WELCOME DANGER   (Paramount, 1929) 9,955'

Director, Clyde Bruckman; story, Bruckman, Lex Neal, Felix Adler; dialog, Paul Gerard Smith; songs, Lynn Cowan; Paul Tits-
worth; sound, George Ellis; camera, Walter Lundin, Henry Kohler.
Harold Lloyd (Harold Bledsoe); Barbara Kent (Billy Lee);
Noah Young (Clancy); Charles Middleton (John Thorne); William Walling (Captain Walton); James Wang (Dr. Gow); Douglas Haig (Roy).

In addition to his big screen antics, hanging from ledges on
high buildings and performing other daredevil stunts, and engaging
in the usual love story, this Harold Lloyd feature also poked fun at
the gangster film, Tong wars, and the narcotics trade.
Lloyd, who produced the picture, plays the son of a San Francisco Police Chief. He is a very meek botanist. Nevertheless, he
is called upon to help stop a war between U.S. and Oriental hoodlums
and on a train meets a girl (Kent) and her crippled brother. The
latter is about to have an operation performed by a Chinese doctor
(Wong). Dr. Gow and John Thorne (Middleton) are among those
complaining about the increased drug traffic, although the latter is
really a top pusher and an underworld leader.
In the nick of time, dexterous Harold rescues the doctor
from Thorne's clutches. By matching fingerprints, he is able to
prove Thorne's overall guilt.

WEST SIDE STORY   (United Artists, 1961) C-155 min.

Producer, Robert Wise; directors, Wise, Jerome Robbins;
based on the musical by Arthur Laurents; screenplay, Ernest Lehman; choreography, Robbins; dance assistants, Tommy Abbott, Mar-
garet Banks, Howard Jeffrey, Tony Mordente; music, Leonard Bern-
stein; songs, Bernstein and Stephen Sondheim; music conductor,
Johnny Green; orchestrators, Sid Ramin, Irwin Kostal; assistant di-
rectors, Robert E. Relyea, Jerome M. Siegel; costumes, Irene
Sharaff; wardrobe, Bert Henrikson; sound, Murray Spivack, Fred
Lau, Vinton Vernon; camera effects, Linwood Dunn; camera, Daniel
L. Fapp; editors, Thomas Stanford, Marshall M. Borden.
Natalie Wood (Maria); Richard Beymer (Tony); Russ Tamblyn
(Riff); Rita Moreno (Anita); George Chakiris (Bernardo); Tucker Smith
(Ice); Tony Mordente (Action); David Winters (A-Rab); Bert Michaels
(Snowboy); Eliot Feld (Baby John); Robert Banas (Joyboy); David Bean
(Tiger); Scooter Teague (Big Deal); Harvey Hohnecker (Mouthpiece);
Tommy Abbott (Gee-Tar); Sue Oakes (Anybodys); Gina Trikonis (Indio);
Eddie Verso (Juano); Jaime Rogers (Loco); Larry Roquemore (Rocco);
Robert Thompson (Luis); Nick Covacebich (Toro); Yvonne Othon (Con-
suelo); Suzie Kaye (Rosalla); Simon Oakland (Lieutenant Schrank);

Richard Beymer and Russ Tamblyn in West Side Story (1961).

William Bramley (Officer Krupke); Ned Glass (Doc); John Astin (Glad Hand); Penny Santon (Madam Lucia).

West Side Story opened at the Winter Garden Theatre on September 26, 1957 and enjoyed a 734-performance run. Adapting Shakespeare's Romeo and Juliet to a contemporary theme, it blended topical racial conflict problems with music and dance. More importantly, as regards this book, it offered a delineation of the juvenile delinquent 1950s-style, the environment-controlled youths who fall into a total life of crime, murder, and disinterest.

Filmed in stark reality (often on the streets of New York), the movie has well staged musical and dance numbers. While the story of two star-crossed lovers, Puerto Rican Maria (Wood) and Polish-descended Tony (Beymer), seems a bit naive today, in its day it had tremendous impact. More impressive than the mooning and crooning of the hero and heroines (their singing was dubbed anyway) were the sequences involving the rival gangs, The Sharks, led by Maria's brother Bernardo (Chakiris), and the Jets, of which Tony is a member. Just as feature films of the Thirties, usually focusing on the Dead End Kids or John Garfield, showed what tenement life could do to a human being's moral outlook, so this new rendition was an indictment of America's indifference to the poverty-filled jungle where nothing (especially human life) is sacred.

The film won several Oscars, including awards for Best Supporting Performers by Chakiris and Rita Moreno (as Bernardo's spitfire girlfriend).

THE WET PARADE (MGM, 1932) 122 min.

Director, Victor Fleming; based on the novel by Upton Sinclair; screenplay, John Meehan; continuity-dialog, John Mahin; camera, George Barnes.

Dorothy Jordan (Maggie May); Walter Huston (Pow Tarleton); Lewis Stone (Colonel Chilcote); Robert Young (Kip); Neil Hamilton

Neil Hamilton, Myrna Loy and Dorothy Jordan in The Wet Parade (1932).

(Roger); Jimmy Durante (Abe Schilling); Wallace Ford (Jerry); Myrna
Loy (Eileen); John Miljan (Doleshals); Joan Marsh (Evelyn); Clara
Blandick (Mrs. Tarleton); Emma Dunn (Mrs. Chilcote); Reginald
Barlow (Major Randolph); Frederick Burton (Judge Brandon); For-
rester Harvey (Mr. Fortesque); Ben Alexander (Dick); Cecil Cunning-
ham (Mrs. Twonbey); Clarence Muse (Tibbs); John Larkin (Moses).

During the Prohibition Era, occasional films were made which
dealt with the problem of drink. MGM presented this leisurely adaptation of Upton Sinclair's novel. The overlong feature attempted to
highlight the evils of excessive drinking while, at the same time,
stating that Prohibition was no answer to the problem. Quite naturally, the criminal element which profited from the bootlegging business
was well represented in this well-mounted production.

The story opens at the beginning of the Prohibition Era following the First World War. It details two families under the thumb of
drinking fathers. Colonel Chilcote (Stone) was a Southern gentleman
who drank excessively, while Pow Tarleton (Huston) was a New York
City alcoholic. When Pow's wife (Blandick) breaks his liquor bottles
he kills her and goes to jail while his son (Young) weds the Colonel's
daughter (Jordan). Kip later becomes an F.B.I. agent fighting lawbreakers. His partner is Abe Schilling (Durante) who is later gunned
down by hoodlums. Meanwhile, the Colonel has committed suicide
and his son (Hamilton) has gone blind by drinking bad liquor.

Besides presenting the domestic dramas of two contrasting
families, The Wet Parade, in its quasi-documentary fashion, showed
how low bootleg liquor was distilled and the resultant crime and
heartbreak that overtook the human beings involved or affected.

WHERE THE SIDEWALK ENDS   (Twentieth Century-Fox, 1950) 95
min.

Producer-director, Otto Preminger; based on the novel Night
Cry by Frank Rosenberg and a book by William L. Stuart; screenplay, Ben Hecht; adaptors, Victor Trivas, Rosenberg, Robert E.
Kent; art directors, Lyle Wheeler, J. Russell Spencer; music director, Lionel Newman; camera, Joseph LaShelle; editor, Louis Loeffler.

Dana Andrews (Mark Dixon); Gene Tierney (Morgan Taylor);
Gary Merrill (Tommy Scalise); Bert Freed (Paul Klein); Tom Tully
(Jiggs Taylor); Karl Malden (Lieutenant Thomas); Ruth Donnelly
(Martha); Craig Stevens (Ken Paine); Robert Simon (Inspector Nicho-
las Foely); Harry von Zell (Ted Morrison); Don Appell (Willis Bend-
er); Lou Krugman (Mike Williams); Grace Mills (Mrs. Tribaum);
Neville Brand (Steve); David Wolfe (Sid Kramer); Steve Roberts (Gil-
ruth); Phil Tully (Tod Benson); Ian MacDonald (Casey); John Close
(Hanson); John McGuire (Gertessen); Lou Nova (Ernie); Oleg Cassini
(Oleg the Fashion Designer); Louise Lorimer (Mrs. Jackson); Lester
Sharpe (Friedman); Chili Williams (Teddy); Robert Foulk (Feeney);
Eda Reiss Merin (Shirley Klein); Mack Williams (Jerry Morris);
Duke Watson (Cab Driver); Joseph Granby (Fat Man); Anthony George,
Barry Brooks (Thugs); Milton Gowman, Fred Graham (Men); Ralph

Peters (Counterman); Bob Patten (Medical Examiner); Robert B. Williams (Detective); Larry Thompson (Riley).

Dana Andrews gave one of his best performances in this film as a policeman whose father is a killer. This policeman accidentally kills a fugitive he is tracking and then tries to pin the murder rap on a well-known gambler (Merrill). The police, however, arrest cabbie Jiggs Taylor (Tully), the fugitive's ex-father-in-law, for the crime and Mark sets out to prove the man's innocence and Scalise's guilt. Eventually he builds a case against the culprit. But, with renewed love for Morgan (Tierney), he confesses to the homicide and she promises to wait for him.

With effective photography and low-keyed direction, this feature (made on the studio lot) captured the flavor of the city in its most alienated aspects. When things go wrong for an accidental malfeasant, there seems little encouragement from anyone or anything around to find a logical, just remedy. Intertwined with this state of affairs are the parallels to the life of the crook (here Merrill's Scalise) who seems to have a plush existence. Unlike the Thirties (or even the Forties) drama, no attempt was made to capitalize on the class distinctions that once were the forte of these tenement-poor folk versus bureaucracy-underworld syndicates-political big shot dramas.

WHILE THE ATTORNEY IS ASLEEP   see   MENS SAGFØREREN SOVER

WHILE THE CITY SLEEPS   (MGM, 1928)   7,231'

Director, Jack Conway; story-screenplay, A. P. Younger; titles, Joseph Farnham; costumes, Gilbert Clark; sets, Cedric Gibbons; camera, Henry Sharp; editor, Sam S. Zimbalist.
Lon Chaney (Dan); Anita Page (Myrtle); Carroll Nye (Marty); Wheeler Oakman (Skeeter); Mae Busch (Bessie); Polly Moran (Mrs. McGinnis); Lydia Yeamans Titus (Mrs. Sullivan); William Orlamond (Dwiggins); Richard Carle (Wally).

A flapper (Page) falls for a dapper hoodlum (Nye) but finds out too much about his boss (Oakman), who in turn threatens to kill her. Myrtle goes to tough detective Dan (Chaney) for help, which he gladly volunteers. Dan, however, falls in love with her. She agrees to marry him, although it is from gratitude and not any romantic feelings on her part. Later, realizing the true situation, Dan reunits Myrtle with Marty, whom he has helped to rehabilitate.
Instead of the love subplot serving as the basic gangster story, it was the other way around in this Jack Conway-directed feature. In this case, the rough detective (Chaney) was a type with whom a girl like Myrtle could not be happy. It was a plot theme (beauty and the beast) that would be frequently repeated in Chaney's motion pictures.
In this film, "the Man of a Thousand Faces" used his own countenance without the usual array of distorting makeup.

WHIPSAW   (MGM, 1935)   83 min.

Director, Sam Wood; story, James Edward Grant; screenplay, Howard Emmett Rogers; camera, James Wong Howe; editor, Basil Wrangell.

Myrna Loy (Vivian Palmer); Spencer Tracy (Ross McBryce); Harvey Stephens (Ed Dexter); William Harrigan (Doc Evans); Clay Clement (Harry Ames); Robert Gleckler (Steve Arnold); Robert Warwick (Wadsworth); Georges Renevant (Monetta); Paul Stanton (Chief Hughes); Wade Boteler (Humphries); Don Rowan (Curly); John Qualen (Dobson); Irene Franklin (Mme. Marie); Lillianne Leighton (Aunt Jane); J. Anthony Hughes (Bailey); William Ingersoll (Mr. Williams); Charles Irwin (Larry King); Edward Peil, Sr. (Bartender); Frank De Voe (Photographer); Bert Moorhouse (Reporter); John Marston, John Kelly, Arthur Loft, William Pawley (Patrolmen); Cyril McLaglen (Detective); Charles Coleman (Doorman); Wallis Clark (Claymore); William Wagner (Waiter); Howard Hickman (Hotel Clerk); Frances Gregg (Nurse); Robin Adair (Cummings); John Sheehan (Joe); Carl Stockdale (Farmer).

One of the most interesting pairings in the gangster genre

Spencer Tracy and Myrna Loy in <u>Whipsaw</u> (1935).

has to be that of Spencer Tracy and Myrna Loy in Whipsaw. This cross-country chase-romance film owed nearly everything to this team of lead players who were so ingratiating in their parts.

Vivian Palmer (Loy) is hopelessly tied up with a gang of thugs who are involved in the theft of federal funds. Ross McBryce (Tracy) pretends to be a fellow criminal and throws in his lot with Vivian after she escapes from the gang with the money. Actually Ross is a G-Man on the trail of the money and the culprits. Due to a storm, the duo are forced to seek refuge in Dobson's (Qualen) farm home. In the middle of the night, Ross risks his life to go for a doctor to aid in the delivery of Dobson's wife's first child-- which turns out to be twins. Vivian acts as a midwife for the doctor and the pleased Dobson names the twins after the visiting couple.

Just as Vivian and Ross are about to leave the farm, they are overtaken by her past cohorts and are taken hostage. Vivian insists to her captors that she left the money in the city. Later, at a roadside cafe, Ross reveals his identity and tries to capture the gang. He is badly injured in the resultant gun battle. However, the police arrive in time to arrest the guilty parties. Later in the hospital, Ross and Vivian admit their mutual love. He promises to testify in her behalf at the pending trial.

Realistically, Miss Loy may have been a bit too glamorous for a moll but she was delightful in her characterization. Another big asset to the production was John Qualen as the excitable expectant father.

WHITE HEAT (Warner Bros. , 1949) 114 min.

Producer, Louis F. Edelman; director, Raoul Walsh; based on the story by Virginia Kellogg; screenplay, Ivan Goff, Ben Roberts; art director, Fred M. MacLean; assistant director, Russell Saunders; music, Max Steiner; orchestrator, Murray Cutner; costumes, Leah Rhodes; makeup, Perc Westmore, Eddie Allen; sound, Leslie Hewitt; special effects, Roy Davidson, H. F. Koenekamp; camera, Sid Hickok; editor, Owen Marks.

James Cagney (Arthur Cody Jarrett); Virginia Mayo (Verna Jarrett); Edmond O'Brien (Hank Fallon--Alias Vic Pardo); Margaret Wycherly (Ma Jarrett); Steve Cochran (Big Ed Somers); John Archer (Phillip Evans); Wally Cassell (Cotton Valetti); Fred Clark (Daniel Winston--The Trader); Ford Rainey (Zuckie Hommell); Fred Coby (Happy Taylor); G. Pat Collins (Herbert the Reader); Mickey Knox (Het Kohler); Paul Guilfoyle (Roy Parker); Robert Osterloh (Tommy Ryley); Ian MacDonald (Bo Creel); Ray Montgomery (Ernie Trent); Jim Toney (Brakeman); Leo Cleary (Fireman); Marshall Bradford (Chief of Police); Milton Parsons (Willie Rolf the Stoolie); Sherry Hall (Clerk); Bob Foulk (Plant Guard); Jim Thorpe (Con); Harry Lauter (Radio Patrolman of Car A).

Reissue title: Sin Street Confidential (1958).

For those who were too young in 1949 to recall the vicious, pulsating gangster entries of the prior decade, White Heat brought back all the flavor/guts/gore of yore. Here James Cagney created

James Cagney, Robert Osterloh, Edward O'Brien and G. Pat Collins
in White Heat (1949).

another definitive interpretation of the neurotic hoodlum who, like
many Cagney punks, has a mother complex.

Bestial killer Cody Jarret (Cagney) is a mental case with an
Oedipus complex. He heads a cutthroat gang being pursued by
T-Men. Cody's girl (Mayo) falls for his henchman (Cochran) and
later double-crosses Cody. Cody hunts down the pair and brutally
murders Big Ed. Meanwhile, T-Men have placed an undercover
agent (O'Brien) in Cody's good graces, and he does his best to keep
his superiors alerted to the criminal's activities. Hank Fallon is
forced to participate with Cody's gang in the robbery of the payroll
office at a chemical plant, but he does manage to warn the police
in time. The factory is surrounded by lawmen and Cody is killed
when bullets cause a gas tank to explode.

The New York Times rated this brutal exercise as "the acme
of the gangster-prison film" and Time said it was in "... the hust-
ling tabloid tradition of the gangster movie of the 30s but its matter-
of-fact violence is a new, post-war style." Life added that it was
"... a wild and exciting mixture of mayhem and madness."

Virginia Kellogg received an Academy Award nomination for
her Best Original Screen Story.

Just as in real life, Cagney was growing too old for the

leading man category onscreen, so in the film he represented an outmolded gangster type, an aging neurotic making his last stand as a representative of the Prohibition-type hoodlum. With the coming of the Fifties, the gangster who was mean just to be mean, or killed for the joy and sake of slaughter, would be replaced by the organized business man of the really big crime syndicates operating on a near global basis. There would be throwbacks, of course, but later gangland studies would always reflect the new order.

Thus the flaming demise of Cody Jarrett accurately paralleled the finale of the Ricos, the Scarfaces, and the Cody Jarretts of before.

THE WHOLE TOWN'S TALKING (Columbia, 1935) 93 min.

Producer, Lester Cowan; director, John Ford; based on the novel by William R. Burnett; screenplay, Jo Swerling, Robert Riskin; assistant director, Wilbur McGaugh; camera, Joseph August; editor, Viola Lawrence.

Edward G. Robinson (Arthur Ferguson Jones/Killer Mannion); Jean Arthur (Wilhelmina "Bill" Clark); Arthur Hohl (Detective Sergeant Mike Boyle); Wallace Ford (Healy); Arthur Byron (District Attorney Spencer); Donald Meek (Hoyt); Paul Harvey (J. G. Carpenter); Edward Brophy (Bugs Martin); Etienne Girardot (Seaver); James Donlan (Detective Sergeant Pat Howe); J. Farrell Macdonald (Warden); Effie Ellsler (Aunt Agatha); Robert Emmet O'Connor (Police Lieutenant Mac); John Wray, Joe Sawyer (Mannion's Henchmen); Frank Sheridan (Russell); Clarence Hummel Wilson (President of the Chamber of Commerce); Ralph M. Remley (Ribber); Virginia Pine (Seaver's Private Secretary); Ferdinand Munier (Mayor); Cornelius Keefe (Radio Man); Francis Ford (Reporter at Dock); Lucille Ball (Girl); Ben Taggart (Traffic Cop); Walter Long (Convict); Mary Gordon (Landlady); Bess Flowers (Secretary); Charles King (Man).

William R. Burnett, who wrote the novel upon which Little Caesar was based, wrote several other works used for gangster films. John Ford directed this vehicle based on yet another Burnett original.

Arthur Ferguson (Robinson) is a timid hardware clerk who is arrested because he looks so much like Public Enemy Number One, Killer Mannion (Robinson), that everyone confuses the two now that Mannion is on the loose. To prove his real identity is not easy, but Arthur does so and is released. Meanwhile, Mannion tracks down his look-alike and advises Arthur that he had better turn over the special I.D. card given him by the District Attorney. Mannion explains that his plan is to have Arthur work by day at his office, and at night, Mannion plans to use Arthur's card to carry out his bank robbing without interference from the law. When the police catch onto what is happening they decide to put Arthur in jail for his own protection. However, Mannion goes in his place to settle an old grudge. The once meek Arthur profits from his strenuous experiences with Mannion and before the finale he has turned the case of mistaken identity to his own advantage, bringing about the downfall of the killer and causing the gang to be captured.

As the New York Herald-Tribune confirmed, it was "... a lively and satisfactory combination of farce and melodrama. " An interesting sidelight of this comedy-drama was the fact that both the killer and the humble good guy were of the same physical types, disproving, at least for the purposes of this plot, the fact that moral-emotional types are determined by physical build.

THE WILD ONE   (Columbia, 1954)   79 min.

Producer, Stanley Kramer; director, Laslo Benedek; based on a story by Frank Rooney; screenplay, John Paxton; art director, Walter Holscher; music, Leith Stevens; camera, Hal Mohr; editor, Al Clark.

Marlon Brando (Johnny); Mary Murphy (Kathie); Robert Keith (Harry Bleeker); Lee Marvin (Chino); Jay C. Flippen (Sheriff Singer); Peggy Maley (Mildred); Hugh Sanders (Charlie Thomas); Ray Teal (Frank Bleeker); John Brown (Bill Hannegan); Will Wright (Art Kleiner); Robert Osterloh (Ben); Robert Bice (Wilson); William Yedder (Jimmy); Yvonne Doughty (Britches); Keith Clarke (Gringo); Gil Stratton, Jr. (Mouse); Darren Dublin (Dinky); Johnny Tarangelo (Red); Jerry Paris (Dextro); Gene Peterson (Crazy); Alvy Moore (Pigeon); Harry Landers (Go-Go); Jim Connell (Boxer); Don Anderson (Stinger); Angela Stevens (Betty); Bruno VeSoto (Simmonds); Pat O'Malley (Sawyer); Timothy Carey (Chino Boy); Wally Albright (Cyclist); Eve March (Dorothy); Mary Newton (Mrs. Thomas); Ted Cooper (Racer).

This famous entry set a new trend in motion pictures by initiating the character of the loner, the young man who uses the law as he sees fit or ignores it completely. The picture also introduced a new type of hoodlum gang, the motorcycle gang, a mobile terrorist-type group still in evidence today.

Based on an actual story of cyclists taking over a small California town in the late 1940s, this feature presented Marlon Brando's Johnny as a new-style, black leather anti-hero. Woven into the new slant on the genre was a more blatant than usual use of sexual attraction and a continuation of the theme of the good girl (Murphy) attracted to the rebel type.

When the Black Rebels are ostracized from a larger motorcycle club, they vent their rage by taking over a small town which has a tiny police force. After mounting tensions and trouble, the citizens band together to combat the hooligans. During the course of the struggle, gang leader Johnny takes a liking to the waitress daughter (Murphy) of a cowardly cop.

Among the scenes that would become de rigeur in later such films were a cycle drag race, a tussle between Johnny and the leader (Marvin) of a rival gang, and an accidental killing (of which Kathie and her dad help to clear Johnny).

At the time of release, this was considered a highly controversial feature. Today it seems tame stuff.

YELLOW CONTRABAND (Pathé, 1928) 5,686'

Director, Leo Maloney; story-screenplay, Ford I. Beebe; camera, Edward A. Kull; editor, Joseph Kane.

Leo Maloney (Leo McMahon/Blackie Harris); Greta Yoltz (Mazie); Moble Johnson (Li Wong Foo); Tom London (Drag Connors); Joseph Rickson (Pierre Dufresne); Robert Burns (Sheriff); Vester Pegg (Dude McClain); Walter Patterson (Ice-House Joe); Bill Patton (Rawhide); Bud Osborne, Frank Ellis, Tom Forman (Dope Runners).

Although big city criminals often came into contact with movie Western heroes, it was a rarity that such activity would dominate an entire feature. An exception to the rule was Yellow Contraband, one of a popular series of sagebrush tales featuring Leo Maloney, who directed them for Pathé release. An obvious asset to the film was the fine script by Ford Beebe.

Maloney took on a dual role in the film, as an Internal Revenue agent and of a Chicago gangster (both of whom resembled each other greatly). When Leo McMahon finds out about plans to ship heroin to Canada he travels Westward, posing as an outlaw. Meanwhile, the underworld figure, Blackie (also Maloney), learns of the agent's plan and returns to Chicago with the drug in his possession. In the big city, Leo recovers the drug with the aid of a policewoman (Yoltz), who has been using the disguise of a gun moll.

YOU AND ME (Paramount, 1938) 90 min.

Producer-director, Fritz Lang; story, Norman Krasna; screenplay, Virginia Van Upp; art directors, Hans Dreier, Ernst Fegte; set decorator, A. E. Freudeman; music, Kurt Weill, Boris Morros; songs, Weill and Sam Coslow; Ralph Freed and Frederick Hollander; music adviser, Phil Boutelje; camera, Charles Lang, Jr.; editor, Paul Weatherwax.

Sylvia Sidney (Helen Dennis); George Raft (Joe Dennis); Harry Carey (Mr. Morris); Barton MacLane (Mickey); Warren Hymer (Gimpy); Roscoe Karns (Cuffy); Robert Cummings (Jim); George E. Stone (Patsy); Adrian Morris (Knucks); Roger Gray (Bath House); Cecil Cunningham (Mrs. Morris); Vera Gordon (Mrs. Levine); Egon Brecher (Mr. Levine); Willard Robertson (Dayton); Guinn Williams (Taxi); Bernadene Hayes (Nellie); Joyce Compton (Curly Blonde); Carol Paige (Torch Singer); Harlan Briggs (Mc Tavish); William B. Davidson (N. G. Martin); Oscar G. Hendrian (Lucky); Edward J. Pawley (Dutch); Joe Gray (Red); Jack Pennick, Kit Guard (Gangsters); Herta Lynd (Swedish Waitress); Matt McHugh (Newcomer); Julia Faye (Secretary); Ernie Adams (Nick the Waiter); Ethel Clayton (Woman); Ellen Drew (Cashier); John McCafferty (Policeman).

This was one of those intriguing cinema ideas that failed to congeal into a proper success. The pre-production problems with this vehicle should have alerted everyone concerned that it was doomed to failure. George Raft and Carole Lombard, who had been

George Raft, Warren Hymer, George E. Stone, Roscoe Karns, Joe
Gray, Kit Guard, Jack Pennick and Bob Cummings in You and Me
(1938).

scheduled to star in the project, rejected the idea of having story
writer Norman Krasna direct the film.   Then Lombard left the project and Sylvia Sidney was contracted for the lead.   However, she
refused the assignment but was persuaded by Fritz Lang, Wallace's
replacement, to follow through on the picture.   Kurt Weill, who did
some of the songs for the picture, also became discouraged part way
through production and left.
      You and Me emerged as a conglomerate of themes, including
melodrama, social drama and a love story with music.   It all added
up to a not very coherent experience for the moviegoers.
      Helen (Sidney) and Joe (Raft) are both ex-convicts employed
at Mr. Morris' (Carey) department store.   Joe has been quite honest
about his past, but Helen keeps her record a secret.   After they
are wed and Joe learns the truth about Helen he becomes discouraged
and joins his old mob, which plans to rob the store.   Helen learns
of the projected caper and gets the store officials to let her handle
the situation.   She gives the would-be robbers a stern lecture on the
economics of crime and sends them on their way.   Joe plans still
to leave Helen, but the lovers are reunited when it is discerned that
she is pregnant.
      Of this bizarre feature, the New Yorker called it "... the
weirdest cinematic hash. "

YOU CAN'T GET AWAY WITH MURDER   (Warner Bros., 1939)
78 min.

Associate producer, Samuel Bischoff; director, Lewis Seiler; based on the play Chalked Out by Warden Lewis E. Lawes, Jonathan Finn; screenplay, Robert Buckner, Don Ryan, Kenneth Gamet; music, Heinz Roemheld; orchestrators, Hugo Friedhofer, Arthur Kay, Rudolph Kopp; assistant director, William Kissel; dialog director, Jo Graham; gowns, Milo Anderson; art director, Hugo Reticker; sound, Francis J. Scheid; camera, Sol Polito; editor, James Gibbon.

Humphrey Bogart (Frank Wilson); Billy Halop (Johnnie Stone); Gale Page (Madge Stone); John Litel (Attorney Carey); Henry Travers (Pop); Harvey Stephens (Fred Burke); Harold Huber (Scappa); Joe Sawyer (Red); Joseph Downing (Smitty); George E. Stone (Toad); Joseph King (Principal Keeper); Joseph Crehan (Warden); John Ridgely (Gas Station Attendant); Herbert Rawlinson (District Attorney); Lane Chandler (Guard); Eddy Chandler (Keeper); Frank Faylen (Spieler); Robert Strange (Detective); Emory Parnell (Cop).

This "B" production concerns a cheap criminal (Bogart) who teaches a boy (Halop) to steal. During a robbery Frank Wilson kills a man with a gun the boy has stolen. The gun's owner (Stephens), fiancé of the boy's sister (Page), goes to the death house. However, Frank forces Johnnie to remain silent. Later the duo are arrested for car theft and are sent to jail. In order to keep the boy quiet, Frank stages a breakout and takes the boy with him, planning to kill the youth later. They are trapped in a boxcar and Frank shoots the kid, but Johnnie lives long enough to confess and to send Frank to the chair. Fred Burke is thus set free.

With the Warners' stock company to draw upon, this assembly-line vehicle took on added dimension, emerging as a slick, if empty, venture. It did emphasize once again the point about impressionable youths being led astray (and this was long before it could be blamed on violent TV shows).

YOU ONLY LIVE ONCE   (United Artists, 1937) 85 min.

Producer, Walter Wanger; director, Fritz Lang; story, Gene Towne; screenplay, Towne, Graham Baker; art director, Alexander Toluboff; music, Alfred Newman; song, Louis Alter and Paul Francis Webster; assistant director, Robert Lee; camera, Leon Shamroy; editor, Daniel Mandell.

Henry Fonda (Eddie Taylor); Sylvia Sidney (Joan Graham); Barton MacLane (Stephen Whitney); Jean Dixon (Bonnie Graham); William Gargan (Father Dolan); Jerome Cowan (Dr. Hill); Charles "Chic" Sale (Ethan); Margaret Hamilton (Hester); Warren Hymer (Muggsy); John Wray (Warden); Jonathan Hale (District Attorney); Ward Bond (Guard); Wade Boteler (Policeman); Henry Taylor (Kozderonas); Jean Stoddard (Stenographer); Ben Hall (Messenger).

This film probably ranks as Fritz Lang's best-directed American crime thriller. It was a gripping tale of a small time crook

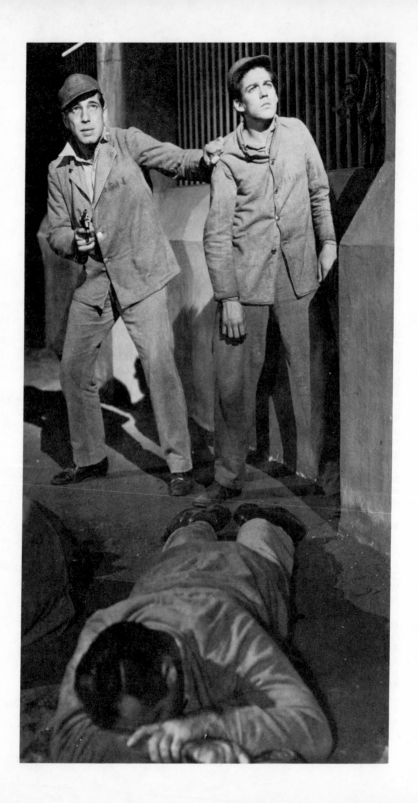

(Fonda) who is framed on a bank-murder job and sent to jail where he goes haywire and kills the priest (O'Brien) who is ironically bringing him news of a pardon.   Eddie then escapes and with his loyal wife (Sidney) tries to reach Canada.   Leaving their baby behind, the duo are pursued by the law and are eventually shot, although they had made it across to Canada.*

This sad Depression era story related how being poor can drive one to criminal acts, and of how society basically ignores such well-intentioned people who go astray.

Beyond the sharply-etched direction, cinematography, and acting, the screenplay hits hard, its social criticism giving dimension to the study of two hounded, lost souls.   Many cinema historians agree that without You Only Live Once there might not have been the later Bonnie and Clyde (1967), q. v.

YOUNG DILLINGER   (Allied Artists, 1965) 105 min.

Producer, Alfred Zimbalist; director, Terry O. Morse; screenplay, Don Zimbalist, Arthur Hoerl.

Nick Adams (John Dillinger); Robert Conrad (Pretty Boy Floyd); Mary Ann Mobley (Elaine); Victor Buono (Professor Hoffman); Dan Terranova (Homer Van Meter); John Hoyt (Dr. Wilson).

When this complicated re-telling of the John Dillinger legend was issued in 1965, star-producer Nick Adams claimed that the film would gross millions.   It did not, mainly due to tepid reviews--"it has all the earmarks of a nine-day cheapie tacked together on a Hollywood back lot" (New York Herald-Tribune)--and poor exploitation.   The film, however, did engender controversy in 1968 when CBS-TV, after an initial showing, shelved the film as "too violent" for network showcase.   Ironically the formula for violence used in the mini feature seemed to have been copied for much more successful Bonnie and Clyde (1967), q. v. , with which it occasionally shared a double bill in later years.

This version had Dillinger as a robber out to obtain the good life for his girl Elaine (Mobley).   After an abortive robbery attempt he is sent to prison and becomes involved with Pretty Boy Floyd (Conrad), Baby Face Nelson (Ashley), and Homer Van Meter (Terranova).   After his release, Dillinger breaks his buddies out of jail. The four go on a series of robberies.   They then decide to graduate to banks and join up with the Professor (Buono), a mastermind at bank holdups.   After one big robbery Dillinger decides to have plastic surgery.   The hack doctor (Hoyt) performs the operation and then tries to rape Elaine.   Dillinger subsequently ties the physician to a wheelchair and pushes him into a lake.

After several more crimes, and an attempted double-cross by the Professor, Elaine has had enough.   She shouts at her

*An alternate ending, filmed but discarded, would have allowed the refugees to escape to freedom.

Opposite: Humphrey Bogart with Billy Halop in You Can't Get Away with Murder (1939).

John Ashley, Nick Adams and Robert Conrad in Young Dillinger
(1965).

boyfriend, "you don't have the guts to live life like a real man. "
For her sake, Dillinger decides to give up his life of crime. However, the F.B.I. surrounds their hideout and Elaine is shot. She
tells him to run for his life. In the film's surprisingly arty finale,
he does just that.

GANGSTER-CRIME-POLICE-DETECTIVE SHOWS
ON RADIO AND TELEVISION

Compiled by Vincent Terrace

RADIO

THE ADVENTURES OF BILL LANCE
With: Gerald Mohr (ABC 1947)*
THE ADVENTURES OF CHARLIE
CHAN With: Walter Connolly,
Ed Begley, Santos Ortega (Blue
Network 1932)
THE ADVENTURES OF CHRISTO-
PHER WELLS With: Les Damon,
Vicki Vola (CBS 1947)
THE ADVENTURES OF ELLERY
QUEEN With: Hugh Marlowe
(CBS 1939)
THE ADVENTURES OF FATHER
BROWN With: Karl Swenson
(Mutual 1944)
THE ADVENTURES OF NERO
WOLFE With: Santos Ortega
(Blue Network 1943)
THE AFFAIRS OF PETER SALEM
With: Santos Ortega, Jack Grimes
(Mutual 1949)
THE ADVENTURES OF PHILIP
MARLOWE With: Van Heflin
(NBC 1947)
THE ADVENTURES OF SAM SPADE
With: Howard Duff, Lurene Tut-
tle (NBC 1949)
THE AFFAIRS OF ANN SCOTLAND
With: Arlene Francis (ABC
1946)
THE AVENGER With: James
Monks, Helen Adamson (Syndi-
cated 1946)
BIG TOWN With: Edward G. Rob-
inson, Claire Trevor (CBS 1937)
THE BISHOP AND THE GARGOYLE
With: Richard Gordon, Ken Lynch
(NBC 1940)
THE BLACK HOOD With: Scott
Douglas, Marjorie Cramer
(Mutual 1943)
BOSTON BLACKIE With: Chester
Morris, Lesley Woods (NBC
1944)
BROADWAY'S MY BEAT With:
Anthony Ross (CBS 1949)
BULLDOG DRUMMOND With:
George Coulouris, Santos Or-
tega (Mutual 1941)
CALL THE POLICE With: Joseph
Julian (NBC 1947)
CANDY MATSON, YUkon 28209
With: Natalie Masters (NBC
1950)
THE CASE BOOK OF GREGORY
HOOD With: Gale Gordon, Bill
Johnstone (Mutual 1946)
CHARLIE WILD, PRIVATE DE-
TECTIVE With: George Petrie
(CBS 1950)
CHICK CARTER With: Bill Lip-
ton (Mutual 1943)
CRIME CASES OF WARDEN LAWES
With: Lewis E. Lawes (Mutual
1946)
THE CRIME FILES OF FLAMOND
With: Everett Clarke (Mutual
1951)
A CRIME LETTER FROM DAN
DODGE With: Myron McCor-
mick, Shirley Eggleston (ABC
1951)
CRIMINAL CASEBOOK With:
Nelson Case (ABC 1948)
DEAR MARGY, IT'S MURDER
With: Mason Adams, Ian Martin
(Mutual 1951)
DRAGNET With: Jack Webb,
Barton Yarborough (NBC 1949)
THE FALCON With: Les Damon,
Joan Banks (Blue Network
1943)
THE FAT MAN With: J. Scott
Smart (ABC 1946)
FLASH GUN CASEY (a. k. a. CASEY,
CRIME PHOTOGRAPHER) With:
Matt Crowley (CBS 1943)
FRONT PAGE FARRELL With:

Staats Cotsworth (Mutual 1941)
GANGBUSTERS With: Lewis J.
Valentine (CBS 1936)
THE GREEN HORNET With: Al
Hodge, Mickey Tolan, Lee Allamn
(Mutual 1938)
THE GREEN LAMA With: Paul
Frees (CBS 1949)
HIGHWAY PATROL With: Michael
Fitzmaurice (Mutual 1943)
I DEAL IN CRIME With: William
Gargan (ABC 1946)
JOHNNY FLETCHER With: Bill
Goodwin (ABC 1948)
THE LINE-UP With: Bill Johnstone
(NBC 1950)
McGARRY AND HIS MOUSE With:
Wendell Corey, Peggy Conklin
(NBC 1946)
THE MAN FROM HOMICIDE With:
Dan Duryea (ABC 1950)
MANHUNT With: Maurice Tarplin,
Larry Haines (Syndicated 1945)
MARTIN KANE, PRIVATE EYE
With: Lloyd Nolan (NBC 1950)
MICHAEL SHAYNE, PRIVATE DE-
TECTIVE With: Jeff Chandler
(CBS 1949)
MISTER CHAMELEON With: Karl
Swenson (CBS 1948)
MR. DISTRICT ATTORNEY With:
Dwight Wiest, Jay Jostyn, Vicki
Vola (NBC 1939)
MURDER IS MY HOBBY With:
Glenn Langan (Syndicated 1946)
NICK CARTER, MASTER DETEC-
TIVE With: Lon Clark, Helen
Choate (Mutual 1943)
PAT NOVAK FOR HIRE With:
Jack Webb (ABC 1949)
POLICEWOMAN With: Mary Sulli-
van (ABC 1946)
RICHARD DIAMOND, PRIVATE DE-
TECTIVE With: Dick Powell
(NBC 1949)
ROGUE'S GALLERY With: Dick
Powell, Barry Sullivan (NBC
1944)
SCOTLAND YARD With: Basil
Rathbone (Mutual 1947)
THE SHADOW With: Orson Welles,
Brett Morrison, Agnes Moorehead,
Grace Matthews, Lesley Woods
(Mutual 1936)
SHERLOCK HOLMES With: Richard
Gordon, Nigel Bruce (NBC 1930)
SPECIAL AGENT With: James
Meighan, Lyle Sundrow (Mutual

1948)
THE THIN MAN With: Les Tre-
mayne, Claudia Morgan (CBS
1946)
TRUE DETECTIVE MYSTERIES
With: Frank Dunne (Mutual
1944)
UNDER ARREST With: Craig
McDonald (Mutual 1946)
YOURS TRULY, JOHNNY DOLLAR
With: Charles Russell (CBS
1949)

TELEVISION

ADAM-12 With: Martin Milner,
Kent McCord (NBC 1968)*
THE AFRICAN PATROL With:
John Bentley (Syndicated 1957)
AMY PRENTISS With: Jessica
Walter (NBC 1974)
ARCHER With: Brian Keith
(NBC 1975)
THE ASPHALT JUNGLE With:
Jack Warden, Arch Johnson, Bill
Smith (ABC 1961)
BANYON With: Robert Forster,
Richard Jaeckel, Joan Blondell
(NBC 1972)
BARNABY JONES With: Buddy
Ebsen (CBS 1973)
BARNEY BLAKE, POLICE RE-
PORTER With: Gene O'Donnell
(NBC 1948)
THE BIG STORY With: narrators
Ben Grauer, Burgess Meredith
(Syndicated 1951)
BIG TOWN With: Patrick McVey,
Mark Steven, Margaret Hayes,
Mary K. Wells, Jane Nigh,
Beverly Tyler, Trudy Wroe,
Julie Stevens (CBS 1950)
BOSTON BLACKIE With: Kent
Taylor, Lois Collier, Frank
Orth (NBC 1951)
BOURBON STREET BEAT With:
Andrew Duggan, Richard Long
(ABC 1959)
BRENNER With: Edward Binns,
James Broderick (CBS 1959)
BURKE'S LAW With: Gene Barry,
Gary Conway, Regis Toomey
(ABC 1963)
CADE'S COUNTY With: Glenn
Ford, Edgar Buchanan (CBS
1971)
CANNON With: William Conrad

(CBS 1971)

THE CASE OF THE DANGEROUS ROBIN With: Rick Jason (Syndicated 1960)

THE CASES OF EDDIE DRAKE With: Don Haggerty, Patricia Morison (CBS 1949)

(CASEY) CRIME PHOTOGRAPHER With: Richard Carlyle, Darren McGavin (CBS 1951)

CHARLIE WILD, PRIVATE DETECTIVE With: John McQuade, Kevin O'Morrison, Cloris Leachman (ABC 1951)

CHECKMATE With: Anthony George, Doug McClure, Sebastian Cabot (CBS 1959)

THE CHICAGO TEDDY BEARS With: Dean Jones, John Banner (CBS 1971)

CHICAGOLAND MYSTERY PLAYERS With: Gordon Urquhart (Dumont 1949)

CITY DETECTIVES With: Rod Cameron (Syndicated 1953)

CHOPPER ONE With: Jim McMullan, Dirk Benedick (ABC 1974)

COLONEL MARCH OF SCOTLAND YARD With: Boris Karloff (Syndicated 1958)

COLUMBO With: Peter Falk (NBC 1971)

CORONADO 9 With: Rod Cameron (Syndicated 1959)

CRIME DOES NOT PAY Anthology (Syndicated 1960)

THE D.A.'S MAN With: John Compton, Ralph Menza (NBC 1959)

DAN AUGUST With: Burt Reynolds, Norman Fell (ABC 1970)

DECOY With: Beverly Garland (Syndicated 1957)

THE DETECTIVES With: Robert Taylor, Tige Andrews, Adam West, Ursula Thiess (ABC 1959)

THE DETECTIVE'S WIFE With: Donald Curtis, Lynn Bari (CBS 1950)

DIAL 999 With: Robert Beatty (Syndicated 1959)

DICK TRACY With: Ralph Byrd, Joe Devlin (NBC 1950)

DOORWAY TO DANGER With: Stacy Harris (Syndicated 1950)

DRAGNET With: Jack Webb, Ben Alexander (NBC 1951)
Jack Webb, Harry Morgan (NBC

1967)

87th PRECINCT With: Robert Lansing, Norman Fell, Ron Harper (NBC 1961)

ELLERY QUEEN With: Richard Hart, Lee Bowman, Hugh Marlowe, George Nader, Lee Philips (Dumont 1950)

THE F.B.I. With: Efrem Zimbalist, Jr. (ABC 1965)

FABIAN OF SCOTLAND YARD With: Bruce Seton (Syndicated 1951)

FARADAY AND CO. With: Dan Bailey (NBC 1973)

THE FELONY SQUAD With: Howard Duff, Dennis Cole, Ben Alexander (ABC 1966)

THE FILES OF JEFFREY JOMES With: Don Haggerty, Gloria Henry (Syndicated 1955)

THE FOUR JUST MEN With: Vittorio De Sica, Jack Hawkins, Richard Conte, Dan Dailey (Syndicated 1959)

FRONT PAGE DETECTIVE With: Edmond Lowe, Frank Jenks (ABC 1951)

GANGBUSTERS (a. k. a. CAPTURED) With: Chester Morris (NBC 1952)

GIDEON, C. I. D. With: John Gregson (Syndicated 1966)

GRIFF With: Lorne Greene, Ben Murphy (ABC 1973)

HARBOR COMMAND With: Wendell Corey (ABC 1957)

HAWAII FIVE-O With: Jack Lord, James MacArthur (CBS 1968)

HAWAIIAN EYE With: Connie Stevens, Anthony Eisley, Robert Conrad (ABC 1959)

HAWK With: Burt Reynolds (ABC 1966)

HIGHWAY PATROL With: Broderick Crawford, William Boyett (Syndicated 1956)

I COVER TIMES SQUARE With: Harold Huber (ABC 1950)

I'M THE LAW (a. k. a. THE GEORGE RAFT CASEBOOK) With: George Raft (Syndicated 1953)

THE INFORMER With: Ian Hendry, Jean Marsh (Syndicated 1965)

INSPECTOR FABIAN OF SCOTLAND YARD With: Bruce Seton (NBC 1955)

INTERNATIONAL DETECTIVE

With: Arthur Fleming (Syndicated 1959)

IRONSIDE With: Raymond Burr (NBC 1967)

IT HAPPENS IN SPAIN With: Scott McKay, Elena Barra (Syndicated 1958)

JOHNNY MIDNIGHT With: Edmond O'Brien (Syndicated 1960)

JOHNNY STACCATO With: John Cassavetes (NBC 1959)

KHAN! With: Khigh Dhiegh (CBS 1975)

LOCKUP With: Macdonald Carey (NBC 1959)

M SQUAD With: Lee Marvin (NBC 1957)

McCLOUD With: Dennis Weaver (NBC 1970)

McMILLAN AND WIFE With: Rock Hudson, Susan Saint James (NBC 1972)

MAN AGAINST CRIME (a. k. a. FOLLOW THAT MAN) With: Ralph Bellamy, Frank Lovejoy (CBS 1949)

MAN BEHIND THE BADGE With: Charles Bickford (CBS 1955)

MAN WITH A CAMERA With: Charles Bronson (ABC 1958)

MANHUNT With: Victor Jory, Patrick McVey (Syndicated 1959)

MANHUNTER With: Ken Howard (CBS 1974)

MARTIN KANE, PRIVATE DETECTIVE With: Lee Tracy (later) Lloyd Nolan, William Gargan, Mark Stevens (NBC 1949)

MIKE HAMMER With: Darren McGavin (NBC 1958)

MR. & MRS. NORTH With: Richard Denning, Barbara Britton (CBS 1952)

MISTER DISTRICT ATTORNEY With: Jay Joslyn, (later) David Brian (CBS 1951, 1954)

MYSTERIES OF CHINATOWN With: Marvin Miller (ABC 1949)

MYSTERY THEATRE (a. k. a. UNCOVERED) With: Tom Conway (Syndicated 1951)

N. O. P. D. With: Stacy Harris, Lou Sirgo (Syndicated 1956)

N. Y. P. D. With: Jack Warden, Frank Converse, Robert Hooks (ABC 1967)

NAKED CITY With: John McIntire, James Franciscus (later) Paul

Burke, Nancy Malone, Horace McMahon (ABC 1958, 1960)

THE NEW BREED With: Leslie Nielsen, John Beradino (ABC 1961)

OFFICIAL DETECTIVE With: Everett Sloane (Syndicated 1958)

PARIS PRECINCT With: Louis Jourdan, Claude Dauphin (Syndicated 1955)

PETE KELLY'S BLUES With: William Reynolds, Connie Boswell (NBC 1959)

PETER GUNN With: Craig Stevens Lola Albright, Herschel Bernardi (NBC 1958)

THE PLAINCLOTHESMAN With: Ken Lynch (Syndicated 1950)

POLICE CALL Anthology (Syndicated 1955)

POLICE STORY With: Norman Rose (CBS 1952)

POLICE WOMAN With: Angie Dickinson, Earl Holliman (NBC 1974)

THE PROTECTORS With: Leslie Nielsen, Hari Rhodes (NBC 1969)

PUBLIC DEFENDER With: Reed Hadley (Syndicated 1955)

RACKET SQUAD With: Reed Hadley (CBS 1951)

RACKETS ARE MY RACKET With: Sergeant Audley Walsh (Dumont 1948)

RICHARD DIAMOND, PRIVATE DETECTIVE With: David Janssen Mary Tyler Moore, Barbara Bain, Regis Toomey (CBS 1957)

THE ROARING 20'S With: Dorothy Provine, Donald May, Rex Reason (ABC 1960)

ROCKY KING, DETECTIVE With: Roscoe Karns, Todd Karns (Dumont 1950)

SABER OF LONDON With: Donald Gray (NBC 1957)

77 SUNSET STRIP With: Efrem Zimbalist, Jr. , Roger Smith, Edd Byrnes (ABC 1965)

SHAFT With: Richard Roundtree (CBS 1973)

THE SILENT FORCE With: Ed Nelson, Linda Day George (ABC 1971)

THE SNOOP SISTERS With: Helen Hayes, Mildred Natwick (NBC 1973)

STATE TROOPER With: Rod
Cameron (Syndicated 1957)

SURFSIDE 6 With: Troy Donahue,
Lee Patterson, Van Williams
(ABC 1960)

TARGET: THE CORRUPTORS
With: Stephen McNally, Robert
Harland (ABC 1961)

TENAFLY With: James McEachin
(NBC 1973)

THE THIN MAN With: Peter Lawford, Phyllis Kirk (NBC 1957)

TIGHTROPE! With: Michael Connors (CBS 1959)

TREASURY MEN IN ACTION With:
Walter Greaza (Syndicated 1953)

21 BEACON STREET With: Dennis
Morgan, Joanna Barnes (NBC
1959)

THE UNTOUCHABLES With: Robert
Stack, Paul Picerni, Abel Fernandez, Walter Winchell (ABC 1959)

THE WALTER WINCHELL FILE
With: Walter Winchell (ABC
1957)

WANTED With: Walter McGraw
(CBS 1955)

---

*Year and network of the program's first airing is given.
Much more so than with the feature films detailed in the previous
section of this volume, it is extremely difficult to draw the fine line
separating crime versus detective entries, especially since there
have been so few radio or television programs in which the gangster
and not the law enforcer or detective is the primary focus.

ABOUT THE AUTHORS AND THE STAFF

JAMES ROBERT PARISH, New York based free-lance writer, was born in Cambridge, Massachusetts. He attended the University of Pennsylvania and graduated Phi Beta Kappa with a degree in English. A graduate of the University of Pennsylvania Law School, he is a member of the New York Bar. As president of Entertainment Copyright Research Co., Inc., he headed a major researching facility for the film and television industries. Later he was a film reviewer-interviewer for Motion Picture Daily and Variety. He has been responsible for such reference volumes as The American Movies Reference Book: The Sound Era and The Emmy Awards: A Pictorial History. He has co-authored The MGM Stock Company: The Golden Era, Vincent Price Unmasked, and The Glamour Girls, among others, and has authored such volumes as The Fox Girls, The RKO Gals, and Hollywood's Great Love Teams. He recently compiled Actors' Television Credits (1950-1972), and with Michael R. Pitts prepared The Great Spy Pictures and Film Directors: A Guide to Their American Pictures.

MICHAEL R. PITTS is a journalist and freelance writer. A graduate of Ball State University, with a B.S. in history and a Master's Degree in journalism, he is the former entertainment editor of the Anderson (Ind.) Daily Bulletin. Besides writing, Mr. Pitts currently works as a researcher for the Madison County Council of Governments, a local planning and advisory agency, and he is film reviewer for Channel 7 in Anderson, where he resides. He has been published in cinema journals both here and abroad and with Mr. Parish he has written The Great Spy Pictures, Film Directors: A Guide to Their American Films, and the forthcoming The Great Western Pictures. Formerly in public education, Mr. Pitts has also had material published by various wire services.

T. ALLAN TAYLOR, godson of the late Margaret Mitchell, has long been active in book publishing and is currently production manager of one of the largest abstracting and technical indexing services in the United States. He was editor on The Fox Girls, The RKO Gals, Liza!, The Great Movie Heroes, The Great Spy Pictures, The Debonairs and other volumes.

Since an early age, Brooklynite JOHN ROBERT COCCHI has been viewing and collating data on motion pictures and is now regarded
430

as one of America's most thorough film researchers. He is the
New York editor of Boxoffice magazine. He was research associate
on The American Movies Reference Book: The Sound Era, The
Paramount Pretties, The Cinema of Edward G. Robinson, Hollywood's Great Love Teams, and many other books. He has written
cinema history articles for such journals as Film Fan Monthly and
Screen Facts and has currently written a movie quiz book on Western films.

EDWARD MICHAEL CONNOR was born in Willimansett, Massachusetts. Later he moved to New York and joined the staff of the
Pius Xth School of Liturgical Music. Thereafter, he trained choirs
in New York and New Jersey. He joined the National Board of Review in 1954 and the National Catholic Office for Motion Pictures in
1959. He has contributed many articles on motion pictures to Films
in Review, Screen Facts, and Screen Careers, and for several years
was musical editor of Films in Review. He has had two books published, Prophecy for Today and Recent Apparitions of Our Lady.
An avid cinemagoer, Mr. Connor resides in Manhattan.

New York-born FLORENCE SOLOMON attended Hunter College and
then joined Ligon Johnson's copyright research office. Later she
was appointed director for research at Entertainment Copyright Research Co., Inc. and is presently a reference supervisor at
ASCAP's Index Division in New York City. Ms. Solomon has col-
laborated on such works as TV Movies, The American Movies Reference Book, The George Raft File, and Film Directors Guide:
Western Europe. She is the niece of the noted sculptor, the late
Sir Jacob Epstein.

VINCENT TERRACE, a native New Yorker, is a graduate of the New
York Institute of Technology, possessing a Baccalaureate Degree in
Fine Arts. He is the author of The Complete Encyclopedia of Tele-
vision Programs: 1947-1974 and is presently preparing volumes on
Charlie Chan: A Definitive Study and The Complete Encyclopedia of
Radio Programs: 1920-1960. He previously assisted Mr. Parish
and Mr. Pitts with media information on The Great Spy Pictures.